Academic
Literacy

Academic Literacy

READINGS AND STRATEGIES
Fourth Edition

Jill Lewis, Ed.D.
NEW JERSEY CITY UNIVERSITY

Houghton Mifflin Company

Boston · New York

In memory of Gray Lewis, a loving husband and father whose love of reading was surpassed only by his compassion for others.

Publisher: Patricia Coryell
Sponsoring Editor: Joann Kozyrev
Editorial Associate: Peter Mooney
Associate Project Editor: Eric Moore
Composition Buyer: Chuck Dutton
Associate Manufacturing Buyer: Brian Pieragostini
Executive Marketing Manager: Annamarie Rice
Marketing Associate: Andrew Whitacre

Cover image: © Leo Kundas/images.com

Printed in the U.S.A.

Library of Congress Control Number: 2006922358

Instructor's examination copy
    ISBN-10: 0-618-73204-7
    ISBN-13: 978-0-618-73204-3
For orders, use student text ISBNs
    ISBN-10: 0-618-63946-2
    ISBN-13: 978-0-618-63946-5

23456789-MV-10 09 08 07

Contents

To the Instructor   xv

To the Student   xix

Part 1   Handbook for Reading and Studying Strategies   1

Chapter 1   *Taking Control of Your Reading*   3
Assessing Your Academic Self-Esteem   3
Taking Control of Your Learning   6
Taking Control of Your Learning Environment   6
Taking Control of Your Comprehension   10
Preparing for Tests   31
Chapter Summary   33
Extended Application   34

Chapter 2   *Strategies for Increasing Vocabulary: Using Context Clues, Word Parts, and the Dictionary*   36
What Do We Mean By Context?   37
How Will Context Help You Read Academic Text?   37
What Is the Process for Using Context Clues?   40
What Are the Most Useful Types of Context Clues?   42
Word Structure: A Clue to Word Meaning   54

Intelligent Use of the Dictionary   61
Chapter Summary   70
Extended Application   71

Chapter 3   Strategic Reading for Topics, Subtopics,
             and Main Ideas   72

What Is the Topic of a Reading Selection?   73
Recognizing Topics and Subtopics   74
Just What Is the Main Idea?   83
Purposes for Creating Main-Idea Sentences   89
The Process for Creating Main-Idea Sentences   90
Other Considerations for Creating Main-Idea Sentences   93
Testing Your Main-Idea Sentences   99
Chapter Summary   105
Extended Application   106

Chapter 4   Understanding Details   107

Why Are Details Needed?   107
Understanding Types of Details   111
Details as Answers to Questions   118
Major and Minor Details   123
Chapter Summary   135
Extended Application   136

Chapter 5   Understanding Organizational Patterns
             in Academic Texts   137

Reviewing What You Already Know   138
How Can Patterns Be Identified?   140
Relationships Among Main Ideas, Details, and Patterns   154
Recognizing Patterns of Organization   155
Using Patterns to Help You Remember   164
Chapter Summary   179
Extended Application   180

Chapter 6 ⁙ *Strategies for Critical Reading and Thinking:*
Fact/Opinion; Point of View; Style,
Mood, and Tone 182

What Is Critical Reading? 183
Distinguishing Statements of Fact from Statements of Opinion 189
Evidence for Statements of Opinion 197
Additional Criteria for Judging Facts and Opinions 201
Identifying Author's Style, Mood, and Tone 207
Chapter Summary 219
Extended Application 220

Chapter 7 ⁙ *Reading Critically to Make Inferences,*
Draw Conclusions and Analyze
Web-Based Materials 221

Inferences in Everyday Life 222
Finding Support for Your Inferences 222
Drawing Conclusions from Your Reading 229
Analyzing Web-Based Material 236
Chapter Summary 244
Extended Application 245

Chapter 8 ⁙ *Strategies for Reading Visual Aids*
in Texts 246

What Are Visual Aids? 246
What Are the Various Types of Visual Aids? 249
How Do Visual Aids Facilitate Comprehension? 257
What Are Effective Strategies for Reading Visual Aids? 262
Previewing Visual Aids 262
Noting Details 272
Connecting Visual Aids to Text 277
Making Inferences from Visual Aids 281
Drawing Conclusions from Visual Aids 285

Chapter Summary   290

Extended Application   291

Chapter 9 ⋅ *Strategies for Active Listening and Notetaking*   292

Becoming a Good Listener   292

Indicators of Positive Listening   296

Effective Notetaking from Books and Lectures   304

A Process for Effective Notetaking   305

Identifying Usable Notes   305

Notetaking Basics   310

Notetaking Systems   312

Using Your Notes Effectively   318

Preparing Graphics from Lectures and Texts   323

Underlining and Marking Textbooks   323

Chapter Summary   331

Extended Application   332

Chapter 10 ⋅ *Assessing Your New Knowledge*   333

PART 2 ⋅ Background Essays for Academic Literacy   337

Cross-Reference to Handbook for Reading and Study Strategies   338

Chapter 11 ⋅ *Psychology: The Science of Mind and Behavior*   339

Key Concepts for the Study of Psychology   340

SELECTION 1

The Education Directorate and the Office of Public Communications of the American Psychological Association, *What Psychology Is*   341

Preview   341

Reading Selection   342

Comprehension of the Discipline 347
Critical Thinking: Reaction and Discussion 349
Using Technology for Further Understanding 349
Guidelines for Reading Psychology 349

SELECTION 2

Randy Borum, *Understanding the Terrorist Mind-Set* 352
Preview 352
Reading Selection 355
Postreading Comprehension Development 359
Critical Thinking: Reaction and Discussion 364
Using Technology for Further Understanding 364

SELECTION 3

Monica Ramirez Basco, *The "Perfect" Trap* 365
Preview 365
Reading Selection 366
Postreading Comprehension Development 371
Critical Thinking: Reaction and Discussion 375
Using Technology for Further Understanding 376

SELECTION 4

Robert Kubey and Mihaly Csikszentmihalyi, *Television Addiction
Is No Mere Metaphor* 377
Preview 377
Reading Selection 379
Postreading Comprehension Development 385
Critical Thinking: Reaction and Discussion 389
Using Technology for Further Understanding 390

Chapter 12 ⁒ *Sociology: The Science of Societies and Their Effects on Human Behavior* 391

Key Concepts for the Study of Sociology 392

SELECTION 5

James M. Henslin, *The Sociological Perspective*   394

   Preview   394

   Reading Selection   395

   Comprehension of the Discipline   399

   Critical Thinking: Reaction and Discussion   402

   Using Technology for Further Understanding   402

   Guidelines for Reading Sociology   406

SELECTION 6

Donna Harrington-Lueker, *Blown Away by School Violence*   408

   Preview   408

   Reading Selection   409

   Postreading Comprehension Development   412

   Critical Thinking: Reaction and Discussion   418

   Using Technology for Further Understanding   418

SELECTIONS 7 AND 8 ALTERNATIVE VIEWPOINTS:
SAME-SEX MARRIAGE

Andrew Sullivan, *Here Comes the Groom* • Viewpoint 1   419
Robert Sokolowski, *The Threat of Same-Sex Marriage* •
Viewpoint 2   419

   Preview   419

   Viewpoint 1   420

   Viewpoint 2   423

   Postreading Comprehension Development   427

   Critical Thinking: Reaction and Discussion   431

   Using Technology for Further Understanding   432

Chapter 13 ⁙ *The Sciences: Knowledge of the
Physical World*   434

Key Concepts for the Study of the Sciences   435

SᴇʟᴇᴄᴛɪᴏN 9

American Association for the Advancement of Science,
The Nature of Science 436

> Preview 436
>
> Reading Selection 438
>
> Comprehension of the Discipline 442
>
> Critical Thinking: Reaction and Discussion 445
>
> Using Technology for Further Understanding 446
>
> Guidelines for Reading the Sciences 446

SᴇʟᴇᴄᴛɪᴏN 10

Dustin Stephens and Robert Dudley, *The Drunken Monkey Hypothesis* 449

> Preview 449
>
> Reading Selection 450
>
> Postreading Comprehension Development 455
>
> Critical Thinking: Reaction and Discussion 460
>
> Using Technology for Further Understanding 463

SᴇʟᴇᴄᴛɪᴏN 11 Preview

Natural Disasters: Earthquakes and Tsunamis 464

> Preview 464
>
> Reading Selections 466
>
> Postreading Comprehension Development 470
>
> Critical Thinking: Reaction and Discussion 476
>
> Using Technology for Further Understanding 476

Chapter 14 ⁙ *Business: The Activities of Groups or*
Individuals Who Develop, Produce, and
Distribute Goods and Services 477

Key Concepts for the Study of Business 478

SᴇʟᴇᴄᴛɪᴏN 12 Preview

Roger E. Herman and Joyce L. Gioia, *Making Work Meaningful:*
Secrets of the Future-Focused Corporation 480

> Preview 480

Reading Selection   481

Comprehension of the Discipline   488

Critical Thinking: Reaction and Discussion   490

Using Technology for Further Understanding   490

Guidelines for Reading Business   490

SELECTION 13

Jack Bishop, *Who Are the Pirates? The Politics of Piracy, Poverty, and Greed in a Globalized Music Market*   492

Preview   492

Reading Selection   493

Postreading Comprehension Development   498

Critical Thinking: Reaction and Discussion   503

Using Technology for Further Understanding   504

SELECTION 14

Paul Klebnikov, *Coke's Sinful World*   505

Preview   505

Reading Selection   506

Postreading Comprehension Development   511

Critical Thinking: Reaction and Discussion   516

Using Technology for Further Understanding   517

SELECTION 15

Tyce Palmaffy, *El Millonario Next Door*   518

Preview   518

Reading Selection   519

Postreading Comprehension Development   526

Critical Thinking: Reaction and Discussion   531

Using Technology for Further Understanding   532

Chapter 15 ∴ *History: A Record or Explanation of Past Events*   533

Key Concepts for the Study of History   534

SELECTION 16

F. Otnes, compiler, *Why History?* 535

Preview 535

Reading Selection 536

Comprehension of the Discipline 542

Critical Thinking: Reaction and Discussion 547

Using Technology for Further Understanding 547

Guidelines for Reading History 547

SELECTION 17

Olaudah Equiano, *Kidnapped, Enslaved, and Sold Away* (c. 1756) 550

Preview 550

Reading Selection 551

Postreading Comprehension Development 555

Critical Thinking: Reaction and Discussion 560

Using Technology for Further Understanding 561

SELECTION 18

Brenda Fowler, *A Place Without History* 562

Preview 562

Reading Selection 563

Postreading Comprehension Development 568

Critical Thinking: Reaction and Discussion 573

Using Technology for Further Understanding 574

Chapter 16 ∴ *Political Science: A Social Science Analyzing Political Processes and Institutions* 575

Key Concepts for the Study of Political Science 576

SELECTION 19

W. Phillips Shively, *Politics: Setting the Stage* 577

Preview 577

Reading Selection 578

Comprehension of the Discipline 583

Critical Thinking: Reaction and Discussion 588

Using Technology for Further Understanding 588
Guidelines for Reading Political Science 588

SELECTION 20
James Q. Wilson, *What Should We Know About American Government?* 591
Preview 591
Reading Selection 592
Postreading Comprehension Development 597
Critical Thinking: Reaction and Discussion 602
Using Technology for Further Understanding 604

SELECTIONS 21 AND 22 ALTERNATIVE VIEWPOINTS:
ILLEGAL IMMIGRATION

Mark Krikorian, *The Way to Go on Immigration* • Viewpoint 1 605
Edwin Meese III, James Jay Carafano, Ph. D., Matthew Spalding, Ph. D.
and Paul Rosenzweig, *Not Amnesty, but Attrition: The Way to Go on
Immigration* • Viewpoint 2 605

Preview 605
Viewpoint 1 606
Viewpoint 2 610
Postreading Comprehension Development 616
Critical Thinking: Reaction and Discussion 619
Using Technology for Further Understanding 619

APPENDIX   READABILITY LEVELS FOR ESSAYS 621

CREDITS 623

INDEX 625

TO THE INSTRUCTOR

Academic Literacy: Readings and Strategies has evolved as the result of my thirty-plus years of experience teaching students enrolled in developmental reading courses at two- and four-year colleges and assisting high school teachers who are concerned about their students' academic readiness at the start of their college careers. During the past thirty years, our knowledge about the reading process and how students learn has grown considerably; the population we teach has changed; and the academic goals for, and expectations of, students have been re-shaped to include a greater concern for critical thinking and personal response. Many of the readings, strategies, and activities in this text are based on these considerations. Those research-based instructional strategies that have continued to serve students well over the years are also included. Many features of this text make it unique and give students ample opportunity to develop the reading and study strategies they need for academic success. The fourth edition reflects changes in the topics of interest and concern to students since the publication of the third edition as well as the increased foothold technology has gained in the college learning environment.

You will find that this text

❋ **Uses a process-oriented approach to instruction.** Part 1 provides direct instruction in skills. It takes students through the *thinking processes* used to achieve such reading/study goals as recognizing and creating main ideas, making inferences, determining meanings of words from context clues, understanding word structure, drawing conclusions, notetaking, and reading visual aids. There are guidelines for analyzing and using Web-based materials and for recognizing the value of different kinds of evidence authors provide. Students are encouraged to apply these strategies to other coursework and in other contexts throughout the text.

❋ **Includes high-interest and challenging reading material.** Models, practice material, and longer selections are drawn from sources that are commonly assigned to college students. Some selections have a multicultural theme; some are on other topics that are relevant for today's students. Each adds to the knowledge base students will bring to other academic situations. High expectations encourage students and give them a reality-based context in which to practice reading strategies.

❋ **Provides an introduction to many disciplines studied at college.** Part 2 of the text is arranged purposefully so that students learn *about* typical areas of study at college, such as psychology, sociology, and business while they apply strategies to readings in these fields. Concepts common to each field are introduced and the first reading in each section familiarizes students with the nature of the discipline itself.

❋ **Develops metacognitive habits.** In each chapter students reflect on approaches they use for comprehension and self-monitoring. This ongoing practice encourages students to develop the habit of thinking about *how* they are reading *while* they are reading. They develop reading flexibility, adapting their reading style to accommodate the demands of the readings tasks and their purposes. Self-assessment is continuous. Special *Thinking About Your Reading and Writing* activities help students develop metacognitive habits.

❋ **Promotes critical and creative thinking.** Students are frequently asked to justify selected answers or written responses, to evaluate and modify their responses after discussion and review, and to critique the responses of others. Part 1 contains two chapters on critical thinking. Each reading in Part 2 contains a *Critical Thinking: Reaction and Discussion* section by which students extend knowledge gained from that reading to other contexts.

❋ **Facilitates prediction and use of prior knowledge for comprehension.** Chapter and reading previews prepare students for the contents that follow. In Part 2, each reading is preceded by an activity designed to help students recall and organize what they already know about the selection topic. The activities are varied and students learn multiple ways to access their prior knowledge before reading, a habit necessary to academic success.

❋ **Integrates reading and writing.** We know from research that the processes of reading and writing are mutually supportive. This is demonstrated repeatedly in models throughout this text, and the activities included in each part often engage students in both processes. Students learn to use writing as a complement to their reading and to clarify meaning for themselves.

❋ **Integrates using technology as an instructional tool for developing academic literacy.** Part 2 offers opportunities for students to develop critical and creative thinking through Using Technology activities that suggest technology-based assignments to enhance their text-based reading and learning experiences.

❋ **Provides for partner and collaborative activities.** Every chapter of Part 1 has several stopping points at which students compare their responses to questions with those of a peer or a group. This offers additional opportunities to think about their reading processes and to understand their personal responses to what they have read, as well as to understand different perspectives. These Working Together activities are identified by many activities in Part 2, including those in each *Critical Thinking: Reaction and Discussion* section, which are designed for collaboration.

❋ **Supports a variety of learning styles.** Questions and activities throughout the text are varied. Part 1 contains many visual models to accompany explanations of concepts. The many built-in occasions to discuss strategies, concepts, and interpretations with peers provide another avenue for learning. As students use the language of the text, they gain confidence in the use of new discourse patterns, concepts, sentence structures, and vocabulary that are common in academic settings.

❋ **Gives students responsibility for their own learning.** This text puts students in control of their reading. Instead of reading author-determined chapter summaries in Part 1, students create their own, based on ideas that will be useful to them. This process encourages students to take ownership of the ideas and to think about their wider application.

❋ **Provides alternative assessment opportunities for the instructor.** The *Extended Application* section at the end of each chapter in Part 1 invites students to apply developing strategies to whole texts. Every activity in Part 2 can be used for ongoing assessment. These options give instructors a fuller view of student progress than do traditional multiple-choice and standardized tests.

❋ **Lends itself to a variety of curriculum formats and teaching styles.** You may prefer to use this text in a straightforward way, progressing from one chapter to another, starting with Part 1 and gradually proceeding to Part 2; on the other hand, you might prefer to alternate between both parts of the text: students might apply the strategies from Part 1 to chapters in Part 2, as needed, or you might prefer to give more direction to the coordination between the two parts. You might also assign different chapters to different students, based on their learning styles, self-assessments, and areas of interest. Classroom activity may be largely independent, or you may want to convert independent assignments in each part into group and peer activities in order to increase the number of these already available.

However you decide to use this text, I hope it will meet your needs and serve your students well.

Acknowledgments

I wish to thank the many reviewers whose advice at different stages of the development of the fourth edition of this text assisted me: Dianne S. Cates, Central Piedmont Community College; Vicki Combs, Brescia University; Stephen R. Koelle, Rio Hondo College; Robert S. Mann, Des Moines Area Community College–Urban Campus; Myra M. Medina, Miami Dade College; and Marie A. Stokes, Stark State College.

Many individuals contributed to the efforts and encouragement necessary for completion of this book. In particular, at Houghton Mifflin my thanks to Lisa Kimball, Senior Sponsoring Editor, who played a key role in helping to define the final shape of the fourth edition text, and to Peter Mooney, Editorial Associate, whose meticulous attention to detail and guidance through development were greatly valued. Other individuals at Houghton Mifflin who made significant contribution to this edition are Andrew Whitacre, Marketing Associate; Annamarie Rice, Executive Marketing Manager; Eric Moore, Associate Project Editor; and Joann Kozyrev, Sponsoring Editor. I am also indebted to project manager, Merrill Peterson of Matrix Productions for ongoing assistance during the production stage. I owe much appreciation to my colleagues, especially Freda Wasserstein Robbins at New Jersey City University, and Gary Moorman at Appalachian State University, who helped me to select materials and develop apparatus to accompany the text. My students, too, are thanked for their revision suggestions for the fourth edition. I would also like to express my continuing gratitude to my friends, my children Allison and Miles, and my mom and sisters for their ongoing support and encouragement.

Jill Lewis
New Jersey City University

TO THE STUDENT

Imagine that you are driving in your car in an unfamiliar town, perhaps trying to get to a doctor's new office. You don't recognize street names or where to turn. You don't have any idea of the distance from one point to the next. And, even more distressing, landmarks known to local residents are totally unfamiliar to you and you cannot use them as reference points. A map with clearly labeled street names and understood landmarks would certainly help you find your way around this unknown territory.

Reading unfamiliar text is similar, in a number of respects, to driving in such a situation. If you don't know the subject matter you need to read, if you are uncertain about which comprehension strategies will help you with interpreting the material, or if you are unfamiliar with the writing style commonly used in a certain discipline, you are at a disadvantage compared to students who have prior knowledge and reading experience with that subject. Students who are equipped with a variety of strategies to use in different reading situations and who are already familiar with basic concepts and technical language of the subject will find the reading assignments and related classroom lectures easier to understand.

This book can serve as your *road map* to reading in many disciplines often studied in college. You will learn and apply reading and study strategies necessary to comprehend and retain academic material. The text also will introduce you to areas of study, or *disciplines,* that may be new to you. Your university may require that you take courses in these areas before you begin more specialized study in your major field. You will also learn the special reading requirements of each discipline, and you will participate in a number of activities that will serve as checkpoints for you in your travels through academic literacy.

The *Table of Contents* of this textbook identifies the "points of interest" on this map that you will encounter on your journey through this text. It also gives you the general picture of where you are. If you take a quick look at it now, you will notice that this text is divided into two parts, each of which has a different purpose.

Scan the entries for Part 1: *Handbook for Reading and Study Strategies,* to see what topics will be discussed. No doubt you are already familiar with much of the language in the chapter headings of this section, such as *topic, main idea, details, inference*. These are critical elements of text that form the basis for reading comprehension. Your ability to take notes and listen to lectures is also important for success in college.

Numerous *Activities* in the *Handbook* let you apply the reading and study strategies that are discussed in this section of the text. Although short reading passages are used within the *Handbook* for most of this practice, the *Extended Application* section at the end of each chapter asks you to apply the strategies to the complete articles found in Part 2. You will find opportunities for working with your classmates, sharing and refining your understanding of the strategies, and evaluating your success with applying them. Such *Working Together* activities are identified by ��� .

This *Handbook* is different from traditional skills development materials. It is based on the idea that it is more important for you to know *how* to do something than it is for you to get the right answer to every *Activity* question. You are frequently asked to think about the processes you are using to answer questions and to consider whether you need to make refinements in the strategies you use. This kind of practice will help you to transfer strategies you learn in the *Handbook* to your college readings assignments.

Another difference you will note is that in this book you are often asked to assess your ideas while you read and to write about what you notice about your reading process. In this way your reading and writing abilities are used to support each other. 🖊 indicates such *Thinking About Your Reading and Writing* activities. In many *Activities* you are also asked to justify, or to prove, your answers. To do this, you must think about *why* your answer is adequate or correct. You will need to look for evidence in the material. Making this self-analysis when you read is similar to what you do when you drive with a destination in mind. You make logical choices about which direction to take at each turn in the road. You also have goals when you are comprehending text. As you work with the *Activities* in the *Handbook,* it will not be sufficient just to select an answer. You will need reasons for your choices, and you will need to be able to explain them.

Return to the *Table of Contents* and note the organization of Part 2: *Background Essays for Academic Literacy*. This part is organized by discipline. These areas of study have been included because they are often required as part of the general studies programs college students must complete, and/or because of their popularity as major fields of study in college. Each chapter in Part 2 has a similar organization. Each discipline begins with a section titled *Key Concepts*. There are also *Guidelines for Reading* and several essays within the chapter. The *Key Concepts* section gives you background to prepare you for reading the essays and helps you to establish a focus for the specific subject area. It also enables you to form conclusions about the sorts of questions that might be investigated by people who work in particular fields.

The first reading introduces you to the subject area. From this essay, you will learn what someone who works in that field does or how such a person thinks. This is followed by a section with guidelines for reading the particular discipline. Here you are informed about the writing style or organization that is typically used in that field, the perspective from which authors generally write, or the reading pitfalls common to the discipline that you, as a reader, will want to avoid. These *Guidelines* differ from strategies presented in Part 1 because they are discipline specific. The remainder of the essays in each chapter of this text provide a sampling of issues, events, or concerns of that discipline.

Each essay includes a *Preview*. Here is a brief introduction to the essay, and you will be asked to consider a question, complete a diagram, or work with a partner on some activity related to the forthcoming reading. The major purpose for most of these prereading experiences is to help you recall what you *already* know about the topic of the essay to be read. Students who can *activate prior knowledge* have more information to use when reading to help them understand the new material.

A section titled *Postreading Comprehension Development* follows each essay. Within this section you will have an opportunity to evaluate your own under-standing of the essay. In the case of the introductory essay, you will verify your understanding of the discipline itself. The questions following the other essays verify your understanding of the content of the particular essay. Most of the comprehension questions focus on aspects of textual material that are addressed in the *Handbook*. The *Postreading Comprehension Development* section usually begins with an activity that asks you to evaluate the difficulty of the article and identify the reading strategies you used to comprehend the article. Then you will rewrite some important sentences from the selection, using your own words but keeping the original idea. Some questions have many possible answers. You will be asked to justify yours. A final *Postreading Comprehension Development* activity gives you an opportunity to go beyond the essay and to think critically about some issues related to it through debate, writing, or discussion. You will also be encouraged to use technology to further explore the readings. Often it is sug-gested that you work with a partner or in a small group on these. Opportunities to use technology are also provided.

The essays in this text may be longer and more difficult than those you have usually read. Many are taken from college-level textbooks and other sources that are typically used in college courses. Your ultimate aim is to read with compre-hension and to retain what you have read. You will be working toward this objective. Thus, you should not expect that you will immediately understand everything you read in this text. Consider this text as a starting point. It is the map, or plan, to help you reach academic literacy. But you are the driver. Ultimately you will choose the path to take and will need to figure out how to handle the curves and bumps along the way.

It is my sincere hope that once you have worked with this text you will feel better prepared for academic reading assignments because you can better comprehend academic text *and* because you know more about the various disciplines. You should then be able to experience success and enjoyment as you continue on your journey toward your college degree.

Jill Lewis
New Jersey City University

ABOUT THE AUTHOR

Jill Lewis serves on the board of directors of the International Reading Association (IRA) (2004–2007) and is Professor of Literacy Education at New Jersey City University of Jersey City, NJ, where she has taught developmental reading and teacher education courses in literacy for more than thirty years. She began her teaching career as an English teacher in public junior and senior high schools in Virginia and New York. She quickly realized her students' need to learn reading strategies and pursued an M.A. in Reading and Reading Specialist certification from George Washington University. Her interest in adolescent/young adult literacy extends to the international community. She currently serves as a Volunteer Consultant for the Secondary Education Reform Activity program in Macedonia and was also a volunteer in Macedonia, Kazakhstan, and Albania for IRA's Reading and Writing for Critical Thinking project. Her other contributions to the field are extensive and include chairing many committees for IRA and the New Jersey Reading Association as well as serving on several literacy task forces for New Jersey, including the Middle Grades Task Force and the New Jersey Task Force on Language Arts Literacy Standards. She has authored numerous professional articles and book chapters on adolescent and content literacy, professional development, and advocacy, and is lead author of *Educators on the Frontline: Advocacy Strategies for Your Classroom, Your School, and Your Profession*. Dr. Lewis received her Ed.D. from Rutgers University in New Brunswick, New Jersey, and she presents frequently at state, national, and international literacy conferences.

Handbook
for Reading
and Study
Strategies

CHAPTER ONE

Taking Control of Your Reading

WHEN A PILOT FIRST LEARNS to fly, it is mandatory that an instructor sit alongside the student pilot during flight time. After many hours of practice and a series of demanding tests, the student becomes a licensed pilot who can fly alone and who is totally in charge of what happens in the skies. Occasionally, situations not practiced in flight school might be encountered—perhaps tornadoes or engine trouble. But all the strategies learned in flight school ensure a safe flight.

In much the same way, you have spent many years in school, under the guidance of teachers, perfecting your literacy abilities. You have passed the test—been admitted to college—and are now ready to fly on your own. This chapter will give you some pointers that will help you stay in command as you proceed through what may be some turbulent reading situations—situations that you may not have been prepared for but that you can handle if you have some basic strategies in hand for managing the unexpected.

Assessing Your Academic Self-Esteem

How confident are you about your ability to participate in an academic environment right now? At what level is your academic self-esteem? It is useful to self-assess honestly about these issues when you first begin using this text so that you can immediately set your goals toward improving those areas where you have the least confidence. Through this self-assessment process, you will be able to identify your learning strengths and use them while you develop other areas you target for improvement.

The survey that follows asks a series of questions that you should answer based on your experiences and your knowledge of yourself. Think for a few minutes about each question before you rate yourself. Be as truthful as possible. The information you obtain is to be used for your own benefit. It is not a test! You will not be graded on your answers.

SURVEY OF ACADEMIC SELF-ESTEEM

Directions: For each item, circle the number that you feel best describes you as you are now. (1 = not true of me at all; 4 = very true of me)

1.	I can successfully prepare to take exams.	1	2	3	4
2.	I can figure out what will be asked on tests.	1	2	3	4
3.	I have successful strategies for taking notes on lectures and reading assignments.	1	2	3	4
4.	I know how to preview my textbooks.	1	2	3	4
5.	I know how to come prepared for class.	1	2	3	4
6.	I know how to mark and underline reading material for review purposes.	1	2	3	4
7.	I know how to make predictions when I read.	1	2	3	4
8.	I am able to answer questions in a college classroom.	1	2	3	4
9.	I am able to read a college textbook with understanding.	1	2	3	4
10.	I know when to slow down my reading rate for better comprehension.	1	2	3	4
11.	I know how to use context to get the meaning of unknown words in college-level material.	1	2	3	4
12.	I have good strategies for thinking critically about things I have read.	1	2	3	4
13.	I am able to figure out the main ideas of college-type reading materials (for example, sociology, business, psychology, science).	1	2	3	4
14.	I am able to set purposes for my reading.	1	2	3	4
15.	I can read and interpret maps, graphs, and charts.	1	2	3	4
16.	I know how to create summaries and visual aids to help me remember what I have read.	1	2	3	4
17.	I know how to distinguish between important and unimportant details when I read.	1	2	3	4
18.	I am able to participate successfully in a college classroom.	1	2	3	4

SURVEY OF ACADEMIC SELF-ESTEEM

19. I am able to ask a professor for help when I have a question.	1 2 3 4
20. I believe I will be admitted to the major of my choice.	1 2 3 4
21. I believe I have a lot of knowledge to share with others.	1 2 3 4
22. I believe I will graduate from college.	1 2 3 4
23. I believe I will have a successful future.	1 2 3 4

Let's analyze the results of your survey. The following chart shows the category into which different items fall. Place your ratings on the chart. Then respond to the question in Activity A.

SURVEY ANALYSIS

Category		Question Nos.							
Study Skills		1	2	3	4	6	14	16	
	Your ratings:	___	___	___	___	___	___	___	
Reading Skills		7	9	10	11	12	13	15	17
	Your ratings:	___	___	___	___	___	___	___	___
Participating in College Classrooms		5	8	18	19	21			
	Your ratings:	___	___	___	___	___			
Expecting a Successful Future		20	22	23					
	Your ratings:	___	___	___					

Questionnaire adapted from Jill Lewis, "The Effects of a Precollege Reading Course on the Academic Self-Esteem of Underprepared College Students," *Inquiries in Literacy Learning and Instruction,* College Reading Association Yearbook (Fall 1993): 47–55.

ACTIVITY A: Assessing Your Academic Self-Esteem

1. Based on the information you've obtained from this survey, what are your area(s) of greatest confidence? _____

2. In a few sentences, describe the academic self-esteem goals you would like to achieve this term. _____

_____

_____

Taking Control of Your Learning

Doing this self-analysis is the first step in taking control of your learning. But taking control also involves learning and using strategies that will allow you to achieve to your fullest potential, including how to create the best environment for your learning, how to perform in class so you can gain the most from that experience, how to use your textbooks to your best advantage, and how to read in ways that maximize your comprehension.

Taking Control of Your Learning Environment

One type of self-help tool enables you to examine and then, as far as possible, create your optimal learning environment so that you can complete your reading and other class assignments on time and come to class ready to participate in discussions. You will learn how to do this in this section.

Planning Your Time

As a college student you have many social opportunities, such as clubs, special events on campus, athletics, new friends. These will all compete for your time and attention. You may also have obligations to fulfill, such as a full- or part-time job, family, religion, and other personal commitments. In addition, classes and homework must now be a top priority for you. How can you avoid feeling overwhelmed? A planned approach will enable you to gain control of your time and to accomplish more of what you want to do, along with all of what must be done.

ACTIVITY B: Creating a Schedule

The first thing you can do to take control of your learning environment is to plan a schedule to accomplish all of your obligations—things you have to do no matter what. You will want to determine what your "must" activities are and how much time you need to allocate to each. Some examples of things that must be done daily might include:

Personal hygiene	Transportation to college
Child care	Class attendance
Housekeeping	Sleeping
Time at a job	Eating
Transportation to a job	Religious obligations

In the space provided, make a list of your daily or weekly "must" activities. Notice that this includes the amount of time needed just for attending class.

MUST ACTIVITY   DAILY TIME NEEDED

_____   _____

_____   _____

_____   _____

_____   _____

_____   _____

_____   _____

_____   _____

Next, make a list of the courses you are taking this semester. Then, although it may be too early to tell, and assignments do vary, guess how much time you think you will need to spend on outside assignments for each class. A rule of thumb is that you will need two hours outside time for every one hour in class.

CLASS   DAILY TIME NEEDED FOR OUTSIDE ASSIGNMENTS

_____   _____

_____   _____

_____   _____

_____   _____

_____   _____

Finally comes your wish list of things you would like to be able to do. A few examples are:

Dating   Clubs

Volunteer work   Visiting friends

WISH LIST

_____

_____

_____

_____

_____

_____

WORKING TOGETHER

With a partner, review the lists you have made. Determine whether you need to add or remove any items, or to shift any items from one category to another.

You are now ready to use this information as a self-management tool. By realizing early on how you need to budget your time, you will be able to manage your day-to-day commitments better and reduce stress. You will also feel more in control of your learning environment because you have made an effort to manage it.

Use the full-page grid here to draft a schedule that you will attempt to use for the next two weeks or so. You will revisit it to see how it has worked out for you and will be able to make modifications based on your experience. All the days and hours of the week have been indicated, and hours go from 6:00 A.M. until midnight. You may add additional hours if you start your day earlier or end it later.

Use pencil to record your tentative schedule. As you live with it, you may find that changes are necessary and you can easily make revisions.

Learning About Your Instructor

One of the first things beginning college students often notice about their college classes is that, unlike their teachers in high school, the instructors don't always "follow the book." In high school, your teachers may have reviewed each textbook chapter systematically, page by page. Homework pages were assigned, and class time was spent reviewing it. High school teachers usually have a set

PRELIMINARY SCHEDULE

	SUNDAY	MONDAY	TUESDAY	WEDNESDAY	THURSDAY	FRIDAY	SATURDAY
6:00 a.m.							
7:00 a.m.							
8:00 a.m.							
9:00 a.m.							
10:00 a.m.							
11:00 a.m.							
NOON							
1:00 p.m.							
2:00 p.m.							
3:00 p.m.							
4:00 p.m.							
5:00 p.m.							
6:00 p.m.							
7:00 p.m.							
8:00 p.m.							
9:00 p.m.							
10:00 p.m.							
11:00 p.m.							

curriculum that must be followed by all teachers in that school system (sometimes in that state) who teach a certain subject to a particular grade. In the college classroom, instructors have more leeway with curriculum.

The result may be that your college instructor will address the outside reading you have done only *peripherally,* that is, as a supplement to the other information given through a lecture. Sometimes class lectures may seem to have little connection to the assigned reading. In such cases, you will need to look for relationships. Perhaps the reading and lecture carried the same theme, were about the same period, or were examples of the same principle. You will need to make such connections on your own. On the other hand, many instructors use class time to review outside readings and to clarify areas of confusion. They may ask students to identify points of uncertainty from the reading or question students directly about the assigned reading.

From the start of the term, you will want to learn how each of your instructors will use outside readings during lecture periods. Knowing this will help you to prepare for each class.

Another difference you may find between high school and college is that college instructors may have much higher expectations of their students. You are given much more independence in college—you make many decisions on your own about your personal life—and your instructors expect you to make decisions about your academic life as well. In many cases, instructors don't check to see whether you have completed your assignments or give you detention for coming to class unprepared. Instructors expect that you will do assignments, and do them *well*. But it may not be until you take the final exam that you have an opportunity to show that you have been keeping up with the assignments and that you understood them.

It is critical, then, that you have some strategies for using your textbooks that will help you manage your academic reading on your own.

Taking Control of Your Comprehension

To be a successful reader, you also need to be in charge of what you read, how you read, and what to do when you do not understand something you are required to read. In the remainder of this chapter, you will learn some of these self-help tools for comprehending texts and for checking your understanding. Because you are in charge, however, it will be your decision whether or not to use these strategies. You are in command of your reading development from this point on.

Learning About Your Textbook

For practically every course you take at college, you will have at least one assigned text. You should spend time becoming familiar with each. Most texts have the following features that can assist you with your reading.

INTRODUCTION TO THE STUDENT.   You should thoroughly read this often-overlooked portion of a textbook. It will explain the text's purpose, and it will probably tell you the author's point of view or perspective. By knowing the author's purpose and biases from the start, you are in a better position to evaluate that author's interpretation of events or situations. For example, a liberal-minded person who is writing a critique of the George W. Bush presidency will most likely offer an assessment very different from that of a conservative author.

In the introduction or preface, you may also find the author's suggestions for using the book. The preface may identify different sections of the text that can assist you, and it may give an overview of the text's contents and an explanation of how each part contributes to the whole text.

TABLE OF CONTENTS.   The table of contents provides a map of the entire book. Consider each chapter title as a point of interest along the way. By scanning the table of contents, you will be able to determine the major areas that are covered in the text and the typical length of each chapter. From chapter headings, you can learn the direction the text will take. For instance, information may be arranged topically or chronologically. In the table of contents for some books, you may also find a listing of the subsections within the chapters, which will give you an even better picture of the overall contents.

CHAPTER TITLES AND SUBTITLES.   These two features of textbooks are *organizing aids* that will keep you focused while you read. From a quick scan of these before you read the rest of the chapter, you will know the scope of the topic within the chapter and how the author has organized the information. You will also be able to estimate how familiar you are with the subject. This information will guide the amount of time you should allow for your reading assignment.

CHAPTER INTRODUCTIONS.   An introduction to a chapter prepares you for what you will find in the pages ahead. The introduction may be separated from the rest of the contents and may even appear in a different type style, or it may be integrated with the rest of the contents at the beginning of the chapter. In the latter case, you can often tell that it is the introduction because it doesn't begin with a subheading. The types of information in introductions will vary. Some introductions will give you the major thesis or main points you will be learning in the chapter. You can use each main point like a peg on which to place the details as you proceed through the chapter. Other introductions may be anecdotes intended to spark your interest before you read the chapter. Assess the purpose served by the chapter introductions in each of your texts, and use them accordingly.

CHAPTER SUMMARIES.   The chapter summary is a review of the main points of the chapter. You will be making good use of the summary if you try to recall the details from the chapter that are related to each main point. The summary may be separated from the rest of the text and may even appear in a different type style. Or it may just be at the end of the chapter, integrated with the rest of the text. You should read the chapter introduction and summary before you proceed with more detailed reading. By doing so, you will see the total framework for the chapter. You will understand where the author is headed and will be more able to follow the route, through the details, along the way.

GRAPHIC AIDS.   Many textbooks use graphic materials such as graphs, charts, diagrams, and photographs to clarify information or to serve as examples for material in the text. To use a graphic aid effectively, you will need to analyze how the information on it is organized. Usually, there is a title that tells you what is depicted. *Graphs* usually depict quantitative data, such as percentages. They often show comparisons of the data and frequently comparisons over time. *Charts* may be used to organize information and to show relationships among people, events, and ideas that might otherwise be difficult to explain. For instance, a chart may show the variety of play activities of children in different countries from birth to age twelve, or forms of environmental pollution and the most common causes of them, as well as strategies for eliminating each. *Diagrams* that are clearly labeled can help you visualize information that is otherwise descriptive, such as a diagram showing cell division or one depicting how a television camera works. *Photographs* are subject to different interpretations. However, your textbook author may clarify for you, within the body of the text, what interpretation is preferred. Try to see it from the author's perspective, but don't be afraid to make interpretations of your own. In fact, with any graphic aid, you should try to draw your own conclusions in addition to those that are mentioned in the text.

CHAPTER QUESTIONS.   These are extremely useful for studying textbook material. They let you know what information the author believes students should have gained from their reading and what interpretations and conclusions could have resulted. It is a good idea to read these even before you begin the chapter. As with the titles and subtitles, prereading chapter questions will help keep you focused during your reading.

GLOSSARY.   The glossary is your dictionary for the book. Technical terms, which may or may not have been defined in the chapter where they first occurred, are listed here. Refer to it as you come across terms you do not remember that are important to the subject you are reading.

INDEX.   The index appears at the end of a text and lists topics discussed in the text or references particular people or events, along with their page numbers. It will assist you in finding material quickly.

ACTIVITY C: Assessing Your Textbooks

Complete the checklist for a textbook you are using this term. If your text does not have one of the features listed, note this.

Text: _____

_____

Course: _____

_____

How useful do you think each feature will be? Give reasons for your answer.

Introduction to the student _____

_____

Table of contents _____

_____

Chapter introductions _____

_____

Chapter summaries _____

_____

Chapter titles and subtitles _____

_____

Graphic aids _____

_____

Chapter questions _____

_____

Glossary _____

_____

Index _____

_____

Other features of this text _____

_____

Preparing Yourself to Read

Each time you begin a new text chapter, it is critical that you mentally prepare yourself to read. By doing so, you are again taking charge of your reading—putting yourself in control. Several strategies will help you do this.

ACTIVELY PREVIEW THE CHAPTER.   You will want to know what the chapter contents are before you begin reading the chapter. Does that sound odd? How can you know what it's about before you have read it? Actively previewing the chapter is the key. To preview, you read chapter introductions, summaries, chapter titles and subtitles, questions at the end of the chapter, and graphic aids. Whenever you have to read a new chapter or plan to review one you have already read, begin by skimming these essential parts. As you skim, think about how the chapter is organized, what the main topics are, what kinds of questions you are being asked, what the author's purpose for writing seems to be. Become as familiar as you can with what lies ahead in the chapter.

DETERMINE YOUR PRIOR KNOWLEDGE OF THE SUBJECT.   Ask yourself such questions as: How much do I already know about this subject? What have I read or heard about it? What about it is of interest to me? How might I be able to apply this information to my life? If you recognize your prior knowledge on a subject before you begin reading, your memory will provide information to help you comprehend new material in the text. Your memory will assist you in recalling related concepts, similar situations or characters, and your emotional responses to the subject. You will be able to make connections between the new information and what you already know, and these connections will make the new material easier to learn and more meaningful for you.

SET PURPOSES FOR YOUR READING.   This is another way to prepare for in-depth reading. Before you begin to read, you want to know *why* you are reading. Your reasons for reading can affect your speed and concentration as well as your ability to recall the material at a later time. Six common purposes for academic reading are to:

1. Preview a chapter to determine its contents.
2. Review major points from the previous night's reading before going to class.
3. Read with the intent to share the information with someone else in a study group.
4. Respond personally to what you are reading.
5. Learn everything in a chapter, including the minor details, in preparation for a test.
6. Assess the logic of an argument presented by an author.

Whatever your purpose, you should identify it at the outset.

SET AN APPROPRIATE READING SPEED.   Your reading speeds should vary, and they should be determined by your purpose for reading. Even if you are reading the same material several times, you may need to read it at a different rate each time.

Once you set your purpose, you can begin to assess whether you should skim the material quickly, as you would for purposes 1 and 2, or whether you need to read at a moderate speed, as you would for purposes 3 and 4. For purposes 5 and 6, you would need to use an even slower rate.

An additional factor that influences the speed at which you can read the text with comprehension is the *difficulty level of the material.* After you preread, assess your prior knowledge, and establish your purpose, you will be able to identify any difficulties the material may pose for you. Thus, the level at which the text is written, your background and interest in the material, and your purpose for reading will all influence your reading rate. To achieve an appropriate pace, try the following:

❊ Make an initial guesstimate of how quickly you can read a certain number of pages in the text (for instance, ten pages in one-half hour).

❊ Read at your intended pace, but make sure you are comprehending the material.

- ✳ See whether you reached your target. (Did you read ten pages in one-half hour with comprehension? Did it take more or less time?)

- ✳ Adjust your target accordingly so that you stay at a comfortable speed, maintaining comprehension, while accomplishing your purpose.

ELIMINATE DISTRACTIONS.   Finally, before you start your in-depth reading, identify those things that cause you to take your mind off your reading once you begin. This is sometimes the hardest step to take because it may require big changes in a few of your well-established study habits. Your determination to succeed, though, will get you past this hurdle. To eliminate distractions, you will first need to identify them. Distractions may include phones ringing, people talking, concerns about family or friends, poor lighting, music or television in the background, and other obligations. The list is practically endless. Once you've identified the negative influences on your studying, *develop a plan of attack*. For instance, if you are concerned about noise, music, people talking, or phones ringing, you will obviously need to find a more suitable place to study. Sometimes even libraries are noisy. If this is the case in your library, and noise disturbs you, you will need to look around campus or your neighborhood for a quieter place. You can take the phone off the hook during your study time to eliminate calls. Make a to-do list *before* you begin studying so that you will remember to call family or friends or to take care of other obligations afterward. By making the list before you open the text, you have eliminated the need to remember these things and thus will be more able to remember the text information.

 ## THINKING ABOUT YOUR READING AND WRITING

ACTIVITY D: Strategies for Preparing Yourself to Read

Think about the strategies you have learned for preparing yourself to read. List the strategies you think will be most useful to you. Explain how you will apply each one.

_____

_____

_____

_____

Staying Mentally Active While You Read

Have you ever felt that when you got to the end of a reading assignment, you had no idea what you had read? It's as though you hadn't spent the time reading the material at all! This is a common experience among students. Often it happens because you weren't aware that you weren't comprehending the material while you were reading. Your mind wandered, and you didn't notice this. There are self-monitoring strategies to use to help you avoid this experience, or at least to catch yourself before you are too many pages into the text. These strategies will keep you from having to reread all the material again, will save you time, and will improve your comprehension. What you do *during* your in-depth reading is at least as important as your prereading activities.

SELF-MONITOR.   When you *self-monitor,* you ask yourself questions about the text while you read in order to become more aware of how well you are comprehending the material. As you read and self-monitor, identify those parts of the text that you do or do not understand, note the ideas that seem particularly important to you, and determine whether you are able to see connections between ideas. Ask yourself: Does this make sense? What does this new information have to do with what I have read on previous pages? What can I predict or hypothesize based on this information? What conclusions can I draw? Your responses to these questions will be important indicators of whether you have comprehended the material. The monitoring will also keep you very focused on what you are reading.

CREATE QUESTIONS AND TRY TO ANSWER THEM.   Self-monitoring also involves using the subtitles of the chapters to ask questions *before* you read and then checking whether you can answer your questions *while* you read. For instance, you may read a chapter that includes the subheading, "Successful Television Advertising." The questions you create before you read this portion of the text might include: What are some characteristics of successful television advertising? What are some examples of successful television advertising? After reading this section of the chapter, you immediately verify your understanding of it by attempting to answer your questions.

RESTATE THE AUTHOR'S IDEAS IN YOUR OWN WORDS.   This strategy is critically important to your self-monitoring process. Use your own language to restate the author's ideas. If you are able to answer the questions you've created by restating the author's ideas in your own words, you will know that you have comprehended the material. If you are not able to, there are two possible explanations: (1) You may have had an unsuitable question, or (2) you may not have comprehended. You will need to either revise your question so that you can include the important information in your answer or to reread the material. The benefit of this strategy is that you will have realized your difficulty comprehending the material well before getting to the end of the chapter. Now you can give yourself another chance to understand the section you did not understand before going further with your reading. Some practice in paraphrasing and identifying ideas in sentences is provided in the Activities.

Taking Ownership of Ideas in Texts

A key to improving your comprehension of academic material is to be able to put the author's ideas into your own language. Your goal is to restate the text language well enough to verify that you have understood the main points. If you do not comprehend the material, you will not be able to do this. Furthermore, by restating the ideas in language that is more comfortable for you, you take ownership of those ideas and you will remember them longer. In a sense, you are rehearsing those ideas for a later, final performance in a class discussion or on an exam. When you restate ideas, you need to:

1. Identify the essential ideas in each sentence.
2. Look for important *embedded* ideas within long sentences.
3. Rewrite the ideas so that the main points are clear.

We next describe strategies to help you with each of these three steps.

Identifying Essential Ideas in Sentences

You are no doubt aware that most textbook authors write sentences that are quite different from everyday conversation. Text language is more formal, and ideas are sometimes complicated. A key to understanding academic texts is to apply some of the same language knowledge to reading text that you use when you are having a conversation.

When you listen to someone speak, you are trying to get to the essential meaning of what is being said. The same goal is true for reading. There are things you already know about sentence structure, and you use this knowledge automatically when you listen to someone speak. When you read academic texts, you may need to deliberately apply this knowledge. A brief review of some elements of grammar will help you recall how sentences are structured. Knowing about sentence structure is critical for comprehending text.

To find the essential meaning of a sentence, you will need to determine (1) who or what is being discussed, and (2) what is being said about the *who* or *what*.

These two parts of the sentence are sometimes referred to as the *subject* and *predicate* of the sentence. They provide the fundamental meaning, the basic thought, of the sentence. You may now start to recall some grammatical features of sentences that you have learned in English classes. You should remember that:

1. Some sentences may have more than one subject or verb, and the two subjects or verbs are usually joined by *coordinating conjunctions* such as *or, but, and, for,* and *yet.* Both subjects or both verbs are important.

   Example:

   John Dewey *and* Henry Rousseau had some worthwhile ideas about how children learn.

2. Some sentences have two or more important complete thoughts in them. Each thought has its own subject and verb. Each thought is critical to the meaning of the entire sentence. These two thoughts are also often joined by coordinating conjunctions, and they are separated by a comma. They may also be joined by a semicolon and no coordinating conjunction.

   Example:

   a. We do not know exactly how many regular gamblers are unable to control their gambling, *but* some experienced gamblers estimate that it is as high as 50 percent.

   b. We do not know exactly how many regular gamblers are unable to control their gambling; some experienced gamblers estimate that it is as high as 50 percent.

3. Some sentences will contain two ideas, but they are not equally important. In these cases, one part of the sentence, the most important part, is called the *independent clause.* It makes sense by itself and does not depend on the rest of the sentence for its meaning. The part of the sentence that also has a subject and verb, but that cannot stand alone as a sentence, is called the *dependent clause.* It depends on the rest of the sentence for its meaning. The two clauses are usually separated by a comma. Dependent clauses are often introduced by clause markers such as *because, when, as, since, that, so, although, where, if, unless, who, after, while, even though, which.*

   Example:

   If the union officials could not agree with management on a settlement, there would undoubtedly be a strike by the railroad workers.

🪑 WORKING TOGETHER

With a partner, create one example of each of the three types of sentences described earlier. Identify each type.

More About Predicates

Most sentences have simple as well as complete predicates. The *simple predicate* is the *what,* or the verb itself. It tells what is being said about the subject in the simplest terms. The *complete predicate* consists of the simple predicate plus words that add information necessary for the complete meaning of the sentence. In these cases, the important thought includes the complete predicate, not just the verb. In the following example, the simple predicate is underlined; the complete predicate is the underlined word plus the italicized words. Note the importance of the information in the complete predicate.

> **Example:**
>
> Parent groups <u>tried</u> *to get* more control over TV programming for children.

More About Clause Markers

You now know that clause markers often introduce a dependent clause. They can show the type of relationship that exists between the dependent clause and the independent clause in a sentence. This relationship can often be determined by figuring out the question the dependent clause answers about the independent clause. The marker introduces the answer. Here are some common questions clause markers introduce. The dependent clause is underlined, but the clause marker is italicized.

> 1. Which one (ones)?
>
> **Examples:**
>
> Many businesses *whose* <u>offices were near Ground Zero</u> moved to other locations in Manhattan or in New Jersey.
>
> The plants *that* <u>had not been treated with the chemical</u> showed greater leaf loss over a shorter period of time.

2. When?

    Examples:

    The interest rates on home mortgages were expected to rise *after* the Federal Reserve Bank raised the prime rate.

    When the twentieth century began, America was already an industrialized nation.

3. Who?

    Examples:

    The candidates *who* had presented their views at the open meeting had a good chance of being elected.

    The runner *who* came in last was cheered into the home stretch by the crowd.

4. How?

    Examples:

    The new recruits looked *as if* they were ready to furnish the needed strength.

    The social workers spoke *as though* the family would soon be reunited.

5. Why?

    Examples:

    You will need to take a course in keyboarding *so that* you can type more easily and more accurately.

    It was nearly impossible to identify the origin of the skeleton *because* it was so badly deteriorated.

6. Under what conditions or circumstances?

    Examples:

    If she touched the clay models, the blind girl was able to describe the clothes worn by the Victorians.

    The community resolved to establish its own nightwatch *unless* the police could do a better job keeping the gangs and drug dealers away.

Note that several questions may be answered by several clauses within a single sentence, as in the examples that follow. The clause markers have been italicized.

Examples:

a. Children usually make greater progress in their schoolwork *if* the number of hours of TV they watch is reduced *so that* they have more time for their homework.

b. The teen *who* won the archery contest *that* took place last weekend had been working on her archery skills *since* the age of six.

c. The countries *that* were near the Iraqi border were feeling more threatened recently *because* the United Nations' investigators had not been able to determine Iraq's nuclear power.

d. *After* she had investigated for two months, the anthropologist concluded *that* the shaman was well respected in the village.

WORKING TOGETHER

With a partner, decide which questions are answered by each underlined clause in examples a through d above.

Finding Embedded Ideas in Text

Textbook sentences are often lengthy. This can present a major problem when students attempt to restate main points because several ideas are often stated within, or embedded in, one long sentence. In this kind of sentence, the author is using multiple clauses and phrases. Readers must be able to unravel the sentence in order to identify the several ideas it contains.

It will help you to remember that even very long sentences have at least one independent clause with a main subject and verb, even though the subject and verb may be separated by dependent clauses and modifying phrases. The following two example sentences illustrate this point. In each sentence the independent clause, consisting of the subject and predicate, has been underlined, the clause markers have been circled, and those phrases that only modify either the main clause or a dependent clause have been italicized.

Examples:

1. A number of small businesses, (which) are businesses (that) are usually started *by people* (who) have developed a product or service (that) can be produced and sold only *in a new business* (that) is set up *for that purpose,* often evolve into large corporations.

2. Cognitive psychologists, who developed theories *about* how people learn and remember and who were also studying the thinking processes individuals use when they read and write, <u>made important contributions</u> *to the field of reading.*

Dependent clauses and modifying phrases may also appear at the beginning of the sentence, and in such cases you need to look further on in the sentence to find the main clause.

Example:

When the darkroom and his camera equipment were ready to go, <u>the photographer,</u> who had been asked to submit an entry to a national contest, <u>realized</u> he needed a different type of lens to achieve the effect he desired.

In other long sentences, the subject and a verb are very close to each other, but the sentence length prompts us to look toward the end of the sentence for the main verb. If you do this, you may feel as though you have lost your place in the sentence. This type of sentence is illustrated next. The main clause is underlined.

Example:

<u>The sugars and other organic materials formed by green plants constitute the basic fuels for all of us,</u> for when we walk, pound on a keyboard, or sing a lullaby, we are using the energy released by the combustion of sugars in our body.

Once you have identified the main subject and verb, you can separate out all the key ideas that are embedded in the rest of the sentence, as in the two examples that follow.

Example 1:

As more and more information was collected about the behavior of chimpanzees both in the wild and in captivity, the many similarities in the behavior of chimpanzees and humans became increasingly obvious.

In this sentence, the main idea is that there are *many similarities in the behavior of chimpanzees and humans.* It is stated near the end of the sentence. The following ideas all give important information about this main idea and are embedded in the remainder of the sentence.

Some embedded ideas:

1. A lot of research has been conducted on chimpanzees.
2. Research has been done to compare chimpanzees to humans.
3. Research has been done in the wild.
4. Research has been done in captivity.
5. Conclusions about the behavior of chimpanzees have been drawn from this research.

In the next example, the main subject and verb are near the beginning of the sentence, and they are followed by a series of descriptors that would be important to know if you were studying this material.

Example 2:

After developing and evaluating objectives, *the manager selects the overall policies* that will fulfill the company objective and still satisfy market, industry, and company criteria.

Some embedded ideas:

1. Managers develop objectives.
2. Managers evaluate objectives.
3. Managers select policies that are designed to meet the company objective.
4. Managers also have to consider the market when they set policy.
5. Managers also have to consider the industry when they set policy.

Determining which of the embedded ideas are important is usually a matter of finding those ideas that answer questions about the main subject and verb of the sentence. In Example 1, the question "What are the similarities?" is answered by the embedded ideas that are listed. In Example 2, the main subject and verb phrases generate the question "How does the manager select the policies?" The embedded ideas listed provide answers to these.

ACTIVITY E: Finding Embedded Ideas in Text

For each sentence, list as many important embedded ideas as you can.

1. Cloning could present some complicated issues that will prove difficult to legislate: cloning a child who is dying, cloning a cancer patient for her bone marrow or other organs for transplanting, cloning someone with superior physical or mental attributes, cloning oneself to

achieve immortality, cloning an array of superhuman fighters or workers.

From M. Harris, "To Be or Not to Be?" *Vegetarian Times,* June 1998, pp. 64–69.

EMBEDDED IDEAS:

a. _____

b. _____

c. _____

d. _____

2. Companies make use of general-purpose software such as word processors and database systems as well as more specialized software to manage records, prepare payroll, produce accounting reports, and analyze business finances.

EMBEDDED IDEAS:

a. _____

b. _____

c. _____

d. _____

Rewriting Sentences

Once you have identified the embedded ideas in a sentence and have restated them in your own words, you are ready to create a new, less complicated sentence that restates the author's idea. You will need to determine which of the embedded ideas are most important. You already know that important ideas will answer questions about the main subject and verb. In addition, you should consider the major focus of the paragraph, chapter, or article. This process is outlined in the following example, in which a key sentence has been italicized and then restated.

Example:

When Nelson Mandela spoke to black audiences before his retirement from public life in 1999, he often reminded them that democracy and majority rule in South Africa would not change the material circumstances of their lives overnight. *He rarely practiced the modern politician's art of telling his listeners what he thought they wanted to hear.* His message to white audiences was also sometimes not typical of an elected official who wanted to be reelected. He told the white citizens of South Africa that they must take responsibility for the past and that they would have to accept that their nation would now have majority rule.

Restatement (based on focus of paragraph and important information preceding and following sentence):

Nelson Mandela was not like most politicians because he did not speak to his audiences in ways that would especially please his listeners.

Activity F: Rewriting Key Sentences from Text

Each of the following paragraphs contains an underlined key sentence. Rewrite this sentence, keeping its main idea but simplifying the language. You should refer to the rest of the information in the paragraph.

1. Although school attendance is not compulsory, it is urged by many of the village leaders, and most Hopi boys and girls go to school for a period of from six to ten years. Regularity of attendance differs among Hopi families and Hopi villages, and children in groups that have adopted mainstream cultural values have the highest attendance records. When school interferes too greatly with ceremonial or economic activities, however, the children are likely to drop out for two or three days. To overcome this difficulty, last year the principal of the Polacca Day School persuaded the First Mesa leaders to hold some of the ceremonials on weekends, rather than during the week, and since this time, he reports, regularity of attendance has increased.

   Adapted from Laura Thomas and Alice Joseph, "Youth," *The Hopi Way* (Chicago: University of Chicago Press, 1944), p. 58.

   Your restatement: _____

   _____

   _____

2. The sense of taste conveys information mainly about the general chemical nature of potential food substances. Insects such as flies and moths taste with their legs and mouth parts, the receptors being in bristles on these appendages. In mammals, the taste receptors are taste buds, clusters of elongated ciliated cells set into depressions in the tongue. <u>Some chemicals stimulate buds in different regions of the tongue, and different taste sensations are then perceived.</u> The four primary tastes are sweet, sour, salty, and bitter. Stimulation of buds near the tip of the tongue produces sweet tastes; those at the back, bitter tastes; and those along the tongue edges, sour and salty tastes.

Adapted from Paul B. Weisz and Richard N. Keogh, *Elements of Biology,* 4th ed. (New York: McGraw-Hill, 1977), p. 290.

Your restatement: _____

_____

_____

3. <u>Global Betting & Gaming Consultants says the U.S. was the world's fastest-growing gambling market in the last decade, even though it had plenty of competition for that honor worldwide.</u> Global Betting estimates $900 billion was spent on legal wagers worldwide last year, leaving the industry with a $270 billion take, or gross revenues, after payouts. By the latter score, legal gambling is almost as big a business as steel. This isn't just a phenomenon of relaxed social strictures. There's a reason governments around the world are embracing this vice: to tax it. And few nations are traveling more quickly down this path than the U.S. Windfall: American government received $27 billion in "gambling privilege taxes" in 2000, calculates Christiansen Capital, a 45 percent increase since 1997. Two-thirds was from state-sponsored lotteries. Gambling now generates far more public revenues than either tobacco or alcohol.

From Richard C. Morais, "Casino Junkies," *Forbes,* vol. 169, no.10 (April 29, 2002), p. 66.

Your restatement: _____

_____

_____

THINKING ABOUT YOUR READING AND WRITING

ACTIVITY G: Self-Monitoring Strategies

Think about the strategies you have learned for self-monitoring. List those that you think will be most useful to you. Explain how you will apply each one.

_____

_____

_____

_____

Assessing Your Learning

The practice of checking your comprehension applies not only during reading, but also *after* you have completed the entire reading assignment. In the postreading assessment process, you will concentrate on tying together the main points of the material and connecting them to other knowledge you have. There are several steps you may take to assess what you have learned.

SPEND A FEW MINUTES MENTALLY SUMMARIZING THE ENTIRE CHAPTER.   What were the key points? What details for each key point can you recall? How does each main idea contribute to the whole of the information? Look again at headings, subheadings, and technical terms. Be sure you see the chapter as a whole, not just as bits and pieces of facts. The author has chosen to put all the details into a particular chapter because they have a relationship to one another. Focus on that relationship for a while.

If you still don't understand some part, it is critical that you reread that section for clarification. Again, try to connect the details and main points to see whether there are any remaining areas of uncertainty.

THINK ABOUT HOW THE NEW INFORMATION YOU HAVE LEARNED COMPARES TO WHAT YOU KNEW AT THE START OF YOUR READING.   To do this, you must recall the prior knowledge you had during the prereading phase. Ask yourself: What did I know then? What do I know now? You might also ask: What more would I like to know about this subject? These comparisons will show you how much you have gained from the reading; they also will enable you to connect your prior knowledge to new ideas and to adjust your thinking so that any misconceptions you had before reading will be modified.

CONSIDER THE OPINIONS AND ATTITUDES OF THE AUTHOR AND COMPARE THEM TO YOUR OWN.   This step is especially important if your reading is about a controversial subject. It requires you to make distinctions between facts and the author's opinions, to assess the logic of the author's ideas, to reconsider your opinions, and to identify support for either the author's ideas or your own.

THINK ABOUT HOW YOUR NEW KNOWLEDGE AFFECTS YOU PERSONALLY.   Once you have assessed your knowledge and are clear about the information, you can ask yourself: How can I apply this knowledge to my life? You may be reading about social issues, environmental issues, the economy, philosophical issues and points of view, or business matters. This process will make what you have learned more meaningful for you and will help you remember the material.

 ## THINKING ABOUT YOUR READING AND WRITING

ACTIVITY H: Postreading Assessment Strategies

Think about the strategies you have learned for postreading assessment. List those that you think will be most useful to you. Explain how you will apply each one.

_____

_____

_____

Using Outside Sources to Gain Background Knowledge

Textbook authors have often spent many years learning about a subject before they write their books. You do not have that privilege. You need to learn the information today, this week, or this term. Since the authors are so familiar with their subject, they often assume students have enough background knowledge to help them read the text. This is not always so. When you are confused or feel you can't understand some portion of your assigned reading, you can do many things to get outside assistance. The most obvious is to search the Internet for background information on the subject. There is a very wide range of material on the Web, but only some of it is accurate. In a later chapter, we will discuss how to assess the reliability of Web resources, but for now consider using the Internet to provide assistance when you read unfamiliar material. Here you may find better explanations than those your textbook provides or visuals that depict processes or relationships your textbook author assumes you know. You will find material that will supplement your reading and deepen your understanding.

You might also locate a tutor on campus. Your college probably has many students majoring in the subject that gives you difficulty. Some of these students are probably connected to a tutoring service. Often these services are free of charge and only cost you your time. The only drawback to using the college tutoring service may be that student tutors often lack teaching experience.

Another source of assistance is other books on the subject that may make fewer assumptions about what you already know. Such books may be available at your college library. You may find them at the public library, where the Young Adult section as well as the Adult section may have books about your subject. The past decade has seen an explosion in informational books for young readers, some of which are quite remarkable in their depth and quality. (If you feel embarrassed checking these out, you can always claim it is for a younger relative.)

Also consider people you know who could be sources for information and assistance on particular subjects. A relative who works in an auto factory may have considerable knowledge about air pollution. A friend working at a local restaurant or pharmacy can possibly explain, in simplified terms, some business principles to you. A teacher you know may be able to shed some light on issues raised in sociology or psychology texts. Try to explore every possible avenue for sources.

Once you have gathered all the outside information you need to help you understand the text material, you should sort through it and decide which ideas are more important or worthwhile. Reread the text material, which should now have more meaning for you. Then synthesize your new information with the knowledge you already have from outside sources. You are now ready to record the vital information, in your own language, for later use.

The following list gives you an opportunity to reflect on the outside sources that are available to you for courses you are taking this term.

Outside Source Action List

Course where you may need assistance: _____

Outside sources available to you: _____

_____

_____

Preparing for Tests

Students who have taken charge of their reading also know that tests are a fact of academic life. Examinations are the primary way in which many instructors are able to assess whether you have learned course content. Different instructors may give tests once or twice a term, weekly, or every few weeks. If you have used the strategies described in this chapter, you will be well on your way to success with tests. You will have used all available resources to check and expand your understanding, and you will have recorded what you know in language that is your own so that you have a usable set of study notes. Using these strategies will help to reduce significantly the test anxiety most students feel before taking an important exam. There are, however, still a few remaining things to do as you prepare to take tests. You should use some of these strategies several weeks before the exam. Others you will want to do shortly before the exam. And some are strategies to use during the exam. By following them, you can further reduce your stress level and raise your test scores!

SEVERAL WEEKS BEFORE THE EXAM:

1. Practice distributed review. This means to review your notes at regular intervals throughout the term. Don't wait until just before the exam to begin studying.

2. Identify the type of test you will be taking and prepare with that in mind. Even if you are familiar with the material, knowing the type of exam you will take can further guide your studying. If you are having an essay test, you will want to think of some broad questions that require you to synthesize the material, to argue for a position, to explain historical developments, or to contrast ideas, works of literature, or works of art. Once you have created your questions, practice answering these. Be sure you prepare an outline for each question because it will help you to remember the points you want to make during the exam.

   If your test is to be short answer (multiple choice, true/false), be sure to practice recall of such details that support key points, important dates, steps in processes, key biographical information, historical turning points, literacy devices used, or mathematical formulas.

3. Find a study partner. Study partners can help each other tremendously if they really focus on their task. They can prepare questions for each other to answer, and they can listen to responses to see whether the information is adequate. They can keep each other focused and provide encouragement.

SHORTLY BEFORE THE EXAM:

1. Make a final review of your notes the evening before the exam, including the practice questions you've created. Don't do anything afterward that will interfere with what you have reviewed, such as going to a party.
2. Get up a little earlier than usual the next morning to review your notes once more.
3. Take all materials you will need during the exam. These include a watch as well as any paper and pencils or pens you might need.
4. Be on time for the exam. If you arrive late, you are setting yourself up to do poorly. If you arrive too early, others may distract you.

DURING THE EXAM:

1. Sit in a quiet spot away from talkative and noisy people.
2. Read over all the directions on the exam before you begin. Spend a few minutes thinking about what is required before you begin.
3. Read every question carefully. You probably already know to pay attention to the language in short-answer questions, avoiding saying something is true when words such as *all, none, never,* or *always* are used in the question. For multiple-choice questions, look for such phrases as *most important* or *least important* to help you eliminate choices. Look, too, for distractors in these questions, choices that couldn't possibly be correct, so that you can reduce the number of possible choices you have remaining.
4. If you come to a question you can't answer, remind yourself that you don't need to get *every* answer right in order to pass.
5. Work from your strengths. If there are questions you definitely know, answer these first so that you can feel self-assured before tackling the more difficult questions.
6. Budget your time. Don't spend too much time on any one question.
7. Use all the time allowed to you. There is no need to be the first one finished. If you finish early, use the remaining time to review your answers and to spot and correct careless errors.

THINKING ABOUT YOUR READING AND WRITING

ACTIVITY I: Test-Taking Tips

1. Which of the tips about taking tests will benefit you?

_____

_____

_____

_____

2. What else do you think you can do to improve your test-taking strategies?

_____

_____

_____

_____

Congratulations! If you have been working with the strategies mentioned in this chapter, you have taken control of your reading. You now understand what is necessary for successfully reading academic texts, and you have accepted responsibility for monitoring your own comprehension. You can congratulate yourself on a job well done!

▶ *Chapter Summary*

Based on your reading of this chapter, list at least five ideas it contains that you believe will help you with future reading assignments. Write in complete sentences.

1. _____

_____

_____

_____

2. _____

_____

_____

_____

3. _____

_____

_____

_____

4. _____

_____

_____

_____

5. _____

_____

_____

_____

▶ *Extended Application*

Now that you have worked with the strategies necessary for taking control of your reading, you can practice applying them to full-length reading selections. Choose (or your instructor may choose) a reading selection from Part 2 of this book or another reading selection that is typical of what you will be expected to read for your other college courses, such as an essay or a textbook chapter. Use this selection to practice:

  ❋ Preparing yourself to read

  ❋ Staying mentally active while you read

  ❋ Taking ownership of ideas in text

Decide on the practice strategies you will use. Apply them to your selection. Then write, in a few paragraphs, a description of what you did and how the strategies you used worked for you.

Name of material used: _____

Page numbers: _____

Your description: _____

CHAPTER TWO

Strategies for Increasing Vocabulary: Using Context Clues, Word Parts, and the Dictionary

THREE TEENAGERS ARE IN A BIRDHOUSE-BUILDING competition to see who creates the most beautiful birdhouse in the shortest time. One has a set of directions and some lumber; the second also has directions and a hammer and nails; the third has the directions, hammer and nails, paint, and lumber. Who is most likely to win this competition? Of course, the one with the most tools—assuming he knows how to use them.

Building your vocabulary for academic work is much the same. You need several tools, including knowledge how to use context clues, word parts, and the dictionary. If all three are working for you, you are likely to be able to successfully tackle vocabulary challenges you face with your reading assignments.

Words are the tools with which you think, communicate, and learn. The more words you know, the better you can think, communicate, and absorb knowledge, not just about English, but about everything that is important to you.

In this chapter, we will explore all three tools and you will have opportunities to use each in ways that demonstrate what you've learned. You will find that some of this will be a review for you, but much of the information bears repeating and deeper explanation than you may have received at some other point in your education. Research tells us that one of the primary indicators of a student's ability to successfully comprehend text is that student's vocabulary.

What Do We Mean By Context?

Imagine you have seen a horrible movie on Friday night. The worst ever! Saturday morning, you are startled by a newspaper ad for that same film that includes quotations full of high praise from reviewers, such as "very appealing" and "a sure winner." You wonder how this movie could have gotten such a positive response. A little investigation might reveal that the reviews from which the quotations had come had not been flattering at all. The words quoted in the ad you saw had been taken *out of context.* In fact, the reviewers had actually said, "This movie is not very appealing," and "The director thought he had a sure winner. Boy, was he wrong!" The film advertisers, however, used only parts of sentences from the reviews. The *context,* all the words originally surrounding the quoted portion, conveyed critical information that moviegoers reading the ads did not receive. In much the same way, words in sentences take on particular meanings depending on the context in which they are used. In this chapter, you will learn how to analyze the context as well as some other strategies to help you comprehend the meaning of unfamiliar words.

How Will Context Help You Read Academic Text?

What's the first thing you should do when you come to a word you do not know while you are reading? Do you say, "Look in a dictionary for the meaning"? If so, you might be surprised to learn that this may not be the best course of action. You don't always need the dictionary to define unfamiliar words. In fact, you can often figure out the meaning of such words by using the word's *context.* That is, you can guess at the meaning of one word by thinking about the ideas that are suggested by the other words and sentences near it. This approach to vocabulary, called *using context clues,* lets you continue your reading. You don't interrupt your comprehension, something you would do if you took the time to use a dictionary. In fact, when you use context clues, you are doing some extra thinking about the meaning of what you have read, and you are, therefore, simultaneously developing vocabulary and comprehension skills.

You probably already use context clues even without being aware of it. In this part of Chapter 2, you will increase your ability to use them. To see how you are able to determine the meaning of unfamiliar words by using the context, complete both parts of Activity A.

ACTIVITY A: Learning What Context Clues Can Do for You
Fill in your responses to Parts 1 and 2 in this chart.

PART 1	PART 2	PART 1	PART 2
1. _____	_____	6. _____	_____
2. _____	_____	7. _____	_____
3. _____	_____	8. _____	_____
4. _____	_____	9. _____	_____
5. _____	_____	10. _____	_____
	Your Score:	_____ %	_____ %

Part 1. Here are some words you may not know. For each **boldfaced** word, select what you believe to be the best definition. Place your answers in the chart under Part 1.

1. **myriad** (a) miracle (b) great number (c) skilled person (d) painting
2. **permeated** (a) appointed (b) allowed (c) spread through (d) harmed
3. **castigate** (a) punish (b) support (c) confuse (d) search
4. **indigence** (a) poverty (b) culture (c) innocence (d) knowledge
5. **dogmatic** (a) courageous (b) cruel to animals (c) weak (d) dictatorial
6. **feign** (a) destroy (b) pretend (c) graceful (d) emotional
7. **renounced** (a) rejected (b) announced with force (c) expected (d) encouraged
8. **shun** (a) frighten (b) a Danish coin (c) voice an opinion (d) avoid

9. **replete** (a) full (b) imaginative (c) brightly colored insect (d) cautious

10. **vulnerable** (a) confusing (b) open to attack (c) ready for action (d) scarce

Part 2. Select the meaning for each **boldfaced** word from the choices that appear beneath each sentence. Place your answers alongside your answers for Part 1.

1. Because the sky was so clear, we were able to see a **myriad** of stars.

   (a) miracle (b) great number (c) skilled person (d) painting

2. When the smoke from the cigar **permeated** the lounge, the visitors apologized.

   (a) appointed (b) allowed (c) spread through (d) harmed

3. The dictator said he would **castigate** anyone who opposed him.

   (a) punish (b) support (c) confuse (d) search

4. The family's **indigence** meant they could not afford to buy a house or send their children to college.

   (a) poverty (b) culture (c) innocence (d) knowledge

5. The **dogmatic** leadership style of the chairperson practically guaranteed that she would not be reelected for a second term.

   (a) courageous (b) cruel to animals (c) weak (d) dictatorial

6. If she could **feign** sleep, the child thought that she would not have to take her medicine.

   (a) destroy (b) pretend (c) graceful (d) emotional

7. The new CEO **renounced** some of the previous leader's ideas, considering them too old fashioned for today's consumers.

   (a) rejected (b) announced with force (c) expected (d) encouraged

8. In order to protect himself, the new boy in school had to **shun** the class bully.

   (a) frighten (b) a Danish coin (c) voice an opinion (d) avoid

9. The Christmas tree was **replete** with ornaments that had been collected over a fifty-year period.

   (a) full (b) imaginative (c) brightly colored insect (d) cautious

10. The assemblyman commented, "I don't think there's been any time since the beginnings of Reconstruction or the depths of the Depression that our family structure has been so **vulnerable.**

    (a) confusing (b) open to attack (c) ready for action (d) scarce

The answers to Parts 1 and 2 are b, c, a, a, d, b, a, d, a, b. Check your work. How did you do? Did your context clues help you? In a few sentences, describe the results you found.

_____

_____

_____

_____

What Is the Process for Using Context Clues?

You can best understand the answer to this question if you try to observe yourself and what you do when you read material containing an unfamiliar word. Read the following paragraphs and try to figure out the meaning of the word that is italicized. As you do this, ask yourself, "What am I doing to get the meaning of this word?"

Paragraph 1:

Many researchers initially believed that unusual climatic conditions in the Antarctic atmosphere caused the ozone hole. Intensive studies showed, however, that although climate certainly contributes to the development of the ozone hole, the primary cause of ozone *depletion,* without question, is CFCs, or chlorofluorocarbons. Evidence to support that conclusion came from two intensive studies of the Antarctic stratosphere during the springs of 1986 and 1987.

Adapted from Richard Golub and Eric Brus, eds., *The Almanac of Science and Technology* (Boston: Harcourt Brace Jovanovich, 1990), p. 32.

What do you guess is the meaning of *depletion*?

_____

In a few sentences, explain how you formed this definition.

_____

_____

_____

Paragraph 2:

It is difficult to form generalizations that apply to all Spanish-speaking people in the United States. Since the Hispanics of the Southwest have tended to remain quite rural and isolated until recently, they have encountered very little formal discrimination. The much larger Mexican-American group, however, has been discriminated against in every way, and there is growing impatience and militancy in the barrio, or ghetto. On one hand, there is the desire to merge with the dominant group. Some studies indicate that second- and third-generation Mexican Americans are undergoing rapid *assimilation.* In Los Angeles, for example, Mexican Americans are marrying out of their ethnic community to a much greater extent than ever before. Others, however, are opposed to this trend and prefer to stay within their own cultural group.

What do you guess is the meaning of *assimilation*?

_____

In a few sentences, explain how you formed this definition.

_____

_____

_____

You may find that you have used a combination of strategies to figure out the meanings of unfamiliar words. Some of the strategies are listed next. Check all that you used.

❋ I used my prior knowledge of the word. _____

❋ I tried to pronounce the word. _____

❋ I looked for roots or prefixes in the word. _____

❋ I looked for definitions in the sentence. _____

❋ I looked for words in the sentence that had the opposite meaning. _____

❋ I looked at the other sentences in the paragraph for relationships to the sentence with the unknown word. _____

WORKING TOGETHER

Compare your responses to this checklist with a partner's. Did you use the same strategies? Why do you think your strategies were similar or different?

If you are skilled at using context clues, you will be able to figure out an approximate meaning of the unknown word. There are several different types of context clues. The next section introduces those that are most useful to readers of academic text.

What Are the Most Useful Types of Context Clues?

Several kinds of context clues appear in academic texts. Five that we will review here are:

> **contrast or antonym clues**
>
> **restatement or synonym clues**
>
> **definition clues**
>
> **illustration or example clues**
>
> **experience or common-sense clues**

Each type has certain signal words that are associated with it. *Signal words* alert readers to the type of clue being used. Here are illustrations of these five common types of context clues and the signal words often present with each type.

Contrast or Antonym Clues

One type of context clue is the *contrast clue,* or *antonym clue.* With this type of clue, the author provides you with a word or phrase that is the opposite, or antonym, of the word you may not know. If you know the meaning of the contrasting word, you will be able to figure out the definition of the unknown word. The antonym usually appears in the same sentence as the unknown word, or very close by. Signal words within the sentence containing the antonym may be used to alert you to it. These contrast signal words include *although, on the other hand, however, but, nevertheless, on the contrary, instead, yet, unlike, conversely, in contrast, than* _____. These are often used to indicate contrasts between individual words or concepts. There can also be a contrast between individual words or concepts without the presence of a signal word. In this case, you will rely solely on the context, without the signal word, to help you determine the meaning of the unknown word.

Example:

The mood of the music on the radio was *somber,* unlike the cheerful tunes the child had been singing before she got into the car.

Antonym or contrast clue: <u>cheerful</u>

Meaning of unknown word: <u>sad</u>

Explanation: The word *unlike* is a clue to the contrast between *somber* and *cheerful.* Because we know what *cheerful* means, we can guess at the meaning of *somber.*

Example (without signal word):

The mood of the music on the radio had become *somber.* The cheerful tunes the child had been singing before she got into the car were gone.

Explanation: The contrast is still here, but without the signal word. However, the verb phrase *were gone* indicates the contrast between *somber* and *cheerful.* Because we know what *cheerful* means, we can guess at the meaning of *somber.*

ACTIVITY B: Contrast and Antonym Clues

For each unknown word in italics, indicate the opposite or contrast clue available to you in the sentence(s). Then write the meaning of the unknown word.

1. Melissa was *undaunted* when she had to speak in front of her class but was very fearful about giving a talk before the entire group of freshmen.

   Antonym or contrast clue: _____

   Meaning of unknown word: _____

2. The honor *bestowed* on the athlete was taken away once it was learned he had been on steroids.

   Antonym or contrast clue: _____

   Meaning of unknown word: _____

3. I would have *squandered* my whole week's earnings; however, my best friend encouraged me to save some of the money for next week's dance.

   Antonym or contrast clue: _____

   Meaning of unknown word: _____

4. The old man seemed *eccentric,* but to those who really knew him he was perfectly normal.

   Antonym or contrast clue: _____

   Meaning of unknown word: _____

5. Although the teller was an *underling,* the bank manager treated her with great respect.

   Antonym or contrast clue: _____

   Meaning of unknown word: _____

Restatement or Synonym Clues

A second type of context clue is the *restatement clue,* or *synonym clue.* A word or phrase that has a meaning similar to a word you don't know placed in or near the sentence with the unknown word gives this type of clue. If you recognize the similar word or understand the meaning of the phrase, you will be able to approximate the definition of the word you do not know.

> **Example:**
> She made a *resolution* that she would quit smoking, the fourth time she had made such a promise, so we were not convinced she would really stop.
>
> **Restatement or synonym clue:** promise
>
> **Meaning of unknown word:** promise
>
> **Explanation:** The phrase *such a promise* contains a synonym for *resolution.* The meaning of this phrase refers you to what has just been said. This makes it easy to figure out that *resolution* means *promise.*

ACTIVITY C: Restatement and Synonym Clues

For each unknown word in italics, indicate the clue available to you in the sentence(s). Then write the meaning of the unknown word.

1. Jose's *gratitude* was immeasurable. He couldn't thank his girlfriend enough for helping him find a part-time job.

   Restatement or synonym clue: _____

   Meaning of unknown word: _____

2. After the injury to his leg, the tennis star quickly regained *mobility,* and he could move easily on the court.

   Restatement or synonym clue: _____

   Meaning of unknown word: _____

3. She was so *incensed* at the animal trainer's cruelty that she could not watch any more of the animal acts without being angry.

   Restatement or synonym clue: _____

   Meaning of unknown word: _____

4. There was such a *preponderance* of mail for one member of the jazz band that the others began to be jealous of the huge piles of it that arrived every day.

   Restatement or synonym clue: _____

   Meaning of unknown word: _____

5. During the highly negative campaign, each candidate sought to *discredit* the other.

   Restatement or synonym clue: _____

   Meaning of unknown word: _____

Definition Clues

The *definition clue* is much like the restatement or synonym clue, except that the author *deliberately* provides the meaning of the unknown word. This is often done through the use of punctuation: commas, parentheses, brackets, or dashes that set off the definition. Helping words such as *that is, such as,* or *which means* are also sometimes used to signal the definition.

   Example 1: Definition with commas

   The sculptor's income was *commensurate* with, or equal to, his ability as an artist.

   Clue indicator: commas that set off the definition

   Explanation: The unknown word *commensurate* is defined by the words between the commas.

Example 2: Definition with parentheses

EEGs (tracings of the brain's brain wave activity) were first systematically used in the 1930s when researchers began to study eye movement.

Explanation: The words in parentheses provide a definition of EEGs.

ACTIVITY D: Definition Clues

For each word in italics, indicate how the author signals that a definition is being provided.

1. The *Anasazi,* the group of American Indians living in the Southwest from 1000 to 1300 C.E. (Common Era), lived in cliff dwellings.

   Author's signal: _____

2. It is a *universal* truth—one that all people accept—that success is usually the result of a combination of hard work and good luck.

   Author's signal: _____

3. Our *forbearance,* or patience, made it possible for us to complete the entire experiment properly and to get satisfactory results.

   Author's signal: _____

4. The *petiole* (the stemlike part of the leaf) joins the blade to the stem.

   Author's signal: _____

5. *Photocopying* is the practice of using a copy machine to reproduce parts of books, magazines, newspapers, or pamphlets.

   Author's signal: _____

Illustration or Example Clues

An author may provide *illustration clues,* or *example clues,* to define a complex concept or clarify very important ideas. The reader is able to use these illustrations or examples to create a definition for that concept or unknown word. Words that signal an illustration or example include *for example, for instance, such as, to illustrate.* These phrases are very common in academic text.

Example 1:

Everyone in the scientific community knows that our weather system is *aperiodic.* Nature is full of other examples: animal populations that rise and fall almost regularly, epidemics that come and go on tantalizingly near-regular schedules.

Explanation: The unknown word, *aperiodic,* is explained through the other examples in nature that are given. These examples describe natural events that occur in cycles that are not quite regular. The word *aperiodic,* then, must refer to something that occurs in irregular cycles.

Example 2:

Some people believe that morality in our culture has *retrograded.* For instance, young people are no longer waiting until marriage to have sex. News articles regularly report increases in all kinds of crime. Everywhere one can see growing evidence of crooked politicians. Perhaps the critics are correct.

Explanation: The unknown word, *retrograded,* is clarified through the use of examples. A close look at the examples shows they each refer to changes—change in attitudes toward premarital sex, growth in crime, and increase in crooked politicians. None of these changes are positive. Note also that the first example is introduced by the signal words *For instance.* Using all this information, we can determine that *retrograded* must mean going backward from a higher level in a society.

ACTIVITY E: Illustration and Example Clues

Use the information in each paragraph to define the italicized unknown word. Write your definition in the space provided.

1. Forcing a dominated group to abandon its own language is an important part of *deculturalization.* Culture and values are embedded in language. Educational policymakers in the nineteenth and early twentieth centuries believed that substituting English for Native American languages and for Spanish was the key to *deculturalization.* But the language issue created the greatest resistance by dominated groups. The attempt to change the languages of the groups under consideration may have been the major cause of the limited effectiveness of *deculturalization* programs.

   From Joel Spring, *Deculturalization and the Struggle for Equality,* 3d ed. (New York: McGraw-Hill, 2001), p. 90.

   Your definition: _____

2. A popular way to use imagery is through *mnemonic* devices. The basic process of a mnemonic system consists in taking something that has known imagery content and then associating to its images of things to be learned. Such devices are used by stage magicians to learn the names of people sitting in the audience. A person good at this procedure can learn the names of 100 people after hearing them only once. The famous Roman orator Cicero was the inventor of an early system called the method of loci. He used the images associated with walking to different parts of his garden to learn the order of ideas in his speeches.

Adapted from Anthony F. Grasha, *Practical Applications of Psychology,* 2d ed. (Boston: Little, Brown, 1983), p. 112.

Your definition: _____

3. Managers can improve their efficiency by *delegating* work. Delegating is important for several reasons. First, it frees a manager from some time-consuming duties that can be performed by subordinates. Second, decisions made by lower-level managers usually are more timely than those that go through several layers of management. Third, subordinate managers can reach their potential only if given the chance to make decisions and to assume responsibility for them.

Adapted from Jerry Kinard, *Management* (Lexington, MA: D. C. Heath, 1988), p. 191.

Your definition: _____

4. My eleventh-grade math teacher had few friends among the student body. We considered him a highly *captious* individual. For example, he often put poor-quality homework papers on display and never told the unfortunate souls who wrote them how they could improve their work. If a student saw him in the hall and offered a kindly "hello," Mr. Boise only snapped back an unfriendly grunt along with some suggestion such as, "You're late to class," or "Why don't you get a haircut?"

Your definition: _____

5. My elderly father had become more *sedentary* than I had originally thought. When I went to visit him, the changes in his behavior were clear. He no longer went for his daily walk. He spent many hours sitting on the front porch watching the birds and listening to the rustle of the trees. He didn't visit friends as he used to. My husband and I became so concerned that we finally suggested he might want to come to live with us.

Your definition: _____

Experience or Common-Sense Clues

A fifth type of context clue is the *experience clue,* or *common-sense clue.* In sentences with this type of clue, the author describes a situation that you are probably familiar with or that you can imagine. By using your experience, or by considering what would make sense in the situation described, you will be able to figure out the meaning of the unknown word.

> **Example:**
>
> The low temperatures and cloudy sky *foreshadowed* the snowstorm that was soon to come.
>
> **Unknown word:** foreshadowed
>
> **Experience or common-sense clue:** low temperatures; cloudy sky
>
> **Meaning of unknown word:** suggested; indicated beforehand
>
> **Explanation:** In this sentence, the reader is told about three things: low temperatures, a cloudy sky, and a coming snowstorm. If the reader asks, "What is the relationship among these three things?" it makes sense to say that the low temperatures and cloudy sky are signs of the storm. Thus, *foreshadowed* must mean they are signs of, they suggest, they indicate beforehand.

ACTIVITY F: Experience and Common-Sense Clues

For each unknown word in italics, indicate the clue given in the sentence. Then write the meaning of the unknown word.

1. The accused was *exonerated* of all charges after the judge learned that the lab work performed on the fingerprint found at the crime scene was faulty.

   Experience or common-sense clue: _____

   Meaning of unknown word: _____

2. I was *repulsed* by the stories of conditions in the concentration camps during the Holocaust.

   Experience or common-sense clue: _____

   Meaning of unknown word: _____

3. The typical *surrogate* mom is 28, married, employed, and solidly middle class and wants to help people have families.

   Experience or common-sense clue: _____

   Meaning of unknown word: _____

4. The *cherished* photographs were wrapped carefully in tissue paper and placed in a velvet-lined trunk, which would be kept safely in the attic.

   Experience or common-sense clue: _____

   Meaning of unknown word: _____

5. Using statistics from last year, the World Wildlife Fund has been able to *conjecture* the rate at which humans will slash and burn tropical forests this year

   Experience or common-sense clue: _____

   Meaning of unknown word: _____

THINKING ABOUT YOUR READING AND WRITING

ACTIVITY G: Reviewing Context Clues

Review each of the five types of context clues explained in this section. Then answer the following questions.

1. Which of these clues were most familiar to you?

   _____

   _____

2. How can knowledge of these clues help you with your writing?

   _____

   _____

   _____

   _____

ACTIVITY H: Defining Words Without Using a Dictionary

Without the use of a dictionary, define each of the italicized words or phrases in the following paragraphs. Then, in the space provided, indicate how you obtained the definition. In some cases, something other than, or in addition to, context may have helped. If you used context clues, indicate which one(s) helped you.

1. It was soon common knowledge that Washington intended to appoint Hamilton as secretary of the treasury. Undoubtedly, this knowledge was the primary motivation when Congress passed legislation that would prevent the president from granting the secretary too much power. The opponents of strong government feared Hamilton's views and his undoubted abilities, and they wished to *hamstring* him from the start.

   Word or phrase to define: *hamstring*

   Your definition: _____

   The process you used: _____

   _____

   _____

2. Fat babies have been thought to be healthy ones, which is not necessarily so. Fat babies are sometimes praised for being good babies because they seem to fuss less and are less active than thinner babies. Studies have shown that physical activity is habit forming. If we are in the habit of being active, we feel restless when inactive. If we are inactive and *lethargic,* we feel more comfortable that way. Babies should be encouraged to be active and to play so that they will get into the habit of being dynamic rather than vegetative. This will definitely aid in fat prevention.

   Word or phrase to define: *lethargic*

   Your definition: _____

   The process you used: _____

   _____

   _____

3. As long as parents don't abuse or neglect their children, U.S. law gives them the authority to make their own decisions about their children's welfare. However, parents' authority is not *absolute.* Children do not have to obey parents who order them to do something dangerous or illegal. Parents who mistreat their children can be charged with child abuse. Moreover, parents cannot allow their children to run wild or do anything they want. If they do, the parents can be charged with contributing to the delinquency of a minor. For example, a father who encourages his son to use drugs could be convicted of this crime.

From Edward T. McMahon et al., *Street Law: A Course in Practical Law,* 3d ed. (St. Paul, MN: West, 1986), p. 219.

Word or phrase to define: *absolute*

Your definition: _____

The process you used: _____

_____

_____

4. In farming their unstable and harsh country, the Ifugao have acquired a thorough familiarity with local drainage patterns. Their understanding of hydraulic technology, combined with excellent stonemasonry skills and the simplest of hand tools, have enabled them to create the world's most extraordinary system of *rice terracing.* Ifugao rice terraces are sturdy stone walls that can reach as high as 50 feet, and are constructed along the land's natural contours. When finished, the terraces are backfilled and another wall at a slightly higher elevation is constructed. By repeating this process from valley floor to mountain peak, the Ifugao are able to construct their rice fields on the steepest of slopes. But sites are selected carefully, because the terraces require an elevated water source to flood the fields during the growing season. An elevated water source is also of great assistance during initial construction. The dammed water can be released to assist in moving the many tons of boulders, stones, and earth required in a new terrace. Irrigation water is frequently brought from great distances by ingenious stone-lined channels and hollow log or bamboo aqueducts that cross canyons and chasms and snake around the sides of mountains.

From John Fowler, *The Ifugao: A Mountain People of the Philippines.* From http://www.tribalsite.com/articles/ifugao.htm. Retrieved June 6, 2002. Reprinted by permission of the author.

Word or phrase to define: *rice terracing*

Your definition: _____

The process you used: _____

_____

_____

5. How do animals such as homing pigeons have such an amazing navigational ability? Experiments suggest that many animals use earth's magnetic field for guidance. People do the same with compasses, and many animals seem to have internal compasses. Embedded in their bodies are tiny crystals of an iron oxide called *lodestone*. Like iron filings attracted to a bar magnet, these crystals *orient* in the direction of earth's magnetic poles. By sensing this orientation, homing pigeons can determine the direction to their loft.

Word or phrase to define: *lodestone*

Your definition: _____

The process you used: _____

_____

_____

Word or phrase to define: *orient*

Your definition: _____

The process you used: _____

_____

_____

WORKING TOGETHER

Compare your responses with those of a partner.

1. Which of your definitions were similar?

2. In what ways were the processes you used for defining words similar or different?

3. What reasons can you give to explain the similarities or differences in the processes you each used for defining words?

Word Structure: A Clue to Word Meaning

What are the origins of the English language? A look at its history can be quite fascinating. Some of our words in English can be traced to a remote past; some have histories that began yesterday or are even beginning today. Sometimes there are swift new coinages of science or slang, as with such phrases as *text messaging*.

When we study word structure, we analyze *affix*es (which are *prefixes* and *suffixes*) and *word roots,* sometimes referred to as *base words*. *Affix*es are word parts that appear at either the beginning of words (*prefixes*), or the end of words (*suffixes*). The word *undeniable* has two affixes, a prefix (*un-*) and a suffix (*-able*). We are able to form many words from word roots or base words. For example, the word *graph* is a base word. Using it as a base, we are able to form the words *phonograph, graphic, grapheme, autograph, spectrograph, monograph, photograph,* and so on.

Many of these word parts have their origins in other languages. Anyone trying to learn a second language knows that when words of the language being studied share a common affix with your native language, it is easier for you to determine the meaning of the foreign word. Many English words, for instance, have their origin in other languages; 60 percent of these root words are Latin or Greek. When prefixes and suffixes are attached to the root to create other words, these are always some variation of the root word. Note how, in the example that follows, the meaning of the root *scribere* remains central to the meaning of a wide number of other words in which it appears. All of the words, in one way or another, have to do with writing.

root:	*scribere* (L), to write
scribe	[n] an official or public secretary or clerk; a copier of manuscripts
	[v] to work as a scribe; write
transcribe	to make a copy of (dictated or recorded matter) in longhand or on a machine
subscribe	to pledge or contribute; to sign one's name at the end of a document
inscribe	to write, engrave, or print as a lasting record
describe	to represent or give an account of in words
prescribe	to write or give medical prescriptions, to lay down a rule

All of these examples have prefixes before the root. It is possible for a word to have more than one prefix. When this occurs, the meaning of each prefix is needed to arrive at the complete meaning of the word. Note how the prefixes are combined for meaning in the following examples. The original root word is also indicated.

> **redistribute**   to divide among several or many again
> *re:* again
> *dis:* apart
> (root: French *tribere*—to allot; to give)
> **undiscernible**   unable to recognize as separate and distinct
> *in:* not
> *dis:* apart
> (root: French *cervere*—to shift; to sort)
> **inconclusive**   leading to no conclusion or definite result
> *in:* not
> *con:* with, together, thoroughly
> (root: French *claudere*—to shut)

The suffix appears at the end of a word. Suffixes have a grammatical function. They can, for instance, be used to change the part of speech, the tense, the plurality of a word. The following chart shows some of the most common suffixes for nouns, verbs, adjectives, and adverbs.

COMMON SUFFIXES

Noun suffixes	-dom , -ity, -ment, -sion, -tion, -ness, -ance, -ence, -er, -or, -ist, -ade, -ization
Verb suffixes	-en, -ize, -ify, -fy
Adjective suffixes	-ive, -en, -ic, -al, -able, -y, -ous, -ful, -less, -ette
Adverb suffixes	-ly

Notice how some of these changes occur in these examples:

> **dramatization**   the art or act of dramatizing, as of a literary work
>
> **dramatize**   to adapt (a literary work) for performance
>
> **dramatic**   of or relating to drama or the theater
>
> **dramatically**   with expression or emotion

ACTIVITY I: Understanding Word Parts

For each word part listed, think of a word that uses the same word part. On the lines provided, explain how your word keeps the word part's meaning. In each case you are told whether the word part is a prefix, suffix, or base or root word, and you are given its meaning.

      Example: -cide   (suffix meaning *kill[ing]*)

      Your word: herbicide

      How this word relates to the word part: A herbicide kills garden insects so plants can live.

    1. inter- (prefix meaning *between*)

      Your word: _____

      How this word relates to the word part: _____

      _____

    2. gene (base word meaning *genetic material*)

      Your word: _____

      How this word relates to the word part: _____

      _____

    3. cred- (prefix meaning *believe*)

      Your word: _____

      How this word relates to the word part: _____

      _____

    4. audi (root meaning "hear")

      Your word: _____

      How this word relates to the word part: _____

      _____

    5. homo- (root meaning "same")

      Your word: _____

      How this word relates to the word part: _____

      _____

ACTIVITY J: Recognizing and Using Word Structure

For each word listed, (a) identify the prefix, root, and suffix, as indicated, and provide a definition for the word. Then (b) think of another word that uses the same prefix and write its definition. Then think of another word with the same root and write its definition. Your definitions may be approximations. Determine the part of speech that the suffix creates and write this information. If you can't answer one part of the question, continue to the next. Answers to later questions may help you with earlier ones you did not know. Write your answers in the space provided.

Example: *biographical*

a. **Prefix:** bio

Prefix meaning: life

Root: graph

Root meaning: to write; to make a record of something

Suffix: ical

Part of speech: noun

Definition of this word: a written work about a life

b. **Another word with the same prefix:** biology

Its definition: the science of life and living organisms

Another word with the same root: autograph (noun)

Its definition: to write your own name

1. *monotonous*

a. **Prefix:** _____

Prefix meaning: _____

Root: _____

Root meaning: _____

Suffix: _____

Part of speech: _____

Definition of this word: _____

b. **Another word with the same prefix:** _____

Its definition: _____

Another word with the same root: _____

Its definition: _____

2. *unfairness*

    a. Prefix: _____

    Prefix meaning: _____

    Root: _____

    Root meaning: _____

    Suffix: _____

    Part of speech: _____

    Definition of this word: _____

    b. Another word with the same prefix: _____

    Its definition: _____

    Another word with the same root: _____

    Its definition: _____

3. *prediction*

    a. Prefix: _____

    Prefix meaning: _____

    Root: _____

    Root meaning: _____

    Suffix: _____

    Part of speech: _____

    Definition of this word: _____

    b. Another word with the same prefix: _____

    Its definition: _____

    Another word with the same root: _____

    Its definition: _____

4. *tricyclist*

    a. Prefix: _____

    Prefix meaning: _____

Root: _____

Root meaning: _____

Suffix: _____

Part of speech: _____

Definition of this word: _____

   b. **Another word with the same prefix:** _____

Its definition: _____

Another word with the same root: _____

Its definition: _____

THINKING ABOUT YOUR READING AND WRITING

ACTIVITY K: Your Conclusions About Word Structure

What conclusions can you now draw about using word structure to help you with meanings of unknown words?

_____

_____

_____

_____

It is useful to know that certain academic subjects, particularly some of the sciences, have many words that share a common prefix or root. If you learn some of the most common prefixes and roots in the subjects you study, you will have a good start at defining many unfamiliar words. For instance, the prefix *gen* is used often in biology or courses dealing with the human body. The examples that follow illustrate how this prefix is used.

prefix:

gen (also *gene*), born

words:

gene   a unit of hereditary information

genetic engineering	the use of recent technologies to "cut and paste" genes from one organism to another, introducing new genes and new characteristics into organisms
genetic map	a presentation of the physical locations of genes on a chromosome
genetics	a branch of biology that deals with the heredity and variation of organisms
genotype	an organism's hereditary makeup

From Joseph S. Levine and Kenneth R. Miller, *Biology,* 2d ed. (Lexington: D. C. Heath, 1994), p. A25.

Some roots, prefixes, and suffixes appear quite often in academic texts. These word parts can be combined into a small number of *master words* that, if memorized, can serve as a reference tool for you for new words. The list on page 62 contains fourteen master words, each of which has a prefix and a root that form a part of many words in the English language. In fact, if you learn this chart, you will have the key to unlocking the meanings of more than 100,000 words!

ACTIVITY L: Applying Your Knowledge of Word Structure

Review the Key to 100,000 Words on page 62. Then, in the space provided below, write any other words you know that have the same prefix or root as the master word. Write your definitions for each word. Develop your definitions from your knowledge of word parts as well as from your prior experience with using each word.

MASTER WORD	DEFINITION	WORD YOU KNOW	DEFINITION

_____

_____

_____

_____

Using Context and Word Parts Together

On their own, word parts may not give you the word meaning you seek. For instance, if you look at the word *trilogy*, you know the meaning of the two parts that comprise this word: *tri-*, the prefix meaning three, and *-logy*, the suffix meaning the study of something. However, the word's meaning cannot be derived from this knowledge. The prefix helps, because the word actually refers to a group of three dramatic or literary works that are related in subject or theme. You can view or read a trilogy, but you might not necessarily be studying it. But what if the word appeared in this sentence: "The making of the *Lord of the Rings* trilogy may constitute one of the greatest stories in film"? Here you would be able to derive the meaning by using both the context and your knowledge of word parts. Using your knowledge of prefixes, suffixes, and roots combined with using context is the most effective way of determining a word's meaning in many situations.

Intelligent Use of the Dictionary

Although being able to use context clues and word parts will often enable you to determine the meaning of many unknown words, a good dictionary is still an essential tool for academic success.

There are several different types of "standard" dictionaries, dictionaries that contain alphabetical listings of words along with their pronunciations and definitions. One type, an *unabridged dictionary*, contains a great many words of the language as well as information about the origin and use of words. These huge dictionaries include more than 400,000 words. They are expensive and impractical for everyday use. Libraries typically have at least one unabridged dictionary.

Abridged dictionaries contain about half the number of words as unabridged ones. This type of dictionary serves college students extremely well for a number of reasons. They are usually hardbound, which makes them durable, and they contain all the general vocabulary information you are most likely to need for your academic study. Most of the information in this section is based on the typical elements of abridged dictionaries.

KEY TO 100,000 WORDS

Prefix	Its Other Spellings	Its Meaning	Master Words	Root	Its Other Spellings	Its Meaning
1. *de-*	—	down or away	detain	*tain*	*ten, tin*	have, hold
2. *inter-*	—	between	intermittent	*mitt*	*miss, mis, mit*	send
3. *pre-*	—	before	precept	*cept*	*cap, capt, ceiv, cip, ceit*	take or seize
4. *ob-*	*oc, of, op*	to, toward, against	offer	*fer*	*lat, lay*	carry, bear
5. *in-*	*il, im, ir*	into	insist	*sist*	*sta*	stand endure
6. *mono-*	—	one, alone	monograph	*graph*	—	write
7. *epi-*	—	over, upon, beside	epilogue	*log*	*ology*	speech science
8. *ad-*	*a, ad, ag, al, an, ap, ar, as, at*	to, toward	aspect	*spect*	*spec, spi*	look
9. *un-*	—	not	uncomplicated	*plic*	*play, plex, ploy, ply*	fold
com-	*co, col, con, cor*	with, together				bend
10. *non-*	—	not	nonextended	*tend*	*tens, tent*	stretch
ex-	*e, ef*	out, formerly				
11. *re-*	—	back, again	reproduction	*duct*	*duc, duit*	lead, make shape
pro-	—	forward, in favor of				
12. *in-*	*il, im, ir*	not	indisposed	*pos*	*pound, pon, post*	put place
dis-	*di, dif*	apart from				
13. *over-*	—	above	oversufficient	*fic*	*fac, fact, fash, feat*	make, do
sub-	*suc, suf, sur, sus*	under				
14. *mis-*	—	wrong(ly)	mistranscribe	*scribe*	*script, scriv*	write
trans-	*tra, tran*	across, beyond				

Source: Paul D. Leedy, "Key to 100,000 Words," *A Key to Better Reading* (New York: McGraw-Hill, 1968), p. 19. Reproduced with permission of The McGraw-Hill Companies.

Pocket dictionaries, are, as the name implies, very small and thus are not as useful for students. They have only one-quarter to one-half the number of words found in an abridged dictionary. Because these books are smaller, the definitions are shorter. Pocket dictionaries also contain less information about a word's origin or use. They are a handy spelling reference, though, and students often carry pocket dictionaries, along with their own reference materials, when they are preparing to write papers.

Specialized dictionaries are devoted to the language of a particular field, such as music or technology. Such a dictionary may become useful to you when you start to take upper-level courses in your major.

A good dictionary is perhaps the most effective tool to use when you want to:

* Define words that cannot be defined from the context.
* Check pronunciation.
* Verify spellings.
* Determine parts of speech.
* Verify word usage.

Before we look at each of these intelligent uses of the dictionary, we should review some of the basic facts about this learning tool. No doubt you already know a great many of these facts from your earlier education. To determine your prior knowledge about the dictionary, complete Activity M.

ACTIVITY M: Identifying Your Prior Knowledge About the Dictionary

Several questions about standard dictionaries follow. For each, list any information that you already know. Include any details that come to mind, even if they seem unimportant to you.

1. What are some of the things you can learn about an individual word in a dictionary entry in addition to the word's definition(s)?

   _____

   _____

   _____

   _____

2. In what order is the information about a word usually listed in a dictionary entry?

_____

_____

3. What is a good strategy for locating words in the dictionary?

_____

_____

4. What is a good strategy for figuring out how to pronounce words in the dictionary?

_____

_____

5. What should you do when more than one meaning is given for a word in the dictionary?

_____

_____

6. What else, besides information about individual words, might you find in a good dictionary?

_____

_____

WORKING TOGETHER

Share your knowledge with a partner. Add to your answers any information that your partner helped you recall.

How much were you able to recall? Probably quite a bit. You may have mentioned most of the following facts about dictionaries and dictionary entries:

* The word being defined, the *entry word,* is written in boldface type. It is also written to show *end-of-line divisions.* These indicate where to hyphenate if this word must be broken at the end of a line you are writing.

* Entries give the correct pronunciation for the word being defined. *Diacritical markings* are used to show how it is pronounced. Alternative accept-

able pronunciations are also given. A key to the diacritical markings usually appears at the bottom of the page.

❋ Dictionary entries also tell the function and usage of the word. A descriptor explains how the defined word usually functions grammatically. You may find, for instance, that the word is usually used as a noun [*n*] or as an adjective [*adj*]. This information usually appears immediately following the pronunciation. Words that are no longer used in a language are noted as *obs,* meaning obsolete. If a word is seldom used, the entry reads *archaic.* In some cases, the entry about usage may indicate that a word's use is limited to a specific region of the United States (such as [New Eng] or [Northwest]) or to another part of the world (such as [chiefly Irish] or [Brit]). Word usage comments also may inform you that a word is *slang* or *nonstandard.* Words or expressions that are slang, such as the expression *main squeeze,* are used only for very informal writing or speaking situations. If the descriptor *nonstan* appears in the entry, it means that the word is disapproved of by many people. Try to avoid using slang and nonstandard words in your formal writing assignments.

❋ Entries also inform you about word origin, or *etymology.* Often, you can understand the current usage of a word by knowing the word's history. Abbreviations are used to show the origins, the most common of which are [Gr.] Greek; [L.] Latin; [ME.] Middle English; [OE.] Old English; and [Fr.] French. If the exact date or the century when the word was first used in a particular way is known, this may be shown, as in (12c) or (1599). If the word is no longer in use, the period when it was used may be indicated.

❋ The definition, or definitions, of a word is, of course, also part of the entry. Some words have multiple meanings. The entry gives all of these; you will then need to refer to the context in which the word was used to determine the appropriate meaning for your purposes. In some dictionaries, synonyms for the word are noted as well.

❋ *Inflected* forms of the entry word are often included. This part of the entry shows how the word is written in another form, as in a different tense or number. The entire word with the changed inflection is sometimes completely written. For instance, the inflected forms for the word *carry* may be shown as *carried, carrying.* Sometimes, though, only the added portion is shown, as in *-ried; -rying.* An inflected form may also be listed as a separate entry.

The following model illustrates how these parts of entries are arranged in one abridged dictionary for the word *tax.* Note that there are two different entries, each for a different part of speech. As you study this entry, note any additional information about dictionary entries that you did not have on your original list in Activity M.

tax (tăks) *n.* **1.** A contribution for the support of a government required of persons, groups, or businesses within the domain of that
government. **2.** A fee or dues levied on the members of an organization to meet its expenses. **3.** A burdensome or excessive demand; a
strain. ❖ *tr.v.* **taxed, tax·ing, tax·es 1.** To place a tax on (income, property, or goods). **2.** To exact a tax from. **3.** *Law* To assess (court costs,
for example). **4.** To make difficult or excessive demands upon: *taxed
my patience.* **5.** To make a charge against; accuse. [ME < *taxen,* to tax
< OFr. *taxer* < Med.Lat. *taxāre* < Lat., to touch, reproach, reckon, freq.
of *tangere,* to touch. See **tag-** in App.] —**tax´er** *n.*

tax– *pref.* Variant of **taxo–**.

The American Heritage College Dictionary 4/e Entry,

❋ Dictionaries may vary slightly in the order in which the entry contents
appear, but the pronunciation, part of speech of defined word, and word
origin are always near the beginning of the entry.

❋ You also probably noted in your answers to Activity M that *guide words*
appear at the top of each page of a dictionary. Guide words show the first
and last words on the page and enable you to locate words quickly.

❋ Many abridged dictionaries also include some very useful and interesting
information in sections that are set apart from the definitions portion of the
book. Within a single abridged dictionary, you may find such sections as:

The English Language (a history of its development)

Common Abbreviations (this section may also include symbols for chemical elements)

Foreign Words and Phrases

Biographical Names (names of notable persons, both living and dead)

Geographical Names (this section often includes basic information about
the countries of the world and their most important regions, cities, and
physical features)

Signs and Symbols (especially those used in the sciences and math)

A Handbook of Style (which discusses general rules for punctuation and
grammar as well as models for writing bibliographies)

Forms of Address (which show the title to use in letters to officials in
various capacities, such as an archbishop or ambassador)

Activity N: Recognizing Functions of
Entries in Dictionaries

Here are some dictionary entries from an abridged dictionary. Several items on the entry have been labeled with a letter. In the space provided, identify the function of each lettered item.

a.

1. **trans·la·tion** \tran(t)s-ˈlā-shən, tranz-\ *n* (14c)   **1 :** an act, process, or instance of translating: as   **a :** a rendering from one language into another; *also* : the product of such a rendering   **b :** a change to a different substance, form, or appearance: CONVERSION   **c (1) :** a transformation of coordinates in which the new axes are parallel to the old ones   **(2) :** uniform motion of a body in a straight line   **2 :** the process of forming a protein molecule at a ribosomal site of protein synthesis from information contained in messenger RNA—compare   TRANSCRIPTION   **3**—**trans·la·tion·al** \-shnəl,-shə-nəl*adj*

b.

c.

a. _____

b. _____

c. _____

a.

2. **in·sol·vent** \(ˌ)in-ˈsäl-vənt, -ˈsȯl-\ *adj* (1591)   **1 a (1) :** unable to pay debts as they fall due in the usual course of business   **(2) :** having liabilities in excess of a reasonable market value of assets held   **b :** insufficient to pay all debts <an ~ estate>   **c :** not up to a normal standard or complement : IMPOVERISHED   **2 :** relating to or for the relief of insolvents — **in·sol·ven·cy** \-vən(t)-sē\ *n*—**insolvent** *n*   b.

c.

a. _____

b. _____

c. _____

a.   b.

3. ¹le•ver\\le-vər, ¹lē-\ *n* [ME, fr. MF *levier,* fr. *lever*\to raise, fr. L *levare,* fr. *levis* light in weight — more at LIGHT] (14c)   **1 a** : a bar used for prying or dislodging something   **b** : an inducing or compelling force :—TOOL <u>use food as a political</u> ~ —*Time*>   **2 a** : a rigid piece that transmits and modifies force or motion when   c. forces are applied at two points and it turns about a third; *specif* : a rigid bar used to exert a pressure or sustain a weight at one point of its length by the application of a force at a second and turning at a third on a fulcrum   **b** : a projecting piece by which a mechanism is operated or adjusted

a. _____

b. _____

c. _____

Using the Dictionary to Define Words

Intelligent use of the dictionary for the purpose of defining words means that you are able to make choices about which words to look up. If you have searched for context clues to meaning within the material you are reading but have not found any, perhaps you should refer to a dictionary. This does not mean that you should look up *every* word you do not know. Your decisions should be guided by your answers to these two questions.

1. Is the word essential to your comprehension of the material? Essential words usually (a) are repeated often in the material, or (b) have specific technical definitions, or (c) are important to the main ideas in the material.

   As a general rule of thumb, look up words that cannot be defined through context whenever the flow of ideas is interrupted for you because you do not know the word's meaning or whenever the word is a technical term.

2. Does your text have a glossary that can provide the definition? Glossaries of technical terms are often included in textbooks. When they are, you are better off using the glossary instead of the dictionary because the author tells you precisely how a term is being used in *that* text.

Using the Dictionary to Check Pronunciation

Do you need to be able to pronounce every word you read? If your goal is to read material quickly and to obtain meaning, you can temporarily ignore your questions about pronunciation. Keep your reading going, and use a temporary pronunciation for the unpronounceable word. When you complete your reading, you can decide whether you should check pronunciation. If you believe that it will be important for you to be able to use the word in class discussions, you should learn how to pronounce it. Knowing the pronunciation of a word will also help you spell it.

Using the Dictionary to Check Spelling

Your instructors will grade your papers, in part, on your spelling and grammar. If too many words are misspelled, the worth of your ideas may be overlooked. The dictionary is a wonderful spelling reference. Use it to verify spellings whenever you are in doubt. Some students have begun to rely on spelling checkers that are included in many computer word processing programs. Spelling checkers compare the words in a document you write with words in an electronic dictionary that contains as many as 100,000 words. The user usually can add additional words. The spelling checker runs through your document, comparing each word to the words in the dictionary. If a match is found, it moves on to check the next word. If it does not find a match, the spelling checker either marks the word for later correction or asks the user to correct the error immediately. Some programs even offer suggested corrections, guessing at what the word is supposed to be. Spelling checkers have limitations, though, and should be used with caution. For instance, if the word *are* was typed instead of *art,* the spelling checker would not catch the error because both are legitimate words.

Adapted from Helene G. Kershner, "Using the Dictionary to Check Spelling," *Computer Literacy,* 2d ed. (Lexington, MA: D. C. Heath, 1992), p. 302. Reprinted by permission of the author.

Using the Dictionary to Check Word Usage

Every adult has four vocabularies: speaking, reading, listening, and writing. As adults, our speaking and writing vocabularies tend to be smaller than our reading and listening vocabularies. Thus, the words we use in our writing are ones we already have in our listening vocabulary. If you are uncertain whether a word can be used in a particular form, perhaps as an adjective, you will need to decide if this use of the word is correct. The first way to verify usage is to listen to how the word sounds in the sentence with the word form you intend to use. If it sounds correct to you, it probably is. If you are still uncertain, though, check the dictionary. A pocket dictionary may not give you this information; you may need to use either an abridged or an unabridged one.

THINKING ABOUT YOUR READING AND WRITING

ACTIVITY O: Personal Use of the Dictionary

Under what circumstances might you use a dictionary, even if you can define a word from the context? List any situations you can think of.

_____

_____

_____

_____

▶ Chapter Summary

Based on your reading of this chapter, list at least five ideas that you believe will help you with future reading assignments. Write in complete sentences.

1. _____

_____

_____

2. _____

_____

_____

3. _____

_____

4. _____

_____

_____

5. _____

_____

_____

_____

▶ Extended Application

Now that you have worked with the strategies necessary for using contextual clues and other strategies for increasing vocabulary, you can practice applying them to full-length reading selections. Choose (or your instructor may choose) a reading selection from Part 2 of this book or another reading selection that is typical of what you will be expected to read for your other college courses, such as an essay or a textbook chapter. Use this selection to practice:

❋ Identifying a variety of contextual clues

❋ Getting meanings of words from context

❋ Determining meanings from word structure

❋ Using the dictionary for a variety of purposes

Decide on the practice strategies you will use. Apply them to your selection. Then, in a few paragraphs, write a description of what you did and how the strategies you used worked for you.

Name of material used: _____

Page numbers: _____

Your description: _____

CHAPTER THREE

Strategic Reading for Topics, Subtopics, and Main Ideas

HAVE YOU EVER TRIED TO PUT TOGETHER a jigsaw puzzle? Some people find them extremely frustrating. There are so many pieces! The key to success is to figure out the relationship of each piece to all the other pieces of the puzzle. For instance, if your puzzle is a seascape, some pieces will be part of the sky, others part of the ocean. One major help provided is the puzzle box cover. This gives you the whole picture; it tells you what the final product should look like. Some puzzlers use the box cover picture to help them cluster the pieces in piles related to a particular section of the puzzle, such as the sky.

In some ways, comprehending texts is like working a jigsaw puzzle. There are many details, topics, main ideas. Good readers need to figure out how the various parts of the text are related to each other. To do this, they usually sort out the topics and main ideas and think about how the details within the text are related to these. This chapter and the next introduce you to strategies for accomplishing this task.

What's the first thing you do when you turn on your television? Do you start your viewing by switching channels? If you do, you are not alone. You probably want to know the different possibilities on TV and how much they interest you before you make your final choice. Most of us channel-surf our TVs to find the topic most appealing to us. A channel that has few viewers will probably go off the air. Authors, like television producers, must find ways to appeal to their audience. When authors choose topics that are interesting to their readers, their readers stay tuned to the text a little longer. Sometimes, though, it is difficult for readers to figure out what the topic is. When this occurs, how can you know if the text will interest you? This section will show you some strategies for identifying topics in any type of reading material. You will then be able to make more informed choices about your reading.

What Is the Topic of a Reading Selection?

The *topic* is, essentially, the subject matter the author has chosen to write about. It can be a situation, a feeling, an event, a person, a hobby, a scientific principle, a belief, a particular country, a design element of a piece of art, an exercise routine, a type of plant. Anything. The list is endless. Anything you think about, feel, touch, read about, experience, or hear about can be the topic of a reading selection.

Some topics that college students often read and write about include:

career choices

football games

trust

relations with foreign countries

bioterrorism

peer pressure

drunk driving

the environment

video games

race relations

music

What are some topics you might like to read or write about that aren't listed here?

_____

_____

_____

Recognizing Topics and Subtopics

Knowing the topic of a piece of writing you are preparing to read will help you in a number of ways. First, it will help you stay focused. If you remind yourself periodically of the topic while you are reading, you will have little difficulty staying focused. Even if your mind wanders, it will be easy for you to get back on track. Second, if you know the topic, you will be better able to see how several ideas in a reading selection are connected. All the important ideas will be saying something about the same topic. This will make it easier for you to pick out important ideas from less important ones. Ideas that have little relationship to the topic may have been included to add interest to the material or to serve as examples, but they are of less importance than those ideas that have a clear relationship to the topic. When you know the topic, you are also in a better position to make predictions about the content. You may be able to anticipate some of the subtopics, the smaller but related parts of the topic, that will be discussed. Then you can mentally prepare yourself for your reading. Each of these advantages of knowing the topic is explained more fully in the following sections.

Narrowing Topics

Topics can be very broad. To write all there is to write about a single topic might take many pages, even volumes. Therefore, writers must decide the general topic to discuss, but they also must choose what aspect of the topic to focus on. That is, they must decide how to narrow the topic. For instance, instead of writing a book about myths from all over the world, one might be written that concentrated only on *Native American Myths*. The author writing this book could then further divide this topic into smaller units, or chapters, such as these:

Tales of Human Creation

Tales of World Creation

Tales of the Sun, Moon, and Stars

Monsters and Monster Slayers

War and the Warrior Code

Tales of Love and Lust

Stories of Animals and People

Ghosts and the Spirit World

As another example, instead of writing a text on all facets of photography, an author might choose to narrow the topic of the book to unique photography tricks. The author might divide this text, titled *Creative Photography,* into the following chapters:

Viewpoints: Wide Angles, Telephotos, and Composition

Color, Grain, and Contrast

Color Effects

Filter Effects

Mixing Images

Adding Color

Photographic Tricks

Even when the topic of a book title sounds very broad, the author narrows the topic by dividing the contents so that there is a particular focus to the book. Not everything about the topic is discussed in the single text. A book titled *American Government,* for instance, is divided into the following chapters. Despite the broad title, the author discusses primarily the *structure* of American government; there is, for example, no chapter with the title "Corruption in American Government," "Women in American Government," or "Government Controls on American Businesses."

BOOK TITLE:

American Government

CHAPTERS:

1. What Should We Know About American Government?
2. The Constitution
3. Federalism
4. Civil Liberties and Civil Rights
5. Public Opinion and the Media
6. Political Parties and Interest Groups
7. Campaigns and Elections
8. Congress
9. The Presidency

10. The Bureaucracy
11. The Judiciary
12. American Government: Continuity and Change

In the preceding examples, a very broad topic has been narrowed to become the topic of an entire book. And, further, each chapter focuses on a smaller part of the larger topic. The divisions within books are usually called *chapters.* Divisions within the chapter itself, or within a single article, are usually called *subtopics.*

Recognizing Topics by Previewing

Recall our discussion of previewing in Chapter 1. Previewing is a particularly useful strategy when you begin a new reading assignment. As the previous examples illustrate, by previewing chapter titles of a book you will know the author's focus. Similarly, if you preview titles of a textbook chapter, essay, or magazine article you will have direction for your reading. For example, one chapter title from a text on American government is called "Civil Liberties and Civil Rights." This title is quite broad. Based on it, the chapter could discuss such things as what these terms mean, what the civil rights and liberties of individuals are, how the civil rights and liberties have changed over time, and landmark cases that have given people civil rights and liberties. If you next preview the subtitles, you will learn the specific parts of the topic that will actually be discussed in this chapter. This is illustrated in the example that follows.

CHAPTER TITLE:

Civil Liberties and Civil Rights

SUBTITLES:

Freedom of Expression

Church and State

Crime and Due Process

Equal Protection of the Laws

As you can see from these subtitles, each mentions one area or aspect of civil liberties or civil rights. We can safely predict that in the "Freedom of Expression" section the author will discuss the connections among civil liberties and civil rights and freely communicating your ideas to others. Most probably the "Church and State" section will discuss such rights as the freedom of religion. The title and subtitle work together and enable us to predict the nature of the contents we will be reading.

This next example is from a magazine article. Here, too, the topic is fairly broad. We know that the topic is *nutrition.* Consider, though, how the subtitles help you better understand and prepare for the contents of the article because they direct your attention to particular parts of the topic. The explanation following the outline describes the relationship between the topic and subtopics, which is what you will want to think about each time you look at a chapter outline.

ARTICLE TITLE:

Treat Yourself to Nutrition

SUBTITLES:

From Scarcity to Plenty

The Food We Eat

Nutrition and Disease

Nutrition at Every Age

Everyday Nutrition

Because the article is about how you can enjoy nutrition, you can expect that each subtitled section will say something about that. You may not be certain what the first section is about, but the others are pretty clear. The section titled "The Food We Eat" will probably discuss the typical diets we have and may mention their nutritional value (or absence of it). The section on "Nutrition and Disease" will obviously give information about the role good eating plays in staying healthy. By looking for these connections even before you begin reading in depth, you can have a good idea of the direction the text will take, and you can prepare mentally for the rest of it.

There are many other clues to a topic of a selection that you can look for while you preview, in addition to the title and subtitles. These are introductory and concluding paragraphs, chapter questions, and visual aids. Previewing a chapter or article for the purpose of identifying the topic should be done at a rapid reading rate. You are not trying to learn the details or even the main idea. Your goal at this point is to be able to answer the question "What is this about?" With this answered, you are better prepared to do an in-depth reading. Once you identify the topic, you can use your understanding of the relationship between title and subtitles, or topics and subtopics, to help you predict the contents of the material.

ACTIVITY A: Identifying Topic and Subtopic Relationships

For each list, identify the topic (T) and the subtopics (S). Then, in your own words, explain the relationship between them. These headings are typical of what might appear in a textbook chapter or in an article a professor might assign to you.

LIST 1

S	Social Strata in Afghanistan	S	Early Political Parties in Afghanistan
S	Ethnic Groups	S	Islam in Afghanistan
S	Afghanistan		
T	The Problems of Economic Development in Afghanistan		

In your own words, explain the relationship between the topic and subtopics in this list.

The Topics tell you about the whole chapter; but subtopics only explain about that one little paragraph.

LIST 2

S	Jawless Fishes	T	Amphibians
T	Vertebrate Evolution	S	Reptiles
S	Cartilaginous Fishes	S	Birds
S	Bony Fishes	S	Mammals

In your own words, explain the relationship between the topic and subtopics in this list.

The topic explains that they are going to be talking about vertebrates, and the subtopics explain what kind of vertebrates there is.

LIST 3

_S_	The Importance of Memory	_S_	Uncommon Memory
_S_	Aging and Memory		Conditions
_T_	Memory	_S_	Improving Memory
_S_	Why People Forget		

In your own words, explain the relationship between the topic and subtopics in this list.

The topic gives you one word about what the whole section is going to talk about

THINKING ABOUT YOUR READING AND WRITING

ACTIVITY B: Chapter Subtopics

You have already seen how the chapter on civil liberties was divided for a political science book. What are some subtopics the author might use for the chapter titled "Campaigns and Elections"?

- How a campaign works. ~~chapters~~
- Difference between campaigns and elections.

The source from which this chapter is taken actually divides the chapter into the following sections: Political Participation, Historical Voting Patterns, Explaining—and Improving—Turnout, Political Campaigns, The Effects of Campaigns, Opinion and Voting, Election Outcomes, Modern Technology and Political Campaigns, Elections and Money, The Effects of Elections on Policy. Were you able to predict any sections similar to these?

Using Your Prior Knowledge to Make Predictions

Another strategy for identifying topics and subtopics is to use your prior knowledge to make predictions. For instance, if your instructor had told you that you were assigned to read an article on homelessness, you could think about what you already know about this topic before you begin your reading, and then guess how the author might have narrowed the topic. The chart that follows illustrates the thinking process that might have occurred. On the left are things you might already know about homelessness. You might have spent some time using your prior knowledge to consider how each of these ideas could have been developed into a narrower topic. On the right are some narrowed topics that might have occurred to you. Any one of these topics, or any several of them, might actually be the topic of the assigned reading. Once you begin to read, you would be able to verify your predictions.

TOPIC: HOMELESSNESS

WHAT YOU ALREADY KNOW	NARROWED TOPICS
It is a big problem.	Seriousness of the problem
It occurs in most major cities.	
There is not enough low-income housing.	Causes of the problem
There are not enough places for the mentally ill to live.	
Some children are living on the streets.	Effects of the problem
Street crime activity has increased.	
The homeless are losing touch with their extended families.	
More homeless are becoming ill.	
Cities should build more shelters for the homeless.	Solutions to the problem
There should be more affordable housing.	

Thinking about all these issues related to homelessness before you read gives you momentum, or intellectual energy, for reading. Once your mind is charged with information, you are ready to go.

This process is similar to starting your car on a cold morning. You can press on the gas pedal immediately, in which case you'd probably experience the sluggishness of your car's cold start. You might even have a number of false starts. Or you can leave your car in park and let the engine idle for a while until it warms up. Then, after a few minutes, you can press on the gas and take off to a smooth start. If you warm up to your reading assignments by tapping into your prior knowledge first, your in-depth reading will go more smoothly.

Looking for Repetition

Even in short reading selections, or those without subtitles or other aids, identifying the topic and subtopics is fairly easy because the author keeps repeating the idea, person, place, or feeling being discussed. For instance, in the paragraph that follows, notice how many times the author refers to *myotonic dystrophy*. Notice, too, that the word *symptoms* occurs twice.

> Myotonic dystrophy, the most common form of muscular dystrophy affecting adults, strikes roughly 1 in every 8,000 persons worldwide. Symptoms of myotonic dystrophy include muscle spasms and wasting, particularly in the head and neck. Whereas mildly affected people may simply have difficulty unclenching a fist, those with more severe forms of myotonic dystrophy cannot walk and have difficulty swallowing. The disorder's other symptoms include cataracts, premature balding, shrunken ovaries or testicles, and mental retardation.
> Adapted from *Science News* 141: 7 (February 15, 1992): 103.

The same principle of repetition also applies to longer selections. Thus, a textbook's structure might look like this:

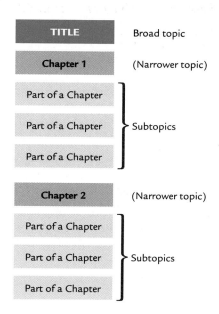

ACTIVITY C: Composing Questions to Check Comprehension Before and During Reading

Based on what you now know about topics, narrowed topics, and subtopics, what are some questions you could ask yourself before reading and during reading? You should ask questions that you believe would be beneficial; in other words, the answers to your questions should provide enough information to let you know whether you are comprehending what you are reading.

Before reading, I could ask: what is the paragraph about? What I need to know? why is this important?

During reading, I could ask: How did it happen? when did it happen? who was involved?

WORKING TOGETHER

Compare your ideas with those of a partner. Add any questions that you feel would improve your list.

Being able to identify the topic and subtopics of what you are reading is a good starting point for effective comprehension, but anything you read is *more* than just a listing of topics and subtopics. For example, you are probably familiar with the play *Romeo and Juliet*. If you were asked what it was about and you replied "the deaths of two young lovers," you would be naming the topic, but think about how much you would be leaving out! Authors have major points they want to make about topics. These major points are often called *main ideas*. In this section, you will learn how to identify and restate main ideas in text and how to infer them and create your own main idea sentences when the author doesn't directly state them for you.

Just What Is the Main Idea?

Perhaps the most important thing to remember about the main idea is that it is an *idea,* not a single word or phrase. It is *at least one sentence that contains a particular point of view or theory.* Most ideas cannot be stated in a single word. Notice, in the list that follows, the difference between the single word (topics) and the statements (main ideas) about the topics.

Topic	Statement (Main Idea)
Writing poetry	a. Poetic style and theme are closely related.
	b. Many different poetic forms can be used to express an idea.
	c. Good poetry is difficult to write.
Washington, D.C.	a. There are some wonderful places to visit in Washington, D.C.
	b. Washington, D.C. has undergone major demographic changes in the last twenty years.
	c. Some residents of Washington, D.C. would like their city to have full status as the fifty-first state.
Taking photographs	a. Different lenses will create different photographic effects.
	b. Photography can be an expensive hobby.
	c. Doing fashion photography is quite different from taking photos on a trip.

THINKING ABOUT YOUR READING AND WRITING

ACTIVITY D: Distinguishing Between Topics and Main Ideas

1. What are some differences that you notice between topics and main ideas?

   _____

   _____

2. What does an author have to think about in order to get from the topic to the main idea?

_____

_____

Progressing from Topics to Main Ideas

If your answer to question 2 in Activity D suggested that an author's thinking has to progress from a broad topic to a narrowed topic to the main idea, you are correct. You learned earlier that a broad topic is narrowed when the author selects the part of the topic to discuss. Once that choice is made, the author needs to determine the major or key point to make about it. The result is the main idea. This is the author's *focus.*

If you are able to identify the narrowed topic or focus, you have the starting point for figuring out the author's main idea. This holds no matter what type of material you are reading. To further clarify the relationship among broad topic, narrowed topic, and main idea, let's look at this process from the reader's rather than the author's perspective.

Suppose you read an article whose main idea was that Tom Cruise's childhood was a difficult one. If someone asked you what you had read about and you said, "Tom Cruise," you would have stated only the *topic.* If you said "Tom Cruise's childhood," you would have stated the *narrowed topic* or *focus* and given more information.

But if you went a step further and said you had read about "some of the difficulties Tom Cruise had when he was growing up," your listener would have a much more accurate picture. You would have been very close to stating the *main idea* of the selection.

Here are two more examples of how broad topics are narrowed, followed by a particular statement about the narrowed topic—that is, the main idea. A different focus is also suggested.

Topic: Sports events

Focus: Pay-per-view television

Author's main idea: Cable television companies benefit considerably from pay-per-view sports events.

Another suggested focus: Ticket scalping

Topic: Commuting to work

Focus: Car pools and commuting to work
Author's main idea: Companies that arrange car pools for their employees have made it easier for people to commute to work.
Another suggested focus: Public transportation

ACTIVITY E: Identifying Topics of Main-Idea Sentences

A number of main-idea sentences follow. For each, indicate the broad topic and focus. Then suggest another focus for the same broad topic. It should be one that you think would make for interesting reading.

Example:

Main idea: Antiquing has became an enjoyable pastime for millions of Americans.

Topic: Antiquing

Focus: enjoyable pastime

Your suggested focus: Making costly mistakes

1. **Main idea:** *Some experts agree that drinking one glass of red wine each day can be beneficial to your health.*

   Topic: _____

   Focus: _____

   Your suggested focus: _____

2. **Main idea:** *Computer experts can change jobs frequently without risking unemployment.*

   Topic: _____

   Focus: _____

   Your suggested focus: _____

3. **Main idea:** *Genes are located in particular positions on chromosomes.*

   Topic: _____

   Focus: _____

   Your suggested focus: _____

4. **Main Idea:** *Once the chronology of the start of the Vietnam War was made known, many thought there could have been a way, besides war, to resolve the internal political struggles of the country.*

   Topic: _____

   Focus: _____

   Your suggested focus: _____

5. **Main idea:** *Recent investigations into domestic violence have increased the willingness of husbands and wives to file charges against each other.*

   Topic: _____

   Focus: _____

   Your suggested focus: _____

WORKING TOGETHER

With a partner, create main idea sentences for the suggested focus for two paragraphs in Activity E. Verify that your sentences state your idea or viewpoint about your focus.

ACTIVITY F: Summing It Up

In a sentence or two, explain what you have learned about the relationship between focus and main ideas.

_____

_____

_____

ACTIVITY G: Locating Main-Idea Sentences

Now that you can distinguish among topic, focus, and main idea, read the following paragraphs and underline the main idea in each. Be prepared to explain your selection.

1. When voters cast their votes in our current plurality system, they are allowed to select only a single candidate for each office. That is far better than no choice at all, of course, but it is nowhere near as good as also being allowed to specify a second and third choice, or beyond.

Current voting rights are therefore incomplete. Complete voting rights would allow voters to vote according to their convictions and principles without wasting their vote on a candidate with little or no chance of winning. The rules for determining the winner would be slightly more complicated than they are now, but they would be based on elementary mathematics and should be understandable by virtually anyone old enough to vote.

From "Condorcet: A Better Election Method" From *http:www.electionmethods.org/ Condorcet.html.* Retrieved April 4, 2005.

2. That nonprofit organizations have so sizable a presence even in countries with substantial government social welfare spending is due to the way these organizations are financed. Contrary to popular belief, private giving is not the largest source of nonprofit revenue. Nearly half of all nonprofit revenue in 26 countries for which there are data comes from service fees and charges. Government, however, is a close second, accounting on average for 39 percent of nonprofit revenue. Philanthropy, by contrast, is third, providing just 10 percent of the cash income. Even in the relatively generous United States, philanthropy composes less than 20 percent of total nonprofit income, even with religious congregations included. The West European countries, which have the highest nonprofit employment, also record the highest proportions of nonprofit revenue from government. The European "welfare state," it turns out, is not a welfare state at all but a welfare partnership that relies heavily on private, nonprofit groups.

From Lester M. Salamon, "Social Engagement," *Foreign Policy* 130 (May/June 2002): 30. Copyright 2002 by Foreign Policy. Reproduced with permission in the format Textbook via Copyright Clearance Center.

3. At the outbreak of World War I, census officials fueled anti-immigrant fervor by reporting that one-third of America's foreign-born residents had come from "enemy" countries. Immigration policy became a wartime weapon. And the Justice Department found ways to strip "disloyal" German-Americans of their U.S. citizenship. It also unofficially deputized citizen-spy groups to investigate acts of alleged disloyalty. The department rounded up 500 suspected Communist aliens after the war. The Farmers National Congress recommended that the department "burn a brand in the hide of those fellows when you deport them so that if they ever dare return, the trademark will tell its tale and expose them."

From Siobhan Gorman, "The Endless Flood, " *National Journal* 36:6 (February 7, 2004): 378.

4. The family physician has a legal obligation to obtain informed consent from the patient and a duty to inform the patient of the news, unless the patient refuses. Ideally, the physician can take advantage of the knowledge of the family to promote a congenial family alliance. Asking the family why they don't want to tell the patient can uncover relational issues and dysfunctional family dynamics. The family physician must be prepared for the wide range of emotions available for the patient and the family. These may vary from loving acceptance to anger and rage. When emotions are communicated to the patient, it is important to listen quietly and intently, with specific attention to the emotional description of feelings. In addition to verbal communication, nonverbal communication, including open body language, is important. It is essential for family physicians to be culturally sensitive to the patient and the family when discussing such important news. Having appropriate family members or other support personnel present is important.

   From Michael L. Sparacino, "Breaking Bad News: The Many Roles of the Family Physician," *American Family Physician* 64:12 (December 15, 2001): 1946.

5. Some neurons are well connected at birth, giving us the ability to breathe, unconsciously regulate our body temperature, and control certain muscles. But trillions of neurons are not yet connected at birth. These connections are dependent on learning. From a biopsychological perspective, learning takes place when new dendrites are formed and connect with new receptor sites. In humans, many of the brain's neuron connections are formed at birth. This fact suggests that, rather than being designed to behave only in ways dictated by our genes, we are genetically built to learn. Our experiences change the structure of our brains by affecting the neuron connections formed.

   Adapted from Laura Uba and Karen Huange, *Psychology* (New York: Longman, 1999), p. 177.

6. Seriously disordered eating is often difficult to identify, but teachers can be vigilant for certain signs. Any student who seems unusually cognitively slowed and tired for a prolonged period should probably be investigated. These symptoms can, of course, represent multiple problems, from a nasty flu to depression to substance abuse to difficulties with friends or family. But if a girl is rapidly losing weight, restricting her intake of food, or making frequent bathroom requests, then extra scrutiny is in order. Instructors might speak with the school nurse or the guidance counselor about how best to talk with the stu-

dent. If the teacher's relationship with the student is strong, then the teacher might gently approach the student.

From Steven C. Schlozman, "The Shrink in the Classroom," *Educational Leadership* 59:6 (March 2002): 86.

7. Nothing is private. There is no such thing as private e-mail correspondence. Even when a message is deleted, many software programs and online services can access messages on the hard drive. Before you click on "send," consider what may happen if the message is read by someone else. The general rule of thumb is not to send very personal or confidential e-mails. Better safe than sorry. You certainly wouldn't want a patient's secrets revealed or your off-color joke to be read by the wrong person. If you use antagonistic words or critical comments—known as "flames" in cyberspeak—it can hurt people and cause awkward situations. In general, it's not a good idea to "diss" patients, employees, or fellow doctors via e-mail.

From Marjorie Brody, "Addressing Proper Email Etiquette," *Review of Ophthalmology* 8:7 (July 2001): 24.

WORKING TOGETHER

Compare your responses with two other members of your class. Discuss how you identified the main idea sentence and which paragraphs posed the most difficulty. How did you narrow down your choices to one sentence?

Purposes for Creating Main-Idea Sentences

In Chapter 1 you learned about the importance of putting the author's complicated sentences into your own language. This strategy also applies to main ideas. Main ideas that are directly stated in the material you are reading are sometimes worded in formal language. This can make remembering the ideas difficult. By restating the main ideas in your own words, you are more likely to retain the information. This is partly because the language is your own and partly because creating a new sentence requires that you think about the meaning of the original statement of the main idea. The following example shows how a main idea can be simplified.

Original main idea:

Many adolescents would like to get through their teen years quickly in order to gain entry into adulthood and many of its benefits.

Student's reworded version:

Many teens are in a great hurry to grow up and gain the benefits of adult life.

Creating your own main-idea sentences will be important in other academic reading situations, including:

❋ *Reading situations where the main idea is not stated.* Writers frequently state their main ideas in a sentence, sometimes referred to as a *topic sentence.* These often appear as the first or second sentence of a paragraph, but they may be located elsewhere. Sometimes, however, the main idea is not stated at all. When there is no main-idea sentence, you will need to create one to be sure you are able to explain how the details in the selection are related to one another. The process you use to create a main-idea sentence gives you a chance to verify that you understand what you are reading.

❋ *Reading situations in which several paragraphs relate to a single main idea.* In these cases, even if the main idea is stated, it will probably appear in only one of the related paragraphs. The other paragraphs may provide illustrations or descriptions to support the main idea. In this situation, you should first try to create a main-idea sentence on your own. Then reread the material to see whether a sentence in the text actually states the main idea. If there is such a sentence, and if it has the same meaning as your own sentence, you have verified your comprehension.

❋ *Reading situations where your goal is to comprehend a lengthy essay or article.* In this type of situation, the author may have several main ideas, all of which are tied together by a single *thesis,* or controlling idea. The *thesis statement,* like the main idea, consists of a particular slant, angle, or point of view about the narrowed topic. In fact, thesis statements sound much like main ideas. But the author may discuss the thesis over a number of pages, and it may be developed through a discussion of several main ideas with supporting details for each. In such cases, you will need to look at the entire array of main ideas in the article to see how they are related to one another; then you will need to create your own thesis statement if the author hasn't directly stated one.

The Process for Creating Main-Idea Sentences

The process for creating main-idea sentences is not complicated. To create a main-idea sentence:

1. Identify the narrowed topic or focus of the topic.
2. Decide what is the most important idea the author wants to tell you about this topic or focus.
3. Create a sentence that describes the most important idea the author wants to tell you about this narrowed topic or focus.

You've already practiced the first step in several of the previous exercises. Just keep in mind that identifying the focus is a critical part of creating main ideas.

How do you figure out what is most important? The paragraph that follows also contains several important ideas, all related to a single topic. The paragraph map drawn here illustrates the relationship. Study the map, and then read the explanation beneath it, which describes the connection between the ideas.

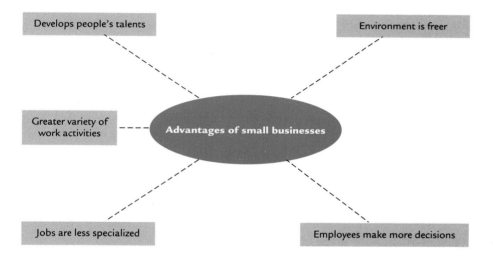

A unique advantage of small businesses is that they develop people as well as goods and services. Their freer, less specialized environment enables employees to strive for more balanced, well-rounded development than they could hope for in larger firms. People in small firms have to be more versatile, and they have a greater variety of work activities than they would if they were working in specialized jobs in larger companies. Instead of just being cogs in the corporate machine, employees have greater freedom to learn by making decisions and living with the results. This freedom, in turn, lends zest and interest to work, trains people to become better leaders, and encourages more effective use of individual talents and energies.

Adapted from Leon C. Megginson, *Business* (Lexington, MA: D. C. Heath, 1984), p. 97.
Copyright © 1984 by Houghton Mifflin Company. Reprinted with permission.

Look at the map and ask yourself: How are these ideas connected? What do they have in common? They obviously have the topic *advantages of small businesses* in common. But the author could have gone in several different directions with this topic. For instance, the author could have discussed the economic advantages of small businesses by describing some of the profit benefits that small businesses have; the author could have focused on the interpersonal relationship advantages that result for people who work in small businesses; or the author could have emphasized the advantages to consumers when they patronize small businesses. Instead, the author has chosen to discuss the advantages of small businesses to *the employees.* The first sentence of the paragraph states this main idea, along with some additional information. The sentence reads, "A unique advantage of small businesses is that they develop people as well as goods and services." Note that the rest of this sentence is not necessary to the main idea. "Goods and services" are not discussed in the paragraph, only the development of people.

You are now ready to create a main-idea sentence for this paragraph. We will use a "main-idea starter" to help you with this. Notice that the starter is a partial sentence that you will complete.

Main-idea starter:

What the author really wants me to understand about the narrowed topic is that _____.

For our example paragraph, your main-idea starter might read this way: What the author really wants me to understand about the narrowed topic is that *small businesses offer many advantages to their employees.* This sentence works as the main idea. In fact, if you put this sentence at the center of the map instead of the topic that is now there, you would see that it connects to all the other sentences; it ties them together, as this map illustrates.

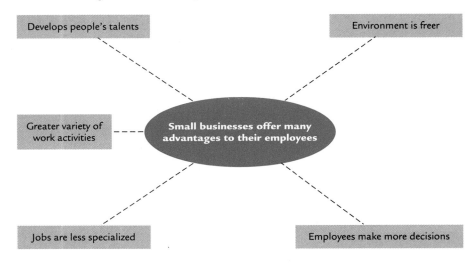

Other Considerations for Creating Main-Idea Sentences

❋ Your main-idea sentence must contain both the topic and the statement the author is making about the topic. This requires that you keep an open mind when you read. If the author's main idea is unusual, or if it differs significantly from your own views, keeping an open mind might be difficult. Your prior knowledge should be used to help you understand the material. And your viewpoints, whether they agree or disagree with the author's, can help you evaluate the author's ideas. But a major goal for students is to learn the information, ideas, and viewpoints presented by the author. At least initially, you will need to set aside your own attitudes and concentrate on determining those of the author.

❋ Because a main idea is an *idea* about the narrowed topic or focus, and because ideas are complete thoughts, your main-idea sentence must be a *complete* sentence. Your main-idea sentence, including the starter portion, should read as a complete sentence. A complete sentence should result when you fill in the space that follows the main-idea starter.

> What the author really wants me to understand about the focus of the topic is that _____.

This will work only if what you write to follow the main-idea starter fits grammatically with the starter. When you read the entire sentence aloud, including the starter, it must flow naturally, as though you were speaking it. It must sound grammatical. If you begin your completion with a question word (*how, what, why,* and the like), you will not have a complete sentence.

Example:
The author wants me to understand that *many wealthy Americans are choosing to put their money into foreign investments.*

(Not: The author wants me to understand that *how many wealthy Americans are choosing to put their money into foreign investments.*)

Remember that whatever you write on the line should be able to serve as a sentence by itself. Using the starter will help you avoid fragments and incomplete sentences.

In summary, to identify main ideas and create main-idea sentences:

1. Identify the broad topic being discussed.
2. Identify the focus.
3. Decide what is the most important thing the author wants to tell you about that focus.

4. Complete the main-idea starter: What the author really wants me to understand about the selected focus of the topic is that:

_____ .

THINKING ABOUT YOUR READING AND WRITING

ACTIVITY H: Main Ideas in Longer Selections

Finding main ideas is more complicated in longer reading selections than in shorter ones. Why do you think this is so?

_____

_____

_____

_____

In your answer, you may have correctly noted that longer reading material often has several main ideas. Or you may have said that sometimes the main idea is not stated, so it must be inferred. (Remember, the main idea might not be stated in shorter essays, either.) Finally, you may have suggested that in the longer essays there could be several main ideas, all or most of which are related to a single thesis. For all these reasons, it is sometimes more difficult to identify main ideas in longer selections. On the other hand, readers are given more information in longer selections than in shorter ones, and this extra information gives you more material to use to verify your thinking about the main ideas.

ACTIVITY I: Creating Main-Idea Sentences

For each of the following paragraphs, identify the broad topic and the focus. Then create a main-idea sentence for each paragraph.

1. Chinese immigration to the United States began in the mid-nineteenth century, following the news of a California gold rush. Chinese men also came as miners and were imported as cheap labor for building the transcontinental railroad. Initially unable to bring their wives, they formed an almost exclusively male society; many took advantage of this situation to establish such small businesses as laundries and restaurants.. Many Americans felt that by accepting low wages the Chinese were competing unfairly with white laborers; their

success as small businessmen was also resented. Following several incidents of lynchings and other violence directed against them, the U.S. government passed legislation in 1882 to restrict Chinese immigration. These restrictions were not lifted until 1952 and 1965.

Topic: _____

Focus: _____

Main-idea sentence: _____

_____

_____

2. Harry Harlow (1971) studied rhesus monkeys to test the effect of lack of normal mothering. Infant monkeys were reared in an apparatus where a "wire" mother (a wire mesh arrangement with a simulated head on top) *provided food* (in a bottle in the mesh), and a warm terrycloth mother *provided nothing* except "her" presence. The infant monkeys spent the great bulk of their time with the terrycloth mother, going only to the wire mother to eat. They would venture away from the terrycloth mother but would scamper back when startled. This behavior runs contrary to theories that stress that infants become attached to those who satisfy their hunger-thirst-pain needs.

Adapted from Robert C. Beck, *Applying Psychology: Understanding People,* 2d ed. (Englewood Cliffs, NJ: Prentice-Hall, 1986), p. 123.

Topic: _____

Focus: _____

Main-idea sentence: _____

_____

_____

3. There was no record of eruptive activity on Tristan da Cunha during historic times, so it was not on the list of active volcanoes. Then in the summer of 1961 some mild earthquakes began shaking in the village. By mid-September, they had become more severe. The people began keeping track of them. In one five-day period, they counted

eighty-nine shocks. They also found that the shocks seemed to be localized near the settlement. At the same time, they began to notice other effects. Doors jammed tight and then were released. Walls cracked, then closed. Cracks appeared in the ground, grew bigger, and then closed. Some of the ground cracks were within 600 feet of the nearest house. One crack was rather startling: on one side, the ground remained stationary; on the other, it lifted more than ten feet, creating a cliff. The villagers thought some enormous pressure must be forcing up the ground. They were right.

From Dan L. Leet and Florence Leet, *Earthquake: Discoveries in Seismology* (New York: Dell, 1964), p. 111.

Topic: _____

Focus: _____

Main-idea sentence: _____

_____

_____

4. Most astronauts do have the right stuff, at least until they come back down to earth. Then, many get dizzy and lightheaded when they simply stand in one place for a while. This unsettling effect can last for days or weeks. "When astronauts come back to Earth, a lot of stuff goes haywire," says Janice V. Meck of the Life Sciences Research Laboratories at NASA's Johnson Space Center in Houston. What makes them dizzy is a temporary dysfunction of their circulatory system. Though probably no more than an inconvenience for astronauts, the phenomenon has led to a better understanding of a longer lasting condition that, for some people, makes just standing up a challenge all the time. People with the condition, now usually called orthostatic intolerance, may experience accelerated heartbeat, faintness, nausea, or dizziness when they stand.

From Damaris Christensen, "Standing Up to Gravity," *Science News* 161:24 (June 15, 2002): 376.

Topic: _____

Focus: _____

Main-idea sentence: _____

_____

_____

5. Free speech zones first emerged in the late 1980s. And since then they have grown increasingly common at America's public universities. Berkeley, the cradle of student activism, now restricts where and how campus demonstrations take place. Kansas State, Iowa State, and the universities of Houston, Mississippi, Central Florida, Southern California, and West Virginia—to name but a few—also restrict and regulate the location of speech. At these schools, the administration has selected certain (usually small) places, often located in obscure corners of the campus—safely out of sight of deans, donors, and the general public—as free speech zones. The conduct code at West Virginia University, for example, provides students with two out-of-the-way patches of ground, each about the size of a small classroom, on which to demonstrate. At the University of Mississippi, only the limited space in front of Fulton Chapel is available for student assembly. "Used to be we had a sea of freedom with some islands of restriction," comments Rick Johnson, a Tallahassee civil rights lawyer who attended FSU in the 1960s. "Now the campus is a sea of restriction with some islands of free speech."

From Diane Roberts, "Zoned Out," *New Republic* 226:18 (May 13, 2002): 14. Reprinted by permission.

Topic: _____

Focus: _____

Main-idea sentence: _____

_____

6. According to the government, there are now 66.6 million handguns in circulation in the United States. Most of these are kept, according to their owners, to protect themselves against random crime. Fatalities from these are now the second-highest cause of death among high-school children, half of whom say they can get guns easily. Shocking as

these figures are, they still do not cause Americans to call for tighter controls. Even the doctors who swab the wounds say merely that the figures should be treated as a "public-health crisis." The comparison they draw is with road deaths, caused by consumer durables that everyone should still be free to buy, own, and enjoy.

From *The Economist* 323:7764 (June 20, 1992): 17.

Topic: _____

Focus: _____

Main-idea sentence: _____

_____

_____

ACTIVITY J: Creating Main-Idea Maps for Paragraphs

Either on your own or with a small group, select two paragraphs from those in Activity I and create a map that shows the relationship between the main idea and several other sentences in the paragraph. To recall how this is done, refer to the model earlier in this chapter. If you work with a group, you will first need to reach agreement on the main-idea sentence for each of the two paragraphs you choose. You may also see that you need to revise your topic and focus.

    1. Paragraph no. _____

Map

2. Paragraph no. _____

Map

WORKING TOGETHER

With a partner, discuss the following chart. What do you think it shows? Write your response in the space beneath the chart.

TOPIC	FOCUS	MAIN IDEA
1. AIDS	1. Prevention	1. People are not practicing safe sex.
2. AIDS	2. Research	2. The money spent on AIDS research significantly increased in the 1990s.
3. AIDS	3. Epidemic	3. AIDS is a global problem.

_____

_____

_____

Testing Your Main-Idea Sentences

Good readers use certain strategies to verify that a main-idea sentence they created really states the main idea of the selection. Making maps, such as you did in Activity J, is a good starting point. But there is even more you can do to make sure your sentence is *a statement of the most important thing the author wants to tell you about the narrowed topic.* You can test your sentence in this way:

1. Determine what questions are raised by your main-idea sentence.

2. Determine whether most of the reading selection's details provide answers to those questions.

A main-idea sentence must be fairly general for it to cause the reader to ask questions. For instance, a sentence such as, "Scientists have learned much about the relationship of the moon to earth," is general or broad. It generates questions in the reader's mind such as, "What is the relationship?" and, "What have scientists learned?" On the other hand, a sentence such as, "It is 93 million miles to the moon," does not generate many questions. It is too specific. Both of these sentences might appear in the same paragraph, but the second sentence answers something about the first. If other sentences in the paragraph also answer questions about the statement, "Scientists have learned much about the relationship of the moon to earth," then you have probably identified the main idea sentence.

Your ability to distinguish between general and specific statements in related text (within a text? or really, nothing at all sounds better) obviously plays a major role in the quality of the main-idea sentences you create.

ACTIVITY K: Distinguishing between General and Specific Sentences

Each pair of sentences could appear in the same paragraph. Indicate which of the pair is general (G), because it raises questions, and which is specific (S), because it provides at least a partial answer to a question raised by the sentence you said was *general*.

1. A reduction in the military budget was one of the items that was under serious consideration. _____

   At a meeting in the White House, the president's top national security advisers considered alternative options for reducing the deficit.

   _____

2. The report said there was substantial evidence that peer pressure can cause students to do better in school than they would do without such pressure. _____

   Friends can influence us both negatively and positively. _____

3. The college had found a few remedies for the shortage in student housing. _____

   A twelve-story student housing complex was being built in the downtown area. _____

4. Just as there are popularity cycles in fashion, there are similar cycles in literature. _____

   During the last few decades, the "tell-all" story about famous people has been popular. _____

5. Most of the advances in electronics, including the ever-smaller chips and faster computers, have been made possible by a process called *photolithography*. _____

   Photolithography involves etching intricate electronic circuit designs on microchips by passing a light through a stencil-like mask cut into the shape of the circuit. _____

6. Abandoned by his mate shortly after the laying of their egg, the male emperor penguin sits on the egg for two beak-chilling months, huddled together with other forlorn males against the shrieking Antarctic winds. _____

   Nature is not kind to the male emperor penguin. _____

7. Japanese economists were pessimistic about their country's prospects for economic recovery this year. _____

   Fifty-one percent of the heads of Japan's one hundred largest corporations predict that land prices, already down 30 percent in some areas from the previous year, will continue to fall. _____

8. The act of writing helps people understand things better. _____

   If you are a student of history and you write about historical theories, data, issues, and problems, you will begin to sort out those theories, data, issues, and problems more clearly. _____

The second step for testing your main-idea sentences is to determine whether most of the details of the reading selection provide answers to the questions raised by your sentence. In the next paragraph, the main idea has been underlined. See what questions it brings to mind.

Like condominiums and cooperatives, mobile homes have become more popular as single-family homes have risen in price. However, there are certain drawbacks to mobile home ownership. First, mobile homes are financed more like cars than houses. Mobile home loans are typically for a shorter period than are home mortgages, and buyers are usually charged a higher rate of interest. Second, after buying a mobile home, the owner must find someplace to put it. This is sometimes a problem because many cities restrict the areas where mobile homes may be located. Finally, because some mobile homes are poorly constructed, buyers should carefully check out the dealer's reputation for service and the warranty that accompanies the mobile home.

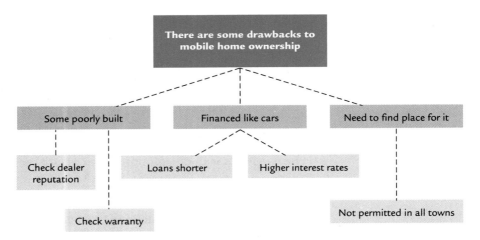

This main-idea sentence raises several questions, including, "What are mobile homes?" and "What are the drawbacks to mobile homes?" In the main-idea map for this paragraph, note that the phrases connected directly to the main-idea answer the second question. They are major details that support the main idea. This map verifies that the main idea has been correctly identified. Also included on the map are some minor details that elaborate on the major details. In Chapters 4 and 5, you will learn more about details as well as some other mapping formats.

You can use the same process for verifying stated main ideas to check any main-idea sentences you infer or create. In the following paragraph, there is no main-idea sentence. One that the reader has inferred and then created has been written beneath the paragraph. In the space provided, write the questions that this main idea sentence brings to your mind. Then look at the supporting sentences in the paragraph. Ask yourself whether they answer most of the questions generated by the main-idea sentence. Write the answers you find.

Many retailers use hand-held tag readers that enter sales information into the register automatically. Some firms are using newer systems that can use the data entered to update inventory and automatically print out purchase orders when new merchandise is needed. Large supermarkets use laser scanners to read the universal product codes printed on almost all grocery items. The sales tape prints out for the customer the items that were actually bought. Simultaneously, the data entered in the computer system help management analyze which products are selling well. Some of the latest systems are even saying, "Thank you for shopping with us."

Main-idea sentence:

Many retailers are using technology to provide them with sales information.

Questions (based on main-idea sentence): _____

_____

_____

_____

Answers to your questions provided by this paragraph: _____

_____

_____

_____

WORKING TOGETHER

Compare your questions with those of a partner. Are they similar? Refer to the paragraph to see whether each of your questions was answered.

What about the main-idea sentences you created in Activity I? Do they raise questions? Are the questions answered by the details in the passage? To test some of your own main-idea sentences, complete Activity L.

ACTIVITY L: Testing Your Main-Idea Sentences

Return to Activity I, in which you created some original main-idea sentences. Select two of your main-idea sentences. Then, in the spaces provided, (1) indicate the paragraph you are using; (2) write the main-idea sentence you created for that paragraph; (3) write the questions raised by your sentence; (4) write at least two details from the passage that provide answers to your sentence; and (5) if your main-idea sentence does not meet the test, revise your sentence, repeating steps (1), (2), and (3).

1. Paragraph being used _____

   Your original main-idea sentence for that paragraph:

   _____

   _____

Questions raised by your main-idea sentence:

_____

_____

Answers to your questions provided by the paragraph:

_____

_____

Do you need to revise your main-idea sentence?   Yes_____ No_____

(If you answered yes, return to the paragraph and create a new one. Then repeat the preceding steps.)

2. Paragraph being used _____

Your original main-idea sentence for that paragraph:

_____

_____

Questions raised by your main-idea sentence:

_____

_____

Answers to your questions provided by the paragraph:

_____

_____

Do you need to revise your main-idea sentence?   Yes_____ No_____

(If you answered yes, return to the paragraph and create a new one. Then repeat the preceding steps.)

THINKING ABOUT YOUR READING AND WRITING

ACTIVITY M: Using Main Ideas to Raise Questions

In your own words, explain the reasons your main-idea sentence should be one that raises questions.

_____

_____

_____

_____

_____

▶ *Chapter Summary*

Based on your reading of this chapter, list at least five ideas that you believe will help you with future reading assignments. Write in complete sentences.

1. _____

_____

_____

_____

2. _____

_____

_____

_____

3. _____

_____

_____

_____

4. _____

_____

_____

_____

5. _____

_____

_____

_____

▶ Extended Application

Now that you have worked with the strategies necessary for identifying and remembering topics and main ideas, you can practice them to full-length reading selections. Choose (or your instructor may choose) a reading selection from Part 2 of this book or another selection that is typical of what you will be expected to read for your other college courses, such as an essay or a textbook chapter. Use this selection to practice:

❋ Identifying topics and subtopics

❋ Composing questions before and during reading

❋ Identifying main ideas

❋ Creating main ideas

❋ Mapping main ideas

Decide on the practice strategies you will use. Apply them to your selection. Then, in a few paragraphs, write a description of what you did and how the strategies you used worked for you.

Name of material used: _____

Page numbers: _____

Your description: _____

CHAPTER FOUR

Understanding Details

Y OUR FIRST RESPONSE TO AN ATTRACTIVE PERSON might be based on an overall impression. That is, the person may seem well groomed or appear to have a good personality. After a while, you might notice *particular* features of the person, such as an interesting way of dressing, a hairstyle that is particularly suited to the person, or a laugh that has some special sparkle. Readers may experience main ideas and details in much the same way. At first, the reader gets the big picture, the main idea. Then the details might be examined for how they contribute to the total effect of the text. In this chapter, we explore connections between main ideas and details.

Why Are Details Needed?

If you have ever spoken with friends who have just returned from a trip, you know how excited they were to give you the details of what they saw, where they went, and so on. Without these details, you might not be convinced that the trip was so terrific. The details are necessary to give the fullest meaning to the statement, "Our vacation was really wonderful." The main idea is supported by the details as the following outline illustrates. Notice how each detail mentions some "wonderful" aspect of the trip.

Main idea:	Our vacation was really wonderful.
Details:	The temperature never went above 80 degrees, and it was always sunny.
	Our hotel room overlooked the bay.
	There was so much unusual and delicious food, it was hard to decide what to eat.
	The prices on gold jewelry were much better than the prices back home.
	The museums and galleries had exhibits of work of the natives from nearby villages.

The same principles that apply to sharing information when you speak apply to most of the writing assignments you will have in college, including when you write personal narratives about your experiences, theoretical papers in which you give researched evidence for some idea, and argumentative or persuasive papers in which you provide arguments for or against something. In all cases, support for your ideas is provided by the details. Without the details, your readers would have only the basic statement (the main idea or thesis). Your readers would never fully understand your theory or your experience, nor would they be able to agree or disagree with your arguments.

Sentences that provide details are usually referred to as *supporting sentences.* They may provide facts and statistics, offer reasons, give examples, add description, give steps or procedures, or in some other way answer questions about the main idea.

Activity A: Adding Supporting Sentences to Paragraphs

In each of the following paragraphs, the main idea is underlined. To each paragraph, add a sentence of details that you think would lend support for the main idea. Draw an arrow to the place in the paragraph where this additional sentence of details would go. It should not go at the end or you may find your sentence is a concluding sentence and not a detail. (*Note:* What you add does not have to be true. Use your imagination.)

Example:

Visitors to Hawaii are often surprised to hear that English is not the only language spoken there. Even today, Hawaiians include much of their mother tongue, Hawaiian, in their speech. <u>It is an interesting language to study.</u> It is very musical. It is one of a number of Polynesian languages spoken throughout the Pacific. Hawaiian contains only twelve letters. Each vowel in a word is pronounced separately and distinctly.

A detail you could add: The language also uses one of the letters, the letter *h,* in 50 percent of its words.

1. People tend to overrely on doctors for advice about the care of newborns. One study showed that new mothers leaving the hospitals with their babies asked their doctors an average of nine questions about caring for their newborn. Questions ranged from concerns about how to diaper the baby to how often to feed it. Some parents wanted to know about the proper dress for the infant in various types of weather conditions. A very popular question was, "How often shall I feed my baby?" Let's hope these new parents remembered what they were told or sought help elsewhere once they left the hospital.

   A detail you could add: _____

   _____

2. Sales of hair color for men hit $113.5 million last year, reports Information Resources Inc., triple the amount a decade ago. One in twelve American men today color their hair, according to NFO Research, and they defy the usual stereotypes. A disproportionate number of guys who dye are in their thirties and forties, single or divorced, and lead active social lives. They're more likely than average Americans to work out, go to bars, attend the theater, and take adult education courses (like painting and drawing). They tend to be upper middle class, but not rich enough to let money alone make a first impression.

   From "Father's Day Special: Guys Who Dye," *American Demographics* 21:5 (June 1999): 20.

   A detail you could add: _____

   _____

3. Until the Industrial Revolution, workers in Europe were mostly independent. Then they became dependent on someone else—especially absentee owners—for their livelihood. This arrangement led to many abuses because employees were forced to work long hours at hard labor in dingy, windowless, and unventilated factories in return for low pay and no job security. Children were also unfairly exploited. Children as young as seven years of age were forced to lift heavy loads and work

twelve to fourteen hours a day. When workers were hurt in an accident or became too old or sick to work, they were fired, with no pension.

A detail you could add: _____

_____

4. A new tattoo is an injury to your skin. It's a lot like a scrape. Typically, when the artist finishes, he or she will cover the new tattoo with some sort of bandage. In the old days, this might have been gauze, but now we have nonstick bandages that are much better. Some will use clear plastic sheet, such as Saran Wrap (TM). This is all right and has the advantage that you can look at your new tattoo without having to lift the bandage. The bandage is largely to protect the tattoo and your clothes, since new tattoos ooze a lot. Also note that tattoos will ooze ink along with the other fluids, and it is not unusual to find an imprint of your new tattoo on the inside of the bandage when you take it off. This is normal. Also, it is normal for the oozing to go on for about 24 hours.

From *http:www.cs.uu.nl/wais/html/na-dir/bodyart/tattoo-faq/part6.html* Retrieved March 2, 2005.

A detail you could add: _____

_____

5. The small helicopter lands in the heart of the tundra, not far from the nomad camp. At the end of May, the snow in Siberia has thawed, but the far north is still in the depths of winter. A line of fur tents, called chum, is the only landmark in the endless wilderness of ice and frozen lakes. People come out of the tents and approach the spot where the helicopter has landed. The Nenets look the visitor over for a few more minutes and then turn around and go back to their chum. The temperature is freezing and a harsh wind blows. Nobody invites the visitor into their home. Familiar with the Nenets' customs from an earlier visit to the tundra, anthropologist David Dektor knows that an outsider cannot enter a tent without an invitation from its owner.

From Debbie Hershman, David Dektor, et al. "Last of the Nomads," *Geographical Magazine* 70:9 (September 1998): 6.

A detail you could add: _____

_____

THINKING ABOUT YOUR READING AND WRITING

ACTIVITY B: Describing the Process

Describe the process you used to create sentences of details for the paragraphs in Activity A.

_____

_____

_____

_____

WORKING TOGETHER

Share your additional sentences of details with those of a partner. Decide if your sentence and your partner's sentence could both be added to the same paragraph. Could they both be used in the same paragraph? Why or why not? What do you think accounts for this result?

Understanding Types of Details

Important details in an article or textbook chapter may serve different purposes. Depending on the main idea, authors may include details to:

* Offer reasons or arguments.
* Provide description.
* Outline steps or procedures.
* Give single or multiple examples or illustrations.
* Cite facts or statistics.

It is also possible that within a single paragraph the author will use a combination of these types of details in order to lend support to the main idea. Notice how these various alternatives have been applied in the following example paragraphs. The main ideas have been underlined.

Details That Offer Reasons or Arguments

Increasingly, the disposal of used materials has become a problem. Some used materials, such as organic wastes, can be returned safely to the environment—although as the population grows, the task becomes more difficult and more expensive. But some materials, such as plastics, are not easily recycled; nor do they degrade quickly when returned to the environment. Still other used materials—radioactive waste being the most dramatic but not the only example—are so hazardous for such a long time that how best to dispose of them is not clear and is the subject of widespread controversy. Solving these problems of disposal will require systematic efforts that include both social and technological innovations.

From American Assn. for the Advancement of Science, *Project 2061: Science for All Americans* (Washington, DC: AAAS, 1989), p. 92.

Details That Provide Description

Looking out my window, I clearly knew that I was a long way from home. Outside my window the skyscrapers stood side by side against the gray sky. The marble edifice of the art museum I had briefly visited yesterday faced me, and to its left was the post office from which I had mailed the fateful postcard to Sandy saying, "I won't be coming back." Down the street, I could see the shopkeepers beginning to open their stores—so many of them. Not at all like the small-town Main Street to which I had become so accustomed.

Details That Outline Steps or Procedures

Homeowners can do home repair work themselves and save a great deal of money. For instance, hanging wallpaper is not difficult. The first step for hanging wallpaper is to select your pattern. You want to be sure that it does not clash with your floor design. After you have made your selection and it has been delivered to you, you will have to gather the tools you will need for hanging. For prepasted paper, you will need a sponge, scissors, a ruler, an edge roller, and an edge cutter or single-edge razor blade. Next, you should be sure you have a large bucket or a tub filled with water for dipping the paper. You will also need a large table on which you can cut the paper to the proper sizes. Once you have gathered your materials, you can finally begin to hang the paper, starting with an edge of a door and working your way around a room until all the areas have been covered. The process is easy, and the results are very satisfying.

Adapted from Ed Ezor and Jill Lewis, *From Paragraph to Essay: A Process Approach to Beginning College Writing* (New York: McGraw-Hill, 1984), p. 89. Reprinted by permission of the authors.

Details That Give Single or Multiple Examples or Illustrations

SINGLE

The Swiss psychologist Jean Piaget found that around the age of seven or eight, children reach the step of "concrete operations." This stage is marked by the appearance of an ability that Piaget called *conservation*. An example of conservation is demonstrated with an activity using some beakers and water. Before age seven or eight, children believe that the amount of water in a short, wide glass changes when it is poured into a tall, thin beaker—they think there is more water in the beaker because it is higher, or less because it is thinner. An eight-year-old is able to "conserve" the amount of water and understands it remains constant despite the change in shape.

MULTIPLE

Social Security has relieved children of the obligation to support their parents. Public schools and various public agencies have taken over many traditional parental responsibilities. In general, the social and economic ties between parents and children and grandchildren have loosened a great deal in America. People are far less likely than they once were to live in extended family units. Age groups have segregated themselves: children in the suburbs, single adults in fashionable city enclaves, older people in the Sunbelt retirement communities. Generations are less dependent on one another than in past decades, and this has allowed Americans pursuing their dreams to focus much more sharply on the present—on their own problems and interests.

Details That Cite Facts or Statistics

In 1996, nearly 15,000 people were employed as registered Washington lobbyists, with 3,750 of these serving as officers of 1,900 trade and professional organizations, including labor unions; another 1,500 employed by individual corporations; and about 2,500 representing organizations ranging from the National Right to Live Association to the Sierra Club. In addition, the six major national political-party committees, three Republican and three Democratic, headquartered in Washington, now employ roughly 1,200 people. And the creation and expansion of such ideological think tanks as the Heritage Foundation, the Center for National Policy, the Urban Institute, the American Enterprise Institute, the Cato Institute, and the Hoover Institution on War, Revolution, and Peace have established whole networks of influential public policy entrepreneurs specializing in media relations and in targeted position papers. The number of special interest groups that have set up offices in Washington, D.C., is simply astounding.

Paragraphs That Combine Types of Details

Recent reports indicate that two out of every five women over thirty-five who are pregnant are now opting for genetic screening. Just ten years ago, this figure was one out of every five. Increasingly, women are opting for genetic screening during pregnancy, screening that enables physicians to detect some fetal abnormalities. The reasons for such increases are, perhaps, best understood by examining what can be learned from the tests that are done. Tests can reveal the condition of fetuses carried by women known to be at risk for specific diseases—such as women in their late thirties, who are more likely to have a child with Down's syndrome, a mental retardation caused by an abnormal number of chromosomes. Another disease that can be detected is Tay-Sachs disease, a fatal degenerative disorder of the nervous system. Doctors can use a number of procedures to make these genetic determinations, including blood examinations, ultrasound imaging, and amniocentesis. One woman reported that because of the early testing, her son was able to have a prebirth life-saving heart operation.

ACTIVITY C: Recognizing Types of Details

In each of the following paragraphs, identify the type of support provided by each of the numbered sentences. Be prepared to justify your answers. The main idea sentence has been underlined in each case, and an example has been done for you.

Reasons or arguments

Steps or procedures

Description

Single or multiple examples or illustrations

Facts or statistics

Combination (indicate what combination is being used)

> **Example:**
>
> (1) Until the mid-1980s, most states and the federal government had no formal statutes focusing on computer crime. (2) Most computer criminals were charged with illegal use of phone lines. (3) In 1984, at least partially in response to the computer invasions caused by the Milwaukee 414ers, the Federal Computer Fraud and Abuse Act was passed, making it illegal to tamper in any way with the federal government's computer systems. (4) This act was expanded in 1986 to include computer crimes against most private computers. (5) In addition, the 1986 Electronic Communications Privacy Act was passed, making it illegal to intercept electronic information including bank transactions and electronic mail. (6) This new law also made it a federal crime to transfer information obtained through computer break-ins. (7) Providing others with computer information such as phone numbers, passwords, and the like became the equivalent of trafficking in stolen goods.
>
> From Helene G. Kershner, "Specialized Technology," *Computer Literacy,* 2d ed. (Springfield, IL: D. C. Heath, 1992), p. 243.
>
> **Type of support provided by sentence 3:** Example (of what has happened since the mid-1980s) and reason (why law was passed)
>
> **Type of support provided by sentence 5:** Example (of what has happened since the mid-1980s)
>
> **Type of support provided by sentence 7:** Reason (why it is considered a crime)

1. (1) Many questionable claims have been made for vitamin C that haven't been proved entirely. (2) Probably the most widely acclaimed value for vitamin C is that it is a preventive and cure for the common cold when taken in massive doses. (3) Famed chemist Linus Pauling, who wrote a small book on the subject, was largely responsible for this claim. (4) He recommended taking one or two grams of vitamin C a day to prevent colds and four grams a day to cure them. (5) His work was based mainly on subjective feelings about how he felt after he took the vitamin.

   Adapted from Norman S. Hoffman, *A New World of Health,* 2d ed. (New York: McGraw-Hill, 1977), p. 185.

   Type of support provided by sentence 2: _____

   Type of support provided by sentence 4: _____

2. (1) If a particular genetic defect is known to cause a disease in humans, and if the same gene is knocked out in a mouse, the mechanism of the disease and the potential effectiveness of drugs and gene therapies can all be studied in the mouse model. (2) Knockout mice make great animal models for human diseases. (3) Last year, for instance, three research groups reported knocking out the gene that, when damaged, causes cystic fibrosis. (4) The knockout mice displayed some of the symptoms of the "human knockout": clogged lungs, digestive disorders, and early death.

   From Marcia Baringa, "Knockout Mice Offer First Animal Model for C.F.," *Science* 256 (August 9, 1992): 1046.

   Type of support provided by sentence 1: _____

   Type of support provided by sentence 3: _____

3. (1) The activity and prosperity of America's retirees have not gone unnoticed by the advertising industry. (2) There was a time when advertisers behaved as though no one past middle age ever bought anything more durable than pantyhose. (3) No more. (4) Few marketing experts can ignore the fact that Americans over fifty earn more than half the discretionary income in the country. (5) Magazine publishers are betting on the favorable demographics. (6) Norman Lear's former wife Frances recently began publishing a glossy, upscale bimonthly magazine for women over forty. (7) Major firms are forming special groups to study the senior market, and at least one company that offers ageless ads has opened.

Type of support provided by sentence 4: _____

Type of support provided by sentence 6: _____

4. (1) After food is ingested, digestion in different parts of an alimentary tract is achieved by mechanical and chemical means. (2) Mechanical digestion, carried out, for example, through muscular grinding by teeth and stomach, achieves a progressive physical subdivision of ingested materials into fine particles suspended in water. (3) Chemical digestion then reduces these particles to molecular dimensions. (4) In the process, usable ions and molecules become separated out, and more complex molecules are broken up into smaller, usable ones.

From Paul N. Weisz and Richard N. Keogh, *Elements of Biology,* 4th ed. (New York: McGraw-Hill, 1977), p. 172.

Type of support provided by sentence 2: _____

Type of support provided by sentence 3: _____

5. (1) Dr. George Cierny III, orthopedic surgeon at Atlanta's St. Joseph's Hospital, studied the time it took twenty-nine patients to recuperate from leg-bone surgery. (2) His findings: Patients who smoked regained their ability to walk an average of six months later than nonsmokers. (3) "It may be that people smoking a pack a day mend their broken bones only while they sleep," says Cierny. (4) Research indicates that when a bone fractures, cells near the break produce a fibrous substance called collagen that patches the fissures. (5) The carbon monoxide and nicotine in cigarette smoke limit the amount of oxygen that reaches those cells, hindering their collagen-making ability.

Type of support provided by sentence 1: _____

Type of support provided by sentence 3: _____

Type of support provided by sentence 5: _____

6. (1) Designed by the same architectural firm that designed the National Gallery of Art, the Thomas Jefferson Memorial was built in the style of Jefferson's own Rotunda at the University of Virginia. (2) Surrounding the statue are floors of Tennessee marble, walls of Georgia marble, and a coffered ceiling of Indiana limestone. (3) Each spring, the circular dome is framed by a ring of Japanese cherry trees on the banks of the Tidal Basin. (4) Restoration is currently taking place, but the 29-foot bronze statue of the brilliant statesman and excerpts from his

famous works are still visible. (5) This memorial is truly a testimony to Jefferson's greatness.

Type of support provided by sentence 2: _____

Type of support provided by sentence 3: _____

7. (1) Lionell Portell is eight years old. (2) He has spent four hours every day watching TV for seven days per week, since he was two. (3) This is a total of 8,760 hours he has already spent viewing cartoons, sitcoms, and whatever else has attracted his eye. (4) There ought to be a limit on how much television a kid can watch. (5) It's bad for the eyes. (6) It's bad for the brain. (7) Little mental exercise is required. (8) There is an absence of problem solving and creative thinking, and communication is totally one way. (9) There are better ways for kids to spend their out-of-school time.

Type of support provided by sentence 2: _____

Type of support provided by sentence 8: _____

Type of support provided by sentence 9: _____

Details as Answers to Questions

In Chapter 3, you learned that main-idea sentences are fairly broad sentences; they are more general than sentences whose primary purpose is to provide details as support for the main-idea. Recall also that these broad sentences raise questions in the mind of the reader and that the details often answer them. In Chapter 3, you were able to verify the accuracy of the main-idea sentences you created by comparing details in the paragraphs to the questions raised by your main idea. You knew your main-idea sentence was usable if the details answered some or most of the questions that resulted from your sentence.

You can also use the questions raised by main ideas to predict the content of the details in a reading passage. Because the main idea is often stated near the beginning of a reading selection, after you identify it you should spend a few moments thinking about the information that probably will follow. In the next example, the main idea is stated in the first sentence. Before you read the remainder of the paragraph, predict what will follow. What type of information can you expect to proceed from this main idea? Then read the rest of the paragraph to verify your predictions.

Example:

You may be surprised to learn that Buenos Aires resembles a European capital. At first glance, the comparisons are evident: There are tidy plazas with Rodin statues in them, sidewalk cafés, *prêt-à-porter* windows where beautiful women gaze simultaneously at the clothes and their own reflections. A huge obelisk looms in the middle of the Avenida Nueve de Julio, and on either side are heavy-limbed subtropical trees and Parisian-style office buildings. You are in the heart of South America, but you can drink tap water and eat raw salads and buy almost any new magazine or exquisite cosmetic. Throughout her convulsive and sometimes bloody history, Buenos Aires has kept her eyes fixed lovingly on Europe.

If you predicted that the example paragraph would contain details about Buenos Aires that illustrate its similarity to European cities, you were, of course, correct. Your prediction prepared you for the reading ahead and kept you focused while you read.

When you read with a questioning attitude, your goal is to find the relationship between some of the more general sentences in the material you are reading and the remaining sentences. You search for those details that elaborate on the questions raised by the more general sentences. And you understand how those details provide support for the main idea. In Activity D, you will have an opportunity to think about this aspect of the reading process.

ACTIVITY D: Predicting Details from Main-Idea Sentences

In these exercises, the main-idea sentence is noted separately above the paragraph. Beneath this is a space for you to make predictions about the content of the details. You should base these on the questions the main idea raises for you. Make as many predictions as you can. After you read the paragraph, decide how accurate your predictions were. Note this in the space provided below the paragraph. An example has been done for you.

Example:

Main-idea sentence: Francis Bacon was known for his writing, his politics, and his influence on the scientific community.

Predicted content of details: The paragraph will discuss his writing and his politics as well as how he influenced the scientific community.

Francis Bacon was known for his writing, his politics, and his influence on the scientific community. He was a gifted writer and was recognized as an outstanding essayist. Some scholars also consider him as the true author of the plays attributed to William Shakespeare. Bacon is reported to have been an ambitious and unscrupulous politician. Between 1618 and 1621, he was lord chancellor of England, under James I of England. Convicted of accepting bribes, he was dismissed and died in disgrace. Bacon is perhaps best remembered, however, as an early propagandist for the Scientific Revolution. His *New Organon* (1620), designed to replace Aristotle's logical works collectively called the *Organon,* called for a new approach to the study of nature. Science for Bacon was the means by which men could gain power over nature and use it for their own purposes. To do this, they needed a new instrument, a new method of approach. This new method was *empiricism.*

Adapted from Mary Ann Frese Witt et al., *The Humanities*, 3d ed., vol. 2 (Lexington, MA: D. C. Heath, 1989), pp. 8–9.

Accuracy of your prediction: The details did discuss what had been predicted.

1. **Main-idea sentence:** How a person handles space in dating others is an obvious and very sensitive indicator of how he or she feels about the other person.

   Predicted content of details: _____

   _____

   _____

How a person handles space in dating others is an obvious and very sensitive indicator of how he or she feels about the other person. On a first date, if a woman sits or stands so close to a man that he is acutely conscious of her physical presence inside the intimate-distance zone, the man usually construes it to mean that she is encouraging him. However, before the man starts moving in on the woman, he should be sure what message she's really sending; otherwise, he risks bruising his ego. What is close to someone of northern European background may be neutral or distant to someone of Italian heritage. Also, a woman sometimes uses space as a way of misleading a man, and there are few things that put men off more than women who communicate contradictory messages, such as women who cuddle up and then act insulted when a man takes the next step.

From Edward T. Hall and M. R. Hall, "The Sounds of Silence," *Playboy*, June 1971, p. 138ff.

Accuracy of your prediction: _____

2. **Main-idea sentence:** <u>Marketing strategies involving sales promotions must be used wisely, or serious consequences can occur.</u>

Predicted content of details: _____

_____

_____

As the automakers have learned, once a pattern of sales incentives is begun, it is extremely difficult to turn off. Marketing strategies involving sales promotions must be used wisely, or serious consequences can occur. Managers should be aware that sales promotion devices work in the same way as narcotics. They are so potent as reinforcers that consumers become dependent on them. Consumers simply stop buying when the incentives are removed. Furthermore, sales promotion devices can act as a large drain on profits. The extremely poor financial performance of General Motors during the fall of 1986, when the company employed a massive sales promotion campaign, illustrates this point.

Accuracy of your prediction: _____

3. **Main-idea sentence:** <u>Intermediate stages in evolution may occur very rapidly and may even be difficult to identify.</u>

Predicted content of details: _____

_____

_____

People think of evolution of a system as proceeding gradually, with a series of intermediate states between the old and the new. This does not mean that evolutionary change is necessarily slow. Intermediate stages in evolution may occur very rapidly and may even be difficult to identify. Explosions, for example, involve a succession of changes that occur almost too rapidly to track—whether the explosions are electric as in lightning, chemical as in automobile engines, or nuclear as in stars. What is too rapid, however, depends on how finely the data can be separated in time. Consider, for example, a collection of fossils of fairly rare organisms known to have existed in a period that lasted many thousands of years. In this case, evolutionary changes that occurred within a thousand years would be impossible to track precisely. And some evolutionary changes do occur in jumps. For instance, new biological developments do not arise only by successive rearrangement of existing genes but sometimes by the abrupt mutation of a gene into a new form. On an atomic scale, electrons change from one energy state to another with no possible intermediate states. For both the gene and the electron, however, the new situation is limited by, and explicable from, the previous one.

From American Association for the Advancement of Science, *Project 2061: Science for All Americans* (Washington, DC: AAAS, 1989), p. 13.

Accuracy of your prediction: _____

4. **Main-idea sentence:** It is obvious that Yom Kippur is a day that Jews anxiously await.

   Predicted content of details: _____

   _____

   _____

To the Jewish people, Yom Kippur, the Day of Atonement, is the most solemn religious holiday of the year. It is a day of great importance, the day they "heed the call of the shofar" and ask God to forgive them for their sins and transgressions. It is obvious that Yom Kippur is a day that Jews anxiously await. Sociologist David Phillips discovered something extremely interesting about Yom Kippur and the people who observe it. Studying the mortality records for Jews in New York and Budapest, he found a notable drop in the death rate just before the Day of Atonement. There was no such drop among non-Jews before the High Holy Day. Carrying his investigation further, Phillips also examined the mortality patterns around people's birthdays. What he discovered tied in nicely with his Yom Kippur findings: There was a significant dip in deaths before birthdays and a significant peak in deaths thereafter—which all means, according to Phillips, that "some people look forward to witnessing certain important occasions and are able to put off dying in order to do so."

From Lewis Andrews and Marvin Karlins, *Psychology, What's in It for Us?* 2d ed. (New York: Random House, 1975), p. 147.

Accuracy of your prediction: _____

Major and Minor Details

Have you ever stopped to ask for directions when you were driving to an unfamiliar location? If you have, you are surely aware that some people are better direction givers than others. One thing that can distinguish a good set of directions from a poor set is the kind of information provided. Two different sets of directions for the same destination, a local movie theater, follow. They are being given from the same location, a local gas station. As you read each set, think about which set you prefer, and why.

1. As you leave from the station, make a right. Turn left after you pass the Fiesta Food store, which you'll see because it has a new brick facing on it and the prices are really low, and then you go past a school for grades two through five; keep going, but don't turn left yet. You see there's a large ball field, and across from that is the Central gas station. After that, you come to a red house on the right and a bowling alley next to it. Then there's the first traffic light. Turn left here. Go up about three blocks. You'll see a white mailbox and a sign reading "Katie's Kennels" on the first block. An ice cream store and drug store are on the next block. When you get to the third block, you'll see a big sign saying "Theater Parking." Go in there, and you'll be at the theater.

2. As you leave from the station, make a right. Turn left at the first traffic light. Go up about three blocks. Then you'll see a big sign saying "Theater Parking." Go in there, and you'll be at the theater.

If you are like most people who ask for directions, you would prefer the second set. It is short, to the point, and easy to remember. In fact, most of the information given in the first set is unnecessary. Although the first example is interesting and does help to create a picture for you of the town, all you need to know to get to the theater is what is mentioned in the second example. It contains only the major details, whereas the first set contains many minor details.

WORKING TOGETHER

What are some of the minor details in the first set of directions? With a partner, underline all that you can locate.

Major and Minor Details in Sentences

Which would you prefer to watch: a major league or minor league baseball game? Probably the major league game, because it is a more important game with better-known players. The terms *major* and *minor* can also be applied to the level of importance details have in reading selections. A sophisticated reader of textbook material spends time sorting out important, or major, details from unimportant, or minor, ones in order to focus on those that really matter. Major details contribute directly to the main idea. They can raise questions, and answers to these can usually be considered minor details. The minor details may provide more information about the main idea, but it won't be as important as the information provided by major details. Minor details also often elaborate on a major detail. For example, the paragraph that follows contains several major details and some minor ones. These are pointed out to you to the right of the paragraph. As you look at this example, Note the questions the major and minor details answer. Ask whether the minor detail adds information about the major detail or more information about the main idea, but in a less important way.

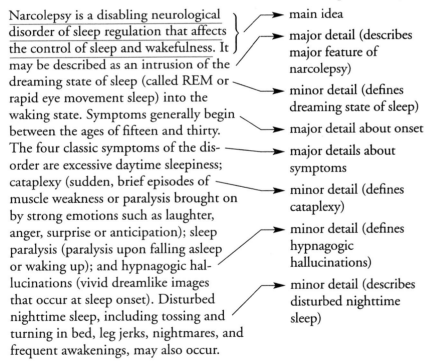

Narcolepsy is a disabling neurological disorder of sleep regulation that affects the control of sleep and wakefulness. It may be described as an intrusion of the dreaming state of sleep (called REM or rapid eye movement sleep) into the waking state. Symptoms generally begin between the ages of fifteen and thirty. The four classic symptoms of the disorder are excessive daytime sleepiness; cataplexy (sudden, brief episodes of muscle weakness or paralysis brought on by strong emotions such as laughter, anger, surprise or anticipation); sleep paralysis (paralysis upon falling asleep or waking up); and hypnagogic hallucinations (vivid dreamlike images that occur at sleep onset). Disturbed nighttime sleep, including tossing and turning in bed, leg jerks, nightmares, and frequent awakenings, may also occur.

main idea

major detail (describes major feature of narcolepsy)

minor detail (defines dreaming state of sleep)

major detail about onset

major details about symptoms

minor detail (defines cataplexy)

minor detail (defines hypnagogic hallucinations)

minor detail (describes disturbed nighttime sleep)

From National Institute of Neurological Disorders and Stroke, *http://www.ninds.nih.gov/disorders/narcolepsy/narcolepsy.htm* Retrieved March 2, 2005.

ACTIVITY E: Distinguishing between Major and Minor Detail Sentences

Here you will find main ideas paired with two sentences. In each pair, identify the major (Maj) and minor (Min) detail by determining how important the information is to understanding the main idea.

1. **Main-idea:** On the average, Americans eat a diet in which about 36 percent of the calories come from fat.
   Details:

   _____ a. The rest come from other sources.

   _____ b. The Dietary Guidelines suggest a goal of 30 percent or less of total calories from fat.

2. **Main-idea:** Shortly before midnight on March 24, 1934, Nellie Madison, a Montana rancher's daughter, pumped five bullets into her husband Eric as he lay in bed in the couple's Burbank, California, apartment.
   Details:

   _____ a. Police arrested her two days later hiding in the closet of a remote mountain cabin and brought her back to Burbank where she was questioned, jailed, and charged with first-degree murder.

   _____ b. Fifty reporters who sat in on her interrogation nicknamed her the "enigma woman" for her oddly detached and inscrutable demeanor and her refusal to talk.

3. **Main-idea:** The general perception is that mixed-sex classes are harder to teach than single-sex classes.
   Details:

   _____ a. Pupils agree with that assessment.

   _____ b. As one girl says, "With boys you don't talk much because sometimes you feel embarrassed about what you're going to say."

4. **Main-idea:** Many nations are using eco-labels for a variety of products.
   Details:

   _____ a. The Blue Angel plan was in response to a recommendation adopted by the Council of The Organization for Economic

Cooperation & Development and high environmental awareness among West Germans in the late 1970s.

_____ b. In 1978, West Germany established an official eco-label procedure, the Blue Angel plan, long before other nations.

ACTIVITY F: Identifying Questions Answered by Details

The following paragraphs contain several major details. For each one listed beneath the paragraph, indicate the question the detail answers about the main idea. The main idea has been underlined. Then identify whether you think this is a major or minor detail.

1. Some 11 percent of adults who have ever been married or cohabited have been unfaithful to their partner, according to the results of a national survey. In the first analysis of its kind to examine a constellation of factors that have not previously been studied simultaneously, the investigators assessed the influence of adults' opportunities for meeting additional sex partners, sexual values and tastes, current relationship, and demographic characteristics on the odds of being unfaithful. When these factors were analyzed together, thinking about sex several times a day, having had a high number of prior sex partners, living in a central city, being male or black, and having been part of a couple for a long time were all associated with an increased risk of infidelity. Disapproving of sexual infidelity and sharing social networks with one's partner were associated with reduced odds of having been unfaithful.

From I. Olenick, "Odds of Spousal Infidelity Are Influenced by Social and Demographic Factors," *Family Planning Perspectives* 32:3 (May/June 2000): 148.

a. **Detail:** Eleven percent of adults who have ever been married or cohabited have been unfaithful to their partner.

Question this detail answers: _____

(circle one)   Maj   Min

b. **Detail:** Disapproving of sexual infidelity was associated with reduced odds of having been unfaithful.

Question this detail answers: _____

(circle one)   Maj   Min

c. **Detail:** Living in a central city was associated with an increased risk of infidelity.

Question this detail answers: _____

(circle one)   Maj   Min

2. <u>College campuses are seeking ways to reduce student drinking.</u> Some schools have signed on to national programs to combat heavy drinking. Ten schools, including Lehigh and the University of Vermont, take part in a program called A Matter of Degree, which tries to change campus cultures to cut drinking. Some schools are studying whether they're scheduling too few classes on Fridays, which might spur Thursday-night partying. They're also restricting tailgating and stadium beer sales. The U.S. Department of Education has begun highlighting innovative anti-drinking practices; high school guidance offices now have a brochure listing model schools. Other colleges are trying a "social norms" approach, spreading the message to students that their peers drink less than they think, in an attempt to make heavy drinking less socially acceptable.

Adapted from Daniel McGinn, "Scouting a Dry Campus," *Newsweek* 136:22 (November 27, 2000): 83.

   a. **Detail:** Some schools have signed on to national programs to combat heavy drinking.

   Question this detail answers: _____

   (circle one)   Maj   Min

   b. **Detail:** Other colleges are trying a "social norms" approach.

   Question this detail answers: _____

   (circle one)   Maj   Min

   c. **Detail:** Some schools are studying whether they're scheduling too few classes on Fridays.

   Question this detail answers: _____

   (circle one)   Maj   Min

3. Television has been central to [Generation] Xers' lives, and TVs will likely be found throughout their entertainment-based and technology-driven homes. <u>But above all, the Xer home will be practical and utilitarian; pragmatic concerns will outweigh "home as showplace" considerations.</u> A generation largely unfamiliar with cooking from scratch will have kitchens that are less about cooking and more about unpacking, processing, heating and storing. Indeed, many homes are now being built with two dishwashers (one for clean dishes and one for dirty dishes)—the utilitarian convenience of never having to unload a dishwasher outweighs the desire to display china. The days of the dining room appear numbered, a victim of Xer lifestyle components: fast-paced lives, multitasking (consuming food and media simultaneously), and the proliferation of what the food industry calls

"home meal replacement" options. The demise of the dining room signals a broader trend away from rooms dedicated to a single purpose. Futurists predict "great rooms" that can be used for many purposes and occasions, and it seems likely that Generation Xers (the multitasking generation that grew up doing homework in front of the TV set) will usher this trend into mainstream home design.

From Stephen J. Krause, "Gen Xers' Reinvented 'Traditionalism,'" *Brandweek* 41:23 (June 5, 2000): 28. Reprinted by permission.

   a. **Detail:** Kitchens will be less about cooking and more about unpacking, processing, heating, and storing.

   Question this detail answers:_____

   (circle one)   Maj   Min

   b. **Detail:** Xers are largely unfamiliar with cooking from scratch.

   Question this detail answers:_____

   (circle one)   Maj   Min

   c. **Detail:** The days of the dining room appear outnumbered.

   Question this detail answers:_____

   (circle one)   Maj   Min

WORKING TOGETHER

Compare your responses with a partner. If you disagreed on any question, return to the paragraph to see if you can reach agreement or determine whether it is possible for a detail to answer more than one question. Also see whether you agreed on whether a detail was major or minor.

As Activity F illustrates, an entire sentence may be a major or a minor detail. But a single sentence may also include both major and minor details. The following examples illustrate this possibility.

In the first example, the sentence containing the main idea is underlined twice. The sentence underlined once contains both major and minor details. The major detail is in boldface type; the minor details are italicized. The major detail in this sentence answers the question, "How does ginseng help to improve mental functioning?" The minor detail answers the question, "Which workers?" Two other italicized sentences in this paragraph are also minor details. The first of these provides an example of how ginseng is used. The second offers a use for ginseng that is somewhat different from the main point of the article, ginseng's ability to improve mental functioning.

Example 1: Major and Minor Details in a Single Sentence

Unlike most stimulants, ginseng improves mental ability without disturbing your sleep pattern, even when it is taken over an extended time. In fact, it actually helps you sleep sounder. It's all in the dose. True to its adaptogenic properties, large quantities of Asian ginseng tend to be sedative while small ones are stimulating. Ginseng increases oxygen not only to muscles, but also to the brain where they help rebuild nerve cells that relay brain messages throughout the body. *Nerve reflexes return faster in anesthetized hospital patients when they take Asian ginseng beforehand.* Ginseng may not actually make you smarter, **but people working under stressful conditions,** *such as telegraph operators,* **have found their work efficiency and hearing improve** when taking ginseng. If you notice your mental functions declining due to age, illness, stress, or hardening of the arteries, then ginseng may be your answer. *In addition, European doctors prescribe Asian ginseng to also treat mood disorders such as depression, especially in the elderly.*

From Kathi Keville, "Ginseng," *Better Nutrition,* 63:5 (May 2001): 48. Reprinted by permission of the author.

In the second example, there are two sentences that state the main idea; these are underlined twice. The major details are in boldface. They explain, "How?" or, "What kind of negative and positive influences?" The remaining sentences give specific examples and are only minor. The map following the paragraph illustrates this relationship.

Example:

There is no question that groups can exert both negative and positive influences over an individual's behavior. *They can be used to extinguish human spirit and encourage antisocial acts, yet they can also be employed to expand individual freedom and social responsibility.* Groups can encourage an individual to take drugs; to commit violent crimes; even to disrupt platform speakers at a rally or convention. On the other hand, groups can also be effective in working to build shelters for the homeless, encouraging AIDS research, or maintaining safety at a concert. Clearly, group power is similar to atomic power: It can be used to improve or to hamper the quality of life. In the final analysis, it is up to us to decide how group power will be exercised.

Adapted from Lewis M. Andrews and Marvin Karlins, *Psychology: What's in It for Us?* 2d ed. (New York: Random House, 1975), p. 115.

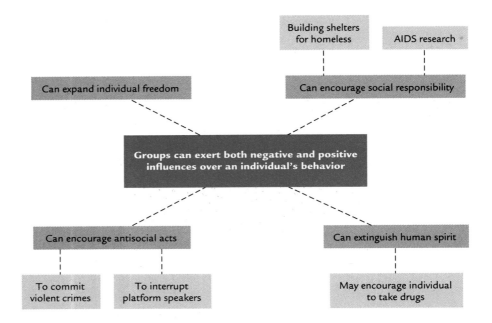

ACTIVITY G: Recognizing Major and Minor Details in Paragraphs

Each paragraph below includes a stated main idea, which is underlined, as well as sentences containing major and minor details. In the spaces following the paragraph, write whether each detail listed is major (Maj) or minor (Min). Be prepared to justify your answer.

1. When used strategically, camera movement at different angles can enhance the quality and effects of a film. A *pan* (short for panorama) or *panning shot* is a revolving horizontal movement of the camera from left to right or right to left. To achieve this shot, the motion picture camera is mounted on a tripod and simply pivots sideways in either direction to follow the subject. A *tilt* or *tilt shot* is similar to a pan except that the camera moves up and down. In a *tracking shot* (also referred to as a *dolly shot* or *trucking shot*), the camera moves with the subject. The camera is mounted on a *dolly,* a special cart, or on any moving device or vehicle. For a *boom shot,* the camera and its operator are usually placed on a *boom,* a large supporting arm or pole that can move in any direction. Boom shots were used in *Field of Dreams* (1989), so that the audience could see the baseball field from a high

angle. In *Honey, I Shrunk the Kids* (1989), directors Joe Johnston and Rob Minkoff used a boom shot to peer through giant blades of grass at shrunken kids struggling to find their way out of their backyard.

From Jan Bone and Ron Johnson, *Understanding the Film,* 5th ed. (Lincolnwood, IL: NTC Publishing Group, 1996), p. 90.

   a. A *pan* shot involves revolving, horizontal movement. _____

   b. In a *pan* shot, the camera is mounted on a tripod. _____

   c. The *tilt* shot is similar to the *pan* shot. _____

   d. In the *tilt* shot, the camera moves up and down. _____

   e. A *tracking* shot is also referred to as a dolly or trucking shot. _____

   f. In a *tracking* shot, the camera moves with the subject. _____

   g. A *boom* is a large supporting arm or pole that can move in any direction. _____

   h. Boom shots were used in *Field of Dreams.* _____

2. In the United States a man cannot have more than one wife at a time, even if (as once was the case with Mormons) polygamy is thought desirable on religious grounds. For religious reasons, you may oppose being vaccinated or having blood transfusions, but if the state passes a compulsory vaccination law or orders that a blood transfusion be given a sick child, the courts will not on grounds of religious liberty prevent such things from being carried out. Many young children, however, have had to wait for transfusions until their case was heard in court. And in an issue that remains bitterly controversial to this day, the courts have allowed local authorities to close down schools operated by fundamentalist religious groups if the schools were not accredited by the state. This has upset many parents who feel their religious needs could not be met by the public schools. Having the right to exercise your religion freely in this country does not mean that you are exempt from laws binding other citizens, even when the law goes against your religious beliefs.

   From James Q. Wilson, *American Government,* 2d ed., brief version (Lexington, MA: D. C. Heath, 1992), p. 59.

      a. Many Mormons once believed it was proper to have more than one wife. _____

      b. In this country, a man cannot have more than one wife, even if it is not opposed by his religion. _____

  c. Hospitals will give life-saving transfusions even if it is against the patient's religion. _____

  d. Some fundamentalist parents are dissatisfied with public schools. _____

  e. Some fundamentalist schools were not accredited. _____

  f. Some fundamentalist schools were closed down because they were not accredited. _____

  g. There are religions that oppose vaccinations. _____

  h. States may pass compulsory vaccination laws. _____

3. The federal government has initiated no programs for battered women since 1984; and Minnesota, which has one of the most progressive and best-funded abuse prevention programs in the country, spends less to help battered women than to kill mosquitoes. Federal and state funding for battered women's shelters and related services is pitifully short-lived and small. One result is that there are only about a thousand shelters for battered women in the United States. Everywhere, women in need are turned away. In Philadelphia, Women Against Abuse rejects 75 percent of the women who seek shelter. In New York City, Sanctuary for Families turns away one hundred battered women and their children every week. In Seattle, five hundred men are arrested for battering every month, but only thirty-nine shelter beds are available for battered women. In Massachusetts, women's shelters turn away 71 percent of the women in need of shelter and 80 percent of the children. In all areas of the country, demand for temporary shelter, court advocacy, and peer support groups is rising, and budgets are being cut. Some shelters have had to discontinue support programs for children, while others have had to drop court advocates. Everywhere paid workers have cut their own salaries to make the money stretch farther; many carry on as volunteers. One Midwestern shelter laid off its custodian for lack of funds; later, when the shelter was criticized publicly for being dirty and unsanitary, she wrote to the local newspaper: "Until government and society commit themselves to ending violence in the home, there will always be battered women's shelters, they will always be full and there will always be dishes to wash and bathroom floors to mop. Token laws and band-aid funding are the real problem. If we're looking for solutions, why aren't we putting batterers in shelters and letting the women and children stay at home?"

From Ann Jones, *Next Time, She'll Be Dead: Battering and How to Stop It* (Boston: Beacon, 1994), pp. 229–231.

a. There have been no new federal programs for battered women since 1984. _____

b. In New York City, Sanctuary for Families turns away 100 battered women and their children every week. _____

c. In all areas of the country, demand for temporary shelter is rising.
_____

d. Some shelters have had to discontinue support for children.
_____

e. One Midwestern shelter laid off its custodian for lack of funds.
_____

f. Minnesota spends less to help battered women than to kill mosquitoes. _____

g. There are only about a thousand shelters for battered women in the United States. _____

h. In Seattle, 500 men are arrested for battering every month.
_____

4. <u>Since the beginning of time, it seems, roses have been the flowers of love, the true flowers of Venus.</u> Cleopatra carpeted a room with red rose petals so that their scent would rise above Mark Antony as he walked toward her. Dionysius, the tyrant of Syracuse, filled his house with roses for the frequent compulsory orgies he held with the young women of his city; Nero used millions of the blooms to decorate a hall for a single banquet, and rose water–saturated pigeons fluttered overhead to sprinkle the guests with scent. In fact, roses were so popular in ancient times that they actually became a symbol of the degeneracy of later Roman emperors, and it took the Church, to which the rose became a symbol of purity, to rescue it from oblivion during the Dark Ages. According to one ancient story, a number of noble Romans were suffocated under tons of rose petals dropped on them during one of Emperor Heliogabalus's orgies. The Romans so loved the flower that they imported bargefuls of rose petals and hips from Egypt, where the growing season was longer, and they believed in the flower's powers so fervently that they used rose water in their fountains. Long before this, the Greek physician Galen had used a full pound of rose oil in a facial cosmetic he invented, and "attar of roses" remains a much-valued cosmetic ingredient to this day. For centuries, the rose has been employed to invoke love in some rather strange ways. Persian women thought that rose water was a philter that would bring back straying lovers; one old Chinese love recipe drunk during the fourth-month rose festivals

consisted of prunes, sugar, olives, and rose petals; and colonial ladies made "rose wine" to stimulate their lovers by marinating rose petals in brandy. Finally we have Napoleon's empress Josephine, who, when her teeth turned bad, always carried a rose in her hand with which to cover her mouth when she laughed.

From Robert Hendrickson, *The Facts on File Encyclopedia of Word and Phrase Origins* (New York: Facts On File/Quality Paperback Book Club, 1997), pp. 578–79. Copyright © 1997 by Robert Hendrickson. Reprinted by permission of Facts On File, Inc.

a. Mark Antony filled his house with roses for his orgies. _____

b. Roses became a symbol of the degeneracy of later Roman emperors. _____

c. The Church rescued the rose from oblivion during the Dark Ages. _____

d. The Romans so loved the flower that they imported bargefuls of rose petals and hips from Egypt. _____

e. Galen used a full pound of rose oil in a facial cosmetic he invented. _____

f. Dionysius was the tyrant of Syracuse. _____

g. There is a Chinese love recipe that uses rose petals. _____

h. Persian women thought rose water would bring back straying lovers. _____

THINKING ABOUT YOUR READING AND WRITING

ACTIVITY H: Understanding Your Thought Process

Describe the thought process you used to determine whether a detail in Activity G was major or minor.

_____

_____

_____

_____

WORKING TOGETHER

With a partner, return to the paragraphs in Activity G. Create maps for two paragraphs that show the relationships between the major and minor details in each.

▶ *Chapter Summary*

Based on your reading of this chapter, list at least five ideas that you believe will help you with future reading assignments. Write in complete sentences.

1. _____

_____

_____

_____

2. _____

_____

_____

_____

3. _____

_____

_____

_____

4. _____

_____

_____

_____

5. _____

_____

_____

_____

▶ *Extended Application*

Now that you have worked with the strategies necessary for understanding details, you can practice applying them to full-length reading selections. Choose (or your instructor may choose) a reading selection from Part 2 of this book or another reading selection that is typical of what you will be expected to read for your other college courses, such as an essay or a textbook chapter. Use this selection to:

❋ Recognize supporting sentences.

❋ Understand types of details.

❋ Understand relationships between main ideas and details.

❋ Distinguish between major and minor details.

Decide on the practice strategies you will use. Apply them to your selection. Then, in a few paragraphs, write a description of what you did and how the strategies you used worked for you.

Name of material used: _____

Page numbers: _____

Your description: _____

CHAPTER FIVE

Understanding Organizational Patterns in Academic Texts

T HINK ABOUT THE LYRICS OF A SONG you enjoy hearing. Is there a beginning, a middle, and an end to the song? Does each part connect logically to the next? How does the song's structure affect your enjoyment of the lyrics? Through their music, composers intentionally convey particular moods and ideas. They do this in part by selecting certain notes or combinations and sequences of sounds, but their choices of these are often guided by a larger consideration— the type of music they are writing.

Certain patterns for organizing musical elements are associated with classical music, others with jazz, rap, and so on. These patterns give the musical score cohesiveness, or unity. The parts fit together to create a well-coordinated whole. Writers of prose also need organizational patterns so that the various sections of their text fit together in a way that makes sense or so that there is cohesiveness. Such a plan is often referred to as the *writer's organization*. In this chapter, you will learn how writers achieve organization and how this contributes to their overall success in conveying a message.

Reviewing What You Already Know

You have already learned that a relationship exists between the main idea and the remainder of the text you are reading. You now know that the main idea or thesis provides the focus of the reading material and that details essentially explain, describe, support, or in some other way elaborate on the main idea. Authors of expository text organize their main ideas and details around patterns.

The design of an essay or paragraph, then, might look like the following illustration.

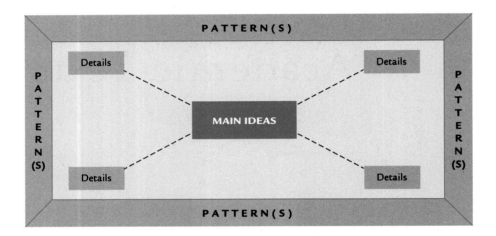

Organizational patterns are extremely beneficial to writers. They provide the framework for connecting the main idea and details of an essay. They help writers assist readers in understanding the development of ideas, stay on target and avoid digressions from the main point, and provide variety in their writing and maintain audience interest. Writers can choose from a number of ways to organize their ideas. There are six common organizational patterns:

1. Simple listing
2. Definition and explanation
3. Comparison and contrast
4. Thesis and proof or opinion and reason
5. Cause and effect
6. Problem and solution

ACTIVITY A: Recognizing What You Already Know About Patterns

In this exercise, list the pattern(s) with which you are familiar. For each one you list, indicate what you know about it or in what kinds of writing situations it might be useful. Also note any signal words you can recall that are associated with the particular pattern. Don't worry if you can't do too much with this activity. We will explain each pattern in this chapter.

1. Pattern I know: _____

   What I know about it: _____

   _____

   Signal words I know for this pattern: _____

   _____

2. Pattern I know: _____

   What I know about it: _____

   _____

   Signal words I know for this pattern: _____

   _____

3. Pattern I know: _____

   What I know about it: _____

   _____

   Signal words I know for this pattern: _____

   _____

A single essay may be structured around one pattern, such as thesis and proof or comparison and contrast. This is the primary pattern of the essay. But within such an essay, individual paragraphs may have their own patterns or arrangements of details. One paragraph may also contain several patterns, but one pattern may seem more primary or dominant. As you will learn later in this chapter, the author's purpose for writing, along with the main idea or thesis to be developed through the essay, plays a key role in determining what patterns, and how many patterns, he or she will use.

The patterns discussed in this chapter are used more frequently in expository writing (such as essays or informative writing like textbooks) than in narrative writing (such as plays, novels, short stories, and poems). Narrative writing most often uses other mechanisms, such as dialogue and plot, for creating cohesiveness.

Knowledge of patterns of organization also offers benefits to readers. If *before* and *during* your reading you search for the organizational structure, you may be able to:

* Follow the development of an author's ideas.
* Stay focused on the main ideas.
* Make predictions about what might be the next topic of discussion or next set of details.
* See relationships between details.
* Remember information (using the pattern as the organizing structure for memory).
* Create visuals to help you remember the information.

How Can Patterns Be Identified?

The following sections contain more detailed explanations of each pattern. You will learn about *signal words* that are often associated with each pattern, sample sentences that suggest the pattern the author will probably use, and example paragraphs. A signal word does not need to be used every time a new pattern begins. However, you should be alert to these words because when they are used you will be able to predict the way the material will be organized and to follow the author's thinking while you read.

Simple Listing

In this pattern, a number of details are given in list order. The list may be written in order of importance, chronologically, spatially, or enumerated in no particular order.

SIGNAL WORDS FOR SIMPLE LISTING

Order of importance: most important, less important, least important

Chronological: first, second, and so on; next, then, today, yesterday, finally; 1991, 1992, and so on; after, before, previously, once, meanwhile

Spatial: to the right, to the left, on top, inside

Enumeration: also, in addition, further, another, furthermore, moreover, besides, a number of, several

EXAMPLES OF SENTENCES THAT SUGGEST A SIMPLE LISTING PATTERN

1. Over the last five years, New Jersey taxpayers have expressed increasing dissatisfaction with the state government. *You would expect a listing of the dissatisfactions, perhaps in chronological order.*

2. There are several important steps to take when you are planning to apply for a job in a new field. *You would expect a listing of the steps, perhaps in order of importance.*

Sample paragraph: simple listing pattern (chronological) (with signal words underlined)

The history of rap music can be traced to many sources. Pop culture historians say that rap draws on the tradition of urban street jive, a form of speech that developed in Chicago, Ill., in the 1920s. More directly, critics say that rap music first appeared in New York City in the mid-1970s. Jamaican immigrant Clive Campbell, also known as DJ Kool Herc, mixed up music by using records playing on two turntables, switching rapidly from one to the other to mix and match beats between songs. In addition, Campbell introduced the art of Jamaican "toasting" in which the DJ speaks with humor and syncopation over the rhythm of instrumental versions of music. The first rap hit was "Rappers Delight" (1979), released by a group of rappers from Brooklyn, N.Y., called the Sugarhill Gang. "Rappers Delight" reached number 36 on Billboard's Top 40 music chart. In the early 1980s, DJ Afrika Bambaataa popularized the use of drum machines and synthesizers to produce a new "techno sound." As rappers attracted more listeners in the 1980s, they also began to address economic inequalities in the U.S. In the late 1980s, a brutal brand of rap developed known as "gangsta rap." Gangsta rap often glorified misogyny and violence and elicited an outcry from critics.

From "Getting a Bad Rap?" *Current Events* [Teacher's Ed.] 100:17 (February 2, 2001): 2. Copyright © 2002 by Weekly Reader Corporation. Used by permission.

Sample paragraph: simple listing pattern (spatial) (with signal words underlined)

The Sri Lakshmi Temple is a popular center for the worship of the goddess Lakshmi, known for her graciousness and generosity. Tamil-speaking Hindu priests perform the daily and festival rituals while Hindus young and old come from neighboring towns to beg her favor and celebrate her glory. To Lakshmi's left is her spouse Vishnu, Lord of the universe; <u>to her right</u>, the popular elephant-headed god Ganesh; <u>around the temple's central space</u> stand Shiva, the mysterious and gracious destroyer of illusions, the loving and playful Murugan, the welcoming Ayappan who is child of both Vishnu and Shiva, and the beloved monkey god Hanuman. <u>Downstairs</u> there are regular lectures, concerts and weddings.

From Francis X. Clooney, "The Mosque Next Door," *America* 185:16 (November 19, 2001): 21.

Sample paragraph: simple listing pattern (order of importance) (with signal words underlined)

Since the 1970s, some interesting studies have been done on teachers' attitudes toward girls in the classroom. Perhaps <u>the most important</u> finding is that stereotypes about girls influenced teacher expectations about acceptable classroom behavior and academic performance. Girls were expected to be "ladylike" and to "control themselves." Aggressive behavior by girls was discouraged. <u>Also significant</u> were the findings concerning specific subject areas. Many teachers believed that girls are likely to "love" reading and to "hate" mathematics and science. Girls were not expected to think logically or to understand scientific principles. <u>It was also noted in many studies</u> that if there were student-organized activities, boys were typically in charge, with girls assisting, in the stereotyped role of secretary. Today's educators have worked hard to eliminate these sex biases in the classroom.

Definition and Explanation

This pattern is used to define a new term or concept, or to explain or describe a topic, idea, or process that the author thinks may be unclear to the reader. An entire paragraph may be written in this pattern. The definition may be straightforward and may sound almost like a dictionary entry. Or the definition may include *classification* of the unknown term or concept. For instance, an author might define the musical style of a new group by defining the type of music it plays, such as *techno*. Or an animal may be defined by such classifications as its *phylum, genus,* and *species*. Readers can understand a new term or concept by associating it with one they already know when the classification is given.

This pattern also refers to paragraphs of elaborate explanation, such as an explanation of how personal computers work or how to use a high-speed drill.

SIGNAL WORDS FOR DEFINITION AND EXPLANATION

this is

for example

in other words

such as

for instance

which means

EXAMPLES OF SENTENCES THAT SUGGEST A DEFINITION
AND EXPLANATION PATTERN

1. The *big bang theory,* a contemporary explanation of how the universe began, is being challenged by some scientists. *You would expect a definition or explanation of the big bang theory and then a discussion of the kinds of challenges it is facing.*

2. It is not difficult to use a single-lens reflex camera. You would expect a definition of single-lens reflex camera. Then you would hope for an explanation of how to use it, perhaps in a chronological, spatial, or order-of-importance listing pattern.

Sample paragraph: definition and explanation pattern (with signal words underlined)

The control unit is the computer's internal police officer. This CPU component maintains order and controls all the internal activities of the machine. The control unit sends out electronic signals directing the computer to perform specific tasks such as moving data between memory and the CPU, activating the ALU, receiving data and sending information. The control unit manages the flow of data throughout the machine based on the instructions it receives from programs. No instructions are processed by the control unit. Rather, it directs other parts of the computer to perform their functions in a specific order, at a specific time.

From Helene G. Kershner, *Computer Literacy,* 2d ed. (Lexington, MA: D. C. Heath, 1992), p. 77.

What term in this paragraph did the author think needed to be defined for readers? _____

Explain what the author did to help the reader understand this term.

_____

_____

Comparison and Contrast

This pattern is used to show similarities (*comparisons*) or to show differences (*contrasts*). Writers use this pattern when they want to show how something or someone is similar to or different from something or someone else. Often, both similarities and differences are included within a single comparison and contrast paragraph. Signal words associated with this pattern are then used to let the reader know a shift in focus is occurring.

SIGNAL WORDS FOR COMPARISON AND CONTRAST

COMPARISON	CONTRAST	
in the same way	although	instead
similarly	on the other hand	yet
likewise	however	unlike
both	but	conversely
in comparison	nevertheless	in contrast
	on the contrary	

EXAMPLES OF SENTENCES THAT SUGGEST
A COMPARISON AND CONTRAST PATTERN

1. The Mets fans behaved better than those who were rooting for the Yankees. *You would expect a contrast to be made between the two groups of fans.*

2. Moderate exercise for a few minutes every day is more beneficial than doing a whole day of strenuous physical exercise once a week. *You would expect a contrast between the two exercise regimens to be made in order to show why one is better than the other.*

3. Yasmine's taste in closthing was just like her mom's. *You would expect a comparison to be made between Yasmine and her mom.*

Sample paragraph: comparison pattern (with signal words underlined)

Roberto Corelli, the main character in the story "Rise Up and Fall Down," reminds me of my maternal grandfather in several respects. Roberto came to America in 1900, a penniless nine-year-old orphan. He was apprenticed to a brutal uncle in Chicago who kept him out of school and put him to work in a blacksmith's shop. My grandfather sailed to America in steerage just a few years after 1900. <u>Like</u> Roberto, he had little chance for formal education. As soon as he had learned to read, write, and add, he was taken out of his second-grade class by his impoverished parents and made to sell newspapers on the Boston streets. Roberto ran away, joined a circus, and at the age of twenty-one became the Strong Man in a sideshow set. My grandfather started to practice boxing at the YMCA and by the age of eighteen was a promising light heavyweight. <u>Both</u> Roberto and my grandfather eventually fell in love with immigrant girls, married, and settled down as local shopkeepers—Roberto as a butcher and my grandfather as a news-dealer. <u>Similarities such as these</u> continued to occur to me as I read "Rise Up and Fall Down," making it easy for me to give Roberto the understanding and compassion that his life's story was intended to evoke.

From Ed Ezor and Jill Lewis, *From Paragraph to Essay: A Process Approach for Beginning College Writing* (New York: McGraw-Hill, 1984), p. 255. Reprinted by permission of the authors.

Sample paragraph: contrast pattern (with signal words underlined)

America's population has increased 13.2 percent since the 1990 census, which is <u>more than</u> was predicted. We enter the new millennium with a record total of 281,421,906 people. <u>By contrast,</u> the Russia State Statistics Committee reports that Russia's population has been declining by about 750,000 annually since the Soviet collapse in 1991, bringing it down to 145 million. This means the vast territory does not have much more than half the population of the United States. Russia is expected to shrink by another 11 million people in the next 15 years. That would move it from the seventh most populated country in the world to the 14th. <u>Conversely,</u> in our country, according to the National Center for Health Statistics, life expectancy in 1998 was 76.7 years, up from 74.9 a decade earlier. That means an American can expect to live 10 years longer <u>than</u> a Russian. And it means that the oldest of the 79 million baby boomers, who have reached the age of 54, can count on an active life for many more years to come.

Adapted from Daniel Schorr, "A Study in Contrasts," *New Leader* 84:1 (January/February 2001): 5. Reprinted with permission of *The New Leader.* Copyright © the American Labor Conference on International Affairs, Inc.

Sample paragraph: comparison and contrast pattern (with signal words underlined)

Shamika's college adviser told her that she possessed many of the traits similar to those reported in accounts of successful businesswomen, and he suggested that she should consider majoring in business. Shamika had excellent rapport with other people. She was a good public speaker and had shown leadership skills when she served as one of the key organizers for the college's first Environmental Awareness conference. On the other hand, she had some traits that her adviser thought might hinder her chances for success. For instance, she was often late with her assignments, and she was impatient with herself when things took longer to do than expected. She also needed to improve her math skills. Her adviser suggested that Shamika consider all that he had said before she selected a major.

Thesis and Proof or Opinion and Reason

This pattern is used to persuade readers to accept an idea. The idea may be one that is factual or well researched, supported by substantial evidence, or supported by information drawn from authoritative sources. The author may have conducted a research study and have cited evidence or findings from this study to support the *thesis.* Or the material may be a statement of *opinion,* supported by unresearched reasons, personal beliefs, or information from unauthoritative sources. The sentence that states the opinion or the thesis serves as the main idea for the paragraph or essay. The author offers *proof* for the thesis and *reasons* for the opinion. The proof or reasons are intended to convince the reader that the author's view is correct. These arguments may be enumerated and may be listed in ascending or descending order.

SIGNAL WORDS FOR THESIS AND PROOF OR OPINION AND REASON

it is widely known	one must consider
the reasons for this	in my opinion
there is evidence	evidently
it should be accepted	as proof
it is believed	

EXAMPLES OF SENTENCES THAT SUGGEST A THESIS AND PROOF OR OPINION AND REASON PATTERN

1. The city council argued that the town pool should be built immediately. *You would expect several sentences to give the reasons that the council argued this way.* This suggests an opinion and reason pattern.
2. It has been established that dinosaurs were both herbivores and carnivores. *You would expect sentences to show how this has been "established."* This suggests a thesis and proof pattern.

Sample paragraph: opinion and reason pattern (with signal words underlined)

Dog owners ought to accept more responsibility for their animals. They should not let their dogs run wild because dogs can be very destructive to other people's property. Further, dogs sometimes carry rabies, and if they bite another dog, or worse, a human, the dog or human can develop rabies and die. Dog owners also have responsibility for their pets' own welfare. If dogs are allowed to run loose, they can get killed by cars or hurt by wild animals such as raccoons and squirrels.

Sample paragraph: thesis and proof pattern (with signal words underlined)

Although we used to believe that folk medical remedies were merely forms of superstition, now we know otherwise. Biomedical research has shown that the active ingredient in many folk remedies is the same as in the medicines doctors prescribe. There is also new evidence that supports the view that the prohibition of many foods in folk medicine was based on sound biological principles.

Cause and Effect

Text may be written that describes only the *causes* of something: what made something happen. Or text may be written that describes only the *effects*, or *results*, of some action. These two terms are often confused. It may help you remember the distinction between them if you bear in mind that the *cause* results in the *effect*. The *cause* may show what led up to the event or idea—that is, what caused it to become what it is now. The consequences of the event or idea are the *effects* of it. *Cause* or *effect* paragraphs are sometimes written separately; in this case, one paragraph will state the causes, and the other will give the effects. Often, though, both the *cause* and the *effect* are combined into a single paragraph.

SIGNAL WORDS FOR CAUSE AND EFFECT

CAUSE	EFFECT	COMBINED
because	as a result	if (cause), then (effect)
since	thus	(cause) resulted in (effect)
as	consequently	because of (cause), (effect)
the reason for this	so	happened
a cause	hence	a result (effect) is caused by
	therefore	
	one outcome	
	effect (affect)	

EXAMPLES OF SENTENCES THAT SUGGEST A CAUSE AND EFFECT PATTERN

1. The sudden rise to fame and fortune for some professional athletes may result in financial and personal problems for them. *This suggests an effect pattern. You would expect a discussion of the effects of sudden fame and fortune on the finances and personal lives of athletes. The cause is given.*

2. Advances in technology have caused some major changes in the way industries operate today. *You would expect a discussion of the advances (causes) and the changes (effects) of technology on business.*

Sample paragraph: cause pattern (with signal words underlined)

Farming has become a much easier occupation in recent years. <u>One reason</u> for this is that cows are now milked by automatic pumps rather than by hand. Eggs are hatched in incubators instead of by the hens themselves, which <u>also results</u> in less work for the farmers, who no longer have to keep nesting hens warm or watch over them to make sure they don't damage the eggs. The temperature and humidity in the hen houses are controlled by thermostats, not by nature's whim; and the amount of feed chickens get each day is determined by a computer rather than by a farmhand's estimates. <u>Another factor</u> that <u>makes</u> farming easier is that the farmhouse itself probably features an electronic range in place of the old coal kitchen stove. Unlike farmers of olden days, today's farmer can actually take a vacation and leave all the work to the brain of a computer, which will sense when each chore must be done and will signal the technological innovation that will accomplish it.

Adapted from Ed Ezor and Jill Lewis, *From Paragraph to Essay: A Process Approach for Beginning College Writing* (New York: McGraw-Hill, 1984), p. 255. Reprinted by permission of the authors.

This paragraph gives causes of:

_____

_____

Two causes mentioned are:

1. _____

_____

2. _____

_____

Sample paragraph: effect pattern (with signal words underlined)

People's social and cultural environments <u>affect</u> their thoughts and feelings about themselves, including their self-esteem and their self-concept. When people have no objective criteria by which to judge themselves, they look to others as the basis for social comparison. Such comparison can <u>influence</u> their self-evaluation or self-esteem. Categories of people that are habitually used for social comparison are known as reference groups. Comparison to reference groups sometimes <u>produces</u> relative deprivation, which in turn can <u>cause</u> personal and social turmoil.

From Douglas A. Bernstein and Peggy W. Nash, *Essentials of Psychology,* 2d ed. (Boston: Houghton Mifflin, 2001), p. 527.

This paragraph gives effects of:

_____

_____

Two effects mentioned are:

1. _____

_____

2. _____

_____

Sample paragraph: cause and effect pattern (with signal words underlined)

Until World War I, the United States had always been a debtor nation. This means we owed more money to foreign nations than they owed us. This was partly <u>because</u> the value of the goods and services we imported often exceeded the value of goods we sold to foreigners. Also, foreigners were investing far more in the United States than Americans were investing in other countries. <u>Thus</u> we had to pay interest and dividends to investors abroad. During World War I, the situation was reversed. The war-torn nations of Europe needed U.S. goods, <u>so</u> our exports more than doubled, while the value of the goods we imported declined. By 1919 we had become a creditor nation—foreign nations owed more to the United States than the United States owed to them. This position continued until 1985, when the United States once again became a net debtor nation. The value of our imports greatly exceeded the value of our exports, and foreigners were investing heavily in U.S. securities, largely because of the relatively high interest rates here. [*Note:* A chronological listing is also evident in this paragraph, but the cause and effect relationship of the events is the major emphasis.]

Adapted from Sanford D. Gordon and George G. Dawson. *Introductory Economics,* 7th ed. (Lexington, MA: D. C. Heath, 1991), p. 433.

This paragraph gives causes of:

_____

_____

Two causes mentioned are:

1. _____

_____

2. _____

_____

This paragraph gives effects of:

_____

_____

Two effects mentioned are:

1. _____

_____

2. _____

_____

Problem and Solution

The *problem and solution* pattern is used to explain a problem and to offer recommendations. Most often the causes and effects of the problem are also stated, which means this pattern may not be clear until you have read several sentences or paragraphs. The statement of the problem is usually at or near the beginning of the paragraph or essay, and this should alert you to look for this pattern in the text that follows.

SIGNAL WORDS FOR PROBLEM AND SOLUTION

PROBLEM	SOLUTION
unfortunately	clearly
the problem	consequently
a difficulty	obviously
	to solve
	one solution

EXAMPLES OF SENTENCES THAT SUGGEST
A PROBLEM AND SOLUTION PATTERN

1. People who rent apartments must find ways to deal with landlords who sometimes ignore tenants' needs. *You would expect an explanation of the solutions to the problem already stated.*

2. Multinational corporations must regain support from customers after being accused of taking advantage of workers in Third World countries. *You would probably expect some suggestions for regaining support and a more detailed explanation of the accusations.*

Sample paragraph: problem and solution pattern (with signal words underlined)

Parents often have difficulty deciding how much allowance to give their children. One reason for this is that they are torn between believing their children should have an opportunity to budget their money and the feeling that their children will not use their allowance wisely and will continue to ask for additional money. Parents also have trouble deciding what to include in the child's list of items that the allowance must pay for. The result of such dilemmas is that children are often given too little or too much allowance, with little clear guidance about how it is to be spent. The rules keep changing. One way to solve this problem is for parents and children to confer regularly about how allowance is being spent and to establish clear guidelines, with revisions being made every so often as the child's needs and interests change.

The problem that is stated is:

_____

_____

The cause(s) given for the problem is (are):

_____

_____

The effect(s) of the problem is (are):

_____

_____

_____

The solution(s) offered is (are):

_____

_____

Note that each part you've listed could be developed into its own paragraph. If you added introductory and concluding paragraphs, the result could be a complete essay.

WORKING TOGETHER

With a partner, write one sentence that you believe could suggest each of the types of paragraphs listed below.

1. Simple listing
   Order of importance

   _____

   _____

   Chronological

   _____

   _____

   Spatial

   _____

   _____

2. Definition and explanation

   _____

   _____

3. Comparison and contrast

_____

_____

4. Thesis and proof or opinion and reason

_____

_____

5. Cause and effect

_____

_____

6. Problem and solution

_____

_____

Relationships Among Main Ideas, Details, and Patterns

In the preceding section you saw how single sentences could indicate the pattern that would probably be used by the author. These sentences could have been main-idea sentences for paragraphs or entire essays. The main idea often suggests how the material will be organized—what pattern, or patterns, will be used. The writer's choice of organizational patterns is often based on a decision about which questions raised by the main idea, or thesis statement, will be answered. The example main-idea sentence that follows illustrates this point.

Example:
There are at least three good reasons people should participate in community service activities.

The author of this sentence will certainly need to give at least three reasons for this belief about community service activities. The sentence lends itself immediately to two patterns: (1) *opinion and reason,* and (2) *simple listing.* The next example suggests a different pattern of organization even though the sentence is about the same topic as the previous example.

Example:

Teenagers who participate in community service activities have greater self-esteem than those who don't.

Although the author will probably be giving opinions again, the comparison and contrast introduced in the main-idea sentence needs elaboration. This sentence lends itself to a *comparison and contrast* essay, which may easily incorporate a simple listing format. In the next example, also on the same topic, the author will probably use a different pattern of organization to develop the idea.

Example:

Community service means different things to different people.

Very likely, this author will use a *definition* pattern to explain the different meanings.

To some extent, then, the main idea controls the form the essay will take. After you identify a stated main idea or thesis, you should be able to predict the pattern that will be used. You can use your knowledge of patterns to help you follow the development of the main idea or thesis while you read; you will know to look for certain kinds of information, such as definitions, reasons, and comparisons. In cases where the author does not state the main idea, you will be able to create one that suits the organization of the reading material. Your knowledge of patterns will also help you remember the information and comprehend how the different details are related to each other and to the main idea.

Recognizing Patterns of Organization

Four steps will help you recognize what pattern is being used, whether it provides the organizing structure for an entire essay or is the basis for a single paragraph.

1. Identify the stated main idea or thesis, or create one.
2. Make a prediction about the pattern that might be used as the author elaborates on this main point.
3. Locate key words within the supporting sentences that suggest a pattern.
4. Verify your prediction. For example, if you had predicted an *opinion and reason* pattern, you should be able to find opinions or reasons in the content. If you had predicted a problem and solution pattern, you should find each of these as well as, perhaps, some causes and effects of each.

Keep each of these steps in mind as you complete Activities B and C.

ACTIVITY B: Identifying Patterns in Text

For each paragraph, decide the dominant pattern of organization being used. Consider the main idea of the paragraph as well as the details when making your decision. Circle any signal words within the paragraph that are associated with the pattern you select. In the space provided, also list any secondary patterns that you find in the paragraph and be prepared to explain why you feel this secondary pattern is also evident.

PATTERN CHOICES

a. Simple listing	d. Thesis and proof	g. Problem and solution
b. Definition and explanation	e. Opinion and reason	
c. Comparison and contrast	f. Cause and effect	

1. Just how willing and able people are to make intimate commitments may depend on their earlier attachment relationships. Researchers have discovered that young adults' views of intimate relationships parallel the patterns of infant attachment. If their view reflects a secure attachment, they tend to feel valued and worthy of support and affection; develop closeness easily; and have relationships characterized by joy, trust, and commitment. If their view reflects an insecure attachment, however, they tend to be preoccupied with relationships and may feel misunderstood, underappreciated, and worried about being abandoned; their relations are often negative, obsessive, and jealous. Alternatively, they may be aloof and unable to commit or trust. Video-tapes produced by researchers reveal that as anxiety increases, people with a secure attachment style increase their requests for support from their partners, whereas those with an insecure style decrease support-seeking behaviors. In another study, insecurely attached individuals were found to engage in more one-night stands and less cuddling than did those whose attachment style was secure.

   Adapted from Douglas A. Bernstein and Peggy W. Nash, *Essentials of Psychology,* 2d ed. (Boston: Houghton Mifflin, 2001), p. 337.

   Primary Pattern(s): _____

   Secondary Pattern(s): _____

Your explanation: _____

_____

_____

2. Winston Churchill once said, "We build our buildings and then they build us." A society's success is ultimately based on its culture. A society whose culture builds productivity, hard work, education, and scientific research will build wealth. A culture that encourages hedonism, sloppy work, poor worker motivation, and illiteracy will be eclipsed. A nation whose culture easily obtains from its citizens cooperation, discipline, and self-sacrifice has a cultural foundation much firmer than those countries whose work ethic has been eroded, whose sense of mission is undercut, and whose destiny is less manifest.

Primary Pattern(s): _____

Secondary Pattern(s): _____

Your explanation: _____

_____

_____

3. In May 1779, the First Company of Philadelphia Artillery petitioned the Assembly about the troubles of the "midling and poor" and threatened violence against "those who are avariciously intent upon amassing wealth by the destruction of the more virtuous part of the community." That same month, there was a mass meeting, an extralegal gathering which called for price reductions and initiated an investigation of Robert Morris, a rich Philadelphian who was accused of holding food from the market. In October came the "Fort Wilson riot," in which a militia group marched into the city and to the house of James Wilson, a wealthy lawyer and Revolutionary official who had opposed price controls and the democratic constitution adopted in Pennsylvania in 1776. The militia were driven away by a "silk stocking brigade" of well-off Philadelphia citizens.

From Howard Zinn, *A People's History of the United States* (New York: Harper & Row, 1980), p. 79.

Primary Pattern(s): _____

Secondary Pattern(s): _____

Your explanation: _____

_____

_____

4. Psychological problems sometimes take somatic form, or the form of a bodily disorder, even though there is no physical cause. One type of somatoform disorder is **hypochondriasis** (pronounced "hye-pohkon-DRY-a-sis"), a strong, unjustified fear that one has, or might get, cancer, heart disease, AIDS, or some other serious medical problem. The fear prompts frequent visits to doctors and reports of numerous symptoms. Their preoccupation with illness often leads hypochondriacs to become "experts" on their most feared diseases. In a related condition called **somatization disorder**, individuals make dramatic, but vague, reports about a multitude of physical problems rather than any specific illness. Pain disorder is marked by complaints of severe, often constant pain (typically in the neck, chest, or back) with no physical cause.

Adapted from D. A. Bernstein and P. W. Nash, *Essentials of Psychology*, 3d ed. (Boston: Houghton Mifflin, 2005), p. 150.

Primary Pattern(s): _____

Secondary Pattern(s): _____

Your explanation: _____

_____

_____

5. Today's business people live in an overcommunicated world. There are too many Web sites, too many reports, too many bits of information bidding for their attention. The successful ones are forced to become deft machete wielders in this jungle of communication. They ruthlessly cut away at all the extraneous data that are encroaching upon them. They speed through their tasks so they can cover as much ground as possible, answering dozens of e-mails at a sitting and scrolling past dozens more. After all, the main scarcity in their life is not

money; it's time. They guard every precious second, the way a desert wanderer guards his water.

From David Brooks, "Time to Do Everything Except Think," *Newsweek* 137:18 (April 30, 2000): 71.

Primary Pattern(s): _____

Secondary Pattern(s): _____

Your explanation: _____

_____

_____

6. Just think of the many people you know who wanted to be something really special when they reached adulthood, and seemed to have the ability to achieve this goal, who are now in seemingly dead-end jobs. Most people begin and end their working years willing, even anxious, to compromise their career goals with what they assume to be the harsh realities of the marketplace. Often this shift in career goals results from an attitude developed during childhood. Sometimes it is the result of an unpleasant interview during their twenties. Parental pressure, financial strain, or lack of patience can all contribute to this unnecessary tragedy. It might also result from unpleasant work experiences early on in a career, such as difficulties with coworkers or a boss. But it is never too early or too late to correct this situation and to find yourself the job that you desperately want and deserve.

Primary Pattern(s): _____

Secondary Pattern(s): _____

Your explanation: _____

_____

_____

7. Essential oils have long been known to relax the body and rejuvenate the nervous system. To get the most out of their healing properties, add a few drops into the bath or a vaporizer, or just apply as you would perfume. For a case of cabin fever, consider floral oils, such as geranium, rose or jasmine, which are known for their balancing and

restorative properties. Citrus oils, including bergamot and mandarin, are great for boosting the spirit and clearing the mind. And for a raging case of the doldrums, try the essential oils of chamomile, marjoram or ylang-ylang, all of which encourage emotional peace and have a calming effect on both body and spirit.

From M. Rabat, "Got the Fever?" *Vegetarian Times* 295 (March 2002), p. 16.

Primary Pattern(s): _____

Secondary Pattern(s): _____

Your explanation: _____

_____

_____

8. Although the use of marijuana for medical purposes has been recorded for centuries, it has become of intense interest only in recent times. There are active initiatives in several western countries designed to make marijuana legally available for medical purposes. In view of the controversy surrounding the recreational use of marijuana, it is not surprising that there has been intense debate about marijuana's potential as a therapeutic agent. Advocates describe medical marijuana as a highly effective treatment for a vast array of diseases that are refractory to all other medications. Moreover, they stress that terminally ill patients are being denied a valuable medication that is without adverse effects. These arguments have resonated with the public, the result of which is laws in several countries that sanction medical marijuana. Others counter that marijuana has not been proven to be effective for any disorder and that it poses serious health risks.

From Billy R. Martin, "Medical Marijuana—Moving beyond the Smoke," *Lancet* 360:9326 (July 6, 2002), p. 4.

Primary Pattern(s): _____

Secondary Pattern(s): _____

Your explanation: _____

_____

_____

9. There are many choices of colleges in the United States, and they vary in size, academic program, and quality of life offered to students. At one college, the fine arts program may be very strong. It may also have wonderful athletic programs and lots of options in the humanities. But the science facilities may not be as good, and the business programs may be weaker than those found at other colleges. Unless students know what they want, they may have difficulty choosing which college to attend. Students today have so many options—what music to listen to, what movies to see, what books to read—they can end up feeling overwhelmed and unable to make a decision. Some colleges provide a small, closely knit community, in which students live in the dorms and know practically everyone on campus. At other institutions, the campus is so big that buses transport students from one class in one building to another. Tuition also varies quite a bit from college to college. The cost of tuition is not always a reflection of the quality of the academic program, either. Every year, one popular magazine lists those campuses that give students a lot for their money.

   Primary Pattern(s): _____

   Secondary Pattern(s): _____

   Your explanation: _____

   _____

   _____

10. Until recently, archaeologists were able to pin only a few firm dates on the ancient human remains that had been discovered in the Americas. Part of the reason was that the existing dating technology required that large samples—sometimes an entire bone—be destroyed, and so the process was infrequently applied. But in the past decade several new analytical methods have emerged: DNA typing of ancient biological material, comparative skull measurements and accelerator mass spectrometry, a radiocarbon-dating technique that requires only minuscule amounts of bone. Those new techniques have made it possible to accurately determine the ages of skeletal remains, as well as to classify the various human ethnic groups far more precisely than ever before. Moreover, in recent years a few very ancient and well-preserved new skeletons have been unearthed. Those discoveries, combined with the new analyses, have led archaeologists to some startling conclusions—

including the possibility that modern-day Native Americans are not descended from the earliest people who colonized the Americas.

From Robson Bonnichsen and Alan L. Schneider, "Battle of the Bone," *Sciences* 40:4 (July/August 2000), p. 40.

Primary Pattern(s): _____

Secondary Pattern(s): _____

Your explanation: _____

_____

_____

ACTIVITY C: Patterns in Multiparagraph Essays

Essays often use a variety of patterns. This adds interest to the writing and enables the writer to accomplish a number of purposes within a single essay. In a single essay, for instance, an author may wish to present a problem, along with solutions; give a number of examples; compare one aspect of the problem with some other aspect; and describe in chronological order how the problem developed. Multiparagraph essays usually have an introductory paragraph that introduces the topic and, perhaps, states the main idea to be developed. They often also have a concluding paragraph that restates the main idea and summarizes major points.

Read the following multiparagraph essay to see how many different patterns within it you can find. Look for signal words. See also whether there is an introductory or concluding paragraph.

1. What makes you see red? For most people, it's light with a wavelength just a shade over 550 nanometers (billionths of a meter). But what you call red and what I call red may be horses (or apples) of a different hue. The color you perceive, researchers have discovered, may differ subtly, but significantly, from the color someone else sees. What's more, they've traced the mechanism for this color mismatch right down to a single amino acid sequence in our genes.

2. Color perception begins when light strikes specialized cone-shaped receptor cells in the retina. The cones are called red, blue, and green because proteins embedded in them respond selectively to different wavelengths of light. But the terms are misleading; in fact, each pro-

tein responds to a wide range of colors. "Color perception is a comparative system," explains molecular biologist Jeremy Nathans of Johns Hopkins. "A red apple illuminated by the afternoon sunlight is giving off all wavelengths of light. But it mostly reflects red wavelengths while absorbing blue and green and, to a lesser extent, yellow wavelengths. That distribution of light will excite the eye's red pigment most, the green somewhat less, and the blue least of all. That distribution is what your brain gets, and it says, 'That ratio means red.'"

3. But figuring out just how colors appear to people has always been a problem. "We couldn't get inside people's heads," says Nathans. "All we could do is design a test and ask, 'Do these two colors look identical or do they look different?'" Along with colleague Shannath Merbs, Nathans figured out a way to determine at least which colors a person was capable of perceiving. Nathans first analyzed DNA from a number of people and then genetically engineered the proteins found in their red, green, and blue cone cells. Using a spectrometer, he measured the precise wavelengths of light absorbed by the so-called pigment proteins. He then plotted the results and came up with a bell curve representing the absorption spectrum—or range of responses—for each pigment. In effect, he found a way of seeing the same colors other people saw, using their own color receptors.

4. It was in the course of sequencing the DNA that Nathans found a surprising natural variation. The string of amino acids on the chromosome that codes for the red pigment protein came in two slightly different forms. "It happened to be position number 180," says Nathans. "Some people have an alanine there, some people have a serine." Color receptors with the amino acid serine at site 180, he found, respond most strongly to light with a wavelength of 557 nanometers; those with alanine prefer a wavelength of 552.

5. To determine the effect of this difference in the actual eyes of beholders, Samir Deeb and colleagues at the University of Washington put people from both the serine and alanine groups through standard color-matching tests. "Those with serine would be more sensitive to red light," says Nathans. "When asked to mix ingredients to form a standard color, they would require less red." Further studies then determined how frequently each variation appeared in a population of normally sighted men: approximately 60 percent had serine at site 180, and 40 percent had alanine.

6. It may come as no surprise that we each color our world somewhat differently, that even normally sighted people don't always see eye to eye. What is remarkable, however, is the ability to trace this difference right down to a single amino acid, making a direct link between gene and brain.

From Beth Ann Meehan, "Seeing Red: It's Written in Your Genes," *Discover* (June 1993): 66.

What patterns did you find? List the patterns and the paragraphs in which you found them. Circle the signal words that support your findings.

_____

_____

_____

WORKING TOGETHER

Compare your answers with those of a partner. Make any revisions to your answers that you believe are needed.

Using Patterns to Help You Remember

You can use the knowledge you now have about the relationships among main ideas, paragraph patterns, and details, and about distinctions between major and minor details to help you create visual displays of the information you read. These displays, sometimes referred to as *graphic organizers,* are frameworks that illustrate the important conceptual relationships between ideas in text. They will help you organize and recall information, and they are valuable study aids. The process of creating them will give you an opportunity to verify that you have understood the connections between ideas. (In Chapter 8, you will learn how to interpret and create graphic organizers that are used primarily for displaying statistics.)

There are different types of graphic organizers. We discuss several types in the following sections. The patterns used in the text direct you toward the type of organizer to create.

Concept Maps (for Key Vocabulary)

Recall that the definition/explanation pattern introduces new terms or concepts. Once you establish that the primary purpose of a section of the material you are reading is to define or explain a new term or concept, you can think about preparing a *concept map* for it. The basic layout for a concept map is shown in the figure. Notice that the term, or concept, is placed in the middle of the map. The broad definition for it appears at the top. On the right is space for indicating characteristics or properties of the term or concept. At the bottom is room for examples of it. On the left is space for writing another term or concept that is different from the one in the center but that will help you make comparisons with the new term.

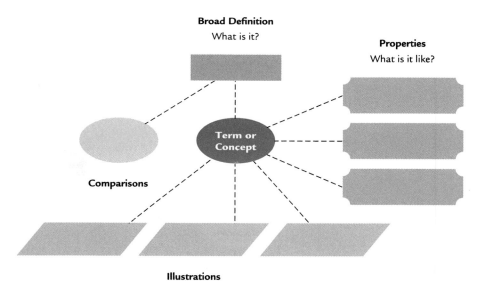

Here is an example of material for which a concept map could be created. Read the material, and while you do so think about what such a map would look like for this selection. Then study the example map that follows.

Example:

Optical Fibers

The revolution in ground-based communications has depended not only on the invention of the laser but also on the development of the *optical fiber.* An optical fiber is a hair-thin, flexible thread of ultra clear glass one-tenth of a millimeter in diameter. Optical fibers also are known as *lightguides* because they serve as pipelines or conduits for laser light.

A glass optical fiber is made from silicon, the same material that is used to make microchips. Silicon is the main ingredient in sand, so it is very plentiful. An optical fiber has a glass inner *core* with an outer layer called the *cladding.*

The cladding is composed of a slightly different glass from the core. It acts like a mirror, totally reflecting the light beam traveling through the optical fiber back into the core of the fiber. The trapped light beam cannot escape from the optical fiber until it comes to the other end. For this reason, laser light traveling through an optical fiber does not lose its brightness.

Optical fibers have many advantages over copper wires for voice, information, or data transmission. Much more information can be sent by laser beam over a single optical fiber than by electricity over one copper wire. A single optical fiber can carry the same amount of information as a telephone cable containing 256 pairs of wires. A spool of optical fiber weighing only four and one-half pounds is capable of transmitting the same number of messages as 200 reels of copper wire weighing over eight tons!

Though an optical fiber looks fragile, it is stronger than steel and can withstand over 600,000 pounds of pulling force per square inch. Unlike ordinary glass, optical fibers are not brittle or easily broken. An optical fiber is flexible enough to be tied into a loose knot and still transmit laser light flawlessly.

The first commercial application of lasers and optical fibers to connect telephones in the United States was in 1978 at Disney World in Orlando, Florida. Vista-United Telecommunications linked telephones throughout the thousands of acres of the park using fiber optic trunk lines. In addition, alarm systems and lighting systems in the park use optical fibers.

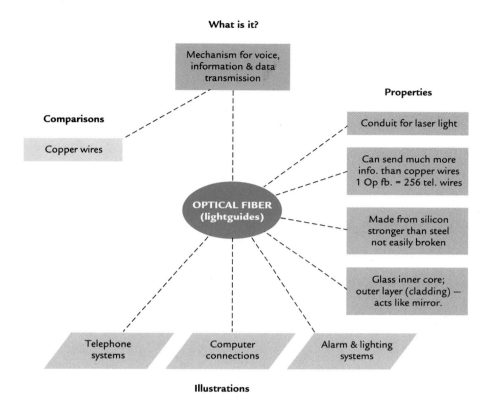

Semantic Webbing

If you decide to create a *semantic web* from text, it means that you believe the author's purpose for the material you are diagramming is to give a considerable amount of information about an event, process, or situation. The semantic web is useful as a self-monitoring tool, particularly if you create your web immediately after reading the material and without referring to the text. The semantic web is especially useful when several patterns are evident or for the problem/solution pattern. Once you have drawn it, you can verify that your web contains the important points made in the selection and that the relationship between these points has been clearly drawn. To identify prior knowledge they have on a topic, students sometimes create semantic webs before reading new material. This is always a good idea.

Read the example text. Then study the web above it. Notice how the lines drawn on the web show how the ideas are connected.

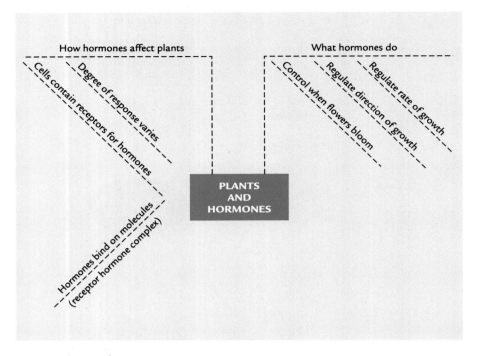

Example:

Plants and Hormones

Plants are able to use hormones to regulate their rate and direction of growth, to control the time at which they produce flowers and drop leaves, and even to coordinate the functions associated with germination. A hormone does not necessarily affect every cell of an organism in the same way. In fact, many cells cannot respond to a hormone message at all. In order to respond to the message carried by a particular hormone, a cell must contain a *receptor* for that hormone. Receptors are molecules to which hormones bind, forming a *receptor-hormone complex* that then affects cellular metabolism. Cells cannot respond to a hormone unless they contain the proper receptor. Those cells that do contain the receptor are known as *target cells,* and it is to such cells that the hormonal message is directed. The nature of the response depends on the amount of hormone that reaches the target cell, and it may also be influenced by the presence of other hormones that affect the same cell.

From Joseph S. Levine and Kenneth Miller, *Biology,* 2d ed. (Lexington, MA: D. C. Heath, 1994), p. 654.

Notice that the topic is in the middle of this map. Each important point (main idea) that is discussed and that is related to the topic is noted separately, and a line is drawn from it to the topic. The major details pertaining to each main idea have also been noted; lines extend between the detail and main idea. Minor details are drawn on lines that extend from the major details. Even someone who had not read the text would be able to see the relationship between the ideas on this web.

Hierarchical Array

When an author presents ideas in order of importance (one type of simple listing pattern), you can diagram these relationships on a *hierarchical array.* This type of visual display is illustrated in two figures. In the example text, on which both displays are based, signal words tell you to expect that some details will have greater importance than others. This should alert you to read actively and to try to visualize the hierarchy while you read so that you are prepared to create the array immediately afterward.

Example:

Death Aboard Slave Ships

Death in the crossing was due to a variety of causes. The biggest killers were gastrointestinal disorders, which were often related to the quality of food and water available on the trip, and fevers. Bouts of dysentery were common and the "bloody flux," as it was called, could break out in epidemic proportions. The increasing exposure of the slaves to dysentery increased both the rates of contamination of supplies and the incidence of death. It was dysentery that accounted for the majority of deaths and was the most common disease experienced on all voyages. The astronomic rates of mortality reached on occasional voyages were due to outbreaks of smallpox, measles, or other highly communicable diseases that were not related to time at sea or the conditions of food and water supply, hygiene, and sanitation practices. It was this randomness of epidemic diseases that prevented even experienced and efficient captains from eliminating very high mortality rates on any given voyage.

Although time at sea was not usually correlated with mortality, there were some routes in which time was a factor. Simply because they were a third longer than any other routes, the East African slave trades that developed in the late eighteenth and nineteenth centuries were noted for overall higher mortality than the West African routes, even though mortality per day at sea was the same or lower than on the shorter routes. Also, just the transporting together of slaves from different epidemiological zones in Africa guaranteed the transmission of a host of local endemic diseases to all those who were aboard. In turn, this guaranteed the spread of all major African diseases to America.

From Herbert S. Klein, "Profits and the Causes of Mortality," in David Northrup, ed., *The Atlantic Slave Trade* (Lexington, MA: D. C. Heath, 1994), p. 118.

In Model A, the hierarchy is noted by the size of the print as well as the order in which the items have been placed beneath the heading. In Model B, the distance of each item from the heading indicates its relative importance.

This type of diagram also works well for material that includes classifications. An essay about Indo-European languages, for instance, might result in your creation of a hierarchical array similar to Model C that follows.

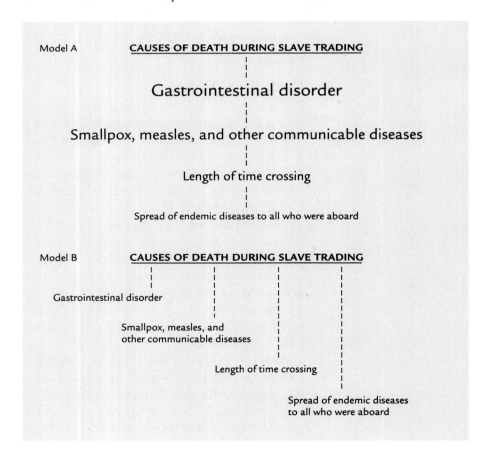

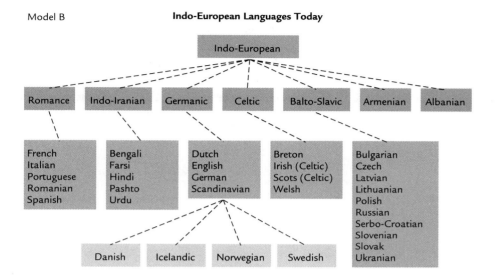

Model B — Indo-European Languages Today

Linear Array

A linear array, sometimes called a *flowchart,* may also be used to show a sequence of events, as in the simple listing chronological pattern, or a process, as in the definition/explanation pattern when used to explain how something occurs. The example text discusses a process, and the linear array for the details appears beneath the text. Notice on the array that the connections between the parts of it are made clear by lines and arrows. It would be possible to understand the information on this visual without reading the text. When you create a visual such as this, be sure that you have included all the steps of the process.

Example:

Organizational communication is a complex system involving people's feelings, attitudes, relationships, and skills as well as the goals of management and the process of change, adaptation, and growth. Individuals can both send and receive information. Both the receiver and sender have their own personal frame of reference, developed over time. Each also uses his or her own communication skills, such as reading, writing, and listening abilities, that either strengthen or lessen understanding.

In the communication process between a manager and another organizational member, the receiver accepts the message and transmits either verbal or nonverbal feedback, thereby becoming the sender. Verbal feedback is a written or spoken response. Nonverbal feedback is a body movement or actions. Noise is the interference or the barriers that may occur at any point in the process, distorting understanding. The organizational environment also affects sending, receiving, and interpreting the message. The communication process is successful only when the sender and receiver understand the message to the same degree. Feedback permits clarification and repetition until the message is fully understood.

Adapted from Jerry Kinard, *Management* (Lexington, MA: D. C. Heath, 1988), p. 349.

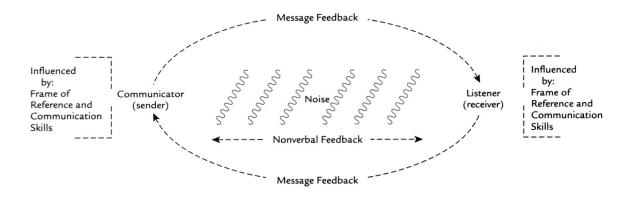

Visual Aids to Show Comparisons and Contrasts

You can also use visuals to illustrate comparison and contrast patterns. This will help you to determine whether you really know the comparisons or contrasts made. If you do not know them, you will not be able to complete all parts of the visual aid that would indicate that you need to reread the material. In this section we show two ways to prepare visuals for text that includes comparisons and contrasts.

COMPARISON AND CONTRAST BOX.   Read the example text to note the contrasts being discussed. Think about the specific points made and try to visualize how you might place this information inside a box. Then look at the model to see how it has been done.

Example:

Probably the basic disagreement on the causes of income inequality is between those who emphasize flaws in the economic system and those who emphasize flaws in those who are poor. Thus, many liberals, those on the political left, assert that the nation's economic system does not always create enough jobs, or the proper mix of jobs, so that all able-bodied individuals who want to work can find jobs at which they earn enough to provide adequately for those dependent upon them. On the other hand, many conservatives, those on the political right, tend to stress the disabilities that keep poor people from lifting themselves out of their poverty: low aspirations, low motivation, weak commitment to a conviction that one should work. They point to behaviors that make upward mobility impossible: dropping out of school, poor job performance, early parenthood, alcohol and drug abuse. They point out the obvious barrier created by lack of skills. Emphasizing the persistence of poverty despite more than twenty years of a war on poverty, some go so far as to argue that the very programs designed to reduce poverty had operated to perpetuate it.

From Bertha Davis, *Poverty in America: What We Do About It* (New York: Franklin Watts, 1991), p. 23.

Note that the information in the box is written in short phrases; not everything has been written—just the most important points.

Issue: Causes of Income Inequality	
Left Point of View	**Right Point of View**

Flaws in the system:
  not enough jobs
  wrong types of jobs
  jobs don't pay enough
	Flaws in the people:
	  low aspirations
	  low motivation
	  behaviors —
	    dropping out of school
	    drug and alcohol abuse
	    early pregnancies
	    ineffective social programs

VENN DIAGRAMS.   A second way to illustrate comparison and contrast information from text is by creating a diagram that illustrates both points of commonality and points of difference. This diagram, called a *Venn diagram,* is shown following the example text.

Example:

The one thing that all crystals have in common is that they are built up of repeated patterns. In other ways, crystals may differ widely. Some shatter easily. Others do not. Some are very hard. Some crumble at a touch.

These different properties of crystals are due to many causes. Let's look at some of them.

The way the atoms are arranged in a crystal affects its properties. Two crystals may be made up of the same kind of atom and yet have very different properties. The difference is caused by the way the atoms are arranged in each crystal.

The "lead" in a pencil is really a kind of crystalline material called graphite. Graphite is a form of the element carbon, so graphite crystals are made up entirely of carbon atoms.

Diamond is another form of carbon. Diamond crystals are also made up entirely of carbon atoms.

Diamond and graphite appear to be as different as Dr. Jekyll and Mr. Hyde. Or, as one scientist has put it, they are "beauty and the beast among crystals."

Diamond is the hardest material known. This is another way of saying that diamond will scratch or cut through all other materials. Diamond drills and saws are used to cut through rock. Diamond dust is used to grind and shape metal tools. Diamond crystals when cut and polished make brilliant gems.

Graphite is usually dull black in color and has a greasy feel. It is a very soft material. Like mica, graphite can be sliced easily into very thin sheets. The fact that thin sheets of graphite slide past each other very easily makes it useful for "oiling" moving parts in machines and makes it work in a pencil.

The difference between graphite and a diamond is the result of one extra atom of carbon in the building block of the diamond. Let's take a look at the building block of graphite first.

From Malcolm E. Weiss, *Why Glass Breaks, Rubber Bends, and Glue Sticks* (New York: Harcourt Brace Jovanovich, 1974), p. 24. © 1977 by Malcolm E. Weiss, reprinted by permission of Facts On File, Inc.

The center part of the Venn diagram on the next page shows how the two types of crystals are similar; hence, the circles overlap. The left and right parts list the differences. This diagram could not have been prepared unless the reader understood the material.

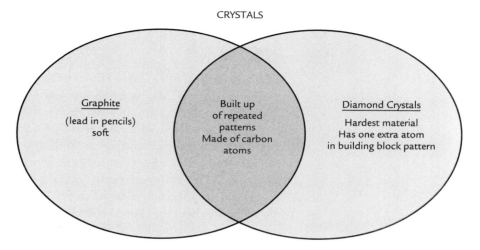

CRYSTALS

Graphite

(lead in pencils)
soft

Built up
of repeated
patterns
Made of carbon
atoms

Diamond Crystals

Hardest material
Has one extra atom
in building block pattern

WORKING TOGETHER

With a partner, decide which type of visual aid would be best for each of the following passages. Then work together to create a visual aid for one of them.

1. DECISION-MAKING STRATEGIES

There are two different schools of thought on the decision process—*analytical* and *intuitive*. **Analytic,** or **systematic, decision making** (sometimes called *scientific decision making*) is based on the theory that problem solving can be reduced to a systematic selection process. Proponents insist that decision theory should construct an ideal procedure for rational choice—a step-by-step, logical sequence for picking the best alternative as a solution to a business problem.

Intuitive decision making is based on the belief that good decision making is an art, not a science. Proponents contend that sound problem solving is largely intuitive and unconscious. They argue that good problem diagnosis and decision making result from an esoteric blend of experience, imagination, intelligence, and feeling joined almost unconsciously.

Considerable evidence suggests that managers use both approaches in solving problems and in making decisions. The analytical approach is more orderly, logical, and systematic; the intuitive approach is more prone to trial and error, or haphazard decisions. Studies reveal significant differences in how the two types of decision makers approach problems.

Adapted from Jerry Kinard, *Management* (Lexington, MA: D. C. Heath, 1988), p. 142.

Type of visual aid to create for this text: _____

2. Chinese Medicine

"Chinese medicine," often called "Oriental medicine" or "traditional Chinese medicine (TCM)," encompasses a vast array of folk medical practices based on mysticism. It holds that the body's vital energy (*chi* or *qi*) circulates through channels, called *meridians*, that have branches connected to bodily organs and functions. Illness is attributed to imbalance or interruption of *chi*. Ancient practices such as acupuncture, Qigong, and the use of various herbs are claimed to restore balance.

Traditional acupuncture, as now practiced, involves the insertion of stainless steel needles into various body areas. A low-frequency current may be applied to the needles to produce greater stimulation. Other procedures used separately or together with acupuncture include: moxibustion (burning of floss or herbs applied to the skin); injection of sterile water, procaine, morphine, vitamins, or homeopathic solutions through the inserted needles; applications of laser beams (laserpuncture); placement of needles in the external ear (auriculotherapy); and acupressure (use of manual pressure). Treatment is applied to "acupuncture points," which are said to be located throughout the body. Originally there were 365 such points, corresponding to the days of the year, but the number identified by proponents during the past 2,000 years has increased gradually to about 2,000. Some practitioners place needles at or near the site of disease, whereas others select points on the basis of symptoms. In traditional acupuncture, a combination of points is usually used.

Qigong is also claimed to influence the flow of "vital energy." Internal Qigong involves deep breathing, concentration, and relaxation techniques used by individuals for themselves. External Qigong is performed by "Qigong masters" who claim to cure a wide variety of diseases with energy released from their fingertips. However, scientific investigators of Qigong masters in China have found no evidence of paranormal powers and some evidence of deception. They found, for example, that a patient lying on a table about eight feet from a Qigong master moved rhythmically or thrashed about as the master moved his hands. But when she was placed so that she could no longer see him, her movements were unrelated to his. Falun gong, which China recently banned, is a Qigong varient claimed to be "a powerful mechanism for healing, stress relief and health improvements."

Most acupuncturists espouse the traditional Chinese view of health and disease and consider acupuncture, herbal medicine, and related practices to be valid approaches to the full gamut of disease. Others reject the traditional approach and merely claim that acupuncture offers a simple way to achieve pain relief. The diagnostic process used by TCM practitioners may include questioning (medical history, lifestyle), observations (skin, tongue, color), listening (breathing sounds), and pulse-taking. Six pulse aspects said to correlate with body organs or functions are checked on each wrist to determine which meridians are "deficient" in *chi.* (Medical science recognizes only one pulse, corresponding to the heartbeat, which can be felt in the wrist, neck, feet, and various other places.) Some acupuncturists state that the electrical properties of the body may become imbalanced weeks or even months before symptoms occur. These practitioners claim that acupuncture can be used to treat conditions when the patient just "doesn't feel right," even though no disease is apparent.

TCM (as well as the folk medical practices of various other Asian countries) is a threat to certain animal species. For example, black bears—valued for their gall bladders—have been hunted nearly to extinction in Asia, and poaching of black bears is a growing problem in North America.

From Stephen Barrett, "Acupuncture, Qigong, and 'Chinese Medicine.'" *http:www.quackwatch.org/01QuackeryRelatedTopics/acu.html.* Retrieved March 8, 2005.

Type of visual aid to create for this text: _____

Weight Control: Which Sex's Perception Is Right?

You probably have heard the statement that men are from Mars and women are from Venus when it comes to relationships. Well, the same is true with dieting. A national survey conducted for the Calorie Control Council found differences between women and men in terms of why they diet, use low-calorie and reduced-fat foods, and can't lose those unwanted pounds. The Council takes a biannual look at American eating and weight control habits and has tracked dieting trends for more than 20 years.

The survey revealed that women blame themselves for not being able to lose weight, while men are more likely to give external excuses. Forty-one percent of women attribute their weight loss failures to a lack of self-discipline, compared with 30% of men. Women (36%) are more than twice as likely to say they "often eat for emotional reasons such as boredom, stress, or lack of family support" as men (16%) do. Men are more likely to indicate they don't eat properly at restaurants or often overeat at mealtimes.

The survey also revealed that physical appearance is a top contender among females as a reason for using low-calorie and reduced-fat (or "light") products, but males ranked this reason much lower. Nearly half of all women give "maintaining physical appearance" as a reason to use these products, while one-third of men cite it. More women than men indicate "feeling better about the way I look" as a reason for using light products.

Men also face another issue—eating away from home. Dining out has become a problem for many Americans, but especially for men. In fact, it may be a contributing factor to obesity in this country. A Department of Agriculture report states that the number of meals consumed away from home has almost doubled over the last 25 years and almost half of Americans are restaurant patrons on any given day.

The Calorie Control Council survey demonstrated that there are some things men and women do agree on that affect their eating habits and weight control efforts. Both agree that lack of exercise is the number-one reason for being overweight. Many health professionals and health organizations report that exercise and physical activity is a key to losing weight as well as maintaining a healthy weight. Former U.S. Surgeon General C. Everett Koop has urged Americans to make fitness a national health priority. Experts estimate that approximately 60% of Americans are not physically active on a regular basis, and 25% are not active at all.

However, there are some bright spots. It seems that both men and women are trying to watch what they eat. The survey reveals that most check the nutrition label on food packages to determine the amount of calories and fat and the type of ingredients they are consuming. Overall, males and females feel that they are eating a healthier diet than they were just three years ago. Moreover, because of the many low-calorie, reduced-sugar, and reduced-fat foods available, both sexes feel that they are able to control and balance their total caloric intake better.

Males and females alike seem to be getting the message that they are simply too big, with 66% of women and 51% of men stating they need to lose weight. With approximately 114,000,000 Americans overweight, 24% (or almost 50,000,000 Americans over the age of 18) are dieting. Men and women are realizing that short-term diets do not work, but making long-term lifestyle commitments to better eating and regular physical activity can result in successful weight loss. Weight-conscious individuals are realizing that fad diets, diet pills, crash diets, and fasting are counterproductive. These weight management methods were used the least, by either sex.

Both men and women are consuming a healthier diet and seem to be aware of the importance of a healthy lifestyle and a healthy weight. They know the methods that help them succeed in losing and controlling their weight, as well as those obstacles that stand between successful maintenance or weight loss, but such knowledge is merely half the battle. Although men and women may face different obstacles, the challenge is the same—to lose those unwanted pounds or maintain a healthy body weight.

"The survey confirms that successful weight loss means adopting sensible behaviors," notes Lyn O'Brien Nabors, executive vice president of the Caloric Control Council. "Pills, fad diets, and cutting out certain foods and food groups just aren't working—and consumers finally understand this. To lose pounds, you've basically got to lighten up and also get moving."

There is nothing like a national survey to identify public awareness and perceptions. It remains to be seen if both men and women, whether they are from Mars or Venus, can put their knowledge into action. That's a very earthly challenge.

Adapted from Beth Brown, "Weight Control: Which Sex's Perception Is Right?" *USA Today Magazine* 129:2670 (March 2001): 62–63. Reprinted by permission.

Type of visual aid to create for this text: _____

▶ Chapter Summary

Based on your reading of this chapter, list at least five ideas that you believe will help you with future reading assignments. Write in complete sentences.

1. _____

_____

_____

_____

2. _____

_____

_____

3. _____

_____

_____

4. _____

_____

_____

5. _____

_____

_____

▶ *Extended Application*

Now that you have worked with the strategies necessary for understanding paragraph patterns, you can practice applying them to full-length reading selections. Choose (or your instructor may choose) a reading selection from Part 2 of this book or another reading selection that is typical of what you will be expected to read for your other college courses, such as an essay or a textbook chapter. Use this selection to practice:

❋ Identifying paragraph patterns

❋ Predicting paragraph patterns

❋ Using patterns to create visual aids

Decide on the practice strategies you will use. Apply them to your selection. Then, in a few paragraphs, write a description of what you did and how the strategies you used worked for you.

Name of material used: _____

Page numbers: _____

Your description: _____

Strategies for Critical Reading and Thinking: Fact/Opinion; Point of View; Style, Mood, and Tone

WHAT MADE YOU DECIDE TO ATTEND THIS SCHOOL? You probably investigated many colleges thoroughly before making your choice. In the process, you most likely reviewed such facts as costs, course offerings, housing, and tuition assistance opportunities. You may have used information gathered by talking with college representatives or reading college catalogs to help you with your choice. Perhaps you also sought opinions from students already attending this school. Once you had all this information, you could weigh the positive and negative points, think about what people said about the school, as well as what was suggested by what was said, and sort out reliable from unreliable sources. Then you made your decision. This process required you to engage in critical reading, thinking, and listening. All critical reading, thinking, and listening experience involves similar analytical and reflective processes: you make judgments about what you read, see, or hear. In this chapter and Chapter 7, you will learn the types of criteria to use for making these judgments and how to apply these criteria to academic situations. In this chapter, we will define critical reading and then focus on recognizing fact, opinion, point of view, style, mood, and tone.

What Is Critical Reading?

There are many definitions of critical reading, but all of them involve evaluating what you read for its:

* Logic
* Truth or accuracy
* Merit of the ideas
* Usefulness of the ideas

Evaluating texts in this way requires analysis beyond simply identifying main ideas and details. Authors choose what information to give readers and how this information will be presented. They also determine which ideas to state directly and which to suggest indirectly. Critical readers draw conclusions and form judgments about what they read on the basis of what they are told as well as how the information is presented. They also examine the underlying ideas that are suggested by both of these. Critical readers consider the logic of the ideas as well as how the information coincides or conflicts with prior knowledge and personal beliefs. Further, critical readers are aware that there are many viewpoints from which even a single subject or event can be discussed. Clearly, if you hear only one side of an argument or read about an event that is written from only one perspective, you are limiting your understanding and your ability to critically analyze it. The critical reader is an investigative reader. The value of being able to read with a critical eye is illustrated in Activity A.

ACTIVITY A: Critical Analysis of Three News Articles

Three accounts of the same event, each from a different newspaper, follow. Read all three news stories, then answer the questions.

1. QUEENS WOMAN IS STABBED TO DEATH IN FRONT OF HOME (*NY Times*)

A 28 year old Queens woman was stabbed to death early yesterday morning outside her apartment house in Kew Gardens.

Neighbors who were awakened by her screams found the woman, Miss Catherine Genovese of 82–70 Austin Street, shortly after 3 A.M. in front of a building three doors from her home.

The police said that Miss Genovese had been attacked in front of her building and had run to where she fell. She had parked her car in a nearby lot, the police said, after having driven it from the Hollis Bar where she was day manager.

The police, who spent the day searching for the murder weapon, interviewing witnesses and checking automobiles that had been seen in the neighborhood, said last night they had no clues.

From *The New York Times*, March 14, 1964, p. 26. © 1964 by the New York Times Company.

2. "HELP" CRY IGNORED, GIRL DIES OF KNIFING (*NY Herald Tribune*)

ROBERT PARRELLA

The neighbors had grandstand seats for the slaying of Kitty Genovese.

And yet, when the pretty diminutive 28 year old brunette called for help, she called in vain.

It wasn't until she had been stabbed 12 times and had crawled into a vestibule, that somebody called police, and even then Kitty lay for 10 minutes, bleeding and unbefriended, before they arrived.

"I wonder how many lives could be saved in this City if people who ask for help were not ignored?" Magistrate Bernard J. Dublin mused yesterday in Queens Criminal Court. "How many people could have been saved from death if when they call for help other persons did not run away."

Karl Ross, 31, a poodle clipper, of 82–65 Austin Street, Kew Gardens, a neighbor of Kitty's, finally did call police.

Mr. Ross had just testified that he recognized the girl, bleeding profusely after she had staggered into the vestibule of his apartment house. He returned to his apartment, he said, and called the police, and remained in the apartment until he heard them arrive, some ten minutes later.

A charge of breach of the peace was leveled against Mr. Ross later in the day by Detective Mitchell Sang, who said Mr. Ross tried to prevent him from questioning one of Miss Genovese's roommates, Mary Ann Zielonko.

Mr. Ross was sentenced to pay a $25 fine and serve five days on the breach of peace charge which was reduced from interference with an officer. The jail term was suspended.

Detectives on the case say that at least half a dozen neighbors heard Miss Genovese scream for help on Austin Street at about 3:30 A.M. yesterday. Several of the witnesses told police they saw a man bending over the girl, straighten up and run away.

The girl, they said, then staggered around the corner onto 82nd Street. Her slayer reappeared at that point, and then, not finding his victim, disappeared again. Finally, Miss Genovese returned to Austin Street and collapsed in the vestibule about 30 yards from her own apartment door.

Police, called by Mr. Ross, summoned an ambulance, and the girl was taken to Queens General Hospital, where she died a short time later. Assistant Queens Medical Examiner, Dr. William Bennison, said she had suffered 12 stab wounds in the chest, abdomen and back, inflicted by a very strong killer armed with a slender knife.

Police said Miss Genovese was manager of Ev's 11th Hour, a tavern at 1293–14 Jamaica Avenue, Hollis, and shared her apartment with Miss Zielonko and another waitress from the establishment.

Detectives are seeking to question a patron at the tavern with whom Miss Genovese had had dinner earlier in the evening. Although the girl's wallet was not found at the stabbing scene, investigators said they did not believe the motive was robbery.

From *The New York Herald Tribune,* March 14, 1964, p. 10.

3. QUEENS BARMAID, STABBED, DIES (*NY Daily News*)

THOMAS PUGH AND RICHARD HENRY

An attractive 28 year old brunette who had given up a more prosaic life for a career as a barmaid and residence in a tiny Bohemian Section of Queens was stabbed to death early yesterday.

Catherine (Kitty) Genovese, 5 feet 1 and 105 pounds was stabbed eight times in the chest and four times in the back and she had three cuts on her hands, probably inflicted as she tried to fight off her attacker near her apartment in an alley way, at 82–70 Austin Street at Lefferts Boulevard, Kew Gardens.

Late yesterday, police said the 30 detectives assigned to the case had not come up with any clues or a possible motive for the savage murder.

Had Teen Nuptial Annulled

Police of the Richmond Hill Precinct said Kitty had had her teenage marriage annulled two months after her wedding and, when her large family moved to Connecticut, she stayed in New York on her own.

She worked for an insurance firm, but gave that up for a barmaid's career. In August 1961, her travels with a "fast crowd" contributed to her arrest on a bookmaking rap.

Police pieced together this account of her last hours at 6 P.M. Thursday; she left Ev's Eleventh Hour Tavern, 193–14 Jamaica Avenue, Hollis, where she had been a barmaid and co-manager for one and a half years.

She and a male patron went on a dinner date to Brooklyn, and returned to Ev's at midnight. Her escort left (he was questioned by cops yesterday and his alibi freed him of suspicion in the crime).

Three Girls Shared Apartment

Kitty left the bar at 3 a.m. and drove her Fiat sports car seven miles to her home. She parked in the Long Island Railroad's parking lot next to the group of buildings where she and two other girls shared an apartment.

She walked along Austin Street, instead of going more directly to the apartment via a walkway at the rear of the building. Police said she apparently walked out front to have the protection of the street lights.

Gasps *"I've Been Stabbed!"*

Neighbors suddenly heard screams and the roar of an auto driving off. Leaving a trail of blood, Kitty staggered back toward the parking lot, around the rear of the structures, and collapsed in the doorway of 892–60 Austin Street, next to her home.

***"I've Been Stabbed! I've Been Stabbed!"* the Brunette Gasped**

Kitty died in an ambulance en route to Queens General Hospital, Jamaica.

From *The New York Daily News*, March 14, 1964, p. 10.

1. How does each author want you to feel about the event?

   Article 1: _____

   _____

   Article 2: _____

   _____

Article 3: _____

_____

2. What does each author do to get you to feel this way?

Article 1: _____

_____

Article 2: _____

_____

Article 3: _____

_____

3. What does the author of each article want you to feel about the person who is primarily involved?

Article 1: _____

_____

Article 2: _____

_____

Article 3: _____

_____

4. How do you know the author wants you to feel this way?

Article 1: _____

_____

Article 2: _____

_____

Article 3: _____

_____

5. Which article has left the biggest impression on you? Why do you think it has?

_____

_____

_____

WORKING TOGETHER

With a partner, discuss how a reader's reactions to this event might differ depending on which news story he or she has read.

THINKING ABOUT YOUR READING AND WRITING

ACTIVITY B: Your Conclusions About Content and Language
What conclusions can you draw from Activity A about the ways in which an author's content and language can influence a reader's beliefs and knowledge?

_____

_____

_____

_____

It is not wrong for an author to try to influence others. Authors write because they have something to say. They expect their readers to understand their ideas and, they hope, to agree with them. But critical readers and listeners will evaluate the ideas before accepting them. In the remainder of this chapter and the next, you will learn strategies for making such evaluations. These strategies will enable you to recognize:

❅ When an author's content is factual and when ideas are based on opinion.

❅ How to judge the authoritativeness of opinions.

* When an author's content and language reflect certain points of view or perspectives.

* When these points of view or perspectives are justified by reasons and evidence.

* How the author's attitudes are similar to or different from your own and those of others.

We introduce these strategies separately so that you can have a clear picture of how to use each. However, these features of communication work simultaneously, in combination with one another, to produce the final effect on the reader or listener. For instance, if the newspaper articles in Activity A had differed from one another by only one sentence, the effect of any single article on you would probably not have been very different from that of any other single article. It was the totality—the headlines, the events discussed, the descriptions—that caused the striking contrasts.

Distinguishing Statements of Fact from Statements of Opinion

Ideas you read and hear usually contain both factual information as well as opinions. Statements of opinion in academic text and lectures are also sometimes referred to as *thesis statements, theories,* or *hypotheses.* If you can distinguish between opinion statements and factual statements, you will be better able to determine the value and truthfulness of the ideas expressed. As a critical reader and listener, you will recognize ideas that are accurate, logical, and worthy of serious consideration, as well as those that you must question because they are unsupported, illogical, or seem inaccurate. Further, you will be more aware of whether your own opinions about what others say are grounded in fact or opinion or in a combination of these.

Factual statements are distinguished from statements of opinion in several ways:

* Facts can be proved to be true.

* Facts cannot be disputed. There is evidence to prove their truth.

* Facts are easily agreed-on ideas or are concepts that are held by everyone or that can easily be proved, such as, "The sun sets in the west" or "Maine is in the northeastern part of the United States."

* Facts are based on direct evidence or actual observation. Examples, statistics, original documents, reports from research experiments, or eyewitness accounts are used to verify them.

＊ Facts are things that have occurred. They are not predictions.

＊ The truthfulness of facts can change over time. For instance, at one time it was thought that AIDS could be contracted only by homosexual males.

＊ Factual statements often begin with such expressions as, *The evidence for this is*_____; _____ *found; Statistical evidence for this appeared in a study by* _____

Opinions are one person's, or perhaps one group's, view of the truth. They are not clear cut or right or wrong, as are facts. Your academic reading and experiences in classrooms will expose you to many areas of controversy where opinions are voiced strongly. It is possible for people to disagree endlessly about an opinion and never reach a conclusion. For instance, one person might say assisted suicide is a good idea; another might say assisted suicide should not be permitted.

Frequently, there are opposing viewpoints or theories in academic writing. For example, there is disagreement over such issues as capital punishment and the seriousness of global warming. Psychologists and others have disagreed over the extent to which a person's genetic makeup influences his or her other personality and intelligence, compared to his or her environment. (These are called nature–nurture theories.) Critical readers recognize the possibility of such disagreements and will draw conclusions based on whatever evidence and facts they can find. Statements of opinion, then, have several features that will help you distinguish them from facts:

＊ Statements of opinion cannot be conclusively verified. Even if you agree with the author's opinion, it is still just an opinion even though there may be good evidence for that opinion.

＊ Statements of opinion are often an expression of someone's values, personal beliefs, attitudes, or feelings. These are often based on hunches, inferences, or guesses. It is when you agree with the author's point of view that it is more difficult to make the distinction between fact and opinion statements. Try to avoid letting your own opinions influence your ability to determine which is which.

＊ Statements of opinion are subjective. The language of opinion statements is often vague or persuasive. The words used to convey the opinion may be open to many interpretations, like *love, peace, beneficial, dangerous.*

＊ Opinion statements often begin with such expressions as *I believe, It appears, It seems, All would agree, I think* _____ *is true because, In my opinion* . . .

＊ It is possible for a single word to turn a statement of fact into a statement of opinion. For example, the phrase *sixteenth-century music* is a factual phrase. The descriptor, *sixteenth-century,* is factual because one could prove whether the music was of that period. However, the phrase *beautiful music* is a statement of opinion. Its descriptor, *beautiful,* is a matter of opinion to the listener.

ACTIVITY C: Creating Fact and Opinion Descriptors

For each pair, write one descriptor that makes a phrase factual and one that makes it an opinion. An example is done for you. Be prepared to justify your answers.

FACTUAL		OPINION	
Sunday	picnic	*enjoyable*	picnic
_____	damage	_____	damage
_____	country	_____	country
_____	parents	_____	parents
_____	holiday	_____	holiday
_____	highway	_____	highway

THINKING ABOUT YOUR READING AND WRITING

ACTIVITY D: Evaluating What You Know

What are some features of facts and opinions that you think will be useful for you to remember as you listen to lectures and do your reading assignments?

_____

_____

_____

_____

_____

_____

ACTIVITY E: Personal Facts and Opinions

In the space provided, write some factual and some opinion statements about yourself. As you do this, think about the criteria you are using to distinguish between fact and opinion.

FACTUAL STATEMENTS ABOUT YOU:

_____

_____

_____

_____

_____

OPINION STATEMENTS ABOUT YOU:

_____

_____

_____

_____

_____

WORKING TOGETHER

Have a partner look at your personal factual and opinion statements in Activity E. Discuss whether they meet the criteria for each.

At this point, you are ready for some good news and some bad news. The good news is that by now you have developed some useful strategies for determining whether an idea is a statement of fact or opinion. The bad news is that many statements that appear in academic text are neither all fact nor all opinion. Very often a statement contains a portion of fact *and* a portion of opinion. This is a particularly useful technique for writing an argumentative or persuasive essay, one in which an author is trying to convince the reader to accept a certain idea or viewpoint. The author's opinions are mingled with the facts, so the sentence sounds factual. But, in reality, only that portion that states a fact is verifiable. The rest of it must be considered opinion and open to disagreement.

For example, a sentence may read: *Web pages that require user names and passwords safeguard our information, but at the same time they are annoying for the forgetful.* The part of this sentence that is fact is, *Web pages that require user names and passwords safeguard our information.* The rest, which reads, *but at the same time they are annoying for the forgetful,* is the author's opinion. Many people, even the forgetful, may be grateful that their personal information is being protected and don't mind the small inconvenience of having to recall their passwords and user names.

Here's another example: *Although the Navajo have told and retold many myths, none is as popular as that of the Big Fly, which has been part of the culture for centuries.* Which part is fact? You should have recognized that there are two factual parts in this sentence: *the Navajo have written many myths* is a fact. Further, the segment of the sentence that reads, *which has been part of the culture for centuries,* is a fact. One can check to see whether the Navajo have, indeed, told and retold many myths and whether this particular myth has been part of the culture for so long. The rest of the sentence is definitely opinion. It would be hard to prove that one myth is more popular than another, and views on methods to use to judge popularity would vary.

Fact and opinion also can become intermingled when someone else's opinion is quoted. The quotation marks give the opinion the appearance of fact, and it is a fact that someone made the quoted statement, but often the idea within the quotation marks is an opinion. For example, consider the statement, *"The United States should consider a complete halt in nuclear power plant construction because of unresolved safety questions," an Atomic Energy Commission safety expert said on September 21, 1974.* An individual made this statement when he resigned from the Atomic Energy Commission because he felt the Commission was ignoring questions of safety. It is a fact that the AEC safety expert made this statement, and perhaps one could argue that it is a fact that there were *unresolved safety questions* when the statement was made. But the solution recommended, *a complete halt in nuclear power plant construction,* is an opinion.

In Activity F, you will have a chance to identify those parts of sentences that are fact and those that are opinion.

ACTIVITY F: Recognizing Segments of Fact and Opinion in Sentences

In each sentence, *underline* those portions that you believe to be fact. Remember that you are claiming that what is not underlined is opinion. More than one part of a sentence may be factual. Be prepared to justify your answers.

1. Although everyone feels sad now and then, 4 to 8 million Americans are treated yearly for clinical depression, and about 250,000 of these require hospitalization.

2. By 1885, fewer than one thousand buffalo were left on the Midwest plains, and clearly there was little concern that the once numerous quadrupeds were facing an inevitable complete extermination.

3. Ten years ago, John Graves Fletcher, a distinguished painter, designed the colorful, modernistic murals in our student union building, which houses all clubs, fraternities, and sororities as well as a number of auditoriums and conference rooms.

4. *Austin Powers in Goldmember,* a movie that dazzled audiences with its clever comedy and mischievous mayhem, was the third film in actor Mike Myers's spy spoof series.

5. Some scholars have spent decades studying the unplanned effects of social reform, and they have now reached the conclusion that everything has been tried, but nothing has worked.

WORKING TOGETHER

Compare your answers to Activity F with those of a partner. If you disagree, try to reach agreement by reviewing the criteria for factual statements. Then read the two paragraphs that follow. Beneath them, on the lines provided, list the facts and opinions that you find in each. Remember that one sentence may contain segments of both.

1. Shorter people are always within a minority amongst any group because we are—by simple definition—shorter than average within that group. In *any* group of people who are not of identical height, there will be an average, with some shorter and some taller than the average. Mass cloning is the only way not to get "short" people; in a society where the average is 6'4", a six footer will be considered short. An insidious move in this direction is practiced by some private sperm banks that exercise a minimum height requirement in donors. This will ensure the most advantaged sections of society, who can pay money for such treatments, will almost guarantee their child can assume a privileged position due to their anticipated height. Nobody is under illusions as to why this should be favorable.

From Glenn Beard, "Understanding and Living with Height Discrimination," March 2004. *http:www.shortsupport.org/Essays/GlennBeard1.html#Whatis.* Retrieved March 10, 2005. Copyright 2000-2005, Short Persons Support, *editor@shortsupport.org.*

FACTUAL STATEMENTS IN THIS PARAGRAPH:

_____

_____

_____

_____

_____

OPINION STATEMENTS IN THIS PARAGRAPH:

_____

_____

_____

_____

2. *"Never doubt that a small group of thoughtful, committed citizens can change the world. Indeed, it's the only thing that ever has."* That was Margaret Mead's conclusion after a lifetime of observing very diverse cultures around the world. Her insight has been borne out time and again throughout the development of this country of ours. Being allowed to live life in an atmosphere of religious freedom, having a voice in the government you support with your taxes, living free of lifelong enslavement by another person. These beliefs about how life should and must be lived were once considered outlandish by many. But these beliefs were fervently held by visionaries whose steadfast work brought about changed minds and attitudes. Now these beliefs are commonly shared across U.S. society.

   From Bonnie Eisenberg and Mary Ruthsdotter, "Living the Legacy: The Women's Rights Movement 1848–1998." *http:www.legacy98.org/move-hist.html.* Retrieved March 9, 2005. © By Bonnie Eisenberg and Mary Ruthsdotter, the National Women's History Project, 1998.

FACTUAL STATEMENTS IN THIS PARAGRAPH:

_____

_____

_____

_____

_____

OPINION STATEMENTS IN THIS PARAGRAPH:

_____

_____

_____

_____

THINKING ABOUT YOUR READING AND WRITING

ACTIVITY G: Reviewing Your Decision-Making Processes

Describe the thought process you used in Activities F to distinguish between fact and opinion. List as many of the steps you used in this procedure as you can.

_____

_____

_____

_____

_____

_____

_____

Evidence for Statements of Opinion

Just because something you read or hear is an opinion, it does not mean you should think it is worthless. Even though an opinion cannot be absolutely verified, it can be supported with evidence in a way that strengthens its force and makes it more believable. Critical readers will examine the type of evidence given for opinions to determine its value as support for the ideas that are suggested. We next discuss several types of evidence commonly used in academic writing to support opinions.

Expert Opinion

Expert opinion differs from other opinions because the person expressing the opinion knows quite a bit about the subject being discussed. Examples include Eastern European historians discussing the end of communism in Eastern Europe, music historians discussing the influence of the Beatles on contemporary music, economists discussing a recession, and a doctor giving medical testimony. When support for an opinion or theory is provided by an expert rather than by someone who knows little about the subject, that opinion carries more weight.

Informed Opinion

Authors and speakers preparing arguments or developing a thesis frequently conduct research or seek information from other sources that will help them prove their points. Informed opinions may include statistical reference, historical reference, the use of visual aids, and the use of personal experience.

REFERENCE TO STATISTICS OBTAINED THROUGH RESEARCH. For instance, if someone has the opinion that gun control legislation deters crime, statistics from states that have passed gun control legislation may be used to provide evidence that in these states there has been a reduction in crime. If someone wants to argue that one method of teaching mathematics to children is superior to another, the argument can be bolstered by citing mathematics test scores of the children using the favored method or by comparing these test results to those of children who were taught by a different method.

Here is one note about using facts in this way. Since in both examples a number of factors affect the situation being discussed, the facts cited as evidence are only partially useful. They do not give the whole picture. For example, crime might have dropped in cities that had passed gun control laws because the economy in those states was up, or children who were using the favored math approach might have been in school systems that also had very small classes. When statistics are used to support arguments, they must be considered with caution. The person voicing the opinion has chosen to include only particular statistics. Other statistics may support an equally strong argument against it.

HISTORICAL REFERENCE.   The use of history to prove one's point is a fairly common strategy for creating the impression of an informed opinion. Phrases such as *history tells us* or *we know from the past* convince us that the opinion expressed is based on fact. Reference to historical documents, diaries, or speeches may be used as well. Critical readers will notice such references and will try to verify that the history as presented is both factually correct and portrayed fairly.

THE USE OF VISUAL AIDS.   Photographs, charts, and diagrams make arguments seem valid. After all, the reasoning goes, if it can be graphically depicted, it must be true. Consider, however, the photos on the covers of supermarket tabloids. Wonderful graphics can be made on computers as well. But how valid is what they portray? Further, you must analyze whether there is any relationship between what is on the graphic display and the idea under discussion. For instance, if one is presenting an argument in favor of gun control legislation, one might use a graphic of a baby who has just been caught in the crossfire between two drug dealers. The impact on you is powerful. But how much support, beyond emotional appeal, does this photo lend to the key point? The critical reader will examine the source of the visual aid as well as the relationship between the graphics and the argument or theory itself.

THE USE OF PERSONAL EXPERIENCE.   How often have you remarked that you knew something to be true because you experienced it yourself? Perhaps you have said this when expressing an opinion that the food in a particular restaurant is bad, a certain band has a great sound, or someone you know is a terrific athlete. When you gave your opinion, did everyone agree with you? It is very common to use personal experience as evidence for personal theories or opinions, but critical thinkers will not rely too heavily on this type of evidence for judging the merit of ideas. People interpret their experiences differently. Personal experience is subjective, as are opinions themselves. When personal experience is used as evidence, it is really a case of using subjective evidence to support a subjective idea.

Unsupported Opinion

Unsupported opinions often consist of *sweeping generalizations* and *stereotypes*. These are even less reliable than opinions based on personal experience. For example, to give support to the argument that towns ought to have curfews for teenagers, one might say: *Today's parents have little time for disciplining their chil-*

dren. This statement is not backed by any statistical evidence or facts. It is a personal opinion intended to give strength to the argument that towns need curfews. Or if one is arguing that the news media should be controlled by the government, one might also say: *The stories in many local newspapers encourage crime.* This claim is unsupported. It is merely an unsupported personal opinion. Even a seemingly noncontroversial view—for example, that the Industrial Revolution had a major effect on the family life of Americans—would not be well defended if the only support given for such a statement was: *Men worked in factories for long hours and came home too tired to pay attention to their wives and families.* How is this known? It remains just an unsupported opinion unless some evidence is offered, such as statistics, entries from diaries of people living at the time, or findings from other research studies.

ACTIVITY H: Identifying Support for Opinions

Several statements of opinion follow. Beneath each opinion statement are two other sentences that provide support for the opinion. Based on the type of support given, indicate whether the opinion is an expert opinion (EO), informed opinion (IO), or unsupported opinion (UO). Be prepared to justify your answers.

1. Sexual harassment in the workplace is far more common than most people suppose. _____

   ❋ One worker said she was sexually harassed by her boss nearly every day for six years.

   ❋ The American Civil Liberties Union noted that more than two hundred cases of sexual harassment are reported to them every day.

2. Politicians have become extremely self-centered. _____

   ❋ Elected officials are more occupied with their own plans for reelection than with the public interest.

   ❋ Senators obviously spend more time campaigning in their home states than voting on important issues in Congress.

3. Prior to 1870, American children were not encouraged to think independently. _____

   ❋ One popular children's magazine I investigated, *Youth's Companion,* published from the mid-1800s until 1910, told children in 1856 to spend their time "thinking of ways they could achieve salvation."

   ❋ Another American periodical I examined, *Juvenile Miscellany,* first published in 1826, contained numerous stories of children who lived in fear of the dire consequences they would face if they did anything contrary to established rule.

4. Some actors and actresses pay a heavy price for stardom.
   _____

   ❊ It is rumored that the legendary Greta Garbo once said she never married because "all those damn photographers would just follow us around then, maybe even to the bedroom."

   ❊ The public craves all the latest gossip on their favorite stars, making them the target of tabloid smear campaigns.

5. Through the training of their young, not only all humans but apparently all other primates as well pass on strong convictions of what is proper food and what is not. _____

   ❊ Dietary laws of certain groups of Hindus and Buddhists prohibit eating meat of any kind.

   ❊ DeGarine (1974) reports that in Polynesia in former times all species of fish that were offered to the gods, as well as all meat except poultry, were forbidden to women.

WORKING TOGETHER

With a partner, provide different types of support to make each of the following statements an expert opinion, informed opinion, and unsupported opinion. Write your support in the space provided. (Be creative. Make up the support for an expert opinion and informed opinion if you wish.)

Statement 1:   Small businesses provide service for their customers that larger businesses just cannot offer.

Support to make this an expert opinion: _____

_____

Support to make this an informed opinion: _____

_____

Support to make this an unsupported opinion: _____

_____

Statement 2:   People who watch their diet will be happier than people who eat whatever they choose.

Support to make this an expert opinion: _____

_____

Support to make this an informed opinion: _____

_____

Support to make this an unsupported opinion: _____

_____

Additional Criteria for Judging Facts and Opinions

As you evaluate ideas presented in texts and lectures, you should consider some additional factors.

The Author's Qualifications

Some authors are more knowledgeable about a subject than others because of the length of time they have been doing research, the experience they have had in the subject, and/or the formal training they have received in the subject. In textbooks, information about the author can often be found in the introduction or foreword. Periodicals sometimes offer a brief biography of the author.

The Source of the Material

Hundreds of articles appear monthly in magazines, journals, and newspapers that are published by special-interest groups: religious organizations, groups with particular leanings, senior citizens' organizations, women's rights associations, labor unions, environmental protection organizations, and so on. Publication affiliations are identified in the editorial box, which is usually placed in the first few pages of the publication. The critical reader understands that an article that discusses whether parents should be concerned about the type of music today's teenagers listen to would be very different if it appeared in *Good Housekeeping* magazine than if it appeared in *Spin.* The special interests of the publisher and the audiences for those two magazines are quite different; they play an important role in the content and method of presentation of information. Critical readers consider this when they evaluate the ideas presented.

The *recency of the information* must also be considered. If the material was published some time ago, its age may affect its value. In many fields, such as the sciences, history, and anthropology, new information continually updates older theories and research findings.

The Author's Point of View and Perspective

When we express an opinion on a subject, we are stating our position or attitude toward it. A single word can suggest much about your opinion toward a person or situation. For instance, if you refer to a person as a *dedicated worker,* you are saying something positive. But if you call that same person a *workaholic,* you are conveying a negative attitude about the same set of behaviors. Following a class debate, you might comment to a friend that the class debate was *stimulating,* or you might call it *argumentative.* One city dweller visiting a small town might call it *dull,* another person visiting the same town might describe it as *peaceful.* In each case the descriptive word suggests a reaction to the same experience, and in each case the reaction is clearly different.

Opinions are most often derived from an individual's *perspective* or *point of view*—the position from which the author considers a subject. A person may express a point of view on a very controversial topic, such as whether there should be mandatory testing for AIDS in the workplace. This topic might be considered from the perspective of an AIDS patient, a doctor, a parent of someone with AIDS, a medical researcher, an insurance company, an employer. You can see how, depending on a person's situation or role, the perspective on this topic might differ. As another example, a citizens' group might be discussing *proposed legislation to pass a property tax increase so there is more funding for the local public schools.* You might hear opinions from the following individuals, each of whom is addressing this topic from a different perspective:

residents living in private homes

senior citizens living on fixed incomes

parents of school age children

children who attend school

It is also possible to simultaneously represent several points of view; in the first example, for instance, you could be a medical researcher who is living with

AIDS; in the second example, you might be a senior citizen who lives in a private home.

Readers may sometimes recognize that an author's point of view differs from their own. It is always worthwhile to consider how an author's own experience and background have influenced his or her point of view and to assess how your own experience and background influence the position you take on the same subject. You also need to consider what other points of view are possible.

Sometimes the author won't express a personal point of view; instead, you might be shown several different points of view on the same subject. That is, the author will present information from several different perspectives. For example, an author may offer several perspectives to discuss a plan by New York City's mayor to overhaul the city's mass transit system. You might be shown the perspective of someone who lives in the city and who regularly uses the system; the perspective of a Rochester, New York, resident who would have to pay toward the system but who does not use it; and the perspective of a senior citizen who doesn't use the system but lives in New York City and would pay increased taxes. Or the author may write from just a single perspective, such as that of a regular transit user who is fed up with paying for poor service. In this case, a critical reader would need to consider other perspectives that might be possible, such as some of those suggested here.

Whatever our individual point of view, we all use facts and opinions (ours and others) that best support our ideas. We might also include different viewpoints in our discussion, but only to show why they are incorrect.

ACTIVITY I: Determining Point of View

Read each paragraph to identify the point of view, and then answer the questions that follow. Where you are asked to give evidence to support your own point of view, it may be from some source other than the paragraph.

1. A report released by the U.S. Bureau of Justice Statistics in 1997 indicated that in 1994, 29 percent of persons whose most serious conviction offense was a drug-trafficking felony got probation instead of incarceration; so did 31 percent of those whose most serious conviction offense was a weapons crime felony. Weapons offenders were thus slightly more likely than drug merchants to escape incarceration and get probation. In Massachusetts and several other states, about half of probationers are under supervision for a violent crime, while half of those in prison for drug law violations have no official record of violence. From a crime control perspective, forcing drug-only offenders

behind bars while violent offenders beat feet to the streets is just plain batty.

From John J. DiIulio Jr., "Against Mandatory Minimums," *National Review* 51:9 (May 17, 1999): 46.

What is the subject? _____

_____

What is the author's point of view toward this subject? _____

_____

What evidence is there that this is the author's point of view? _____

_____

How does this point of view compare to your own? _____

_____

What evidence do you have to support your viewpoint? _____

_____

What other points of view are possible? _____

_____

2. The Web has a reputation as a self-publisher's medium, offering a worldwide audience to anyone with a computer, a text editor, and an FTP connection to an Internet service provider. That's all the equipment you'll need if you're publishing a family newsletter or a fanzine, but if you're offering a service to commercial clients, things get a lot more complicated. Creating today's database-driven, dynamically updated, 1000-page-plus commercial sites means working on a team—made up of individualistic, creative, entrepreneurial people like yourself. These individuals—temperamental, driven—are brought together from a variety of professional backgrounds: engineering, publishing, television, advertising, and other fields related to technology and media, each with its own culture. Imagine the bar scene in *Star Wars* and you get the picture.

    From Darcy DiNucci, "Yay, Teamwork," *Print* 53:3 (May/June, 1999): 26.

What is the subject? _____

_____

What is the author's point of view toward this subject? _____

_____

What evidence is there that this is the author's point of view? _____

_____

How does this point of view compare to your own? _____

_____

What evidence do you have to support your viewpoint? _____

_____

What other points of view are possible? _____

_____

3. The corporation is a relatively new form of business ownership that didn't become really popular until about a century ago. Yet today it's the best-known and most powerful form of business ownership in the country. Although less than 15 percent of all U.S. businesses are corporations, they account for over 86 percent of revenues each year and receive 75 percent of all profits. Small business owners recognize that this staggering financial record gives corporations tremendous economic and political clout. Corporations even influence campaigns by forming political action committees (PACs) to contribute to favored candidates.

   From Leon C. Megginson et al., *Business* (Lexington, MA: D. C. Heath, 1985), p. 66. Reprinted with permission.

What is the subject? _____

_____

What is the author's point of view toward this subject? _____

_____

What evidence is there that this is the author's point of view? _____

_____

How does this point of view compare to your own? _____

_____

What evidence do you have to support your viewpoint? _____

_____

What other points of view are possible? _____

_____

WORKING TOGETHER

Compare your responses to Activity I with those of a partner. Look for differences in point of view.

THINKING ABOUT YOUR READING AND WRITING

ACTIVITY J: Personal Response to Point of View

Do you think it is more interesting to read ideas that are similar to or that are different from your own? Explain your answer.

_____

_____

_____

_____

_____

_____

_____

_____

Identifying Author's Style, Mood, and Tone

Critical readers are aware that several important features of a written work contribute to its overall effect. These features include the author's *style, mood,* and *tone.* We discuss each separately in this section, but as with all the elements of an article or essay discussed thus far in this textbook, they work simultaneously to create a single effect on the reader. Style, mood, and tone describe *how* something has been written, whereas events or ideas could be considered the *what* of an article or essay. *How* something has been written affects the reader's response to the text.

Identifying Author's Style

The author's style refers to the *types of words and sentence construction* the author uses in order to appeal to a particular type of audience. Some writers want to appeal to a wide audience and will use fairly common expressions, slang, or easy-to-read sentences. Other authors address their comments to a more educated group. Their sentences tend to be longer, and their choice of words more sophisticated. They may use a number of metaphors or historical references and might include many citations. A writer who expects the audience to have a great deal of knowledge of the subject may use more technical language. Authors who want to persuade their audience to respond in a certain way will use emotional language; others will not make any effort to appeal to their readers' emotions. Their purpose, then, influences the language authors use.

Writers, of course, generally do not tell their readers what style they are using. The reader must know what to look for within the text itself in order to determine the author's style. The process is similar to the one you used to search for evidence to make other types of inferences.

> **Example 1:**
>
> Long-haul drivers, away from family and hearth for weeks at a time, put in longer hours to make a decent living than any other workers in America. From up high in a big truck we can look down into your little cars and scope out the "seat covers" (passengers). Despite what

we sometimes see, we often wish we were in this other, more normal world. We can watch couples argue with each other, watch ladies try to drive to work and paint their faces at the same time, watch the less affluent people with their windows rolled down in the summer (no AC) but looking so proud: black T shirt, the driver's beefy arm hanging out the window with the radio blasting. (It's amazing how healthy the males look and how sparky the females in those noisy, hot cages.) Our TV screen is the windshield and yes, we male drivers do leer sometimes, enjoying the view as we observe the multiethnic, sultry femucopia of south Florida, the aggressive, preening go-getters driving the D.C. beltway, the Chicago working girls as we pass the train platforms alongside I-94, or the sunbathers along any beach highway. But what every driver likes even more, when he can get it, is a little respect.

From J. Aalborg, "The View from the Big Road," *Newsweek,* December 20, 1993, p. 10. Reprinted by permission of the author.

The author of this paragraph does not use a very extensive vocabulary, and the language is informal. Words such as *scope out* and *AC* contribute to this informality. The sentences are not complicated, either. They are short and easy to read. The intended audience is probably, then, a large general audience—perhaps all of us who have wondered about the life of the long-haul driver. The style is very natural, down to earth. The examples that illustrate what the drivers see—all of us—connect the author to all of us. By relating so personally to us, the driver is able to keep our attention to the end when he asks for *respect*. The author's style, then, helps accomplish the author's purpose.

Example 2:

When an external magnetic field is applied to a diamagnetic substance, such as bismuth, the only magnetic moments included in the substance are aligned *against* the external field. Correspondingly, a diamagnetic substance has a *negative* susceptibility. Furthermore, one finds that a diamagnetic sample is *repelled* when placed near the pole of a strong magnet (in contrast with a paramagnetic sample, which is *attracted*). Although the effect of diamagnetism is present in all matter, it is weak compared with paramagnetism and ferromagnetism.

The language of this passage is extremely technical. The author assumes that readers are quite familiar with the subject already. The sentences are fairly long and complex, but the author believes that this educated audience will be able to follow. Because the language is unemotional, the author's intention is probably just to convey information. By writing with a straightforward style, the author is able to accomplish this purpose.

Critical readers who are sensitive to an author's style will have another measure by which to evaluate the usefulness of an author's ideas. You will be able to select material that is suitable for your own purposes. For instance, if you are writing a research paper, you would want to use material that has itself been researched and has used authoritative sources to support personal opinions. On the other hand, if you are reading for pleasure, you might prefer material written for a wide general audience rather than a specialized one. Many authors are sensitive to their audiences. A textbook author who is aware that students are taking an introductory course in the particular discipline, for example, will often use examples they can relate to in order to help them comprehend the subject matter. This is often not the case in textbooks written for advanced students, who are expected to have more knowledge of the field.

Keep in mind, too, that an author's style should have a bearing on your reading rate. If the language is very technical, you will need to slow down. If the writing style is more like that of the first example, you can go at a faster pace.

ACTIVITY K: Identifying Author's Style

Read each paragraph, noting the style in which it is written, such as formal, informal, or technical. Then answer the questions that follow.

1. Our nation's economy today is a far cry from what the classical economists envisioned. In Chapter 9, we will survey and discuss the changes in size and influence of our various levels of government. Today, a third of the market value of all the production in the United States, called the *gross national product* (GNP), is spent by our local, state, and national governments.

   Who is the intended audience? _____

   How do you know? _____

   Is there any evidence that the author is trying to appeal to your emotions? If so, what is it? _____

   _____

2. In sixteen of the past seventeen Gallup polls on education, poor public discipline has been the most frequent criticism leveled against public

schools. One may wonder if better discipline codes and more home-work are adequate remedies for our current school problems or whether these dysfunctions are more profound and should be treated with more sensitive and complex remedies. Although literacy and student diligence are unquestionably worthy of pursuit, they are only part of the process of communicating serious morality. If we want to improve the ways we are now transmitting morality, it makes sense to analyze the way morality was transmitted before youth disorder became such a distressing issue.

Who is the intended audience?

How do you know?

Is there any evidence that the author is trying to appeal to your emotions? If so, what is it?

3. Many people came in contact with Elinor, including some people of power and influence. Many tried to assist her. Could not someone, some agency, have done something to alter the course of her seemingly inevitable destruction? In many ways, Elinor chose the way she lived, she chose to stay in the terminal. But that's just too simple: she was a victim.

Who is the intended audience?

How do you know?

Is there any evidence that the author is trying to appeal to your emotions? If so, what is it?

4. Cotton was grown in the American South, sold to English factories, where it was made into clothing, and then sent back to the United States, where it was bought by Americans. By the 1850s, tariffs on the clothing that was brought into the country greatly reduced the profits that the English could make on their products. As a result, the English naturally bought less cotton from the South. Southerners complained bitterly about the tariffs but could do nothing about them.

Who is the intended audience?

How do you know? _____

Is there any evidence that the author is trying to appeal to your emotions? If so, what is it? _____

_____

5. Any viewer of the United States who watched regularly the television reporting from Vietnam—and it was from television that 60 percent of Americans got most of their war news—would agree that he saw scenes of real-life violence, death, and horror on his screen that would have been unthinkable before Vietnam. The risk and intrusion that such filming involved could, perhaps, be justified if it could be shown that television had been particularly effective in revealing the true nature of the war and thus had been able to change people's attitudes to it. Is there any evidence to this effect?

   From Phillip Knightley, "The First Televised War," in Nancy R. Comley et al., eds. *Fields of Writing,* 3d ed. (New York: St. Martin's, 1975), p. 632.

Who is the intended audience? _____

How do you know? _____

Is there any evidence that the author is trying to appeal to your emotions? If so, what is it? _____

_____

6. Correctly placing and securing a helmet on the head is important to maximize protection. Because four helmet sizes exist and models fit slightly differently, your child should try on several sizes and models to find the best fit when you are purchasing a helmet. Correct fit involves positioning the helmet on the head so it sits low on the forehead and is parallel to the ground when the head is held upright (the wearer should be able to see its lower brim when looking all the way up); installing or removing inside pads to make the helmet snug; and adjusting the chin strap so it is comfortably snug (i.e., tight with room for only two fingers to be inserted between the strap and the chin). When in place with the chin strap secure, the helmet should not come off or shift over the eyes when the wearer tries to shake it loose.

   From "Bicycle Helmets," *Pediatrics* 108:4 (October 2001): 1030.

Who is the intended audience?_____

How do you know? _____

Is there any evidence that the author is trying to appeal to your emotions? If so, what is it? _____

_____

7. Simply put, a career path combines related occupations into a general category or cluster. Workers in these occupations share similar interests and strengths, but may have achieved different levels of education and training. For example, two of the occupations in the health sciences career path are pediatrician and medical assistant. While both professions require an interest in helping people get well, the specific job-related educational requirements differ. Doctors train nearly 10 years, but medical assistants sometimes enter the field after less than a year of specialized courses. The variety of job requirements and responsibilities within each career path will allow you to pick out occupations that fit you best.

   From Janice Arenofsky, "Creating Your Career Path," *Career World* 30:1 (September 2001): 6.

Who is the intended audience?_____

How do you know? _____

Is there any evidence that the author is trying to appeal to your emotions? If so, what is it? _____

_____

WORKING TOGETHER

Compare your answers to Activity K with those of a partner. Did you agree on which paragraphs made emotional appeals to readers?

Identifying Mood and Tone

Words can be powerful descriptors of feeling. Mood and tone refer to the emotional atmosphere conveyed through written language. When readers analyze narrative text (short stories, poetry, plays, and novels), the terms *mood* and *tone* may be used interchangeably. A character's dialogue, for instance, may simultaneously suggest a tone and create a mood, as in the case of a dying soldier who bids a passionate farewell to his lover. However, when readers analyze expository text (essays, newspaper or periodical articles, and textbook chapters), the term *tone* is generally used. As with other elements of writing we have already studied in this chapter, the author may not tell you directly what mood or tone is present in the writing. You will need to analyze the word choice and the details of the writing to arrive at an understanding of its mood or tone. You will be able to further appreciate and understand mood and tone by looking at some everyday examples of them.

Your experiences communicating with others have no doubt made you sensitive to differences in tone of voice. If a friend is troubled, you might listen and talk sympathetically. If you are speaking to someone who has damaged your property, you probably sound angry. If a new co-worker asks you to explain some work-related procedure, you probably use an instructional or serious tone of voice. If you have very strong feelings in an argument, you may be passionate when you explain your point of view. We adjust our tone of voice to suit the situation and our purpose, as well as to convey our feelings in the situation. Authors of expository text, or narrators of a literary work, use tone to reflect serious, angry, sympathetic, instructional, argumentative or persuasive, humorous, or ironic attitudes.

Tone can influence our personal reactions to a piece of writing or toward a character. Consider, for instance, the difference in your reactions to someone who requests a favor and sounds sweet and grateful, compared to someone who sounds demanding and insistent. You should recognize that your response to what you read may be similarly influenced by its tone. Thus, to read critically, you will need to be able to separate the content of what is said from the manner in which it is said. Then you will be able to honestly assess whether the ideas have merit.

As a critical reader, you should try to match your purpose for reading to the author's purpose for writing. Doing this will help your comprehension. For instance, if an author writes an essay suggesting that people should never own pets and does so in a humorous vein, the reader who recognizes the humor will read it as a humorous piece and won't criticize the author for having outrageous ideas. However, readers who think this author is serious will misinterpret the entire essay. To accomplish this reader-writer match in purpose, it is essential to determine the author's tone. The box that follows lists various kinds of tone you can encounter in text.

EXAMPLES OF TONE

Formal	Resigned
Informal	Indifferent
Romantic	Hateful
Serious	Passionate
Humorous	Cheerful
Amused	Optimistic
Angry	Pessimistic
Playful	Thoughtful or pensive
Neutral	Enthusiastic
Satirical	Argumentative
Fearful	Pleading
Suspicious	Matter-of-fact
Gloomy	Informative
Monotonous	Persuasive
Suspenseful	Wistful
Sad	Tense

The mood of a written work may refer to the frame of mind of a character, as reflected through the character's actions, dialogue, and tone of voice. Mood also refers to the general atmosphere that surrounds an incident or scene; it is created by description and details or events. To further understand this element of a writer's craft, imagine that you are getting ready for a first date with someone you find pretty exciting. Your date has planned the entire evening. You hope for candlelight and champagne; instead, you are treated to hot dogs and a football game. Obviously, there is a difference in the mood or atmosphere created by the details used to describe each of these situations.

Authors of narrative text use details for a variety of purposes, one of which is to create a particular mood for their story. The details work together to create an overall effect. Some examples of mood that you might find in narrative text are suspense or mystery, horror, gaiety or joyfulness, sadness, gloominess, anticipation or adventure, romance, loneliness, hopefulness, and frustration.

If an author has been successful at creating a particular mood, it will inspire the desired feeling in the reader. Notice the contrast between the following two example paragraphs, both of which are about the same event. One has been written with carefully chosen details so as to create a certain mood; the other seems flat by comparison. Note the difference in the effect each has on you, the reader.

Example 1:

It was unbelievably wonderful to be home. The first thing she did was to race upstairs, tear off her uniform, and put on some proper clothes—an old cotton skirt, a well-worn white shirt left over from school, her favorite red sweater. Nothing had changed; the room was just the way she had left it, only tidier and shiningly clean. When, bare legged, she ran downstairs again, it was to go from room to room, a thorough inspection, just to make sure that there, as well, everything was exactly the same. Which it was.

Example 2:

It was good to be home. She first went upstairs, took off her uniform, and put on some proper clothes—a cotton skirt, a white shirt left over from school, a red sweater. Her room was as she had left it, only cleaner. After dressing, she went downstairs again to go through the house to make sure that there, as well, everything was the way she had left it. Which it was.

What mood is created by example 1? _____

What details contribute to its effectiveness? _____

_____

_____

There is an air of excitement in the first example that isn't present in the second. Some of the details that help create this mood are the phrases *unbelievably wonderful* and *nothing had changed*. We can tell how glad the girl is to be home and to be putting on her *favorite red sweater*. These details, and others you may have noticed, work together to create the mood.

ACTIVITY L: Identifying Author's Mood and Tone

In the space provided, indicate the tone or mood that has been used in each paragraph. Then explain why you believe this is the tone or mood of the passage.

Example:

All health-care workers must follow universal precautions and established infection control procedures to reduce infection risks to patients and themselves. Appropriate use and disposal of needles and sharp instruments are the most important risk reduction strategy. In addition, universal precautions include the use of gloves, masks, eye protection, and other barriers as needed for procedures that involve contact with blood and body fluids.

Mood or tone: informative; serious

Explanation: A good deal of information is given. There is not much emotional language.

1. Every new advance in medicine—every new drug, new operation, new therapy of any kind—must sooner or later be tried on a living being for the first time. That trial, controlled or uncontrolled, will be an experiment. The subject of that experiment, if not an animal, will be a human being. Prohibiting the use of live animals in biomedical research, therefore, or sharply restricting it, must result either in the blockage of much valuable research or in the replacement of animal subjects with human subjects. These are the consequences—unacceptable to most reasonable persons—of not using animals in research.

   Mood or tone: _____

   Explanation: _____

   _____

2. I speak from experience when I say that cigar smokers have suffered the scorn of Americans who think our habit is vile. We have seen the steady disappearance of places where cigar smoking is acceptable. Now we are being told that the federal government wants to raise taxes on our cigars to help finance health care. Eventually, cigars will cost nothing because if the prices keep going up and there's nowhere to smoke them, nobody's going to smoke them. The whole thing nauseates me.

   Mood or tone: _____

   Explanation: _____

   _____

3. As terrible as the fear of existence is, the fear of nonexistence is even worse. Maybe if we only knew what happened to us after we died, it would all be easier.

   One speculation is that we go to the Land of the Umbrellas. You've probably seen them at the end of every rainstorm. Lying in the gutter, crumpled, skeletal, inside out, bereft of personal history. Who did these umbrellas belong to? Where are they going? What use are they now?

   Others say that after death we go to the Land of the M&M's—the place where the M&M's go after they fall behind the cushions on the sofa. Or some say it's the Land of the Other Shoe. (Ever drive along the road and see only one shoe lying on the pavement and wonder how it got there? You never see *both shoes;* the other shoe has gone to join the umbrellas and the M&M's.)

   In the end, it is probably foolish to speculate about such matters. In ancient times, the biggest fear was that you would have a terrible life and be reincarnated, and the next life would be even worse. Nowadays, life is Hollywood, and if your life's been bad, you don't have to worry about there being a sequel. Not if Part I didn't make any money.

   From Stephanie Brush, "Life: A Warning," in William Novak and Moshe Waldoks, eds., *The Big Book of North American Humor* (New York: HarperCollins, 1990), p. 178.

   Mood or tone: _____

   Explanation: _____

   _____

4. He sat on a bench here, watching the leafy trees and the flowers blooming on the inside of the railing, thinking of a better life for himself. He thought of the jobs he had had since he had quit school—delivery boy, stock clerk, runner, lately working in a factory—and he was dissatisfied with all of them. He felt he would someday like to have a good job and live in a private house with a porch on a street with trees. He wanted to have some dough in his pocket to buy things with, and a girl to go with, so as not to be so lonely, especially on Saturday nights. He wanted people to like and respect him.

   Bernard Malamud, "A Summer's Reading," in Raymond Harris, ed., *Best Short Stories: Advanced Level,* 2d ed. (Providence, RI: Jamestown Publishers, 1990), p. 91.

Mood or tone: _____

Explanation: _____

_____

5. She gazed up at him, the wide, young eyes blazing with light. And he bent down and kissed her on the lips. And the dawn blazed in them, their new life came to pass, it was beyond all conceiving good, it was so good, that it was almost like a passing-away, a trespass. He drew her suddenly closer to him.

Mood or tone: _____

Explanation: _____

_____

6. Alfred lowered the gun. One shot, and he would be cornered like a rabbit at harvest time. If he was going to kill the man, he would have to do so silently. With the Colt in his right hand, he pulled off his shoes and crept cautiously across the tiles. A chimney stack obstructed his view for part of the way. By the time he rounded it, Snits had raised the rifle to his shoulder and was settling himself into a firing position.

Mood or tone: _____

Explanation: _____

_____

THINKING ABOUT YOUR READING AND WRITING

ACTIVITY M: Mood and Tone in Films

Think about some movies or videos you have seen. In a few sentences, discuss what you notice about how filmmakers create mood.

_____

_____

_____

_____

_____

_____

_____

_____

_____

WORKING TOGETHER

With a partner, discuss some films you have seen where the mood has been an important part of the film's effect on you. Compare the types of moods you prefer.

▶ *Chapter Summary*

Based on your reading of this chapter, list at least five ideas that you believe will help you with future reading assignments. Write in complete sentences.

1. _____

_____

_____

_____

2. _____

_____

_____

_____

3. _____

_____

_____

_____

4. _____

_____

_____

_____

5. _____

_____

_____

_____

▶ *Extended Application*

Now that you have worked with the strategies necessary for critical reading and think-ing, you can practice applying them to full-length reading selections. Choose (or your instructor may choose) a reading selection from Part 2 of this book or another reading selection that is typical of what you will be expected to read for your other college courses, such as an essay or a textbook chapter. Use this selection to practice:

※ Distinguishing between fact and opinion

※ Evaluating evidence for statements of opinion

※ Identifying point of view

※ Identifying mood, tone, and style

Decide on the practice strategies you will use. Apply them to your selection. Then, in a few paragraphs, write a description of what you did and how the strategies you used worked for you.

Name of material used: _____

Page numbers: _____

Your description: _____

Reading Critically to Make Inferences, Draw Conclusions, and Analyze Web-Based Materials

HAVE YOU EVER DECIDED whether or not to see a movie based on the reactions of people coming out of the theater? Many people find this a useful way to judge whether or not to spend their money on seeing a film. Because strangers coming out of the theater most likely won't just come out and tell you their opinions, it is useful to know what to look for as audience indicators of a good movie: people laughing or crying (depending on the movie content) or people excitedly talking about it. Based on your observations, you make inferences and draw conclusions about your interest in seeing the movie.

Authors, like moviegoers, also don't often directly tell you everything. Critical readers, like critical observers, look for ideas that are *suggested* in text as well as for those that are directly stated. In Chapter 6, you discovered how the author felt about the subject being discussed by looking for words or phrases that suggested an opinion or point of view. The author's mood, tone or style contributed to the information on which you based your findings. You were doing *inferential reading.* In this chapter, we discuss strategies for making other types of inferences: inferences about events, characters, or ideas that are suggested by the information stated in the text. You will also learn how to draw conclusions from these inferences and the other information the text provides. In Chapter 6, you also learned some criteria to use for judging the accuracy and value of opinions you find in text. This chapter continues that discussion and adds information about how to evaluate resources you find on the Internet.

Inferences in Everyday Life

We are constantly making guesses, or *inferences,* about things we see, hear, and read. Imagine, for instance, that your attention is caught by a front-page photo in this morning's newspaper: A Jeep is turned over; shattered glass is all around it. The middle of the Jeep looks crushed. A car is close behind it. Standing beside the car is a young man looking off into the distance. Also next to the car is a firefighter. Across the street is a fire truck, its hose extending to the Jeep. Without reading the caption, you can already infer what has happened: a serious accident. Clearly, this was not some stunt being performed or some advertising ploy designed to capture the attention of Jeep buyers. Only one driver is in the photo, near the car; maybe the driver of the Jeep is trapped inside or has been taken to a hospital. That driver probably didn't survive. You wonder if there were any passengers. You also guess that there was a fire in the Jeep, caused when it flipped over. The man standing by the Jeep may have driven the car and may have caused the accident. It is hard to tell. But he doesn't look hurt. You are hypothesizing all this information through your interpretation of the picture. You still have not read any text. Now you read the article beneath the photo. It confirms some of your hypotheses and denies others: there was an accident and a fire; a young boy, not the driver, was killed. Making inferences from text, without photos, works in much the same way.

Finding Support for Your Inferences

An inference is an "informed guess" you make about something you read or experience. Your guess is based on what you know from your *prior experience* as well as from the *information given* in the text, photograph, cartoon, letter, situation, or dialogue about which you are making inferences. What you know (the factual details in the text as well as your prior knowledge) is considered to be the evidence or support for your guess. The inferences you make must follow logically from the available information. As more information becomes available, you may need to modify your original thinking. The following example illustrates how the process of making inferences works and how new information may cause you to reject inferences you made earlier. Read sentence 1. Then decide which statements beneath it could be appropriate guesses, based on the information in that sentence as well as on your prior knowledge.

> **Sentence 1:** The surgeon removed his gloves and quickly scanned the chart on the wall.

> **Possible inferences:** [Decide which inferences are logical. More than one can be selected. Put the letter(s) of your choice(s) in the space provided.]

> _____ a. The surgeon had just completed surgery.

> _____ b. The surgeon felt the surgery had gone poorly.

> _____ c. The surgeon was getting ready for his next patient.

> _____ d. The surgeon was in a hurry.

> _____ e. The surgeon had been cold.

> _____ f. The surgeon was an experienced pilot.

Supported inferences: _____

There is evidence that supports sentences a, c, d, and e. For sentence a, the evidence is that he was taking off gloves. You know that surgeons wear gloves. For sentence c, the evidence is that he is looking at a chart, which might be a chart of patients and surgery schedules. You know that hospitals use charts for patients. For sentence d, the evidence is the word *quickly,* which describes how the gloves were being removed. For sentence e, the evidence is that the surgeon was wearing gloves. He might have come inside from where he had been cold and then taken off the gloves.

Now read sentence 2, which gives additional information. From your choices of inferences that seemed logical based on sentence 1 and your prior knowledge, eliminate those that no longer make sense. In the space provided, list only those inferences that can now be supported.

> **Sentence 2:** The airport where he was now waiting for his departure was freezing cold.

Supported inferences: _____

The sentences to be eliminated as logical inferences are a and c. In both cases, the sentences are contradicted by the fact that the surgeon is at an airport. You know that surgery is not performed at airports.

The sentence to be added as a logical inference is f. Sentence f is a logical inference because he is at an airport, and it is possible he will fly a plane. The charts he is looking at in sentence 1 might be connected to his flight. You know that airports keep various charts and records of flight schedules. We now have sentences d, e, and f as inferences that can be supported based on the information from the first two sentences.

Now read sentence 3, which gives additional details. Repeat the procedure you used with sentence 2.

Sentence 3: From the chart, he learned which instructor he had been assigned to for his first flying lesson ever.

Supported inferences: _____

What sentences did you say are now suitable as inferences? Only d and e remain as logical inferences. Sentence 3 contradicts choice f, which, based on sentence 2, initially seemed possible.

You can see how important it is not to jump to conclusions. Every sentence *before and after* the sentence from which you make an inference contains information that will assist you in determining the extent to which your inference is valid. You will need to reject your inference if you can't find support for it in the material and if you have no prior knowledge to support it.

This process of making inferences while you read is applicable to any kind of text, regardless of length or subject matter. It works for both nonfictional (expository) and fictional (narrative) reading material. Activity B offers additional practice in applying this reading and thinking strategy.

THINKING ABOUT YOUR READING AND WRITING

ACTIVITY A: Understanding How to Make Inferences

In your own words, explain the process for making inferences.

_____

_____

_____

_____

_____

Activity B: Identifying Possible Inferences

Beneath each paragraph are several possible inferences. For each possible inference, indicate whether it is supported (S) or contradicted (C) by the information given in the paragraph. If there is no information either supporting or contradicting the possible inference, write (?) to indicate that the inference is neither supported nor contradicted by the paragraph. Be prepared to cite evidence for your answers. Your evidence may include your prior knowledge but should also include information from the passage.

Example:

Major advertisers, eager to tap the estimated $134 billion in spending power wielded by Spanish-speaking Americans, have ventured into Spanglish to promote their products. In some cases, attempts to sprinkle Spanish through commercials have produced embarrassing mistakes. An ad for now-bankrupt Braniff airlines that sought to tell Spanish-speaking audiences they could settle back *en* (in) a luxurious *cuero* (seat), for example, mistakenly said they could fly without clothes (*encuero*).

Possible inferences:

_S_ a. Corporations will write specific ads for specific audiences.
(The first sentence supports this inference.)

_S_ b. Large corporations are willing to spend huge sums of money on advertising.

(The first sentence also supports this inference.)

_?_ c. Spanish-speaking Americans object to having ads made that are designed to appeal especially to them.

(There is no information about this in the paragraph.)

_S_ d. It is sometimes difficult to translate concepts from one language to another.

(The example given illustrates this inference.)

_C_ e. Braniff intended its ad to be humorous.

(It is suggested that this was an "embarrassing mistake.")

1. Benedict Arnold had long considered himself unjustly treated by Congress. Time and again, his brilliant gifts had been overlooked and less able officers promoted over his head. Such had also been the lot of other competent commanders in the army, yet none turned traitor to his country. Arnold, however, feeling mistreated and suffering financial

embarrassment because of his own reckless expenditures and the extravagances of his pretty wife, the former Peggy Shippen, entered into secret negotiations with Sir Henry Clinton. On the promise of a large sum of money and a command in the British army, he agreed to surrender West Point, key fortress to the Hudson River Valley and vital to communication lines between New England and the other states.

Possible inferences:

_____ a. Benedict Arnold easily forgave people.

_____ b. Benedict Arnold knew his negotiations with the British army were wrong.

_____ c. Benedict Arnold's wife encouraged him to be a traitor.

_____ d. Benedict Arnold was guided by his feelings more than by his intellect.

_____ e. Sir Henry Clinton knew of Benedict Arnold's financial problems.

2. When Mr. Pontellier learned of his wife's intention to abandon her home and take up residence elsewhere, he immediately wrote her a letter of unqualified disapproval and remonstrance. She had given reasons which he was unwilling to acknowledge as adequate. He hoped she had not acted upon her rash impulse; and he begged her to consider first, foremost, and above all else, what people would say. He was not dreaming of scandal when he uttered this warning; that was a thing which would never have entered into his mind to consider in connection with his wife's name or his own. He was simply thinking of his financial integrity. It might be noised about that the Pontelliers had met with reverses, and were forced to conduct their menage [household] on a humbler scale than heretofore. It might do incalculable mischief to his business prospects.

From Kate Chopin, "The Awakening," in Lewis Leary, ed., *The Awakening and Other Short Stories* (New York: Holt, 1970), p. 313.

Possible inferences:

_____ a. Mr. Pontellier was concerned about his status.

_____ b. Mr. Pontellier loved his wife.

_____ c. Mr. Pontellier and his wife were wealthy.

_____ d. Mrs. Pontellier was having an extramarital affair.

_____ e. Mr. Pontellier did not want his wife to leave.

3. The ethical code that all doctors recite when they join the medical profession today goes back at least two thousand years. The Hippocratic oath defines what ethical behavior is when a physician works with his or her patients. The oath describes not only the methods that doctors should and should not use in treating the ill but also the code of conduct they should follow in working with patients. One part of the code says, for example, "Whatever, in connection with my professional practice, or not in connection with it, I see or hear, in the life of men which ought not to be spoken of abroad, I will not divulge as reckoning that all such should be kept secret."

Possible inferences:

_____ a. Ethical problems in medicine have concerned men and women for a long time.

_____ b. The concern for ethics in medicine originated in the United States.

_____ c. Some patients prefer doctors who have not taken the Hippocratic oath.

_____ d. Part of the ethical behavior of doctors is to respect a patient's right to privacy.

_____ e. Today, graduates of medical schools in Europe do not have to take the Hippocratic oath.

4. Flying solo isn't necessarily a lonely ride, says Duane Alwin, a University of Michigan expert on single living and mental health. A large body of research indicates that unmarried people suffer more from depression, anxiety, and ill health than those who are married—the theory being that close relationships protect the married against stresses the unmarried face alone. But Alwin argues that solitary living itself can't be held responsible. People need strong ties with others to be happy, he says, but it can't be assumed that living alone prevents those ties from forming.

From J. Seligman, "The Art of Flying Solo," *Newsweek* (March 1, 1993): 70.

Possible inferences:

_____ a. Duane Alwin is married.

_____ b. The longer a person is married, the less he or she will feel depressed.

_____ c. Unmarried people are incapable of forming strong ties with others.

_____ d. Flying solo refers to being unmarried.

_____ e. Sometimes there is disagreement about psychological theories.

5. Several aspects of Brazilian social structure impede the economic advancement of lower-class Brazilians. Most obvious are obligations associated with kinship. Men who through hard work have become more successful within the community are expected to share their wealth with a larger number of people. Obligations associated with marriage also drain wealth from the enterprising man. In Brazil, the union with the most prestige is one that has been sanctified by both church and state. Poorer couples are generally involved in common-law unions wherein there is no written legal joining of the couple. Upwardly mobile young men may have civil and religious ceremonies when they marry. If they do this, however, they undertake obligations to care for the wife's relatives, which do not exist with the common-law union. Because there is no divorce in Brazil, these obligations are for life.

Possible inferences:

_____ a. Parents whose children are in common-law marriages will not have the same protection in their later years as parents whose children have sanctified marriages.

_____ b. There are fewer sanctified marriages in Brazil than anywhere else in the world.

_____ c. Brazilian culture encourages concern for others who are less well off.

_____ d. It is acceptable for Brazilian men who are wealthy to be critical of relatives who ask for money.

_____ e. The church and state have a close connection in Brazilian culture.

📘 THINKING ABOUT YOUR READING AND WRITING

ACTIVITY C: Contrasts in Processes for Inferences and Main Ideas

In a few sentences, explain how the thought processes you use to make inferences differ from those you use to find main ideas.

_____

_____

_____

_____

_____

_____

Drawing Conclusions from Your Reading

Critical readers often draw conclusions from what they read. Some of these conclusions are probability statements based on the information in the text. Others are suggestions of how an author's ideas can be applied to different situations. In this section, you will learn how to form conclusions and how to decide whether your conclusions reasonably follow from the text and from your prior knowledge.

What Are Conclusions?

We draw conclusions about our everyday experiences all the time. For instance, we go into Sam's music store and notice that the price of a popular CD is $11.99, which is $2 higher than in Lonny's music store. From this, we might conclude that Sam's has high prices on CDs. Our conclusion is verified by other instances of higher prices on CDs at Sam's. We try to remember whether Lonny's was having a sale when we looked at its prices. If it was not, we can predict, or conclude, that anytime we come to Sam's the prices on CDs will be higher. If a sale was being held at Lonny's, however, we cannot conclude this.

In drawing conclusions about CD prices, we are stating that something is a *probable outcome* based on evidence we have gathered. Drawing conclusions from texts or lectures uses the same process: We look at the facts or reasons (which may include opinions), we judge how accurate and unbiased they are, and we eliminate particularly biased or irrelevant information.

A conclusion may explain or predict what will probably happen, or what will result, based on what you already know. It is a *reasonable guess about what an outcome will be.* Conclusions are based on facts and well-supported opinions. For a conclusion to be probable, it should follow logically from this information. When you draw a conclusion, you are tying together the various pieces of information you have into a broad statement of probability. When you draw conclusions, you are moving beyond the text with your predictions. If you insert the word *Therefore* before your conclusion, it will serve as a reminder that you are making a guess about an outcome based on the information you have been given. The information you use to draw your conclusion may come from several sources, as in Example 1. Or it may come from a single source, as in Example 2.

Example 1:

Conclusion: In your search for a family dog, you have decided that *the golden retriever is the best kind of dog for a family to own.* Your reasons are:

a. The American Kennel Club rates the golden retriever as the dog with the best disposition.

b. A friend of yours says his golden retriever has never destroyed any of his property.

c. You have read a newspaper account of a golden retriever who rescued a baby who had fallen into a pool.

Example 2:

Conclusion: As a result of your reading about the code of medieval chivalry, you have concluded that *the honor of being called a chivalrous gentleman could be bestowed on only a few men.* The basis for this conclusion is the information in the following passage: A chivalrous gentleman was brave, straightforward, and honorable; loyal to his monarch, country, and friends; unfailingly true to his word; ready to take issue with anyone he saw ill treating a woman, a child, or an animal. He was a natural leader of men, and others unhesitatingly followed his lead. He was fearless in war and on the hunting field and excelled at many sports, but however tough with the tough, he was invariably gentle to the weak; above all, he was always tender, respectful, and courteous to women regardless of their rank. He put the needs of others before his own.

In each example, the conclusion logically follows from the information gathered. They are acceptable conclusions, or statements of probability. It may be that at a later date some other information will become known that will refute these conclusions, but since it is not now available, these conclusions are considered probable or likely to be true.

ACTIVITY D: Identifying Conclusions

Select the conclusion that *logically follows* for each paragraph. Remember to mentally insert the word *Therefore* as a reminder that you are connecting pieces of the text together. Underline all the information in the paragraph that you believe supports your conclusion. Be prepared to justify your answers.

1. The skillful blending of different textures in a room is just as important to the success of the scheme as the choice of colors and the mixing and matching of patterned and plain surfaces, yet it is often a neglected subject. Textures are all too often put together haphazardly even when the rest of the scheme has been carefully balanced. The selecting of textures needs even more care and attention when a room is being decorated with mostly plain colors on the larger areas of walls, floor, windows, and on upholstered furniture. If all these surfaces are of the same texture, the final effect will be boring even if the colors are different. Just as a successful scheme in mainly warm or cool colors needs a sharp contrast from the opposite side of the color wheel to bring it to life, so textures need contrast for emphasis.

   Adapted from Jill Blake, *Colour and Pattern in the Home* (London: Design Council, 1978), p. 50.

   a. The textures in a room can have a major impact on the final effect of its appearance.

   b. When colors in a room are of the same hue, the effect is dramatic.

   c. Textures and colors can be used to reflect certain period styles.

   d. To give rooms a lavish appearance, you should use velvet and satin textures.

2. During World War II, when great numbers of trained technicians were in demand, it was assumed that those who had mechanical aptitude would make good airplane mechanics. A careful analysis of this

assumption proved otherwise. It turned out that a good shoe clerk in civilian life would become a better mechanic for military purposes than someone who had fixed cars most of his life and learned on a Model-T Ford. The critical trait was not mechanical aptitude but the ability of the trainee to follow instructions. The Army then worked out its instruction manuals so meticulously that the best recruit turned out to be a mildly obsessional person who could read and follow directions. The last thing they wanted was someone with his own ideas on how to fix equipment.

From Edward T. Hall, *The Silent Language* (New York: Anchor, 1981), p. 71.

    a. The Army is not a good place for an engineer.

    b. Instruction manuals printed by the Army are designed for people who do not read very well.

    c. Specialized skills are not needed by the Army.

    d. The Army gives careful consideration to job requirements.

3. Scientists had believed that natural chemical cycles involving nitrogen and hydrogen controlled the stratospheric ozone amounts in this part of the earth's atmosphere. Observations made by NASA's high-altitude ERO2 plane, however, detected much lower levels of nitrogen oxides (NOx) than scientists expected. The measurements also showed higher than anticipated levels of chlorine monoxide (ClO), known to play a key role in destroying ozone in the polar regions.

    a. Scientists had overemphasized the importance of chlorine monoxide and its effect on the ozone layer.

    b. Scientists had overemphasized the importance of the nitrogen cycle in its effect on the ozone layer.

    c. NASA was reluctant to conduct this study.

    d. The ERO2 plane is unreliable.

4. Because we live in a highly specialized society, different social tasks are entrusted to different groups of individuals. Government, for example, is held responsible for safeguarding the public's health. This, in turn, makes government officials dependent on the skills and commitment of a certain category of medical person; if the latter cannot be induced to perform their tasks—such as, for example, finding a cure for AIDS—tens of thousands of citizens will find their lives endangered. Similarly, if the government wishes to develop more advanced nuclear weapons, put a man on the moon, or design a strategic defense, it

makes itself dependent on the relative handful of individuals who possess the appropriate scientific and technical skills. Indeed, since the number of each of these is far smaller than the number of business-men, each of them is proportionately more powerful than is each businessman. And unlike those who currently occupy the role of busi-nessman, they cannot be readily replaced.

From David Vigel, "The New Political Science of Corporate Power," *Public Interest* 87 (Spring 1987): 63–79.

    a. Businessmen feel pressured to increase their scientific knowledge.

    b. In highly specialized societies, people are more interdependent.

    c. Medical science has advanced over the years because of increases in government funding.

    d. The government should feel responsible when small businesses fail.

5. Toward the end of March, Alice Manfred put her needles aside to think again of what she called the *impunity* of the man who killed her niece just because he could. It had not been hard to do; it had not even made him think twice about what danger he was putting himself in. He just did it. One man. One defenseless girl. Death. A sample-case man. A nice, neighborly, everybody-knows-him man. The kind you let in your house because he was not dangerous, because you had seen him with children, bought his products and never heard a scrap of gossip about him doing wrong. Felt not only safe but kindly in his company because he was the sort women ran to when they thought they were being followed, or watched, or needed someone to have the extra key just in case you locked yourself out. He was the man who took you to your door if you missed the trolley and had to walk night streets at night. Who warned young girls away from hooch joints and the men who lingered there. Women teased him because they trusted him. He was one of those men who might have marched down Fifth Avenue—cold and dignified—into the space the drums made. He knew wrong wasn't right, and did it anyway.

From Toni Morrison, *Jazz* (New York: Knopf, 1992), pp. 73–74.

    a. Alice Manfred thought her niece had been unwise.

    b. The man who killed Alice Manfred's niece had escaped.

    c. Alice Manfred feels very unsafe now.

    d. Alice Manfred felt that the courts were ignoring the horror of her niece's death.

THINKING ABOUT YOUR READING AND WRITING

ACTIVITY E: Reflecting on Drawing Conclusions

In a few sentences, describe the thought process you used to reject or accept conclusions in Activity D.

_____

_____

_____

_____

_____

_____

ACTIVITY F: Evidence for Conclusions

The sentences that follow offer conclusions that could have been drawn from academic texts or lectures. In the space provided, indicate what type of evidence you would want to have before you accepted this conclusion. Be specific.

Example:

Conclusion: Increasingly, the Mundurucu people of the Amazon's rain forest are becoming Westernized.

Evidence you would need to accept this conclusion: Reports from anthropologists who have been there.

1. **Conclusion:** Women have an easier time moving into executive positions today than they did twenty-five years ago.

Evidence you would need to accept this conclusion: _____

_____

2. **Conclusion:** When he assassinated John F. Kennedy, Lee Harvey Oswald was acting alone.

   Evidence you would need to accept this conclusion: _____

   _____

3. **Conclusion:** America's wilderness and sensitive animal life are not threatened by big business, but by government.

   Evidence you would need to accept this conclusion: _____

   _____

4. **Conclusion:** Children who are adopted by gay couples fare as well in life as those who grow up with heterosexual couples.

   Evidence you would need to accept this conclusion: _____

   _____

5. **Conclusion:** Skateboarding is the fastest growing sport in America.

   Evidence you would need to accept this conclusion: _____

   _____

6. **Conclusion:** A run-down, negative environment can have a negative influence on community behavior.

   Evidence you would need to accept this conclusion: _____

   _____

WORKING TOGETHER

Compare your answers to Activity F with those of a partner. What differences were there in the evidence you each wanted? Add any of your partner's ideas that you liked to your own.

 THINKING ABOUT YOUR READING AND WRITING

ACTIVITY G: Your Conclusions About Conclusions

What are some conclusions you can draw about how critical reading and thinking will benefit you in your college career?

_____

_____

_____

_____

_____

_____

_____

_____

_____

Analyzing Web-Based Material

Many college professors now require their students to demonstrate that they are able to conduct research using Web-based materials. Fortunately, most students have had several years of practice searching the Internet in high school, so finding the sources seems easy. However, beware! Some sources are more trustworthy than others and thus more appropriate for use in academic research reports, such as term papers or oral presentations. In this section, you will learn how to critically evaluate the sources you find on the Web in order to determine how authoritative, accurate and useful they are.

Once you know your goal and purpose for your study and have formulated the questions or problems you want to research, you can begin your search. Your initial search should help you develop a point of view you can defend with reliable materials you find on the Web.

Here are some examples of sites you might be directed to if you did a search on the topic of *women in the military.* Consider the point of view that each site might reflect as well as the authoritativeness of the information that each might provide. Then answer the questions below the list.

a. **American Women in Uniform, Veterans Too! Military women**—a history of military women from the Revolutionary War to present day. Information about combat issues, current women veterans issues, and extensive information about military women, past and present. coelacanth.aug.com/captbarb - 54k - *Cached - More from this site*

b. **Women in Vietnam**
Interviews, articles, first person accounts, and announcements of events of interest and research requests.
www.illyria.com/vnwomen.html - 24k - *Cached - More from this site*

c. **Women in the United States Military**
Women make up about 20 percent of today's military. Information and resources concerning women in the United States military, both in the past and the present. . . . Higher Positions for Women in the Military. Women are rising to increasingly higher levels in the Defense . . . show that officer and enlisted women on active duty increased from 13 . . .
usmilitary.about.com/od/womeninthemilitary - 40k - *Cached - More from this site*

d. **Women Veterans . . . Women Veterans Comprehensive Health Centers. Women in the Military.** VA Benefits and Services. . . . Gains made by women in the military continue through the 1970's and that trend remains . . .
www1.va.gov/womenvet - 54k - *Cached - More from this site*

e. **Hot Topics - visionforum.org**
If certain federal lawmakers have their way, your eighteen-year-old daughters will be registered for selective service and drafted for combat by the next war. . . . Christians have long since abandoned the issue of women in the military. Sadly, far too many pastors and . . . by permitting and perpetuating the practice of women in the military. . . .
www.visionforumministries.org/sections/hotcon/ht/ womeninmilitary - 26k - *Cached - More from this site*

f. **GenderGap: Women & the Military**
GenderGap: Women & the Military GenderGap: Women & the Military. This is one woman's study of women around the world who have gone into combat during the last 6,000 years—now available online. Site includes a section on American Women and the . . .
www.gendergap.com/military.htm - *More from this site*

g. **Linda Chavez: Sexual tension in the military**
Townhall.com. $200,239 as of 2:15 PM Monday. More on National Security. Today's Opinion. Monday. Sexual tension in the military. Linda Chavez (archive) May 5, 2004 Admit it, the increased presence of women in the military serving in integrated units has made military . . . While some advocates of women in the military have argued that women's . . .
www.townhall.com/columnists/lindachavez/lc20040505.shtml - 57k - *Cached - More from this site*

h. **NARA | ALIC | Military Resources: Women in the Military**
Access to information on American history and government, archival administration, information management, and government documents to NARA staff, archives and records management professionals, and the general public. . . . Military Resources: Women in the Military. African-American Women in Military History. From the Air University Library . . . World War II. Women in Military Service for America Memorial
archives.gov/research_room/alic/.../women_in_military.html - 55k - *Cached - More from this site*

i. Untitled Document
Their Own Self. FRED Columns. Women In the Military. More Letters From The Field. About our policy of putting women into military jobs for which they are not suited: It isn't working. It isn't coming close. . . . telling the politicians what they want to hear: that women in the military are working out . . .
www.fredoneverything.net/MoreWomenLetters.shtml - 22k - *Cached - More from this site*

1. Which of the websites listed here might include very positive remarks about women serving in the military? Circle all that you think apply. Be prepared to justify your answers.
   a.   b.   c.   d.   e.   f.   g.   h.   i.

2. Which of the websites probably contain more opinion than fact? Circle all that you think apply. Be prepared to justify your answers.

   a.   b.   c.   d.   e.   f.   g.   h.   i.

3. Which of the websites probably contain a good deal of statistical information? Circle all that you think apply. Be prepared to justify your answers.

   a.   b.   c.   d.   e.   f.   g.   h.   i.

4. Which of the websites probably give primarily historical information about women in the military as well as information about this issue in the present? Circle all that you think apply. Be prepared to justify your answers.

   a.   b.   c.   d.   e.   f.   g.   h.   i.

5. Which of the websites are most likely to represent the U.S. government's view about women in the military? Circle all that you think apply. Be prepared to justify your answers.

   a.   b.   c.   d.   e.   f.   g.   h.   i.

6. Which of the websites most likely limits its content to one war?

   a.   b.   c.   d.   e.   f.   g.   h.   i.

Answering these questions required you to do several things. First, you needed to look at the title of the website. Then you needed to read the website description to determine content and its viewpoint. You also needed to look at the web address because some contained information about the source of the website material, such as the U.S. government. If you have done all of these things, then you probably arrived at the following answers for each question:

1. a, c, d, i
2. b, e, g, i
3. a, c, d
4. a, h
5. d, h
6. b

If you were uncertain about the content of any website listed, you could have gone directly to the site to verify your impressions. This is what you will need to do when you use the Internet for research. Remember that website content, like other text content, may be attempting to persuade you to believe a certain way about something. Think of persuasive arguments at websites similar to TV or radio commercials—some are credible, some are not. One way to decide if the information is believable is to look closely at all the material at that site. Is the webmaster or author of the text material an authority on the subject? How do you know? If not, are you given research data for the content, along with source information for that research, and are these trustworthy sources, such as professional peer-reviewed journals? Perhaps the site indicates it is affiliated with a respected organization, and this builds your confidence in the information provided. All information about the website ownership should be provided, including details of the organization that owns the site—street address, phone numbers, and the like. If the site asks you for something, such as a donation, be suspicious unless you know that the organization making this request is reputable.

You will also want to verify that the information is up to date. In most academic fields, new research constantly updates our knowledge of the field. Be sure you have researched for the most current information available. Even if the current date appears on a webpage, the page could be set up for a date change to occur automatically. You will need to look carefully at the information itself for its recency. Look back at the sites on women in the military. You will notice that most say the information is *cached*. This means that it is stored in the files of the search engine you are using, such as Google or Yahoo. The webmasters for those engines will sometimes direct you to another location that might contain more up-to-date information. If you click on to the word *cached* for material stored at Google, for instance, you might find a comment from the webmaster.

Some web pages, particularly those of a personal nature, contain grammatical and spelling errors. If there are many of these at one site, the source is probably unsuitable for scholarly research. Some organization-sponsored web pages will advise you of their connections to other groups that address similar topics and might even provide links to these. Such linkages often demonstrate good faith on the part of the webmaster to provide you with the best research available on your topic.

Another way to determine whether you are looking at well-supported fact or personal opinion is to do some further investigation by locating other material, perhaps at another website, that supports what you have found at the first one. Your own knowledge of the subject you are researching will also help you to determine whether or not to trust the ideas presented at the website. You cannot know everything, but if the site makes claims about ideas that seem far fetched to you, such as claims about UFO sightings, move cautiously.

If you critically analyze Web material as you do other text material, you will be able to recognize author assumptions and biases, make valid inferences, and determine if conclusions drawn by authors are logical. But websites are not just pages of connected text, as a novel might be. They also have visual material that must be analyzed for fairness, point of view, accuracy. In Chapter 8 we will discuss how to analyze visual material, including material from websites by noting details, making inferences, and drawing conclusions.

ACTIVITY H: Comparing Websites on the Same Subject

Select two websites on one topic that interests you. Both sites should be on the same topic. Review, compare and comment the two sites with regard to each of the website features listed below. Then decide which site will provide you with the best information for a research report on that topic.

Topic:

Web address 1: _____

Web address 2: _____

1. Analysis of Features
   a. believability

   Website 1:

   _____

   _____

   Website 2:

   _____

   _____

   b. authoritativeness

   Website 1:

   _____

   _____

Website 2:

_____

_____

c. recency

Website 1:

_____

_____

Website 2:

_____

_____

d. links to other sources

Website 1:

_____

_____

Website 2:

_____

_____

e. grammar and spelling

Website 1:

_____

_____

Website 2:

_____

_____

f. author's assumptions and biases

Website 1:

_____

_____

Website 2:

_____

_____

g. visual content

Website 1:

_____

_____

Website 2:

_____

_____

2. Conclusions

In a few sentences, describe the usefulness of each site for writing an academic research paper.

Website 1:

_____

_____

_____

_____

Website 2:

_____

_____

_____

_____

▶ *Chapter Summary*

Based on your reading of this chapter, list at least five ideas that you believe will help you with future reading assignments. Write in complete sentences.

1. _____

_____

_____

_____

2. _____

_____

_____

_____

3. _____

_____

_____

_____

4. _____

_____

_____

_____

5. _____

_____

_____

_____

▶ *Extended Application*

Now that you have worked with the strategies necessary for reading critically to make inferences, draw conclusions and analyze Web-based materials, you can practice applying them to full-length reading selections. Choose (or your instructor may choose) a reading selection from Part 2 of this book or another reading selection that is typical of what you will be expected to read for your other college courses, such as an essay or a textbook chapter. Use this selection to practice:

❋ Reading for inferences

❋ Identifying conclusions

❋ Analyzing Web-based materials

Decide on the practice strategies you will use. Apply them to your selection. Then, in a few paragraphs, write a description of what you did and how the strategies you used worked for you.

Name of material used: _____

Page numbers: _____

Your description: _____

CHAPTER EIGHT

Strategies for Reading Visual Aids in Texts

D O YOU LIKE TO TAKE photographs? Why? Why do so many people take cameras with them when they go on vacation or to special events? Most say they enjoy taking photos because then they can share with others what they've seen. It also helps them remember the places they've visited and the people they've met. Although reading a textbook isn't exactly like going on vacation, authors often include visual information in their texts for some of the same reasons: to help explain information to the readers and to help them remember what they have read. In Chapter 5, you were shown how to make visuals, or graphic organizers, for your own purposes. In this chapter, you will learn strategies for reading visual aids that authors provide and how these strategies can help you with reading comprehension.

What Are Visual Aids?

Pictorial displays, or visual aids, are often included in textbook chapters. They can be of great assistance to readers who know how to use them effectively.

ACTIVITY A: Determining the Value of Visual Aids

Read Example 1 and Example 2. Then answer the questions that follow under the heading *Reflection*.

Example 1:

Auction sales turnover 2004 / weight by country

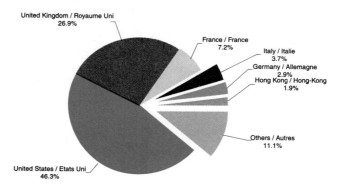

Example 2:

ART MARKET PLACES

NEW YORK REMAINS THE LARGEST MARKET

With turnover of $ 1,322 million for some 30,000 lots sold, the United States dominated the art market once again in 2004. US auction houses accounted for 46.3% of the global fine art market compared with 42% in 2003, and total turnover generated in the United States rose 45% in one year.

A number of factors contributed to this substantial rise: an increase in sales volume (+15%), a dramatic cumulative rise in prices (+18.5% on the New York market) and the growing number of lots sold for over a million dollars (229 works in New York, compared with 132 in 2003). Intense competition among the leading auction houses enhanced further the quality of works that changed hands in 2004, with New York benefiting the most from this race for the finest pieces. The Big Apple is by far the best market for selling works in the seven-figure range.

Underlying this dynamic increase is a combination of factors: the inevitable wider accessibility of the art market, resumed growth on the financial markets, the dollar's depreciation and the search for alternative investments.

While an investment of $ 100 in the US art market in 1994 yielded 60% in 2004, it was a completely different story in France: an art investment of € 100 only yielded on average 2% in 10 years.

THE CHANGING FACE OF THE EUROPEAN MARKET

With a 26.9% market share, London is number two worldwide and number one in Europe for fine art auctions. London's market climate is very similar to that of New York. All the indicators in 2004 showed an upward trend: prices: +14% over twelve months, volume of transactions: +9%, turnover: +22%.

Sixty-nine lots exceeded the million-pound mark. A Vermeer painting, Young Woman seated at the Virginals, fetched the highest price on the London market at £ 14.5 million. This sale strengthened London's position as leader of the Old Master category, as these auctions in London always prove a huge success.

In view of the much less favourable economic climate together with the impact of the euro weighing on the French art market, works sold in France did not benefit from the growth in the US market. In 2004, prices of artwork sold in Paris decreased by 2% to July 2000-levels, just prior to the first signs of the stock market crisis. Against this backdrop, it is not surprising that France is one of the only markets whose turnover contracted in 2004 (-1% compared with 2003). France's total market share fell from 9.2% to 7.2% between 2003 and 2004. Nonetheless, known for its deep reserve of art

works, France still boasts the largest market by the volume of transactions (19.4%).

Italy's share of the global fine art market rose to 3.7% in 2004, moving it up to fourth position in the Artprice ranking of countries by turnover, just ahead of Germany, which was relegated to fifth position. While the two countries still ran neck and neck in 2004, so far this year Germany only accounts for 2.9% of the market. Revenue generated at fine art auctions in Italy was up 32% on the previous year, whereas in Germany sales were up only 8%. In addition to slow growth in volumes (+3%), we note a general decline in prices in Germany. Sales volumes have remained virtually unchanged, with some 25,000 lots sold. What distinguishes the German market is its dominance of multiple series works. In Germany, prints make up one-third of transactions, whereas in other markets, this segment generally only accounts for 15% of lots sold. Furthermore, prints are the only medium where prices have shrunk over recent months.

Reflection:

What are some differences between the approaches you used to read Example 1 and Example 2? _____

_____

Which presentation of this information do you prefer? Why?

_____

_____

Which presentation do you think will help you remember this information longer? Why? _____

_____

In what way was the visual aid helpful? _____

_____

WORKING TOGETHER

Compare your answers to Activity A with those of a partner. What differences do you find in your responses?

What Are the Various Types of Visual Aids?

There are several common types of visual aids. Each type has its own unique features and purposes.

Charts

Charts summarize information through a combination of words and graphics. Often they show relationships between the items on the chart or comparisons between them. Charts enable the writer to explain complex ideas more concretely, and they enable the reader to visualize the relationship between abstract concepts.

TREE CHARTS. *Tree charts* look like trees with branches. A tree chart showing the relationship between the sales division of a large company and the rest of the company might look like the following:

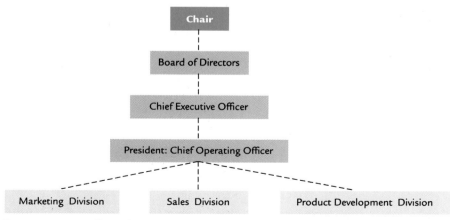

RELATIONSHIP OF SALES DIVISION TO LARGER ORGANIZATIONAL STRUCTURE

FLOWCHARTS.   *Flowcharts* show movement between events (a process) and may depict stopping out or correction points in this process. A flowchart designed to show the process for eating lunch might look like the diagram that follows. The

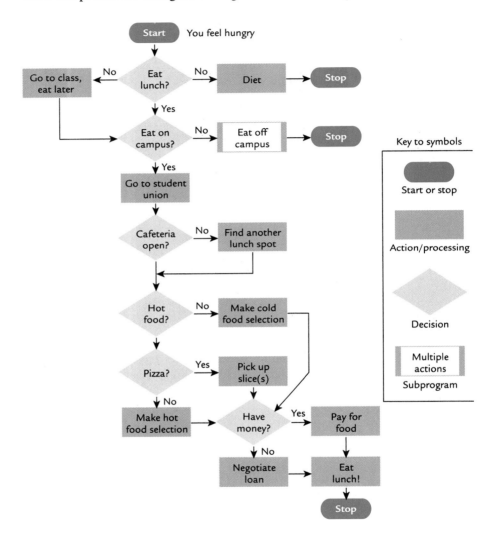

"EATING LUNCH" FLOWCHART

Source: Adapted from Helene G. Kershner, *Computer Literacy,* 2d ed. (Lexington, MA: D. C. Heath, 1992), p. 169. Reprinted by permission of the author.

symbols on the chart are explained in a key or legend alongside the chart. Notice that several decision points can cause the flow to stop or to continue. These *stopping* or *rerouting points* are common on flowcharts and are one reason they are useful for depicting processes.

Timelines

To show how something has progressed in stages or how something has evolved over time, a *timeline* is particularly effective. Timelines often appear in scientific writing and may illustrate how scientific discoveries progressed from one stage, perhaps the stage where an illness is first identified, to a later stage, perhaps when a cure is found. More frequently, they are used to show progressive events in chronological order, as in the timeline shown here.

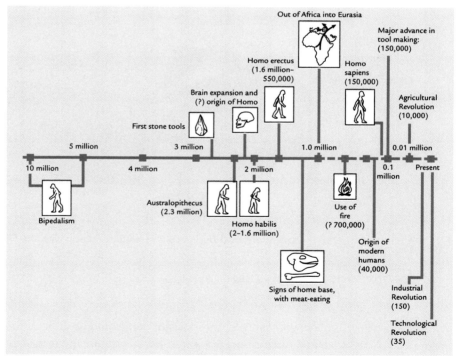

APPROXIMATE TIMELINE FOR THE MAJOR EVENTS IN HUMAN EVOLUTION
Source: Philip G. Zimbardo and Ann L. Weber, *Psychology.* Published by Allyn and Bacon, MA. Copyright © 1994 by Pearson Education. Reprinted by permission of the publisher.

Graphs

Graphs, especially *circle* (or *pie*), *bar,* and *line* graphs, are also commonly found in textbooks. The purpose of a graph is most often to show comparisons of quantitative information. There is always text, either directly on or surrounding the graph, and this information tells the reader what is being depicted. The reader then needs to see the relationship between the different pieces of information and determine the significance of it. For instance, by looking at the *circle graph,* we can see the differences in influences on individuals' satisfaction with air travel. The information outside the graph tells us what each part of the circle represents. We can draw several conclusions from the data—for instance, that individuals were more concerned with creature comforts once they got on the plane than almost anything else except "On-time performance." We might also wonder if travelers would respond differently today, given the changed nature of air travel.

Ten Factors Drive Overall Airline Satisfaction

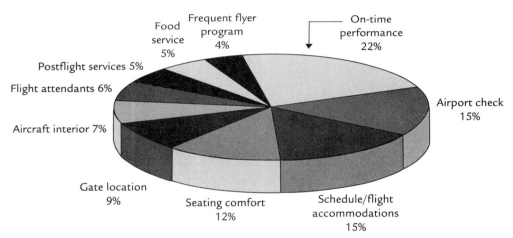

Percent of Contribution to Overall Satisfaction with the Flight

Source: Courtland L. Bouvée and John V. Thill, *Business Communications Today,* 6th ed. (Upper Saddle River, NJ: Prentice Hall, 2000), p. 410. Reprinted by permission of Pearson Education, Inc.

Bar graphs depict information that would be difficult for readers to follow in a textual discussion; they also make it easy for the reader to compare data, as bar graph Example 1 illustrates. Notice that the meanings of the various shadings are provided. On the bar graph, several relationships are shown. The reader can compare different ethnic groups to the total population and any vitamin or mineral

Example 1:

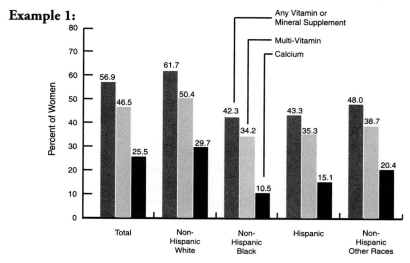

VITAMIN AND MINERAL SUPPLEMENTATION AMONG WOMEN AGED 18 AND OLDER BY RACE/ETHNICITY CHART

Source: National Health Interview Survey. http://mchb.hrsa.gov/pages/page_23.htm. Retrieved June 10, 2005.

Example 2:

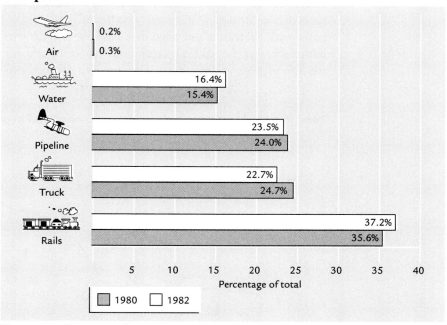

VOLUME OF DOMESTIC FREIGHT CARRIED BY EACH TRANSPORTATION MODE

Source: Leon C. Megginson et al., *Business* (Lexington, MA: D. C. Heath, 1985), p. 414. Reprinted with permission.

supplement, multivitamin, and calcium supplement within and across ethnic groups.

Bar graphs may also be drawn horizontally, as in Example 2 on page 253. Once again, several comparisons are shown. One is a comparison over time of the form of transportation that has been used to carry domestic freight. Another is the comparison between types of carriers, namely, air versus truck. In addition to the bar itself, which illustrates differences, the specific percentage volume contributed by each type of carrier to the total volume of domestic freight is given in the notations alongside the chart and a scale drawing of percentages is located at the bottom of the "Rails" bar.

Line graphs are useful for showing trends over time. Because line graphs can show small increases and decreases, they are sometimes considered the most accurate type of graph. As in all graphs, the information outside the graph is critical for you to read. It explains what the information on the graph represents. The line graph has two lines that show a comparison between the total amount of petroleum exports and the exports to Canada and Mexico between 1960 and 2000. We can see that the total number has risen significantly, growing from less than 300 thousand barrels per day to more than 900 thousand. Exports to Canada and Mexico have more than tripled, growing from almost zero in 1960 to approximately 600 thousand barrels per day in 2000. On this graph, different types of lines are used to distinguish between "Total" and "Canada and Mexico" exports, with the former indicated by a solid line and the latter by a dotted line. The information to the left designates thousands of barrels per day that are exported; the information on the bottom is used to plot the total exports every five years.

Total Petroleum Exports and Exports to Canada and Mexico, 1960–2000

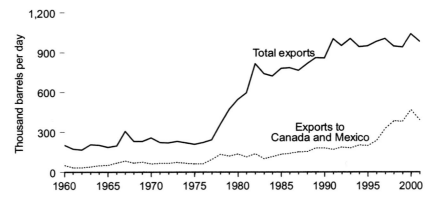

Source: From *http://www.eia.doe.gov/emeu/aer/pdf/pages/sec5_14.pdf.* Retrieved July 21, 2002.

Tables

Tables are used to classify or categorize information, particularly when there are many numbers or several categories. The information on a table is usually arranged in columns, with the categories listed horizontally across the top and the items falling into each category listed vertically. As in the example that follows several comparison points are often made on a single table. Footnotes also frequently appear on tables to give further explanation for some of the items. The chart shown here has such a footnote.

PRIMARY AND SECONDARY SYPHILIS RATES 2000 VS. 1999

No.	City	Cases 2000	Rate Per 100,000 Population, 2000	Rate Per 100,000 Population, 1999	Percent Change
1.	Nashville, TN	200	37.7	47.2	−20.1%
2.	Indianapolis	301	37.1	50.2	−26.1%
3.	Baltimore	218	34.5	38.9	−11.3%
4.	Memphis, TN	246	28.2	29.6	−4.7%
5.	Detroit	274	21.9	15.1	45.0%
6.	Oklahoma City	82	20.0	27.8	−28.1%
7.	Norfolk, VA	37	16.4	8.9	84.3%
8.	Atlanta	116	15.6	28.6	−45.5%
9.	Newark	28	9.9	7.8	26.9%
10.	Chicago	292	9.8	9.5	3.2%
11.	Louisville, KY	57	8.5	10.0	−15.0%
12.	*San Francisco	53	7.1	3.9	82.1%
13.	Washington, DC	37	7.1	8.7	−18.4%
14.	Charlotte, NC	45	6.9	8.2	−15.9%
15.	San Juan, PR	68	6.5	5.8	12.1%
16.	Phoenix	172	6.0	6.8	−11.8%
17.	*Miami	126	5.8	3.8	52.6%
18.	*San Antonio	67	4.9	2.3	113.0%
19.	Dallas	100	4.8	7.3	−34.2%
20.	New Orleans	22	4.8	11.1	−56.8%

*Not among the 20 most affected cities in 1999. The following cities were among the 20 most affected cities in 1999, but were not in 2000: Tulsa (2.1 rate in 2000, 11.7 rate in 1999, −82.1% change); St. Louis (3.3 rate in 2000, 15.3 rate in 1999, −78.4% change); Richmond (2.6 rate in 2000, 6.9 rate in 1999, −62.3% change).

Source: Rebecca Goldsmith, "Newark's Syphilis Cases Rise as Nation's Continue to Fall," *Star Ledger,* March 6, 2002, p. 6.

Photographs

Another popular type of visual aid in texts is the photograph. Some photographs depict situations that are true to life, such as urban street scenes, children in classrooms, or athletes in training. Art books depend heavily on photos of paintings. Other photos may be the result of special effects, such as photos of cells as seen from under a microscope or photos that are the result of computer graphic effects.

Diagrams

Technological or scientific writing often depends on drawings to explain complicated processes, structures, or sequences described in the text. On page 257, a drawing has been used to help the reader understand the structure of the ear. Each part is clearly labeled.

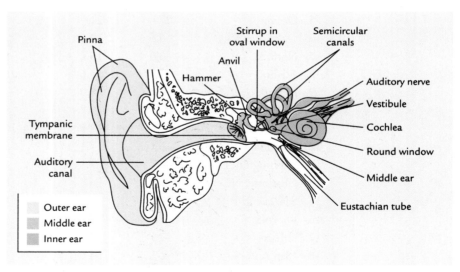

PHONORECEPTORS: THE MAMMALIAN EAR *Note ear bones in the middle ear cavity. The semicircular canals are a part of the inner ear that detects changes in head and body position.*
Source: Sylvia Mader, *Biology: Inquiry into Life* (Dubuque, IA: Wm. C. Brown Publishers, 1976), fig. 17.16. Reproduced with permission of The McGraw-Hill Companies.

📗 THINKING ABOUT YOUR READING AND WRITING

ACTIVITY B: Your Prior Experience with Visual Aids

In the past, what types of visual aids have you found the most useful?

_____

_____

What types have been most difficult for you to read?

_____

_____

What do you do when you encounter a difficult one?

_____

_____

_____

ACTIVITY C: Creating a Visual Aid Reference Table

Using the information from the preceding section, create your own table for handy reference to visual aids. In the space provided, create separate columns to list (1) the type of visual aid, (2) why it is used, and (3) its distinguishing features. Include all types of visuals discussed so far in this chapter. Give a title to your table. When you have completed it, compare your table with a partner's.

How Do Visual Aids Facilitate Comprehension?

Perhaps you commented in Activity A of this chapter that it would be easier for you to recall information when it was presented in table format rather than in paragraph form. Most people would agree with you. Even when the paragraphs and sentences give valuable information, visuals allow us to organize that information in a way that is often easier to remember.

Another advantage of visuals is the effect they have on reader response to the information. The visual impact of an idea can be much more impressive than an idea stated in words. An author who wants to impress the reader with an idea or to make a more powerful statement, might want to use a visual aid. Notice the difference in the effect between the two presentations of the same idea that follow.

Example 1:

Students received almost $90 billion in financial aid in 2001–2002, an increase of 11.5 percent over the preceding year, or 10.0 percent after adjusting for inflation. Grant aid has doubled in real terms, while education loan volume has tripled. By 2001–2002, loans increased to constitute 57 percent of student aid and grants were only 42 percent. However, because of the addition of tuition tax credits to the total aid pool in 1998, loan aid has declined to 54 percent of total aid, while grants are 39 percent; tax credits are 6 percent; and work aid is only 1 percent of the total. Unsubsidized borrowing, by students (Stafford unsubsidized) as well as parents (PLUS), now accounts for almost $22 billion, over half of federal education loan volume.

Nonfederal borrowing totaled $5.6 billion in 2001–2002, up 34 percent in real terms over the previous year. While the amount of nonfederal borrowing is small relative to the $42 billion in federal education loans, the rapid growth since 1995–1996 reflects a growing reliance on alternative methods of paying for college. Institutional grants account for nearly 20 percent of total available aid.

Example 2:

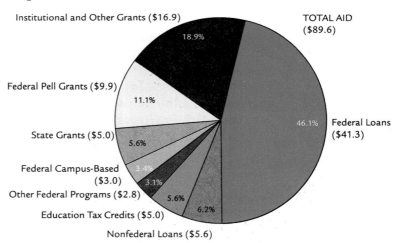

ESTIMATED STUDENT AID BY SOURCE FOR ACADEMIC YEAR 2001–2002 (CURRENT DOLLARS IN BILLIONS)

Source: College Board, *Trends in Student Aid 2002*, p. 4. From *http:www.collegeboard.com/ press/cost02/html/CBTrendsAid02.pdf#search='Federal%20Aid%20to%20college%20students, %20data'*. Retrieved June 8, 2005.

▮ THINKING ABOUT YOUR READING AND WRITING

ACTIVITY D: Responding to Visual Aids

What is the visual impact of the preceding visual (Example 2) on you? Why do you think it has this impact?

_____

_____

_____

_____

_____

_____

_____

_____

_____

Visual information can also help clarify material that sounds complex when stated in sentence form. Read the following paragraph. Then look at the diagram accompanying the text. Notice how the diagram helps the reader understand the complex process described in the text.

Example:

The tick vector of Lyme disease has a two-year life cycle in which it requires three blood meals. The larval form becomes infected from small animals, usually field mice, then enters a dormant stage until the following spring. Then it molts into a nymph, which is still infected. This is the stage at which it is most likely to infect humans. It is crucial to the maintenance of the cycle in the wild that the spirochete be able to remain viable in small animals to reinfect the larvae the following year. The field mouse is well adapted to this. The third feeding, by the infected adults that develop from the nymph, is taken from the deer. After this, the adults lay eggs, which are uninfected, that over winter develop into larvae the following spring.

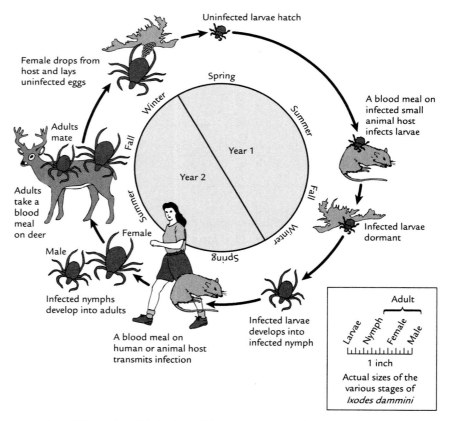

Source: Gerard J. Tortora, Berdell R. Funke, and Christine L. Case, *Microbiology: An Introduction,* 4th ed. (Redwood City, CA: Benjamin/Cummings, 1992), p. 571. Copyright © 1992 by The Benjamin/ Cummings Publishing Company, Inc. Reprinted by permission of Pearson Education, Inc.

Visual aids can also substitute for written information. There is a saying that "a picture is worth a thousand words." For readers, pictures often can convey much more than words could ever describe. See how this effect might apply to the photo shown here.

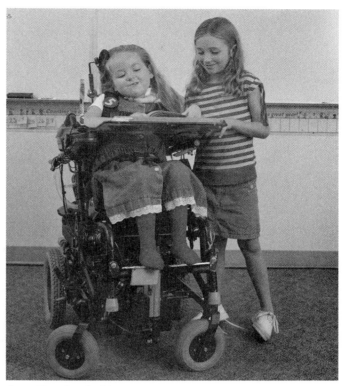

Source: Photodisc Blue/Getty Images

THINKING ABOUT YOUR READING AND WRITING

ACTIVITY E: Assessing the Impact of a Photo

Do you think this visual aid is worth a thousand words? Why or why not?

_____

_____

_____

What Are Effective Strategies for Reading Visual Aids?

For successful reading of visual aids, you should:

1. Preview the visual aid to get an overall impression and to make predictions.
2. Note details to gain more information and to verify your predictions.
3. Make connections between the visual aid and the text to see how each part is supported or extended by the other.
4. Make inferences from the visual aid to elaborate on your interpretation of the data and to see whether there is confirmation of your inferences in the rest of the text.
5. Draw conclusions from the visual aid to determine any wider application of the information and to see how your conclusions are further supported by information anywhere else in the reading selection.

In the remainder of this chapter, you will note that the strategies for reading visual aids differ somewhat from those you use for reading texts that do not contain visual aids. There are also common factors, however, and you will be able to apply your prior knowledge about reading strategies to the activities in this section.

Previewing Visual Aids

Visual aids, like information conveyed through sentences and paragraphs, can be previewed. During your preview, your goal is to obtain an overall idea of the purpose of the visual and to determine how the data on it are organized. You also hope to be able to predict what sort of details you will find once you examine the visual aid more closely.

Previewing Graphs

To preview a graph, you need to:

1. Read the title of the graph. Treat it in the same way you would treat the title of a chapter or article.
2. Examine the lengths of the bars, divisions of a circle graph, or shape of the line(s). These features of a graph are similar to subtitles in texts. They convey an overall impression of the information that will be provided through the details.

3. Look along the sides and bottom of the graph for any headings or labels that tell you more about the details displayed.

4. Look for any keys, legends, or footnotes on the graph that identify codes the author is using.

5. Make predictions about what you will find when you read the information on the graph more closely.

On the first bar graph about occupations of men and women, 1880–1920, some details have been eliminated. Follow the steps for previewing a graph to see what information you can obtain and what predictions you can make about the contents of the rest of the graph.

Distribution of Occupational Categories Among Employed Men and Women, 1880–1920

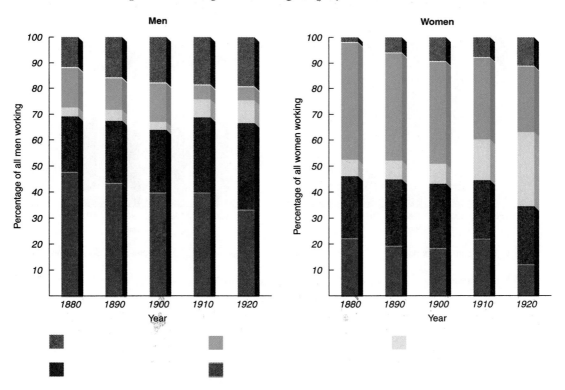

Source: Mary Beth Norton, David M. Katzman, David W. Blight, Howard P. Chudacoff, Thomas G. Paterson, William M. Tuttle, Jr., and Paul D. Escott, *A People and a Nation: A History of the United States,* 6th ed. (Boston: Houghton Mifflin, 2001), p. 496.

What information can you obtain from the graph in its present form?

_____

_____

_____

Now look at the second version of the graph, below, that has added details.

Distribution of Occupational Categories Among Employed Men and Women, 1880–1920

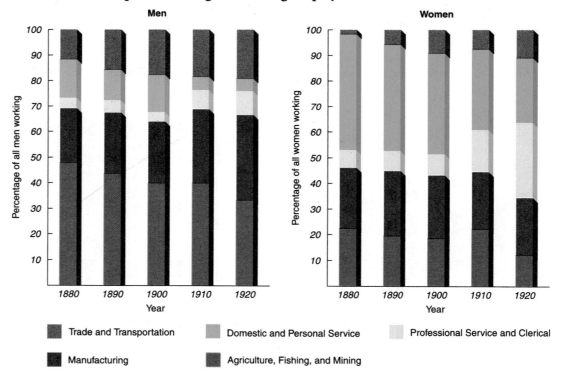

Source: Mary Beth Norton, David M. Katzman, David W. Blight, Howard P. Chudacoff, Thomas G. Paterson, William M. Tuttle, Jr., and Paul D. Escott, *A People and a Nation: A History of the United States,* 6th ed. (Boston: Houghton Mifflin, 2001), p. 496.

What additional information do you learn about occupations of men and women during the years 1880–1920?

_____

During your preview, you were able to recognize that this graph would be about the kinds of jobs men and women had between 1880 and 1920, and how these were distributed. You could also tell that there were differences in the jobs men and women held. You might have predicted that the jobs where men and women seemed equally employed were less risky than those held significantly by men.

Once the details were added, your additional information should have included the following: Fewer women were employed in agriculture throughout this period; men were increasingly employed in manufacturing; work in transportation continued to increase. (You may recognize that this was the period of industrialization.)

Previewing Tables

The aids for previewing that you will find on tables include the title of the table (often appearing at the top) and the subheadings that appear above each column on the table. These parts of the table should be treated in the same way as titles and subtitles in texts. Thus, to preview a table, you would:

1. Read the title.
2. Read the subheadings.
3. Use the title and subheadings to determine the focus of the table.
4. Look for any keys, legends, or footnotes on the table that identify any codes or symbols the author is using.
5. Make predictions about the specifics of the data in the table.

In the next example, you are first presented with a table that contains only the title and vertical and horizontal subheadings. Examine it to see what you learn from your preview. Then answer the questions that follow.

What is this table about?

What information does the title provide?

How are the title and the subheadings on this table related to one another?

_____

_____

What kinds of details are you most likely to find on this visual?

_____

_____

Monitoring the Future Study: Trends in Prevalence of Various Drugs for 8th-Graders, 10th-Graders, and 12th-Graders, 2001–2004[1]

	8th-Graders				10th-Graders				12th-Graders			
	2001	2002	2003	2004	2001	2002	2003	2004	2001	2002	2003	2004
Any Illicit Drug Use												
lifetime												
annual												
30-day												
Marijuana/Hashish												
lifetime												
annual												
30-day												
daily												
Inhalants												
lifetime												
annual												
30-day												
Hallucinogens[2]												
lifetime												
annual												
30-day												
Cocaine												
lifetime												
annual												
30-day												
Tranquilizers[3]												
lifetime												
annual												
30-day												

	8th-Graders				10th-Graders				12th-Graders			
	2001	2002	2003	2004	2001	2002	2003	2004	2001	2002	2003	2004
Alcohol												
lifetime												
annual												
30-day												
daily												
Cigarettes (any use)												
lifetime												
30-day												
½ pack+/day												
Steroids												
lifetime												
annual												
30-day												

[1]"Lifetime" refers to use at least once during a respondent's lifetime. "Annual" refers to an individual's drug use at least once during the year preceding their response to the survey. "30-day" refers to an individual's drug use at least once during the month preceding their response to the survey.

[2]For hallucinogens, in 2001 "other psychedelics" was changed to "other hallucinogens" on the MTF survey forms, and mushrooms ("shrooms") was added. For 2001, half the students sampled received the original survey question and the other half the revised question. To trend the findings from 2000 to 2001, the researchers used the old item in the 2001 data; to trend from 2001 to 2002, they used the new item. In the table above, the researchers show a break between 2000 and 2001, indicating a technical discontinuity.

[3]For tranquilizers, in 2001 "Miltown" was removed and "Xanax" was added on the MTF survey forms. For 2001, half the students sampled received the original survey question and the other half the revised question. To trend the findings from 2000 to 2001, the researchers used the old item in the 2001 data; to trend from 2001 to 2002, they used the new item. In the table above, the researchers show a break between 2000 and 2001, indicating a technical discontinuity.

Source: Adapted from National Institute on Drug Abuse, U.S. Dept. of Health and Human Services, from Monitoring the Future Study; Trends in Prevalence of Various Drugs for 8th-Graders, 10th-Graders, and 12th-Graders, 2002-2005. Revised March 2006.

Based on your prior knowledge, what do you expect the data to show (for instance, increases, decreases)? Why do you expect this?

_____

_____

Look now at the complete table that follows, which includes all the previously missing details. How accurate were your predictions?

_____

_____

What additional information have you learned now that you have studied the details of this table?

_____

_____

During your preview, you no doubt recognized that this title would be about changes in drug use for a variety of drugs during the years 2001 and 2004 among different age groups. From the information beneath the title, you could tell that the details would be percentages by age groups. One prediction you might have made, based on your prior knowledge of this topic, is that more youths were using hard drugs in 2001. You may also have predicted the percentages would be higher for older students. Once you could view the details, your additional information should have included the facts that although usage did increase for some drugs, it declined for others, especially for cigarettes in all age groups. What other details did you find?

Monitoring the Future Study: Trends in Prevalence of Various Drugs for 8th-Graders, 10th-Graders, and 12th-Graders, 2001–2004[1]

	8th-Graders				10th-Graders				12th-Graders			
	2001	2002	2003	2004	2001	2002	2003	2004	2001	2002	2003	2004
Any Illicit Drug Use												
lifetime	26.8	24.5	22.8	**21.5**	45.6	44.6	41.4	**39.8**	53.9	53.0	51.1	**51.1**
annual	19.5	17.7	16.1	**15.2**	37.2	34.8	32.0	**31.1**	41.4	41.0	39.3	**38.8**
30-day	11.7	10.4	9.7	**[8.4]**	22.7	20.8	19.5	**18.3**	25.7	25.4	24.1	**23.4**
Marijuana/Hashish												
lifetime	20.4	19.2	17.5	**16.3**	40.1	38.7	36.4	**35.1**	49.0	47.8	46.1	**45.7**
annual	15.4	14.6	12.8	**11.8**	32.7	30.3	28.2	**27.5**	37.0	36.2	34.9	**34.3**
30-day	9.2	8.3	7.5	**[6.4]**	19.8	17.8	17.0	**15.9**	22.4	21.5	21.2	**19.9**
daily	1.3	1.2	1.0	**0.8**	4.5	3.9	3.6	**3.2**	5.8	6.0	6.0	**5.6**
Inhalants												
lifetime	17.1	15.2	15.8	**[17.3]**	15.2	13.5	12.7	**12.4**	13.0	11.7	11.2	**10.9**
annual	9.1	7.7	8.7	**9.6**	6.6	5.8	5.4	**5.9**	4.5	4.5	3.9	**4.2**
30-day	4.0	3.8	4.1	**4.5**	2.4	2.4	2.2	**2.4**	1.7	1.5	1.5	**1.5**
Hallucinogens[2]												
lifetime	5.2	4.1	4.0	**3.5**	8.9	7.8	6.9	**6.4**	14.7	12.0	10.6	**9.7**
annual	3.4	2.6	2.6	**2.2**	6.2	4.7	4.1	**4.1**	9.1	6.6	5.9	**6.2**
30-day	1.6	1.2	1.2	**1.0**	2.1	1.6	1.5	**1.6**	3.3	2.3	1.8	**1.9**

	8th-Graders				10th-Graders				12th-Graders			
	2001	2002	2003	2004	2001	2002	2003	2004	2001	2002	2003	2004
Cocaine												
lifetime	4.3	3.6	3.6	**3.4**	5.7	6.1	5.1	**5.4**	8.2	7.8	7.7	**8.1**
annual	2.5	2.3	2.2	**2.0**	3.6	4.0	3.3	**3.7**	4.8	5.0	4.8	**5.3**
30-day	1.2	1.1	0.9	**0.9**	1.3	1.6	1.3	**1.7**	2.1	2.3	2.1	**2.3**
Tranquilizers[3]												
lifetime	5.0	4.3	4.4	**4.0**	9.2	8.8	7.8	**7.3**	10.3	11.4	10.2	**10.6**
annual	2.8	2.6	2.7	**2.5**	7.3	6.3	5.3	**5.1**	6.9	7.7	6.7	**7.3**
30-day	1.2	1.2	1.4	**1.2**	2.9	2.9	2.4	**2.3**	2.9	3.3	2.8	**3.1**
Alcohol												
lifetime	50.5	47.0	45.6	**43.9**	70.1	66.9	66.0	**64.2**	79.7	78.4	76.6	**76.8**
annual	41.9	38.7	37.2	**36.7**	63.5	60.0	59.3	**58.2**	73.3	71.5	70.1	**70.6**
30-day	21.5	19.6	19.7	**18.6**	39.0	35.4	35.4	**35.2**	49.8	48.6	47.5	**48.0**
daily	0.9	0.7	0.8	**0.6**	1.9	1.8	1.5	**1.3**	3.6	3.5	3.2	**2.8**
Cigarettes (any use)												
lifetime	36.6	31.4	28.4	**27.9**	52.8	47.4	43.0	**[40.7]**	61.0	57.2	53.7	**52.8**
30-day	12.2	10.7	10.2	**9.2**	21.3	17.7	16.7	**16.0**	29.5	26.7	24.4	**25.0**
½ pack+/day	2.3	2.1	1.8	**1.7**	5.5	4.4	4.1	**[3.3]**	10.3	9.1	8.4	**8.0**
Steroids												
lifetime	2.8	2.5	2.5	**[1.9]**	3.5	3.5	3.0	**[2.4]**	3.7	4.0	3.5	**3.4**
annual	1.6	1.5	1.4	**[1.1]**	2.1	2.2	1.7	**1.5**	2.4	2.5	2.1	**2.5**
30-day	0.7	0.8	0.7	**0.5**	0.9	1.0	0.8	**0.8**	1.3	1.4	1.3	**1.6**

[1]"Lifetime" refers to use at least once during a respondent's lifetime. "Annual" refers to an individual's drug use at least once during the year preceding their response to the survey. "30-day" refers to an individual's drug use at least once during the month preceding their response to the survey.

[2]For hallucinogens, in 2001 "other psychedelics" was changed to "other hallucinogens" on the MTF survey forms, and mushrooms ("shrooms") was added. For 2001, half the students sampled received the original survey question and the other half the revised question. To trend the findings from 2000 to 2001, the researchers used the old item in the 2001 data; to trend from 2001 to 2002, they used the new item. In the table above, the researchers show a break between 2000 and 2001, indicating a technical discontinuity.

[3]For tranquilizers, in 2001 "Miltown" was removed and "Xanax" was added on the MTF survey forms. For 2001, half the students sampled received the original survey question and the other half the revised question. To trend the findings from 2000 to 2001, the researchers used the old item in the 2001 data; to trend from 2001 to 2002, they used the new item. In the table above, the researchers show a break between 2000 and 2001, indicating a technical discontinuity.

Source: Adapted from National Institute on Drug Abuse, U.S. Dept. of Health and Human Services, from Monitoring the Future Study; Trends in Prevalence of Various Drugs for 8th-Graders, 10th-Graders, and 12th-Graders, 2002-2005. Revised March 2006.

WORKING TOGETHER

Compare your findings with those of a partner. Did you notice the same details? What information did your partner find that was also important?

Previewing Other Types of Visual Aids

All visual aids contain elements that can be studied for making predictions before you make a closer inspection. In previewing timelines and flowcharts, for instance, you can first read the major headings and the beginning and ending notations to see the period covered or the starting and finishing points of the process that are included in the visual aid. With a diagram or photo, you should first identify those features that stand out from the rest, then use these to make predictions about the remaining details. When you are reading a tree chart, you will want to notice the overall organization of the chart—such as how the hierarchy is arranged and how many branches stem from each of the major branches—before you read the individually boxed headings. You will always want to look for keys, legends, or footnotes to the visual aid and to take note of any special effects the author has used to make distinctions, such as colors or shadings.

Whenever and whatever you preview, your goal is to obtain a general sense of the material before you do more extensive analysis. In this way, you are mentally preparing yourself for the detailed reading and analysis ahead. Try this with the pie chart that follows.

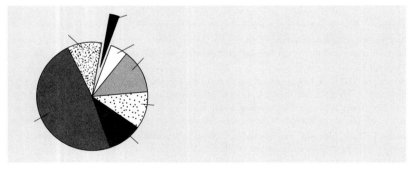

WHO DO YOU THINK STATE GOVERNMENT SERVES?

Source: The Boston Globe, September 3, 1990, pp. 1, 8–9.
Reprinted courtesy of *The Boston Globe.*

Predictions:

Based on your prior knowledge, what information do you expect to find next to the lines by each section of the circle?

What significant points do you expect this new information to prove?

_____

_____

How are the different sections of the circle related to one another?

_____

_____

The visual below includes all the previously missing details. How accurate were your predictions?

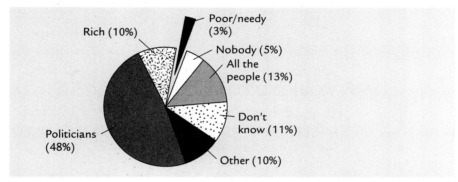

WHO DO YOU THINK STATE GOVERNMENT SERVES?

Source: The Boston Globe, September 3, 1990, pp. 1, 8–9. Reprinted courtesy of *The Boston Globe.*

Closer Analysis:

What additional information have you learned now that you have studied the details of this visual aid?

_____

_____

 THINKING ABOUT YOUR READING AND WRITING

ACTIVITY F: Sharing What You Know with Others

What advice can you now offer to another student about strategies to use when previewing visual aids?

_____

_____

_____

_____

_____

_____

_____

_____

WORKING TOGETHER

Compare the advice you have written in Activity F with that of a partner. Discuss the value of each suggestion. Make any additions to your original thoughts that you now think should be included.

Noting Details

When you complete your preview of a visual aid, your next step will be to analyze all its details. As you do this, you will want to:

1. Identify any special effects the author uses to make distinctions between the various elements on the visual aid. Consider some of the methods used in the previous section:

   Colors, shadings, or patterns. The visual on occupations of men and women, 1880–1920, illustrates how various patterns are used to separate one type of occupation from another. You may also recall maps you have read that use different colors to reflect different temperature zones or topographical features.

   Broken or solid lines. If a line graph contains several lines, the author may distinguish between what each line represents by using a combination of broken and solid lines or by varying line thicknesses. In this chapter, the graph on petroleum exports used broken and solid lines to make distinctions.

2. Establish the nature or types of details included. Details may be names, dates, percentages, whole numbers, qualities, or almost anything. Often a combination of these details is provided. As you have seen in this chapter, when numbers are too large to express completely, the author may use a shortened form, which is then explained elsewhere on the visual.

3. Determine how the details are related to one another. In diagrams, each label may represent part of a whole. On a tree chart, they may show a hierarchy of importance. Details on a timeline or flowchart show a sequence over time. Numbers may be used to show comparisons such as those between cities, ethnic groups, gender, age, or years.

4. Determine whether the details are presented in any particular order. This is obvious on tree charts or flowcharts and timelines, but on tables you often must determine an order for yourself, such as size, chronology, increases, or decreases.

5. Determine whether some details have more significance than others. For example, on the pie chart on state government, many more respondents thought the government served the politicians than served the poor.

ACTIVITY G: Understanding Details on Visual Aids

Preview each visual aid then answer the questions that appear beneath it.

1.

TWENTY-ITEM CHECKLIST CONSISTING OF REASONS FOR AND REACTIONS TO SHOPLIFTING
PERCENT OF RESPONDENTS CHECKING EACH ITEM PRE- AND POSTGROUP (N = 143)

Items	Pregroup		Postgroup	
	Number	Percent	Number	Percent
You felt remorseful when caught.	85	59	76	53
You do not understand why you shoplifted.	73	51	31	22
You shoplifted because you couldn't afford the items.	56	39	48	34
You were surprised that you were arrested for the shoplifting offense.	51	36	45	32
You shoplifted because you were frustrated.	50	35	76	53
You shoplifted because you don't have enough money to support yourself and/or your family.	44	31	39	27
You shoplifted because it was so easy to get away with it.	43	30	45	32

(continued)

1. *continued*

Items	Pregroup		Postgroup	
	Number	Percent	Number	Percent
You shoplifted because you felt angry.	38	27	58	41
You knew you were going to be caught shoplifting.	37	26	51	36
You shoplifted because you felt sorry for yourself.	29	20	55	39
You shoplifted because you didn't see it as a serious crime.	26	18	32	22
You were relieved when you were caught.	25	18	51	36
You are very lonely.	24	17	29	20
You shoplifted because it was exciting.	20	14	32	22
You shoplifted because you wanted revenge.	20	14	33	23
You shoplifted because you felt that stores make too much money anyway.	13	9	17	12
You wanted to be caught.	11	8	26	18
You started shoplifting as a teenager and have continued to shoplift as an adult.	6	4	8	6
You shoplifted because you felt that you wanted to humiliate yourself.	5	4	5	4
You shoplifted because you had been drinking or using drugs.	4	3	9	6

Source: Anita Sue Kolman and Claudia Wasserman, "Theft Groups for Women: A Cry for Help," *Federal Probation* 55:1 (March 1991): 49.

Why was this research done? _____

_____

What did the researchers find out? _____

_____

What do the details tell you? _____

_____

What special effects, if any, does the author use to make distinctions between details? _____

_____

_____

How are the details related to one another? _____

_____

Which details, if any, give information that you consider to be particularly significant? _____

_____

2.

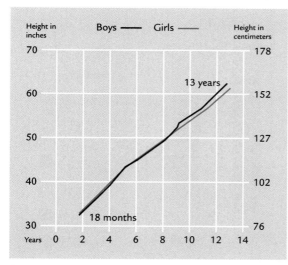 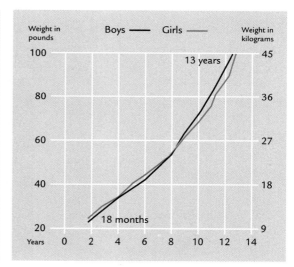

AVERAGE HEIGHT AND WEIGHT FOR CHILDREN

Source: National Center for Health Statistics, U.S. Public Health Service, adapted by *The World Book Encyclopedia.* © 2000 World Book, Inc. By permission of the publisher. *www.worldbook.com.*

Why was this research done? _____

What did the researchers find out? _____

What do the details tell you? _____

_____

What special effects, if any, does the author use to make distinctions between details? _____

_____

How are the details related to one another? _____

_____

Which details, if any, give information that you consider to be particularly significant? _____

_____

3.

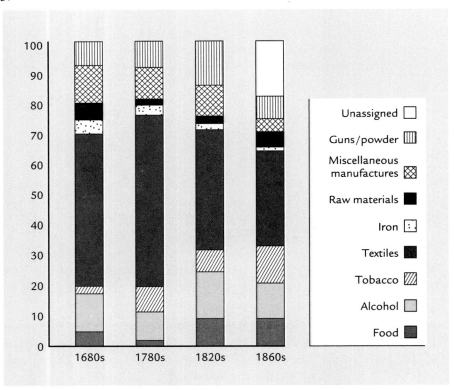

ESTIMATED RELATIVE VALUE OF IMPORTS INTO WESTERN AFRICA IN SELECTED DECADES, 1680S—1860S

Source: David Eltis, "The Economics of African Participation in the Slave Trade," in David Northrup, ed., *The Atlantic Slave Trade* (Lexington, MA: D. C. Heath, 1994), p. 166. Reprinted by permission of Houghton Mifflin Company.

Why was this research done? _____

What did the researchers find out? _____

What do the details tell you? _____

_____

What special effects, if any, does the author use to make distinctions between details? _____

_____

How are the details related to one another? _____

_____

Which details, if any, give information that you consider to be particularly significant? _____

Connecting Visual Aids to Text

Visual aids most often accompany text for one of the following reasons:

* *To give evidence for a point made in the text.* For instance, the text may make the claim that poverty rates have increased in urban areas during the last decade. A table with poverty rates in urban areas during the last several decades would illustrate this point.

* *To clarify or explain a complicated idea.* The diagram of the life cycle of Lyme disease, which appeared earlier in this chapter, is an example. The idea presented is complicated because of the number of stages and species involved in the two-year period of the cycle. The visual aid helped clarify the events during the cycle.

* *To add interest to the text.* Sometimes visual aids do not add a great deal of information to the reading material, but they do help maintain reader involvement. Photographs are frequently used for this purpose.

Whenever a visual aid is included in your reading material, you should decide its purpose. Visual aids that give evidence or explain complicated ideas are often as important to know for exams as the text itself.

ACTIVITY H: Connecting Visual Aids and Text

Look at each visual and read the text that accompanies it. Decide whether the purpose of the visual is to (1) give evidence, (2) clarify or explain a complicated idea, or (3) provide interest.

The Earth's General Circulation

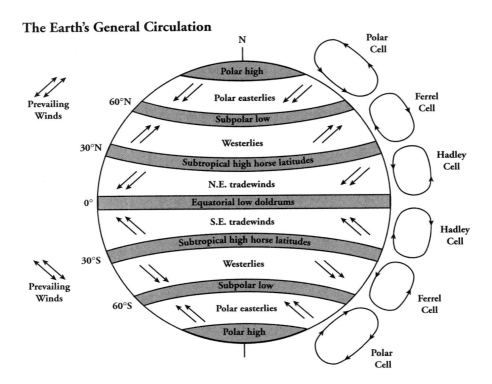

PLANETARY WINDS

MAJOR CIRCULATION CELLS

The Earth's global winds are the result of contrasting pressure and temperature belts that exist on a semipermanent or permanent basis. Earth's major wind circulation patterns occur because warm air at the equator rises and migrates to the poles, and cold air at the poles sinks and moves toward the equator. The circulation slowly changes with the seasons, as the Sun's rays differentially heat the Earth.

There are three major cells that carry air currents in both hemispheres.

Named after English meteorologist George Hadley, the *Hadley cells* (tropical cells) are caused by the rising and sinking of heated and cooled air, respectively. The heated air rises near the equator, travels toward the poles, and sinks again at 30° north and south latitudes.

With the *Polar cells,* heated air rises about 30° north and south latitudes and sinks at the respective pole.

Named after American meteorologist William Ferrel, the *Ferrel cells* exist between the two tropical (Hadley) and Polar cells. The Ferrel cells circulate in the reverse direction from the Hadley and Polar cells: cold air rises at 60° north and south latitudes, and warm air descends at 30° north and south latitudes. These cells act as slight brakes on the general circulation. They cause heavy precipitation between latitudes 40 and 60° (ascending circulation), and arid conditions in the subtropics (descending circulation).

PREVAILING WINDS

The *prevailing winds* are produced by the global patterns of barometric pressure, both at the surface and aloft. The prevailing winds are influenced by the Earth's rotation (Coriolis effect), with the northern winds curving to the east, and the southern winds to the west. The prevailing winds are the polar high, polar easterlies, subpolar lows, westerlies, subtropical high horse latitudes, and trade winds in both the Northern and Southern Hemispheres. These northern and southern prevailing wind bands are mirror images of each other. The equatorial low doldrums are found along a belt at the equator.

Source: Patricia Barnes-Svarney, ed., *The New York Public Library Science Desk Reference* (New York: Macmillan, Stonesong Press, 1995), pp. 423–424. Copyright © 1995 The Stonesong Press, Inc. and The New York Public Library.

The purpose of this visual aid is to: _____

---

2. Reasons for U.S. Households Discontinuing Internet Access, Percent Distribution, 2000

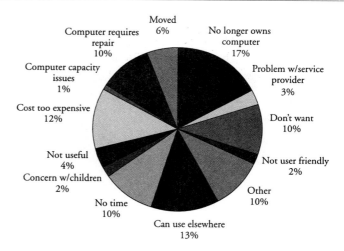

WHY HOUSEHOLDS WITH COMPUTERS HAVE DISCONTINUED INTERNET ACCESS

In August 2000, there were 4.0 million Internet "drop-offs" (i.e., those households that once had but do not currently have electronic access). That number is essentially unchanged from the 4.1 million "drop-offs" in December 1998.

Respondents to the August 2000 survey cited several principal reasons for their households' decisions to discontinue their Internet access (see the figure). The leading factor noted was "no longer owns computers" (17.0%). Next in importance were "can use anywhere" (12.8%) and "cost, too expensive" (12.3%). The other key reasons were "don't want it" (10.3%), "not enough time" (10.0%), and "computer requires repair" (9.7%). Also provided as reasons were "moved" (6.1%), "not useful" (4.2%), "problems with ISP" (2.9%), "concern with children" (2.3%), "not user friendly" (1.5%), and "computer capacity issues" (1.2%). "Other" reasons—those that are too heterogeneous to be included elsewhere—were also given by respondents (9.8%).

These results reflect changes from the answers given in the December 1998 survey. In 1998, respondents identified "cost, too expensive" (15%) as the most important reason for dropping off the network. In 1998, the reason "no longer owns computer" ranked second (14%) and "can use anywhere" ranked fourth (9%). "Not enough time to use it" registered a higher percentage (10% vs. 9%) in 2000 but slipped from third in 1998 to fourth in 2000. Respondents accorded "computer requires repair" about double the response rate from December 1998 (5%) to August 2000 but had the same ranking (sixth). "Don't want it" was the fifth most popular reason in 1998 (7%).

A more disaggregated look at the August 2000 survey results reveals additional insights.

As a reason for discontinuing Internet access, "no longer owns a computer" ranked number one and cost is the number two reason for all income brackets except the highest ($75,000+). The most affluent income category respondents led with "can use elsewhere," "computer requires repair," "don't want it," and "not enough time."

Source: Gregory L. Rohde and Robert J. Shapiro, "Falling Through the Net: Toward Digital Inclusion," (Washington, DC: U.S. Department of Commerce Economics and Statistics Administration, National Telecommunications and Information Administration, October 2000). *http:/www.ntia.doc.gov/ ntiahome/fttn00/falling.htm.* Retrieved July 29, 2002.

The purpose of this visual aid is to: _____

_____

Coca-Cola in Bengali

Coca-Cola in Cyrillic

Coca-Cola in Turkish

Coca-Cola in Thai

Coca-Cola in Amharic

Coca-Cola in Arabic

KOKA-KOΛA
Coca-Cola in Greek

Coca-Cola in Hebrew

Coca-Cola in Chinese

Coca-Cola in Japanese

Coke in Japanese

Coca-Cola in South Korean

Fanta in Bengali

Fanta in Chinese

Fanta in Japanese

Fanta in Thai

Fanta in Amharic

Sprite in Amharic

Sprite in Japanese

Sprite in Thai

A MULTINATIONAL COMPANY MUST OFTEN COPE WITH A WIDE VARIETY OF WORK CUSTOMS AND EVEN LANGUAGES.

Source: Richard Lachmann, ed., *The Encyclopedic Dictionary of Sociology,* 4th edition, © 1991, Dushkin. Reproduced with permission of the The McGraw-Hill Companies.

The purpose of this visual aid is to: _____

_____

Making Inferences from Visual Aids

 ### THINKING ABOUT YOUR READING AND WRITING

ACTIVITY I: Applying Your Prior Knowledge
About Inferences

1. How might the strategies you learned in Chapter 7 for making inferences be applied to reading visual aids?

   _____

   _____

   _____

   _____

2. What should the reader of the visual aid do to make an inference?

   _____

   _____

   _____

   _____

WORKING TOGETHER

Compare your answers in Activity I with those of a partner. Do you suggest similar strategies? Refer to Chapter 7 after you make your comparisons and see what else you can add. Then make your revisions to Activity I.

In Chapter 7, you learned that inferences are statements about the unknown based on what is known. With your partner, you probably agreed that you can make inferences from visual aids in the same way that you make inferences from text. When you make them from visual aids, of course, the numbers or features on graphs and tables, parts of the diagram, points on the timeline, or details on the photograph become the evidence to support the inference in the same way that details in sentences or paragraphs provide evidence to support an inference about written material. The following figure illustrates this point. Although not stated on the graph, it is obvious that once the measles vaccine was licensed and people realized its value, they took advantage of it, which resulted in the sharp drop in the number of measles cases.

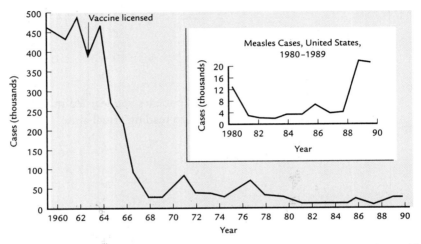

Source: Gerald J. Tortora, Berdell R. Funke, and Christine L. Case, *Microbiology: An Introduction,* 4th ed. (Redwood City, CA: Benjamin/Cummings, 1992), p. 527. Copyright © 1992 by The Benjamin/Cummings Publishing Company, Inc. Reprinted by permission of Pearson Education, Inc.

ACTIVITY J: Making Inferences from Visual Aids

Use the details on each visual to make at least one inference about it. Beneath your inference, indicate your evidence.

1.

TEN LARGEST CITIES IN THE UNITED STATES, 1820, 1900, AND 1970

1820		1900		1970	
New York, NY	123,706	New York, NY	3,437,202	New York, NY	7,771,730
Philadelphia, PA	63,802	Chicago, IL	1,698,575	Chicago, IL	3,325,263
Baltimore, MD	62,738	Philadelphia, PA	1,293,697	Los Angeles, CA	2,782,400
Boston, MA	42,541	St. Louis, MO	575,238	Philadelphia, PA	1,926,529
New Orleans, LA	27,176	Boston, MA	560,892	Detroit, MI	1,492,914
Charleston, SC	24,780	Baltimore, MD	508,957	Houston, TX	1,213,064

1. *continued*

1820		1900		1970	
Washington, DC	13,247	Cleveland, OH	381,768	Baltimore, MD	895,222
Albany City, NY	12,630	Buffalo, NY	352,387	Dallas, TX	836,121
Providence, RI	11,767	San Francisco, CA	342,782	Washington, DC (est.)	764,000
Salem, MA	11,346	Cincinnati, OH	325,902	Indianapolis, IN	742,613

Source: Melvin L. De Fleur et al., *Sociology: Man in Society,* brief ed. (Glenview, IL: Scott Foresman, 1972). Data from U.S. Bureau of the Census.

Your inference from this visual aid:

_____

Your evidence:

_____

2.

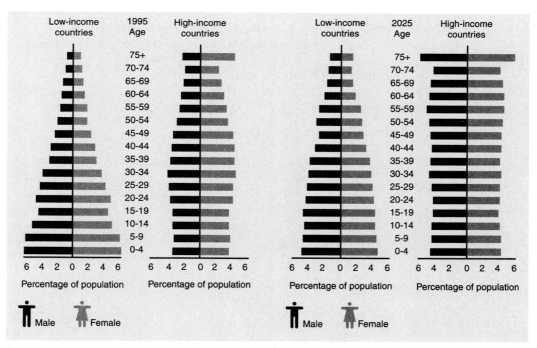

POPULATION PYRAMIDS FOR LOW- AND HIGH-INCOME COUNTRIES, 1995 AND 2025
Source: World Bank, *Beyond Economic Growth: Meeting the Challenges of Global Development,* 2000. *http:www.worldbank.org/depweb/beyond/beyondbw/begbw_08.pdf.* Retrieved June 1, 2005.

Your inference from this visual aid:

_____

Your evidence:

_____

3.

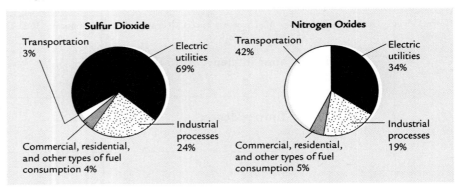

SOURCES OF ACID RAIN POLLUTANTS CREATED BY HUMAN ACTIVITIES

Source: World Book, Science Year, 1993, p. 210. From U.S. National Acid Precipitation Assessment Program.

Your inference from this visual aid:

_____

Your evidence:

_____

Drawing Conclusions from Visual Aids

 ## THINKING ABOUT YOUR READING AND WRITING

ACTIVITY K: Using Your Prior Knowledge About Drawing Conclusions

1. How might the strategies you learned in Chapter 7 about drawing conclusions be applied to reading visual aids?

   _____

   _____

   _____

2. What should someone reading a visual aid do to draw a conclusion?

   _____

   _____

   _____

WORKING TOGETHER

Compare your answers to Activity K with those of a partner. Do you suggest similar strategies? Refer to Chapter 7 after you make your comparisons to see what else you can add. Then make your revisions to Activity K.

As you work with visual aids in texts, you will need to draw your own conclusions from them. You will look for likely outcomes based on the data that are given. Conclusions move you beyond the text to thinking about applications and logical consequences or results that you can expect in the future based on the data given. Authors may state their conclusions from the data directly within the body of the text, but the visual aid will enable you to see how such conclusions were reached. Additionally, you may be able to draw other conclusions that the author does not state explicitly. These are often the most interesting conclusions because they are truly your own ideas, and the visual aid proves why your ideas are logical. The example on page 286 illustrates how information on visual aids leads to a variety of conclusions and applications.

MULTIMEDIA AUDIENCES—SUMMARY: 2001

[In percent, except total (201,715 represents 201,715,000). As of spring. For persons 18 years old and over. Represents the percent of persons participating during the prior week, except as indicated. Based on sample and subject to sampling error; see source for details.]

Item	Total Population (1,000)	Television Viewing	Television Prime Time Viewing	Cable Viewing[1]	Radio Listening	Newspaper Reading	Accessed Internet[2]
Total	**201,715**	**93.6**	**82.5**	**73.1**	**84.4**	**79.3**	**52.1**
18 to 24 years old	26,356	90.5	73.5	67.4	92.2	75.3	64.4
25 to 34 years old	38,298	92.3	80.3	72.0	90.0	75.6	63.3
35 to 44 years old	44,981	92.7	80.8	75.4	91.0	81.1	61.2
45 to 54 years old	36,085	94.3	85.4	76.1	88.7	82.5	60.2
55 to 64 years old	23,293	95.3	86.7	76.5	77.8	80.4	41.8
65 years old and over	32,702	96.9	88.6	70.1	62.4	80.3	14.7
Male	96,590	94.1	81.9	74.1	86.3	79.9	53.0
Female	105,125	93.1	83.1	72.1	82.6	78.9	51.2
White	168,905	93.5	82.6	74.4	84.3	79.5	53.8
Black	23,919	94.8	83.0	67.4	87.6	81.2	37.4
Asian	5,649	91.5	80.2	64.9	79.7	74.9	67.2
Other	3,241	93.5	76.9	59.0	71.9	64.6	45.0
Spanish speaking	23,046	94.0	82.4	61.0	86.8	66.5	41.5
Not high school graduate	34,691	92.0	80.1	60.0	74.3	61.3	16.3
High school graduate	66,416	95.1	84.9	74.1	82.5	78.8	36.8
Attended college	54,127	93.5	81.3	76.7	89.1	82.9	66.6
College graduate	46,481	93.5	82.8	77.6	89.2	86.5	76.5
Employed:							
Full time	112,508	92.8	81.2	75.6	91.7	81.9	64.3
Part time	19,483	92.9	79.9	72.2	87.9	79.7	64.0
Not employed	69,725	95.1	85.4	69.3	71.6	75.1	28.9
Household income:							
Less than $10,000	13,333	92.4	81.5	53.8	73.4	65.6	18.1
$10,000 to $19,999	23,325	93.9	83.5	58.4	72.4	69.1	18.5
$20,000 to $29,999	24,853	93.6	82.7	66.3	79.0	73.1	28.0
$30,000 to $34,999	11,984	93.6	81.5	68.0	82.8	77.4	34.8
$35,000 to $39,999	11,487	93.2	81.3	70.4	85.2	78.4	46.1
$40,000 to $49,999	21,354	94.2	82.8	75.6	87.0	78.4	53.5
$50,000 or more	95,378	93.6	82.6	81.6	89.8	86.0	73.9

[1] In the past 7 days. [2] In the last 30 days.

Source: Mediamark Research, Inc., New York, NY. *Multimedia Audiences.* Copyright © Spring 2002. *http:www.census.gov/prod/2003pubs/02statab/infocom.pdf.* Retrieved June 11, 2005.

Some conclusions that can logically be drawn from this table are: (1) More people enjoy watching television than using any other form of multimedia. (2) The older you are the less time you will spend using multimedia. (3) Ethnic groups differ in their use of multimedia. (4) There is a relationship between people's education and their use of the Internet. (5) Multimedia use is an important part of American culture.

ACTIVITY L: Drawing Conclusions from Visual Aids

Beneath each of the following visual aids, write as many conclusions as you can draw from the information provided. Then indicate why you think these are logical conclusions.

1.

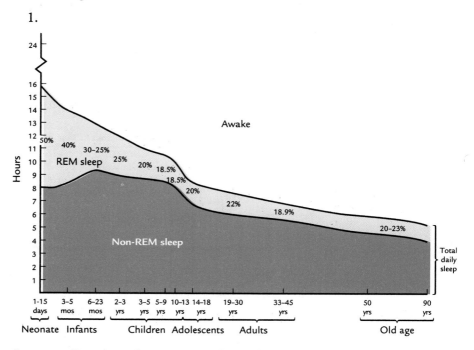

SLEEP AND DREAMING OVER THE LIFE SPAN

Source: Douglas A. Bernstein et al., *Psychology,* 4th ed. (Boston: Houghton Mifflin, 1997), p. 172.

Your conclusions:

_____

_____

_____

Why is each conclusion logical?

_____

_____

_____

2.

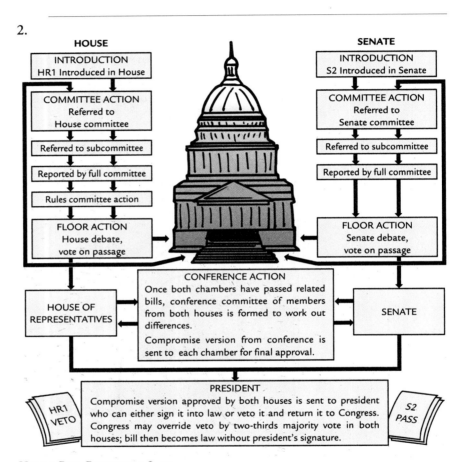

HOW A BILL BECOMES A LAW

Source: James Q. Wilson, *American Government,* brief version, 2d ed. (Lexington, MA: D. C. Heath, 1990), p. 201. Copyright © 1990 by Houghton Mifflin Company. Reprinted with permission.

Your conclusions:

_____

_____

_____

Why is each conclusion logical?

_____

_____

3.

DIVISION OF LABOR BY GENDER: A CROSS-CULTURAL COMPARISON

	Number of Cultures Dominated By				
	Men Always	**Men Usually**	**Either Gender Equally**	**Women Usually**	**Women Always**
Hunting	166	13	0	0	0
Herding	38	4	4	0	5
Fishing	98	34	19	3	4
Planting	31	23	33	20	37
Harvesting	10	15	35	39	44
Cooking	5	1	9	28	158
Carrying water	7	0	5	7	119

Source: Thomas R. Dye, *Power and Society,* 7th ed. (Belmont, CA: Wadsworth, 1996), p. 57.

Your conclusions:

_____

_____

_____

_____

Why is each conclusion logical?

_____

_____

_____

_____

▶ *Chapter Summary*

Based on your reading of this chapter, list at least five ideas that you believe will help you with future reading assignments. Write in complete sentences.

1. _____

_____

_____

_____

2. _____

_____

_____

_____

3. _____

_____

_____

_____

4. _____

_____

_____

_____

5. _____

_____

_____

_____

▶ *Extended Application*

Now that you have worked with the strategies necessary for reading visual aids, you can practice applying them to full-length reading selections. Choose (or your instructor may choose) a reading selection that is typical of what you will be expected to read for college courses, such as an essay or a textbook chapter, which also contains visual aids. Use this selection to:

※   Preview visual aids.

※   Note details of visual aids.

※   Make connections between visual aids and text.

※   Make inferences from visual aids.

※   Draw conclusions from visual aids.

Decide on the practice strategies you will use. Apply them to your selection. Then, in a few paragraphs, write a description of what you did and how the strategies you used worked for you.

Name of material used: _____

Page numbers: _____

Your description: _____

CHAPTER NINE

Strategies for Active Listening and Notetaking

H OW MIGHT YOU EXPERIENCE a football game differently if you were a player in the game or a spectator watching it? In which situation would you obtain the greatest inside knowledge about what had happened during particular plays? Which experience would result in more information about why your team won or lost the game? In which circumstance would you have greater connection to the emotions and reactions of the other team members? No doubt you realize that in answer to most or all of these questions, being in the game would give you an advantage over watching it. College students have a choice to make when they attend classes and do their reading assignments they can be in the game, or they can be spectators. The experiences and knowledge you gain as a student will largely depend on which choice you make. In this chapter, you are introduced to strategies for listening and notetaking that will help you become an active player in academic life.

Becoming a Good Listener

Good listening does not come automatically to most people. It is a skill that is learned, practiced, analyzed, and practiced some more. We are constantly bombarded with noises that compete for our attention. We *hear* all these sounds. But when we *listen,* we make a decision about which sounds will get our attention. Hearing that is purposeful and directed is called *listening.*

In your earliest grades in school your teachers tried to instill in you the habit of being a good listener. Consider, for instance, how many times you sat in a circle in the classroom while the teacher told you and your classmates to "Shhh." Can you recall some special signals your teacher may have used to tell you that it was time to listen? Maybe the lights were momentarily turned off, or two fingers were raised, or perhaps your teacher rang a small bell that sat on his or her desk. These school practices were designed to help children learn that there was time to talk and time to listen. In some families, listening is very important, and children are frequently told they must listen to their elders. In other families, it appears that no one listens to anyone else—everyone seems to be talking all the time without concern for whether they are being heard.

In adulthood, our needs and interests in various situations guide our listening habits. We are more aware that listening is a voluntary activity and that we can deliberately tune in or tune out as we choose. When we tune out, communication stops and messages sent to us become undeliverable. But when we choose to listen, all sorts of knowledge and understanding become possible for us. Your decision whether or not to be an effective listener can have a major impact on your success in college and career.

The amount of time college students spend listening in classes, as opposed to other in-class activities, is considerable. Some estimates suggest that students spend more than 50 percent of class time listening to their instructors. Given this situation, you can understand why it is necessary to develop effective listening strategies.

 ## THINKING ABOUT YOUR READING AND WRITING

ACTIVITY A: Your Listening Habits

Think about the listening habits you developed in your early life. How have they helped or hindered your ability to listen in a college classroom?

_____

_____

_____

_____

_____

_____

_____

_____

_____

_____

ACTIVITY B: How Good a Listener Are You?

Here are some characteristics of listeners. Rate yourself on each item by placing a check in the column that most applies to you.

	Always True of Me	Sometimes True of Me	Never True of Me
When I Listen, I			
1. Look at the speaker.			
2. Make predictions about what will be said.			
3. Think about what I already know about the topic.			
4. Look at the speaker's body language.			
5. Intend to understand.			
6. Stay awake.			
7. Ask for clarification when I don't understand.			
8. Select what is important.			
9. Take notes.			
10. Become distracted easily.			
11. Try to restate what the speaker has said in my own words.			
12. Fake attention.			

	Always True of Me	Sometimes True of Me	Never True of Me
13. Evaluate my personal biases on the topic.			
14. Focus on the speaker.			
15. Summarize what's being said.			
16. Daydream.			
17. Listen for the speaker's organization.			
18. Use speaker's pauses as time to think.			
19. Try to identify the speaker's purpose.			
20. Concentrate on content, not delivery.			
21. Listen for speaker bias.			
22. Set a purpose for listening.			

 ## THINKING ABOUT YOUR READING AND WRITING

ACTIVITY C: Analyzing Your Listening Strengths

How did you do? Put the item numbers you placed in each category on the following lines:

Always true of me_____

Sometimes true of me_____

Never true of me_____

    Only items 10, 12, and 16 suggest *negative listening behaviors*. They are behaviors that interfere with effective listening. All the other statements are *positive listening behaviors*. You can evaluate your own listening behavior by noting the number of the positive behaviors that are true of you sometimes or all the time. We explain the reasons these are considered positive behaviors in the next section.

What do you notice about your listening behaviors? Which listening behaviors, if any, would you like to change? Write your answers on the following lines.

_____

_____

_____

Indicators of Positive Listening

Connecting with the Speaker

Communication is a two-way process between speaker and listener or reader and author. Speakers often look at their audience for evidence that their ideas are being communicated successfully. One source of evidence is the audience's actions while listening. Listeners who make eye contact with the speaker, who sit in an attentive posture, who nod in recognition of some ideas, or who take notes signal that they are connecting with the speaker and that speaker-listener communication is occurring. Professors are usually aware of those students who are making an effort to become involved in the lecture or discussion and those who are dozing off or who seem inattentive. Students may try to fake attention, but they can easily be detected. Even though these students may appear to be looking at the speaker, their eyes are often glazed over, and it is clear to the observer that these listeners' minds are elsewhere.

If you analyze the speaker's body language, it may help you stay engaged. Your analysis may also reveal particular body language signals that the speaker uses to send important messages to listeners. For instance, if the speaker is pacing back and forth across the front of the room but suddenly stops to face the audience, it probably signals that an important point will be made. If the speaker's hand makes a pounding or other forceful type of motion, this, too, is to emphasize an important idea. Sometimes speakers will move closer to the audience when they really want to get a point across. Arms folded across the speaker's chest may mean a disagreement with an idea being suggested, one that the speaker will refute in later remarks. Voice changes, such as increased volume, or a slowed rate of speech, or repetition of a point, also signal key points.

You will find that many benefits result from effective listening. The extent to which you try to stay engaged with the speaker can affect the speaker's own enthusiasm and effort to *keep* you interested. This give-and-take between listener and speaker builds mutual rapport. Speakers are more willing to answer questions and to provide requested clarifications for an attentive audience. Further, your efforts to stay involved with the speaker will have a bearing on how much you will remember of what you have heard. In a college classroom, this may have a tremendous impact on your grades; tests often measure what was discussed in class as well as what you have read. The rapport you establish with your professor by being a good listener can also carry over into the other facets of classroom activity and may be the basis for your instructor to have a positive feeling toward you as a student.

Maintaining Concentration

Positive listeners are able to stay focused on the speaker, no matter what is occurring in the surrounding environment. Often the environment in which a lecture is given is not ideal—construction, bad weather, or loud conversation may be occurring outside the classroom. Imagine how distracting such noise is for someone trying to lead a discussion or to give a lecture. Of course, it is equally difficult for listeners to pay attention to what is happening inside the classroom when distractions such as these are outside. Nevertheless, both speaker and listener are obligated to attempt to stay focused and to ignore the distractions. How can you do this? *Concentration* is the key to success in such a situation. This means you must be able to focus your attention on a single task—in this case, on the speaker.

We have become so used to being able to "change the channel" when we don't like the program before us that we sometimes have difficulty concentrating when a lecture seems boring or unrelated to other things that are more meaningful for us. Recently, students have tried to do text messaging to friends during class recitations. This will definitely interfere with a student's ability to focus on the instructor, and the instructor might also find it rude. Some strategies to help you keep focused while listening follow.

THINK ABOUT HOW THE INFORMATION YOU HEAR RELATES TO WHAT YOU ALREADY KNOW ABOUT A SUBJECT.   Some instructors assume their students have considerable background on a topic, either because of students' prior knowledge or because they believe students have completed related assigned reading. We have discussed the importance of prior knowledge at many points in this text. If you connect new knowledge from a lecture to information you already have, it will help you understand and remember it.

WHILE YOU LISTEN, SORT OUT MAIN POINTS FROM LESSER ONES.   We have already mentioned some ways in which you can do this:

1. Look for body clues that are signals to important ideas.
2. Follow the organizational plan to identify shifts in topic or focus or details to support key points.

3. Notice whether the speaker uses a different tone of voice to signal important points.

4. Recognize a speaker's special efforts to point out major ideas. Sometimes visual aids are used to clarify or emphasize these.

5. Note when your professor refers to pages in the text that may further explain some point being made or when you are given such hints as, "This would be a good topic of discussion for a test."

STAY FOCUSED BY MAKING PREDICTIONS ABOUT WHAT WILL BE SAID NEXT.   As you try to follow the speaker's direction of thought, you may be able to make some predictions about key points to be made, types of supporting evidence that will be used, and point of view. You will keep mentally active as you listen for verifications.

FORM QUESTIONS WHILE YOU LISTEN.   Active listening includes active questioning, either about points that seem unclear or about which you would like more information or about arguments being made that could be refuted by other evidence.

IDENTIFY THE SPEAKER'S POINT OF VIEW, OR OPINION, EVEN WHEN IT ISN'T EXPRESSED DIRECTLY.   This will require *listening between the lines*. Your speaker may not tell you directly the point of view being taken, but body language signals, as well as remarks about other opinions on the same subject, are indicators you can use to determine the speaker's position. You will need to listen actively as you seek evidence to verify your conclusions about the speaker's opinions..

EVALUATE THE MESSAGE.   Your analysis of the value of a speaker's remarks should proceed in much the same way as if you were evaluating an author's writing. If the talk is anything more than mere recitation of facts, you will want to analyze the evidence offered as proof of the speaker's ideas. As you learned in Chapter 6, evaluation of messages includes noting whether the proof provided is merely more opinion or whether the factual evidence is available, and it involves asking yourself such questions as: How authoritative is the source? What other opinions on this subject are possible?

TAKE NOTES.   Notetaking is an important skill in college, one that we discuss later in this chapter. It is one of the best ways to maintain your concentration during a lecture and to keep yourself actively involved in what is being said.

Listening with the Intent to Learn

Listeners who have positive attitudes will enter the lecture hall or classroom each time with an *intent* to listen. This intention requires that several things occur before and during the lecture:

COME PREPARED TO LISTEN AND LEARN.   This means you should do the assigned readings before you arrive in class, and you should have brought the tools necessary for effective listening: your text and either a course notebook and pen or pencil, or a laptop for writing important ideas during the lecture.

BE AWARE OF BARRIERS TO EFFECTIVE COMMUNICATION DURING THE LECTURE AND TRY TO REMOVE THESE.   One barrier might be that of dialect or accent. When the speaker's native language is different from the listener's yet the speaker is using the listener's language, it is up to the listener to make every effort to identify the pronunciation differences that occur regularly so as to be able to quickly make listening accommodations.

Another barrier might be the physical appearance of the speaker. If the speaker's appearance is somehow disturbing, or if he or she seems very nervous or uncomfortable, the listener will need to focus on what is being said and shut out the physical distractions caused by the speaker. Being aware of distractions is the first step toward ignoring them.

Technical language used by the speaker can also be a barrier to communication. In such cases, advance reading and awareness of context are the two best strategies for overcoming the difficulty. If you have done these but still are unable to understand some of the language used, it may be appropriate to ask for clarification.

It may also be the case that you are unfamiliar with the speaker's style. When the speaker is one of your professors, you do have the advantage of having many class sessions during which you can adjust to the particular approach and language used. One area of difference may be the way in which the speaker organizes the lecture. Chapter 5 introduced you to organizational patterns in writing. These patterns are also often used in speaking situations. Although the speaker may digress from time to time, you may still be able to discern an overall pattern of organization that, once identified, will help you follow the speaker's ideas. Another difference you will notice is that some professors will use long, complex sentences with many embedded ideas. You will need to process this information rather rapidly, sorting out important ideas from unimportant ones. Fortunately, rate of speech is slower than rate of thinking, so you will have some time to weigh the importance of each element of the lecture. Some instructors may help you process information by identifying what the lecture goals are at the start of each class session. This kind of preview will certainly facilitate communication.

A final barrier to communication may be the result of the instructional style the speaker uses, particularly if it is different from what you have been used to. Different instructors include student activities in their course presentations to different extents. Some classes require a great deal of collaboration, and students will be expected to learn important concepts of the course as a result of these activities and exchanges with other students. At the other extreme, the professor remains at the center of activity and students participate actively only as listeners. In all instructional settings you need to ask yourself: What is the instructor expecting me to do to learn the major concepts of this course?

KEEP AN OPEN MIND WHEN THE SPEAKER'S IDEAS ARE DIFFERENT FROM YOUR OWN.   The intent to learn requires that the listener believe there is something to be gained from listening. How do you typically respond to a speaker whose ideas are in total disagreement with yours? If you are like most of us, you get angry and want an opportunity to explain to everyone why the speaker is wrong. This tactic is not one that promotes good listening because your mind is so focused on your rebuttal that you really don't listen to what the speaker is saying. The speaker's ideas may contain either some points you haven't considered or points that serve your interests because you can easily argue against their logic or significance. But if you don't listen to the speaker, if you are too wrapped up in developing your plan of attack, you will miss the opportunity to hear these other ideas. College students frequently discover that their ways of thinking about events change from the time they first enter their academic program to the time they graduate. There are many influences on your attitudes. Your personal biases are the result of your experiences and your memories of them. These are valuable sources of evidence for your present perceptions and biases. However, your instructors may have some new insights to offer that will help you rethink your ideas and, perhaps, modify them. By keeping an open mind, you are allowing yourself to find support for your beliefs or to change your ideas to more defensible and logical ones. Intelligent responses are easier when you have listened to what has already been said.

RECOGNIZE CONFUSIONS.   Because effective listeners plan to learn from lectures or discussions, they must recognize when they are confused and thus when learning is not taking place. In most classrooms and lecture halls students are given the opportunity to ask questions. Don't hesitate to ask them. Some professors assign "one-minute papers" after a lecture in which students write some of the main ideas they obtained from the lecture as well as any questions they still have about the topic that was discussed. Use this opportunity to give feedback to your instructor and to ask for further explanation. If there is no chance to ask questions during the class session, make an appointment to see your instructor afterward. You will show yourself to be a serious student. You will be respected for seeking clarification, and you will demonstrate that you are working hard at reaching understanding.

THINKING ABOUT YOUR READING AND WRITING

ACTIVITY D: Controlling Your Listening Experience

Based on what you now know about indicators of positive listening, to what extent do you believe listeners are in control of how much they benefit from a learning situation? Write your response in the space provided. Be specific.

_____

_____

_____

_____

_____

_____

_____

_____

_____

WORKING TOGETHER

Compare your ideas in Activity D with those of a partner. How do you differ in your definition of what it means to be in control of a learning situation? Make any changes to your response in Activity D that you feel are appropriate.

ACTIVITY E: Analyzing Instructional Styles

Complete this activity for two of your instructors. For each category, write a few sentences that characterize each instructor. Then explain how this instructional style affects you as a listener.

1. Instructor A (name not required)

   Speech complexity:_____

   _____

   _____

Body language: _____

_____

_____

Assumptions about prior knowledge of students: _____

_____

_____

Clarity of presentation: _____

_____

_____

Organization: _____

_____

_____

Opportunities for student involvement: _____

_____

_____

Listening strategies I should use in this class: _____

_____

_____

Overall characterization of style: _____

_____

_____

_____

How this instructional style affects me: _____

2. Instructor B (name not required)

   Speech complexity:

   Body language:

   Assumptions about prior knowledge of students:

   Clarity of presentation:

   Organization:

   Opportunities for student involvement:

   Listening strategies I should use in this class:

Overall characterization of style: _____

_____

_____

_____

How this instructional style affects me: _____

_____

_____

Effective Notetaking from Books and Lectures

One noticeable difference between academic life in high school and college is the extent to which students are expected to be independent learners. Your high school teachers may have put a lecture outline on the chalkboard, and they may have deliberately pointed out important points for you. This is often not the case in college. Usually, you must decide for yourself what notes to take and how to write them. Further, in some college courses, outside reading assignments are never discussed in class. Nevertheless, you are expected to read, understand, and remember information from them, and these assignments may form an important basis for exams and class lectures on related topics. The overall result is that your ability to effectively mark your textbooks and to take notes from them can have an impact on your course grades.

Because notetaking and textbook marking skills are seldom taught to students, you may believe that there aren't any specific strategies to use. It may appear as though some students just have a knack for good notetaking and others don't. This, however, is seldom so. There are numerous strategies for effective marking of textbooks and taking notes. This section describes those found to be most beneficial to college students. As you work with them, you should adapt them to your own purposes and learning needs so that they will be most useful for you.

ACTIVITY F: Your Current Notetaking Strategies

You may have already found a useful way to take lecture notes. In the space provided, list some ways you take notes.

1. _____

2. _____

3. _____

Others:

_____

_____

In the next section you will be introduced to some research-based strategies for effective notetaking.

A Process for Effective Notetaking

Earlier you read that effective listeners think about what they hear before they write anything. A listener can use the *wait time,* the time between a speaker's thought and actual speech, to think about and then to write down the important ideas, as shown here.

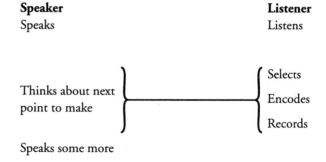

Speaker	**Listener**
Speaks	Listens
	Selects
Thinks about next point to make	Encodes
	Records
Speaks some more	

During wait time you *select,* from all the information the speaker has delivered, that which is most important. Then you *encode,* or translate, these important ideas into language that is more like your own. Finally, you *record* these ideas. This process of listening, selecting, encoding, and recording continues until the lecture ends.

Identifying Usable Notes

Imagine that you are preparing for a test in the introductory psychology course you are taking. You are studying your lecture notes from a session on memory. Two examples of notes from part of that lecture follow. Which set would you prefer to have available to you as you study?

Example 1:

Memory

Laboratory studies of memory show how much you know later as compared to how much you know right away. Really, memory study is study of forgetting.

In lab studies the subject is given task and then scientist measures how much learning occurred. Subject does activity to keep him/her from thinking about the new information. Later is tested again to see what of the new information is remembered.

Recall is reproduction of the learned material. Sometimes it is rote or verbatim, which means remembering it in the exact form. Recognition is recognizing something that was previously experienced, such as faces of friends. Relearning involves both recall and recognition. Scientist finds out how long it takes to learn the material as measured on a test. After an interval of time, the subject relearns it. (may test subject on it till he can pass the same test equally well on two occasions)

Ebbinghaus did first important studies on retention; used nonsense syllables. List of nonsense syllables had to be remembered in serial order. Found there was a rapid initial loss, followed by a gradual slower decline. (Memory Curve)

Why we forget? trace decay theory says knowledge we have learned just fades away, and the longer it remains unused, the greater we decay. interference theory—other learnings interfere with memory of a previous learning. Trace transformation theory—memory is active process; information stored is automatically transformed to make it more consistent with other knowledge we are remembering. Repression theory—believes that the things we remember and the things we forget are related to their value and importance to us. (Freud)

Adapted from Floyd L. Ruch and Philip G. Zimbardo, *Psychology and Life,* 8th ed., brief version (Glenview, IL: Scott Foresman, 1971).

Example 2:

Memory

11/4/95

Lab studies of Memory
 —show how much you know later as compared to how much you know right after learning.
 —Mem. study is really a study of forgetting.
Lab procedures
 (1) subject given task & scientist measures how much learning occurred.
 (2) Subj. does activity—kept from thinking about new info.
 (3) Subj. tested again later to see what new info is remembered.
Terms About Memory
 Recall—
  reproduction of the lrnd material.
  Sometimes rote or verbatim (remembering it exactly)
 Recognition—
  recognizing something that was experienced before, i.e. faces of friends.
 Relearning—   see text
  involves both recall and recognition.   pg. 247
 (1) Scientist finds out how long it takes to learn the material (may give a test)
 (2) Later subj. relearns it. (may be tested till he can pass the same test equally well on two occasions)
STUDIES
 Ebbinghaus
  —first imp. studies on retention
  —used list of nonsense syllables
  —syllables had to be remembered in serial order
  —Found rapid loss at beginning, followed by gradual slower decline.

Example 2: *continued*

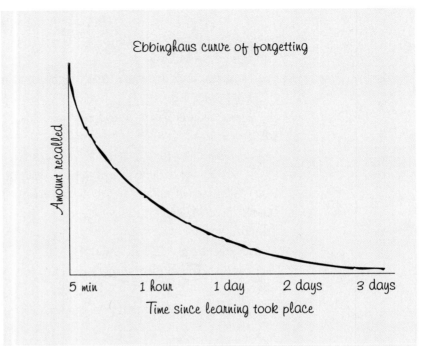

Ebbinghaus curve of forgetting

Amount recalled

5 min   1 hour   1 day   2 days   3 days

Time since learning took place

Source: Hermann Ebbinghaus, "Curve of Forgetting," *Psychology: An Elementary Text-Book* [1908], trans. and ed. Max Meyer (New York: Arno, 1973).

THEORIES of WHY WE FORGET

trace decay theory:

what we lrnd just fades away,

the longer it remains unused, the greater it decays.

interference theory:

other lrngs interfere with mem. of previous lrng.

trance transformation theory:

mem is active process

? information stored is automatically transformed to

make it more consistent with other knowledge we are remembering.

repression theory:

things we remember and things we forget are related to their value

and importance to us. (Freud)

📓 THINKING ABOUT YOUR READING AND WRITING

ACTIVITY G: Your Notetaking Preferences

1. Which set of notes do you prefer? Why?

2. What differences do you see between the two examples?

3. How is the example you prefer different from your current notetaking system?

Notetaking Basics

If you had considered that the notes you chose were to be used to study for a test, you should have chosen the second example. Perhaps you recognized some of the following elements in this example, which are features of a good set of lecture notes.

1. *The notes are dated.* Dating the notes serves as a reference for you. You will be able to compare a set of lecture notes from a particular date with those of another student. Further, if your notes get out of sequence for some reason, it will be easy to restore order to them if they have been dated. Ideas from earlier lectures may have a bearing on those of lectures later in the semester.

2. *The notes are organized so that the relationships between ideas are clear.* This clarity results from the writer's systematic approach to notetaking. Main topics can readily be distinguished from minor ones because they have been placed apart from the details, and the margin of the page serves as the starting place for writing the main topics. Each new important topic is written on a separate line. Details and subtopics are indented under the main ideas to which they relate. Major details are distinguished from minor ones by indenting the minor details even further.

3. *Important terms are quickly seen.* A system of circling new terminology has been used. This will make it easy to go back to this notebook and to locate where new vocabulary has been introduced.

4. *Only a few words are used to convey ideas.* Because it is impossible, and also not a good idea, to write everything that is said word for word, effective note takers learn to condense whole sentences into shorter phrases that convey the same meaning. This saves time and gives you an additional opportunity to reflect on the meaning. This is part of the process of encoding the material.

5. *There is space for additional information.* Even with the advantage of wait time, there is still the possibility that other related ideas or information will occur to you well after you have taken your original set of notes. In the second example, space has been left for such entries.

6. *A personal shorthand system has been used for repeated and common words.* The author of these notes recognizes that some words, like *subject* and *memory,* occur over and over again in this course. Having this system of abbreviations (for example, *subj.* and *mem.*) reduces writing time.

7. *Areas of uncertainty are noted.* By using a question mark to reflect areas needing further investigation, the author of these notes processes the

ideas of the speaker during the lecture; the note taker has asked himself, Am I understanding this? while the lecture is in progress. A question mark enables areas of uncertainty to be easily located later, and you will be able to seek assistance and clarification.

8. *Diagrams have been carefully drawn.* We cannot tell whether the student taking these notes drew the diagram without direction from the instructor to do so or copied it from the board or display. The important point, though, is that all parts are clearly labeled, and it will be a useful study aid during the semester.

9. *References to pages in the textbook have been noted and are easily spotted.* Again, we do not know whether the student independently noted this reference to the textbook or whether the instructor had pointed it out. But it is clear that the student will be able to refer to the text for further elaboration on this point. If the instructor made the reference and the student had not noted it, he would have lost out on this opportunity.

10. *The notes are legible.* All the information is easy to read. Some students who incorporate many of the basics of effective notetaking into their study skills repertoire still have a serious problem when they try to study from their notes because they can't read what they have written. This may result from writing too fast, which can occur if you try to write the lecture word for word. Carefully selecting what to write means that you will need to write less; this, in turn, means that you can take the time to write legibly so that you can successfully use notes later for review. Bear in mind that excessive doodling can also make useless an otherwise good set of notes.

THINKING ABOUT YOUR READING AND WRITING

ACTIVITY H: Analyzing Your NoteTaking Processes

1. Which notetaking basics mentioned here do you already use?

_____

_____

_____

_____

2. Which basics mentioned here might be hard for you to apply? Why?

_____

_____

_____

_____

Notetaking Systems

There are more ways than one to take good notes from lectures and textbooks. In this section we describe two of the most popular notetaking systems, the *Cornell method* and the *Outline method*. You should examine each and then decide which system will work best for you, which will most satisfactorily help you achieve your own notetaking objectives. You will need to keep an open mind as you try your selected approach. You might start using one system but later decide that you need to try another approach because your first strategy is not working for you.

The Cornell Method

This notetaking method, developed by Walter Pauk, is highly recommended by study skills experts. Although it is a little more structured than the notes in Example 2 that you reviewed earlier, it is popular with students because it is easy to use, and it encourages reflection about the material both during and after the lecture or initial reading. To use the Cornell method, you will need a full-size (8½ x 11-inch) notebook that has an extra-wide left margin (legal ruled or summary ruled). Such notebooks are available in bookstores, or you may rule the margins yourself. The Cornell method involves a two-phase process of notetaking. During the lecture or initial reading of the assignment, you write information in a right-hand (6-inch) column. Write each main idea on a separate line, and write supporting details beneath each of these. A set of notes written this way for a lecture in a business course is illustrated next.

Cornell method example (phase 1):

February 19, 1996
Careers in Marketing

Mktg. is a broad field; many opportunities
  Can be involved with product any time—from creation til after
    sale, incl. service & maintenance
  1983—demand for sales & mktg. execs. rchd 5 yr. high, esp in
    Southeast & Midwest
  Over 1/2 labor force in service is in some aspect of mktg.
  Career opp. in selling, advertising, sales promotion, publ. rela,
    product mngmnt, mktg resrch, retailing, wholesaling, physical
    distrib, mktg mngmnt.
Selling has many opportunities
  more employees than any other mktg. occup
  some salespeople are own boss; most work for others
  most jobs routine—structured work schedule, regular pay
  ed. & trng vary
    for standardized goods & svcs—only h.s.dip.;
      e.g. Retail trade sales—interest cust. in product;
      demonstrate prod., prep sales slips, receive cash, give
      change and receipt—reg. h.s. dip.
    for manufacturers salespeople—college degree req.
      e.g. sell to factories, banks, wholesalers, schools,
      hospitals, libraries
Advertising jobs very competitive; good starting salary
  Jobs are in advertising depts. of producers and intermediaries; ad
  agencies; w/media firms.
  e.g. adv. mgr—directs program; decides allocation of $, type of
  ad and ad agcy to use.
    rsrch directors—survey cust buying habits; test sample ads.
    production mgr—arranges for printing ads (or film, t.v.,
    radio)
Jobs in Public Relations
      req. college deg. in jrnlism, communications, or pub rela
      helps orgs. build & maintain positive pub image; must
      underst. pub concerns & communicate this info. to mngmnt

Adapted from Leon C. Megginson, Lyle R. Trueblood, and Gayle M. Ross, *Business* (Lexington, MA: D. C. Heath, 1985), pp. 420–23. Copyright © 1984 by Houghton Mifflin Company. Reprinted with permission.

In the second phase of using the Cornell method, you review the information that is in the center of the page and then edit and summarize it. In editing you may correct spelling, insert punctuation, delete or add words, and improve the organization of the notes, perhaps by numbering ideas. When you summarize, you want to make it easy to find the key topics that were discussed and to state the main ideas. To do this, you write on the left-side margin (the remaining one-third page) any key words, phrases, or questions that summarize the main ideas and pull together important facts from the right side of the page. These summary notes will serve as important cues when it is time for you to review for subsequent readings or lectures or to study for exams. As a part of your summary, you also write one or two sentences that state the main idea of the lecture. This summary is written at the bottom of your final page of notes. You create the space to write it by drawing an additional line at the bottom of the notebook page, 2 inches up from the edge. When you summarize ideas in this way, you are giving yourself an additional opportunity to review and reflect on the lecture and to organize it into meaningful units of information. The next example illustrates this second step.

Cornell method example (phase 2):

Job Opportunities	*February 19, 1996* *Careers in Marketing*
	Mktg. is a broad field; many opportunities
	Can be involved with product any time—from creation til after sale, incl. service & maintenance
Where are they located?	1983—demand for sales & mktg. execs. rchd 5 yr. high, esp in Southeast & Midwest
	Over 1/2 labor force in service is in some aspect of mktg.
What type of jobs?	Career opp. in selling, advertising, sales promotion, publ. rela, product mngmnt, mktg resrch, retailing, wholesaling, physical distrib, mktg mngmnt.
	Selling has many opportunities
Opportunities in Selling	more employees than any other mktg. occup
	some salespeople are own boss; most work for others
	most jobs routine—structured work schedule, regular pay
	ed. & trng vary

variety and requirements	for standardized goods & svcs—only h.s.dip.; e.g. Retail trade sales—interest cust. in product; demonstrate prod., prep sales slips, receive cash, give change and receipt—reg. h.s. dip. for manufacturers salespeople—college degree req. e.g. sell to factories, banks, wholesalers, schools, hospitals, libraries
Advertising	Advertising jobs very competitive; good starting salary Jobs are in advertising depts. of producers and intermediaries; ad agencies; w/media firms.
variety	e.g. adv. mgr—directs program; decides allocation of $, type of ad and ad agcy to use. rsrch directors—survey cust buying habits; test sample ads. production mgr—arranges for printing ads (or film, t.v., radio)
Public Relations requirements variety	Jobs in Public Relations req. college deg. in jrnlism, communications, or pub rela helps orgs. build & maintain positive pub image; must underst. pub concerns & communicate this info. to mngmnt

Summary: There are many job opportunities in marketing, including jobs in selling, advertising and public relations. The jobs have different education requirements and involve different types of responsibilities

Adapted from Leon C. Megginson, Lyle R. Trueblood, and Gayle M. Ross, *Business* (Lexington, MA: D. C. Heath, 1985), pp. 420–23. Copyright © 1984 by Houghton Mifflin Company. Reprinted with permission.

The Outline Method

You may find that in some instances an outline format is more useful for note-taking from lectures and texts. This is particularly true when a lecturer or text is very well organized, provided you are comfortable with numbering each topic and detail as the lecture or reading proceeds. Outlines may be written using only topics, sentences, or paragraphs. However, outlines often use a combination of main-idea sentences and subtopics supporting each main idea. The importance of each idea in relation to each other is shown on the outline through the use of either a roman or an arabic number-and-letter system or a decimal numbering system. The first outline, which is based on a class lecture, illustrates the roman numeral system. The decimal system is illustrated in the second outline.

Example Outline A:

THE HUMAN NERVOUS SYSTEM

I. Divisions
   A. Central Nervous System (CNS)
      1. Housed in skull and vertebral column
      2. Consists of brain and spinal cord
   B. Peripheral Nervous System (PNS)
      1. Distributed throughout the body
      2. Consists of afferent and efferent fibers and sense organs.
II. Interactions
   A. The two systems interact constantly
   B. Both systems are necessary for voluntary actions and involuntary actions
III. Activities of Central Nervous System
   A. Reception
      1. From motor (efferent) divisions of PNS
      2. From sensory (afferent) divisions of PNS
   B. Integration
      1. Of information about internal and external environments
      2. Decides on course of action
   C. Action
      1. Distributes "instructions" to effector organs
      2. Effector organs may be glands, blood vessels, fingers and toes, etc.

Example Outline B:

THE HUMAN NERVOUS SYSTEM

1. Divisions
   1.1 Central Nervous System (CNS)
      1.1.1 Housed in skull and vertebral column
      1.1.2 Consists of brain and spinal cord
   1.2 Peripheral Nervous System (PNS)
      1.2.1 Distributed throughout the body
      1.2.2 Consists of afferent and efferent fibers and sense organs

2. Interactions

    2.1 The two systems interact constantly

    2.2 Both systems are necessary for voluntary actions and involuntary actions

3. Activities of Central Nervous System

    3.1. Reception

        3.1.1 From motor (efferent) divisions of PNS

        3.1.2 From sensory (afferent) divisions of PNS

    3.2. Integration

        3.2.1 Of information about internal and external environments

        3.2.2 Decides on course of action

    3.3. Action

        3.3.1 Distributes "instructions" to effector organs

        3.3.2 Effector organs may be glands, blood vessels, fingers and toes, etc.

THINKING ABOUT YOUR READING AND WRITING

ACTIVITY I: Selecting a Notetaking System

Of the two notetaking systems introduced in this section, which do you believe will be the best one for you? Why have you selected this approach?

_____

_____

_____

_____

_____

_____

_____

_____

_____

_____

_____

_____

🪑 WORKING TOGETHER

Compare your responses to the questions in Activity I with those of a partner. How are your notetaking system needs similar? How are they different?

ACTIVITY J: Creating Notes from Lectures and Textbooks

Select a textbook chapter or a lecture to attend for notetaking practice. Take notes using the notetaking method you prefer. Then write a one-page analysis of how the method worked for you and what changes, if any, you think you should make in your approach.

Using Your Notes Effectively

Once you have a good set of notes, you will want to make the best possible use of them. We outline six strategies for effective use of notes in this section. As you read these strategies, see whether you have used any of them before. Also try to identify any suggestions that you would like to use from now on.

Edit Your Notes

Edit immediately after a lecture or after completing a reading assignment while the ideas are still fresh in your mind. Your goal for editing is to create a set of notes that you will understand weeks, or even months, after you have heard the lecture or completed the reading. While editing, you should:

1. Be sure everything is legible.
2. Add any punctuation that is needed for clarity.
3. Check your abbreviations and write out the complete words for abbreviations that you do not frequently use.

4. Check the spelling of technical terms and proper names.
5. Check the accuracy of dates.
6. Be sure the hierarchy of ideas is clearly seen from your layout.

Cross-Reference Text Notes with Class Notes, and Vice Versa

Class and text notes should support each other; that is, one should add more information to the other. Textbook or other assigned readings often address the same subject as lectures. Note in your reading material the lecture dates that address the same subject, and write in your lecture notes the related text page numbers.

Check Your Notes for Accuracy

While you are editing your notes, you may find that you are unclear on some points or that information seems incomplete. In such cases:

1. Get clarification on the ideas and terminology about which you are uncertain. To do this, you can refer to the relevant portions of your text, compare your notes with others, discuss the material with your instructor, or refer to other materials on the same subject.

2. If you are describing a sequence of events, a procedure, or any series that you will need to remember in order, be certain you have included all parts of the sequence. If there appear to be gaps in the sequence you have recorded in your notes, you will again need to check others' sources to make your notes complete.

Summarize Key Points

Do this as soon as you feel you have reviewed a chunk of related information. Write down your summaries. When you put ideas on paper, you can see whether you really are able to state a few sentences that will express the main points of the lecture of reading, or whether there are some points on which you are uncertain. Follow these steps to write an effective summary:

1. Consider the entire lecture you have heard or text material you have read. Be sure the meaning is clear to you. Review what you have underlined and highlighted or noted as being a major point.

2. If a thesis was stated that connected the main points of the text or lecture, write it as the first sentence of your summary.

3. Write a sentence that states each key point of the lecture or reading. These are really statements of main ideas. For an hour's lecture, there may be only three or four main points.

4. Identify the major supporting details for each point that the lecturer or author has included. Try to consolidate these major details into one or two sentences, and then add them to your summary, following each main idea. The result will be a paragraph of perhaps seven to ten sentences, written in your own words.

5. Return to the material you have summarized to compare it to your summary. Be certain you have not omitted key points or changed the essential meaning.

Practice Distributed Review

How much of what you heard in class last week do you still remember? What about what you heard three or four weeks ago? There is so much information coming into the sensory storage area of our brain that it is impossible for it to stay there for more than just a few seconds. During this time, we need to decide whether to retain the information and transmit it to our short-term memory or to discard it. Information that we transfer to short-term memory we will retain for only a few seconds—20 or less—unless we rehearse it, deliberately, as we might do with a shopping list or telephone number. Information that we wish to keep in permanent storage for a long time, such as ideas from lectures and textbooks, must be reviewed regularly, or it will be difficult to retrieve. Research shows that without such periodic review, we quickly forget what we learned. Three days after learning something, we forget most of it if we make no effort to remember it. The curve of forgetting that appeared earlier in the memory lecture notes is shown again here. It illustrates the point that if you periodically review your notes, you will keep the information fresh in your mind and significantly reduce the amount of material you will need to relearn. It will be easier for you to retrieve the ideas for tests and class discussion or as prior knowledge to help you comprehend later material.

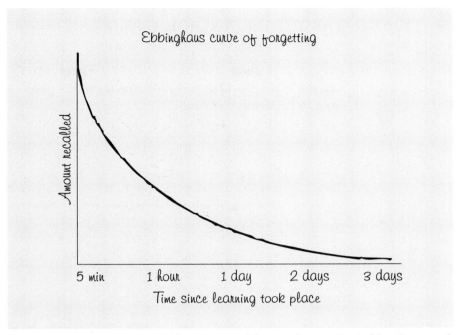

Source: Hermann Ebbinghaus, "Curve of Forgetting," *Psychology: An Elementary Text-Book* [1908], trans. and ed. Max Meyer (New York: Arno, 1973).

Formulate Questions from Your Notes

See how many different ways you can ask a question that will yield similar information. This will get you used to hearing requests for the information in different ways, and you will then be more likely to know when your instructor's question is calling for certain information. To create and work with your questions:

1. Use the headings you have written in the left column (Cornell method) or the topical headings of your outline.

2. Make as many questions from the headings as you can so that you will have the chance to include all of what you have studied in your responses.

3. Use question words such as *how* and *why.* Questions worded in this way require more thorough answers than those beginning with *what, who, when,* or *where.*

4. Be sure you can answer your questions. Refer to your notes for verification, and be honest with yourself. If you don't know the answer during your review, you certainly won't know it for an exam.

THINKING ABOUT YOUR READING AND WRITING

ACTIVITY K: Making Personal Decisions about Notetaking

In the space provided, write a summary of the points made about notetaking so far in this chapter.

_____

_____

_____

_____

_____

_____

_____

Which of the suggestions for using your notes effectively are new ideas for you? Which of these new suggestions do you think you will try?

_____

_____

_____

_____

_____

_____

_____

ACTIVITY L: Making Notes Usable

Choose a set of notes that you have taken on a previous lecture or reading assignment. Make whatever revisions you believe are needed. Keep your original notes. On a separate sheet of paper, explain what you have done to

make your notes more usable. Attach your original notes to the revised notes and your explanation.

⋈ WORKING TOGETHER

Review your revised notes with a partner. Can your partner suggest anything else to improve them?

Preparing Graphics from Lectures and Texts

One way to record information from lectures and textbooks that we have not yet discussed in this chapter is to make a graphic that shows the relationship between ideas. In Chapters 3 and 5, you worked with graphics that organized main ideas and details. In Chapter 8, you practiced creating and interpreting graphics that illustrated other types of relationships. You can create any of these graphics, such as timelines, circle charts, tables, flowcharts, semantic maps, or Venn diagrams, to express visually the ideas from lectures and texts. If you found the work with graphics in the previous chapters to be beneficial, you should consider using this strategy often.

ACTIVITY M: Creating a Graphic from Lecture or Text Notes

Select a set of notes you have taken from a lecture or reading assignment, and prepare a graphic to show the relationship between ideas or data. Choose the graphic format that best fits the data or information you have chosen to graphically illustrate. Be prepared to discuss why it is the best type of visual aid for the information.

Underlining and Marking Textbooks

Did you experience "sticker shock" at the bookstore this semester when you purchased your textbooks? Most freshmen have not had to pay for textbooks in the past, and they are usually astonished at the prices. Once the shock is over, though, you can think about some of the advantages of owning the books, an advantage most students did not have in high school, where the books are typically owned by the school.

Owning your textbooks allows you to underline and make notations in them. If you use effective underlining and textbook notation strategies, you will be able to find important information and to review it more easily. Study the examples of textbook page notations that appear in the next three examples. All the examples have been taken from the same textbook page, but the notations were made by three different readers. See what differences you can find in how each reader has interacted with the text.

Example 1:

The Supreme Court in Action

If your case should find its way to the Supreme Court—and the odds are that it will not—you will be able to participate in one of the more impressive, sometimes dramatic, ceremonies of American public life. The Court is in session in its white marble building for thirty-six weeks out of each year, from early October until the end of June. The nine justices read briefs in their individual offices, hear oral arguments in the large, stately courtroom, and discuss their decisions with one another in a conference room where no outsiders are allowed.

Most cases come to the Court on a writ of certiorari. The lawyers on each side may then submit their **briefs**—documents summarizing the lower-court decision, giving the arguments for their side, and discussing the other cases that the Court has ruled on that bear on the issue. Then the lawyers are allowed to present their oral arguments in open court. These usually summarize the briefs or emphasize particular points in them, and are strictly limited in time—usually to no more than half an hour. The oral arguments give the justices a chance to question the lawyers, sometimes searchingly.

for decisions

Since the federal government is a party—as either plaintiff or defendant—to about half the cases the Supreme Court hears, the government's top trial lawyer, the solicitor general of the United States, appears frequently before the Court. The solicitor general decides what cases the government will appeal from lower courts and personally approves every case that the government presents to the Supreme Court.

In addition to the arguments made by lawyers for both sides, written briefs and even oral arguments may also be offered by "a friend of the court," or **amicus curiae.** An amicus brief is from an interested party not directly involved in the suit. For example, when Allan Bakke complained that he had been the victim of reverse discrimination when he was denied admission to a University of California medical school, fifty-eight amicus briefs were filed supporting or opposing his position. Before such briefs can be filed, both parties must agree or the Court must grant permission. These documents are a kind of polite lobbying of the Court which, though they sometimes offer new arguments, generally are a declaration of what interests are on which side. The ACLU, the NAACP, the AFL-CIO, and the United

involved

States government itself have been among the leading sources of such briefs.

These briefs are not the only source of influence on the justices' views. Leading legal periodicals, such as the *Yale Law Journal* and the *Harvard Law Review,* are frequently consulted and cited in decisions, so that the outside world of lawyers and law professors can help shape, or at least supply arguments for, the justices' conclusions.

The justices retire to their conference room every Friday, where in complete secrecy they debate the cases they have heard. The chief justice speaks first, followed by the other justices in order of seniority. After the arguments they vote, traditionally in reverse order of seniority. In this process an able chief justice can exercise considerable influence— in guiding or limiting debate, in setting forth the issues, and in handling sometimes temperamental personalities. In deciding a case, a majority of the justices must be in agreement: if there is a tie, the lower-court decision is left standing. (There can be a tie among the nine justices if one is ill or disqualifies himself or herself because of prior involvement in the case.)

Though the vote is what counts, by tradition the Court usually issues a written decision, the **Opinion of the Court.** Sometimes this opinion is brief and unsigned (called a **per curiam opinion**); sometimes it is quite long and signed by the justices agreeing with it. If the chief justice is in the majority, he will either write the opinion or assign it to a justice who agrees with him. If he is in the minority, the senior justice on the winning side will decide who writes the Court's opinion. There are four kinds of signed opinions: *unanimous, majority* (the majority opinion of the Court when it is divided), **concurring** (an opinion by one or more justices who agree with the majority's conclusion but for different reasons that they wish to express), and **dissenting** (the opinion of one or more justices on the losing side).

Example 2:

The Supreme Court in Action

If your case should find its way to the Supreme Court—and the odds are that it will not—you will be able to participate in one of the more impressive, sometimes dramatic, ceremonies of American public life. The Court is in session in its white marble building for thirty-six weeks out of each year, from early October until the end of June. The nine justices read briefs in their individual offices, hear oral arguments in the large, stately courtroom, and discuss their decisions with one another in a conference room where no outsiders are allowed.

Most cases come to the Court on a writ of certiorari. The lawyers on each side may then submit their briefs—documents summarizing the lower-court decision, giving the arguments for their side, and discussing the other cases the Court has ruled on that bear on the issue. Then the lawyers are allowed to present their oral arguments in open court. These usually summarize the briefs or emphasize particular points in them, and are strictly limited in time—usually to no more than half an hour. The oral arguments give the justices a chance to question the lawyers, sometimes searchingly.

Since the federal government is a party—as either plaintiff or defendant—to about half the cases the Supreme Court hears, the government's top trial lawyer, the solicitor general of the United States, appears frequently before the Court. The solicitor general decides what cases the government will appeal from lower courts and personally approves every case that the government presents to the Supreme Court.

In addition to the arguments made by lawyers for both sides, written briefs and even oral arguments may also be offered by "a friend of the court," or **amicus curiae.** An amicus brief is from an interested party not directly involved in the suit. For example, when Allan Bakke complained that he had been the victim of reverse discrimination when he was denied admission to a University of California medical school, fifty-eight amicus briefs were filed supporting or opposing his position. Before such briefs can be filed, both parties must agree or the Court must grant permission. These documents are a kind of polite lobbying of the Court which, though they sometimes offer new arguments, generally are a declaration of what interests are on which side. The ACLU, the NAACP, the AFL-CIO, and the United States government itself have been among the leading sources of such briefs.

These briefs are not the only source of influence on the justices' views. Leading legal periodicals, such as the *Yale Law Journal* and the *Harvard Law Review,* are frequently consulted and cited in decisions, so that the outside world of lawyers and law professors can help shape, or at least supply arguments for, the justices' conclusions.

The justices retire to their conference room every Friday, where in complete secrecy they debate the cases they have heard. The chief justice speaks first, followed by the other justices in order of seniority. After the arguments they vote, traditionally in reverse order of seniority. In this process an able chief justice can exercise considerable influence—in guiding or limiting debate, in setting forth the issues, and in handling sometimes temperamental personalities. In deciding a case, a majority of the justices must be in agreement: if there is a tie, the lower-court decision is left standing. (There can be a tie among the nine justices if one is ill or disqualifies himself or herself because of prior involvement in the case.)

Though the vote is what counts, by tradition the Court usually issues a written decision, the **Opinion of the Court.** Sometimes this opinion is brief and unsigned (called a **per curiam opinion**); sometimes it is quite long and signed by the justices agreeing with it. If the chief justice is in the majority, he will either write the opinion or assign it to a justice who agrees with him. If he is in the minority, the senior justice on the winning side will decide who writes the Court's opinion. There are four kinds of signed opinions: *unanimous, majority* (the majority opinion of the Court when it is divided), **concurring** (an opinion by one or more justices who agree with the majority's conclusion but for different reasons that they wish to express), and **dissenting** (the opinion of one or more justices on the losing side).

Example 3:

The Supreme Court in Action

If your case should find its way to the Supreme Court—and the odds are that it will not—you will be able to participate in one of the more impressive, sometimes dramatic, ceremonies of American public life. The Court is in session in its white marble building for thirty-six weeks out of each year, from early October until the end of June. The nine justices read briefs in their individual offices, hear oral arguments in the large, stately courtroom, and discuss their decisions with one another in a conference room where no outsiders are allowed.

1. Most cases come to the Court on a writ of certiorari. The lawyers on each side may then submit their briefs—documents summarizing the lower-court decision, giving the arguments for their side, and discussing the other cases that the Court has ruled on that bear on the

2. issue. Then the lawyers are allowed to present their oral arguments in open court. These usually summarize the briefs or emphasize particular points in them, and are strictly limited in time—usually to no more than half an hour. The oral arguments give the justices a chance to question the lawyers, sometimes searchingly.

job of sol. gen.

Since the federal government is a party—as either plaintiff or defendant—to about half the cases the Supreme Court hears, the government's top trial lawyer, the solicitor general of the United States, appears frequently before the Court. The solicitor general decides what cases the government will appeal from lower courts and personally approves every case the government presents to the Supreme Court.

3.

In addition to the arguments made by lawyers for both sides, written briefs and even oral arguments may also be offered by "a friend of the court," or amicus curiae. An amicus brief is from an interested party not directly involved in the suit. For example, when Allan Bakke complained that he had been the victim of reverse discrimination when he was denied admission to a University of California medical school, fifty-eight amicus briefs were filed supporting or opposing his position. Before such briefs can be filed, both parties must agree or the Court must grant permission. These documents are a kind of polite lobbying of the Court which, though they sometimes offer new arguments, generally are a declaration of what interests are on which side. The ACLU, the NAACP, the AFL-CIO, and the United States government itself have been among the leading sources of such briefs.

amicus curiae →

These briefs are not the only source of influence on the justices' views. Leading legal periodicals, such as the *Yale Law Journal* and the *Harvard Law Review,* are frequently consulted and cited in decisions, so that the outside world of lawyers and law professors can help shape, or at least supply arguments for, the justices' conclusions.

also ←

4.

order of voting

The justices retire to their conference room every Friday, where in complete secrecy they debate the cases they have heard. The chief justice speaks first, followed by the other justices in order of seniority. After the arguments they vote, traditionally in reverse order of seniority. In this process an able chief justice can exercise considerable influence— in guiding or limiting debate, in setting forth the issues, and in handling sometimes temperamental personalities. In deciding a case, a majority of the justices must be in agreement: if there is a tie, the lower-court decision is left standing. (There can be a tie among the nine justices if one is ill or disqualifies himself or herself because of prior involvement in the case.)

5.

① ②
③

④

Though the vote is what counts, by tradition the Court usually issues a written decision, the **Opinion of the Court.** Sometimes this opinion is brief and unsigned (called a per curiam opinion); sometimes it is quite long and signed by the justices agreeing with it. If the chief justice is in the majority, he will either write the opinion or assign it to a justice who agrees with him. If he is in the minority, the senior justice on the winning side will decide who writes the Court's opinion. There are four kinds of signed opinions: unanimous, *majority* (the majority opinion of the Court when it is divided), **concurring** (an opinion by one or more justices who agree with the majority's conclusion but for different reasons that they wish to express), and **dissenting** (the opinion of one or more justices on the losing side).

From: James Q. Wilson, "The Supreme Court in Action," *American Government,* brief version, 5th ed. (Lexington, MA: D. C. Heath, 2000), pp. 298–300.

🔖 THINKING ABOUT YOUR READING AND WRITING

ACTIVITY N: Evaluating Notations

Which of the three examples do you think has the most effective notations? Why?

_____

_____

_____

_____

You may have noticed some of the following about each example:

> **Example 1:** Very little has been marked. Only single words and short phrases have been underlined, and they have little relationship to one another. The meaning of marginal notes is unclear.

> **Example 2:** A great deal has been underlined. It is hard to distinguish between important ideas and details.

> **Example 3:** Symbols have been used. Technical terms have been circled. Main ideas have been underlined, and related details are numbered. This is the most effectively marked page. This page is useful for study purposes because the important ideas and technical vocabulary stand out from the rest. The reader will not have to reread the entire page to get the most from it.

There are a few guidelines to follow when you are deciding what to mark on textbook pages. These guidelines also apply to any other reading materials that you will later need to reread and study. These guidelines incorporate principles of good textbook reading and good note-taking from lectures and textbooks. At this point, they should sound very familiar to you:

> 1. *Make predictions about chapter content before and while you read the chapter.* You will then know, at the outset, the most important concepts to be discussed. You may want to review the process for predictions and previewing discussed in Chapters 2 through 5. As you preview, be sure that you analyze the introductory and concluding paragraphs, headings, and subheadings, as well as graphics and questions that may appear at the end of the chapter.

2. *Read sections of information before you do any marking.* It is surprising how many students think that if they have highlighted something they've read, they will remember it. The mere act of highlighting does not ensure memorization. Some students' textbooks are filled with high-lighted page after highlighted page. It is clear that little reflection actually went into deciding what to mark since all of it was considered important. The three-step process for highlighting or underlining is to:

Read with your marker or pen down.

Think which of the many ideas are the most important.

Mark the ideas you selected as important.

3. *Develop a marking system.* Students use a variety of these, but features of the most popular ones include:

Double underlining—for main ideas

Double vertical lines—for very long main ideas

Single underlining—for important details

Arrows—to show connections

Marginal notes—for personal comments on an idea (if these are very long, you may want to write them on an adhesive note and attach this to your page)

Question marks—to indicate uncertainty

Brackets or circling—to note important terms

Numbers—to note a sequence or a listing of details related to a main idea

4. *Review your notated pages regularly.* Treat your marked textbook pages as you would your notes from lectures and texts. Review them periodically so that you can easily recall the material when you prepare for tests and class discussion.

ACTIVITY O: Underlining and Marking Textbooks

Select two or three pages of a reading assignment that interests you. Mark the material, following those guidelines described that you believe will be most helpful to you. On another sheet of paper, indicate which guidelines you followed.

WORKING TOGETHER

Review your notations with a partner. See whether your partner can quickly spot the important information on the page. Does your partner have any additional suggestions for making your notations?

▶ *Chapter Summary*

Based on your reading of this chapter, list at least five points that were made that you believe will help you with future academic assignments.

1. _____

_____

_____

2. _____

_____

_____

3. _____

_____

_____

4. _____

_____

_____

5. _____

_____

_____

_____

▶ Extended Application

Now that you have worked with the strategies necessary for active listening and note-taking, you can practice applying them to other academic situations. Choose (or your instructor may choose) a reading selection from Part 2 of this text, or another reading selection, or a classroom listening experience that is typical in a college setting. Use this selection or lecture to practice:

* Using active and positive listening
* Creating a set of usable notes
* Creating a graphic from lecture or text notes
* Using your notes effectively
* Underlining and marking textbooks

Decide on the practice strategies you will use. Apply them to your selection. Then, in a few paragraphs, write a description of what you did and how the strategies you used worked for you.

Name of material used: _____

Page numbers: _____

Your description: _____

CHAPTER TEN

Assessing Your New Knowledge

CONGRATULATIONS! YOU HAVE NOW PRACTICED using all the major reading and study strategies necessary for meeting many of the literacy challenges you will face at college. It is time to reconsider how you feel about your ability to meet these challenges. You may recall that you completed the following survey when you started to use this textbook. Complete it again, and then you will have an opportunity to analyze your pre- and post study survey results.

SURVEY OF ACADEMIC SELF-ESTEEM

Directions: For each item, circle the number that you feel best describes you as you are now (1 = not true of me at all; 4 = very true of me).

1. I can successfully prepare to take exams.	1	2	3	4
2. I can figure out what will be asked on tests.	1	2	3	4
3. I have successful strategies for taking notes on lectures and reading assignments.	1	2	3	4
4. I know how to preview my textbooks.	1	2	3	4
5. I know how to come prepared for class.	1	2	3	4
6. I know how to mark and underline reading material for review purposes.	1	2	3	4
7. I know how to make predictions when I read.	1	2	3	4
8. I am able to answer questions in a college classroom.	1	2	3	4
9. I am able to read a college textbook with understanding.	1	2	3	4
10. I know when to slow down my reading rate for better comprehension.	1	2	3	4
11. I know how to use context to get the meaning of unknown words in college-level material.	1	2	3	4
12. I have good strategies for thinking critically about things I have read.	1	2	3	4
13. I am able to figure out the main ideas of college-type reading materials (for example, sociology, psychology, science).	1	2	3	4
14. I am able to set purposes for my reading.	1	2	3	4
15. I can read and interpret maps, graphs, and charts.	1	2	3	4
16. I know how to create summaries and visual aids to help me remember what I have read.	1	2	3	4
17. I know how to distinguish between important and unimportant details when I read.	1	2	3	4
18. I am able to participate successfully in a college classroom.	1	2	3	4
19. I am able to ask a professor for help when I have a question.	1	2	3	4
20. I believe I will be admitted to the major of my choice.	1	2	3	4
21. I believe I have a lot of knowledge to share with others.	1	2	3	4
22. I believe I will graduate from college.	1	2	3	4
23. I believe I will have a successful future.	1	2	3	4

Let's analyze the results of this poststudy survey. The following chart shows the category into which different items fall. Place your ratings on the chart. Then respond to the questions in Activity A.

SURVEY ANALYSIS

Category		Question Nos.							
Study Skills		1	2	3	4	6	14	16	
	Your ratings:	___	___	___	___	___	___	___	
Reading Skills		7	9	10	11	12	13	15	17
	Your ratings:	___	___	___	___	___	___	___	___
Participating in College Classrooms		5	8	18	19	21			
	Your ratings:	___	___	___	___	___			
Expecting a Successful Future		20	22	23					
	Your ratings:	___	___	___					

ACTIVITY A: Assessing Your Academic Self-Esteem

1. Based on the information you've obtained from this survey, in which area(s) do you seem particularly strong?

   _____

   _____

   _____

   _____

2. Look at the responses you gave to these areas in Chapter 1. How have you changed?

   _____

_____

_____

_____

_____

3. In a few sentences, describe the academic self-esteem goals you feel you have achieved this term.

_____

_____

_____

_____

_____

4. What are some of the areas of academic literacy you would like to continue to develop?

_____

_____

_____

_____

_____

You should now be able to recognize that you have gained a great deal of knowledge and self-esteem concerning your ability to read and study academic material. You should also realize that these changes would not have occurred if you had not taken responsibility for your learning and had not applied yourself seriously to the material in this text. This is true for any learning situation. It is up to you to decide how much you will get out of it.

Remember: You are in control!

Background Essays for Academic Literacy

Cross-Reference to Handbook for Reading and Study Strategies

You may wish to refer to the Handbook chapters listed here to help you recall strategies for answering particular types of questions.

Type of Question (Part 2)	Related Handbook Chapter
Sentence Rewrite	1
Identifying Topics	3
Identifying Subtopics	3
Recognizing Main Ideas	3
Identifying Important Details	4
Identifying Patterns of Organization	5
Recognizing Author's Purpose	6
Using Context Clues	2
Making Inferences	7
Recognizing Mood and Tone	6
Recognizing Point of View	6
Drawing Conclusions	7
Critical Thinking	6, 7
Interpreting Visual Aids	8

CHAPTER ELEVEN

Psychology
The Science of Mind and Behavior

There are few things more exciting to me . . .
than a psychological reason.

—Henry James
The Art of Fiction (1888)

Derivation: *psych*   —life, soul
                 -ology   —science

Key Concepts for the Study of Psychology

Before you read this list of concepts, think about some issues or topics that you might study if you took courses in psychology. In the space provided, list your ideas.

_____

_____

BEHAVIOR.   The response of an individual, group, or species to its environment. Psychologists study and may try to change the behavior of others.

ENVIRONMENT.   The circumstances, objects, or conditions by which one is surrounded. A psychologist may study behavior within a single environment such as home or school.

MOTIVATION.   The stimulus or influence that causes a person to act. Motivations may be from within the individual (internal) or from an outside source (external). Psychologists try to learn what motivates particular behaviors.

PERCEPTION.   Observation; physical sensation interpreted in the light of experience. Our perceptions help us identify and interpret stimuli obtained from people, objects, or events in our lives. Our perceptions may be influenced by experiences, motives, emotions, attitudes, abilities, and personality.

HYPOTHESIS.   A tentative assumption made in order to draw out and test its logical or empirical consequences. The psychologist may conduct research to find out whether a hypothesis is correct.

Now that you have read this list, what are some additional issues or topics that you might study if you took courses in psychology? In the space provided, list your ideas.

_____

_____

_____

● # SELECTION 1

What Psychology Is

■ THE EDUCATION DIRECTORATE AND
THE OFFICE OF PUBLIC COMMUNICATIONS
OF THE AMERICAN PSYCHOLOGICAL
ASSOCIATION

Preview

In the following selection, you will learn about what psychologists do and the kinds of questions that interest them. You will also learn about some differences between several groups of psychologists. The authors will tell you about the process psychologists use for conducting their research, and you may come to see how the study of psychology can be of value to you in your daily life.

To Think About Before You Read

Imagine that you are a high school senior and you have the opportunity to interview a college freshman who is attending the college you plan to attend. You want to know about the people who are on campus. Prepare a list of five to eight questions you would like to ask this student. Under your list, answer this question: How will knowing this information about the "human factor" on campus help you when you attend the college? Your questions:

1. _____
2. _____
3. _____
4. _____
5. _____

How will knowing this information about the "human factor" on campus help you when you attend the college?

_____

_____

Why people do the things they do is an age-old question. However, psychology—the science concerned with behavior, both human and animal—is only about one hundred twenty-five years old. Despite its youth, it is a broad discipline, essentially spanning subject matter from biology to sociology. Biology studies the structures and functions of living organisms. Sociology examines how groups function in society. Psychologists study two critical relationships: one between brain function and behavior, and one between the environment and behavior. As scientists, psychologists follow scientific methods, using careful observation, experimentation, and analysis. But psychologists also need to be creative in the way they apply scientific findings.

2   Psychologists are frequently innovators, evolving new approaches from established knowledge to meet changing needs of people and societies. They develop theories and test them through their research. As this research yields new information, these findings become part of the body of knowledge that practitioners call on in their work with clients and patients. Psychology is a tremendously varied field. Psychologists conduct both basic and applied research, serve as consultants to communities and organizations, diagnose and treat people, and teach future psychologists and other types of students. They test intelligence and personality. They assess behavioral and mental function and well-being, stepping in to help where appropriate. They study how human beings relate to each other and also to machines, and they work to improve these relationships. And with America undergoing large changes in its population makeup, psychologists bring important knowledge and skills to understanding diverse cultures.

3   Many psychologists work independently. They also team up with other professionals—for example, other scientists, physicians, lawyers, school personnel, computer experts, engineers, policy makers, and managers—to contribute to every area of society. Thus we find them in laboratories, hospitals, courtrooms, schools and universities, community health centers, prisons, and corporate offices.

Psychologists traditionally study both normal and abnormal functioning, and also treat patients with mental and emotional problems. Today, they are increasingly concentrating on behaviors that affect the mental and emotional health and mental processes of healthy human beings. For example, they work with business executives, performers, and athletes to combat stress and improve performance. They advise lawyers on jury selection and collaborate with educators on school reform. They show up immediately following a disaster such as a plane crash or bombing, to help victims and bystanders recover from the trauma, or shock, of the event. They team with law enforcement and public health officials to analyze the causes of such events and prevent their occurrence. Involved in all aspects of our fast-paced world, psychologists must keep up with what's happening all around us. When you're a psychologist, your education never ends.

Psychology is a discipline with a bright future. Among fields requiring a college degree, it is expected to be the third fastest-growing field in America through the year 2005 and to continue to grow steadily for at least another dozen years after that.

Opportunities for work in psychology are expanding in number and scope. The move toward preventing illness, rather than merely diagnosing and treating it, requires people to learn how to make healthy behavior a routine part of living. Indeed, many of the problems facing society today are problems about behavior, for example, drug addiction, poor personal relationships, violence at home and in the street, and the harm we do to our environment. Psychologists contribute solutions to problems through careful collection of data, analysis of data, and development of intervention strategies—in other words, by applying scientific principles, the hallmark of psychology.

7   In addition, an aging America is leading to more research and practice in adapting our homes and workplaces for older people. The promises of the electronic revolution demand more user-friendly technologies and training. More women in the workplace calls for employers to accommodate the needs of families. Psychologists are helping employers to make the changes that are needed. The diversity of America today calls for psychologists to develop and refine therapies to meet the unique needs of different ethnic groups. Furthermore, research advances in learning and memory, and the integration of physical and mental health care, make psychology more exciting than ever.

8   Most psychologists say they love their work. They cite the variety from day to day and the flexibility of their schedules. They are thrilled by the exciting changes taking place in the field, from working with primary care physicians to using computers. Most of all, they are committed to helping people manage the ups and downs of daily life.

9   The study of psychology is also good preparation for many other professions. Many employers are interested in the skills that psychology majors bring to collecting, analyzing, and interpreting data, and their experience with statistics and experimental design.

SOME OF THE SUBFIELDS IN PSYCHOLOGY

Psychologists specialize in a host of different 10 areas within the field and identify themselves by many different labels. A sampling of those focal areas is presented below to give you an idea of the breadth of psychology's content as well as the many different settings in which it is found. Additionally, many psychologists teach psychology in academic institutions from high schools to graduate programs in universities.

    The field of psychology encompasses both 11 *research,* through which we learn fundamental things about human and animal behavior, and *practice,* through which that knowledge is applied in helping to solve human problems. In each of the subfields there are psychologists who work primarily as researchers, others who work primarily as practitioners, and many who do both (scientist-practitioners). Indeed, one of psychology's most unique and important characteristics is its coupling of science and practice, which stimulates continual advancement of both.

    Clinical psychologists assess and treat mental, 12 emotional, and behavioral disorders. These range from short-term crises, such as difficulties resulting from adolescent rebellion, to more severe, chronic conditions such as schizophrenia.

    Some clinical psychologists treat specific 13 problems exclusively, such as phobias or clinical depression. Others focus on specific populations: youngsters, ethnic minority groups, gays and lesbians, and the elderly, for instance.

    Counseling psychologists help people to accom- 14 modate to change or to make changes in their lifestyle. For example, they provide vocational and career assessment and guidance or help someone come to terms with the death of a loved one. They help students adjust to college, and people to stop smoking or overeating. They also consult with physicians on physical problems that have underlying psychological causes.

15   *Developmental psychologists* study the psychological development of the human being that takes place throughout life. Until recently, the primary focus was on childhood and adolescence, the most formative years. But as life expectancy in this country approaches 80 years, developmental psychologists are becoming increasingly interested in aging, especially in researching and developing ways to help elderly people stay as independent as possible.

16   *Health psychologists* are interested in how biological, psychological, and social factors affect health and illness. They identify the kinds of medical treatment people seek and get; how patients handle illness; why some people don't follow medical advice; and the most effective ways to control pain or to change poor health habits. They also develop health care strategies that foster emotional and physical well-being.

17   Psychologists team up with medical personnel in private practice and in hospitals to provide patients with complete health care. They educate medical staff about psychological problems that arise from the pain and stress of illness and about symptoms that may seem to be physical in origin but actually have psychological causes.

18   Health psychologists also investigate issues that affect a large segment of society, and develop and implement programs to deal with these problems. Examples are teenage pregnancy, substance abuse, risky sexual behaviors, smoking, lack of exercise, and poor diet.

19   *Industrial/organizational psychologists* apply psychological principles and research methods to the work place in the interest of improving productivity and the quality of work life. Many serve as human resources specialists, helping organizations with staffing, training, and employee development and management in such areas as strategic planning, quality management, and coping with organizational change.

20   *Rehabilitation psychologists* work with stroke and accident victims, people with mental retardation, and those with developmental disabilities caused by such conditions as cerebral palsy, epilepsy, and autism. They help clients adapt to their situation, frequently working with other health care professionals. They deal with issues of personal adjustment, interpersonal relations, the work world, and pain management. Rehabilitation psychologists have also become more involved in public health programs to prevent disabilities, especially those caused by violence and substance abuse. And they testify in court as expert witnesses about the causes and effects of a disability and a person's rehabilitation needs.

21   *School psychologists* work directly with public and private schools. They assess and counsel students, consult with parents and school staff, and conduct behavioral intervention when appropriate. Some school districts employ psychologists full time.

22   *Sports psychologists* help athletes refine their focus on competition goals, become more motivated, and learn to deal with the anxiety and fear of failure that often accompany competition. The field is growing as sports of all kinds become more and more competitive and attract younger children than ever.

23   What all psychologists have in common is a shared interest in mind and behavior, both human and animal. In their work, they draw on an ever-expanding body of scientific knowledge about how we think, act, and feel, and apply the information to their special areas of expertise. Among psychologists, researchers spend most of their time generating knowledge; practition-

ers apply the knowledge; and some psychologists do both.

PSYCHOLOGISTS CONDUCT RESEARCH

24 Many psychologists conduct research that runs the gamut from studies of basic brain functions to the behavior of complex social organizations. Subjects of such scientific study include animals, human infants, well-functioning and emotionally disturbed people, elderly people, students, workers, and just about every other population one can imagine. Some research takes place in laboratories where the study conditions can be carefully controlled; some is carried out in the field, such as the workplace, the highway, schools, and hospitals, where behavior is studied as it occurs naturally.

25 Much of the laboratory research is conducted in universities, government agencies (such as the National Institutes of Health and the armed services), and private research organizations. Whereas most psychological scientists are engaged in the actual planning and conduct of research, some are employed in management or administration—usually after having served as active researchers.

PSYCHOLOGISTS STUDY AND CONTRIBUTE TO THE WORK ENVIRONMENT

26 Anywhere people work, and anything they do while at work, is of interest to psychologists. Psychologists study what makes people effective, satisfied, and motivated in their jobs; what distinguishes good workers or managers from poor ones; and what conditions of work promote high or low productivity, morale, and safety.

27 Some psychologists design programs for recruiting, selecting, placing, and training employees. They evaluate, monitor, and improve performance. They help make changes in the way the organization is set up.

28 Others help design the actual tasks, tools, and environments with which people must deal when doing their jobs. These specialists can also help design the products that organizations turn out and conduct research related to product design. For example, they play a big role in making computer hardware and software more user friendly, which in turn contributes both to operator performance in the workplace and product acceptability in the marketplace.

29 Psychologists with training in mental health and health care also deal with the health and adjustment of individuals in the work setting. They work with employee assistance plans that provide help with drug or alcohol addiction problems, depression and other disorders; they also foster healthy behavior.

PSYCHOLOGISTS HELP PEOPLE LEARN

30 Psychologists provide a number of services—both direct and indirect—to children, youth, and families in schools at all levels, from nursery school through college. Many focus on improving the effectiveness of teaching and student learning, frequently by studying motivation and cognitive processes in the classroom.

31 School psychologists also provide counseling and crisis intervention services. They help students with learning or behavior problems, learning disabilities, and cognitive deficits. They work with students in schools to prevent violence and other disruptive behaviors. They also serve on interdisciplinary teams that develop individual educational plans for students with

special needs. Psychologists work within specialty areas of learning, too, such as the arts and sports.

PSYCHOLOGISTS PROMOTE PHYSICAL AND MENTAL HEALTH

32 Psychologists as health providers span a large and diverse spectrum of subfields. Today, many psychologists work alone, with patients and clients coming to the psychologist's office.

33 Increasingly, however, psychologists in independent practice are contracting on either a part-time or a full-time basis with organizations to provide a wide range of services. For example, a psychologist can join a health practice and work with a team of other health care providers, such as physicians, nutritionists, physiotherapists, and social workers to prevent or treat illness. This team approach, which is likely to become more common in the future, frequently includes efforts to change unhealthy behaviors and ensure that patients follow the recommended treatment. The team also helps patients cope with stress.

34 Psychologists also instruct students who are training to become health care professionals, such as physicians and nurses, about the psychological factors involved in illness. And they advise health care providers already in practice about the psychological bases of much illness so that symptoms that are psychological in origin can be better diagnosed and treated.

35 Psychologists involved in health care teams typically work in hospitals, medical schools, outpatient clinics, nursing homes, pain clinics, rehabilitation facilities, and community health and mental health centers.

PSYCHOLOGISTS WORK IN THE COMMUNITY

36 Work in the community draws a wide range of psychologists. They advise our human services, court, prison, and youth services systems. They also design programs for Boys' and Girls' Clubs, Ys, and community centers.

37 Some psychologists working in the community study the behavior of adult and juvenile law offenders and develop methods of modifying their behavior. They diagnose and counsel youthful offenders to bring about important behavior changes that keep these offenders out of prison. They provide counseling services within jails or other correctional facilities so that inmates can return to society with better coping skills. They also work in the legal system.

38 Psychology graduates are generally pleased with the way what they studied in school helped prepare them for both life and work. A woman who opened her own business shortly after earning a baccalaureate in psychology explains, "After all, psychology is the business of life." Psychology graduates continue to be excited by the changes taking place in the field that relate to what they are now doing.

Evaluation of the Article
Difficulty Rating   □ 1 □ 2 □ 3 □ 4 □ 5
(1 = easy; 5 = difficult)

What reading difficulties did you encounter? _____

_____

How did you handle these difficulties? _____

_____

Comprehension of the Discipline

1. Which of the following describes the major interest of psychologists?
   a. Methods for storing data
   b. The origins of the universe
   c. The growth and development of plants
   d. Causes and changes in human and animal behavior

2. Which of the following situations would a psychologist be most likely to study?
   a. A comparison of the length of time it would take two individuals to reach San Diego, California, one riding a bicycle and one riding a jeep
   b. An analysis of how identical twins, separated at birth by adoption, are different from or similar to each other as adults
   c. A critical review of the most notable books in the "humor" section of a public library
   d. The effectiveness of one method of pollution control in the auto industry compared with another

3. Identify each of the following statements as either true (T) or false (F) based on the information given in this article. Be prepared to justify your answers.
   _____ a. A knowledge of psychology is useful only for "sick" people.
   _____ b. Scientific methods are used by psychologists.
   _____ c. The work of psychology benefits, primarily, those who are emotionally disturbed.

___T___ d. Psychologists do not concern themselves with the physical environment.

___F___ e. Psychologists use primarily subjective interpretations to make their conclusions about human behavior.

___T___ f. All psychologists use the same questions to study human behavior.

___F___ g. The methods psychologists use for research are similar to those used by other scientists.

___F___ h. Psychology is useful for predicting human behavior.

4. Predictions that psychologists make are considered *probability statements*. Why do you think they are given this name?

Because it is a probability and not a fact

5. Is the heading "Psychologists Promote Physical and Mental Health" appropriate for the discussion that follows it? Give your opinion in the following space.

Yes because that's what the topic discusses.

6. How do the authors feel about the study of psychology? What evidence can you cite to support your answer?

7. What is some new information you've learned about the work of psychologists from reading this article?

That phycologist work with humans and animals

Critical Thinking: Reaction and Discussion

1. With a small group, do the following:

   Compare with your group the interview questions you developed before you read this selection that were intended for a student on a campus you might visit. Did you all want to know the same things about the people on campus? Discuss with your group why you might have had the same or different questions. Prepare a final list of 7–8 questions that would give you good insight into the "human factor" on campus.

2. Some people think that seeing a psychologist to discuss personal problems is a sign of weakness. Do you agree? In an essay of at least 250 words, discuss your point of view on this issue.

3. Review the psychology section of your college's catalog, and write a response to each of the following questions:

   a. What courses in psychology are offered to undergraduates?

   b. What courses listed under psychology are you surprised to see? What is surprising about this?

   c. How do the courses reflect the interdisciplinary nature of this field?

   d. What psychology courses sound interesting to you?

USING TECHNOLOGY FOR FURTHER UNDERSTANDING

Look up the word *psychology* on the World Wide Web, using several different search engines.

1. What are some of the differences you find in the sources and types of sources each engine provides?

2. What do you notice about the various fields related to psychology that are not mentioned in this article?

3. What else do you find that interests you?

Guidelines for Reading Psychology

Much of the writing in psychology is research based. That is, many of the articles from psychology that you will read are reports of research that has been conducted. To read this type of material successfully, you should:

❋   Look for the organizational structure of the material.

1. A statement about some feature of human behavior will often begin the article. For example, a psychologist might write, "Children who come from homes where there is an alcoholic parent are likely to have periods of depression and to suffer from low self-esteem." This statement states a point of view for which the author will most likely give evidence.

2. Reports of research done by other psychologists might be cited, or named, to support this writer's viewpoint. You will be given a summary of the supporting research, and you will be told its source in a citation. The citation might be written as follows: (Stern, 1987). This tells you the name of the researcher and when the research was published. A more complete reference may appear at the end of the reading selection. Evidence to support the idea that children of alcoholic parents are depressed or have low self-esteem, for instance, might include results of interviews a psychologist has conducted with such children or results of questionnaires a researcher has given to them.

3. The author might next provide a detailed description of his or her own research. The author may have looked at a population that was different from those studied by others, may have used different methods of obtaining information, or may have found different results.

4. Conclusions are drawn that are based on findings of the author's research. An author's own study, for instance, may find that children of alcoholic parents have developed sophisticated survival skills.

5. The author makes logical recommendations based on the conclusions. The author might suggest, for instance, that teachers should receive more education on indicators of children growing up in alcoholic homes.

❋ Look for signals to the various parts of the article. Subtitles are frequently used to separate hypotheses, related research, methods used in the present study, findings, conclusions, and recommendations. Use these divisions to help you follow the discussion.

❋ Identify the author's perspective. There are controversies in psychology, including different "schools of thought" about how people come to be what they are and how behavior can be changed. These differences are important to know because an author's perspective, or theoretical orientation, will influence the approach to the topic that is taken, including what research is cited and what methods for changing behavior are suggested.

❋ Note the scope of the materials you have been assigned to read. The range of topics in the field of psychology is enormous. Whole texts have been written on what appear to be narrow topics, such as a single emotional disorder like depression, perception, the psychology of language, and learning processes. Introductory psychology courses, however, usually cover many topics.

* Give attention to the technical vocabulary. As in any field, psychology has its own technical vocabulary, words that have specific meanings in the study of psychology. These need your careful attention.

Keep these guidelines in mind as you read the remaining articles from the field of psychology.

● # SELECTION 2

Understanding the Terrorist Mind-Set

■ RANDY BORUM

Preview

Have you ever watched one of those TV crime shows where a psychologist, part of a crime investigation team, tries to develop a psychological profile of the criminal? The psychologist's work helps the team understand the criminal, anticipate future behaviors, and track him or her down. In this article, the author offers his view of what we should consider when we are trying to understand the behavior of terrorists.

To Think About Before You Read

Here is an Anticipation/Reaction Guide that you should complete now, before you read this selection. You will complete it again after your reading. Think about each statement and indicate whether you agree or disagree with it. Then write one or two sentences that explain your reason for your opinion.

ANTICIPATION/REACTION GUIDE
1. Even before the bombing of the World Trade Center on September 11, 2001, most Americans were deeply afraid that terrorism would be committed on American soil.

   Before reading:

   _____ Agree _____ Disagree

   Reasons for agreeing or disagreeing with this idea: _____

   _____

   _____

   After reading:

   _____ Agree _____ Disagree

Reasons for agreeing or disagreeing with this idea: _____

_____

_____

2. Most terrorist groups use the same methods to develop extremist ideas that justify acts of violence.

   Before reading:

   _____ Agree _____ Disagree

   Reasons for agreeing or disagreeing with this idea: _____

   _____

   _____

   After reading:

   _____ Agree _____ Disagree

   Reasons for agreeing or disagreeing with this idea: _____

   _____

   _____

3. Terrorists often commit suicide bombings because they believe that after the bombing their lives will be meaningless.

   Before reading:

   _____ Agree _____ Disagree

   Reasons for agreeing or disagreeing with this idea: _____

   _____

   _____

   After reading:

   _____ Agree _____ Disagree

Reasons for agreeing or disagreeing with this idea:_____

_____

_____

4. Some terrorists are actually just criminals just looking for a cause.

   Before reading:

   _____ Agree _____ Disagree

   Reasons for agreeing or disagreeing with this idea:_____

   _____

   _____

   After reading:

   _____ Agree _____ Disagree

   Reasons for agreeing or disagreeing with this idea:_____

   _____

   _____

5. Law enforcement has found the psychological profiles of terrorists all over the world to be quite similar.

   Before reading:

   _____ Agree _____ Disagree

   Reasons for agreeing or disagreeing with this idea:_____

   _____

   _____

   After reading:

   _____ Agree _____ Disagree

Reasons for agreeing or disagreeing with this idea: _____

_____

_____

Terms to Know Before You Read

Caliphate (17) A political group that originally formed under Muhammad

While nothing is easier than to denounce the evildoer, nothing is more difficult than to understand him.

—DOSTOEVSKY

The terrorist attacks on America on September 11, 2001, shocked millions who perhaps before did not realize there were people in the world that would take such violent actions, even those resulting in their own deaths, against innocent civilians. It dismayed and puzzled them that such individuals could hate Americans with such fervor that they would commit these large-scale acts of lethal aggression.

2   After the attacks, many Americans saw terrorism as a real hazard for the first time. However, extremist ideology and its use to justify violence are not at all new. Although the use of the term terrorism did not emerge until the late 18th century (identified with the French government's "Reign of Terror," the idea of terrorizing civilians to further a particular political, social, or religious cause has existed for centuries.

3   As professionals in the law enforcement and intelligence communities increasingly direct their energies and resources to countering and preventing this type of extreme violence, they are working to acquire new knowledge and skills. In learning about terrorism, they not only should consider the specific ideology of those who commit or advocate acts of terrorism but also gain an understanding of the process of how these ideas or doctrines develop, as well as the various factors that influence the behavior of extremist groups and individuals.

4   An investigator might reasonably wonder why such an understanding is important. The answer lies in the old military adage "know your enemy." In one of the many translations of The Art of War, Sun Tzu, a well-known Chinese general, is quoted as saying, "Know your enemy and know yourself; in a hundred battles you will never be in peril."

CONSIDERING IDEOLOGICAL ORIGINS

5   There likely is no universal method in developing extremist ideas that justifies terroristic acts of violence. However, four observable stages appear to frame a process of ideological development

common to many individuals and groups of diverse ideological backgrounds. This four-stage process—a model designed as a heuristic (trial and error) to aid investigators and intelligence analysts in assessing the behaviors, experiences, and activities of a group or individual associated with extremist ideas—begins by framing some unsatisfying event or condition as being unjust, blaming the injustice on a target policy, person, or nation, and then vilifying, often demonizing, the responsible party to facilitate justification for aggression.

6   To begin with, an extremist individual or group identifies some type of undesirable event or condition ("it's not right"). This could be, for example, economic (e.g., poverty, unemployment, poor living conditions) or social (e.g., government-imposed restrictions on individual freedoms, lack of order or morality). While the nature of the condition may vary, those involved perceive the experience as "things are not as they should be." That is, "it's not right."

7   Next, they frame the undesirable condition as an "injustice"; that is, it does not apply to everyone ("it's not fair"). For example, members of a police bargaining unit may feel that their low pay scale is "not right"; however, when they learn that other, perhaps less skilled, city workers are making more money, they also consider the circumstance "unfair." In this regard, some use the United States as a comparison point to create a sense of injustice about economic deprivation; this holds true for some people in Middle Eastern countries who see the United States as a caricature of affluence and wasteful excess. For those who are deprived, this facilitates feelings of resentment and injustice.

8   Then, because injustice generally results from transgressive (wrongful) behavior, extremists hold a person or group responsible ("it's your fault"), identifying a potential target. For example, racially biased groups in the United States often use this tactic in directing anger toward minority groups. Members of these groups seek out young white men whose families are poor. They then point to examples of minorities receiving economic assistance or preferences in employment as the reason the white family is suffering.

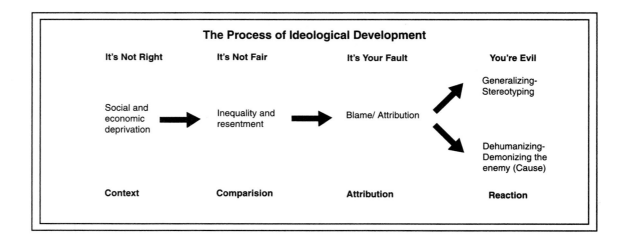

The Process of Ideological Development

It's Not Right	It's Not Fair	It's Your Fault	You're Evil
Social and economic deprivation	Inequality and resentment	Blame/ Attribution	Generalizing-Stereotyping / Dehumanizing-Demonizing the enemy (Cause)
Context	**Comparision**	**Attribution**	**Reaction**

9   Last, they deem the person or group responsible for the injustice as "bad" ("you're evil"); after all, good people would not intentionally inflict adverse conditions on others. This ascription has three effects that help facilitate violence. First, aggression becomes more justifiable when aimed against "bad" people, particularly those who intentionally cause harm to others. Second, extremists describe the responsible party as "evil"; dehumanizing a target in this regard further facilitates aggression. Third, those suffering adverse conditions at the hands of others do not see themselves as "bad" or "evil"; this further identifies the responsible person or group as different from those affected and, thus, makes justifying aggression even easier.

10   When looking at the behaviors of emerging extremists in this way, investigators may better identify persons who represent desirable candidates for recruitment ("it's not fair"), possible sites of indoctrination ("it's not right," and "it's your fault"), and extremists or groups that may use violent tactics ("you're evil"). The operational objective for this analysis and increased understanding is not to sympathize with or excuse terrorism but to comprehend and, thereby, prevent acts of terrorism. Thus, "the challenge for the analyst is to learn why the terrorists are doing what they're doing and how deep it runs, then to look at the moral side and explain why we can't approve of the politics of terrorism even when the motives of some involved are comprehensible."

UNDERSTANDING MOTIVE

11 Fully "knowing one's enemy," specifically, understanding, anticipating, and forecasting another's behavior, demands not only an ideological understanding but a behavioral one as well. Gaining insight as to how someone may resolve a particular dilemma or handle a given situation requires a consideration of the person's entire perspective as influenced not only by their values and beliefs but by other factors, such as the information they have been exposed to, their assumptions, and their life experiences—in short, how they view the world. All people operate on their own internal "map" of reality, not reality itself. This is a mental-behavioral phenomenon that psychologists refer to as "social cognition." If people understand their opponents' "maps," it becomes easier to understand and to anticipate their actions.

12   A good example of how this principle might apply involves considering the common misunderstanding of the tactic of "suicide bombings" used by Islamic extremists. The use of the term *suicide* to characterize these attacks reflects an outsider's view. Those who commit or encourage these attacks do not associate these acts with suicide. Instead, they consider them heroic acts of martyrdom. What is the difference? The motive, thoughts, feelings, responses of others, and preincident behaviors likely will differ for an act of suicide and an act of martyrdom.

13   People usually associate suicide with hopelessness and depression. The desire to end intense and unbearable psychological pain typically motivates the actor to commit such an act. Others who care for the actor typically view suicide as an undesirable outcome. Family and loved ones attempt to discourage the behavior and often struggle with feelings of shame if suicide does occur.

14   By contrast, people typically associate martyrdom with hopefulness about afterlife rewards in paradise and feelings of heroic sacrifice. The desire to further the cause of Islam and to answer the highest calling in that religion motivates the actor. Others who care for the actor see the pending act as heroic. Family and loved

ones typically support the behavior, and, if the event occurs, the family is honored. Not only does the family of a martyr gain forgiveness of their sins in the afterlife but the supporting community often cares for them socially and financially. If investigators consider these attacks acts of suicide, the result could involve erroneous assumptions about how to anticipate the behavior and misguided ideas about how best to prevent it.

ATTRIBUTING IDEOLOGY AS THE SOLE MOTIVE

15 Another investigative issue related to motive is the often-presumed role of ideology as the sole cause for a particular violent act of extremism. Generally, when someone or some group that supports a radical idea commits such an act, the ideology is assumed to be the motive. In some cases, this attribution may be overly simplistic. In others, it simply may be wrong.

16 Some violent people, predisposed to criminality or aggressive behavior, simply use a particular cause or ideology to justify their acts. In the scheme of classifying terrorists as criminals, crazies, and crusaders, these are the criminals. Threat assessment experts have referred to these individuals as murderers in search of a cause.

17 Others truly do believe in extreme ideas, but the motive for a given act or series of acts may be broader. For example, in some Islamic fundamentalist movements, there is significant struggle for power that mixes with the religious ideas; specifically, conflicts exist over establishing the Caliphate that will unite dar al Islam. In this regard, an Islamic fundamentalist leader may wish to support Islam and to defeat those

who oppose the kingdom of Allah on earth, but his actions also may insert him in the Caliphate power struggle. From the perspective of strategic intelligence, it would prove inaccurate to see only the holy warrior and to miss the influence that the dynamics of this religious power struggle might have on, for example, decisions to act, target selection, and relationships between key figures or groups. Stated simply, the ideology may be a factor, but not necessarily the factor in determining motive.

CONCLUSION

18 Professionals in the law enforcement and intelligence communities would do well to gain an understanding of how extremist ideas develop. By using a framework to organize behavioral information, counterterrorist analytic and threat assessments can become more accurate and more sophisticated.

19 Also, it is important to understand that analyzing counterterrorist intelligence requires an understanding of behavior, not just ideology. Investigators and analysts who must attempt to understand and anticipate how a person will act in a given situation should seek to understand that individual's "map," or perception, of the situation. Ideology may be a part of that, but other important dynamics and behavioral factors may contribute as well.

20 Extremist ideology is not at all new, although many Americans did not give the subject of terrorism proper attention until September 11, 2001. Those facing the task of safeguarding this nation and its interests, particularly important in this day and age, will do so most effectively when armed with a thorough understanding of terrorist ideology and behavior.

Evaluation of the Article

Difficulty Rating □ 1 □ 2 □ 3 □ 4 □ 5
(1 = easy; 5 = difficult)

What reading difficulties did you encounter? _____

_____

How did you handle these difficulties? _____

_____

Postreading Comprehension Development

Sentence Rewrite

To check your understanding of some of the key concepts of this essay, rewrite each of the following sentences in your own words, keeping the original idea. (See Chapter 1.)

1. . . . extremist ideology and its use to justify violence are not at all new. (2)

   _____

   _____

2. All people operate on their own internal "map" of reality, not reality itself. (11)

   _____

   _____

3. Some violent people, predisposed to criminality or aggressive behavior, simply use a particular cause or ideology to justify their acts. (16)

   _____

   _____

Author's Main Idea

(See Chapter 3.)

1. Using the following starter sentence, state the author's main idea:
The author wants me to understand that:

_____

_____

2. The author's purpose for writing this article is most clearly stated in
paragraph:

 a. 1

 b. 2

 c. 3

 d. 4

3. How clearly related is the title of the article to the main idea?

_____

_____

4. What title would have been equally, or more, appropriate?

_____

5. How does paragraph 4 contribute to your understanding of the
author's purpose for writing this article?

_____

_____

6. How does paragraph 11 relate to the main idea of this selection?

_____

_____

7. In paragraph 17, the author remarks, *"Stated simply, the ideology may
be a factor, but not necessarily the factor in determining motive."* How
does this idea contribute to the author's purpose for writing this article? Write your opinion on the lines that follow.

_____

_____

Inferences, Metaphors, and Vocabulary in Context
(See Chapters 2, 6, and 7.)

1. The audience for whom this article is written is:

   a. the general public.

   b. terrorists.

   c. the federal government.

   d. law enforcement officials.

2. The purpose of paragraph 5 is:

   a. to explain a universal method.

   b. to define a four-stage process.

   c. to prepare the reader for learning about a four-stage process.

   d. to let terrorists know that their extremist ideas are no mystery to anyone.

3. What is meant by the phrase "ideological development" as it is used in paragraph 5?

   _____

   _____

4. What is meant by the phrase "a caricature of affluence and wasteful excess" as it is used in paragraph 7?

   _____

   _____

5. After reading paragraphs 6 through 9, what is your understanding of how each of the following contributes to acts of terrorism? Write your responses on the lines provided.

   a. sense of injustice

   _____

   _____

b. groups targeted for terrorist acts of aggression

_____

_____

c. justifiable aggression

_____

_____

_____

6. What is meant by the phrase "operational objective" as it is used in paragraph 10?

_____

_____

_____

7. Which of the following does the author imply in paragraphs 12–14? Be prepared to justify your answer.
   a. People do not understand motives for suicide bombings.
   b. People need to know that suicide bombers feel hopeless.
   c. Families of suicide bombers try to discourage the terrorism.
   d. Acts of martyrdom and suicide are very similar in meaning.

8. One assumption we can make from the *Conclusion* section of this article is that
   a. The author is confident that law enforcement officials will pay closer attention to the mind-set of terrorists since 9/11.
   b. There are better ways to understand terrorists than the methods currently being used by law enforcement officials.
   c. It is beyond our capacity to understand terrorist behavior.
   d. It is best to wait until after a terrorist act has been committed before we try to understand terrorist behavior.

9. Using only the context and your knowledge of word structure, define each of the following words. Do not use a dictionary.
   a. dismayed (1)   _____
   b. fervor (1)   _____
   c. ideology (2)   _____
   d. heuristic (5)   _____

      e. vilifying (5)   _____

      f. ascription (9)   _____

      g. indoctrination (10)   _____

      h. erroneous (14)   _____

      i. predisposed (16)   _____

Recalling Details

(See Chapters 4 and 5.)

1. Which of the following are factual statements in this article? Which are opinions? Use (F) or (O) for your response. For those you label opinion, write any support for the opinion that is given in this article.

      _____ a. After the attacks, many Americans saw terrorism as a real hazard for the first time.

      _____ b. There is likely no universal method in developing extremist ideas that justifies terroristic acts of violence.

      _____ c. An investigator might reasonably wonder why such an understanding is important.

      _____ d. This is a mental-behavioral phenomenon that psychologists refer to as "social cognition."

      _____ e. Threat assessment experts have referred to these individuals as murderers in search of a cause.

      _____ f. . . . specifically, conflicts exist over establishing the Caliphate that will unite dar al Islam.

2. Indicate whether each of the following items is a major (MAJ) or minor (MIN) detail of this article. Be prepared to justify your answers.

      _____ a. After the attacks, many Americans saw terrorism as a real hazard for the first time.

      _____ b. . . . the use of the term terrorism did not emerge until the late 18th century.

      _____ c. An investigator might reasonably wonder why such an understanding is important.

      _____ d. All people operate on their own internal "map" of reality, not reality itself.

      _____ e. Others who care for the actor see the pending act as heroic.

_____ f. Another investigative issue related to motive is the often-presumed role of ideology as the sole cause for a particular violent act of extremism.

_____ g. Threat assessment experts have referred to these individuals as murderers in search of a cause.

Critical Thinking: Reaction and Discussion

1. Refer back to the Anticipation/Reaction Guide you completed in the Before You Read section of this article. Complete the After Reading section for each question. Where your answer changes, add the information that resulted in this change. Where your answer remains the same, add any new support you can find for your original answer.

2. In an essay of at least 250 words, respond to the following questions: *How has the threat of terrorism changed us as a nation and as individuals? And how should it change us in the future?*

3. On October 1, 2005, Secretary Michael Chertoff, U.S. Department of Homeland Security, said, "If we are going to arrive at a day when terrorism no longer casts a dark cloud over the civilized world, we have to be prepared to advance international cooperation to hitherto unseen heights."

   With a group, discuss this comment and then create a five-point plan that describes how, if you were President of the United States, you would *advance international cooperation to hitherto unseen heights.* For each point, explain why it would be important and include specific steps describing how the point would be implemented.

USING TECHNOLOGY FOR FURTHER UNDERSTANDING

1. Identify a country that interests you and has recently experienced terrorism, such as Great Britain, the Philippines, Japan, or Jordan. On the Internet, locate information about how this country has responded to the terrorism and comment on your view of the effectiveness of this response.

2. Use the Internet to learn how civil uprisings differ from terrorist attacks. Using what you learn, create a Venn diagram to show similarities and differences between these two types of events.

● SELECTION 3

The "Perfect" Trap

■ MONICA RAMIREZ BASCO

Preview

Perfectionism is one personality trait studied by psychologists. What is it? How does it affect those who have it? And what is its impact on others? Find out by reading the following article, written by a psychologist.

To Think About Before You Read

Honestly rate the level at which you believe each of these statements, with 100% indicating complete agreement and 0% indicating that you do not believe it at all.

_____ I must be perfect or I will be rejected.

_____ If I make a mistake, it will be horrible.

_____ If I do it perfectly, then I will be accepted.

_____ I must be perfect or I will be embarrassed.

_____ If I make a mistake, I will be humiliated.

_____ When I get it right, I will finally accept myself.

_____ When I achieve perfection, I will find inner peace.

_____ If I do it perfectly, then it will be rewarded.

_____ If others do not approve of me, then I am not okay.

_____ If I make a mistake, then I am worthless.

_____ I'm not good enough. I must keep trying.

_____ I must be perfect or others will disapprove of me.

_____ If I do it perfectly, then everything will work out right.

_____ I'll never be good enough.

_____ If others approve of me, then I must be OK.

_____ If I do it perfectly, then everyone will notice.

_____ I must be perfect or I will fail.

_____ Things should be done the right way.

_____ There is a right way and a wrong way to do things.

_____ It is possible to do things perfectly.

What do you think your responses tell you about yourself?

Term to Know Before You Read

existential (29) abstract; intangible

If you're always worried that no matter how hard you try it is never good enough, or you're constantly disappointed in the people you live or work with, you may be caught in a sneaky snare. Here's how to break free.

2 Susan, an interior designer, had been working frantically for the last month trying to get her end-of-the-year books in order, keep the business running, and plan a New Year's Eve party for her friends and her clients. Susan's home is an advertisement of her talent as a designer, so she wanted to make some changes to the formal dining room before the party that would be particularly impressive. It all came together in time for the party and the evening seemed to be going well, until her assistant, Charles, asked her if Mrs. Beale, who owned a small antique shop and had referred Susan a lot of business, and Mr. Sandoval, a member of the local Chamber of Commerce and a supporter of Susan's, had arrived.

3 Susan felt like her head was about to explode when she realized that she had forgotten to in-

vite them to the party. "Oh, no," she moaned. "How could I be so stupid? What am I going to do? They'll no doubt hear about it from someone and assume I omitted them on purpose. I may as well kiss the business good-bye." Though Charles suggested she might be overreacting a little, Susan spent the rest of the night agonizing over her mistake. She is an inwardly focused perfectionist. Although it can help her in her work, it also hurts her when she is hard on herself and finds error completely unacceptable. Like many people, she worries about what others will think of her and her business. However, in Susan's case her errors lead to humiliation, distress, sleepless nights and withdrawal from others. She has trouble letting go and forgiving herself because, in her mind, it is OK for others to make mistakes, but it is not OK for her to make mistakes.

4 Tom, on the other hand, is an outwardly focused perfectionist. He feels OK about himself, but he is often disappointed in and frustrated with others who seem to always let him down. Quality control is his line of work, but he cannot always turn it off when he leaves the office.

5 Tom drove into his garage to find that there was still a mess on the workbench and floor that his son Tommy had left two days ago. Tom

walked through the door, and said to his wife in an annoyed tone of voice, "I told Tommy to clean up his mess in the garage before I got home." His wife defended their son, saying, "He just got home himself a few minutes ago." "Where is he now?" Tom demanded. "He better not be on the phone." Sure enough, though, Tommy was on the phone and Tom felt himself tensing up and ordering, "Get off the phone and go clean up that mess in the garage like I told you." "Yes, sir," said Tommy, knowing that a lecture was coming.

6   For Tom, it seems like every day there is something new to complain about. Tommy doesn't listen, his wife doesn't take care of things on time, and there is always an excuse. And even when they do their parts it usually isn't good enough, and they don't seem to care. It is so frustrating for Tom sometimes that he does the job himself rather than ask for help, just so he doesn't have to deal with their procrastination and excuses.

7   Tom's type of perfectionism causes him problems in his relationships with others because he is frequently frustrated by their failure to meet his expectations. When he tries to point this out in a gentle way, it still seems to lead to tension, and sometimes to conflict. He has tried to train himself to expect nothing from others, but that strategy doesn't seem to work either.

THE PERSONAL PAIN OF PERFECTIONISTS

8   The reach for perfection can be painful because it is often driven by both a desire to do well and a fear of the consequences of not doing well. This is the double-edged sword of perfectionism.

9   It is a good thing to give the best effort, to go the extra mile, and to take pride in one's per-

formance, whether it is keeping a home looking nice, writing a report, repairing a car, or doing brain surgery. But when despite great efforts you feel as though you keep falling short, never seem to get things just right, never have enough time to do your best, are self-conscious, feel criticized by others, or cannot get others to cooperate in doing the job right the first time, you end up feeling bad.

10   The problem is not in having high standards or in working hard. Perfectionism becomes a problem when it causes emotional wear and tear or when it keeps you from succeeding or from being happy. The emotional consequences of perfectionism include fear of making mistakes, stress from the pressure to perform, and self-consciousness from feeling both self-confidence and self-doubt. It can also include tension, frustration, disappointment, sadness, anger or fear of humiliation. These are common experiences for inwardly focused perfectionists.

11   The emotional stress caused by the pursuit of perfection and the failure to achieve this goal can evolve into more severe psychological difficulties. Perfectionists are more vulnerable to depression when stressful events occur, particularly those that leave them feeling as though they are not good enough. In many ways, perfectionistic beliefs set a person up to be disappointed, given that achieving perfection consistently is impossible. What's more, perfectionists who have a family history of depression and may therefore be more biologically vulnerable to developing the psychological and physical symptoms of major depression may be particularly sensitive to events that stimulate their self-doubt and their fear of rejection or humiliation.

12   The same seems to be true for eating disorders, such as anorexia nervosa and bulimia. Several recent studies have found that even after treatment, where weight was restored in

malnourished and underweight women with anorexia, their perfectionistic beliefs persisted and likely contributed to relapse. Perfectionism also seems to be one of the strongest risk factors for developing an eating disorder.

13   Sometimes the pain of perfectionism is felt in relationships with others. Perfectionists can sometimes put distance between themselves and others unintentionally by being intolerant of others' mistakes or by flaunting perfect behavior or accomplishments in front of those who are aware of being merely average. Although they feel justified in their beliefs about what is right and what is wrong, they still suffer the pain of loneliness. Research suggests that people who have more outwardly focused perfectionism are less likely than inwardly focused perfectionists to suffer from depression or anxiety when they are stressed. However, interpersonal difficulties at home or on the job may be more common.

HOW DID I GET THIS WAY?

14   There is considerable scientific evidence that many personality traits are inherited genetically. Some people are probably born more perfectionistic than others. I saw this in my own children. My oldest son could sit in his high chair, happily playing with a mound of spaghetti, his face covered with sauce. My second son did not like being covered in goo. Instead, he would wipe his face and hands with a napkin as soon as he was old enough to figure out how to do it. As he got a little older, he kept his room cleaner than his brother. When he learned to write, he would erase and rewrite his homework until it was "perfect."

15   Parental influences can influence the direction or shape that perfectionism takes. Many perfectionists, especially inwardly focused perfectionists, grew up with parents who either directly or indirectly communicated that they were not good enough. These were often confusing messages, where praise and criticism were given simultaneously. For example, "That was nice, but I bet you could do better." "Wow, six As and one B on your report card! You need to bring that B up to an A next time." "Your choir performance was lovely, but that sound system is really poor. We could hardly hear you."

16   Unfortunately, with the intention of continuing to motivate their children, these parents kept holding out the emotional carrot: "Just get it right this time and I will approve of you." Some psychological theories suggest over time the child's need to please her parents becomes internalized, so that she no longer needs to please her parents; she now demands perfection from herself.

17   Some perfectionists tell stories of chaotic childhoods where they never seemed to have control over their lives. Marital breakups, relocations, financial crises, illnesses, and other hardships created an environment of instability. One of the ways in which these people got some sense of order in their otherwise disordered lives was to try to fix things over which they had some control, such as keeping their rooms neat and tidy, working exceptionally hard on schoolwork, or attempting to control their younger brothers and sisters. As adults, however, when their lives were no longer in flux, they may have continued to work hard to maintain control.

ARE YOU A PERFECTIONIST?

18   Perfectionists share some common characteristics. They are usually neat in their appearance and are well organized. They seem to push themselves harder than most other people do. They also seem to push others as hard as they push themselves. On the outside, perfectionists

usually appear to be very competent and confident individuals. They are often envied by others because they seem to "have it all together." Sometimes they seem perfect. On the inside they do not feel perfect, nor do they feel like they always have control over their own lives.

19   Let's look at some of these characteristics more closely and how they interfere with personal and professional life. Terry, 34, a divorced working mother of two, is a high achiever with high career ambitions. But she can sometimes get hung up on the details of her work. She is not good with figures, but does not trust her staff enough to use their figures without checking them herself. She gets frustrated with this mundane work and makes mistakes herself and then becomes angry with her subordinates for doing poor work.

20   Perfectionists also tend to think there is a right way and wrong way to do things. When Joe, a retired Marine Corps drill sergeant, takes his boys fishing, they have a routine for preparation, for fishing, and for cleanup. It is time-efficient, neat, organized. The boys think the "fishing ritual" is overdone and they resent having to comply.

21   Expecting people to do their best is one thing. Expecting perfection from others often means setting goals that can be impossible to achieve. Brent, 32 and single, has been looking for Ms. Right for 12 years but cannot seem to find her. He does not have a well-defined set of characteristics in mind. He just has a general impression of an angel, a sex goddess, a confident, independent, yet thoroughly devoted partner. Blond is preferable, but he's not that picky.

22   Perfectionists can have trouble making decisions. They are so worried about making the wrong one that they fail to reach any conclusion. If the person is lucky, someone else will make the decision for them, thereby assuming responsibility for the outcome. More often the decision is made by default. A simple example is not being able to choose whether to file income tax forms on time or apply for an extension. If you wait long enough, the only real alternative is to file for an extension.

23   Along with indecision, perfectionists are sometimes plagued by great difficulty in taking risks, particularly if their personal reputations are on the line. Brent is in a type of job where creativity can be an asset. But coming up with new ideas rather than relying on the tried and true ways of business means making yourself vulnerable to the criticism of others. Brent fears looking like an idiot should an idea he advances fail. And on the occasions when he has gone out on a limb with a new concept he has been overanxious. Brent's perfectionism illustrates several aspects of the way that many perfectionists think about themselves. There can be low self-confidence, fear of humiliation and rejection, and an inability to attribute success to their own efforts.

BREAKING FREE

24   To escape the tyranny of perfectionism, you need to understand and challenge the underlying beliefs that drive you to get things "just right."

25   Each of us has a set of central beliefs about ourselves, other people and the world in general and about the future. We use these beliefs or schemas to interpret the experiences in our life, and they strongly influence our emotional reactions. Schemas can also have influence on our choice of actions.

26   Perfectionists tend to have the beliefs listed in the To Think About Before You Read section that introduced this article. But under every perfectionist schema is a hidden fantasy that some really good thing will come from being

perfect. For example, "If I do it perfectly, then . . . I will finally be accepted. . . . I can finally stop worrying . . . I will get what I have been working toward . . . I can finally relax." The flip side of this schema, also subscribed to by perfectionists, is that "If I make a mistake," there will be a catastrophic outcome ("I will be humiliated. . . . I am a failure . . . I am stupid . . . I am worthless").

27   Changing these schemas means taking notice of the experiences you have that are inconsistent with, contrary to, or otherwise do not fit with them. June, who prides herself on being a "perfect" homemaker and mother, believed with 90% certainty that "If I do it perfectly, I will be rewarded." Yet she does a number of things perfectly that others do not even notice. June would tell herself that there would be a reward from her husband or her children for taking the extra time to iron their clothes perfectly. Her son did not even realize his shirts had been ironed. When Mother's Day came, she got the usual candy and flowers. No special treats or special recognition for her extra efforts.

28   When June begins to notice the inaccuracy of her schema, she begins to reevaluate how she spends her time. She decides that if it makes her feel good, then she will do it. If it is just extra work that no one will notice, then she may skip it. She is certain that there are some things she does, such as iron the bedsheets, which no one really cares about. As a matter of fact, June herself doesn't really care if the sheets are ironed. However, she does like the feel of a freshly ironed pillow cover, so she will continue that chore. June has modified her schema. Now she believes that "If you want a reward, find a quicker and more direct way to get it."

29   If your schema centers around more existential goals, like self-acceptance, fulfillment or inner peace, then you must employ a different strategy. If you believe that getting things just right in your life will lead to acceptance, then you must not be feeling accepted right now. What are the things you would like to change about yourself? What could you do differently that would make you feel better about who you are? If you can figure out what is missing or needs changing, you can focus your energies in that direction.

30   Or you may be motivated to take a different, less absolute, point of view. Instead of "I must have perfection before I can have peace of mind," consider "I need to give myself credit for what I do well, even if it is not perfect." Take inventory of your accomplishments or assets. Perhaps you are withholding approval from yourself. If your schema is that other people's opinions of you is a mirror of your self-worth, you must ask yourself if you know when you have done something well, if you are able to tell the difference between a good performance and a poor performance. If you are capable of evaluating yourself, you do not really need approval from others to feel like you are a valuable worker or a good romantic partner.

31   In general, you must treat your perfectionistic schemas as hypotheses rather than facts. Maybe you are right or maybe you are wrong. Perhaps they apply in some situations, but not in others (e.g., at work, but not at home), or with some people, such as your uptight boss, but not with others, such as your new boyfriend. Rather than stating your schema as a fact, restate it as a suggestion. Gather evidence from your experiences in the past, from your observations from others, or by talking to other people. Do things always happen in a way that your schemas would predict? If not, it is time to try on a new basic belief.

32　One of my patients described the process as taking out her old eight-track tape that played the old negative schemas about herself and replacing it with a new compact disc that played her updated self-view. This takes some practice, but it is well worth the effort.

Evaluation of the Article

Difficulty Rating □ 1 □ 2 □ 3 □ 4 □ 5

(1 = easy; 5 = difficult)

What reading difficulties did you encounter? _____

_____

How did you handle these difficulties? _____

_____

Postreading Comprehension Development

Sentence Rewrite

To check your understanding of some of the key concepts of this essay, rewrite each of the following sentences in your own words, keeping the original idea. (See Chapter 1.)

1. In many ways, perfectionist beliefs set a person up to be disappointed, given that achieving perfection consistently is impossible. (11)

_____

_____

2. These were often confusing messages, where praise and criticism were given simultaneously. (15)

_____

_____

3. Along with indecision, perfectionists are sometimes plagued by great difficulty in taking risks, particularly if their personal reputations are on the line. (23)

_____

_____

Author's Main Idea

(See Chapter 3.)

1. What is the topic of this article?

_____

2. What is the author's focus on this topic?

_____

3. Using the following starter sentence, state the author's main idea:

The author wants me to understand that:

_____

_____

4. The author develops the main idea primarily through:
   a. anecdotes.
   b. research studies.
   c. statistics.
   d. her personal experience
5. The author's main point is most clearly stated in:
   a. paragraph 8.
   b. paragraph 9.
   c. paragraph 10.
   d. paragraph 11.

Inferences, Metaphors, and Vocabulary in Context

(See Chapters 2, 6, 7.)

1. In your own words, explain why the author refers to perfectionism as "a double-edged sword."

   _____

   _____

2. Check each statement with which you think the author would agree. Be prepared to justify your answers.

   _____ a. Inwardly focused perfectionists are likely to feel depressed.

   _____ b. Tom has a job that suits his personality.

   _____ c. It would be fun to go on a trip with a perfectionist.

   _____ d. It is difficult to tell that a perfectionist is having psychological problems.

   _____ e. Perfectionism may be inherited.

   _____ f. Parenting styles can influence the development of perfectionist tendencies.

   _____ g. Perfectionists have unrealistic expectations of the outcomes that result from their behavior.

   _____ h. Perfectionist tendencies cannot be overcome.

3. Using only the context and your knowledge of word structure, define each of the following words. Do not use a dictionary.

   a. snare (1) _____

   b. emitted (3) _____

   c. vulnerable (11, 23) _____

   d. flux (17) _____

   e. mundane (19) _____

   f. schemas (25, 28, 29) _____

   g. inconsistent (27) _____

   h. employ (29) _____

4. Which of the following can you infer from paragraph 14? Be prepared to justify your answer.

   a. Children of the same parents are likely to inherit the same perfectionist tendencies.

b. The author's younger son would eventually exhibit perfectionist tendencies.

c. It is difficult for parents to identify perfectionist tendencies in their children.

d. Children who are not perfectionists are still careful with their homework.

5. As used in paragraph 23, the expression "going out on a limb" means

   a. failing at something.

   b. avoiding something new.

   c. blaming others.

   d. taking a risk.

6. The author's tone throughout most of this essay is

   a. humorous.

   b. argumentative.

   c. informative.

   d. doubtful.

7. Which of the following can you infer from paragraph 12? Be prepared to justify your answer.

   a. It is more difficult for perfectionists to overcome eating disorders than it is for others.

   b. People who have anorexia nervosa will develop perfectionism.

   c. Teenagers are more likely to have anorexia nervosa as a result of perfectionism than any other cause.

   d. People with perfectionist beliefs should not worry that they will develop anorexia or bulimia.

Recalling Details
(See Chapters 4 and 5.)

1. Indicate which of the following are major (MAJ) or minor (MIN) details of this selection. Be prepared to cite evidence for your answers.

   ____ a. Susan's home is an advertisement of her talent as a designer.

   ____ b. Susan is an inwardly focused perfectionist.

   ____ c. Tom's type of perfectionism causes him problems in his relationships with others.

_____ d. Perfectionists are more vulnerable to depression when stressful events occur

_____ e. Some perfectionists tell stories of chaotic childhoods where they never seemed to have control over their lives.

_____ f. Terry, 34, is a high achiever with high career ambitions.

_____ g. Brent, 32 and single, has been looking for Ms. Right for 12 years but cannot seem to find her.

_____ h. Perfectionists can have trouble making decisions.

_____ i. Under every perfectionist schema is a hidden fantasy that some really good thing will come from being perfect.

_____ j. In general, you must treat your perfectionistic schemas as hypotheses rather than facts.

2. The overall pattern of organization used in this essay is:

   a. comparison and contrast.

   b. thesis and proof.

   c. problem and solution.

   d. definition and explanation.

3. What new information about perfectionism did you gain from reading this article?

   _____

   _____

   _____

   _____

Critical Thinking: Reaction and Discussion

1. Review your responses to the questionnaire you took in the Preview section of this article. What do you now think your responses tell you about yourself?

2. Ask a good friend to take this survey to learn whether you have common perfectionist tendencies and/or whether the tendencies either of you have complicates your friendship.

READING

3. With a group, discuss the following question. Prepare to share your responses with your classmates.

   In your view, is perfectionism helpful or harmful to athletes?

 USING TECHNOLOGY FOR FURTHER UNDERSTANDING

Search the World Wide Web for some self-help sites for perfectionists. What types of groups or individuals have created these sites? What advice is given? How useful do you think these sites would be? Explain your answer.

●　SELECTION 4

Television Addiction Is No Mere Metaphor

■ ROBERT KUBEY AND
MIHALY CSIKSZENTMIHALYI

Preview

Do you spend a lot of time watching TV? How is this affecting you? In this article the authors describe several research studies conducted on TV viewing and explain how this form of media might be impacting on our lives.

To Think About Before You Read

1. Indicate whether you agree or disagree with each of the following statements. In the space provided, give your reasons for each of your opinions.

    a. Television viewing can have a harmful effect on memory.
       _____ Agree _____ Disagree

    Your reasons:_____

    _____

    b. TV viewing can be addictive. _____ Agree _____ Disagree

    Your reasons:_____

    _____

    c. Watching a lot of TV can raise energy levels.
       _____ Agree _____ Disagree

    Your reasons:_____

    _____

d. TV helps people feel relaxed._____ Agree_____ Disagree

Your reasons:_____

_____

e. People find that watching a lot of TV is a rewarding experience.
    _____ Agree_____ Disagree

Your reasons:_____

_____

f. People feel guilty if they watch a lot of TV.
    _____ Agree_____ Disagree

Your reasons:_____

_____

g. Watching TV provides more mental stimulation than reading.
    _____ Agree_____ Disagree

Your reasons:_____

_____

h. Most people watch TV longer than they intend to.
    _____ Agree_____ Disagree

Your reasons:_____

_____

2. Check the statement that is true about you and give your reasons in
    the space provided.
    _____ I am addicted to TV.   _____ I am not addicted to TV.

Your reasons:_____

_____

Terms to Know Before You Read

ironic (1, 12) contrary to what was expected or intended

uniquity (2) existence or apparent existence everywhere at the same time

laden (4) weighed down with a load; burdened

per se (5) of, in, or by itself or oneself

dysphoric (10) anxious; depressed; restless

rumination (10) the act of pondering; meditation

Perhaps the most ironic aspect of the struggle for survival is how easily organisms can be harmed by that which they desire. The trout is caught by the fisherman's lure, the mouse by cheese. But at least those creatures have the excuse that bait and cheese look like sustenance. Humans seldom have that consolation. The temptations that can disrupt their lives are often pure indulgences. No one has to drink alcohol, for example. Realizing when a diversion has gotten out of control is one of the great challenges of life.

2 Excessive cravings do not necessarily involve physical substances. Gambling can become compulsive; sex can become obsessive. One activity, however, stands out for its prominence and ubiquity—the world's most popular leisure pastime, television. Most people admit to having a love-hate relationship with it. They complain about the "boob tube" and "couch potatoes," then they settle into their sofas and grab the remote control. Parents commonly fret about their children's viewing (if not their own). Even researchers who study TV for a living marvel at the medium's hold on them personally. Percy Tannenbaum of the University of California at Berkeley has written: "Among life's more embarrassing moments have been countless occasions when I am engaged in conversation in a room while a TV set is on, and I cannot for the life of me stop from periodically glancing over to the screen. This occurs not only during dull conversations but during reasonably interesting ones just as well."

Scientists have been studying the effects of 3 television for decades, generally focusing on whether watching violence on TV correlates with being violent in real life [see "The Effects of Observing Violence," by Leonard Berkowitz, *Scientific American,* February 1964; and "Communication and Social Environment," by George Gerbner, September 1972]. Less attention has been paid to the basic allure of the small screen—the medium, as opposed to the message.

The term "TV addiction" is imprecise and 4 laden with value judgments, but it captures the essence of a very real phenomenon. Psychologists and psychiatrists normally define substance dependence as a disorder characterized by criteria that include spending a great deal of time using the substance; using it more often than one intends; thinking about reducing use or making repeated unsuccessful efforts to reduce use; giving up important social, family or occupational activities to use it; and reporting withdrawal symptoms when one stops using it.

5   All these criteria can apply to people who watch a lot of television. That does not mean that watching television, per se, is problematic. Television can teach and amuse; it can reach aesthetic heights; it can provide much needed distraction and escape. The difficulty arises when people strongly sense that they ought not to watch as much as they do and yet find themselves strangely unable to reduce their viewing. Some knowledge of how the medium exerts its pull may help heavy viewers gain better control over their lives.

A BODY AT REST TENDS TO STAY AT REST

6   The amount of time people spend watching television is astonishing. On average, individuals in the industrialized world devote three hours a day to the pursuit—fully half of their leisure time, and more than on any single activity save work and sleep. At this rate, someone who lives to 75 would spend nine years in front of the tube. To some commentators, this devotion means simply that people enjoy TV and make a conscious decision to watch it. But if that is the whole story, why do so many people experience misgivings about how much they view? In Gallup polls in 1992 and 1999, two out of five adult respondents and seven out of 10 teenagers said they spent too much time watching TV. Other surveys have consistently shown that roughly 10 percent of adults call themselves TV addicts.

7   To study people's reactions to TV, researchers have undertaken laboratory experiments in which they have monitored the brain waves (using an electroencephalograph, or EEG), skin resistance or heart rate of people watching television. To track behavior and emotion in the normal course of life, as opposed to the artificial conditions of the lab, we have used the Experience Sampling Method (ESM). Participants carried a beeper, and we signaled them six to eight times a day, at random, over the period of a week; whenever they heard the beep, they wrote down what they were doing and how they were feeling using a standardized scorecard.

8   As one might expect, people who were watching TV when we beeped them reported feeling relaxed and passive. The EEG studies similarly show less mental stimulation, as measured by alpha brain-wave production, during viewing than during reading.

9   What is more surprising is that the sense of relaxation ends when the set is turned off, but the feelings of passivity and lowered alertness continue. Survey participants commonly reflect that television has somehow absorbed or sucked out their energy, leaving them depleted. They say they have more difficulty concentrating after viewing than before. In contrast, they rarely indicate such difficulty after reading. After playing sports or engaging in hobbies, people report improvements in mood. After watching TV, people's moods are about the same or worse than before.

10   Within moments of sitting or lying down and pushing the "power" button, viewers report feeling more relaxed. Because the relaxation occurs quickly, people are conditioned to associate viewing with rest and lack of tension. The association is positively reinforced because viewers remain relaxed throughout viewing, and it is negatively reinforced via the stress and dysphoric rumination that occurs once the screen goes blank again.

11   Habit-forming drugs work in similar ways. A tranquilizer that leaves the body rapidly is much more likely to cause dependence than one that leaves the body slowly, precisely because the user is more aware that the drug's ef-

fects are wearing off. Similarly, viewers' vague learned sense that they will feel less relaxed if they stop viewing may be a significant factor in not turning the set off. Viewing begets more viewing.

12   Thus, the irony of TV: people watch a great deal longer than they plan to, even though prolonged viewing is less rewarding. In our ESM studies the longer people sat in front of the set, the less satisfaction they said they derived from it. When signaled, heavy viewers (those who consistently watch more than four hours a day) tended to report on their ESM sheets that they enjoy TV less than light viewers did (less than two hours a day). For some, a twinge of unease or guilt that they aren't doing something more productive may also accompany and depreciate the enjoyment of prolonged viewing. Researchers in Japan, the U.K. and the U.S. have found that this guilt occurs much more among middle-class viewers than among less affluent ones.

GRABBING YOUR ATTENTION

13 What is it about TV that has such a hold on us? In part, the attraction seems to spring from our biological "orienting response." First described by Ivan Pavlov in 1927, the orienting response is our instinctive visual or auditory reaction to any sudden or novel stimulus. It is part of our evolutionary heritage, a built-in sensitivity to movement and potential predatory threats. Typical orienting reactions include dilation of the blood vessels to the brain, slowing of the heart, and constriction of blood vessels to major muscle groups. Alpha waves are blocked for a few seconds before returning to their baseline level, which is determined by the general level of mental arousal. The brain focuses its attention on gathering more information while the rest of the body quiets.

14   In 1986 Byron Reeves of Stanford University, Esther Thorsen of the University of Missouri and their colleagues began to study whether the simple formal features of television—cuts, edits, zooms, pans, sudden noises—activate the orienting response, thereby keeping attention on the screen. By watching how brain waves were affected by formal features, the researchers concluded that these stylistic tricks can indeed trigger involuntary responses and "derive their attentional value through the evolutionary significance of detecting movement. . . . It is the form, not the content, of television that is unique."

15 The orienting response may partly explain common viewer remarks such as: "If a television is on, I just can't keep my eyes off it," "I don't want to watch as much as I do, but I can't help it," and "I feel hypnotized when I watch television." In the years since Reeves and Thorson published their pioneering work, researchers have delved deeper. Annie Lang's research team at Indiana University has shown that heart rate decreases for four to six seconds after an orienting stimulus. In ads, action sequences and music videos, formal features frequently come at a rate of one per second, thus activating the orienting response continuously.

16 Lang and her colleagues have also investigated whether formal features affect people's memory of what they have seen. In one of their studies, participants watched a program and then filled out a score sheet. Increasing the frequency of edits—defined here as a change from one camera angle to another in the same visual scene—improved memory recognition, presumably because it focused attention on the screen. Increasing the frequency of cuts—changes to a new visual scene—had a similar effect but only up to a point. If the number of cuts exceeded 10 in two minutes, recognition dropped off sharply.

17   Producers of educational television for children have found that formal features can help learning. But increasing the rate of cuts and edits eventually overloads the brain. Music videos and commercials that use rapid intercutting of unrelated scenes are designed to hold attention more than they are to convey information. People may remember the name of the product or band, but the details of the ad itself float in one ear and out the other. The orienting response is overworked. Viewers still attend to the screen, but they feel tired and worn out, with little compensating psychological reward. Our ESM findings show much the same thing.

18   Sometimes the memory of the product is very subtle. Many ads today are deliberately oblique: they have an engaging story line, but it is hard to tell what they are trying to sell. Afterward you may not remember the product consciously. Yet advertisers believe that if they have gotten your attention, when you later go to the store you will feel better or more comfortable with a given product because you have a vague recollection of having heard of it.

19   The natural attraction to television's sound and light starts very early in life. Dafna Lemish of Tel Aviv University has described babies at six to eight weeks attending to television. We have observed slightly older infants who, when lying on their backs on the floor, crane their necks around 180 degrees to catch what light through yonder window breaks. This inclination suggests how deeply rooted the orienting response is.

"TV IS PART OF THEM"

20   That said, we need to be careful about overreacting. Little evidence suggests that adults or children should stop watching TV altogether. The problems come from heavy or prolonged viewing.

21   The Experience Sampling Method permitted us to look closely at most every domain of everyday life: working, eating, reading, talking to friends, playing a sport, and so on. We wondered whether heavy viewers might experience life differently than light viewers do. Do they dislike being with people more? Are they more alienated from work? What we found nearly leaped off the page at us. Heavy viewers report feeling significantly more anxious and less happy than light viewers do in unstructured situations, such as doing nothing, daydreaming or waiting in line. The difference widens when the viewer is alone.

22   Subsequently, Robert D. McIlwraith of the University of Manitoba extensively studied those who called themselves TV addicts on surveys. On a measure called the Short Imaginal Processes Inventory (SIPI), he found that the self-described addicts are more easily bored and distracted and have poorer attentional control than the nonaddicts. The addicts said they used TV to distract themselves from unpleasant thoughts and to fill time. Other studies over the years have shown that heavy viewers are less likely to participate in community activities and sports and are more likely to be obese than moderate viewers or nonviewers.

23   The question that naturally arises is: In which direction does the correlation go? Do people turn to TV because of boredom and loneliness, or does TV viewing make people more susceptible to boredom and loneliness? We and most other researchers argue that the former is generally the case, but it is not a simple case of either/or. Jerome L. and Dorothy Singer of Yale University, among others, have suggested that more viewing may contribute to a shorter attention span, diminished self-restraint and less patience with the normal delays of daily life. More than 25 years ago psychologist Tannis M. MacBeth Williams of the University

of British Columbia studied a mountain community that had no television until cable finally arrived. Over time, both adults and children in the town became less creative in problem solving, less able to persevere at tasks, and less tolerant of unstructured time.

24   To some researchers, the most convincing parallel between TV and addictive drugs is that people experience withdrawal symptoms when they cut back on viewing. Nearly 40 years ago Gary A. Steiner of the University of Chicago collected fascinating individual accounts of families whose set had broken—this back in the days when households generally had only one set. "The family walked around like a chicken without a head." "It was terrible. We did nothing—my husband and I talked." "Screamed constantly. Children bothered me, and my nerves were on edge. Tried to interest them in games, but impossible. TV is part of them."

25   In experiments, families have volunteered or been paid to stop viewing, typically for a week or a month. Many could not complete the period of abstinence. Some fought, verbally and physically. Anecdotal reports from some families that have tried the annual "TV turn-off" week in the U.S. tell a similar story.

26   If a family has been spending the lion's share of its free time watching television, reconfiguring itself around a new set of activities is no easy task. Of course, that does not mean it cannot be done or that all families implode when deprived of their set. In a review of these cold-turkey studies, Charles Winick of the City University of New York concluded: "The first three or four days for most persons were the worst, even in many homes where viewing was minimal and where there were other ongoing activities. In over half of all the households, during these first few days of loss, the regular

routines were disrupted, family members had difficulties in dealing with the newly available time, anxiety and aggressions were expressed. . . . People living alone tended to be bored and irritated. . . . By the second week, a move toward adaptation to the situation was common." Unfortunately, researchers have yet to flesh out these anecdotes; no one has systematically gathered statistics on the prevalence of these withdrawal symptoms.

27   Even though TV does seem to meet the criteria for substance dependence, not all researchers would go so far as to call TV addictive. McIlwraith said in 1998 that "displacement of other activities by television may be socially significant but still fall short of the clinical requirement of significant impairment." He argued that a new category of "TV addiction" may not be necessary if heavy viewing stems from conditions such as depression and social phobia. Nevertheless, whether or not we formally diagnose someone as TV-dependent, millions of people sense that they cannot readily control the amount of television they watch.

SLAVE TO THE COMPUTER SCREEN

28   Although much less research has been done on video games and computer use, the same principles often apply. The games offer escape and distraction; players quickly learn that they feel better when playing; and so a kind of reinforcement loop develops. The obvious difference from television, however, is the interactivity. Many video and computer games minutely increase in difficulty along with the increasing ability of the player. One can search for months to find another tennis or chess player of comparable ability, but programmed games can immediately provide a near-perfect match of challenge to skill. They offer the psychic pleasure—what one

of us (Csikszentmihalyi) has called "flow"—that accompanies increased mastery of most any human endeavor. On the other hand, prolonged activation of the orienting response can wear players out. Kids report feeling tired, dizzy and nauseated after long sessions.

29   In 1997, in the most extreme medium-effects case on record, 700 Japanese children were rushed to the hospital, many suffering from "optically stimulated epileptic seizures" caused by viewing bright flashing lights in a Pokemon video game broadcast on Japanese TV. Seizures and other untoward effects of video games are significant enough that software companies and platform manufacturers now routinely include warnings in their instruction booklets. Parents have reported to us that rapid movement on the screen has caused motion sickness in their young children after just 15 minutes of play. Many youngsters, lacking self-control and experience (and often supervision), continue to play despite these symptoms.

30   Lang and Shyam Sundar of Pennsylvania State University have been studying how people respond to Web sites. Sundar has shown people multiple versions of the same Web page, identical except for the number of links. Users reported that more links conferred a greater sense of control and engagement. At some point, however, the number of links reached saturation, and adding more of them simply turned people off. As with video games, the ability of Web sites to hold the user's attention seems to depend less on formal features than on interactivity.

31   For growing numbers of people, the life they lead online may often seem more important, more immediate and more intense than the life they lead face-to-face. Maintaining control over one's media habits is more of a challenge today than it has ever been. TV sets and computers are everywhere. But the small screen and the Internet need not interfere with the quality of the rest of one's life. In its easy provision of relaxation and escape, television can be beneficial in limited doses. Yet when the habit interferes with the ability to grow, to learn new things, to lead an active life, then it does constitute a kind of dependence and should be taken seriously.

Evaluation of the Article

Difficulty Rating ☐ 1 ☐ 2 ☐ 3 ☐ 4 ☐ 5
(1 = easy; 5 = difficult)

What reading difficulties did you encounter? _____

_____

How did you handle these difficulties? _____

_____

Postreading Comprehension Development

Sentence Rewrite

To check your understanding of some of the key concepts of this essay, rewrite each of the following sentences in your own words, keeping the original idea. (See Chapter 1.)

1. The term "TV addiction" is imprecise and laden with value judgments, but it captures the essence of a very real phenomenon. (4)

   _____

   _____

2. To some commentators, this devotion simply means that people enjoy TV and make a conscious decision to watch it. (6)

   _____

   _____

3. It is part of our evolutionary heritage, a built-in sensitivity to movement and potential predatory threats. (13)

   _____

   _____

4. He argued that a new category of "TV addiction" may not be necessary if heavy viewing stems from conditions such as depression and social phobia. (27)

   _____

   _____

Author's Main Idea

(See Chapter 3.)

1. What is the topic of this article?

   _____

2. How do the words "No Mere" in the title prepare you for this main idea?

_____

3. Using the following starter sentence, state the authors' main idea:

The authors want me to understand that: _____

_____

_____

4. How well do the authors support their main idea? Be specific in your response.

_____

_____

_____

Inferences, Metaphors, and Vocabulary in Context
(See Chapters 2, 6, and 7.)

1. How do you think the authors want the reader to feel after reading the last paragraph of this selection? What are the reasons for your beliefs?

_____

_____

_____

2. Which of the following can be inferred from paragraph 15? Be prepared to justify your answer.
   a. Most TV viewers can control their viewing habits.
   b. Reeves and Thorson had a large body of research on television viewing to use as background for their own studies.
   c. Advertisers use their knowledge of orienting when creating ads.
   d. The orienting stimulus creates anxiety in TV viewers.

3. Which of the following can be inferred from paragraph 19? Be prepared to justify your answer.
   a. The effects of TV can be studied at all ages.
   b. Dafina Lemish believes babies comprehend TV programs.
   c. Orienting responses do not occur during adolescence.
   d. Television is watched less frequently in Tel Aviv than in the U.S.

4. From paragraph 20 the reader can predict that:
   a. The authors will discuss their personal experiences with TV viewing.
   b. The authors will explain adults and children should not watch TV.
   c. The authors will discuss the harmful effects of prolonged TV viewing.
   d. The authors will argue the need for more research on TV viewing.

5. In paragraph 22 the authors imply that:
   a. McIlwraith did not believe there was any such thing as a TV addict.
   b. Participation in sports is a good thing.
   c. TV addicts were unwilling to spend time completing surveys on their viewing habits.
   d. TV addicts feel guilty about their viewing habits.

6. In paragraph 23 the authors raise a question. Explain whether you believe this is an important question for researchers to answer, and provide reasons for your views.

   _____

   _____

   _____

7. The authors' tone throughout most of this essay is:
   a. sarcastic.
   b. depressed.
   c. hopeful.
   d. informative.

8. Using only the context, define each of the words below. Do not use a dictionary.

a. sustenance (1) _____

b. diversion (1) _____

c. allure (3) _____

d. aesthetic (5) _____

e. depleted (9) _____

f. begets (11) _____

g. depreciate (12) _____

h. predatory (13) _____

i. oblique (18) _____

j. untoward (29) _____

9. The authors' point of view about television is that:

a. TV and computers are okay in moderation.

b. Congress should spend more money to help TV addicts.

c. TV addiction is worse than computer addiction.

d. Parents should control their children's viewing habits.

Recalling Details

(See Chapters 4 and 5.)

1. Which of the following are factual statements in this article? Which are opinions? Use (F) or (O) for your response. For those you label opinion, write any support for the opinion that is given in this article.

_____ a. Infants have an orienting response to TV.

_____ b. People spend more time watching TV than on any other leisure-time activity.

_____ c. The amount of time people spend watching television is astonishing.

_____ d. Survey participants commonly reflect that television has somehow absorbed or sucked out their energy.

_____ e. Annie Lang's research team at Indiana University has shown that heart rate decreases for four to six seconds after an orienting stimulus.

_____ f. Many ads today are deliberately oblique.

_____ g. If a family has been spending the lion's share of its free time watching television, reconfiguring itself around a new set of activities is no easy task.

_____ h. Maintaining control over one's media habits is more of a challenge today than it has ever been.

2. Use the information in this selection as well as your own knowledge to create a Venn diagram for the following two phrases: "TV Addiction" and "Addiction to Hard Drugs." Put your diagram on separate paper.

Match the following researchers with the major findings from their study.

_____ Gary A. Stiener

_____ Robert D. McIlwraith

_____ Gallup polls

_____ Reeves and Thorson

_____ Lang

_____ Lemish

_____ Lang and Sundar

a. Study of amount of time spent viewing TV

b. Study of effect of formal features of TV on memory

c. Responses to Web sites and number of links

d. Study of TV addicts versus non-addicts

e. Study of orienting response to formal features of TV

f. Study of babies' responses to TV

g. Study of families whose TVs had broken

4. Which details from this selection did you find most interesting? Be prepared to discuss why.

_____

_____

Critical Thinking: Reaction and Discussion

1. In an essay of at least 250 words discuss how this article supports the definition of psychology as a science.

2. Return to the To Think About Before You Read section of this article and decide which answers you would change. Discuss your changes with a small group.

3. With a small group, prepare a survey to investigate some of the issues about TV viewing discussed in this article. Each member of your group should give this survey to 5–7 college students and others. Be sure to include the age and sex of each person you interview. Compare your findings with each other and with the class.

USING TECHNOLOGY FOR FURTHER UNDERSTANDING

1. Watch one of your favorite TV shows. Observe your viewing behavior. What did you notice about yourself that confirms or refutes some of the information in this article?

2. Visit a local store that sells televisions. What features do new models have, or how are these newer sets being advertised, that might be designed to appeal to some of the specific aspects of viewing behavior that were discussed in this article?

CHAPTER TWELVE

Sociology
The Science of
Societies and Their
Effects on
Human Behavior

*It is easy in the world to live after the world's opinion; it is easy in
solitude to live after our own; but the great man is he who in the
midst of a crowd keeps with perfect sweetness the independence of
solitude.*

—Ralph Waldo Emerson

Derivation: *socio-*   —society, social

           -ology   —science

Key Concepts for the Study of Sociology

Before you read this list of concepts, think about some issues or topics that you might study if you took courses in sociology. In the space provided, list your ideas.

_____

_____

NORM.   A pattern or trait taken to be typical in the behavior of a social group. A principle of right action binding on the members of a group and serving to guide, control, or regulate proper and acceptable behavior. All cultural groups have norms they expect their members to follow.

SOCIALIZATION.   A learning process through which the individual is made fit for or is trained for a social environment. The family is the most important agent of socialization for young children.

ROLE.   A socially expected behavior pattern usually determined by an individual's status in a particular society. The role of a president in our society is different from that of a college student.

DEVIANT BEHAVIOR.   Behavior that departs significantly from the behavioral norms of a particular society. Burglarizing a home is an example of deviant behavior.

SOCIAL INSTITUTION.   Every society has five basic types of social institutions: familial, religious, economic, educational, and political. More complex societies may have others, such as military and scientific. For each there is a complex pattern of cultural traits and social organization, which result in a recognizable and stable form in a given society. Every social institution has its own well-defined roles, norms, beliefs, and values.

CLASS.   A group sharing the same economic or social status. The typical suburban family belongs to the middle class.

ALIENATION.   A withdrawing or separation of a person or a person's affections from an object or position of former attachment, such as from the values of one's society and family. Teenagers often feel alienated from their parents.

MICRO-LEVEL SOCIOLOGY.   A way to study society by focusing on patterns of social interaction at the individual level. A study of a single Navajo family in order to make generalizations about Navajo culture is an example of micro-level sociology.

MACRO-LEVEL SOCIOLOGY.   A way to study society by focusing on major structures and institutions. A study of the Irish Republican Army and its impact on the Catholics in Northern Ireland is an example of macro-level sociology.

PARTICIPANT OBSERVATION.   One way a sociologist can study a group. The sociologist who is a participant observer temporarily becomes a member of the group being studied.

Now that you have read this list, what are some additional issues or topics that you might study if you took courses in sociology? In the space provided, list your ideas.

_____

_____

_____

● # SELECTION 5

The Sociological Perspective

■ JAMES M. HENSLIN

Preview

In the following article, you will learn what sociologists do and how this discipline is different from some other fields of study, such as psychology. You will also discover some of the issues that are particularly interesting to sociologists.

To Think About Before You Read

Decide how you think each of the following groups might feel about the issue of *violence in movies.* Compare your answers with those of other members of your class. Make a chart for your group responses.

> parents of preschoolers
>
> members of the National Rifle Association
>
> teenagers
>
> police officers
>
> priests/ministers/rabbis
>
> movie producers
>
> senior citizens

Term to Know Before You Read

Perspective(title) point of view

Even from the dim glow of the faded red-and-white exit sign, its light barely reaching the upper bunk, I could see that the sheet was filthy. Resigned to another night of fitful sleep, I reluctantly crawled into bed—tucking my clothes firmly around my body, like a protective cocoon.

2   The next morning, I joined the long line of disheveled men leaning against the chain-link fence. Their faces were as downcast as their clothes were dirty. Not a glimmer of hope among them.

3   No one spoke as the line slowly inched forward. When my turn came, I was handed a styrofoam cup of coffee, some utensils, and a bowl of semiliquid that I couldn't identify. It didn't look like any food I had seen before. Nor did it taste like anything I had ever eaten.

4   My stomach fought the foul taste, every spoonful a battle. But I was determined. "I will experience what they experience," I kept telling myself. My stomach reluctantly gave in and accepted its morning nourishment.

5   The room was eerily silent. Hundreds of men were eating, but each was sunk deeply into his own private hell, his head aswim with disappointment, remorse, bitterness.

6   As I stared at the styrofoam cup holding my solitary postbreakfast pleasure, I noticed what looked like teeth marks. I shrugged off the thought, telling myself that my long weeks as a sociological observer of the homeless were finally getting to me. "That must be some sort of crease from handling," I concluded.

7   I joined the silent ranks of men turning in their bowls and cups. When I saw the man behind the counter swishing out styrofoam cups in a washtub of water, I began to feel sick at my stomach. I knew then that the jagged marks on my cup really had come from a previous mouth.

8   How much longer did this research have to last? I felt a deep longing to return to my family—to a welcome world of clean sheets, healthy food, and "normal" conversations.

THE SOCIOLOGICAL PERSPECTIVE

9   Why were these men so silent? Why did they receive such despicable treatment? What was I doing in that homeless shelter? (After all, I hold a respectable, secure professional position, and I have a home and family.)

10   Sociology offers a perspective, a view of the world. The **sociological perspective** (or imagination) opens a window onto unfamiliar worlds, and offers a fresh look at familiar worlds. In this text you will find yourself in the midst of Nazis in Germany, chimpanzees in Africa, and warriors in South America. But you will also find yourself looking at your own world in a different light. As you look at other worlds, or your own, the sociological perspective casts a light then enables you to gain a new vision of social life. In fact, this is what many find appealing about sociology.

11   The sociological perspective has been a motivating force in my own life. Ever since I took my first introductory course in sociology, I have been enchanted by the perspective that sociology offers. I have thoroughly enjoyed both observing other groups and questioning my own assumptions about life. I sincerely hope that the same happens to you.

Seeing the Broader Social Context

12   The sociological perspective stresses the broader context of life in society. To find out why people do what they do, sociologists look at

From James Henslin, *Sociology: A Down-to-Earth Approach,* 4/e. Published by Allyn and Bacon, Boston, MA. Copyright © 1999 by Pearson Education. Reprinted by permission of the publisher.

social location, where people are located in history and in a particular society. Sociologists focus on such characteristics of people as their jobs, income, education, gender, and race. At the center of the sociological perspective is the question of how people are influenced by **society**—a group of people who share a culture and a territory. Take, for example, how growing up identified with a group called females or a group called males affects people's ideas of what they should attain in life.

13   Sociologist C. Wright Mills (1959b) said that the sociological perspective enables us to grasp the connection between history and biography. Because of its history, a society has certain broad characteristics—such as its commonly accepted ideas of the proper roles of men and women. By biography, Mills meant the individual's specific experiences in society. This intersection of history and biography results in people having particular values, goals, aspirations, and even self-concept. In short, in the sociological view people don't do what they do because of some sort of inherited internal mechanism, such as instincts. Rather, external influences—people's experiences—become internalized, become part of an individual's thinking and motivations.

14   An example will make this point obvious. If we were to take a newborn baby away from its U.S. parents today and place that infant with a Yanomamo Indian tribe in the jungles of South America, you know that when that child begins to speak, his or her sounds will not be in English. You also know that the child will not think like an American. He or she will not grow up wanting credit cards, for example, or designer jeans, a new car, and the latest video game. Equally, the child will unquestioningly take his or her place in Yanomamo society—perhaps as a food gatherer, a hunter, or a warrior—and

will not even know about the world left behind at birth. And, whether male or female, that child will grow up, not debating whether to have one, two, or three children, but assuming that it is natural to want many children.

15   People around the globe take their particular world for granted. Something inside us Americans tells us that hamburgers are delicious, small families attractive, and designer clothing desirable. Yet something inside some of the Sinai Desert Arab tribes used to tell them that warm, fresh camel's blood makes a fine drink and that everyone should have a large family and wear flowing robes (Murray 1935; McCabe and Ellis 1990). And that something certainly isn't an instinct. As sociologist Peter Berger (1963) phrased it, that "something" is "society within us."

16   Although obvious, this point frequently eludes us. We often think and talk about people's behavior as though it is caused by their sex, their race, or some other factor transmitted by their genes. The sociological perspective helps us to escape from this cramped personal view by exposing the broader social context that underlies human behavior. It helps us to see the links between what people do and the social settings that shape their behavior.

SOCIOLOGY AND THE OTHER SCIENCES

17   Just as humans today have an intense desire to unravel the mysteries around them, people in ancient times also attempted to understand their world. Their explanations, however, were not based only on observations, but were mixed with magic and superstition as well.

18   To satisfy their basic curiosities about the world around them, humans gradually developed **science,** systematic methods used to study

the social and natural worlds, as well as the knowledge obtained by those methods. **Sociology,** the scientific study of society and human behavior, is one of the sciences that modern civilization has developed.

19   A useful way of comparing these sciences—and of gaining a better understanding of sociology's place—is to first divide them into the natural and the social sciences.

The Natural Sciences

20 The **natural sciences** are the intellectual and academic disciplines designed to comprehend, explain, and predict the events in our natural environment. The natural sciences are divided into specialized fields of research according to subject matter, such as biology, geology, chemistry, and physics. These are further subdivided into even more highly specialized areas, with a further narrowing of content. Biology is divided into botany and zoology, geology into mineralogy and geomorphology, chemistry into its inorganic and organic branches, and physics into biophysics and quantum mechanics. Each area of investigation examines a particular "slice" of nature (Henslin 1993).

The Social Sciences

21 People have not limited themselves to investigating nature. In the pursuit of a more adequate understanding of life, people have also developed fields of science that focus on the social world. These, the **social sciences,** examine human relationships. Just as the natural sciences attempt to objectively understand the world of nature, the social sciences attempt to objectively understand the social world. Just as the world of nature contains ordered (or lawful) relationships that are not obvious but must be discovered through controlled observation, so the ordered relationships of the human or social world are not obvious, and must be revealed by means of controlled and repeated observations.

Like the natural sciences, the social sciences 22 are divided into specialized fields based on their subject matter. These divisions are anthropology, economics, political science, psychology, and sociology. And the social sciences, too, are subdivided into further specialized fields. Thus, anthropology is divided into cultural and physical anthropology; economics has macro (large-scale) and micro (small-scale) specialties; political science has theoretical and applied branches; psychology may be clinical or experimental; and sociology has its quantitative and qualitative branches. Since our focus is sociology, let us contrast sociology with each of the other social sciences.

POLITICAL SCIENCE *Political science* focuses 23 on politics and government. Political scientists study how people govern themselves: the various forms of government, their structures, and their relationships to other institutions of society. Political scientists are especially interested in how people attain ruling positions in their society, how they then maintain those positions, and the consequences of their activities for those who are governed. In studying a system of government with a constitutional electorate, such as that of the United States, political scientists also focus on voting behavior.

ECONOMICS *Economics* also concentrates on 24 a single social institution. Economists study the production and distribution of the material goods and services of a society. They want to know what goods are being produced at what rate and at what cost, and how those goods are distributed. They are also interested in the choices that determine production and consumption, for example, the factors that lead a society to produce a certain item instead of another.

25 ANTHROPOLOGY *Anthropology,* in which the primary focus has been preliterate or tribal peoples, is the sister discipline of sociology. The chief concern of anthropologists is to understand *culture,* a people's total way of life. Culture includes (1) the group's artifacts such as its tools, art, and weapons; (2) the group's structure, that is, the hierarchy and other patterns that determine its members' relationships to one another; (3) a group's ideas and values, especially how its belief system affects people's lives; and (4) the group's forms of communication, especially language. The anthropologists' traditional focus on tribal groups is now giving way to the study of groups in industrialized settings.

26 PSYCHOLOGY The focus of *psychology* is on processes that occur *within* the individual, within the "skin-bound organism." Psychologists are primarily concerned with mental processes: intelligence, emotions, perception, and memory. Some concentrate on attitudes and values; others focus on personality, mental aberration (psychopathology, or mental illness), and how individuals cope with the problems they face.

27 SOCIOLOGY *Sociology* has many similarities to the other social sciences. Like political scientists, sociologists study how people govern one another, especially the impact of various forms of government on people's lives. Like economists, sociologists are concerned with what happens to the goods and services of a society—but sociologists place their focus on the social consequences of production and distribution. Like anthropologists, sociologists study culture; they have a particular interest in the social consequences of material goods, group structure, and belief systems, as well as in how people communicate with one another. Like psychologists, so-

ciologists are also concerned with how people adjust to the difficulties of life.

28 Given these overall similarities, then, what distinguishes sociology from the other social sciences? Unlike political scientists and economists, sociologists do not concentrate on a single social institution. Unlike anthropologists, sociologists focus primarily on industrialized societies. And unlike psychologists, sociologists stress factors *external* to the individual to determine what influences people.

The Goals of Science

29 The first goal of each science is to *explain* why something happens. The second goal is to make **generalizations,** that is, to go beyond the individual case and make statements that apply to a broader group or situation. For example, a sociologist wants to explain not only why Mary went to college or became an armed robber but also why people with her characteristics are more likely than others to go to college or to become armed robbers. To achieve generalizations, sociologists and other scientists look for **patterns,** recurring characteristics or events. The third scientific goal is to *predict,* to specify what will happen in the future in the light of current knowledge.

30 To attain these goals, scientists must rely not on magic, superstition, or common beliefs but on conclusions based on systematic studies. They need to examine evidence with an open mind, in such a way that it can be checked by others. Secrecy, prejudice, and other biases, with their inherent closures, go against the grain of science.

31 Sociologists and other scientists also move beyond **common sense,** those ideas that prevail in a society that "everyone knows" are true. Just because "everyone" knows something is

true does not make it so. "Everyone" can be mistaken, today just as easily as when common sense dictated that the world was flat or that no human could ever walk on the moon. As sociologists examine people's assumptions about the world, their findings may contradict commonsense notions about social life.

32   Sometimes the explorations of sociologists take them into nooks and crannies that people would prefer remain unexplored. For example, a sociologist might study how people make decisions to commit a crime or to cheat on their spouses. Because sociologists want above all to understand social life, they cannot cease their studies because people feel uncomfortable. With all realms of human life considered legitimate avenues of exploration by sociologists, their findings sometimes challenge even cherished ideas.

As they examine how groups operate, sociologists often confront prejudice and attempts to keep things secret. It seems that every organization, every group, nourishes a pet image that it presents to the public. Sociologists are interested in knowing what is really going on behind the scenes, however, so they peer beneath the surface to get past that sugarcoated image of suppressed facts (Berger 1963). This approach sometimes brings sociologists into conflict with people who feel threatened by that information which is all part of the adventure, and risk, of being a sociologist.

33

Evaluation of the Article

Difficulty Rating □ 1 □ 2 □ 3 □ 4 □ 5
(1 = easy; 5 = difficult)

What reading difficulties did you encounter? _____

_____

How did you handle these difficulties? _____

_____

Comprehension of the Discipline

1. Which of the following describes the major interest of sociologists?
   a. Individual behavior
   b. Group behavior
   c. Infant behavior
   d. Business cycles

2. Which of the following are areas that a sociologist would be likely to study? Check all that apply. Be prepared to explain your reasoning.

____ a. The effect of recent medical breakthroughs on the survival rate of AIDS patients

____ b. The effect of formal education on parenting styles among different socioeconomic groups

____ c. Occupational choices of children of first- versus second-generation immigrants

____ d. Patterns of gang violence in urban versus rural populations

____ e. The amount of profit earned in one year by a particular movie

____ f. The reactions of mice to being without companionship for long periods

3. Indicate whether each of the following statements is true (T) or false (F) based on the information given in this article. Be prepared to justify your answers.

____ a. Sociologists and psychologists differ in how they look at events.

____ b. Some people are not affected by social forces in their environment.

____ c. Because sociology deals with the study of people, it is unscientific.

____ d. Sociologists try to find commonalities in people's behavior.

____ e. Sociology is really just the complicated study of the obvious.

____ f. Sociologists explain individual behavior in terms of group patterns.

4. Read about each event and identify some of its aspects that you think each branch of social science listed would study.
Event: A new film about the war in Iraq, starring Sean Penn, is opening in your town.

a. Political science

b. Economics

c. Sociology

d. Psychology

Event: A church in your community is seeking permission to dig up a cemetery on its property in order to expand the church building. The cemetery dates back more than three hundred years.

    a. Sociology

    b. Economics

    c. Anthropology

    d. Political science

5. How would you explain wife battering or child abuse from a sociological perspective?

    How would this perspective differ from a psychological perspective?

6. Explain what the author probably means when he says you, the reader, "will find yourself looking at your own world in a different light" (10).

7. A sociologist has written an article that explains how a popular singer's music is influenced by the neighborhood where she lived as a child. Discuss why you believe this is an example of seeing the individual in "social location."

8. Using only the context and your knowledge of word structure, define each of the following words. Do not use a dictionary.

a. despicable (9)_____

b. perspective (10)_____

c. intersection (13)_____

d. eludes (16)_____

e. preliterate (25)_____

f. aberration (26)_____

g. recurring (29)_____

h. inherent (30)_____

i. peer (33)_____

Critical Thinking: Reaction and Discussion

1. For each group listed, write one question that you think might be studied by sociologists. Then decide how the concept of "social location" is explored in your question. Compare your questions with those of a partner.

   a. High school valedictorians

   b. Senior citizens

   c. Preschoolers

   d. Musicians

   e. Gang members

2. In an essay of at least 250 words, explain how the findings of one of your questions might benefit others.

USING TECHNOLOGY FOR FURTHER UNDERSTANDING

1. Watch a popular television program intended for a certain age group of people in this country, such as a children's program broadcast in the United States or a program on MTV. In an essay of at least 250 words, discuss the ways in which you feel this program reflects the social location of the group for which the program is intended.

2. On the Internet, review some descriptions of sociology departments at colleges and universities. What kinds of courses do sociology majors take? What else do you learn about the field of sociology from looking at these descriptions?

Sociology and "Common Sense"

The practice of sociology involves gaining knowledge about ourselves, the societies in which we live, and societies different from ours. Sociological findings both disturb and contribute to our common-sense beliefs about ourselves and others. Anthony Giddens, a prominent sociologist, has come up with the following statements about personal beliefs. Consider each statement. Then indicate whether you agree (A) or disagree (D) and explain why. Share your answers with a group.

1. Romantic love is a natural part of human experience and is therefore found in all societies in close connection with marriage. ——

   Your explanation: _____

   _____

   _____

   _____

2. How long people live depends on their biological makeup and cannot be strongly influenced by social differences. ——

   Your explanation: _____

   _____

   _____

3. In previous times, the family was a stable unit, but today there is a great increase in the proportion of "broken homes." ——

   Your explanation: _____

   _____

   _____

4. In all societies, some people will be unhappy or depressed; therefore, rates of suicides will tend to be the same throughout the world. ——

   Your explanation: _____

   _____

   _____

5. Most people value material wealth and will try to get ahead if there are opportunities to do so. _____

    Your explanation: _____

    _____

    _____

6. Wars have been fought throughout human history. If we face the threat of large-scale war today, it is because human beings have aggressive instincts that will always find an outlet. _____

    Your explanation: _____

    _____

    _____

7. The spread of computers and automation in industrial production will greatly reduce the average workday of most of the population. _____

    Your explanation: _____

    _____

    _____

The preceding assertions seem to make sense, but each is wrong or questionable. Knowing why will help us understand the questions sociologists ask, and try to answer, in their work. In the following list, Giddens explains why each preceding statement is incorrect. Do you agree with his explanations?

1. The idea that marriage ties should be based on romantic love is a recent one, not found either in the earlier history of Western societies or in other cultures. Romantic love is actually unknown in most societies.

2. How long people live is very definitely affected by social influences. This is because ways of social life act as "filters" for biological factors that cause illness, infirmity, or death. The poor are less healthy on average than the rich, for example, because they usually have worse diets, live a more physically demanding existence, and have access to inferior medical facilities.

3. If we look back to the early 1800s, the proportion of children living in homes with only one natural parent was probably as high as at present,

because many more people died young, particularly women in childbirth. Today the main causes of "broken homes"—separation and divorce—differ from earlier times, but the overall level has not changed much.

4. Suicide rates are certainly not the same in all societies. Even if we only look at Western countries, we find that suicide rates vary considerably. The suicide rate in the United States, for example, is four times as high as that of Spain, but only a third of that of Hungary. Suicide rates increased quite sharply during the main period of industrialization of the Western societies, in the nineteenth and early twentieth centuries.

5. The value that many people in modern societies place upon wealth and "getting ahead" is for the most part a recent development. It is associated with the rise of "individualism" in the West and the stress which we tend to place on individual achievement. In many other cultures, individuals are expected to put the good of the community above their own wishes and inclinations. Material wealth often is not highly regarded compared to other values, such as religious or family ones.

6. Far from having an aggressive instinct, human beings do not have instincts at all, if "instinct" means a fixed and inherited pattern of behavior. Moreover, throughout most of human history, when people lived in small tribal groups, warfare did not exist in the form it came to have subsequently. Although some such groups were warlike, many were not. There were no armies, and when skirmishes occurred, casualties would often be deliberately avoided or limited. The threat of large-scale war today is bound up with a process of the "industrialization of war" that is a major aspect of industrialization in general.

7. The assumption that computers and automation will mean more free time for everyone is rather different from the others, because it refers to the future. There is in fact good reason to be at least cautious about this idea. The automated industries are still fairly few and far between. Jobs eliminated by automation might be replaced by new ones created elsewhere or by the new automation itself. We cannot as yet be sure. One of the tasks of sociology is to take a hard look at the actual evidence available on issues such as this.

Obviously sociological findings do not always go against common-sense views. Common-sense ideas often provide sources of insight about social behavior. What needs emphasizing, however, is that the sociologist must be prepared to ask of any of our beliefs about ourselves—no matter how cherished—*is this really so?* By this means, sociology also helps to contribute to whatever "common sense" is at any time and place. Much of what most of us today would regard as common sense, "what everyone knows"—for example, that divorce rates have risen greatly over the period since World War II—is in fact due to the work of sociologists and other social scientists. A great deal of research, of a permanent kind, is necessary to produce material from year to year on patterns of marriage and divorce. The same is true of very many other areas of our common-sense knowledge.*

Guidelines for Reading Sociology

Some things to bear in mind when you read sociology are:

❋ *Sociologists study groups.* The impact of the group on a particular individual, or the behavior of the entire group, may be studied. Sociologists often look at a single institution that has many members, such as a school, club, business organization, or political organization. They may also study college students and religious groups, the military, and urban or rural communities. They are interested in how group rules are made, how they are changed, or how an individual's behavior may be affected by the group. They also are interested in lifestyles and practices, such as childrearing practices, and how these change and are affected by certain elements of the social environment, such as the media and the economy.

❋ *The sociologist must remain objective and conduct studies without bias.* Sociologists must find ways to control their personal preferences or prejudices. Think of the sociologist as a scientist who uses society, or an institution or group within the society, as the laboratory in which to conduct research. Statistics play an important role in sociological studies because they can reduce the effects of bias by the researcher and can provide support for any conclusions being drawn.

❋ *You must read actively.* Stay connected to the text you are reading by thinking about it *while* you read. Specifically, you should:

1. *Look for key questions being investigated.* Sometimes the sociologist will include interesting but minor details about social interactions. Good readers will not get lost while reading these.

2. *Notice how the study is designed.* How does the researcher get to know the subject? Was a participant observer approach used?

* From *Introduction to Sociology* by Anthony Giddens. Copyright © 1991 by W.W. Norton & Company, Inc. Used by permission of W.W. Norton & Company, Inc.

3. *Be sure you understand the author's definition of terms used, such as role and norm.* Remember that these terms represent broad concepts. Terminology in sociology is critical and sometimes frustrating for the reader. Often a new name or label must be invented to symbolize some newly discovered phenomenon of group behavior, or a term already popular must be assigned a new meaning by a sociologist who wants to use it in a special way. The term *suburban,* for instance, was not used until recently in sociological research.

4. *Look for generalizations and the support offered for them.* By combining several ideas into a single statement that shows how these ideas are connected to each other, a sociologist forms a generalization. For example, the sociologist might make the following generalization: *As the education level of a family increases, so does its level of income.* Or it might be stated: *There is greater incidence of child abuse among poor families.* You should locate the empirical (factual) evidence in the reading material that supports such statements. The author might present a number of different statistics to demonstrate correlations between education and income levels or between child abuse and income.

5. *Recognizing the theoretical model underlying the author's point of view.* Sociologists generally develop their theories based on one of three major theoretical models. The three models used are (1) (structural) functionalism, (2) conflict, and (3) symbolic interactionism. Depending on which of these models is adopted by the author, the answer to basic sociological questions differs. For instance, the question "What is the role of the sociologist?" would be answered as follows for each model:

(Structural) Functionalism: To explain the elements of society, to show how they are related, and to explain how they affect each other

Conflict: To point out the groups in conflict, to show which groups have power, and to illustrate how power is maintained

Symbolic interactionism: To observe and record, methodically and in detail, the social drama, that is, individuals in society

Keep these guidelines in mind as you read the remaining articles from the field of sociology.

● ## SELECTION 6

Blown Away by School Violence

■ DONNA HARRINGTON-LUEKER

Preview

Although the following article was written in 1992, it addresses an issue that is very much in the minds of Americans today. As you read about this topic, think about the new information you are learning and whether it affects any of your views on this subject.

To Think About Before You Read

This essay is divided into four basic parts, as diagrammed on the structured overview. These divisions are the statement of the problem, the causes of the problem, some of the effects of the problem, and several solutions to the problem. All these parts are connected to the main topic, school violence among children. Think about these parts. Before you read the essay, write in any details that you expect to be mentioned in each part of the essay. Use what you already know about this subject to help you. When you finish reading the selection, you will complete this structured overview by revising your original details and adding others so that the final overview corresponds to the content of the essay.

STRUCTURED OVERVIEW

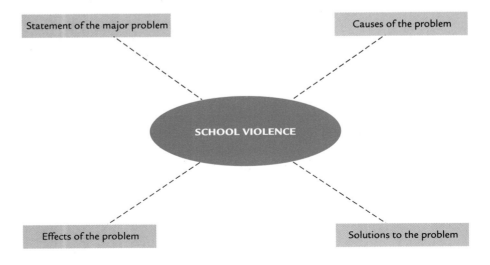

Today, about one in 20 of this country's high-schoolers carries a gun. The number of teenagers aged 15 to 19 who were killed by firearms increased 43 percent between 1984 and 1988; among young black males, firearms are the leading cause of death. Some researchers estimate that more male teenagers died of gunfire in 1988 than of all diseases combined. For schools, the numbers are inescapable. What's behind the rising number of kids with guns?

2 In many communities, the answer is a widespread wave of violence—much of it related to the epidemic of crack cocaine, some of it traceable to continuing gang activity. Some point to America's fascination with violence. "Look at the way we handle problems [such as the Persian Gulf War]—we resolve everything by fighting," notes Clementine Barfield, founder of Save Our Sons and Daughters (SOSAD), a Detroit-based group that combats street violence.

3 America's "Terminator 2" entertainment industry comes in for part of the blame, too. "Every week kids see their favorite TV star blown away one minute and out of the hospital the next," says Vanessa Scherzer, of the Center to Prevent Handgun Violence, in Washington, D.C. "They don't see what family members go through [as a result of a shooting], they don't see a kid in a wheelchair, and they don't even see the legal ramifications."

4 Others speak of well-founded fear. Some 80 percent of the youngsters in Detroit's public schools have either lost someone to gun violence or know of someone who has, says Barfield, who founded SOSAD after her own 15- and 16-year-old sons were shot on the street, one fatally. "This is the world they know," Barfield says. "Ask them why they carry a gun, and they'll tell you it's for protection. . . . They'll say they have to get the other guy before he gets them."

Concurring is Edward Muir, director of 5 school safety for the United Federation of Teachers, New York City's teachers union. In several of this year's shootings, says Muir, younger teens squared off against older classmates who had a history of intimidating them. "It's like the Old West," concludes Muir. "The gun becomes the equalizer."

EQUALIZER

And as the year's police reports suggest, it's an 6 equalizer teenagers are using to solve the most mundane problems: a beef over something someone said, a fallout over a girl, a suspected slight, a pair of sneakers, a Raiders' jacket. And it's an equalizer boys use more often than girls.

"In many cases it's a question of being 7 macho—'Nobody will mess with me; I'll resolve the problem with my piece,'" explains Larry Burgan, security chief of the Baltimore City Public Schools. Still other factors include alcohol and drug use, both of which cloud a teenager's fledgling sense of judgment.

But the most potent ingredient in this volatile 8 mix of kids and guns is the proliferation of guns—and the ease with which teenagers can acquire them. "We're the distribution end of the cheap handgun industry," says Muir. "I've had teachers tell me that in some areas of the city, it's easier to buy a gun than a book."

Those numbers translate into opportunity. 9 At a minimum, youngsters can bring guns from home—a classic scenario, says William Pollack, of the Howard County, Maryland, police. "At elementary school level," says Pollack, "a kid will see a gun and bring it in for show-and-tell with his friends." School security experts and law enforcement officials estimate that 80 percent of the guns youngsters tote come from home.

But guns can also be borrowed from friends, 10

bought by proxy, or stolen. Other guns can be bought on the street, where the trade can be brisk and the dealers unconcerned about the age of their customers. Costs vary, but after changing hands a couple times, "old" guns might sell for as little as $25 or $50. "That's money some kid can easily get his hands on," says Jack Killorin, of the Bureau of Alcohol, Tobacco, and Firearms.

11   Once a kid has a gun, bringing it to school is easy. "These guns are so small—so inconspicuous—that there's just no way we can keep them off campus," says Doug McVicker, a retired public school principal and current member of the Albuquerque school board. "I know the National Rifle Association [NRA] says that guns don't kill people, people kill people," continues McVicker, a former member of the NRA, the nation's most powerful gun lobby. "But guns do kill. And they kill very efficiently." After all, asks McVicker in exasperation, "when was the last time you heard of a drive-by knifing?"

12   Others share McVicker's frustration. Stricter gun-control laws are the obvious answer, say children's advocates, public health officials, and gun-control groups. "Stopping the flow of guns is important," says Joshua Horwitz, of the Education Fund to Prevent Handgun Violence, in Washington, D.C. "You can't really stop the flow to kids unless you stop the flow [of guns] overall."

13   Among the measures advocated are waiting periods for the purchase of guns, background checks for gun buyers, and even an outright ban of certain categories of weapons—such as handguns and assault rifles. Still others argue the need for laws that make parents responsible for their children's use of guns and for the creation of so-called gun-free zones around schools. (A little-known provision of the 1990 federal anti-crime bill designates any public or private school as a "gun-free zone" and allows a maximum five-year prison sentence and a $5,000 fine.)

14   But such measures often ignite a political firestorm—as some state legislatures found when they considered bills that would impose stricter penalties for carrying guns on school property. In Washington state, for example, public school officials and members of the state's gun lobby collided this past February over a proposal to bar anyone—not just students—from bringing guns to school. Guns rights advocates objected, arguing the proposal was unnecessary infringement on their constitutional rights, and the proposal was tabled in the legislature.

15   Without such controls, schools must fall back instead on locker searchers, weapons sweeps, million-dollar police forces, and even metal detectors. Another option—increasing the number of separate alternative schools for youths with a history of violent and abusive behavior—is also attracting attention, though such schools remain controversial.

16   "They're just a euphemism for where we're going to put the blacks," says one school security director dismissively. "Our task force [on alternative schools] is cognizant of the fact that such schools could become dumping grounds," allows another whose school system is considering that option in the wake of a recent shooting.

17   Security experts and child advocates also advise schools to incorporate programs to prevent gun violence into their curricula. Such programs, experts agree, must deal directly with attitudes and actions that endanger kids most and not simply with gun safety.

18   Teens on Target in Oakland, California, is one such program, says program director Deane Calhoun, who helps a cadre of 30 teens from some of the city's most drug-ravaged neighborhoods spread the word about the dangers of

gun violence. But getting the message out isn't easy, says Calhoun, because the romance of guns often outweighs reality. "The kids here pictured that, if you got shot, you died," says Calhoun. "They don't think you could end up in a wheelchair for the rest of your life with a spinal cord injury. . . . The assumption is, you die in glory."

19   Her job—and that of the students she works with—is to dispel such romance. Tell youngsters that every gun injury amounts to more than $33,000 in medical costs—exclusive of doctor's fees—and kids do a double take, Calhoun says. Point out that the anesthesia doesn't always take effect before an emergency room physician starts probing for a bullet, and they pay attention. Rather than give in to the law of the street, students are encouraged to stay in school, to explore jobs and careers, and to become leaders.

20   Students in Charlotte-Mecklenburg, North Carolina, and Dade County, Florida, receive a similar message via videotapes that realistically detail the consequences of carrying a gun. In one video, a young victim discusses what it's like to be a paraplegic; another shows a former high school sports star undergoing physical therapy after a bullet wound to the head. Both include conversations with youngsters in prison. (Contact both school systems for more information.) "Kids need to know it's not like on TV," says Dade County, Florida, school security chief Red McAllister.

21   The Center to Prevent Handgun Violence will test a K–12 gun violence prevention curriculum called "Straight Talk About Risks" in five big-city school systems: New York, San Diego, Los Angeles, Oakland, and Dade County. The curriculum, developed in cooperation with Dade County schools, teaches youngsters how to stay safe around guns, how to resist peer pressure, and how to differentiate between what happens on TV and on the street.

22   Changing a teenager's behavior can be difficult, though, says Jacqueline Brown, a professor at Bowie State University, in suburban Maryland, and director of a violence prevention project. She says many youngsters must juggle three sometimes conflicting "cultures," or codes of conduct: the culture of the home, the culture of the street, and the culture of the school. "The street definitely has a mystique, an image that kids can buy into," says Brown. "They know that culture will deal them death, but they know also that it provides them with a sense of psychological and social well-being."

23   "I'm someone with my boys," kids tell Brown. "And I'm not to people at school."

24   Until individual schools establish a strong enough cultural identity of their own, the street culture will continue to rule school corridors, Brown says; "The school's come-hither is just so weak." Taking action, though, is essential, she concludes, echoing the recommendation that has also been heard from other children's advocates. "The surprising thing is how much kids blame us for going to sleep at the wheel."

Education Digest, November 1992, pp. 50–53.

Evaluation of the Article
Difficulty Rating □ 1 □ 2 □ 3 □ 4 □ 5
(1 = easy; 5 = difficult)

What reading difficulties did you encounter? _____

_____

How did you handle these difficulties? _____

_____

Postreading Comprehension Development

Sentence Rewrite

To check your understanding of some of the key concepts of this essay, rewrite each of the following sentences in your own words, keeping the original idea. (See Chapter 1.)

1. For schools, the numbers are inescapable. (1)

_____

_____

2. But such measures often ignite a political firestorm as some state legislatures found when they considered bills that would impose stricter penalties for carrying guns on school property. (14)

_____

_____

3. But getting the message out isn't easy, says Calhoun, because the romance of guns often outweighs reality. (18)

_____

_____

Author's Main Idea

(See Chapter 3.)

1. What is the author's purpose for writing this article?
   a. To present several positions on the issue of gun control in schools
   b. To show how violent our society has become
   c. To express her point of view about gun control and school violence
   d. To discuss the extent of the problem and solutions to school violence

2. Using the following starter sentence, state the author's main idea:
   The author wants me to understand that: _____

   _____

   _____

3. Create another title for this selection that you think would help a reader predict the major focus for this selection. _____

   _____

4. What predictions do you believe a reader could make from your title?

   _____

   _____

5. The author develops the key point primarily through use of:
   a. unreliable sources.
   b. original sources.
   c. secondary sources.
   d. eyewitness reports.

Inferences, Metaphors, and Vocabulary in Context

(See Chapters 2, 6, 7.)

1. Which of the following can be inferred from paragraph 9? Be prepared to justify your answer.
   a. Kids have easy access to guns at home.
   b. Parents encourage children to be violent.

   c. Parents encourage children to bring guns to school.

   d. Teachers and parents have little control over teenage violence.

2. Which word below best describes the main reason for the use of guns by school children?

   a. Fear

   b. Attention

   c. Caution

   d. Retaliation

3. When Muir says, "I've had teachers tell me that in some areas of the city it's easier to buy a gun than a book," he is suggesting that:

   a. teenagers would rather shoot each other than read.

   b. reading encourages violence.

   c. teenagers have easy access to guns.

   d. bookstores sell guns.

4. What evidence is there in this article that handguns for teenagers is a business?

   _____

   _____

5. What evidence is there in this article that gun control is a political issue?

   _____

   _____

6. Describe the relationship between self-esteem and handguns that is implied in this article.

   _____

   _____

7. Using only the context and your knowledge of word structure, define each of the following words. Do not use a dictionary.

   a. ramifications (3) _____

   b. mundane (6) _____

   c. fledgling (7) _____

   d. proliferation (8) _____

   e. proxy (10) _____

f.   tabled (14) _____

g. euphemism (16) _____

h. dispel (19) _____

Recalling Details

(See Chapter 4.)

1. Of 200 high school students, how many probably carry a gun?

    a. Five

    b. Ten

    c. Fifteen

    d. Twenty

2. Which of the following groups have been working to resolve the problems discussed in this article? Check all that apply.

    _____ a. Save Our Sons and Daughters

    _____ b. Center to Prevent Handgun Violence

    _____ c. United Federation of Teachers

    _____ d. Bureau of Alcohol Tobacco and Firearms

    _____ e. National Rifle Association

    _____ f. Mothers Against Drunk Driving (MADD)

    _____ g. Education Fund to Prevent Handgun Violence

    _____ h. Teens on Target

3. Indicate whether each statement is fact (F) or opinion (O). For those you label opinion, list any support for the opinion that is given in this article.

    a. The number of teenagers aged 15 to 19 who were killed by firearms increased 43 percent between 1984 and 1988. (   )

    _____

    _____

    b. America's "Terminator 2" entertainment industry comes in for part of the blame, too. (   )

    _____

    _____

c. Some 80 percent of the youngsters in Detroit's public schools have either lost someone to gun violence or know of someone who has . . . (   )

_____

_____

d. The gun becomes the equalizer. (   )

_____

_____

e. Other guns can be bought on the street, where the trade can be brisk and the dealers unconcerned about the age of their customers. (   )

_____

_____

f. Once a kid has a gun, bringing it to school is easy. (   )

_____

_____

g. Stricter gun control laws are the obvious answer. (   )

_____

_____

h. Security experts and child advocates also advise schools to incorporate programs to prevent gun violence into their curricula. (   )

_____

_____

4. Look at the chart that follows and then explain
   a. What ideas from this article are supported by the chart?

_____

b. What additional information have you learned from this chart?

Rate of Student-Reported Nonfatal Crimes Against Students Ages 12–18 per 1,000 Students, By Type of Crime and Location, 1992–2003

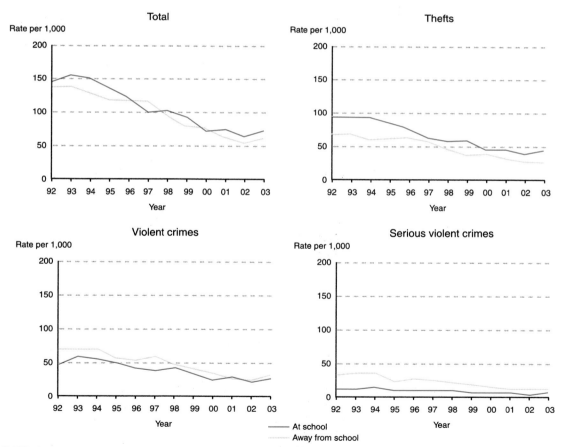

NOTE: Serious violent crimes include rape, sexual assault, robbery, and aggravated assault. Violent crimes include serious violent crimes and simple assault. Total crimes include violent crimes and theft. "At school" includes inside the school building, on school property, or on the way to or from school.

5. Return to the structured overview at the beginning of this selection and add to it any details from the article that further explain the statement of the problem, causes, effects, and solutions.

Critical Thinking: Reaction and Discussion

1. One professor who was interviewed commented, "many youngsters must juggle three sometimes conflicting 'cultures,' or codes of conduct." (22)

   With a group, discuss how this comment reflects your own experiences? What ways have the members of your group found to resolve some of the conflicts you face?

2. With a group, prepare to debate the following question: *Should the media be held accountable for violence among teenagers?*

 ## USING TECHNOLOGY FOR FURTHER UNDERSTANDING

With a group, do the following:

1. Discuss the value of the laws proposed in paragraph 13.

2. This article was published in 1992. Use the Internet to investigate how gun control laws in your state have changed since then, if at all. How have federal laws changed? Do you think these are good changes?

3. Locate any other state or federal laws currently under consideration.

What additional laws would you suggest?

● SELECTIONS 7 AND 8 ALTERNATIVE VIEWPOINTS

Same–Sex Marriage

Andrew Sullivan, *Here Comes the Groom* · Viewpoint 1

Robert Sokolowski, *The Threat of Same–Sex Marriage* ·

Viewpoint 2

Preview

What follows are two articles on the topic of same-sex marriage. Each expresses a different viewpoint. Before you read these, you will have a chance to reflect on your own opinions on this topic.

To Think About Before You Read

What are your views on same-sex marriage? In the space provided, write a sentence that states your opinion. Beneath it write 5 sentences that elaborate on your viewpoint. Each sentence should give a different reason for your opinion.

Your opinion: _____

_____

_____

Your reasons for your opinion: _____

　　　1. _____

　　　2. _____

　　　3. _____

　　　4. _____

　　　5. _____

Terms to Know Before You Read

(Viewpoint 2)

chastened (1) restrained; subdued

enshrining (4) to cherish as sacred

paradigm (5) example, model

arbitrary (6) determined by chance, whim, or impulse

bourgeois (8) a member of the middle class

deconstructionist (10) tearing down of traditional thinking

attenuated (11) made smaller, made less significant

omnipotence (19) the state of being all powerful or having unlimited authority

Viewpoint I

Last month in New York, a court ruled that a gay lover had the right to stay in his deceased partner's rent-control apartment because the lover qualified as a member of the deceased's family. The ruling deftly annoyed almost everybody. Conservatives saw judicial activism in favor of gay rent control: three reasons to be appalled. Chastened liberals (such as the *New York Times* editorial page), while endorsing the recognition of gay relationships, also worried about the abuse of already stretched entitlements that the ruling threatened. What neither side quite contemplated is that they both might be right, and that the way to tackle the issue of unconventional relationships in conventional society is to try something both more radical and more conservative than putting courts in the business of deciding what is and is not a family. That alternative is the legalization of civil gay marriage.

2   The New York rent-control case did not go anywhere near that far, which is the problem. The rent-control regulations merely stipulated that a "family" member had the right to remain in the apartment. The judge ruled that to all intents and purposes a gay lover is part of his lover's family, inasmuch as a "family" merely means an interwoven social life, emotional commitment, and some level of financial interdependence.

It's principle now well established around 3 the country. Several cities have "domestic partnership" laws, which allow relationships that do not fit into the category of heterosexual marriage to be registered with the city and qualify for benefits that up till now have been reserved for straight married couples. San Francisco, Berkeley, Madison, and Los Angeles all have legislation, as does the politically correct Washington, D.C., suburb, Takoma Park. In these cities, a variety of interpersonal arrangements qualify for health insurance, bereavement leave, insurance, annuity and pension rights, housing rights (such as rent-control apartments), adoption and inheritance rights. Eventually, according to gay lobby groups, the aim is to include federal income tax and veterans' benefits as well. A recent case even involved the right to use a family member's accumulated frequent-flier points. Gays are not the only beneficiaries; heterosexual "live-togethers" also qualify.

4   There's an argument, of course, that the current legal advantages extended to married people unfairly discriminate against people who've shaped their lives in less conventional arrangements. But it doesn't take a genius to see that enshrining in the law a vague principle like "domestic partnership" is an invitation to qualify at little personal cost for a vast array of entitlements otherwise kept crudely under control.

5   To be sure, potential DPs have to prove financial interdependence, shared living arrangements, and a commitment to mutual caring. But they don't need to have a sexual relationship or even closely mirror old-style marriage. In principle, an elderly woman and her live-in nurse could qualify. A couple of uneuphemistically confirmed bachelors could be DPs. So could two close college students, a pair of seminarians, or a couple of frat buddies. Left as it is, the concept of domestic partnership could open a Pandora's box of litigation and subjective judicial decision-making about who qualifies. You either are or are not married; it's not a complex question. Whether you are in a "domestic partnership" is not so clear.

6   More important, the concept of domestic partnership chips away at the prestige of traditional relationships and undermines the priority we give them. This priority is not necessarily a product of heterosexism. Consider heterosexual couples. Society has good reason to extend legal advantages to heterosexuals who choose the formal sanction of marriage over simply living together. They make a deeper commitment to one another and to society; in exchange, society extends certain benefits to them. Marriage provides an anchor, if an arbitrary and weak one, in the chaos of sex and relationships to which we are all prone. It provides a mechanism for emotional stability, economic security, and the healthy rearing of the next generation. We rig the law in its favor not because we disparage all forms of relationship other than the nuclear family, but because we recognize that not to promote marriage would be to ask too much of human virtue. In the context of the weakened family's effect upon the poor, it might also invite social disintegration. One of the worst products of the New Right's "family values" campaign is that its extremism and hatred of diversity has disguised this more measured and more convincing case for the importance of the marital bound.

7   The concept of domestic partnership ignores these concerns, indeed directly attacks them. This is a pity, since one of its most important objectives—providing some civil recognition for gay relationships—is a noble cause and one completely compatible with the defense of the family. But the way to go about it is not to undermine straight marriage; it is to legalize old-style marriage for gays.

8   The gay movement has ducked this issue primarily out of fear of division. Much of the gay leadership clings to notions of gay life as essentially outsider, anti-bourgeois, radical. Marriage, for them, is co-optation into straight society. For the Stonewall generation, it is hard to see how this vision of conflict will ever fundamentally change. But for many other gays—my guess, a majority—while they don't deny the importance of rebellion 20 years ago and are grateful for what was done, there's now the sense of a new opportunity. A need to rebel has quietly ceded to a desire to belong. To be gay and to be bourgeois no longer seems such an absurd proposition. Certainly since AIDS, to be gay and to be responsible has become a necessity.

9   Gay marriage squares several circles at the heart of the domestic partnership debate. Unlike domestic partnership, it allows for recognition of gay relationships, while casting no aspersions on traditional marriage. It merely asks that gays be allowed to join in. Unlike domestic partnership,

it doesn't open up avenues for heterosexuals to get benefits without the responsibilities of marriage, or a nightmare of definitional litigation. And unlike domestic partnership, it harnesses to an already established social convention the yearnings for stability and acceptance among a fast-maturing gay community.

10   Gay marriage also places more responsibilities upon gays; it says for the first time that gay relationships are not better or worse than straight relationships, and that the same is expected of them. And it's clear and dignified. There's a legal benefit to a clear, common symbol of commitment. There's also a personal benefit. One of the ironies of domestic partnership is that it's not only more complicated than marriage, it's more demanding, requiring an elaborate statement of intent to qualify. It amounts to a substantial invasion of privacy. Why, after all, should gays be required to prove commitment before they get married in a way we would never dream of asking of straights?

11   Legalizing gay marriage would offer homosexuals the same deal society now offers heterosexuals: general social approval and specific legal advantages in exchange for a deeper and harder-to-extract-yourself-from commitment to another human being. Like straight marriage, it would foster social cohesion, emotional security, and economic prudence. Since there's no reason gays should not be allowed to adopt or be foster parents, it could also help nurture children. And its introduction would not be some sort of radical break with social custom. As it has become more acceptable for gay people to acknowledge their loves publicly, more and more have committed themselves to one another for life in full view of their families and their friends. A law institutionalizing gay marriage would merely reinforce a healthy social trend. It would also, in the wake of AIDS, qualify as a genuine public

health measure. Those conservatives who deplore promiscuity among some homosexuals should be among the first to support it. Burke could have written a powerful case for it.

12   The argument that gay marriage would subtly undermine the unique legitimacy of straight marriage is based upon a fallacy. For heterosexuals, straight marriage would remain the most significant—and only legal social bond. Gay marriage could only delegitimize straight marriage if it were a real alternative to it, and this is clearly not true. To put it bluntly, there's precious little evidence that straights could be persuaded by any law to have sex with—let alone marry—someone of their own sex. The only possible effect of this sort would be to persuade gay men and women who force themselves into heterosexual marriage (often at appalling cost to themselves and their families) to find a focus for their family instincts in a more personally positive environment. But this is clearly a plus, not a minus: gay marriage could both avoid a lot of tortured families and create the possibility for many happier ones. It is not, in short, a denial of family values. It's an extension of them.

13   Of course, some would claim that any legal recognition of homosexuality is a de facto attack upon heterosexuality. But even the most hardened conservatives recognize that gays are a permanent minority and aren't likely to go away. Since persecution is not an option in a civilized society, why not coax gays into traditional values rather than rain incoherently against them?

14   There's a less elaborate argument for gay marriage: it's good for gays. It provides role models for young gay people who, after the exhilaration of coming out, can easily lapse into short-term relationships and insecurity with no tangible goal in sight. My own guess is that most gays would embrace such a goal with as much (if not more) commitment as straights. Even in our society as

it is, many lesbian relationships are virtual textbook cases of monogamous commitment. Legal gay marriage could also help bridge the gulf often found between gays and their parents. It could bring the essence of gay life—a gay couple—into the heart of the traditional straight family in a way the family can most understand and the gay offspring can most easily acknowledge. It could do as much to heal the gay-straight rift as any amount of gay rights legislation.

15   If these arguments sound socially conservative, that's no accident. It's one of the richest ironies of our society's blind spot toward gays that essentially conservative social goals should have the appearance of being so radical. But gay marriage is not a radical step. It avoids the mess of domestic partnership; it is humane; it is conservative in the best sense of the word. It's also about relationships. Given that gay relationships will always exist, what possible social goal is advanced by framing the law to encourage those relationships to be unfaithful, undeveloped, and insecure?

August 28, 1989, *The New Republic.* Copyright © 1989, Andrew Sullivan.

Viewpoint 2

Those who argue against the legalization of same-sex marriages insist that marriage is ordered toward the procreation of children and that the legal supports given to marriage are given with that end in view. Marriage needs the protection of laws because society must be concerned about its own preservation and continuity into the next generation.

2   Those who argue for legalization claim that the abiding friendship between the two persons should be acknowledged by law, and the legal benefits accruing to marriage should be made available to the partners. As a letter in The Wall Street Journal stated, "Marriage is a personal decision of commitment and love, and should be as open to homosexuals as it is to heterosexuals" (3/27/96). The essential point in the argument for legalization is that marriage as an institution sanctions a friendship, not specifically a procreative relationship.

3   Defenders of same-sex marriages often ask their opponents what they fear. What damage will follow from legally recognizing same-sex unions? How will such recognition threaten heterosexual marriages? I would like to address this issue by identifying some of the consequences of giving same-sex marriages full legal status.

I

4   Suppose the laws were to recognize homosexual marriages. Then suppose I were to come along and say: "My uncle and I [or my aunt and I, or my sister and I, or my mother and I, or my father and I, or my friend and I] live together. We are devoted to each other, but we don't engage in mutual sexual conduct. We want to get married in order to get the legal benefits of marriage that affect property rights, taxes, insurance and the like."

5   The reply would probably be negative, at least at first. The laws would say, "You cannot get married." Why not? "Because you don't exchange sex." That is, the homosexual marriage will become the paradigm. The exchange of sex, and specifically nonprocreative sex, will be what defines marriage. This new definition of marriage would be implied by the refusal to let my uncle and me get married, not because we cannot have children but because we do not choose to have sex. A procreative marriage would then only accidentally be a marriage. Procreation would no longer specify what a marriage is.

6   Once this new definition of marriage is in

place, subsequent laws would have to shore it up. What effect would this development have on the public sense of family and marriage? What effect would it have on sex education? It should also be noted that this understanding of marriage would bring the government into the bedroom with a vengeance, because it would be necessary for it to verify that those who are married are indeed having sex.

7   The new reproductive technologies make procreation possible outside of sex, and this reinforces even more the accidentality of procreation to marriage. A partner will be able to make a withdrawal from the sperm bank and have a child, but that partner will be married to no one related to the birth of the child: neither to the sperm donor, nor to the sperm bank, nor to the inseminating health care provider.

8   But suppose the reply of the laws to my demand to marry my uncle or aunt is: "All right, we will declare you married. We have already separated marriage from reproduction, and from now on we will separate marriage from sex entirely. Any two people who live together can get married." After all, if homosexual couples are discriminated against because they cannot get married, why should any two people who live together, even those already related by prior "familial" bonds, such as uncles and nephews, be discriminated against? Any persons who form a house hold should have the right to be married.

9   What effect would this have on the sense of marriage? I could marry my father (even Oedipus was never in danger of doing this, so far have we surpassed the wisdom of the ancients). I could marry someone I plan to live with for a few years, just for the benefit of it all. Suppose I were to move in with my grandfather who is seriously ill, to help him out in his last days. We could get married for the legal benefits and to facilitate the inheritance.

And once this has been done, why not permit polygamy and polyandry? Why discriminate against groups, if just living together is the only requirement for marriage? I could marry not just my mother or father, but both of them together, in a truly deconstructionist gesture, thus joining not with one but with both of the sources of my being.

If this were to occur, there would be very little left of such other familial relationships as those of grandparents, uncles and aunts, cousins and the like. Such relationships have already been attenuated by the prevalence of divorce, remarriage and single parenting: the "network" of relatives is deeply modified when some children in a family have different grandparents and cousins than their siblings do. In cases of artificial insemination by an unknown donor, the child is not related even to his or her biological father and his family. Such a dilution of extended familial relationships is a loss of a great human good; it damages an important dimension of personal identity People become anonymous individuals, left to define themselves instead of being given a role and place in life.

We could even go one step further and ask why people should have to live together to be married. If there are legal and financial benefits to the union, why should they not be available to any people who wish to take advantage of them? The choice to be benefited should override the accidentality of living together, so long as there is a modicum of commitment and friendship among those people.

If "marriage is a personal decision of commitment and love," why should it not be open to whoever is (or says he or she is) committed to and loves anyone else to a greater or lesser degree, whether singly or in a collective?

And why must that love be erotic? The major threat that same-sex marriages pose to traditional unions is that they redefine the institution of marriage.

II

15 Marriage has traditionally been understood to be a human relationship ordered toward reproduction. The "end" of marriage is procreation. To understand this claim, it is important to distinguish between ends and purposes, a distinction introduced by Francis X. Slade.

16 Purposes are goals that human beings have in mind when they act; they are wished-for satisfactions, intentions, things that people hope to obtain through their choices. Purposes arise only where there are human beings who are capable of deliberation and action. Ends, however, are found apart from the intentions and thoughts of human beings. Ends belong to things; they are how things function when they are working according to their own natures, when they reach the perfection that is proper to them. The end of medicine is to preserve or restore health, the end of an axe is to cut. Ends are there apart from human willing. We cannot will even an artifact, like an axe, into being something that it is not.

17 When we use things, purposes and ends interact. A man may pursue many different purposes in practicing medicine. He may strive to become rich, gain a reputation or alleviate suffering, but in all these purposes the end of medicine remains what it is, the preservation or restoration of health. An agent may pursue different purposes in using an axe: he may clear a forest, prepare firewood or attack someone, but cutting remains the end of the axe. Human beings, as they pursue their purposes, may or may not respect the ends inscribed in things. If they fail to respect these ends, they will bring the thing in question to ruin. If medicine is practiced in a way that does not preserve or restore

health, it will die out as an art, and if an axe is used in a manner that contradicts cutting, it will rust, chip or fracture. As Slade has put it, there is an "ontological priority" of ends over purposes.

18 A very important element in our modern culture is the belief that there are no ends in things; there are only purposes. One of the names for this belief is "mastery of nature." We think we can redefine all institutions, relationships and things, because whatever seems to be "natural" to them is really only the result of earlier choices that other agents have made. Their apparent "nature" is only a significance that we have projected onto them. We can introduce new purposes and redefine government, sexuality, birth and death, education, and marriage and the family. We can reinvent anything, because whatever there is has been invented, not discovered, by someone else. There are no ends in nature, so we can use everything according to our own purposes, to satisfy our wants, and nothing in our nature prescribes what we should want. We are free: "At long last our ships may venture out again; . . . the sea, our sea, lies open again; perhaps there has never yet been such an 'open sea'" (Nietzsche, *The Gay Science* [1882], No. 343).

19 It is exhilarating to think that we can redefine everything, ourselves included, in this way. It is easy to address people with rhetoric about "liberating" themselves from the prejudices and restrictions of the past and to encourage them to exercise a kind of small-scale omnipotence. We are invited to choose our own values and define our own understanding of happiness. Furthermore, since people have become used to thinking that things in general do not have natures and ends, it is hard for them to think that sexuality and marriage have ends. Consequently, the proposal to redefine marriage seems appealing to many, especially our cultural elites.

III

20 Sexuality has as its end the procreation of children, but the common use of contraception and the way sex is presented in our popular culture have totally separated sex from procreation in public opinion. Sex is understood as an end in itself. The reigning opinion is that a woman gets pregnant by accident, by not taking precautions, not because sexual activity is procreative and its natural outcome conception. This is a great reversal of nature and accident. Furthermore, it is said that every child must be a wanted child, which implies that the child is loved because the child has been chosen, not because he or she is there.

21 It is often said that we have recently arrived at a new and different sense of sexuality and marriage, but this claim is incorrect; both are what they always were. To say that mutual love is on a par with procreation as an end in marriage is misleading. It is obviously very important, but not as a simply parallel good. Rather, the end of procreation is what specifies this relationship; the physical end of procreation is the first and essential defining character of marriage, and sex is defined as the power to procreate. Then this relationship, so defined, is to be informed with friendship or love, that is, mutual benevolence; but the kind of love it calls for is qualified by the type of relationship it is.

22 Even in the Catholic Church after the Second Vatican Council, people have been quick to introduce mutual love as an end of marriage on a par with procreation. It is, of course, an end of marriage, but not the same kind of end as procreation is. It is not an alternative end, but one based on and specified by the procreative relationship.

23 People who separate sexuality from procreation, whether in their thinking or their actions, live in illusion. They lie about this matter, to themselves and to others. Furthermore, this error occurs not about some human thing, but about the mystery of our own origins. It is an illusion concerning one of the most powerful human emotions and tendencies. Once we live in delusion about such an important issue, we will inevitably be misguided in regard to many other human things: religion, human relations, laws, governmental policies, moral judgments and even our cultural inheritance. The most obvious truths become obscured.

IV

24 The state does not establish legal categories for many different forms of human friendship. Why does it do so for marriage? Because it has an interest in society's next generation. The continuation of the population is a condition for the survival of the body politic. It is this focus on population and reproduction that justifies laws concerning marriage. Even marriages between people who cannot have children, such as older people, depend on procreative marriages for their sense and legal standing. Society has an interest in seeing that there will be a next generation and that it will be brought up to be virtuous, law-abiding and productive. By its actions, therefore, the state has traditionally recognized reproduction as the end of marriage.

25 Proponents of same-sex marriages want to unlink marriage from reproduction and have the laws legalize their friendship because it is a friendship, not because it is procreative. But once the state legalizes one kind of friendship, it cannot stop at that; it will have to legalize any and all friendships for which legalization is sought.

26 The concept of same-sex marriages leads to impossibilities, because it contains a contradiction. Its proponents do not recognize the con-

tradition, because they think that nothing has a natural end, and specifically they think that marriage and sexuality do not have natural ends. They think that choices and purposes are the only things that matter, and that the private choices they make, their "personal decisions of commitment and love," must be ratified and supported by public law.

Msgr. Robert Sokolowski, "The Threat of Same-Sex Marriage," *America,* Vol. 190, No. 19, p. 12. Copyright 2004 American Magazine. All rights reserved. Reproduced by permission of America Press. For subscription information, visit www. americamagazine.org

---

Evaluation of the Articles

Sullivan: Difficulty Rating ☐ 1 ☐ 2 ☐ 3 ☐ 4 ☐ 5
(1 = easy; 5 = difficult)

Sokolowski: Difficulty Rating ☐ 1 ☐ 2 ☐ 3 ☐ 4 ☐ 5
(1 = easy; 5 = difficult)

What reading difficulties did you encounter?

_____

How did you handle these difficulties? _____

_____

Postreading Comprehension Development

1. On the lines provided, write a main idea sentence for each of the two articles, using the starter sentence provided.

   Author: Sullivan

   The author wants me to understand that:

   _____

   _____

   Author: Sokolowski

   The author wants me to understand that:

   _____

_____

_____

2. What are some major details each author gave to support his point of
    view? List 4 major details sentences from each author. Next to each
    detail, identify the type of detail it is.

Author: Sullivan

    a. Major Detail: _____

        Type of detail: _____

    b. Major Detail: _____

        Type of detail: _____

    c. Major Detail: _____

        Type of detail: _____

    d. Major Detail: _____

        Type of detail: _____

Author: Sokolowski

    a. Major Detail: _____

        Type of detail: _____

    b. Major Detail: _____

        Type of detail: _____

    c. Major Detail: _____

        Type of detail: _____

    d. Major Detail: _____

        Type of detail: _____

3. Locate three sentences from each article that you had to reword in order to clarify their meaning. On the lines provided, write the original sentence and beneath that put your revised sentence.

Author: Sullivan

a. Original sentence: _____

_____

_____

Your revised sentence: _____

_____

_____

b. Original sentence: _____

_____

_____

Your revised sentence: _____

_____

_____

c. Original sentence: _____

_____

_____

Your revised sentence: _____

_____

_____

Author: Sokolowski

a. Original sentence: _____

_____

_____

Your revised sentence: _____

_____

_____

b. Original sentence: _____

_____

_____

Your revised sentence: _____

_____

_____

c. Original sentence: _____

_____

_____

Your revised sentence: _____

_____

_____

4. In your opinion, which author did the best job of defending his opinion? Explain your answer on the lines provided.

_____

5. Neither author offered expert opinion to support their point of view. What would you suggest as studies that could be conducted by experts to provide such support? Give an example of one possible study for each author's viewpoint.

   Author: Sullivan

   Author: Sokolowski

6. On separate paper, create a visual array for *each* of the two reading selections. Use a different array style for each. On the lines provided, indicate the style you have chosen for each. Be prepared to discuss the array you used and why you chose that format.

   a. **Author: Sullivan**

   Selected Array Style:

   b. **Author: Sokolowski**

   Selected Array Style:

Critical Thinking: Reaction and Discussion

1. Several states are considering revising some laws to accommodate same-sex partners, even if they aren't married. They are looking at such issues as the partner's rights to health insurance on the other partner's plan, the right to make medical decisions for an ill partner who cannot make them, and designation as "immediate family" to provide visitation rights in hospitals.

   In an essay of at least 250 words, respond to the following statement: *Even if they aren't married, same-sex partners should have the same partner rights as a spouse.*

2. Refer back to the To Think About Before You Read section at the beginning of these articles. Did reading and thinking about these articles have any effect on your opinion? On the lines provided, indicate how these two readings have affected your ideas on this subject.

_____

_____

_____

_____

3. In this activity you will work to reach consensus with a small group. First, you will work with one other person to discuss the question on the Discussion Web that follows. You will discuss your points of view on the central question. Take turns writing down your reasons in two opposite columns. Write the strongest possible arguments on both sides.

Next, pair up with another pair and compare all the reasons listed in both columns on your Discussion Webs. Work toward reaching a consensus on the question. Write a conclusion at the bottom of the Discussion Web. If your group does not reach total consensus (if one or more disagree with the group's conclusion), make note of this to share later.

Decide which three reasons best support your conclusion and select a spokesperson to present to the whole class. Let the class know the process you used to reach consensus and how you handled anyone who was opposed to the group decision.

 USING TECHNOLOGY FOR FURTHER UNDERSTANDING

1. Search the Internet to locate recent state legislation on same-sex marriage in three states in three different regions of the United States. What similarities do you see in the legislation? What are some of the differences? How would each of the two authors respond to each state's legislation?

2. Use the Internet to locate letters to the editor in newspapers on the subject of same-sex marriage. What arguments made differ from those given by Sullivan and Sokolowski?

3. Using the Internet, find information on how other countries are handling the question of same-sex marriage. Discuss any alternatives you find that seem reasonable and explain how they address issues raised in the two articles you read in this section.

DISCUSSION WEB

YES		NO
	Is same-sex marriage a good idea?	
	Conclusions	

CHAPTER THIRTEEN

The Sciences
Knowledge of the Physical World

Science invites us to let the facts in, even when they don't conform to our preconceptions. It counsels us to carry alternative hypotheses in our heads and see which best match the facts.

—Carl Sagan

Derivation: *-ology*   —science

Key Concepts for the Study of the Sciences

Before you read the following list of areas of scientific study, think about some issues and topics that you might study if you took courses in the sciences. In the space provided, list your ideas.

_____

_____

GEOLOGY.   The science that deals with the history of the earth and its life, especially as recorded in rocks; a study of the solid matter of a celestial body (as the moon).

ENVIRONMENTAL SCIENCE.   The science that deals with environmental issues related to the earth, such as air and water pollution, the exhaustion of natural resources, uncontrolled population growth, sound ecological principles, the maintenance of the ozone layer, and global warming.

PHYSICS.   The science that deals with matter and energy and their interactions.

TECHNOLOGY.   The practical application of knowledge; especially in a particular area, engineering.

BIOLOGY.   A branch of knowledge that deals with living organisms and vital processes; the plant and animal life of a region or environment.

ASTRONOMY.   The scientific study of matter in outer space, such as the positions, dimensions, energy, and evolution of stars and planets.

CHEMISTRY.   The science of the composition, structure, properties, and reactions of matter, especially of atomic and molecular systems.

Now that you have read this list, what are some additional issues or topics that you might study if you took courses in the sciences? In the space provided, list your ideas.

_____

_____

_____

● # Selection 9

The Nature of Science

■ The American Association for the
Advancement of Science

Preview

Research done by scientists is usually judged by other scientists who determine whether that research is acceptable—whether it is valid research and whether the findings suggested or the claims made have merit. All scientists use common standards to make these judgments. In the following article, you will learn what attitudes scientists have about their work and scientific knowledge, and what criteria they use to consider the legitimacy of scientific research.

To Think About Before You Read

This article has a number of major and minor headings. To prepare yourself for reading, think about the following questions. They are based on these headings. Write a few sentences in response to each question *before* you read the selection.

1. Why would scientists, perhaps more than other educated people, think that it is possible to understand the world?

    _____

    _____

    _____

2. Do you believe it is possible for scientists to know everything about the world? Why or why not?

    _____

    _____

    _____

3. What example can you think of that illustrates the idea that scientific ideas change over time?

_____

_____

_____

4. When new scientific discoveries are made, should the old ideas be thrown out? Why or why not?

_____

_____

_____

5. Why is it important for scientists to have evidence for their claims?

_____

_____

_____

6. Why do scientists need to have good imaginations?

_____

_____

_____

7. Why is it important for scientists to be open minded and unbiased?

_____

_____

_____

Terms to Know Before You Read

consistent (2) free from variation or contradiction; regular

prevailing (4) generally current; having greater strength or superiority; continuing to be in use

phenomena (5) observable facts or events; facts or events of scientific interest susceptible to scientific description and explanation; rare or significant facts or events

conform (11) to bring into harmony; to be similar

principles (11) rules; comprehensive and fundamental laws

THE SCIENTIFIC WORLD VIEW

1 Scientists share certain basic beliefs and attitudes about what they do and how they view their work. These have to do with the nature of the world and what can be learned about it.

The World Is Understandable

2 Science presumes that the things and events in the universe occur in consistent patterns that are comprehensible through careful, systematic study. Scientists believe that through the use of the intellect, and with the aid of instruments that extend the senses, people can discover patterns in all of nature.

3 Science also assumes that the universe is, as its name implies, a vast single system in which the basic rules are everywhere the same. Knowledge gained from studying one part of the universe is applicable to other parts. For instance, the same principles of motion and gravitation that explain the motion of falling objects on the surface of the earth also explain the motion of the moon and the planets. With some modi-

fications over the years, the same principles of motion have applied to other forces—and to the motion of everything, from the smallest nuclear particles to the most massive stars, from sailboats to space vehicles, from bullets to light rays.

Scientific Ideas Are Subject to Change

4 Science is a process for producing knowledge. The process depends both on making careful observations of phenomena and on inventing theories for making sense out of those observations. Change in knowledge is inevitable because new observations may challenge prevailing theories. No matter how well one theory explains a set of observations, it is possible that another theory may fit just as well or better, or may fit a still wider range of observations. In science, the testing and improving and occasional discarding of theories, whether new or old, go on all the time. Scientists assume that even if there is no way to secure complete and absolute truth, increasingly accurate approximations can be made to account for the world and how it works.

Scientific Knowledge Is Durable

5 Although scientists reject the notion of attaining absolute truth and accept some uncertainty

as part of nature, most scientific knowledge is durable. The modification of ideas, rather than their outright rejection, is the norm in science, as powerful constructs tend to survive and grow more precise and to become widely accepted. For example, in formulating the theory of relativity, Albert Einstein did not discard the Newtonian laws of motion but rather showed them to be only an approximation of limited application within a more general concept. (The National Aeronautics and Space Administration uses Newtonian mechanics, for instance, in calculating satellite trajectories.) Moreover, the growing ability of scientists to make accurate predictions about natural phenomena provides convincing evidence that we really are gaining in our understanding of how the world works. Continuity and stability are as characteristic of science as change is, and confidence is as prevalent as tentativeness.

Science Cannot Provide Complete Answers to All Questions

6There are many matters that cannot usefully be examined in a scientific way. There are, for instance, beliefs that—by their very nature—cannot be proved or disproved (such as the existence of supernatural powers and beings, or the true purposes of life). In other cases, a scientific approach that may be valid is likely to be rejected as irrelevant by people who hold to certain beliefs (such as in miracles, fortune-telling, astrology, and superstition). Nor do scientists have the means to settle issues concerning good and evil, although they can sometimes contribute to the discussion of such issues by identifying the likely consequences of particular actions, which may be helpful in weighing alternatives.

SCIENTIFIC INQUIRY

Fundamentally, the various scientific disciplines 7 are alike in their reliance on evidence, the use of hypotheses and theories, the kinds of logic used, and much more. Nevertheless, scientists differ greatly from one another in what phenomena they investigate and in how they go about their work; in the reliance they place on historical data or on experimental findings and on qualitative or quantitative methods; in their recourse to fundamental principles; and in how much they draw on the findings of other sciences. Still, the exchange of techniques, information, and concepts goes on all the time among scientists, and there are common understandings among them about what constitutes an investigation that is scientifically valid.

Scientific inquiry is not easily described apart 8 from the context of particular investigations. There simply is no fixed set of steps that scientists always follow, no one path that leads them unerringly to scientific knowledge. There are, however, certain features of science that give it a distinctive character as a mode of inquiry. Although those features are especially characteristic of the work of professional scientists, everyone can exercise them in thinking scientifically about many matters of interest in everyday life.

Science Demands Evidence

Sooner or later, the validity of scientific claims 9 is settled by referring to observations of phenomena. Hence, scientists concentrate on getting accurate data. Such evidence is obtained by observations and measurements taken in situations that range from natural settings (such as a forest) to completely contrived ones (such as the laboratory). To make their observations, scientists use their own senses, instruments (such as microscopes) that enhance those senses, and instruments that tap characteristics quite different from what humans can sense (such as magnetic fields). Scientists observe passively (earthquakes, bird migrations), make collections (rocks, shells), and actively probe the world (as by boring into the earth's crust or administering experimental medicines).

10   In some circumstances, scientists can control conditions deliberately and precisely to obtain their evidence. They may, for example, control the temperature, change the concentration of chemicals, or choose which organisms mate with which others. By varying just one condition at a time, they can hope to identify its exclusive effects on what happens, uncomplicated by changes in other conditions. Often, however, control of conditions may be impractical (as in studying stars), or unethical (as in studying people), or likely to distort the natural phenomena (as in studying wild animals in captivity). In such cases, observations have to be made over a sufficiently wide range of naturally occurring conditions to infer what the influence of various factors might be. Because of this reliance on evidence, great value is placed on the development of better instruments and techniques of observation, and the findings of any one investigator or group are usually checked by others.

Science Is a Blend of Logic and Imagination

11   Although all sorts of imagination and thought may be used in coming up with hypotheses and theories, sooner or later scientific arguments must conform to the principles of logical reasoning—that is, to testing the validity of arguments by applying certain criteria of inference, demonstration, and common sense. Scientists may often disagree about the value of a particular piece of evidence, or about the appro-

priateness of particular assumptions that are made—and therefore disagree about what conclusions are justified. But they tend to agree about the principles of logical reasoning that connect evidence and assumptions with conclusions.

12   Scientists do not work only with data and well-developed theories. Often, they have only tentative hypotheses about the way things may be. Such hypotheses are widely used in science for choosing what data to pay attention to and what additional data to seek, and for guiding the interpretation of data. In fact, the process of formulating and testing hypotheses is one of the core activities of scientists. To be useful, a hypothesis should suggest what evidence would support it and what evidence would refute it. A hypothesis that cannot in principle be put to the test of evidence may be interesting, but it is not scientifically useful.

13   The use of logic and the close examination of evidence are necessary but not usually sufficient for the advancement of science. Scientific concepts do not emerge automatically from data or from any amount of analysis alone. Inventing hypotheses or theories to imagine how the world works and then figuring out how they can be put to the test of reality is as creative as writing poetry, composing music, or designing skyscrapers. Sometimes discoveries in science are made unexpectedly, even by accident. But knowledge and creative insight are usually required to recognize the meaning of the unexpected. Aspects of data that have been ignored by one scientist may lead to new discoveries by another.

Science Explains and Predicts

14   Scientists strive to make sense of observations of phenomena by inventing explanations for them that use, or are consistent with, currently accepted scientific principles. Such explana-

tions—theories—may be either sweeping or restricted, but they must be logically sound and incorporate a significant body of scientifically valid observations. The credibility of scientific theories often comes from their ability to show relationships among phenomena that previously seemed unrelated. The theory of moving continents, for example, has grown in credibility as it has shown relationships among such diverse phenomena as earthquakes, volcanoes, the match between types of fossils on different continents, the shapes of continents, and the contours of the ocean floors.

15 The essence of science is validation by observation. But it is not enough for scientific theories to fit only the observations that are already known. Theories should also fit additional observations that were not used in formulating the theories in the first place; that is, theories should have predictive power. Demonstrating the predictive power of a theory does not necessarily require the prediction of events in the future. The predictions may be about evidence from the past that has not yet been found or studied. A theory about the origins of human beings, for example, can be tested by new discoveries of human-like fossil remains. This approach is clearly necessary for reconstructing the events in the history of the earth or of the life forms on it. It is also necessary for the study of processes that usually occur very slowly, such as the building of mountains or the aging of stars. Stars, for example, evolve more slowly than we can usually observe. Theories of the evolution of stars, however may predict unsuspected relationships between features of starlight that can then be sought in existing collections of data about stars.

Scientists Try to Identify and Avoid Bias

16 When faced with a claim that something is true, scientists respond by asking what evidence supports it. But scientific evidence can be biased in how the data are interpreted, in the recording or reporting of the data, or even in the choice of what data to consider in the first place. Scientists' nationality, sex, ethnic origin, age, political convictions, and so on may incline them to look for or emphasize one or another kind of evidence or interpretation. For example, for many years the study of primates—by male scientists—focused on the competitive social behavior of males. Not until female scientists entered the field was the importance of female primates' community-building behavior recognized.

17 Bias attributable to the investigator, the sample, the method, or the instrument may not be completely avoidable in every instance, but scientists want to know the possible sources of bias and how bias is likely to influence evidence. Scientists want, and are expected, to be as alert to possible bias in their own work as in that of other scientists, although such objectivity is not always achieved. One safeguard against undetected bias in an area of study is to have many different investigators or groups of investigators working on it.

Science Is Not Authoritarian

18 It is appropriate in science, as elsewhere, to turn to knowledgeable sources of information and opinion, usually people who specialize in relevant disciplines. But esteemed authorities have been wrong many times in the history of science. In the long run, no scientist, however famous or highly placed, is empowered to decide for other scientists what is true, for none are believed by other scientists to have special access to the truth. There are no preestablished conclusions that scientists must reach on the basis of their investigations.

19 In the short run, new ideas that do not mesh

well with mainstream ideas may encounter vigorous criticism, and scientists investigating such ideas may have difficulty obtaining support for their research. Indeed, challenges to new ideas are the legitimate business of science in building valid knowledge. Even the most prestigious scientists have occasionally refused to accept new theories despite there being enough accumulated evidence to convince others. In the long run, however, theories are judged by their results: When someone comes up with a new or improved version that explains more phenomena or answers more important questions than the previous version, the new one eventually takes its place.

Evaluation of the Article

Difficulty Rating □ 1 □ 2 □ 3 □ 4 □ 5
(1 = easy; 5 = difficult)

What reading difficulties did you encounter? _____

_____

How did you handle these difficulties? _____

_____

Comprehension of the Discipline

1. Check those items that represent areas scientists might study.

   _____ a. The evolution of human use of tools

   _____ b. New stars in the galaxy

   _____ c. How dinosaurs became extinct

   _____ d. The type of car air bags needed to reduce the effect of impacts at particular speeds

   _____ e. Improved methods for teaching writing to college students

   _____ f. The ethnic makeup of a particular religious group

   _____ g. The effect of certain chemicals on the ozone layer

   _____ h. How a particular drug might affect diabetes

   _____ i. New remedies for balding

2. Check those items that represent attitudes scientists have about scientific study. Be prepared to cite evidence from the article to justify your answer.

_____ a. Scientists should share their work with other scientists.

_____ b. Today's scientists should ignore the work of earlier scientists because it is out of date.

_____ c. Scientific study should result in finding absolute truths.

_____ d. All scientific study should be accurate.

_____ e. If a scientific theory is particularly interesting, it doesn't require evidence for proof.

_____ f. Scientific study makes it possible for us to have a better understanding of our universe.

_____ g. Not all branches of science use the same kind of quantitative methods.

_____ h. Scientists should have good imaginations.

3. The methodology scientists use for making a discovery is called

a. investigative reporting

b. scientific inquiry

c. hypothesis analysis

d. prediction sampling

4. In their search for answers, scientists attempt to have which of the following? Check all that apply. Be prepared to justify your answers.

_____ a. Freedom from bias

_____ b. Better instruments

_____ c. As few human subjects as possible

_____ d. Logic

_____ e. Controlled conditions

_____ f. Disagreement with former theories

_____ g. Accuracy

5. Which of the following are characteristics of a good hypothesis? Check all that apply. Be prepared to cite evidence from the article to justify your answer.

_____ a. It is tentative.

_____ b. It is possible to find evidence that supports it.

_____ c. It is illogical.

_____ d. It is agreed to by many other scientists.

_____ e. It is possible to find evidence that argues against it.

6. Several different scientific experiments or activities are listed. Beneath each is an element of scientific inquiry. Explain how that element would be included in the experiment or activity.

   a. Conducting experiments with a new drug by giving some people the new drug and some a placebo, without knowing who is getting which treatment

   Formulation of hypothesis: _____

   _____

   _____

   b. Suggesting new ways to utilize laser technology

   Use of previous research: _____

   _____

   _____

   c. Conducting an experiment on chickens in a laboratory to see how they react to being in a small space for long periods

   Search for evidence: _____

   _____

   _____

7. Indicate whether each of the following is true (T) or false (F) based on the information given in this article. Be prepared to cite the evidence from the article that supports your answer.

   _____ a. Scientists in Japan probably don't share their research with American scientists.

   _____ b. A scientist making a discovery in the year 2050 should expect that by 2100 there would have been a new discovery that would change his or her original findings.

   _____ c. Scientists from different countries use radically different methodology in their research.

_____ d. Controlled studies are probably more accurate in their results than those conducted in uncontrolled situations.

_____ e. A discovery made about the effect of pollutants on the earth's atmosphere in one part of the world is likely to hold for other parts of the world.

_____ f. A scientist who had a very strong belief in a theory would publish the theory in a scientific journal only if there were evidence to support it.

8. Using only the context and your knowledge of word structure, define each of the following words. Do not use a dictionary.

a. modifications (3) _____

b. durable (5) _____

c. stability (5) _____

d. irrelevant (6) _____

e. constitutes (7) _____

f. unerringly (8) _____

g. contrived (9) _____

h. essence (15) _____

i. attributable (17) _____

Critical Thinking: Reaction and Discussion

1. With a small group, prepare a debate on one of the following topics. The people in your group should each represent a particular position or point of view. They may assume different roles: for example, one person could be an American scientist; another could be an owner of a pharmaceutical firm; another could be a representative of the federal government. Be prepared to present the results of your discussion to the class.

a. What moral responsibility do scientists have for the uses to which their discoveries are put? For instance, are they responsible if nations kill people with the poison gas developed by scientists?

b. What kinds of controls, if any, should governments put on the kinds of research that scientists do? Are there some things that should not be researched by scientists?

c. Should there be limits on what research one country's scientists share with another country's scientists? What kinds of information should not be shared?

2. Look at an issue of the *New York Times* Science Times section, or use the Science section of another newspaper or weekly magazine. Find an article about a recent scientific discovery that is of interest to you. Be prepared to discuss what makes it interesting and why you think the discovery is (or is not) beneficial to humanity.

USING TECHNOLOGY FOR FURTHER UNDERSTANDING

Interview a science professor on campus who uses computer simulations in his or her course. Find out why these are used and present your findings to the class.

Guidelines for Reading the Sciences

Although there are several different major branches of science, there are some common ways in which you should handle your reading of scientific material, especially science material that is in your textbook or that is in a popular magazine and has been written to explain a scientific theory, process, or discovery. Some additional things to bear in mind when you read science material follow.

READ SLOWLY.   Scientific material tends to be very detailed. It requires one, or even several, slow readings. How fast you read something should be determined partly by your purpose for reading. If you are reading material for pleasure, you can go rapidly and skip parts of it that don't interest you. If, however, your intention is to learn the material and to read for study purposes, you must go more slowly. Your familiarity with the subject will also influence your reading rate. If you bring a great deal of knowledge to a particular reading assignment in science, you can read at a faster pace than if you bring little or no background information.

PREVIEW THE MATERIAL BEFORE YOU BEGIN TO READ FOR DETAILS. You should always become acquainted with the general outline of the topic before you begin to read in depth. Try to learn from your preview what aspects of a particular topic are going to be discussed in the chapter or article. As part of the preview, you should at least think about:

1. the title
2. major subheadings
3. introductory and concluding paragraphs
4. questions at the end of the chapter
5. charts or diagrams within the chapter or article and the explanations accompanying them

When you are finished previewing, you should be able to identify the concepts that will be discussed by the author.

LEARN THE SPECIALIZED TERMINOLOGY.   The language of science is very precise. For instance, in physics, the terms *speed* and *velocity* have different meanings. A number of new terms are usually within any single science article or chapter. You need to understand and memorize them. To help you with your understanding of this terminology, you can do some of the following:

1. Check the context (the sentences surrounding the new term) to see whether the meaning has been supplied for you directly within the text.
2. If you are working with a textbook, check its glossary for a precise definition if one is not supplied in the context.
3. Try to use the word in class to verify your understanding.
4. Notice how your professor uses the term.

To help with memorization of new terminology, you can:

1. Learn word parts. Often, a particular branch of science will have a large number of words that use the same root or prefix. Learning the meanings of these word parts will help you determine the meanings of new words of similar origin.
2. Create flash cards. On the front of your card, put the word. On the back, write the meaning, and use the word in a sentence. Refer to these cards frequently for review.

STUDY VISUAL AIDS CAREFULLY.   Diagrams, graphs, and charts are frequently included in scientific writing. They help clarify the text material. Be sure you understand the relationship of each part of the visual aid to each other part and that you are clear about what each set of numbers or each label on the visual aid represents. Try recreating the diagram on your own paper.

TRY TO MENTALLY VISUALIZE WHAT YOU READ.   This strategy is especially helpful if you are reading about a process—for example, how food is digested. The picture you create in your mind will assist you with recall at a later date.

CREATE SOME OF YOUR OWN CHARTS, GRAPHS, AND DIAGRAMS TO SHOW RELATIONSHIPS DISCUSSED IN THE MATERIAL.   This strategy encourages you to think about the connections between the different ideas. Again, the concrete visual aid will be easier to recall than the words in the text.

LOOK FOR WRITING PATTERNS WHILE YOU READ.   Science material is frequently organized according to one of four different pattern types:

1. Classification (showing groups and subgroups)
2. Process (how something occurs)
3. Experimental (steps taken to test something)
4. Problem–solution (usually a statement of some problem, its causes, effects, and solutions to the problem)

USE OUTSIDE SOURCES IF SOME IDEAS STILL SEEM UNCLEAR TO YOU. Specialized science encyclopedias and journals, as well as young adult science books, often explain complicated ideas in an easier way than that used in college textbooks. Although using outside resources takes additional study time, it may be time well spent if reading science is especially difficult for you.

TRY TO MAKE PERSONAL CONNECTIONS WITH WHAT YOU READ.   Think about how you may have already observed some topic or theory you are reading about even though you did not completely understand it at the time. Or consider how this information might affect your life.

TRY TO RESTATE IN YOUR OWN WORDS AS MANY OF THE MAIN POINTS AS YOU CAN.   Repeating in your own words what you have read will verify your understanding. This practice will point out areas that you are not sure of and that you will need to reread. You can practice making restatements by writing out your ideas or by discussing with a friend what you have read.

Keep these guidelines in mind as you read the remaining articles from the sciences.

● ## SELECTION 10

The Drunken Monkey Hypothesis

■ DUSTIN STEPHENS AND ROBERT DUDLEY

Preview

Many scientists believe that we can learn about human behavior by looking at primates. In this article you will learn how two scientists who hold this belief, try to better understand alcoholism in humans through their study of primates in their natural environment.

To Think About Before You Read

1. What animal studies do you know that have helped us to better understand human disease or illness?

   _____

   _____

2. Why might scientists be interested in studying alcoholism?

   _____

   _____

3. In your view, do you think federal funds should be spent on this kind of research?
   Explain your answer.

   _____

   _____

4. In your opinion, is alcoholism an emotional, physical, genetic, and/or an ethical issue, or a combination of these?
   Explain the reasons for your views.

   _____

   _____

5. Do you know any positive reasons to drink alcohol? If you do, what are they?

_____

_____

Terms to Know Before You Read

assays (3) analyses or examinations

conferred (4, 14) to invest with (a characteristic, for example)

prehensile (11) adapted for seizing, grasping, or holding, especially by wrapping around an object

inimical (14) injurious or harmful in effect

salubrious (16) conducive or favorable to health or well being

epidemiological study (16) a study that deals with causes

encode (18) specify the genetic code for (a protein molecule, for example)

What can a tipsy howler monkey tell science about humanity's fondness for—and problems with—alcohol? Possibly quite a lot. And that would be a good thing, considering how widespread our problems with alcohol are. In the United States alone, 14 million people are alcoholics, and several millions more are at risk. Although patterns vary from culture to culture, alcoholism is common across the globe, particularly among indigenous groups undergoing modernization, and it comes with tragic consequences: Even in the United States, abuse of alcohol is the third leading cause of preventable death.

2 Studying the evolutionary background of human behaviors that lead to widespread disorders has helped shed light on how those disorders emerged and became established. Similarly, placing alcoholism in an evolutionary frame-work might reveal how our forebears became attracted—and addicted—to alcohol. That's where the tipsy howler monkey comes into the picture. In 2004, one of us (Stephens) observed him feasting on the bright orange fruits of the Astrocaryum palm, in the tropical forest of Panama's Barro Colorado Island. Climbing onto the branches of a neighboring tree to reach the untouched clusters, the forager first sniffed the fruit, then frantically began to eat it, sometimes dropping partly eaten fruits onto the forest floor. Risking a thirty-foot fall and serious injury from the enormous spines of the palm tree, the monkey seemed as fearless as a drunken teenager.

Our assays of the fruit he dropped suggested 3 why: He may, in fact, have been drunk. Our calculations showed that the reckless forager had consumed the monkey equivalent of ten "standard drinks" during his twenty-minute gorging session. This measurement was the first quantitative estimate of the amount of alcohol ingested by a wild primate ever made. It also fitted nicely with the "drunken monkey" hypothesis, developed earlier by one of us (Dudley).

4   The hypothesis proposes that a strong attraction to the smell and taste of alcohol conferred a selective advantage on our primate ancestors by helping them locate nutritious fruit at the peak of ripeness. Millions of years later, in the Middle Ages, people learned to distill spirits, which potently concentrated the natural alcoholic content of fermented fruits and grains. The once advantageous appetite for alcohol became a danger to human health and well-being. Drawing on yeast biology, fruit ripening, biological anthropology, human genetics, and the emerging field of Darwinian medicine, the drunken monkey hypothesis could ultimately contribute to understanding—and perhaps even mitigating—the enormous damage done by alcohol.

5   The drunken monkey hypothesis goes like this: For 40 million years, primate diets have included substantial quantities of fruit. In the warm, humid tropics, where humans evolved, yeasts on the fruit skin and within the fruit convert sugars into various forms of alcohol, the most common being ethanol. Ethanol is a light molecule that disperses readily, and the downwind odor of ethanol is a reliable sign of ripe fruit. In the tropical forests where most primates live, the competition for ripe fruit is intense. For a hungry monkey, then, a good foraging strategy would be to follow the smell of alcohol to the fruit and eat it in a hurry. Natural selection probably favored primates with a keen appreciation for the smell and taste of alcohol. After all, they would have been quicker than their competitors to grab, if you will, the "low-hanging fruit."

6   We want to stress from the outset that the drunken monkey hypothesis is just that—a hypothesis. It remains far from proven, and there are experts who disagree with our assumptions. But we think the hypothesis has great potential for explaining humanity's deep and conflicting relations with alcohol. The logic of the argument, the supporting evidence, and a discussion of the areas where further work is needed all give new evolutionary and biological perspectives on what, until now, has been seen as an issue that is entirely medical and sociological in nature.

7   An impressive body of evidence indicates that contemporary primate diets are dominated by plant materials. In many primate groups those materials take the form of ripe (and probably alcohol-containing) fruits. Fossilized teeth show that fruit has been a major component of the primate diet since the mid to late Eocene Epoch, between 45 million and 34 million years ago. Some of our closest relatives—chimpanzees, orangutans, and certain populations of gorillas—eat diets based primarily on fruit.

8   To be sure, our own ancestors long ago left fruit behind as the main source of their nutrition. By the time the genus Homo appears in the fossil record, between 1 and 2 million years ago, fruit had been marginalized, and largely replaced by meat and by foods such as roots and tubers. But even though our early hominid ancestors stopped relying heavily on fruit, humanity shares a deep evolutionary background with other primates. It seems likely that the taste for alcohol arose during that long shared prologue.

9   Consider the evidence.

10   The place to begin is the relation between ripe fruit and alcohol. Yeasts that occur on fruit consume sugar molecules in the fruit as a

source of energy, in a process known as anaerobic fermentation ("anaerobic," because it takes place in the absence of oxygen). As the fruit ripens, and the yeast enzymes get going, the ethanol content of the fruit rises rapidly. For example, the unripe fruit of the Astrocaryum palm contains no ethanol; ripe hanging fruit is about 0.6 percent ethanol by weight; overripe fruit, often fallen to the ground, can have an ethanol content of more than 4 percent. The howler monkey that Stephens observed on Barro Colorado Island was feasting on fruit near its peak ripeness—when its ethanol content is about 1 percent.

11   What is the evidence that our primate relatives (or other organisms, for that matter) hone in on alcohol as a nutritional signpost? It is known that fruit flies of the genus Drosophila, a laboratory workhorse in genetics, follow increasing concentrations of ethanol vapor as a way to find the ripe fruit within which they lay their eggs. The fruit is an excellent food source for the fly larvae when they hatch.

12   A similar sensory mechanism is likely at play in other species, including primates. Alcohol-driven fruit "binges" similar to the one seen on Barro Colorado have been observed several times in howler and spider monkeys. In each instance, the monkey risked life and limb while eating quickly from bunch after bunch of Astrocaryum fruits, sometimes committing its full weight to a fruit cluster without so much as a prehensile tail secured as a backup. Other observations from the rainforest describe what seems to be fruit-induced intoxication in butterflies, fruit flies, a variety of birds, fruit bats, elephants, and several other primate species.

13   It is possible, of course, that drunken behavior is simply an accident without a deep evolutionary context. Maybe rainforest fauna just like to have fun. But some evidence implies that the connection between alcohol and nutrition is deeper than that, at least for primates. Initial observations of monkeys on Barro Colorado show that they prefer ripe palm fruits with moderate levels of alcohol. They avoid unripe fruits—with no alcohol—as well as overripe fruits—with more alcohol but less sugar (by then, most of the sugar has been converted to alcohol). Anecdotally, we note that people, too, often drink alcohol while eating, suggesting that drink with food is a natural combination. And various experiments have shown that drinking an aperitif increases both the time spent eating and the number of calories consumed at a sitting.

14   If there really is an evolutionary connection between alcohol and primate nutrition, an important conclusion follows: Alcohol—at least in moderation—cannot be entirely inimical to health. If it were, a good nose for alcohol would not have conferred selective advantage on our primate forebears; in fact, it would have damaged them.

15   In any event, a wide range of evidence suggests that moderate consumption of alcohol is healthful for widely divergent organisms. Fruit flies, for instance, live longer and have more offspring when they are experimentally exposed to vapors containing intermediate levels of ethanol than they do when exposed to a lot of it or to none at all. The biological mechanisms underlying those effects remain unclear, but as we noted earlier, the ability to sense and respond to the scent of ethanol plays an important role in the life cycle of the fruit fly. The health benefits of consumption may be connected in some way to the role that ethanol has in the fly's life cycle.

16   In people, too, moderate alcohol consumption seems to be more salubrious than too much or too little. Much of the evidence, how-

ever, for the health benefits of moderate drinking arises out of the risk factors for heart disease, which may not be relevant to the evolutionary argument. (The protection alcohol confers against heart disease may come from counteracting the effects of the high-fat diet we adopted long after our ancestors' fruit-eating days were past.) Still, other evidence suggests, circumstantially at least, that intermediate levels of alcohol consumption have benefits beyond their effects on the heart. A recent epidemiological study of Finnish civil servants showed that the workers who took the fewest official sick days were moderate consumers of alcohol.

17 To prove the drunken monkey hypothesis, it is not enough to show that alcohol is beneficial—or at least not damaging—to health. One also has to demonstrate that a varied group of genes is related to alcohol consumption. Only by operating on a variety of genes could evolution have selected the fittest of our primate forebears. Here we are on firmer ground. There is unquestionably a wide variation among human beings in the genes that underlie alcohol metabolism and, consequently, in individual appetites for alcohol.

18 The genes in question encode two enzymes that metabolize alcohol and its breakdown products; the enzymes are known as alcohol dehydrogenase and aldehyde dehydrogenase. But the genes vary from person to person, and that genetic variation becomes manifest as a wide variation among the gene-encoded enzymes in their efficiency at clearing alcohol or its toxic breakdown product, acetaldehyde, from the blood. Elevated levels of acetaldehyde cause headache, nausea, palpitations, and flushing. Given such a suite of unpleasant effects, it would be surprising if people who have inefficient acetaldehyde-clearing enzymes were eager to get tipsy. And sure enough, studies of East Asian populations, where the less-efficient enzymes are common, confirm that guess. In Japan, alcoholics are more likely to have rapid and efficient versions of the enzymes than nonalcoholics.

19 To sum up: A variety of direct and circumstantial evidence suggests that in our deep evolutionary background, alcohol and nutrition (and consequently, alcohol and survival) were intertwined. For some of our close genetic relatives, rainforest observations show that they remain intertwined to this day. Furthermore, some evidence shows that intermediate levels of alcohol consumption are beneficial to human health. But if evolution has rendered alcohol so good for us, why is it now such a plague?

20 The answer, we think, lies in a mismatch between our species' long evolutionary prelude and the techno-cultural environment we have created in the past few centuries. Until well into the first millennium A.D.—following millions of years of primate evolution—the amount of alcohol our ancestors could consume was strictly limited. As we have noted, even overripe fruits have an ethanol content of only about 4 percent, and they are not the ones favored by monkeys.

21 That picture did not change substantially even when modern humans, some 10,000 years ago, learned to control fermentation. As agriculture took root, barley and wheat became plentiful, which in turn provided good substrates for beer. Archaeological evidence from the same period indicates that wine was also being made. In fact, until industrialization made water filtration practical, alcoholic drinks are thought to have been more widely consumed in many cultures than water was.

22 But the alcoholic drinks of today—and the alcoholism that accompanies them—are, in

evolutionary terms, recent innovations. Yeasts stop making ethanol when its concentration reaches between 10 and 15 percent by weight. Hence drinks made using natural yeasts are limited in alcohol content. Beer and wine made before the invention of chemical distillation (in central Asia around A.D. 700) probably were no more than 5 percent ethanol. No harder stuff was available.

23   The invention of distillation, which had reached Europe in the Middle Ages, radically changed humanity's relationship with alcohol. Drinks whose ethanol content was much higher than 5 or even 12 percent suddenly became widely available. From the vantage of the drunken monkey hypothesis, the results were predictable: wide availability of potent drink led straight to extreme forms of alcohol abuse.

24   From the evolutionary perspective taken by Darwinian medicine, alcoholism is one of the "diseases of nutritional excess" that arises from a mismatch between prehistoric and contemporary environments. Perhaps the most striking example of such a disease is the ongoing epidemic of obesity. In 1962, the late geneticist James Neel predicted that as high-fat, high-calorie Western foods became available to tribal peoples, their incidence of obesity, heart disease, and adult-onset diabetes would sharply increase. The rationale for Neel's hypothesis was that "thrifty" genes, which had been advantageous in sequestering scarce calories, had turned deleterious when fats and sugars become readily available. The high rates of diabetes among Pima

Indians, Micronesian Nauruans and Australian Aborigines have confirmed his predictions.

25   Neel's prescient hypothesis, now clearly relevant to human populations in the developed world as well, fits nicely with the drunken monkey hypothesis. The increased alcohol concentration of booze made possible by industrial distillation played right into a genetically rooted appetite for alcohol that had been present for millions of years—and had served a valuable survival function for our forerunners as they climbed through the rainforest canopy. And just as with obesity, heart disease, and diabetes, alcoholism has become a risk for anyone with access to the fruits of contemporary culture.

26   The drunken monkey hypothesis, like many another productive scientific idea; raises more questions than the evidence so far in its favor can answer. How, precisely, do primates locate ripe fruit? What are the typical alcohol concentrations in the fruits they eat? Does alcohol act as a stimulant for primate feeding? How often do primates become intoxicated as a result of eating fruit? And what are the beneficial effects of alcohol on human beings and related species?

27   We are working to answer some of these questions, and we encourage our colleagues to answer others. It is still just the beginning of what we believe will be (forgive the pun) a fruitful avenue of research into human prehistory. And perhaps the knowledge gained will ultimately suggest strategies for stemming the tragic damage to our species wrought all too commonly by alcoholism.

Evaluation of the Article

Difficulty Rating ☐ 1 ☐ 2 ☐ 3 ☐ 4 ☐ 5
(1 = easy; 5 = difficult)

What reading difficulties did you encounter? _____

_____

How did you handle these difficulties? _____

_____

Postreading Comprehension Development

Sentence Rewrite

To check your understanding of some of the key concepts of this essay, rewrite each of the following sentences in your own words, keeping the original idea. (See Chapter 1.)

1. The hypothesis proposes that a strong attraction to the smell and taste of alcohol conferred a selective advantage on our primate ancestors by helping them locate nutritious fruit at the peak of ripeness. (4)

_____

_____

2. If there really is an evolutionary connection between alcohol and primate nutrition, an important conclusion follows: Alcohol—at least in moderation—cannot be entirely inimical to health. (14)

_____

_____

3. From the evolutionary perspective taken by Darwinian medicine, alcoholism is one of the "diseases of nutritional excess" that arises from a mismatch between prehistoric and contemporary environments. (24)

_____

_____

Author's Main Idea

(See Chapter 3.)

1. What is the topic of this article?

   _____

2. What is the authors' focus on this topic?

   _____

3. Using the starter sentence provided, state the authors' main idea:
   The author wants me to understand that:

   _____

   _____

4. The paragraph in which the authors' main point is most clearly stated is:
   a. 3.
   b. 4.
   c. 13.
   d. 25.

5. How does the discussion about *selective advantage* (4) help serve the authors' purpose for writing this article?

   _____

   _____

   _____

6. How does the information in paragraph 19 contribute to the authors' purpose for writing this article?

   _____

   _____

Inferences, Metaphors, and Vocabulary in Context
(See Chapters 2, 6, and 7.)

1. What assumptions do these scientists make about the origin of man?
    a. Man was on earth well before primates.
    b. Man descended from primates by an evolutionary process.
    c. Man and primates co-existed on earth from the very beginning of time.
    d. An intelligent design of the universe caused man to arrive on earth some time after the primates did.

2. Which of the following does the author imply in paragraph 3? Be prepared to justify your answer.
    a. Most monkeys like to get drunk.
    b. There may be a genetic reason for alcoholism.
    c. A drunken monkey was observed.
    d. Ten "standard drinks" is a vast amount of alcohol.

3. How does this article illustrate the idea that scientists build on the theories of previous scientists? Be specific in your response, citing from the article.

    _____

    _____

4. From paragraph 6 we can conclude that:
    a. The drunken monkey hypothesis has already proven valuable for understanding alcoholism in humans.
    b. The drunken monkey hypothesis has received considerable support from the scientific community.
    c. These scientists will ask other scientists to develop hypotheses about human consumption of alcohol.
    d. These scientists plan to continue their research on this hypothesis.

5. According to the authors, how are primate survival and the smell of alcohol related?

    _____

    _____

6. One assumption we *cannot* make about alcohol consumption is that:

    a. Many animals are attracted to the smell of alcohol.

    b. There appears to be a connection between alcohol and genetics in many insects and mammals.

    c. There are no benefits that drinking alcohol confers on the human race.

    d. There may be similarities between alcoholism and obesity.

7. How does the discussion in paragraph 18 relate to the discussion of *wide variation among human beings* in paragraph 17?

    _____

    _____

8. Which of the following do the authors imply in paragraph 23? Be prepared to justify your answer.

    a. It is the alcoholic content of modern drinks that causes a dilemma for modern man.

    b. Distillation was a positive invention for the human race.

    c. Without the genetic link there would be no alcoholism.

    d. Alcoholism is a genetic problem.

9. In your own words, explain what the authors mean when they say, "The drunken monkey hypothesis, like many another productive scientific idea, raises more questions than the evidence so far in its favor can answer." (26)

    _____

    _____

10. Using only the context and your knowledge of word structure, define each of the following words. Do not use a dictionary.

    a. forager (2) _____

    b. mitigating (4) _____

    c. marginalized (8) _____

    d. anaerobic fermentation (10) _____

    e. forbears (14, 17) _____

f. divergent (15) _____

g. manifest (18) _____

Recalling Details

(See Chapters 4 and 5.)

1. Indicate whether each of the following is true (T) or false (F) based on information in this selection. Be prepared to cite evidence for your answers.

_____ a. Until 200 years ago, the amount of alcohol a human could drink was limited by cultural values.

_____ b. Overripe fruit with an ethanol content of 4% is preferred by monkeys.

_____ c. In humans, inefficient acetaldehyde clearing enzymes cause headaches, nausea, etc., which makes drinking of large quantities of alcohol unpleasant.

_____ d. Alcohol concentrations in modern drinks are much greater than before distillation.

_____ e. Alcohol abuse is caused by evolution.

_____ f. Alcoholism is caused by excessive ethanol content of modern drinks.

_____ g. Yeasts on some fruits convert several sugars into alcohols.

_____ h. The drunken monkey hypothesis has now been proven false by scientists.

2. Which of the following are cited in this article as reasons for alcoholism? Check all that apply.

_____ a. ancient cultures

_____ b. distillation

_____ c. genetics

_____ d. decreased enzyme efficiency

_____ e. health benefits of alcohol consumption on the heart

_____ f. consuming too much fruit

_____ g. environment

_____ h. evolution

3. What new information about *genetics* did you gain from reading this selection?

_____

_____

4. Indicate whether each of the following items is a major (MAJ) or minor (MIN) detail of this article. Be prepared to justify your answers.

_____ a. In the United States alone, 14 million people are alcoholics, and several millions more are at risk.

_____ b. An impressive body of evidence indicates that contemporary primate diets are dominated by plant materials.

_____ c. The fruit is an excellent source of food for the fly larvae when they hatch.

_____ d. Anecdotally, we note that people, too, often drink alcohol while eating, suggesting that drink with food is a natural combination.

_____ e. Only by operating on a variety of genes could evolution have selected the fittest of our primate forebears.

_____ f. . . . some evidence shows that intermediate levels of alcohol consumption are beneficial to human health.

_____ g. The invention of distillation radically changed humanity's relationship with alcohol.

_____ h. In 1962, the late geneticist James Neel predicted that as high-fat, high-calorie Western foods became available to tribal peoples, their incidence of obesity, heart disease and adult-onset diabetes would sharply increase.

Critical Thinking: Reaction and Discussion

1. This article was written from the perspective of the theory of evolution. Intelligent Design (ID) is a competing viewpoint, and its supporters do not believe in Darwin's theory of evolution. They assert that certain features of the universe and of living things exhibit the characteristics of a product resulting from an intelligent cause or agent, not an unguided process such as natural selection.

   With a group, discuss these two perspectives and list three assumptions in the article that suggest an evolution point of view. Then, using your personal experience, knowledge, and/or beliefs, decide how these assumptions might be refuted by individuals who hold an Intelligent Design viewpoint.

2. In this activity you will work to reach consensus with a small group. First, you will work with one other person to discuss the question on the Discussion Web that follows. You will discuss your points of view on the central question. Take turns writing down your reasons in two opposite columns. Write the strongest possible arguments on both sides.

   Next, pair up with another pair and compare all the reasons listed in both columns on your Discussion Webs. Work toward reaching a consensus on the question. Write a conclusion at the bottom of the Discussion Web. If your group does not reach total consensus (if one or more disagree with the group's conclusion), make note of this to share later.

   Decide which three reasons best support your conclusion and select a spokesperson to present to the whole class. Let the class know the process you used to reach consensus or why you were unable to reach a consensus.

DISCUSSION WEB

YES		NO
	Are zoos good places for scientists to study animal behavior?	
	Conclusions	

USING TECHNOLOGY FOR FURTHER UNDERSTANDING

1. Use the Internet to find out what kind of research is being conducted at zoos and how the research findings are being used.

2. Use the Internet to find out more about the controversy between evolutionary theorists and those who believe in Intelligent Design. How has this controversy affected school curriculum in public schools? What other aspects of public life could the disagreements affect?

●   # SELECTION 11

Natural Disasters: Earthquakes and Tsunamis

S. Chernicoff and A. Haydn, *Earthquakes and the Earth's Interior*

National Weather Service, *The Physics of Tsunamis*

Preview

In the material that follows, the authors explain the scientific basis for earthquakes and tsunamis. As you read, think about how different this discussion is from what we read and hear in news accounts of these natural disasters that have been written for the general public.

To Think About Before You Read

Based on recent occurrences of earthquakes in different parts of the world and the tsunami that hit the Indian Ocean nations in 2004, you probably have knowledge about these natural disasters that will help you with reading this article. To activate that knowledge, provide answers as best you can to the questions below.

1. What do you know about earthquakes?

   _____

   _____

2. What do you know about tsunamis?

   _____

   _____

3. What makes some parts of the world more subject to earthquakes than other places?

   _____

   _____

4. What countries have been affected recently by earthquakes and tsunamis?

   _____

   _____

5. How is the tsunami that happened in December 2004 related to an earthquake?

   _____

   _____

6. In your opinion, what can be done to reduce some of the devastating effects of these natural disasters?

   _____

   _____

Terms to Know Before You Read

tectonic plate (5) structural deformation of the earth's crust. The surface of the Earth consists of seven major tectonic plates and many more minor ones.

deform elastically (5) If you pull on a rock, or bend it, or squeeze it, it will deform. If it goes back to its original shape, like a rubber band would, it is said to have deformed elastically. The application of force to change the shape of a rock is called *stress*.

deform plastically (6) When rocks deform plastically, they do not go back to their original shape. This can happen as the result of heat, constant pressure and time. Sometimes rocks are even folded.

period (10) interval of time characterized by the occurrence of a certain condition, event, or phenomenon.

impulsive (10, 14) acting within brief time intervals

shoaling (11, 16) becoming shallow

EARTHQUAKES AND THE EARTH'S INTERIOR

1 From 1985 to 2001, Los Angeles, Oakland–San Francisco, Tokyo, Mexico City, Kobe (Japan), Turkey, Taiwan, Seattle, and many other regions have experienced cataclysmic earthquakes (Fig. 10-1). At 5:46 A.M. on January 17, 1995, a powerful earthquake, calculated at 7.2 on the Richter scale, hit western Japan. The earthquake, which was centered near the port city of Kobe on Awajishima Island, left more than 5000 dead and at least 29,000 injured. Approximately 30,000 residences in and around Kobe were destroyed or severely damaged, leaving 310,000 people homeless. Hanshin Expressway, connecting Kobe and Osaka, 31 kilometers (19 miles) away, collapsed in five places. Rail transportation, including the Shinkansen bullet train service, was disrupted for hundreds of kilometers, and at least seven derailments were reported. The cost of cleanup and restoration in the aftermath of the Kobe earthquake was expected to reach as much as $150 billion.

2 In December 1995, an even more powerful earthquake occurred 5 kilometers (3 miles) off the west coast of Mexico. The quake, which struck some of Mexico's most popular beach resorts, toppled houses and hotels, cracked bridges, opened meter-wide fissures in the main coastal highway, and cut power and phone service throughout the region. Damage was greatest in the resort town of Manzanillo, where the luxury seven-story Costa Real Hotel collapsed, killing at least 20 guests and staff. Even in Mex-

S. Chernicoff and A. Haydn, "Earthquakes and the Earth's Interior," *Essentials of Geology*, 3d ed. (Boston: Houghton Mifflin, 2003), pp. 197–202, including fig. 10-3, "The anatomy of an earthquake." Copyright © 2003 by Houghton Mifflin Company. Reprinted with permission.

ico City, located 335 kilometers (201 miles) to the east, earthquake vibrations caused skyscrapers to sway violently.

3 In the United States, two major earthquakes have occurred relatively recently. The powerful Loma Prieta earthquake struck northern California in 1989, toppling buildings, freeways, and bridges, rupturing gas mains and starting fires, and setting off landslides throughout the San Francisco Bay area. In 1994, another earthquake produced severe damage in the Northridge area of southern California. Together, these two quakes resulted in billions of dollars of damage and caused more than 100 deaths. Even more recently, on February 28, 2001, a magnitude 6.8 earthquake shook the city of Seattle.

4 Here we will discuss what causes earthquakes, see how geologists study, evaluate, and even predict them, and learn how the study of earthquake waves allows us to investigate the Earth's interior.

CAUSES AND CHARACTERISTICS OF EARTHQUAKES

5 An **earthquake** is a trembling of the ground caused, most often, by the sudden release of energy in underground rocks. Most earthquakes occur where rocks are subjected to the stress associated with tectonic plate movement—that is, near plate boundaries. The application of such stress may cause rocks to deform elastically and to accumulate *strain energy*, which builds until the rocks either shift suddenly along preexisting faults or rupture to create new faults. The result—earthquakes.

6 The precise subterranean spot at which rocks begin to rupture or shift marks the earthquake's **focus** (see Figure "The anatomy of an earthquake"). Approximately 90% of all earth-

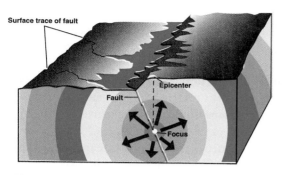

Surface trace of fault

Epicenter

Fault

Focus

THE ANATOMY OF AN EARTHQUAKE.

At the moment an earthquake occurs, pent-up energy is released at the quake's focus and transmitted through the Earth. The point on the Earth's surface directly above the quake's focus is its epicenter.

Retrieved December 29, 2004 from *http:wcatwc.gov/physics.htm* (National Weather Service, West Coast and Alaska Tsunami Warning Center).

quakes have a relatively shallow focus, located less than 100 kilometers (60 miles) below the surface; indeed, the focus of virtually all catastrophic quakes lies within 60 kilometers (40 miles) of the surface. Large earthquakes seldom occur at greater depth because heat has softened rocks there and robbed them of some of their ability to store strain energy. A few earthquakes, however, have occurred at depths as great as 700 kilometers (435 miles). Deeper than this level, higher temperatures and pressures cause stressed rocks to deform plastically, rather than rupture or shift.

7 The point on the Earth's surface directly above an earthquake's focus is its **epicenter.** The greatest impact of a quake is generally felt at the epicenter, with the effects decreasing in proportion to the distance from the epicenter. After a major earthquake, the rocks in the vicinity of the quake's focus continue to reverberate as they adjust to their new positions, producing numerous, generally smaller earthquakes, or *aftershocks*. Aftershocks may continue for as long as one or two years after the main quake, shaking and further damaging already-weakened structures.

8 After an earthquake releases its stored strain energy, the rocks along a fault cease to move and the fault blocks become temporarily locked in place by the friction between them. If the rocks undergo subsequent stress the strain energy again accumulates, sometimes over a period of many decades. Eventually the friction holding the fault blocks is overcome and they lurch, releasing newly accumulated energy in the form of another earthquake.

THE PRODUCTS OF EARTHQUAKES— SEISMIC WAVES

9 When you toss a pebble into a placid lake, the energy from its impact creates small, concentric waves that travel through the water in all directions until they eventually die out some distance from the impact point. Similarly, when underground rocks rupture or shift along a fault, the released energy is transmitted as **seismic waves** that travel at great speeds in all directions through the surrounding rocks. The term *seismic* (from the Greek for "shaking") refers to anything involving earthquakes: A *seismograph* is a machine with which geologists determine the magnitude of an earthquake; *seismology* is the study of earthquakes and the Earth's interior.

THE PHYSICS OF TSUNAMIS

10 The phenomenon we call a tsunami (soo-NAH-mee) is a series of waves of extremely long wave length and long period generated in a body of water by an impulsive disturbance that displaces the water. Tsunamis are primarily associated with earthquakes in oceanic and coastal regions. Landslides, volcanic eruptions, nuclear explosions, and even impacts of objects

from outer space (such as meteorites, asteroids, and comets) can also generate tsunamis.

11   As the tsunami crosses the deep ocean, its length from crest to crest may be a hundred miles or more, and its height from crest to trough will only be a few feet or less. They cannot be felt aboard ships nor can they be seen from the air in the open ocean. In the deepest oceans, the waves will reach speeds exceeding 600 miles per hour (970 km/hr). When the tsunami enters the shoaling water of coastlines in its path, the velocity of its waves diminishes and the wave height increases. It is in these shallow waters that a large tsunami can crest to heights exceeding 100 feet (30 m) and strike with devastating force.

12   The term tsunami was adopted for general use in 1963 by an international scientific conference. Tsunami is a Japanese word represented by two characters: "tsu" and "nami." The character "tsu" means harbor, while the character "nami" means wave. In the past, tsunamis were often referred to as "tidal waves" by many English speaking people. The term "tidal wave" is a misnomer. Tides are the result of gravitational influences of the moon, sun, and planets. Tsunamis are not caused by the tides and are unrelated to the tides; although a tsunami striking a coastal area is influenced by the tide level at the time of impact. Also in the past, the scientific community referred to tsunamis as "seismic sea waves." "Seismic" implies an earthquake-related mechanism of generation. Although tsunamis are usually generated by earthquakes, tsunamis are less commonly caused by landslides, infrequently by volcanic eruptions, and very rarely by a large meteorite impact in the ocean.

13   Earthquakes generate tsunamis when the sea floor abruptly deforms and displaces the overlying water from its equilibrium position. Waves are formed as the displaced water mass, which acts under the influence of gravity, attempts to regain its equilibrium. The main factor which determines the initial size of a tsunami is the amount of vertical sea floor deformation. This is controlled by the earthquake's magnitude, depth, fault characteristics and coincident slumping of sediments or secondary faulting. Other features which influence the size of a tsunami along the coast are the shoreline and bathymetric configuration, the velocity of the sea floor deformation, the water depth near the earthquake source, and the efficiency which energy is transferred from the earth's crust to the water column.

14   A tsunami can be generated by *any* disturbance that displaces a large water mass from its equilibrium position. Submarine landslides, which often occur during a large earthquake, can also create a tsunami. During a submarine landslide, the equilibrium sea-level is altered by sediment moving along the sea-floor. Gravitational forces then propagate the tsunami given the initial perturbation of the sea-level. Similarly, a violent marine volcanic eruption can create an impulsive force that displaces the water column and generates a tsunami. Above water (subarial) landslides and space born objects can disturb the water from above the surface. The falling debris displaces the water from its equilibrium position and produces a tsunami. Unlike ocean-wide tsunamis caused by some earthquakes, tsunamis generated by non-seismic mechanisms usually dissipate quickly and rarely affect coastlines far from the source area.

15   Tsunamis are characterized as shallow-water waves. Shallow-water waves are different from wind-generated waves, the waves many of us have observed on the beach. Wind-generated waves usually have a period (time between two successive waves) of five to twenty seconds and a wavelength (distance between two successive

waves) of about 100 to 200 meters (300 to 600 ft). A tsunami can have a period in the range of ten minutes to two hours and a wavelength in excess of 300 miles (500 km). It is because of their long wavelengths that tsunamis behave as shallow-water waves. A wave is characterized as a shallow-water wave when the ratio between the water depth and its wavelength gets very small. The speed of a shallow-water wave is equal to the square root of the product of the acceleration of gravity (32ft/sec/sec or 980cm/sec/sec) and the depth of the water. The rate at which a wave loses its energy is inversely related to its wavelength. Since a tsunami has a very large wave length, it will lose little energy as it propagates. Hence in very deep water, a tsunami will travel at high speeds and travel great transoceanic distances with limited energy loss. For example, when the ocean is 20,000 feet (6100 m) deep, unnoticed tsunami travel about 550 miles per hour (890 km/hr), the speed of a jet airplane. And they can move from one side of the Pacific Ocean to the other side in less than one day.

16   As a tsunami leaves the deep water of the open sea and propagates into the more shallow waters near the coast, it undergoes a transformation. Since the speed of the tsunami is related to the water depth, as the depth of the water decreases, the speed of the tsunami diminishes. The change of total energy of the tsunami remains constant. Therefore, the speed of the tsunami decreases as it enters shallower water, and the height of the wave grows. Because of this "shoaling" effect, a tsunami that was imperceptible in deep water may grow to be several feet or more in height.

17   When a tsunami finally reaches the shore, it may appear as a rapidly rising or falling tide, a series of breaking waves, or even a bore. Reefs, bays, entrances to rivers, undersea features and the slope of the beach all help to modify the tsunami as it approaches the shore. Tsunamis rarely become great, towering breaking waves. Sometimes the tsunami may break far offshore. Or it may form into a bore: a step-like wave with a steep breaking front. A bore can happen if the tsunami moves from deep water into a shallow bay or river. The water level on shore can rise many feet. In extreme cases, water level can rise to more than 50 feet (15 m) for tsunamis of distant origin and over 100 feet (30 m) for tsunami generated near the earthquake's epicenter. The first wave may not be the largest in the series of waves. One coastal area may see no damaging wave activity while in another area destructive waves can be large and violent. The flooding of an area can extend inland by 1000 feet (305 m) or more, covering large expanses of land with water and debris. Flooding tsunami waves tend to carry loose objects and people out to sea when they retreat. Tsunamis may reach a maximum vertical height onshore above sea level, called a run-up height, of 30 meters (98 ft). A notable exception is the landslide generated tsunami in Lituya Bay, Alaska in 1958 which produced a 525 meter (1722 ft) wave.

18   Since science cannot predict when earthquakes will occur, they cannot determine exactly when a tsunami will be generated. But, with the aid of historical records of tsunamis and numerical models, science can get an idea as to where they are most likely to be generated. Past tsunami height measurements and computer modeling help to forecast future tsunami impact and flooding limits at specific coastal areas. There is an average of two destructive tsunamis per year in the Pacific basin. Pacific wide tsunamis are a rare phenomenon, occurring every 10–12 years on the average.

Evaluation of the Article

Difficulty Rating □ 1 □ 2 □ 3 □ 4 □ 5
(1 = easy; 5 = difficult)

What reading difficulties did you encounter? _____

_____

How did you handle these difficulties? _____

_____

Postreading Comprehension Development

Sentence Rewrite

To check your understanding of some of the key concepts of these essays, rewrite each of the following sentences in your own words, keeping the original idea. (See Chapter 1.)

1. Most earthquakes occur when rocks are subject to the stress associated with tectonic plate movement—that is, near the plate boundaries. (5)

   _____

   _____

2. Similarly, when underground rocks rupture or shift along a fault, the energy is transmitted as seismic waves that travel at great speeds in all directions through the surrounding rocks. (9)

   _____

   _____

3. Since the speed of the tsunami is related to the water depth, as the depth of the water decreases, the speed of the tsunami diminishes (16)

   _____

   _____

Author's Main Idea

(See Chapter 3.)

1. The paragraph in which the authors' main point about earthquakes is most clearly stated is:

    a. 2.

    b. 3.

    c. 5.

    d. 9.

2. The paragraph in which the author's main point about tsunamis is most clearly stated is:

    a. 10.

    b. 13.

    c. 17.

    d. 18.

3. How does the discussion about *epicenter* help serve the author's purpose for writing this material on earthquakes?

    _____

    _____

    _____

4. How does the discussion about *waves* help serve the authors' purpose for writing this material on tsunamis?

    _____

    _____

    _____

Inferences, Metaphors, and Vocabulary in Context

(See Chapters 2, 6, and 7.)

1. Which of the following do the authors imply in paragraph 4? Be prepared to justify your answer.

   a. The importance of this section is to learn about the origins and particulars of earthquakes.

   b. The importance of this section is to learn about how geologists control earthquakes.

   c. The importance of this section is to learn about the geology of the inside of the earth.

   d. The importance of this section is to learn about geology.

2. Which of the following do the authors imply in paragraph 9? Be prepared to justify your answer.

   a. Pebbles can cause earthquakes.

   b. There is no way to measure the strength of an earthquake.

   c. Seismic waves are used to measure only very large earthquakes.

   d. Seismic waves are produced by energy released from an earthquake.

3. In your own words, explain what the authors mean when they say, "The greatest impact of a quake is generally felt at the epicenter, with the effects decreasing in proportion to the distance from the epicenter." (7).

_____

_____

_____

4. Which of the following do the authors of the tsunami reading imply in paragraph 13? Be prepared to justify your answer.

   a. Tsunamis cannot occur unless water and the sea ground are in equilibrium.

   b. Gravity under the ocean is greater than the pull of gravity at the surface of the water.

   c. The initial size of the tsunami is influenced by the depth of the water.

   d. Normally, the water and the sea floor below it are stable.

5. One assumption we can make about *tsunami waves* is that:

   a. they lose significant energy as they travel.

   b. their speed varies with gravity and energy but not with water depth.

   c. their speed varies with water depth but not with gravity.

   d. their speed varies with gravity and with water depth.

6. In your own words, explain the following sentence from paragraph 16:
   As a tsunami leaves the deep water of the open sea and propagates into the more shallow waters near the coast, it undergoes a transformation. (16)

   _____

   _____

   _____

7. What do you think the authors want the reader to understand after reading paragraph 17 ? What are your reasons for thinking this?

   _____

   _____

   _____

8. Paragraph 18 best illustrates which of the following characteristics about science? Be prepared to justify your answer.
   a. Scientific knowledge is durable.
   b. Scientific ideas are subject to change.
   c. Science explains and predicts.
   d. Science demands evidence.

9. One assumption we can make about *seismology* is that:
   a. Everything about earthquakes is already understood by the study of seismology.
   b. The study of seismology will become more valuable as more facts are known.
   c. Everything about the interior of the earth is already understood by the study of seismology.
   d. The study of seismology will become useless once we understand more about earthquakes.

10. Using only the context and your knowledge of word parts, define each of the following words. Do not use a dictionary.
    a. faults (5) _____
    b. plate boundaries (5) _____
    c. focus (6) _____
    d. reverberate (7) _____

e. lurch (8) _____

f. equilibrium (14) _____

g. inversely (15) _____

h. propagates (15, 16) _____

i. imperceptible (16) _____

j. bore (17) _____

Recalling Details

(See Chapters 4 and 5.)

1. Indicate whether each of the following is true (T) or false (F) based on the readings in this selection. Be prepared to cite evidence for your answers.

   _____ a. Rocks subject to plate tectonic movement causing stress is the single cause of earthquakes.

   _____ b. Earthquakes can occur at depths of 700 miles below the earth's surface.

   _____ c. A rationale for studying seismology is to try to reduce the number of lives lost to earthquakes.

   _____ d. The most powerful earthquake mentioned in this article ranked 7.2.

   _____ e. The name of the subterranean spot where the rocks rupture or shift is the epicenter.

   _____ f. Tectonic plate movement and earthquakes are not significantly related.

   _____ g. The energy in a tsunami is always changing as it travels across the ocean to the wave height at shore.

   _____ h. The height of the wave as it reaches the shore depends on gravity.

   _____ i. The wavelength of a tsunami wave is very large.

   _____ j. The energy in a tsunami is always changing as it travels across the ocean, but the wave length is constant.

   _____ k. We can calculate where the next tsunami will occur.

   _____ l. We cannot calculate when the next tsunami will occur.

2. Which of the following are cited as contributing to the strength of a tsunami when it reaches shore? Check all that apply.

_____ a. the temperature of the ocean

_____ b. the depth of the water

_____ c. gravity

_____ d. the tides

_____ e. the height of the wave

_____ f. the position of the sun at the time of the formation of the tsunami

3. Indicate whether each item that follows is a major (MAJ) or minor (MIN) detail of these readings. Be prepared to justify your answers.

_____ a. When you toss a pebble into a lake, the energy creates waves.

_____ b. An earthquake releases stored energy.

_____ c. In the U.S. there were large earthquakes in 1989 and 1994.

_____ d. Earthquakes can cause great devastation.

_____ e. Earthquakes can cause skyscrapers to violently sway.

_____ f. Landslides can generate tsunamis.

_____ g. Tsunamis were once known as tidal waves.

_____ h. The amount of vertical sea floor deformation is critical for tsunami formation.

_____ i. The depth of the coastal water contributes significantly to the height of the tsunami.

_____ j. The speed of the tsunami decreases as the depth of the water decreases.

4. Which of the following are cited as areas that seismologists study? Check all that apply.

_____ a. volcanic activity

_____ b. water content of rocks

_____ c. plate tectonics

_____ d. rainfall levels

_____ e. shift in faults

_____ f. mineral content of mountains on earth

_____ g. fossil remains

_____ h. the wave length and speed of light

5. Match the primary pattern of organization used in each paragraph listed here.

   a. 3   1. simple listing, chronological
   b. 9   2. comparison and contrast
   c. 14   3. definition
   d. 16   4. cause and effect

Critical Thinking: Reaction and Discussion

1. Refer back to the To Think About Before You Read section at the beginning of this selection. Review your original answers and modify them by adding any new information you have learned from these articles.

2. With a group, discuss how these articles illustrate at least three of the ideas about science that are listed here. You may wish to refer back to the reading selection to clarify each idea before your discussion. Be prepared to share your group's ideas with the class.

   a. Scientific Knowledge Is Durable
   b. Scientific Ideas Are Subject to Change
   c. Science Cannot Provide Complete Answers to All Questions
   d. Science Demands Evidence
   e. Science Is a Blend of Logic and Imagination
   f. Science Explains and Predicts
   g. Scientists Try to Identify and Avoid Bias
   h. Science Is Not Authoritarian

3. With a group and using the information from this selection, create a concept map for *tsunami.* Be prepared to explain your visual aid to the class.

USING TECHNOLOGY FOR FURTHER UNDERSTANDING

1. Use the Internet to investigate an earthquake that has occurred in some part of the world. Locate information on the size of the quake, the devastation it caused, the response the United States and other countries made to this devastation, and the recovery progress that has been made.

2. Using the Internet, learn more about the work of seismologists. Locate at least two sites that discuss how seismologists work and problems they encounter.

CHAPTER FOURTEEN

Business
The Activities of Groups or Individuals Who Develop, Produce, and Distribute Goods and Services

Business? It's quite simple.
It's other people's money.

—Alexander Dumas the Younger
La Question d'Argent (1857)

Key Concepts for the Study of Business

Before you read this list of concepts, think about some issues and topics that you might study if you took courses in business. In the space provided, list your ideas.

_____

_____

ASSETS.   Anything of value owned by a business or individual.

BALANCE OF TRADE.   Relationship between the value of a nation's exports and the value of its imports.

COMPETITION.   Rivalry among similar businesses for a share of the same consumer dollars.

CONSUMERISM.   The organized efforts of independent, government, and business groups to protect consumers from undesirable effects resulting from poorly designed and produced products.

ENTREPRENEURS.   Innovative owner-managers who create some new product or service or suggest a better way of using existing products or services.

FIXED COSTS.   Business costs that remain the same regardless of the amount of production, such as property taxes.

LABOR UNION.   An organization of workers banded together to achieve economic goals, especially improved wages, hours, and working conditions.

LAW OF DEMAND.   Economic principle stating that if price goes down, the quantity demanded goes up; if price goes up, the quantity demanded goes down.

MANAGEMENT.   The process of working through people to achieve objectives by means of effective decision making and efficient allocation of scarce resources. Also an individual, an occupational group, or a discipline of study.

MARKETING.   Determination of customers' needs and wants; development of goods and services to satisfy those needs and wants, and then delivery of those goods and services to the customer.

MERGER.   Purchase of one business by a smaller business in which the purchasing company retains its independence and dominance.

ORGANIZATION.   A group of people striving together to reach a common goal and bound together by a set of understood authority-responsibility relationships.

PRODUCTION.   The use of human, physical, and financial resources to produce products or services.

PROFIT.   Income received, minus the costs of operating the business.

REVENUES.   Income from sales of products or services.

Now that you have read this list, what are some additional issues and topics that you might study if you took courses in business? In the space provided, list your ideas.

_____

_____

_____

SELECTION 12

Making Work Meaningful:
SECRETS OF THE FUTURE-FOCUSED CORPORATION

■ ROGER E. HERMAN AND JOYCE L. GIOIA

Preview

All societies, from very primitive to highly technological ones, engage in some sort of business practices. In the United States, these practices are often highly organized and are grounded in some common economic principles. The following introductory essay defines American business and explains some of the basics of business success.

To Think About Before You Read

No doubt you know some people who like their jobs and some who do not like their jobs. In the space provided, think of some reasons for these differences in attitudes. Put your answers in the space labeled **Prereading.** After reading this selection, you will be asked to reconsider your ideas and to record any new thoughts on this subject in the **Postreading** section.

Reasons why some people like their jobs.

Prereading: _____

_____

_____

_____

Postreading: _____

_____

_____

_____

Reasons why some people do not like their jobs.

Prereading: _____

_____

_____

_____

Postreading: _____

_____

_____

_____

Today's worker is no longer willing to work in an authoritarian and dehumanizing environment. Workers want meaning in their work and balance in their lives. Given the amount of time people spend at work, they want opportunities to contribute and to know how their work contributes to the organization. They also want to be valued as individuals with goals and aspirations, not just replaceable drones in the hive.

2   The very nature of organizations can make this change difficult. Every organization has reasons for its existence. A corporation is a structured environment with a purpose—a business purpose. It is an environment established to create wealth, not a natural human social environment. The foundation for building human relationships in such an environment is a mutual respect for what employees contribute to the organization and for the individuals themselves. The evolution to this new, meaningful corporate culture will encompass many changes. These will affect not only the design of work and compensation, but quality of life, environmental accountability, social responsibility, and scope for the human spirit.

CREATING MEANINGFUL WORK

The first step on this evolutionary path is to re- 3 define work. What *is* work? And how do employees relate to the work they do? Research shows that people want to do more than simply "attend" work.

A recent survey by Response Analysis of 4 Princeton, New Jersey, identified employees' top three most important aspects of work. Of the 1,600 people responding, 52% wanted to be responsible for their work and the results it produced, 42% wanted acknowledgment for their contributions, and 39% wanted their tasks matched to their strengths.

Today, and in the future, companies that 5 hope to attract and motivate enthusiastic and dedicated employees will demonstrate their sensitivity to the level of responsibility workers want. They must design work so that employees can take responsibility and be rewarded appropriately. In doing so, these organizations will take a big step toward making work meaningful. Here are some more key elements for redesigning work:

A Valued Part of the Whole

6 Repetitive factory routines and office work that simply moves paper from in-box to out-box are mindless tasks that destroy motivation and productivity. Workers want to know that their work is important and how it fits into the corporate strategy. To make this transition smoothly, organizations must share more information with more people than ever before. Employees want to be responsible for results, so they must have access to the information that will enable them to fulfill that responsibility.

Making an Impact

7 Employees need to know not only how the work they do affects others and the organization's strategic goals, but how they—as individuals—can make an impact. Who knows better how to improve the processes and environment than the people involved on a daily basis? Successful organizations understand and appreciate that this ability to improve workplace effectiveness is part of the intellectual capital of their work force, that what employees know can be even more valuable than what they do.

8 Through their knowledge and experience, workers can provide the organization with a wealth of information that cannot be acquired elsewhere. In order to tap this intellectual capital, the organization must create a culture that encourages and supports collaboration. Employees will contribute their knowledge enthusiastically in a corporate culture that values the individual.

Responsibility for Outcomes

9 Having the responsibility and authority to make decisions increases the meaning of work. Being able to recommend and implement improvements allows individuals to see their impact on the organization. Employees respond positively when they are given clear goals and the authority to make things happen.

10 This kind of exchange can only survive in a culture built on mutual trust. The organization must trust that employees are capable of making the right decisions. Employees, on the other hand, must trust that it is safe to risk making decisions—even wrong ones. This process doesn't take away accountability. It does, however, focus on objective results, and it creates an environment for continuous feedback and improvement.

Measuring Results

11 For workers to be responsible and find their work meaningful, they need direct and timely feedback. Making changes and improving performance comes from an ongoing evaluation process. When workers gain feedback from the customer (internal or external), they can gauge their influence in making things happen, solving company problems, and making appropriate decisions.

12 To assure a continuous flow of valuable feedback, tomorrow's most successful corporations will establish systems for customers to evaluate service performance. They will also provide ongoing coaching for every worker and involve employees in their performance rating, encouraging them to take initiative in improving their work and their results.

13 Every employee's work can be measured in some way. Successful corporations develop those measurements, assure the flow of information

needed to assess progress, and facilitate the evaluative process. Working without feedback is like bowling in the dark: You may put out lots of energy but get no sense of return. Tomorrow's employees—and many of today's—won't tolerate that vacuum.

Meaningful Rewards

14 The profitability of a company is directly related to the quality and efforts of its workers. Therefore, a direct relationship between job performance and reward makes work more meaningful.

15 Compaq Computers enjoys an unusually low turnover rate among its employees. Like many companies in the computer field, Compaq expects its people to work long and hard to achieve big results quickly. In many companies an atmosphere of constant push would inspire people to seek employment with less pressure somewhere else.

16 Instead, high quality people stay with Compaq. The company's culture emphasizes individual responsibility for results and high respect for individuals—from the top of the organization down. This attitude is shown in all sorts of interactions, including providing access to information, resources, and higher management. Both the company and its employees benefit from creating opportunities for every employee to self-actualize and to be rewarded for achievements. By constantly measuring employee performance to assure that contributions are rewarded proportionately, Compaq's empowerment concept achieves its full potential.

Team Effort

17 Even with the focus on individual accomplishment, there is a powerful sense of the team at Compaq Computers. Every employee is expected to support everyone else to serve the customer. The worldwide profit-sharing plan reflects this togetherness: Distribution is based on a balanced formula of customer satisfaction and return on invested capital. All employees benefit from this program.

18 To remain involved and loyal to an organization, employees should share in the profits they create. Workers are reluctant to give 110% only to see executive salaries skyrocketing while their own incomes barely keep pace with inflation.

19 Rewards (financial and other) for a job well done acknowledge the contribution of the individual. Not only are these incentives motivational, they underscore each individual's importance within the organization. Future-focused companies are redesigning compensation to reflect this connection. Performance-based compensation packages can actually help keep payroll costs in line while motivating valuable employees.

20 The Ritz-Carlton hotel and resort company has always been at the forefront of customer service. After winning the Malcolm Baldridge National Quality Award in 1992, Ritz-Carlton established a pilot project of self-directed work teams that embodied many of the components of meaningful work. The pilot was so successful that by 1995, more than 30 Ritz-Carlton hotels and resorts were using the same self-directed work team concepts. By giving frontline workers control over the process and outcomes of their jobs, management taps into employees' problem-solving skills and reinforces their commitment to high level customer service.

21 With self-directed work teams of line employees in control of daily activities, managers have time to provide vision and direction. As a result, Ritz-Carlton has experienced an increase in satisfaction from owners, guests, and employees. Additionally, the team environment allows employees to gain experience in a broad

range of activities. This experience is valuable for recruiting and retaining good employees, since it enables employees to become more marketable both within the Ritz-Carlton group and to other organizations in the hospitality industry.

CREATING A MEANINGFUL ORGANIZATION

22 Meaningful work is just part of what it will take for companies to maintain a high-performance work force and remain competitive in tomorrow's marketplace. Future-focused companies are learning that corporate responsibilities extend beyond their own front door.

23   Increasingly, workers will choose their employers based on how they perceive the organization's aims and values. Their choices will be deliberate, and they will not hesitate to leave employment that they decide isn't "right" for them.

Balancing Work and Family

24 Quality of life, on and off the job, is more important to today's workers than ever before. Parents struggle to balance the requirements of the workplace and the needs of their children and extended families. Some workers care for both children and elderly relatives. Even employees without such responsibilities want time to pursue personal interests. Future-focused companies are finding ways to facilitate a balance between the work and personal lives of their employees. By addressing these issues, employers support a motivated, stable, productive work force.

25   To remain competitive in tomorrow's marketplace, companies must be highly sensitive to employee needs and expectations and be prepared to make a significant investment in the area of personal/professional balance. This makes sense on several levels. Cost/benefit analysis re-

veals a favorable return on such an investment in companies, large and small. Sensitivity to individual employees' concerns outside the workplace can create a meaningful environment conducive to a stable, productive work force. Those companies that fail to address these needs and interests will lose their best and brightest to competitors that offer better quality-of-life programs.

Personal and Professional Growth

Employees also want to develop a meaningful 26 career path that makes them more marketable both internally and externally. To accomplish this, they want opportunities to learn, to increase their responsibility, and to implement solutions. Learning opportunities include both academic and experiential methods and apply to both job training and improving personal skills.

    Companies always benefit when workers 27 are actively engaged in improving their skills or knowledge. Professional development adds meaning to work; personal development adds meaning to the individual. Both build self-confidence and self-esteem. Knowledgeable, confident workers are essential for the lean and meaningful companies of the future.

    Few workers expect to stay in the same job 28 forever. They want to try new kinds of work and to grow, expand their capabilities, and avoid boredom. People who have no opportunity to try different types of jobs with their current employer are likelier to leave in search of something new. So, wherever possible, give people a chance to experiment. Cross-training and cross-experience build understanding and expand an employer's capacity to quickly assign people where they're needed most.

    Workers may resist changing jobs to try 29 something new if there is no safety net in the event they don't like the new work. Can they

Seven Skills for Meaningful Workers

Technical and technological skills will take on greater importance. There will be a growing need for people who can understand and fix systems—from computer systems to product distribution systems to plumbing systems.

Visionary skills will be in demand. The ability to gather and absorb a wide range of input, then use that knowledge, understanding, and perspective to guide organizations into the future, will be vital.

Numbers and measurement will be important, of course, but smoothing the flow from month to month, from quarter to quarter will be essential for highly profitable long-term performance. Practically every company will have to move away from today's obsession with looking ahead only as far as the next financial reporting period.

Ability to organize will definitely be important in the corporation of the future. Everywhere there will be a need to organize something: resources, workflow, marketing mix, financial opportunities, and much more. All will demand high levels of organization—and reorganization.

Persuasive skills will be used in many ways by the corporation of the future. The most effective individuals will be those who know how to present information and ideas so that others can understand and support a particular position. Good salesmanship will be essential in many more interactions than we consider today, especially inside the organization.

Communication skills—careful listening, clear writing, close reading, plain speaking, and accurate description—will be invaluable. In tomorrow's fast-paced business environment there will be precious little time to correct any misunderstandings. Communications breakdown may well become a fatal corporate disease.

Ability to learn will be above everything else in importance—empowering people to grow in effectiveness and help their companies achieve desired objectives. Some of this skill is innate, but many people enhance their ability to learn—and to relate different aspects of learning—through college and university courses. We believe the liberal arts education experience will prove to be the most valuable type of education for tomorrow's leaders.

The top employees of the coming century will be flexible, creative, and motivated toward making a positive difference in the world. They will seek balance, growth, and fulfillment in both their work and home environments. The corporation of the future must respond to these needs and desires; otherwise, they will find themselves hampered by a lack of qualified people to accomplish the organization's work.

say, "no thanks," and return to their former assignments? The Land's End Company, in Dodgeville, Wisconsin, responds to this uncertainty with something they call "job-enrolling." Employees can try a new job temporarily without transferring from their current position. If they like the new work, they can request an official transfer.

Company/Employee Relations

30 Not only prospective employees, but investors and consumers are also coming to judge companies by how they deal with issues like diversity, harassment, hiring and firing, profit sharing, and other labor/management policies. A number of companies recently in the news know all too well the public impact of internal decisions. To cite just two examples, AT&T lost huge image points when it laid off thousands of workers in a year of profits. And Texaco's failure to handle discrimination within its own ranks will remain in the public consciousness for years to come.

31　Prospective employees are reluctant to join a company that has a history of treating its people badly, and current employees are easily lured away to companies with better track records. Investors are also watching companies carefully because the connections between employee retention and profitability have been made quite clear.

32　Diversity is a major concern in corporate America, and it will remain so for years to come. Much more than a racial issue, the emphasis is now on celebrating differences among people and making active use of the varied perspectives that workers from different backgrounds bring to the job.

33　The Hearst Corporation celebrates the unique talents and contributions of all its employees, whether they are high-profile reporters, secretaries, or little-seen printing press operators. When someone at Hearst does something worthy of recognition, flowers are sent—to the employee's spouse. Really special contributions call for a small gift from Tiffany's. Receiving the gifts at home brings the family into the celebration and helps connect the worlds of home-life and work experience.

Corporate Social Responsibility

Employees also want to know that they are 34 working for an ethical company with a mission and a clear set of values they can believe in. Younger workers today are typically more interested in the mission of a company than the price of its stock. Older employees, who have put in their time under the pressures of the old system and weathered the overwhelming changes of the last two decades, are now more cynical and less inclined to give their all to a company they instinctively mistrust.

　To win these valuable workers over, compa- 35 nies that look toward the future will need to live up to their mission statements. Employees and customers are aware of what organizations give back to the community. In a tight labor market, prospective employees will include a company's social report card in their decision process. Thus, how a company is perceived by society will have an impact on its ability to find and keep good employees.

　Customers, shareholders, and other stake- 36 holders are also looking for more than just profit. Companies are being held increasingly accountable for being good corporate citizens. Whether shopping for consumer goods or investing in stock, the general public is becoming more aware of a company's policies and standards, and people are voting with their pocketbooks.

The Company and the Environment

37 Environmental awareness will play a role in any future corporation's image. Whether a company applies environmental considerations at every stage of its operations or ignores these issues unless it gets caught can make a major difference in employee loyalty and market acceptance. A company that takes an active role in protecting the environment, both in its own products and through community involvement, will have a stronger position in tomorrow's marketplace.

Spirituality in the Workplace

38 The human spirit, where hopes, dreams, and aspirations lie, has long been banished from the workplace. Yet there can be no meaning in either work or life when this aspect of human existence is ignored. To be their best, people must be able to express their values, to share their hopes, to tap into their creativity in the workplace. A future-focused corporate culture will make a place for such spiritual expression, which may take many different forms, resulting in benefits ranging from better internal communication to new product design.

PUTTING IT ALL TOGETHER

39 Evolving into a meaningful organization presents some big challenges. Some changes will be easy for companies to adopt; others will be less comfortable. The key will be the *motivation* behind the shift. Sensitivity to the human spirit—in the work environment—will drive the most sincere, longest lasting, and most effective movements into true meaningfulness.

40 Successful future organizations must be mindful of all their relationships and act with integrity at all times. But the core relationship is between a company and its employees. The ability to build strong, collaborative relationships with employees will determine whether a business evolves through time or is lost along the way.

41 With the imperative to find and keep good employees in a shrinking labor market, the efforts made to positively change the relationship of employees, their work, and the organization will be the defining factor in the successful corporation of the future.

Futurist, December 1998, pp. 24–30.

Evaluation of the Article
Difficulty Rating ☐ 1 ☐ 2 ☐ 3 ☐ 4 ☐ 5
(1 = easy; 5 = difficult)

What reading difficulties did you encounter? _____

_____

How did you handle these difficulties?_____

_____

Comprehension of the Discipline

1. Look at this list of key concepts for business, defined earlier in this chapter. Which of these concepts are discussed either directly or indirectly in this article? Check all that apply. Be prepared to justify your answers.

   _____ a. assets

   _____ b. balance of trade

   _____ c. competition

   _____ d. consumerism

   _____ e. entrepreneurs

   _____ f. fixed costs

   _____ g. law of demand

   _____ h. management

   _____ i. marketing

   _____ j. merger

   _____ k. organization

   _____ l. production

   _____ m. profit

   _____ n. revenues

2. Which of the following business practices would be considered future oriented by the author of this article? Check all that apply.

   _____ a. Employees are given 30 minutes for lunch and are docked pay for missed time if they are longer.

   _____ b. Employees are brought into meetings where management is considering new hiring practices.

   _____ c. Employees are encouraged to participate in Bring Your Daughter to Work Day.

   _____ d. The employer gives employees five days per year for "parent care."

   _____ e. Hospitalized employees are visited by management and are told to hurry back to work or they will lose their benefits.

   _____ f. The company holds annual meetings with employees to evaluate how its practices reflect its mission statement.

   _____ g. The company holds a monthly contest for "Best Ideas for Management."

3. How does intellectual capital differ from business profit, and what relationship do they have to each other?

_____

_____

_____

_____

4. What are some experiences you or people you know have had that reflect "meaningful work" and "meaningful organization"? List these in the space provided.

Meaningful work: _____

_____

_____

Meaningful organization: _____

_____

_____

5. What relationship do these authors see between a company's ability to be future oriented and customer satisfaction?

_____

_____

_____

_____

_____

6. Return to the To Think About Before You Read section and see what details you can now add that explain why some people enjoy their work and others do not. Record your new thoughts in the Postreading section.

Critical Thinking: Reaction and Discussion

1. Review the offerings of the business department (or department offering business courses) listed in your college catalog. Write your findings about each of the following:

    a. What are some of the business areas in which students can specialize?

    b. What courses are required outside those in the business department? Why do you think these are required?

    c. What courses sound particularly interesting to you?

    d. What else would you want to know about programs in business before you decided on it as a major?

2. With a group, discuss the Seven Skills for Meaningful Workers. Explore the following questions:

    a. How has your formal education prepared you to have these skills?

    b. What else in your life has contributed to this preparation?

    c. What other skills do you believe are important for future-oriented workers?

USING TECHNOLOGY FOR FURTHER UNDERSTANDING

Compare some classified ads for one type of job, using a newspaper and then the Internet.

1. Are there differences in how that type of job is described on the Internet and in the newspaper? Describe the differences.

2. Is there anything that suggests that the ads are written for different audiences? Explain.

3. Does one medium appear more useful to a job seeker than another? Explain.

4. Is there anything future oriented about the job or the company that is included in the advertising? Explain.

Guidelines for Reading Business

To read articles and textbook chapters related to business, you should bear the following in mind:

BUSINESS MATERIALS OFTEN HAVE THEIR BASIS IN A NUMBER OF OTHER DISCIPLINES, INCLUDING ECONOMICS, PSYCHOLOGY, SOCIOLOGY, LAW AND ETHICS, OR TECHNOLOGY. Be certain you have the appropriate framework in mind when you first approach a business-related reading. Portions of an accounting text, for example, are probably based on principles drawn from economics. On the other hand, theories or practices discussed in a marketing or management text might be rooted in psychology or sociology. If you note the appropriate framework when you begin your reading assignment, you will be able to relate what you know from these broader areas to the text at hand.

YOU CAN USE YOUR EXPERIENCES IN THE REAL WORLD TO ASSIST YOU WITH COMPREHENSION. Many of your life experiences have already connected you to the world of business. You have been a consumer and, perhaps, have been employed or have had financial responsibilities. Your recall of these experiences will contribute to the knowledge pool from which you can draw to make business-related readings more relevant and the comprehension of text easier.

THE LANGUAGE OF BUSINESS IS OFTEN TECHNICAL. Each field within the broad discipline of business has its own language. You will need to pay close attention to the special uses given to common terms, such as *compound, discount,* and *futures,* as well as to those that are used in many business specialties, such as *profit, loss,* and *productivity.*

VISUAL AIDS ARE OFTEN USED TO ILLUSTRATE A WIDE VARIETY OF CONCEPTS AND TO PROVIDE STATISTICAL INFORMATION. Familiarity with visual aids that are common to business materials is critical, including knowing how to read charts, graphs, and tables. These visual aids play an important role in reading business-related materials. They serve to explain complex ideas in a more concrete way, and they will help you visualize the relationships between abstract concepts. Data involving numbers or percentages are remembered more easily when their relationship to other data, such as the relationship between education and household income, is shown in a graphic.

As you work with charts and graphs in business texts, you will need to draw conclusions from them. What do the data tell you? Often the conclusions you draw are the most important points being made in a section of the text you are reading. The author has used the graph to make these points more vivid.

Many specific strategies for reading visual aids are provided in Chapter 7 of this text.

Keep these guidelines in mind as you read the remaining articles from the field of business.

● ## SELECTION 13

Who Are the Pirates? The Politics of Piracy, Poverty, and Greed in a Globalized Music Market

■ JACK BISHOP

Preview

Is downloading music from the Internet ever justifiable? The author of this article provides an interesting sociocultural perspective on this practice that the music industry has fought in the courts.

To Think About Before You Read

The author's title raises a question and mentions three aspects of the globalized music market. In the space provided, write a few sentences about each of these three aspects as you understand their influence or importance to this market. Then write a few sentences in response to the author's question.

ASPECTS:

1. Piracy: _____

_____

_____

2. Poverty: _____

_____

_____

3. Greed: _____

_____

_____

Who Are the Pirates? The Politics of Piracy, Poverty, and Greed . . .   **493**

READING

Your response to author's question, *"Who Are the Pirates?"*

_____

_____

Terms to Know Before You Read

payola (3) bribery of an influential person in exchange for the promotion of a product or service, as bribery of disc jockeys for the promotion of records

unilateral (4) relating to, involving, or affecting only one side

ethnomusicological (5) relating to the scientific study of music of different cultures

In the wake of the aggressive campaign against Napster, in the name of intellectual property rights, the record industry—more precisely the Big 5 labels (BMG, Warner, Universal, Sony, EMI), along with the IFPI (International Federation of the Phonograph Industry), National Academy of Recording Arts and Sciences (NARAS), Latin Academy of Recording Arts and Sciences (LARAS), and Recording Industry Association of America (RIAA)—is on the attack worldwide against CD pirates. The IFPI estimates that, in the year 2000, one in every three CDs purchased throughout the world was pirated. That adds up to more than 1.8 billion units!

2   If this were not such a serious issue, their position might be laughable as the record industry uses the media to cry foul and plead for public support after years of raking artists and consumers over the financial coals. Just last year, the major labels were cited for using pressure tactics against music retailers to keep the cost of CDs higher than necessary. The Federal Trade Commission ruled that the record companies have violated fair trade practices by in-timidating store owners into not advertising CDs below a certain price, leading to antitrust suits being filed by 28 of the 50 United States against the Big 5 ("Musicland"). These practices have added more than $500 million to CD prices since 1997!

In 2001, after an article in the *Los Angeles* 3 *Times* shed light on an all-but-forgotten tactic used by the industry to control airplay—payola—yet another example of the record companies' unfair and unethical trade practices was revealed to the public. Subsequently, the Federal Communications Commission and the Justice Department launched an in-depth investigation into the allegations of payola between independent promoters and radio stations. With such a history of unfairness and one-sided contract negotiations with artists, greed, the lust for power, price gouging, and price fixing, the industry has worked hard to earn its unfavorable reputation.

Now let us consider this coercive industry in 4 control of a universal entity, such as a global music market, with fixed pricing structures applied unilaterally across the board. This raises some complicated issues of how the concept is applied across a variety of nations all with extremely differing economic, cultural, and social realities. With the United States holding the lion's share of the world music market at 37 percent, it has assumed the position of enforcing policies and standards that in many countries are economically unrealistic. The unilateral imposition of these standards upon nations throughout the world is no less than a form of neocolonialism and economic oppression. Unfair price fixing and unilateral policies cause financial hardships for members of the underclasses wishing to consume the product. In Latin America, where music holds such an intrinsic role in cultural expression, purchasing the product at suggested list price is simply impossible for the majority. The idea of a global music market is not a new concept. The international music market has existed for nearly a century. And the record industry has always held control of production and distribution. The world's music consumers were simply forced to pay whatever price was placed on the product. With the adoption en masse of the cassette recorder in the 1970s and CD technology in the 1980s, the playing field began to change. By the mid-1990s, CD technology had advanced to the point where CD burners were coming as standard equipment in personal computers and standalone duplicators were in every stereo store. For the first time in the history of the music industry, consumers could now actually dabble in production. And through Internet file-sharing applications, the consumer could now also achieve a certain amount of distribution that was previously unavailable. With this shifting terrain, the record industry began to feel its stranglehold on consumer music habits being threatened.

5   So, using the defense of intellectual property

rights as their battle flag, IFPI, NARAS, LARAS, and the RIAA have all banded together to "stamp out" music piracy on a global level. Thus far they have been successful in getting the Clinton Administration to issue laws covering the new media of Internet music (No Electronic Theft Act, NET) and other laws that are falling in favor of major record labels and their traditional distribution conglomerates. They are currently seeking the administration to apply political and perhaps economic pressure if necessary on nations where piracy is rampant. From an ethnomusicological perspective, this intercultural dynamic raises some very interesting issues of power structures, ethics, and the relation between greed and poverty. As a preview of a larger project currently underway, this study presents a brief examination of this dynamic between the United States, Mexico, and Brazil, and strives to draw closer to the definitive answer to the question: "Who are the pirates?"

WHAT'S WRONG WITH THIS PICTURE?

In a wash of articles surfacing recently in the 6 newspapers of the world, and in publications by the IFPI, record companies are crying foul and posing as normally benevolent companies falling victim to a technologically changing world. They complain about the increased sale of CD burners, and the quantity of CD-Rs in circulation, but receive a surcharge of $2 and $12 from each CD burner sold and a 2 percent surcharge from the sale of each CD-R. In 1994, these surcharges exceeded $34 million, and every artist with whom I spoke never received any payments from these fees. The industry argues for the protection of their artists' intellectual property rights, rights that they control, and in most cases have been wrested away from their right-

Who Are the Pirates? The Politics of Piracy, Poverty, and Greed . . . **495**

READING

ful owner, the artist. In a guest column on the NARAS website, posted by Miles Copeland, he gives a pathetic plea for a reassessment of the public image of the record industry. Citing a per CD cost of $15 against a wholesale selling price of $10, Copeland paints the record industry as having been unfairly labeled greedy (NARAS). From a purely business perspective, anyone running a record label that consistently loses $5 per CD should most likely consider a career change. But it doesn't stop there.

7   In his open letter to the public, entitled "Building Bridges with Music," in the premier issue of Grammy Latino (1997), the LARAS Magazine, NARAS CEO and President Michael Greene claims that piracy accounts for 50 percent of all music purchases made in Latin America. While piracy is certainly rampant in Latin America, his figure of 50 percent lacks empirical evidence and remains an exaggerated estimate meant to reflect favorably upon an industry that is painting itself as "victimized" by criminals. Greene bases his figures on the imaginary figures provided annually by the IFPI. He continues by claiming "the entire music food chain is starved" as the foreign bandits reap the benefits of piracy. How ridiculous is such a statement coming from a man who, on the periphery of the industry, annually receives an income of nearly $2 million as the director of a nonprofit organization? It is overt mistruths, like this and like Copeland's, that have earned the recording industry its image as a ravenous, heartless vampire. Greene calls for solutions to piracy that "must be tailored to the very specific, yet fluid political and economic environments existing in each country." By this, he is not referring to tailoring the price structure, but to tailoring the means of coercion. In March 2001, the industry was successful in coercing the Brazilian government into a Presidential Decree instituting an "Interministerial" Anti-Piracy Committee, under the Ministry of Justice, aimed at coordinating the country's different enforcement agencies. In his infinite naiveté, Greene goes on to dismiss the existence of a strong middle class in Latin America (an embarrassment in itself for the then-President of LARAS) and cites the disparity of income between the classes as the principal reason for piracy. He is not far off, but at no point does he acknowledge that this class dynamic has been constructed deliberately, on a global level, by the world's wealthy, a class of which he is part, as a means of maintaining power and control.

In the case of Brazil, Greene claims that pi-8 rated recordings account for 45 percent of all sales, and in Colombia the estimate of pirated sales has reached an astonishing 86 percent. Once again, no written records support these percentages aside from the estimated numbers provided by the IFPI. Greene concludes his letter with a call to every citizen in "even the smallest communities" to join in the battle against piracy. In an exuberant display of self-importance, he is essentially requesting that every man, woman, and child on Earth, despite their economic reality, expend their energy and effort to insure the continuity of his luxurious lifestyle. That is what is truly at stake.

Greene cites disparity of wealth and incon-9 sistent enforcement of copyright laws by officials as the main contributors to the situation. Nowhere in his letter does he admit that record executives and publishers are highly overpaid members of an exploitative industry that has historically appropriated the intellectual properties of others and has parlayed them into vehicles with which to satisfy their greed and the lust for power. At no time does Greene admit that perhaps the prices being charged for commercial CDs, which are considered inflated by

US standards, are entirely unrealistic given local economies throughout Latin America. Never does he even consider the high cost of the products as a possible reason for piracy. As a case study let us consider Brazil.

PIRACY MYTHS AND TRUTHS

10 In a *New York Times* article, Larry Rother paints a very different picture of the situation:

> The latest releases of Britney Spears, Madonna, U2 or the Back Street Boys can cost up to R$36.25 (Reais) (US$14.50) in record shops here [Brazil], but that doesn't stop anyone from hearing them. Street vendors, operating from simple metal stands offer the same titles for R$6.87 ($2.75).

11   This phenomenon is not restricted to imported music. The latest releases by the national artists sell for about the same price, averaging R$30. In a nation where the monthly minimum wage is R$140-200 (US$70–100), paying R$36 for a CD is absolutely out of the question. "It is the avarice, the unyielding rapaciousness of the record companies, that foments the violation of recording copyrights in Brazil," said Nehemias Gueiros, Jr., an intellectual property rights lawyer and former record company executive. "When you have a predatory price policy incompatible with the economic reality of a country, then you are simply paving the way for piracy." In regard to the high prices, Antonio Carlos Manfredini, an economist at the Getulio Vargas Foundation, said:

> The higher price for recordings here [Brazil] is maintained not so much with

Brazil itself in mind, but to avoid sales to the United States and Western Europe ; it's simply not worth it to them to threaten their markets in the North by means of aggressive pricing in Brazil.

This statement reveals Brazil's reality of try- 12 ing to deal with the globalized price structure imposed on the world by the US/European/Japanese music industry. As a result of these high prices, record company profit margins in Brazil may be even higher than they are in the United States. Gueiros, an ex-executive at Sony and BMG before opening his own law firm and boutique record label in Rio de Janeiro, calculates that the average producer's cost of a CD in Brazil, which includes royalties, is kept lower than in the United States at less than $3. It is commonly accepted by Brazilian economists and industry forecasters, that profits in Brazil would soar, and piracy would wane, if record companies would trade profit-per-unit for volume sales. In rebuttal to Greene's accusation that local officials are not doing enough, Manfredini states:

> In a low-income country, the regulatory authorities have difficulty protecting the rights of both producers and consumers, and so there is not an institutional structure to control price fixing and other abuses perpetrated by the same companies that complain that their rights are not being protected when piracy results.

This is an interesting statement that reveals 13 the greed of an industry that wants protection for its price gouging and protection from opposition to that gouging. So, in other words, what the industry wants is for governments to oppress the masses in order to preserve their economic pillaging of the lower classes. The painfully obvious truth that seems difficult for the industry to grasp is that in "low-income" societies throughout the world, music pirates are not seen as the bandits Michael Greene and the industry claim them to be. They are, in many cases, Robin Hoods, freeing music from its economic raptors and returning it to the people. Brazil is, after all, a country that defines and expresses itself through song as much as any other in the world, which means that Brazilians view any attempt economically to limit access to music as an attack on their culture and national identity.

MEXICAN PIRATES

14 In another case study, let us consider Mexico. The IFPI released figures in its June 2001 update that state that pirated CDs account for more than 65 percent of all music purchases made in the country during the year 2000. The IFPI states that, owing to "poor coordination between the key enforcement agencies, a lack of commitment to intellectual property offenses by the judiciary and a lack of deterrent sentencing in the courts," piracy continues to grow. Comparing the Mexican gross national product per capita of $4,748 with the $33,933 of the United States (2001), illuminates in dollars and sense the disparity between the social classes of each country. The difference of $29,185 makes selling the same product for the same price in both societies an absurdity. The case of Brazil is even worse, with the difference being $30,496. Third on the list of priorities against piracy, the IFPI claims that Mexican pirates account for annual losses of more than $220 million. What is ironic is that upon closer inspection, Mexico posted a real growth rate in

retail sales of 13 percent compared with that of 6 percent in the United States and to Brazil's depressing −44 percent. Units sold in Mexico during 1999 reached 72.8 million and yielded earnings of $626 million. When combining these figures with the $668.4 million from Brazil, we see that the record industry reaped $1,294,400,000 last year from these two Latin American countries that surprisingly still occupy the third and fourth places on the IFPI's hit list against piracy. The IFPI has stated that their top priority in Mexico is effective antipiracy enforcement. What this actually means has yet to be seen. As in the case of Brazil, Mexico's so-called lack of commitment seems to evidence an unwillingness to be coerced by multinational corporations into enforcing policies that are designed as mechanisms to economically pillage the underclasses of the country. Mexico is no less musical than Brazil, and limiting access to music to those who can pay the price is the same attack on Mexican culture and national identity.

FINAL THOUGHTS

Citing the 80 percent increase in the sale of 15 CD-R blanks in 2000 as the main reason for the increase in piracy, the IFPI has not been as forthcoming with figures on the amount of money raised from the 2 percent surcharge that trickles back to the industry from those CD-Rs, nor the surcharge made from every burner that made the copies. Imagine the revenue generated if the sales of CD-Rs are up 80 percent and in 1994 revenue was $34 million! Yet no distributions were made to the musicians of the member labels of the RIAA. The interesting thing here is that those surcharges are being paid to the RIAA to offset any projected loss in retail sales owing to copies being made by consumers. This was intended to free the listener from these problems. What happened to that agreement? One more note: if piracy is eradicated, will the RIAA stop receiving the surcharges? I doubt it. One thing inherently wrong with the figures thrown around by the industry is that nowhere has it been proved that every CD-R sold is being turned into a pirated product. The main issue here is not the quantity of CD-Rs in circulation, but the reason why so many are used to duplicate music. Apparently the world's music consumer has found an option to the price gouging of the industry. The CD-R offers a previously unavailable choice,

a response to the economic oppression perpetrated against consumers by the world's wealthy. To the "low income" societies throughout Brazil and Mexico, and even the United States, the CD-R represents liberation and freedom of choice. Therefore, it is not necessary to be an economist to see that if we abandon the mind washing we received while growing up that taught us that the normal order of society was for a small faction of the population to control the majority of resources, and for the masses to struggle to obtain them, and we apply a trickle-up rather than a trickle-down theory, it becomes quite clear who the pirates actually are.

Evaluation of the Article

Difficulty Rating ☐ 1 ☐ 2 ☐ 3 ☐ 4 ☐ 5
(1 = easy; 5 = difficult)

What reading difficulties did you encounter? _____

_____

How did you handle these difficulties? _____

_____

Postreading Comprehension Development

Sentence Rewrite

To check your understanding of some of the key concepts of this essay, rewrite each of the following sentences in your own words, keeping the original idea. (See Chapter 1.)

1. The unilateral imposition of these standards upon nations throughout the world is no less than a form of neocolonialism and economic oppression. (4)

_____

_____

2. Greene cites disparity of wealth and inconsistent enforcement of copyright laws by officials as the main contributors to the situation. (9)

_____

_____

3. So, in other words, what the industry wants is for governments to oppress the masses in order to preserve their economic pillaging of the lower classes. (13)

_____

_____

Author's Main Idea

(See Chapter 3.)

1. The paragraph in which the author's main point is most clearly stated is:
   a. 3
   b. 4
   c. 5
   d. 6

2. The sentence in this paragraph which best states the main idea is:

_____

_____

3. How does the discussion about the level of income in Brazil help serve the author's purpose for writing this article?

_____

_____

_____

Inferences, Metaphors, and Vocabulary in Context

(See Chapters 2, 6, and 7.)

1. Which of the following does the author imply in paragraph 6? Be prepared to justify your answer.

   a. Sales of CD burners should be prohibited.

   b. Record companies are cheating recording artists.

   c. The IFPI believes that individuals who download music have a legitimate reason for doing so.

   d. If people downloaded 2 percent less music, the music industry would not object to downloading at all.

2. According to the author, who benefits most from the current policies of the music industry?

   a. recording stars

   b. those who purchase CDs in the United States

   c. the music industry

   d. people who live in poor countries

3. What is the author's view of the music industry's use of "intellectual property rights as their battle flag"? (5)

   _____

   _____

   _____

4. The author's purpose for discussing Larry Rother in the *Piracy Myths and Truths* section is:

   a. to show how people who live in poor countries manage to get things they want.

   b. to complain that people are stealing popular music.

   c. to illustrate how businesses operate in Brazil.

   d. to encourage popular music stars to put a stop to music downloading in Brazil.

5. One inference we can draw from paragraph 13 is that:

   a. The author hopes Greene will use his influence to change the music industry's policies in Brazil.

   b. The author sympathizes with music pirates in Brazil.

   c. Musical expression as a cultural feature is not a reasonable excuse for piracy.

   d. Lower-income Brazilians would be willing to pay the higher price if music were more connected to their culture.

6. Why does the author refer to those who download music from the Internet as Robin Hoods? Do you agree with this description? Explain your answer.

   _____

   _____

7. What answer does the author give to his question, *"Who Are the Pirates"*? Give reasons for your opinion.

   _____

   _____

   _____

8. Using only the context and your knowledge of word structure, define each of the following words. Do not use a dictionary.

   a. en masse (4) _____

   b. intrinsic (4) _____

   c. benevolent (6) _____

   d. periphery (7) _____

   e. expend (8) _____

   f. disparity (9) _____

   g. foments (11) _____

   h. pillage (14) _____

9. How do you think the author wants the reader to feel after reading the *Final Thoughts* section of this selection? What are the reasons for your beliefs?

   _____

   _____

Recalling Details

(See Chapters 4 and 5.)

1. The music industry's reason for not lowering CD prices in countries like Brazil and Mexico is:

   a. People in those countries can afford the CDs.

   b. Recording studios are pressured by recording artists to sell at high prices.

   c. The recording business is expensive.

   d. The recording industry has lost money because of piracy.

2. Which of the following are factual statements in this article? Which are opinions? Use (F) or (O) for your response. For those you label opinion, write any support for the opinion that is given in this article.

   _____ a. The Latin Academy of Recording Artists and Scientists is on the attack worldwide against CD pirates.

   _____ b. If this were not such a serious issue, their position might be laughable. . . .

   _____ c. The idea of a global music market is not a new concept.

   _____ d. In 1994, these surcharges exceeded $34 million, and every artists with whom I spoke never received any payments from these fees.

   _____ e. It is overt mistruths like this and like Copeland's that have earned the recording industry its image as a ravenous, heartless vampire.

   _____ f. In the case of Brazil, Greene claims that pirated recordings account for 45 percent of all sales. . . .

   _____ g. When you have a predatory price policy incompatible with the economic reality of a country, then you are simply paving the way for piracy.

   _____ h. The painfully obvious truth that seems difficulty for the industry to grasp is that in "low-income" societies throughout the world, music pirates are not seen as the bandits.

   _____ i. The difference of $29,185 makes selling the same product for the same price in both societies an absurdity.

   _____ j. The main issue here is not the quantity of CD-Rs in circulation, but the reason *why* so many are used to duplicate music.

3. The author's major criticism of Michael Greene is that:

   a. Greene is a rich man who does not consider poverty of other nations when pricing CDs.

   b. The recording artists are not receiving any of the profits from sales of CDs.

   c. Greene is asking everyone to help fight music piracy.

   d. His profit margins in Brazil may be even higher than they are in the U.S.

4. For each person listed, check those who are opposed (O) to individuals reproducing and selling their own music downloads onto CDs.

   _____ a. Miles Copeland

   _____ b. Manfredini

   _____ c. Nehemias Gueiros, Jr.

   _____ d. Jack Bishop

   _____ e. Michael Greene

5. The pattern of organization used in paragraph 11 is:

   a. opinion and reason.

   b. definition and explanation.

   c. problem and solution.

   d. cause and effect.

6. What new information about downloading music from the Internet did you gain from reading this selection?

   _____

   _____

Critical Thinking: Reaction and Discussion

1. With a group, discuss the following:

   How has music piracy affected your life? Do you think it is reasonable for the music industry to crackdown on those who copy CDs illegally? How did reading this article affect your opinion of music piracy?

2. Assume the role of a recording artist. Decide who you are, what kind of music you make and what the problems discussed in this article

mean to you. Then, in an essay of at least 250 words, discuss the following:

As a recording artist, I propose the following solutions to music piracy because they would be fair to everyone.

USING TECHNOLOGY FOR FURTHER UNDERSTANDING

The article mentions legislation related to music piracy that was passed during the Clinton administration. *What has been passed since? Does the new legislation seem more concerned with protecting the music industry or the consumer? Are their protections for recording artists?* Use the Internet to find answers to these questions.

● SELECTION 14

Coke's Sinful World

■ PAUL KLEBNIKOV

Preview

A leading beverage company encounters many obstacles in its attempts to sell its products in overseas markets. In this article, the author describes some of the challenges Coca-Cola faced and how it addressed them.

To Think About Before You Read

Imagine you manufactured a popular U.S. product that you wanted to sell to other countries with cultures quite different from your own.

1. What are some challenges you might face with regard to each of the following as you try to sell your product in the global marketplace? Be as specific as possible in describing the challenges. Use what you already know about these aspects of life in other parts of the world. List your response in the spaces provided.

    Economic challenges:

    _____

    _____

    Challenges with regard to business practices:

    _____

    _____

    Challenges resulting from cultural differences:

    _____

    _____

2. Bearing these challenges in mind, what are some guidelines you would give your salespeople to follow as they attempted to market your product internationally? Write three guidelines in the space below. Be prepared to discuss why you believe these guidelines would be important for your company to follow in overseas markets.

a. _____

_____

b. _____

_____

c. _____

_____

Terms to Know Before You Read

unorthodox (7) not adhering to what is commonly accepted; customary or traditional

debacle (8) a sudden collapse, downfall, or defeat

equity (11) something that is just, impartial, and fair.

soums (21) Uzbekistan unit of currency; $1 = 1158.28 soums (as of November 2005)

channel-stuffing (24) overdistributing a product that is not needed in order to gain revenue

Coca-Cola Co. has "arguably the strongest and most pervasive marketing and distribution system in the world," Chairman Douglas Daft told investors at the annual shareholder meeting in April. And it does. The Coke empire stretches to more parts of the globe than any other enterprise in the world. The soda is served in more than 200 nations; it's easier to list the markets where Coke isn't: Myanmar, Cuba, Iraq and Syria. Everywhere else—including such tricky markets as Pakistan, Cambodia, Liberia, Zimbabwe and Colombia—Coke is a beloved consumer staple. Nine million stores sell Coke, serving up some 1.2 billion servings a day around the world.

2   That's why overseas sales account for two-thirds of Coke's revenue (expected to total $21 billion this year) and three-quarters of operating income (forecast at $5.8 billion total) and over 90% of the giant brand's profit growth. After a rough patch from 1998 to 2001, Coke is back. In the first nine months of this year Coke has reported a robust 4% rise in volume (the most-watched indicator of the company's health), a 6% increase in revenue and a 12% rise in net income—numbers as good as any Coke has posted since 1997.

3   But here's the part Douglas Daft left out: Building business overseas requires dealing with the devil and other questionable characters—relatives of dictators in the Middle East, Latin American bottlers who allegedly work with assassination squads and Marxist rebels in Colombia.

4   Coke has had to endure that and more as it expands relentlessly into the globe's last nooks and crannies. Since 1999 it has taken charges totaling upward of a billion dollars related to overseas markets and deals gone awry. In February the company was shaken by the murder of a Coke executive by rebels in Colombia. It has been sued in a class action accusing it of forcing "unneeded" beverage concentrate on bottlers to stoke its growth numbers. And Coke has watched a well-funded bottler that was to be its gateway to central Asia wither amid charges of misappropriated funds, tax dodges and cozy inside deals.

5   Coke's chief executive, Daft, declined to be interviewed for this story, and the company refused to make other top executives available. Yet Coke has little choice but to keep prospecting overseas. In the U.S. decades of market dominance have made Coke a low-growth staple: The ten-year compound annual unit-case growth in the U.S. is only 4%.

6   Foreign markets are less flooded with the syrupy soda. The North Africa and Eurasia/Middle East divisions now are among Coke's fastest-growing units, with sales rising two to three times as rapidly as in the U.S. Coke now has hundreds of bottlers outside the U.S. (it doesn't have an exact figure). Historically, it has tried to merge its smaller partners into big "anchor" bottlers, but its success in under-developed markets often depends on small local outfits that know the terrain.

7   And with each such partner it embraces, Coke risks tarnishing its clean-cut image by associating with businesses that may partake in local traditions that can include bribing local officials, paying retailers to shun rival brands and resorting to other unorthodox tactics. "Both Coke and Pepsi try to do business as ethically as possible, but when you have local partners who are not subject to the same governance and scrutiny as in the U.S., then sometimes local behaviors take place," says one former Pepsi executive who worked in Latin America.

8   So far the main thing sparing Coke from a true debacle is the strength of the brand itself. Even the anti-American backlash that swept the Islamic world in recent years has hardly stymied Coke's onward march. French Muslims roll out a politicized anti-Coke called Mecca-Cola, to no noticeable effect on sales. Egypt is swept by a bizarre rumor that the Coca-Cola label (read backwards in Arabic) says "No to Mohammad, No to Mecca." Coke counters by getting the grand mufti of Egypt to issue a fatwa declaring that this is nonsense. And the brand has survived just fine after blows that might have killed another: reports in 1999 in Belgium that a batch of Coke products was giving kids headaches and nausea; and worries in India last August about supposedly high levels of pesticide in the drink.

9   It seems that people who curse the U.S. and condemn it to eternal damnation still want to take time out from politics for the pause that refreshes. The company's fizzy foreign expansion touches thousands of small private businesses—from bottlers and distributors (whom it helps to equip and capitalize) to local grocery stores and roadside vendors (whom it supplies with coolers, shiny display cases and signs).

10   But the linchpin of the success of the business is the far-flung network of independent bottlers who make up the "Coke system." Coke is almost wholly dependent on the bottlers for its own results. They buy secret concentrate from Coca-Cola Co. and add water and sugar to turn it into the world's best-known soda, distributing it in cans and bottles across the world's next developing markets.

11   The biggest bottlers aren't subsidiaries of Coke, nor are they completely independent. Coke effectively controls them by maintaining big equity stakes and a heavy presence on their boards, and by providing their main source of business. Yet it keeps its stakes in the bottlers below 50%, thereby avoiding getting hit with their piles of debt and any unpleasant liabilities.

12   In Brazil price wars are so cutthroat that Coke competes with itself: Its local bottlers use independent distributors that undercut one another to raid retail accounts. It's why a 2-liter bottle of Coke sells for half the price that it does in Mexico. Meanwhile, Pepsi has filed a government complaint in Brazil against Coke for allegedly bugging local Pepsi planning meetings, among other supposed misdeeds. An earlier accusation that a Coke-affiliated brewer had bribed Brazilian antitrust officials to block the merger of two Pepsi-affiliated breweries was never substantiated—because it was never investigated.

In Colombia the company has become un- 13 willingly involved in the long-running civil war between the government and Marxist rebels. Coke's Colombian bottlers have allegedly conspired with right-wing death squads to target six trade union activists at their plants—one was actually assassinated—and intimidate dozens more since 1990. That accusation is laid out in a lawsuit filed in 2001 in U.S. court in Miami by the Colombian food-and-drink union, Sinaltrainal. Earlier this year the judge dismissed the charges against Coca-Cola Co. but allowed the suit against the bottlers to proceed. In February Luisa Fernanda Solarte, a marketing manager for Coke, was killed in a terrorist bombing.

In Coke's Eurasia/Middle East division, suc- 14 cessful market entry has often meant teaming up with the cronies of the local political boss. When Coke entered Iran in 1990, it teamed up with a relative of Iranian president Ali Akbar Hashemi Rafsanjani. Entering the Israeli-occupied West Bank in 1998, Coke jumped into bed with Yasir Arafat's Palestinian Authority.

And in Uzbekistan, the historic centerpiece 15 of Central Asia and its most densely populated market, Coke teamed up with a son-in-law of strongman President Islam Karimov—and came to regret it. Coke saw the former Soviet state as its gateway to the entire region. So in 1993 it signed a deal with one Mansur Maqsudi, an Afghan-American living in New Jersey. He had no previous bottling experience—but he was married to the Uzbek president's eldest daughter, Gulnara Karimova. Together they opened Coca-Cola Bottlers Uzbekistan (CCBU), owned in equal parts by Coke's export subsidiary, Coca-Cola Export Corp., a Maqsudi family trading company and the government of Uzbekistan.

Maqsudi brought in his older brother to 16

help run the operation. CCBU, headquartered in Tashkent, found all doors open to it. Pepsi, which had owned the market in Soviet times, was pushed out, and all of Uzbekistan was soon covered with red Coke logos. In the next eight years CCBU invested over $100 million in new bottling plants, warehouses and a nationwide distribution network. By 1997 the operation was raking in $118 million in sales and recording net profit margins of 29%. CCBU was twice selected by Coke as "Bottler of the Year" for the Eurasia/Middle East region.

17 Then in the summer of 2001 things began to fall apart. Maqsudi's marriage broke up. His estranged wife left New Jersey and took their two children back to Uzbekistan. Maqsudi, still president of CCBU, remained in New Jersey. In August 2001 the Uzbek tax police came calling, unearthing the disturbing fact that CCBU conducted almost all its transactions through companies owned by the Maqsudi brothers.

18 Most of the goods CCBU imported (sugar, bottling equipment, plastic preforms, labels, caps, etc.) went through the Maqsudi-owned companies. And while Coke was paid, often late, in wobbly Uzbek currency that couldn't be taken out of the country, Maqsudi's properties got preferential treatment; they were paid in hard currency, often in advance. From 1998 to 2001, while Coke was struggling to get paid, almost $100 million was wired from Uzbekistan to Maqsudi affiliates, including a Dubai-based trading firm, Valuelink FZE, and various offshore affiliates of Roz Trading (the Maqsudi company that held the family's CCBU stake), according to Uzbek Central Bank records.

19 The Uzbek prosecutor general's office now claims that by overcharging for these imports and taking straightforward trading commissions, the Maqsudis siphoned off much of CCBU's profits and stashed it in offshore accounts to avoid tens of millions of dollars in taxes. In 2002 the Uzbek authorities confiscated the Maqsudis' equity share in CCBU.

20 Mansur Maqsudi counters that he and his family are victims of a political vendetta launched by his ex-wife. He says his companies never made any profits on the Coca-Cola venture and that they played an indispensable role in keeping the CCBU operation afloat. Since CCBU became engulfed in scandal, however, its business has slowed down; this summer it finally stopped altogether. That has hurt Coke's business in Uzbekistan, which had anchored its sales in the entire region.

21 From a purely financial perspective, however, Coke's downside was minuscule, in part because the Uzbek business was tiny on the soda giant's $20 billion-a-year scale. From 1997 to 2000 CCBU made $82 million in net profits, letting Coke add a mere $27 million to its own bottom line. But most of Coke's equity income was reinvested in CCBU, and as much as $40 million was left in an Uzbek bank account, mired in nonconvertible Uzbek soums. "We simply didn't know what to do with the money; we had no place else to put it," says Maqsudi.

22 An internal Coke report compiled by PricewaterhouseCoopers that was rushed out in two weeks pegged Coke's "quantifiable loss" in the Uzbek affair at a mere $3 million, but said the real sum could be much higher; it also made note of possible attempts by a CCBU official to impede the investigation.

23 But Coke continued to do business with CCBU. Maqsudi cites the company's need to keep posting respectable growth. "The pressure at Coke was huge for every division to keep volumes growing, and they understood that this is what they had to do to make their numbers," he

says. By the time he left CCBU in 2001, "we had a year's worth of concentrate in stock," recalls Maqsudi. By contrast, Coke bottlers in the U.S. rarely keep more than a few weeks' supply of concentrate in stock; in remote markets, up to three months' worth is the norm.

24   Similar allegations of channel-stuffing emerged in Japan, which accounts for nearly a fifth of Coke's total worldwide sales, and elsewhere. Some of the details came to light in a shareholder lawsuit filed in U.S. District Court in Atlanta in October 2000. Suing on behalf of several pension funds, lawyers at Milberg Weiss Bershad Hynes & Lerach charged that Coke inflated its 1999 revenue by $600 million and boosted pretax earnings by $400 million by overloading bottlers in Japan, the U.S., Europe and South Africa with "unneeded" concentrate. The lawsuit was filed after Coke reported $1.5 billion in writeoffs and, in the first quarter of 2000, recorded its first quarterly loss in memory.

25   In August the U.S. District Court in Atlanta dismissed the channel-stuffing charges but allowed other parts of the lawsuit to proceed. The law firm has since submitted a much more detailed complaint about channel-stuffing, which the judge is now considering. (The Justice Department is also investigating the matter.)   26

The suit contends Coke induced its Japanese bottlers to take $233 million worth of "excess, unwanted and unneeded" concentrate in 1999; it compensated them with rebates and extra funds to cover marketing and the installation of thousands of new vending machines in underserved locations. Instead of including these payments as a cost in the income statement, Coke spread out the cost over a longer period, classifying it as an investment in retailing assets. In 1999 Coke wrote off its "impaired" Japanese assets. It denies all charges of channel-stuffing.   27

Today signs of a Coke rebound continue on its long march to conquer the world. Coke has built its booming overseas business by teaching thousands of bottlers, distributors and retailers how to sell the world's best-known soda. Now if only the company could teach its overseas partners a thing or two about ethics.

Evaluation of the Article
Difficulty Rating □ 1 □ 2 □ 3 □ 4 □ 5
(1 = easy; 5 = difficult)

What reading difficulties did you encounter? _____

_____

How did you handle these difficulties? _____

_____

Postreading Comprehension Development

Sentence Rewrite

To check your understanding of some of the key concepts of this essay, rewrite each of the following sentences in your own words, keeping the original idea. (See Chapter 1.)

1. It seems that people who curse the U.S. and condemn it to eternal damnation still want to take time out from politics for the pause that refreshes. (9)

_____

_____

2. But the linchpin of the success of the business is the far-flung network of independent bottlers who make up the "Coke system."(10)

_____

_____

3. Its local bottlers use independent distributors that undercut one another to raid retail accounts. (12)

_____

_____

Author's Main Idea

(See Chapter 3.)

1. What is the topic of this article?

_____

2. What is the author's focus on this topic?

_____

3. Using the following starter sentence, state the author's main idea:

The author wants me to understand that:

_____

_____

4. The paragraph in which the author's main point is most clearly stated is:

_____ a. paragraph 1

_____ b. paragraph 3

_____ c. paragraph 5

_____ d. paragraph 7

5. How does the discussion regarding Coke's Colombia help serve the author's purpose for writing this article?

_____

_____

Inferences, Metaphors, and Vocabulary in Context
(See Chapters 2, 6, and 7.)

1. Which of the following does the author imply in paragraph 5? Be prepared to justify your answer.

   a. If Coke lost its overseas markets, it would suffer significant financial loss.

   b. Coke will be careful in the strategies it takes to increase profits.

   c. Coke always knew that getting into overseas markets could be risky.

   d. Other businesses have used Coke as a model for developing their overseas markets.

2. Which of the following does the author also imply in paragraph 5? Be prepared to justify your answer.

   a. Coke's chief executives were on vacation, so they could not answer questions.

   b. Coke felt their chief executives could not be bothered by trivial questioning, so Coke instead hired public relations personnel to answer questions.

c. Coke is unlikely to look to its sales in the U.S. for profit increases.

d. Coke's chief officials were involved in raising the annual unit-case growth and prospecting overseas, which are reasons why they were not available to answer questions.

3. Which of the following does the author imply in paragraph 9? Be prepared to justify your answer.

a. Even though people want to curse the U.S., they are grateful for the business Coke brings to their economy.

b. Coke is despised overseas, but some people are happy about the coolers, shiny display cases, and signs.

c. Coke's foreign expansion is what the majority of people are angry about, because Coke is buying out a lot of small companies and funding leaders who are unethical.

d. Even thought people condemn Coke for its politics overseas, they are happy that Coke is a good company that contributes thousands of dollars to charities.

4. In your own words, explain what the author means when he says, "Building business overseas requires dealing with the devil . . ." (3)

_____

_____

5. What is the relationship between paragraph 2 and paragraph 7 in this article?

6. Which of the following assumptions can be made about Coke's overseas expansion? Check all that apply. Be prepared to justify your answer.

_____ a. Coke will do anything it takes, including murder, to get its product established.

_____ b. Coke will put huge sums of money toward building the best bottling company overseas.

_____ c. Coke will sell its recipe and undercut Pepsi bottlers to get market dominance.

_____ d. Coke will hire the best attorneys to save its reputation from deals gone awry involving overseas markets and Coke's expansion into those markets.

_____ e. Coke will fire overseas bottlers who use unethical business practices.

_____ f. Overseas bottlers must take a course in business ethics in order to get a license to bottle Coke.

7. The author's tone throughout most of this essay is:

   a. cynical regarding Coke and its practices overseas.

   b. neutral regarding Coke and its practices overseas.

   c. optimistic about Coke's practices overseas.

   d. cautious regarding Coke's practices overseas.

8. The pattern of organization used in paragraph 8 is:

   a. comparison and contrast

   b. opinion and reason

   c. simple listing

   d. problem and solution

9. Using only the context and your knowledge of word structure, define each of the following words. Do not use a dictionary.

   a. shareholder (1) _____

   b. pervasive (1) _____

   c. gateway (4) _____

   d. awry (4) _____

   e. stymied (8) _____

   f. intimidate (13) _____

   g. indispensable (20) _____

   h. miniscule (21) _____

Recalling Details

(See Chapters 4 and 5.)

1. Which of the following are factual statements in this article? Which are opinions? Use (F) or (O) for your response. For those you label opinion, write any support for the opinion that is given in this article.

   _____ a. Coke is the strongest and most pervasive marketing and distribution system in the world.

   _____ b. Nine million stores sell Coke.

   _____ c. Building business overseas requires dealing with the devil and other questionable characters.

   _____ d. Foreign markets are less flooded with syrupy soda.

_____ e. People don't seem to mind how Coke infiltrates the overseas market.

_____ f. In February Luisa Fernanda Solarte, a marketing manager for Coke, was killed in a terrorist bombing.

_____ g. Coke bottlers in the U.S. rarely keep more than a few weeks' supply of concentrate in stock.

_____ h. Today, signs of a Coke rebound continue on its long march to conquer the world.

_____ i. Coke is the best-tasting beverage in the world.

_____ j. Douglas Daft did not comment on his questionable business practices overseas.

2. Create a timeline for paragraphs 15–20 that illustrates why the author says Coca Cola "came to regret" its relation with Maqsudi. Use the space provided for your timeline.

3. Which details about Coke's expansion overseas did you find most surprising?

_____

_____

4. Indicate whether each of the following items is a major (MAJ) or minor (MIN) detail of this article.

Be prepared to justify your answers.

_____ a. Coca-Cola has "arguably the strongest and most pervasive marketing and distribution system in the world . . ."

_____ b. It is easier to list the markets where Coke isn't: Myanmar, Cuba, Iraq, and Syria.

_____ c. In the U.S. decades of market dominance have made Coke a low-growth staple.

_____ d. Entering the Israeli-occupied West Bank in 1998, Coke jumped into bed with Yasir Arafat's Palestinian Authority.

_____ e. So far the main thing sparing Coke from a true debacle is the strength of the brand itself.

_____ f. The biggest bottlers aren't subsidiaries of Coke, nor are they completely independent.

_____ g. The North Africa and Eurasia/Middle East divisions now are among Coke's fastest-growing units, with sales rising two to three times as rapidly as in the U.S.

_____ h. The lawsuit was filed after Coke reported $1.5 billion in writeoffs and, in the first quarter of 2000, recorded its first quarterly loss in memory.

_____ i. CCBU was twice selected by Coke as "Bottler or the Year" for the Eurasia/Middle East region.

Critical Thinking: Reaction and Discussion

1. Refer back to the To Think About Before You Read section where you identified challenges and developed business guidelines for your overseas company. With a group, share your ideas and decide:

   a. which of these ideas would you keep?

   b. what guidelines would you delete or add?

With your group, create a final set of guidelines for overseas marketing of products made in the United States.

2. In recent years, many sectors of the United States, including the general public, have expressed concern about the large number of goods from other countries exported to the U.S. Because these goods are less expensive, they appear to have a negative effect on Americans' willingness to purchase goods made at home, and the U.S. has a large negative trade balance that will be felt for generations to come.

   In an essay of 250 words or more, respond to the question: *What can be done in the U.S. to encourage its citizens to purchase more products that have been made in the U.S.?*

USING TECHNOLOGY FOR FURTHER UNDERSTANDING

1. On the Internet, investigate marketing strategies of a product that you like, such as Levi jeans, Diesel, or McDonald's. For instance, look at *http:us.rediff.com/money/2003/aug/09spec.htm* for information about Reebok. How does the company you have chosen attempt to market its products overseas? What is your view of these efforts? How do these efforts compare with strategies Coca-Cola has used?

2. Legislation has been passed in the United States, such as The Foreign Corrupt Practices Act of 1977 (FCPA), and its amendment of 1998, that prohibits a U.S. company as well as certain foreign companies to make a payment to a foreign official for the purpose of obtaining or retaining business for or with, or directing business to, any person. This legislation is viewed by some as putting the U.S. at a disadvantage when it is competing with foreign countries who do not have these ethical standards. Use the Internet to learn more about FCPA and how businesses view this legislation. Then decide whether the law should stay as it is, be modified, or be repealed. Give your reasons for your views.

SELECTION 15

El Millonario Next Door

■ TYCE PALMAFFY

Preview

How do small business entrepreneurs get started? What obstacles do they face, and how do they overcome them? This author describes how one group of minorities is realizing their dreams of being small business owners.

To Think About Before You Read

What are some of the characteristics of successful small business entrepreneurs? For each trait listed, indicate why this might be important for a small business owner's success. Use a dictionary to define traits listed that you do not know.

1. independence _____

   _____

2. perseverance _____

   _____

3. creativity _____

   _____

4. cautiousness _____

   _____

5. friendliness _____

   _____

What other traits do you think would be important? Give reasons for your opinion:

_____

_____

Terms to Know Before You Read

infrastructure (26) an underlying base or foundation, especially for an organization or a system

niche (subtitle; 31) a special area of demand for a product or service

leveraging (31) using power to act effectively

procurement (40) acquisition

beleaguered (46) harassed

Many Americans seem to regard the nation's Hispanics with apprehension. Their high poverty rates, low education levels, and tendency to create separate cultural enclaves feed a perception that Hispanics are not following the upwardly mobile immigrant path worn by their Asian, European, and Middle Eastern predecessors.

2   America, meet Bartolo Lopez.

3   In 1970, at age 17, Lopez crossed the Mexican border into California with barely enough money to pay the "coyote"—immigrants' slang for the guide hired to bring them illegally across the border. At first he, like many Mexican immigrants, labored in the fields of northern California. Finding that wearisome, he began working for a Japanese gardener, who taught him the art of landscape design: skills such as reading blueprints, placing boulders, and creating waterfalls.

4   After earning legal residency as a licensed landscape technician, Lopez joined a landscaping firm in Los Angeles for several years. But when a recession hit in 1982, his salary dropped by half. That setback drove him to start 3 Pinos Landscaping, a landscape design and maintenance firm.

At first he was stuck mowing residential 5 lawns, but within a year he had 10 employees and design projects ranging from $10,000 to $100,000. His business now takes in nearly $2 million in annual revenues serving a predominately upper-middle-class clientele. And Lopez, who once worked dusk to dawn picking strawberries for pennies, now earns nearly $100,000 a year designing and creating opulent backyard Xanadus for the San Fernando Valley's upper crust.

THE FLOWERING

The qualities that prompted Lopez to launch 6 his own enterprise are the same ones that brought him to America in the first place: a penchant for risk-taking and a willingness to sacrifice and work hard in pursuit of a better life. These attitudes are typically strong among immigrants, and they help to explain why a vibrant entrepreneurial culture is developing within the Hispanic community. Indeed, Latinos, more than a third of whom are foreign-born, represent the nation's fastest-growing pool of business owners—a deeply encouraging sign of their desire to join preceding waves of immigrants in pursuit of the American Dream.

7   From 1987 to 1992, the last year for which Census Bureau statistics are available, the number of U.S. businesses owned by Hispanics rose 76 percent, from 490,000 to 863,000. Meanwhile, the number of U.S. firms overall grew by just 26 percent, from 13.7 million to 17.3 million. During the same period, total receipts for Hispanic-owned firms more than doubled, from $32.8 billion to $76 billion, at a time when receipts for all U.S. firms grew by only 67 percent, from $2 trillion to $3.3 trillion. In the space of a decade, from 1982 to 1992, the number of Hispanic-owned firms nearly quadrupled. Assuming similar growth rates since 1992 (a conservative assumption considering the U.S. economy's strong recent performance), the U.S. Hispanic Chamber of Commerce estimates that Hispanics now own 1.3 million U.S. businesses generating more than $200 billion in annual revenues.

8   The overall size of the Hispanic business community is not yet as impressive as its recent growth. Although they are 11 percent of the U.S. population, Latinos owned just 5 percent of all firms in 1992, accounting for 2 percent of gross receipts. Nearly half of all Hispanic-owned businesses earned less than $10,000, and only 15 percent had paid employees. Only two Hispanic-owned firms, Burt Automotive Network and Goya Foods Inc., made Forbes magazine's 1997 listing of the nation's 500 largest privately held companies.

9   That Hispanic entrepreneurs have some

catching up to do should not be surprising. The median age of Latinos is more than a decade younger than America's non-Hispanic whites, and the newly arrived immigrants among them tend to have a limited grasp of English, scant capital, and few sophisticated work skills. They haven't been running firms long enough to expand through reinvesting profits and developing a strong customer base.

10   Hispanic entrepreneurial growth might be compared more usefully with that of other, equally young minority groups, such as Asians and blacks, the other minorities surveyed by the Census Bureau. In 1992, Hispanics in this country owned 43 percent more firms than Asians, widely known for their prolific business formation. The number of Hispanic-owned firms also grew faster than Asian-owned companies between 1987 and 1992. Relatively speaking, however, Asians still come out ahead. They make up only 3 percent of the population, yet their smaller number of firms still generated 26 percent more total receipts than Hispanic-owned concerns.

11   Hispanic business ownership has already surpassed that of blacks, a racial group of similar size, and appears to have done so without as much reliance on government assistance. With 12 percent of the nation's population, blacks as a group owned 242,000 fewer firms in 1992. The average black-owned firm earned only $52,000 that year, slightly more than half the Hispanic average. (This might be partly explained by the fact that blacks tend to own businesses in the low-cost states of the South, Hispanics in relatively high-cost states.)

12   As one of the largest minority business set-aside programs in the federal government, the Small Business Administration's Section 8(a) program is a good indicator of the degree to

which different minority groups depend upon government help. Of the 6,183 firms certified last year to participate in the program, which limits competition for certain government contracts to small, minority-owned firms, blacks owned 45 percent, Hispanics only 25 percent. "When you compare the Hispanic and black business worlds," says Joel Kotkin, a senior fellow at the Pepperdine School of Public Policy, "Hispanics have traditionally been much more tied into the private sector of the economy."

13   The soaring growth of the Hispanic business community is not only lifting Hispanic incomes. It is also revitalizing neglected areas of cities where Hispanics have established a strong presence. Along Florence Avenue in South Central Los Angeles, a once predominately black community, many of the storefronts destroyed during the 1992 riots have been replaced by small, Hispanic-owned retail stores and mini-marts. In Chicago, Hispanic jewelers, restaurateurs, and clothing retailers control commerce along 26th Street, generating sales-tax revenue second only to Michigan Avenue, Chicago's wealthiest retail strip. And, as Peter Beinart reported in the New Republic in 1997, Roosevelt Avenue in Queens, New York, is lined with the small shops established by Ecuadorean, Dominican, Colombian, and Mexican immigrants who have moved in only during the past two decades.

CITY OF LATINOS

14 Just as the blanket terms "Latinos" and "Hispanics" gloss over the variety of races and ethnicities among Latin Americans, aggregate statistics don't even begin to describe the varied character of Latino-owned businesses, from the newer immigrant startups in Los Angeles to the larger and more profitable media firms of Miami.

In Los Angeles, the Hispanic population has 15 grown so large and prosperous that banks have started advertising in Spanish and real-estate firms hire bilingual sales agents to cater to the Latino market. Unsurprisingly, the city boasts the most Hispanic-owned firms of any U.S. metropolitan area, just ahead of Miami. According to UCLA's Center for the Study of Latino Health, the number of businesses in Los Angeles County owned by Latinos—mostly Mexican Americans—has nearly doubled since 1992, from 109,000 to 210,000. If those estimates are correct, nearly one-sixth of all Latino-owned businesses in the U.S. are located in L.A. County.

These businesses range from La Reina Inc., 16 Mauro Robles's $40-million Mexican-food-manufacturing enterprise, to the small tacquerias that dot the city's neighborhoods. In Venice Beach, Latinos occupy small retail stalls that sell everything from sunglasses to Muscle Beach t-shirts; in Reseda, their retail shops dominate the indoor swap meets.

Latinos such as Francisco Pinedo, a furni- 17 ture maker, have also helped to create a boom in light manufacturing, including toys, clothing, and food, that has made L.A. County the largest manufacturing center in the nation. Pinedo's father, a Mexican migrant worker, brought his family to South Central L.A. when Pinedo was 12. A short time later, his father hurt himself and his mother fell ill, leaving Francisco to support the family. He dropped out of the 11th grade and began working full-time at a local upholstery shop.

Soon he became an upholsterer at a larger 18 company, where he worked for nine years. After brief employment at a smaller firm, Pinedo decided it was time to start his own enterprise. "My goal was always to have my own company," he says.

19 At age 27, with about $11,000 in savings, Pinedo opened an upscale furniture-manufacturing firm in a small garage while his wife continued to work to pay the bills. When he was working for the larger company, Pinedo had developed a small but wealthy personal clientele by making custom furniture at night and on the weekends. They became the first clients of Cisco Brothers, his fledgling business. His strategy was to manufacture the sort of sofas, chairs, and loveseats customers would ordinarily purchase from expensive upholstery shops. With the craftsmanship and expertise gleaned from years of factory work, Pinedo figured out how to make high-end furniture at a lower cost than his competitors. "I knew how to make a sofa worth $7,000 for $300," says Pinedo. Since 1990, the firm has grown from two brothers working in a garage to a 125-employee enterprise based in a South Central factory. Last year, Cisco Brothers earned $9 million in revenues.

20 For the most part, Mexican immigrants living in California entered the United States with little formal schooling or English proficiency, and no way of supporting themselves besides grudging factory toil—at best. They want the trappings of middle-class life—a home, furniture, perhaps a car—so they take minimum-wage jobs and do "a lot of work after work," says Pinedo. "They are always building stuff on the weekends to make extra money." Often they move into blighted areas such as South Central. There they find cheap homes, often fixer-uppers, that they share with one or two other families. If all goes well, their children will receive good educations and live easier lives.

21 Their growing numbers and purchasing power—annual estimates range from $250 billion to $350 billion nationwide—have in turn created new market opportunities for Hispanic entrepreneurs. Rising car ownership creates a need for auto mechanics; newly purchased televisions create a need for Spanish-language stations. Economists call this a virtuous cycle: Consumption begets business opportunities, which beget jobs, which beget more consumption, and so on.

22 The growing Latino population has also created a new class of entrepreneurs: Latino middlemen who leverage their education and knowledge of the Latino community into lucrative consulting work for established companies who desire insight into Hispanic consumer behavior. José Legaspi recognized this market before nearly anyone else. In the late 1970s, after stints in real-estate sales, advertising, and insurance, he formed the Legaspi Company, a real-estate development and consulting firm. It combines business with a social mission: establishing firms that provide needed goods, services, and jobs to underserved Latino communities. He began to represent national concerns such as Blockbuster Video and McDonald's. "A lot of national companies did not know how to deal with Latinos" as customers or employees, says Legaspi, a Mexican immigrant himself. "Then need to know what kinds of goods and services to offer and what days are important for an Hispanic worker to take off."

23 They also need to reach the Latino market through advertising, as the Orci family well knows. Together, brothers Roberto and Hector Orci and Hector's wife Norma own and operate La Agencia de Orci & Asociados, a $46-million international advertising agency that specializes in reaching Hispanics. Although Roberto and Hector were born in Mexico, they are not typical Mexican entrepreneurs. They boast master's degrees from top-flight U.S. graduate schools and several years' experience with major advertising firms. The agency started in 1986 when Hector and Norma took

the Hispanic division of a large international firm private; they brought Roberto in two years later. Their first major client, the U.S. government, hired them for an advertising campaign conducted in 48 different languages. Its purpose was to inform illegal immigrants of new laws granting amnesty if they met certain re-24 quirements.

Their clients now include Honda Motors, Pepsi, Allstate, and other national and regional marketers. "There are 30 million Hispanics in the U.S. and they prefer entertainment in Spanish," says Roberto. "Companies hire us to reach that target, and it takes the same level of sophistication and expertise as any other type of marketing."

25 **GATEWAY TO LATIN AMERICA**

Although Latino-owned firms are less numerous in Miami than in Los Angeles, in 1992 their total revenue exceeded that of their L.A. counterparts by more than $4 billion. That's because Miami is the center of a mature business community dominated by Cuban Americans, who owned only 12 percent of Latino firms in the United States but earned more 26 than one-fifth of the revenues.

Unlike most Hispanic immigrants to this country, many of the Cubans fleeing Fidel Castro's Communist regime in the early 1960s were professionals and businessmen. When they settled in Miami, they set about establishing an infrastructure of Latino culture and commerce. More than three decades later, Miami possesses the flavor of a Latin American city and the bus-27 tle of an international trading hub.

This is an environment tailor-made for entrepreneurs like Rafael Puga. Born in Chile, he came to the United States after receiving a degree in biology from the University of Chile. Shortly after he arrived in Miami, a friend in

Chile asked if he could sell 40,000 pounds of fresh grouper. Finding little demand in Florida, he flew to California and worked the yellow pages. Puga moved the entire shipment within a few days, and a new career was born.   28

His business, Beagle Products Inc. (named for Charles Darwin's ship, the *H.M.S. Beagle*), now acts as the nation's primary importer of fresh sea bass, salmon, and swordfish from Chile and Costa Rica. When Puga first started the business in the early 1980s, most imported fish came into the country frozen. He changed that by working with Chilean fishermen to develop new fishing techniques that keep fish fresh longer.   29

Although Puga's firm prepares some value-added products, such as frozen, boneless portions, his main business is quickly packaging and shipping fresh catch to wholesalers and restaurants. After a short stay in Puga's Miami warehouse, the daily cargo is bound for dinner plates in Boston, Houston, and Los Angeles. Puga's success really lies in doing what everyone else thought could not be done. "Nobody had tried bringing fresh fish by plane before," he says. His initial risk now generates $20 million in annual revenues and a host of copycat competitors.   30

Puga, much like José Legaspi and the Orcis, is using his Hispanic heritage to advantage, acting as the middleman between predominately Anglo-run American wholesalers and Chilean fishermen and exporters. There is a lesson here: In a diverse nation and global economy, few skills will be more highly valued than the ability to operate in various cultures and parts of the globe. Firms that shun Hispanic partners will just be hurting their own bottom line. "I have never felt discriminated against as a Hispanic," says Puga. "If I have the right price and the right product, they don't care if I'm American or Chilean."

ESCAPING THE NICHE

31 For every Hispanic businessman who is leveraging his ethnicity, however, there are dozens whose ethnicity has nothing to do with their businesses. Latinos are moving into every field, from major telecommunications firms to candle manufacturers. The most successful ones, like Bartolo Lopez and Francisco Pinedo, acquire skills and business acumen working for larger firms, build their savings, and, often with the help of family and friends, finally go into business for themselves.

32 That's the path Annette and Victoria Quintana took. Annette worked as a sales representative for IBM before deciding, at age 28, that the time was ripe to move into ownership. "I wasn't married, I had no children, the car was paid for, and I could live on $800 a month," says Annette. "I didn't have a whole lot to lose."

33 In 1990, she started Excel Professional Services, a computer consulting firm. She recruited her sister, Victoria, who was then working for MCI as a product manager, to run the business side of operations while Annette drove sales. And drive them she has. Last year, sales reached $22 million, up from $17 million the year before.

34 Based in Denver, Excel hires technical experts to solve computer problems, including the Year 2000 bug, for large corporations such as Lucent Technologies and Time Warner. But at a time when federal agencies are scrambling to fix their ancient computer systems, Annette and Victoria decided to avoid government contracting altogether. "We determined that we would need three times the required administrative staff to fill out the paperwork required for government, while profitability is a half to a third of the private, commercial sector," says Annette.

35 In developing Excel's business plan, Annette and Victoria surveyed dozens of minority firms certified under the federal Small Business Administration's 8(a) program. What scared them away from government contracting was the type of work given to 8(a) companies. "The government will not do 8(a) set-asides on future-oriented business," says Annette. "They don't bring 8(a) companies in to replace old technology, they bring them in to babysit the old system. That's not what you want to build your business or train your employees on." She relates stories of 8(a) firms retaining former high-level government officials to play golf with their old colleagues—to speed up contracts. Instead, the Quintanas hire well-compensated salespeople (on the low end, they earn $100,000 to $160,000 a year) to aggressively cold call the technical and systems divisions of large corporations.

36 On a far smaller scale, there's Norma and David Estrada, owners of Estrada's Carpet & Upholstery Cleaning in Houston, Texas. Neither has a college education; they grew up poor and married early. After they were both laid off by Continental Airlines, David started working for Sears, Roebuck & Co. as a carpet cleaner and soon decided he could better serve customers on his own. With a $500 loan from his parents, the Estradas bought a carpet cleaning machine and—voilà!—they were in business.

37 Their finances remained tight for the first few years—they grossed $7,000 in 1993—so they subsisted on welfare and received a cheap mortgage through the U.S. Department of Housing and Urban Development.

38 Though still cash-strapped, they went off welfare in 1994. "It was just a pain to go down and give the records every month," says Norma. "We had a lot of friends and family members who gave us stuff for garage sales, and we sold half our furniture." They joined the Houston

Hispanic Chamber of Commerce, which has put them in contact with both commercial and government purchasing managers. That helped to secure their largest contract—cleaning carpets at a few federal office buildings at the Port of Houston Authority—as well as contracts with a local country music station and several Marriott hotels in Houston.

39 Their gross revenues have nearly doubled each year to reach $96,000 in 1997, and they have poured most of the money back into the business. "We have what we need to survive and the business is growing," says Norma. "We eat lots of beans and rice, but in Mexico I would be considered rich for what I have now."

GOVERNMENT'S ROLE

40 In some fields, particularly construction, technology, and environmental contracting, affirmative-action policies at the federal, state, and local levels have played a significant role in the growth of many Hispanic-owned businesses. But almost 60 percent of Latino firms and 50 percent of Latino revenues are concentrated in services and retail, sectors largely unaffected by government procurement or contracting. Hispanics have also achieved greater business success in a shorter period of time than blacks despite their more limited ties to government.

41 Many Hispanic firms would depend at least partly on government work, with or without minority set-asides. For instance, Delgado Erectors Inc., a Chicago-area firm with $8 million in annual revenues, erects structural steel for high-rise buildings and bridges. Owner Dominic Delgado, a veteran construction foreman, relies heavily on government contracts because that's who builds bridges and mass-transit systems. Delgado blames nepotism and the "old boy network" in the building trades for his inability to secure much private work. "We can handle almost any project in the city of Chicago," says Delgado, "but private industry doesn't look at us yet; they maintain relationships with their friends for years."

42 The real danger for Hispanic-owned firms that pursue government contracts is failing to diversify. City Wide Security Services Inc., a Latino-owned security firm established in Brooklyn, New York, in the early 1970s, relies almost exclusively on government contracts, from guarding NASA's Goddard Space Flight Center to New York City government buildings. The firm earned $23 million in 1995, but revenues plummeted to $1 million last year after another security company underbid City Wide on its largest contract, the World Trade Center in New York City.

43 That bolsters a point made by Bennett Santana, owner of Business Systems of America, a temporary-staffing service based in Chicago. "Eventually the [government] money runs out and these people need to go out into the market and compete and it's a shock," he says. "The 8(a) program shelter them from what the real world is."

THE FUTURE

44 Whether the Hispanic business community will ever match the success of other immigrant groups will ultimately depend more on their collective competence than on their ability to reap government set-asides. That means improving their general education levels and nurturing their entrepreneurial spirit.

45 Their steady improvement will be important because the nation's economic health will become increasingly tied to Hispanics' well-being. By 2010, they will surpass blacks to become the nation's second-largest racial/ethnic group. In Miami, where Hispanics are already the majority, and California, where Hispanics are

projected to be the largest ethnic group by the year 2025, the health of the regional economy already depends on a vibrant Latino community.

46   Unfortunately, political leaders still insist on treating Hispanics as yet another beleaguered minority in need of preferential treatment. In his famous 1995 "mend it, don't end it" speech to the National Council of La Raza, an Hispanic advocacy group, President Clinton mentioned "affirmative action" 22 times without once acknowledging the tremendous gains Hispanics have made in the business world. This attitude runs the risk of cultivating an entitlement culture rather than one of can-do entrepreneurialism within the Hispanic community. Fortunately, Hispanics generally seem far more intent on self-reliance than on playing racial politics.

Policy Review 90 (July/August 1998): 30–35.

Evaluation of the Article

Difficulty Rating ☐ 1 ☐ 2 ☐ 3 ☐ 4 ☐ 5
(1 = easy; 5 = difficult)

What reading difficulties did you encounter? _____

_____

How did you handle these difficulties? _____

_____

Postreading Comprehension Development

Sentence Rewrite

To check your understanding of some of the key concepts of this essay, rewrite each of the following sentences in your own words, keeping the original idea. (See Chapter 1.)

1. They haven't been running firms long enough to expand through reinvesting profits and developing a strong customer base. (9)

_____

_____

2. With the craftsmanship and expertise gleaned from years of factory work, Pinedo figured out how to make high-end furniture at a lower cost than his competitors. (19)

_____

_____

3. His initial risk now generates $20 million in annual revenues and a host of copycat competitors. (29)

_____

_____

Author's Main Idea

(See Chapter 3.)

1. Is the title for this article appropriate for its content? In the space provided, provide reasons for your answer.

_____

_____

2. How does the opening paragraph serve the author's purpose for writing this article?

_____

_____

3. The paragraph in which the author's main idea is most clearly stated is:
   a. 3
   b. 4
   c. 5
   d. 6

Inferences, Metaphors, and Vocabulary in Context

(See Chapters 2, 6, and 7.)

1. How do you think the author wants the reader to feel after reading the last paragraph of this selection? What are the reasons for your beliefs?

    _____

    _____

    _____

2. The point of view most clearly expressed by the author in paragraph 11 is:

    a. Asians, blacks, and Hispanics have been equally successful in the growth of their businesses.

    b. The amount of revenue minority businesses generate is approximately equal to the percentage of those minorities in the United States.

    c. If there were more Hispanics in the United States, they would be as successful as Asians in their small business ownership.

    d. The size of a minority population cannot predict how much revenue that minority's businesses will generate.

3. Which paragraph provides an example of the "domino effect"?

    a. 12

    b. 13

    c. 14

    d. 15

4. Does the author prove his point that "aggregate statistics don't even begin to describe the varied character of Latino-owned businesses" (14)? Explain your answer on the following lines.

    _____

    _____

    _____

5. From paragraph 26 the reader can conclude:

   a. Cubans arriving in the United States in the 1960s wanted to become as much like Americans as possible.

   b. Cubans arriving in the United States figured the American government would take care of them.

   c. There was considerable resentment by Floridians when large numbers of Cubans arrived in Miami in the 1960s.

   d. Cubans arriving in Miami in the 1960s were resourceful and confident they could be successful.

6. Indicate whether the author would agree (A) or disagree (D) with each of the following statements. Be prepared to justify your answers.

   _____ a. Many Hispanics arrive in the United States with funds to start up a business.

   _____ b. Large numbers of Hispanics are opening their own businesses.

   _____ c. Blacks rely on government loans more than Hispanics.

   _____ d. The number of Hispanic small businesses tend to increase in communities that experience increases in Hispanic residents.

   _____ e. Small business ownership trends vary within the different races and ethnicities among Latin Americans.

   _____ f. Most Latinos eventually get discouraged and give up their small businesses.

   _____ g. There are not enough Hispanics in the United States for them to be considered a significant consumer group.

   _____ h. Few Mexican immigrants are highly educated.

   _____ i. Most Hispanic businesses are aimed at Hispanic consumers.

7. Using only the context and your knowledge of word structure, define each of the following words. Do not use a dictionary.

   a. apprehension (1) _____

   b. opulent (5) _____

   c. penchant (6) _____

   d. vibrant (6) _____

   e. prolific (10) _____

   f. surpassed (11) _____

   g. predominately (13) _____

h. blighted (20) _____

i. lucrative (22) _____

j. acumen (31) _____

k. nepotism (41) _____

8. What is this author's opinion of small government loans? Write your response on the following lines. Be prepared to justify your answer.

   _____

   _____

   _____

9. Which of the following sayings would be most true of the experience of the Hispanic small business entrepreneur? Be prepared to explain your answer.

   a. He who laughs last laughs best.

   b. Good triumphs over evil.

   c. The early bird catches the worm.

   d. Easy come, easy go.

Recalling Details

(See Chapters 4 and 5.)

1. Match each individual listed with the type of business he or she began.

   _____ Bartolo Lopez   a. temporary staffing service

   _____ Francisco Pinedo   b. computer consulting firm

   _____ Bennett Santana   c. fish importer

   _____ Norma and David Estrada   d. carpet cleaning

   _____ Roberto, Hector, and   e. landscape design
         Norma Orci
                                    f. furniture manufacturer
   _____ Rafael Puga
                                    g. real estate development
   _____ Annette and Victoria
         Quintana   h. advertising for an Hispanic
                                       market
   _____ José Legaspi

2. Indicate whether each of the following items is a major (MAJ) or minor (MIN) detail of this article. Be prepared to justify your answers.

_____ a. From 1987 to 1992, the number of U.S. businesses owned by Hispanics rose by 76 percent.

_____ b. At first Lopez labored in the fields of northern California.

_____ c. Blacks tend to own businesses in the low-cost states of the South, Hispanics in relatively high-cost states.

_____ d. The Small Business Administration's Section 8(a) program is a good indicator of the degree to which different minority groups depend upon government help.

_____ e. Pinedo's father, a Mexican migrant worker, brought his family to South Central L.A. when Pinedo was twelve.

_____ f. Hispanic business ownership has already surpassed that of blacks, a racial group of similar size.

_____ g. In Los Angeles, the Hispanic population has grown so large and prosperous that banks have started advertising in Spanish.

_____ h. For the most part, Mexican immigrants living in California entered the United States with little formal schooling or English proficiency.

_____ i. Although Latino-owned firms are less numerous in Miami than in Los Angeles, in 1992 their total revenue exceeded that of their L.A. counterparts by more than $4 billion.

_____ j. Almost 60 percent of Latino firms and 50 percent of Latino revenues are in sectors largely unaffected by government procurement or contracting.

Critical Thinking: Reaction and Discussion

1. With a small group, discuss the following statement: *This article provides examples of advertising done for different ethnic groups. Have you seen or heard examples of this advertising? Is this kind of advertising discriminatory? Should it be permitted?*

2. Survey your neighborhood for examples of small businesses. How are they similar to, or different from, those described in this article? Write your findings in an essay of at least 250 words.

3. Review the descriptions of the entrepreneurs discussed in this article. Which individual is most like yourself? Would you ever like to own your own business? Discuss your response with a partner.

4. Return to the To Think About Before You Read section and consider the entrepreneurs you have read about in this article. Which of these traits do they have? What other traits seem to be important to be successful in your own business? Share your answers with a partner.

USING TECHNOLOGY FOR FURTHER UNDERSTANDING

1. Search the Internet for websites that provide assistance to small business entrepreneurs. What kind of no-cost help is available to them? If you were a small business entrepreneur, which sites would you find useful? How do you think each of these sites would help you?

2. In March 2001, the U.S. Census Bureau issued data from its Survey of Minority-Owned Business Enterprises, from the 1997 Economic Census. Use the Internet to locate the results of this Survey. Review the data to locate information not cited in this article. Print one chart or graphic that contains new information to share with your class.

CHAPTER FIFTEEN

History
A Record or Explanation of Past Events

Anybody can make history.
Only a great man can write it.

—Oscar Wilde
Aphorisms

Derivation: *histor* —knowing
istor learned

Key Concepts for the Study of History

Before you read this list of concepts, think about some issues and topics that you might study if you took courses in history. In the space provided, list your ideas.

_____

_____

AGRARIAN.   Relating to or characteristic of the farmer or his way of life.

EPOCH.   An event or time marked by an event that begins a new period or development; a memorable event or date.

ETHNOCENTRISM.   The attitude that one's own group is superior.

HERITAGE.   Something possessed as a result of one's natural situation or birth.

IMMIGRANT.   A person who comes to a country to take up permanent residence.

INDUSTRIAL REVOLUTION.   A rapid major change in an economy marked by the general introduction of power-driven machinery or by an important change in the prevailing types and methods of use of such machines.

MEDIEVAL.   Of, relating to, or characteristic of the Middle Ages in Western Europe (about C.E. 500 to 1500).

MONARCHY.   Individual rule or absolute sovereignty by a single person; a nation or state having a monarchical government.

NATIONALISM.   Loyalty and devotion to a nation.

REVOLUTION.   A sudden, radical, or complete change; a fundamental change in political organization; especially the overthrow or renunciation of one government or ruler and the substitution of another by the governed.

Now that you have read this list, what are some additional issues and topics that you might study if you took courses in history? In the space provided, list your ideas.

_____

_____

_____

- ## SELECTION 16

Why History?

■ F. OTNES, COMPILER

Preview

The study of history means different things to different people. In the following collection of short answers to the question, "Why history?" you will learn from several scholars what history means to them.

To Think About Before You Read

Imagine that your academic adviser at college has told you that you are required to take one of the courses in American history offered at your school. Answer the questions that follow based on your present thinking.

1. How do you feel about this requirement? Explain your reasons for these feelings.

   _____

   _____

2. Select one period of American history that you think could be developed into a one-semester course that you would enjoy studying. What period would it be?

   _____

3. What are some aspects of this period that you might study in this course?

   _____

   _____

4. Why does this period interest you?

   _____

   _____

5. How do you feel the knowledge you might gain in this history course will help you in your future?

_____

_____

Terms to Know Before You Read

contemplation (2) study

elusive (3) hard to comprehend or define

dissent (6) difference of opinion

exhilaration (11) the feeling of excitement or stimulation

milieu (14) environment; background

contending (20) competing; arguing

fetid (24) having a heavy, unpleasant smell

egalitarian (34) that which is marked by a belief or promoting human equality

The dictionary defines history as "a chronological record of events, as of the life or development of a people or institution," and as "the branch of knowledge that records and analyzes past events."

2 When viewed in its broadest sense, the contemplation of history has universal implications and meaning; virtually everything of value in what we know and possess has been drawn from prior knowledge, experiences, and happenings. Sages since antiquity have advised us that understanding the past is the key to making wise choices in issues affecting the future. "History," wrote Marcus Cicero in the first century B.C., "illumines reality, vitalizes memory, [and] provides guidance in daily life . . . ."

3 Unfortunately, understanding what history has to teach us is not always simple. When we attempt to find meaning in the past we discover that grasping its truths is as elusive as learning "ultimate truth" itself. We face the problem of deciding what in past experiences is important and what is not. The historical record may be incomplete, lacking vital information; or it may so overflow with data that we are overwhelmed. And our view of prior events is always colored by our cultural biases, just as the accounts left by earlier generations were colored by theirs.

4 Yet for all of history's flaws, the quest to understand the lessons of the past remains vital to us as individuals, as a nation, and as a civilization. As this magazine completes twenty-five years of publication, we pause to reflect—through concise essays by ten individuals associated with diverse aspects of history—on some of the meanings, values, and applications of this fascinating, frustrating, instructive, inexact, and most universal of disciplines.

THE BEST GUIDE WE HAVE
WILLIAM H. MCNEILL

5 History tells us who we are and how to behave. Much of it is informal, taking the form of stories and personal memories passed on from parents to children and from veterans to newcomers in all sorts of small, local groups. This is the way we shape private life, learning who we are and what we should do in new situations. Past successes and mistakes guide behavior and make choices comparatively easy. Without this sort of private, informal history, no one would know what to expect or what to do. We would not be human.

6 The sort of history taught in schools and written about in books does the same thing for our public identities. We learn what it is to be an American by reading about what the United States government and what other Americans have done in the past; and we learn what it is to share in other public identities by reading about the history of localities, occupational groups, genders, peoples, churches, civilizations, and humanity as a whole. And transmitted memory of former successes and mistakes is just as important for guiding behavior on the public level as on the private. Leaders frame the issues and choose policies in light of what they know and believe about past triumphs and defeats of the group in question, and followers either concur or dissent (in which latter case the group loses power and vigor, and, in extreme cases, may even dissolve).

7 Quite simply, human life depends on past experience to give it coherence and meaning. The past is all we have. But everything depends on what aspects of the past we choose to remember, because a total recall is impossible. This is where historians (and, for informal, private history, tale-tellers) come into their own.

They organize and simplify the record of the past so that it can be remembered. This means leaving things out, and when new situations and new identities arise, revisionist historians correct the portrait of the past by leaving out some of the things their predecessors thought important and by putting in new data appropriate to new demands.

8 History is therefore a living discipline, reflecting every pulsation of public life, as well as the nuances of everyone's private experience. It provides the best guide we have to effective action. No matter how carefully studied, history is not a very good guide. Witness the innumerable surprises and disappointments of human life. But it is all we have, and as such is endlessly fascinating, offering a persistently ambiguous clue to probable and possible futures.

ENLARGING THE EXPERIENCE OF BEING ALIVE
DAVID MCCULLOUGH

9 Somewhere pretty early, at about age eight I would guess, I discovered that in books I could go back in time. The earliest I remember reading were about Daniel Boone and Abraham Lincoln and a mouse that lived in Ben Franklin's hat. The first book I ever bought on my own was a Modern Library edition of Richard Henry Dana's *Two Years Before the Mast,* which I have still on a shelf where I work. "The 14th of August [1834] was the day fixed upon for the sailing of the brig *Pilgrim,*" it begins. I was fifteen—I know from the flyleaf, where, with my name, I recorded proudly the date of purchase, May 8, 1949. This, I can't help thinking, was perhaps a date "fixed upon" for me for a sailing of a kind. . . .

10 History is about life. That's its pull. The

supposedly dead past is nothing of the kind. Measured beside the present, it is the greater part of human experience by far. Who were those people who braved the storms, who left their marks on cave walls and in revolutionary mathematical theory? What was it like to travel the America Audubon saw? Or to be Gershwin in Paris? Can we ever know enough about the ways the world changed in 1917? Or 1945?

11   I would no more wish to shut myself off from the past than to stay rooted always in the same place. One reads history, just as one travels, primarily to enlarge and intensify the experience of being alive. That really is it, I think; that and the exhilaration of much of the finest writing we have.

A LARGER REALITY

PAUL GAGNON

12   The value of history—that is, of our knowing and understanding as much of it as we can—may be summed up in three phrases: it matures us; it heartens us; it sets us free. How do we grow in maturity, to understand the human condition and ourselves? First, of course, by direct personal experience—in the family, in school, on the street, at work and play, from our own joy and pain. But second, we grow by extending our experiences. Through history, biography, memoirs, imaginative literature, we can know, to some extent, what it meant to be a slave, or fight the battle of Verdun, or work the coal mines, or endure the Holocaust. We can enter a larger reality, place ourselves in time, compare ourselves with others. Indeed we may come to understand what "otherness"—a prime fruit of maturity—means.

13   The wider experience of history is not always cheerful. But neither will it justify despair.

We come to understand what no other study makes so clear: the reality of both tragedy and comedy, of paradox, and of the beauty of work well done, of daily acts of human nature. We observe how hard it has always been to build and keep civilization, or to better human life. But we also observe that these have nonetheless been done by brave people in our past. While history denies us the easy comforts of optimism and pessimism, it gives heartening proof that effort is not always in vain.

Finally, the study of history, more than any 14 other discipline, frees us to choose for ourselves the paths we wish to take as citizens and as private persons. The dignity of free choice can arise only out of knowing the alternatives possible in public and private life, that immense range of approaches people have taken to order their political, economic, and social lives, to pursue personal integrity, creativity, and private happiness. Without historical memory, we are amnesiacs, prisoners of our immediate *milieu*, ignorant of the possibilities for liberation that the past reveals. The first aim of education in a democracy is to confer upon as many people as possible the power to freely choose for themselves. The study of history is the precondition to that power, and to our free search for the larger meaning of human history and life.

WHY STUDY HISTORY?

DIANE RAVITCH

Why study history? The simplest and truest an- 15 swer is that the study of history makes people more intelligent. History is an investigation of causes; it is a way of finding out how the world came to be as it is. Without history, we are without memory and without explanations. Those who do not know history—their own history and that of their society and other societies—cannot comment intelligently on the causes of events—cannot understand their own lives nor the changes in their society and in the world. The person who knows no history is like an amnesiac, lacking a sense of what happened before and therefore unable to tell the difference between cause and effect.

16   Unfortunately, many people get the impression from studying history in school with poorly trained teachers and with boring textbooks that history is nothing more than a recitation of dull facts about battles and kings. Sadly, some states certify people to teach social studies who have never studied a single history course in college; and some districts routinely assign coaches with no history education to teach history. And such teachers tend to use the history textbook as a script that students are supposed to memorize and regurgitate.

17   History ought to be the most exciting course taught in school or college. It ought to be the course that introduces students to great men and women who risked their lives for principle or who committed foul deeds for the sake of power. It ought to be the course that arouses heated discussion about historical controversies, with students contesting different versions of the past or disputing the meaning of events. Just as students need to think about the present, they need to think about the past and to realize that it was just as complicated as the present and not a cut-and-dried affair as the textbooks so often imply.

18   Pick up the newspaper on any day, and the stories presuppose a basic knowledge of history. They refer to events in Eastern Europe or the Soviet Union or Africa or China, assuming that the reader has some knowledge of World War I, World War II, the Russian Revolution, Stalinism, colonialism, imperialism, the postwar decolonization movement, the Universal Declaration of Human Rights, the Solidarity movement, the Chinese revolution, Maoism, the Chinese Cultural Revolution, and so on.

19   The person who has studied history can read the newspapers and magazines with a critical eye; can understand new developments because he or she has a historical context in which to place them; can mentally reject erroneous statements; and is resistant to indoctrination and propaganda.

20   When we teach history, we teach not only what happened in the past, but how to reason, how to weigh evidence, how to analyze continuity and change, and how to assess contending ideas. We need the substance of history, and we need the historical thinking that informs rational judgment. We must teach history in elementary schools, junior high schools, senior high schools, colleges, and universities. But that is not enough. We must teach it on the television and in the movies, in museums and libraries, and around the dinner table.

21   Why study history? To gain the habits of mind and the intellectual tools that are required to be a free person.

A SHIELD AGAINST FATE AND ITS CONSEQUENCES
T. H. WATKINS

22   We live in accelerated times, when the witchery of bytes and bits and megabits and all the other paraphernalia of electronic communication enables us to make mistakes faster than we can correct them. Fashions in clothing, music, literature, movies, diets, and psychotherapy come and go at a dizzying pace. Politicians build careers on the assumption that the attention span of the American people has been reduced to the few minutes it takes to read an airline magazine

article. Nations are convulsed overnight; ideologies die in hours and others rise to take their places; walls come down and walls are built in the space of time it takes to write about them.

23   In such a world, one is asked, of what use is history? How can we indulge the luxury of the time and thought it takes to comprehend the complicated weave of any past that is more distant than yesterday afternoon when it often seems that all the psychic and intellectual energy we possess must be reserved just to maintain our present equilibrium—especially when we continue to live in so dangerous a world that the future may never arrive at all?

24   To such questions, I would answer this: From the unrecorded eons of its beginnings to the overrecorded moments of its present living, humankind has been sustained not merely by its intelligence but by its capacity to hope. It was hope that drove the first neolithic peoples to follow the climate south from the bitter descending edge of the Ice Age; hope that brought the first settlers to the brave new world of the North American continent; hope that enabled thousands to survive even the Holocaust—surely the most fetid demonstration we have yet been given that savagery is as singular a human characteristic as charity.

25   Unlike intelligence, the quality of hope is not genetically programmed into the species; it is a learned characteristic. Like any acquired trait, it can be lost, and without hope we are left with the arid uselessness of nihilism—the darkest corner of an existential state that sees neither value nor possibility in the future.

26   I would insist that the study and remembrance of history remain one of the best ways available to us for nurturing the protocols of hope. How can we not discover hope when we remember the impossible triumph of the "rabble in arms" that challenged Britain in 1776, or

the unlikely melding of minds, interests, convictions, prejudices, and angers that produced the Constitution of the United States in 1789 and the Bill of Rights that followed it? Is it anything less than hope that we find in the story of the men and women who endured the trials of the westering that filled a continent, or in the unspeakable bravery of black men and women who not only endured bigotry but rose up to give new voice, new substance, and new glory to the idea of freedom?

In these days when the shadow of ruin falls 27 on us, it is good to remember that ours is not the first generation to face economic strife and potential war or the consistent testing of the strengths that were designed to make ours the first nation in history to be truly "of the people." In that history there is hope, and in that hope there is a shield against fate and its consequences that can serve us now just as faithfully as it has in the past.

TREE-SLICES OF HISTORY

ALEX HALEY

The graphic meaning and value of history be- 28 gan for me on the morning of my fourth birthday. My parents and grandparents gave me a thick slice from a redwood tree, containing about fifteen small square white markers at different places. My teacher-father, using a pointer, identified the tree's annual growth rings and then explained that each little white marker represented an event that had happened when the tree was that age.

That morning, I first heard such words as 29 "Emancipation Proclamation" and "slavery" and "Civil War," along with the birth year of my maternal great-great-grandfather "Chicken George," and the founding year of Lane College in Jackson, Tennessee, where my parents later met as students—and so on.

30 My "tree-slice" made history for me something that I could feel and touch, and gradually I became immersed in reading (which was my elders' objective), ever seeking new historical events that might qualify for an added cardboard marker on my tree-slice of history. By the time I reached the age of ten, my priority hobby was reading historical books; I truly believe these roots ultimately influenced me toward becoming a self-taught writer whose favorite theme is historical dramas, notably featuring my own ancestry.

31 The intrigue of history that was unfolded for me as a child has become a man's umbilical awareness that the things we do today are involuntarily the history of tomorrow. To paraphrase George Santayana, "Unless we learn from history, we are destined to repeat it." This is no longer merely an academic exercise, but may contain our world's fate and our destiny.

A COHERENT EVOLUTION IN HUMAN THOUGHT

FRANCIS FUKUYAMA

32 As a Hegelian, I believe that the study of history must be subordinated to the study of the architectonic science, philosophy. The "bare facts" of history do not teach us anything meaningful, because we cannot distinguish the important from the trivial. History itself does not supply us with that standard, though the material of history is absolutely crucial for arriving at a philosophical understanding of man and what he has been.

33 Looked at philosophically, history is not simply a record of events, but a coherent evolution in human thought. Most important is thought about how we ought to live, i.e., the best organization of human societies and the regimes that govern them. History is the story of the communities man has chosen to live in, and how they do or do not satisfy the ends of human life. Looked at in this respect, history can be understood as a struggle for the recognition of human dignity and freedom.

34 The struggle for recognition gives coherence and meaning to the different periods of history. It becomes clear that there is a directionality to history: for monarchies, aristocracies, and theocracies have given way to more modern and egalitarian forms of government not arbitrarily, but because the latter solved the problem of recognition more adequately. And if we understand history in the specific sense of a search for the appropriate form of society that is most in accord with human nature, then we must also remain open to the possibility that history itself will one day come to an end.

HISTORY PERMEATES OUR LIVES

JOHN EISENHOWER

35 History—the relating of events past to the present—permeates our everyday lives, more so than most of us realize. Every holiday is a memorial to an event or a person; every baseball statistic a little piece of history. Today, concerned that the Persian Gulf might become another Vietnam, we ask, "Will history repeat itself?"

36 Yet most people, when asked if they enjoy the study of history, will respond negatively, probably because of the uninspired and sometimes biased way in which it was presented to them in school. It was not all the fault of the pedagogues; with so much material to cover, they faced a difficult task in trying to make the

story of the past come to life, to seem applicable to the present.

37 To some professions history is a major tool. The soldier, the statesman, and the economist (to name only three) depend on the study of the past as a guide to their approaches to current situations. To these people, the adage "The Past is Prologue," emblazoned on the front of the National Archives in Washington, D.C., is very real.

38 Those of us who can be called history "buffs," however, simply enjoy the delight of reliving the experiences of those who have gone before us. Their stories make good reading. And history can be part of our everyday lives. For example, an appreciation of the past can make an automobile trip rewarding. A drive from my home on Maryland's eastern shore to some place in the Carolinas can take me by such places as Mount Vernon, Monticello, Fredericksburg, Appomattox, Williamsburg, and Jamestown. Drudgery can become adventure.

The amateur historian knows there are pit- 39 falls. It can be a lonely hobby. Our friends often consider us a bit weird, and we must not flaunt our secret discoveries in their presence. But it is also broadening. History shows us how many ways one subject or event can be viewed, depending on one's perspective. We learn not to be too contemptuous of the mistakes made by some historical figure who, in his or her own way, was trying to accomplish something.

So damn the constraints! Let's read history 40 for the pleasure it brings us and for the way it enriches our lives.

American History Illustrated (March–April 1991): 24–31.

Evaluation of the Article

Difficulty Rating □ 1 □ 2 □ 3 □ 4 □ 5
(1 = easy; 5 = difficult)

What reading difficulties did you encounter? _____

_____

How did you handle these difficulties? _____

_____

Comprehension of the Discipline

1. F. Otnes, the compiler of the material for "Why History?", suggests that there are many problems in studying history.

    _____

    _____

    _____

a. Which of the problems pointed out by him seem particularly important to you? Give your reasons for this choice.

_____

_____

_____

b. How can you use your knowledge of these problems to help you as you read history?

2. According to William H. McNeill, "Human life depends on past experience to give it coherence and meaning." Is there any history that you have read or heard (perhaps family history) that helps you understand McNeill's remark? What was the information? How did it add coherence and meaning to your life?

_____

_____

_____

3. Why does David McCullough say that "The supposedly dead past is nothing of the kind"?

_____

_____

4. There are countries in which newspaper publication is controlled totally by the government and where there are strict regulations on what historical facts may be printed for the public to read. What do you think Paul Gagnon's reactions to such "control of history" would be? Explain.

_____

_____

_____

5. Do you agree with Diane Ravitch's criticism of how history is taught in schools? What might teachers do to make it more interesting? Have you ever been in an exciting history class? What made it that way?

_____

_____

_____

_____

_____

_____

_____

6. According to T. H. Watkins, history can provide us with *hope*. What kind of *hope* does he seem to be talking about?

_____

_____

7. Alex Haley speaks of humanity's "umbilical awareness." Explain why you believe he has used this metaphor to talk about history.

_____

_____

8. The word *coherence* is used by several authors in this collection, including Francis Fukuyama. Why do you think this word appears so often?

_____

_____

9. What constraints might John Eisenhower be damning in his comments on history?

_____

_____

10. Of the several reasons offered in this article for studying history, which ones may have you convinced that it is a worthwhile subject?

_____

_____

11. Based on this article, why do you think it might be important for historians to point out their personal biases to their readers?

_____

_____

12. Are there any reasons you can think of for studying history that have not been mentioned here?

_____

_____

13. Do you think that Otnes did a good job assembling material for this essay? Explain your answer.

_____

_____

_____

14. Look at the following figure and then explain:
    a. What information on this figure do you find interesting?

_____

_____

Nationally, the percentage of women in state legislatures has been rising steadily ...

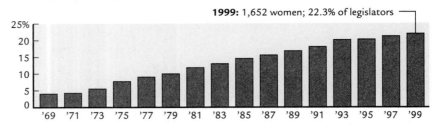

1999: 1,652 women; 22.3% of legislators

... but among states, there are wide differences. The current percentage of women in each legislature:

☐ 7.9% to 14.9%   ☐ 15.0% to 24.9%   ☐ 25.0% to 34.9%   ☐ 35.0% to 40.8%

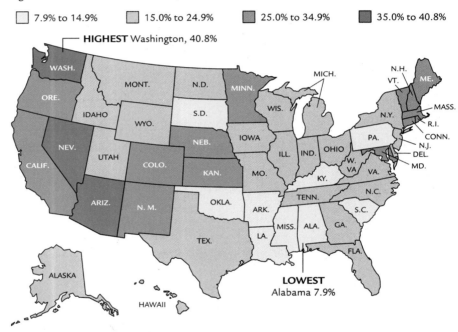

HIGHEST Washington, 40.8%

LOWEST Alabama 7.9%

MORE WOMEN IN THE STATEHOUSE

Source: Reprinted by permission of *The New York Times,* February 4, 1999, p. A18. Copyright © 1990 by the New York Times Co.

b. Does this figure contribute to historical understanding in any of the ways suggested by the authors of this article? Explain your answer.

_____

_____

_____

_____

_____

_____

Critical Thinking: Reaction and Discussion

1. Reconsider your responses to the To Think About Before You Read section. Make any revisions to your original answers that are the result of new thoughts you have had since reading this article.

2. With a group, discuss events that have occurred in the last two years that you believe will have great historical significance for future generations. Then your group should choose the most significant one and prepare to present to the class the reasons for this selection.

USING TECHNOLOGY FOR FURTHER UNDERSTANDING

1. How might some of the technologies now available benefit present-day historians? Discuss this question with a group and prepare a brief response to share with your class.

2. Identify a time period or a historical event that interests you. Search it on the Internet. What can you find out about:

   a. Scholarly groups that are also interested in this time period or event?

   b. Resources for teachers who teach about this time period or event?

Guidelines for Reading History

Some things to bear in mind when you read history are as follows:

YOUR IMAGINATION CAN HELP YOU COMPREHEND WHAT YOU READ. Think about the period (culture, geographic area, and so on) being discussed. Try to imagine this period or culture before you start your reading assignment. Try to make associations with it; for example, think of the music or art of the period; political developments you know about; how people dressed; the industrial or economic conditions; or scientific discoveries of the time.

CAUSE AND EFFECT RELATIONSHIPS ARE OFTEN DISCUSSED. Historians frequently tell their readers that something happened (the effect or the result) because of something else or for some reason (the cause). Authors may discuss immediate causes, which are usually apparent, as well as underlying or less obvious causes. Keep this in mind while you read. You may be able to add to what the author has said and to think of other causes or effects.

MATERIAL IS FREQUENTLY PRESENTED IN CHRONOLOGICAL ORDER. Dates, including centuries, years, or specific "landmark" dates, are important to note when you read history. They help you understand the sequence in which events occurred. You can also assess how long it took for historical changes to occur by knowing significant turning points in history. You can recall these important dates more easily if you create a time line for yourself like the one shown here, which illustrates a chronology of famous musicians.

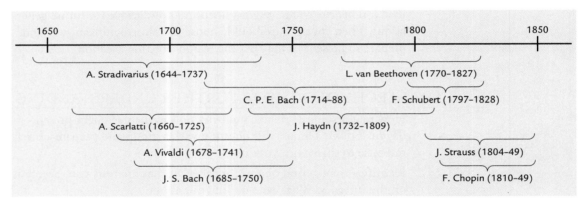

HISTORIANS GET THEIR INFORMATION FROM ONE OF TWO TYPES OF SOURCES. (1) Primary, or original, sources are those that provide firsthand knowledge of the events, such as eyewitness accounts. Such accounts may include reports found in letters, diaries, and interviews. Primary sources also include courthouse records, original government documents, and artifacts at museums or in other collections. (2) Secondary sources include all other materials to which the author refers.

HISTORICAL STUDY IS SCIENTIFIC IN METHODOLOGY. Historians try to use original or primary sources as much as possible. This makes their writing more authentic. If two authors disagree about events, you may want to check the authenticity of their sources.

FOOTNOTES ARE OF PARTICULAR IMPORTANCE IN HISTORICAL WRITING. From these you will learn how the author knows what he or she knows. Footnotes provide verification for the accuracy of the information; they may provide support for the author's interpretation of events.

HISTORICAL WRITING IS USUALLY BOTH DESCRIPTIVE AND INTERPRETIVE. Descriptive writing tells when, where, and who took part. Interpretive writing explains why and how things happened and how these events were interpreted by others.

HISTORIANS WILL NATURALLY TEND TO WRITE ABOUT EVENTS IN TERMS OF THEIR OWN BIAS. However, a good historian will mention this bias, either in the introduction to the text or within the essay itself. When you detect bias, try to consider exactly how it is affecting the writer's interpretation of events. Historians, aware of their own biases, will also try to withhold judgment about an event until all the facts are in. You, as the reader, should try to do the same.

ONCE ALL THE FACTS ARE IN, INSOFAR AS POSSIBLE, THE HISTORIAN MAY FORM A HYPOTHESIS, OR A TENTATIVE CONCLUSION, ABOUT WHAT HAPPENED. This hypothesis or tentative conclusion serves to connect the facts. The facts are then discussed in terms of how they prove or dispute this hypothesis. As a reader, you have the job of finding this hypothesis and determining the authenticity and believability of the facts based on other things you have read or what you know. Then you can determine whether or not the author has proved the hypothesis.

Keep these guidelines in mind as you read the remaining articles from the field of history.

● # SELECTION 17

Kidnapped, Enslaved, and Sold Away (c. 1756)

■ OLAUDAH EQUIANO

Preview

Contemporary U.S. history textbooks include considerable detail about the lives of slaves. Much of this information is drawn from firsthand accounts, such as diaries or journals, written by former slaveholders. But we have fewer such accounts from former slaves, especially accounts of their initial capture and travels to the land where they were to serve as slaves. In the following article, we have such a story, written by a man who lived in Benin until 1755, when he was captured to be sold as a slave at the age of eleven. He was traded several times, and eventually he became a slave in the West Indies to Captain Pascal. The author's African name is given here although his work appears as authored by Gustavus Vassa, the name given to him by Pascal and used by him for the rest of his life.

To Think About Before You Read

Think about the most significant six-month period in your life. Why was it important to you? How did it affect you? How do you think differently about your life or the people in it? In a 250-word essay, tell about that six-month period and why you have selected it as the most important period in your life.

Terms to Know Before You Read

allayed (2) relieved

indulge (5) to give free rein to

windlass (5) any of the various machines for hoisting or hauling; a steam or electric winch with horizontal or vertical shaft and two drums used to raise a ship's anchor

brute (5) beast

pestilential (6) deadly

improvident avarice (6) unwise greediness

fetters (6) chains for the feet

That part of Africa, known by the name of Guinea, to which the trade for slaves is carried on, extends along the coast above 3,400 miles from Senegal to Angola, and includes a variety of kingdoms. Of these the most considerable is the kingdom of Benin, both as to extent and wealth. . . . This kingdom is divided into many provinces or districts: in one of the most remote and fertile of which I was born, in the year 1745, situated in a charming fruitful vale, named Essaka. The distance of this province from the capital of Benin and the sea coast must be very considerable; for I had never heard of white men or Europeans, nor the sea. . . .

2   I have already acquainted the reader with the time and place of my birth. My father, besides many slaves, had a numerous family, of which seven lived to grow up, including myself and a sister, who was the only daughter. As I was the youngest of the sons, I became the favourite with my mother, and was always with her; and she used to take particular pains to form my mind. I was trained up from my earliest years in the arts of agriculture and war: my daily exercise was shooting and throwing javelins; and my mother adorned me with emblems, after the manner of our greatest warriors. In this way I grew up till I was turned the age of eleven, when an end was put to my happiness in the following manner: Generally, when the grown people of the neighbourhood were gone far in the fields to labour, the children assembled together in some of the neighbours [*sic*] premises to play; and commonly some of us used to get up a tree to look out for any assailant, or kidnapper, that might come upon us; for they sometimes took those opportunities of our parents' absence, to attack and carry off as many as they could seize. . . . One day, when all our people were gone out to their works as usual, and only I and my dear sister were left to mind the house, two men and a woman got over our walls, and in a moment seized us both and, without giving us time to cry out, or to make resistance, they stopped our mouths, and ran off with us into the nearest wood. Here they tied our hands, and continued to carry us as far as they could, till night came on, when we reached a small house, where the robbers halted for refreshment, and spent the night. We were then unbound, but were not able to take any food; and, being quite overpowered by fatigue and grief, our only relief was some sleep, which allayed our misfortune for a short time. The next morning we left the house, and continued travelling all the day. For a long time we had kept to the woods, but at last we came to a road which I believed I knew. I now had some hopes of being delivered; for we had advanced but a little way before I discovered some people at a distance, on which I began to cry out for their assistance; but my cries had no other effect than to make them tie me faster and stop my mouth, and then put me in a large sack. They also stopped my sister's mouth, and tied her hands, and in this manner we proceeded till we were out of sight of these people. When we went to rest the following night they offered us some victuals; but we refused them; and the only comfort we had was in being in one another's arms all that night, and bathing each other with our tears. But alas! we were soon deprived of even the smallest comfort of weeping together. The next day proved a day of greater sorrow than I had yet experienced; for my sister and I were separated, while we lay clasped in each other's arms: it was in vain that we besought them not to part us: she was torn from me, and immediately carried away, while I was in such a state of distraction not to be described. I cried and

OLAUDAH EQUIANO. FROM THE 1793 EDITION OF HIS AUTOBIOGRAPHY.

(British Library, London/Bridgeman Art Library, New York)

grieved continually; and for several days did not eat any thing but what they forced into my mouth. At length, after many days travelling, during which I had often changed masters, I got into the hands of a chieftain, in a very pleasant country. . . .

3   I was again sold and carried through a number of places, till, after travelling a considerable time, I came to a town called Timneh, in the most beautiful country I had yet seen in Africa. It was extremely rich, and there were many rivulets which flowed through it, and supplied a large pond in the centre of the town, where the people washed. Here I first saw and tasted cocoa nuts, which I thought superior to any nuts I had ever tasted before; and the trees, which were loaded, were also interspersed among the houses, which had commodious shades adjoining and were in the same manner as ours, the insides being neatly plastered and whitewashed. Here I also saw and tasted for the first time sugar-cane. Their money consisted of little white shells the size of a finger nail. I was sold here for one hundred seventy-two of them by a merchant who lived and brought me there. . . .

4   At last I came to the banks of a large river, which was covered with canoes in which the people appeared to live with their household utensils and provisions of all kinds. I was beyond measure astonished at this, as I had never before seen any water larger than a pond or a rivulet; and my surprise was mingled with no small fear when I was put into one of those canoes, and we began to paddle and move along the river. We continued going on thus till night; and when we came to land, and made fires on the banks. . . . Thus I continued to travel, sometimes by land, sometimes by water, through several different countries, and various nations, till, at the end of six months I had been kidnapped, I arrived at the sea coast. . . .

5   The first object which saluted my eyes when I arrived on the coast was the sea, and a slave ship, which was then riding at anchor, and waiting for its cargo. These filled me with astonishment, which was soon converted into terror, which I am yet at a loss to describe nor the then feelings of my mind. When I was carried on board I was immediately handled, and tossed up, to see if I were sound by some of the crew; and I was now persuaded that I had got into a world of bad spirits, and that they were going to kill me. Their complexions too differ-

ing so much from ours, their long hair, and the language they spoke, which was very different from any I had ever heard, united to confirm me in this belief. Indeed, such were the horrors of my views and fears at the moment, that, if ten thousand worlds had been my own, I would have parted with them all to have exchanged my condition with that of the meanest slave in my own country. When I looked around the ship too, and saw a large furnace or copper boiling, and a multitude of black people of every description chained together, every one of their countenances expressing dejection and sorrow, I no longer doubted of my fate; and, quite overpowered with horror and anguish, I fell motionless on the deck, and fainted. When I recovered a little, I found some black people about me, who, I believed were some of those who brought me on board, and had been receiving their pay; they talked to me in order to cheer me, but all in vain. I asked them if we were not to be eaten by those white men with horrible looks, red faces, and long hair? They told me I was not; and one of the crew brought me a small portion of spirituous liquor in a wine glass; but, being afraid of him, I would not take it out of his hand. One of the blacks therefore took it from him, and gave it to me, and I took a little down my palate, which, instead of reviving me, as they thought it would, threw me into the greatest consternation at the strange feeling it produced, having never tasted any such liquor before. Soon after this, the blacks who brought me on board went off, and left me abandoned to despair. I now saw myself deprived of any chance of returning to my native country, or even the least glimpse of hope of gaining the shore, which I now considered as friendly; and I even wished for my former slavery, in preference to my present situation, which was filled with horrors of every kind, still heightened by my ignorance of what I was to undergo. I was not long suffered to indulge my grief; I was soon put down under the decks, and there I received such a salutation in my nostrils as I had never experienced in my life; so that, with the loathsomeness of the stench, and crying together, I became so sick and low that I was not able to eat, nor had I the least desire to taste any thing. I now wished for the last friend, Death, to relieve me; but soon, to my grief, two of the white men offered me eatables; and, on my refusing to eat, one of them held me fast by the hands, and laid me across, I think, the windlass, and tied my feet, while the other flogged me severely. I had never experienced any thing of this kind before; and, although not used to the water, I naturally feared that element the first time I saw it, yet, nevertheless, could I have got over the nettings, I would have jumped over the side, but I could not; and, besides, the crew used to watch us very closely who were not chained down to the decks, lest we should leap into the water: and I have seen some of these poor African prisoners severely cut for attempting to do so, and hourly whipped for not eating. This indeed was often the case with myself. In a little time after, amongst the poor chained men I found some of my own nation, which in a small degree gave ease to my mind. I inquired of them what was to be done with us? They gave me to understand we were to be carried to these white people's country to work for them. I was then a little revived, and thought if it were no worse than working, my situation was not so desperate: but still I feared I should be put to death, the white people looked and acted, as I thought, in so savage a manner; for I had never seen among any people such instances of brutal cruelty; and this not only shewn toward us blacks, but also to some of the whites themselves. One white man in particular I saw, when we were permitted [*sic*] to be on deck, flogged so unmercifully that he died in consequence of it; and they tossed him over the side as they would have done to a brute. This made me fear these people the more; and I expected nothing less than to be treated in the same manner. . . .

6   The stench of the hold while we were on the coast was so intolerably loathsome, that it was dangerous to remain there for any time, and some of us had been permitted to stay on the deck for the fresh air; but now that the whole ship's cargo were confined together, it became absolutely pestilential. The closeness of the place, and the heat of the climate, added to the number in the ship, which was so crowded that each had scarcely room to turn himself, almost suffocated us. This produced copious perspirations, so that the air became unfit for respiration, from a variety of loathsome smells, and brought on a sickness amongst the slaves, of which many died, thus falling victims to the improvident avarice, as I may call it, of their purchasers. This wretched situation was again aggravated by the galling of the chains, now become insupportable; and the filth of the necessary tubs, into which the children often fell, and were almost suffocated. The shrieks of the women and the groans of the dying, rendered the whole a scene of horror almost inconceivable. Happily perhaps for myself I was soon reduced so low here that it was thought necessary to keep me almost always on deck; and from my extreme youth I was not put in fetters. In this situation I expected every hour to share the fate of my companions, some of whom were almost daily brought on deck at the point of death, which I began to hope would soon put an end to my miseries. Often did I think many

of the inhabitants of the deep much more happy than myself; I envied them the freedom they enjoyed, and as often wished I could change my condition for theirs. Every circumstance I met with served only to render my state more painful, and heightened my apprehensions and my opinion of the cruelty of the whites. One day they had taken a number of fishes, and when they had killed and satisfied themselves with as many as they thought fit, to our astonishment who were on the deck, rather than give any of them to us to eat, as we expected, they tossed the remaining fish into the sea again, although we begged and prayed for some as well as we could, but in vain; some of my countrymen, being possessed by hunger, took an opportunity, when they thought no one saw them of trying to get a little privately, but they were discovered, and the attempt procured them some very severe floggings.

One day, when we had a smooth sea, and 7 moderate wind, two of my wearied countrymen, who were chained together (I was near them at the time), preferring death to such a life of misery, somehow made through the nettings, and jumped into the sea; immediately another quite dejected fellow, who on, account of his illness was suffered to be out of irons, also followed their example; and I believe many more would very soon have done the same, if they had not been prevented by the ship's crew who were instantly alarmed. Those of us that were the most active were in a minute put down under the deck; and there was such a noise and confusion amongst the people of the ship as I have never heard before, to stop her, and get the boat out to go after the slaves. However, two of the wretches were drowned, but they got the other, and afterwards flogged him unmercifully, for thus attempting to prefer death to slavery. In this manner we continued

to undergo more hardships than I can now relate; hardships which are inseparable from this
accursed trade.

The Interesting Narrative of the Life of Olaudah Equiano, or Gustavus Vassa, the African, [London, 1784.], in David Northrup, ed., *The Atlantic Slave Trade* (Lexington, MA: D. C. Heath, 1994), pp. 74–80.

Evaluation of the Article

Difficulty Rating ☐ 1 ☐ 2 ☐ 3 ☐ 4 ☐ 5
(1 = easy; 5 = difficult)

What reading difficulties did you encounter? _____

_____

How did you handle these difficulties? _____

_____

Postreading Comprehension Development

Sentence Rewrite

To verify your understanding of some of the key concepts of this essay, rewrite each of the following sentences in your own words, keeping the original idea. (See Chapter 1.)

1. . . . and my surprise was mingled with no small fear when I was put into one of those canoes, and we began to paddle and move along the river. (4)

   _____

   _____

2. In a little time after, amongst the poor chained men I found some of my own nation, which in a small degree gave ease to my mind. (5)

   _____

   _____

   _____

3. Every circumstance I met with served only to render my state more painful, and heightened my apprehensions and my opinion of the cruelty of the whites. (6)

_____

_____

Author's Main Idea

(See Chapter 3.)

1. If you read the essay "Why History?" that appeared earlier in this chapter, select a quotation from it that captures the effect Olaudah Equiano's story has on you. Explain your reasons for choosing this quotation.

   Quotation: _____

   _____

   _____

   Reasons for your choice: _____

   _____

   _____

2. Why was this set of experiences particularly significant to Equiano?

   _____

   _____

   _____

   _____

3. What evidence is there that Equiano wants to communicate with his readers?

   _____

   _____

   _____

Inferences, Metaphors, and Vocabulary in Context
(See Chapters 2, 6, and 7.)

1. Do you think Equiano ever gained his freedom? On what do you base your opinion?

   _____

   _____

2. What was the reason for selling Equiano more than once?

   _____

3. Why did the crew need to see if he was "sound"? (5)

   _____

4. Why was Equiano beaten for refusing to eat?

   _____

5. What personal qualities does Equiano reveal about himself in this essay? Indicate for each quality the event or remark that suggests this trait.

   a. Trait or quality: _____

      Remark: _____

      _____

   b. Trait or quality: _____

      Remark: _____

      _____

   c. Trait or quality: _____

      Remark: _____

      _____

6. What might the following groups have investigated if they had been "invisible" travelers with Equiano during the experiences he describes in this article?

Sociologists: _____

_____

Psychologists: _____

_____

Businesspeople: _____

_____

7. Using the context and your knowledge of word structure, write your own definition for each of the following words:
   a. considerable (1) _____
   b. victuals (2) _____
   c. besought (2) _____
   d. commodious (3) _____
   e. countenances (5) _____
   f. copious (6) _____
   g. apprehensions (6) _____
   h. unmercifully (7) _____

8. If you had read another account of Equiano's capture, one that had been written by the slave traders, what are some differences that you would expect to see in what the reader is told about this event?

   _____

   _____

   _____

   _____

_____

_____

9. How do you think hearing this story in the first person differs from what its effect on you would have been if it had been written by a third-party observer?

_____

_____

_____

_____

_____

Recalling Details

(See Chapter 4.)

1. How does Equiano's emotional state change from the beginning of this account to the end? Give examples for each shift that you mention.

_____

_____

_____

_____

_____

_____

2. What information from this essay could historians use as facts about slave trading? List each fact and the paragraph in which it is found.

_____

_____

_____

_____

_____

3. What information about slave trading in the 1700s have you learned from this article that you did not previously know?

_____

_____

_____

_____

_____

Critical Thinking: Reaction and Discussion

1. Do some research on the West Indies during the period when Equiano was there, the mid-1700s. In your investigation, try to find out what type of work slaves did in the West Indies and how they were treated. You may recall from the Preview to this article that Equiano was slave to a captain. What kinds of things might Equiano have done in this work situation?

   After you have completed your research, write a 250-word essay about what you have learned. You may also want to compare your findings to what you know about slave life in America.

2. With a partner, discuss the value that an article such as this might have for people of your generation. What can an article such as this do for you? Present the results of your discussion to the class.

3. Write an essay of 250 words or more in which you discuss the reasons Equiano might have written the book from which this article was taken. In your essay, you should answer the question: "In what ways can people who write about their lives benefit from doing so?"

USING TECHNOLOGY FOR FURTHER UNDERSTANDING

Using some of the graphics and/or software for making charts that is available on your computer, make a timeline of the life events Equiano described. (Some of this software may be included in your word-processing program.)

● # SELECTION 18

A Place Without History

■ BRENDA FOWLER

Preview

In the following article you will read about the work of two archeologists in Kenya who are working to learn more about the past of a particular region in the country. Notice how they go about their work and how they draw conclusions about the region's history.

To Think About Before You Read

What objects do you have that are very important to you and that say something meaningful about you? On the lines provided, list five of these objects and explain what you believe someone seeing them would learn about you that would give them insight to who you are.

1. Object: _____ What it says about you _____

   _____

   _____

2. Object: _____ What it says about you _____

   _____

   _____

3. Object: _____ What it says about you _____

   _____

   _____

4. Object: _____ What it says about you _____

   _____

   _____

5. Object: _____ What it says about you _____

_____

_____

Terms to Know Before You Read

indigenous (5) originating and living or occurring naturally in an area or environment

foragers (16, 20) those who look for food or provisions

self-deprecating (19) tending to undervalue oneself

wryly (19) humorously but with a touch of irony or displeasure

morphology (21) the branch of biology that deals with the form and structure of organisms apart from function; the form and structure of an organism or one of its parts

lithics; lithic material (19, 23) consisting of stones or rocks; relating to or characteristic of a specified stage in the use of stone by humans

faunal material (23) remains of animals, especially the animals of a particular region or period, considered as a group

One afternoon in January 2000, Chap Kusimba, an archaeologist at the Field Museum in Chicago, pulled into a little village at the base of forested Mount Kasigau, which rises more than 5,000 feet over the arid Tsavo plain in southeastern Kenya. He and a few students hopped out of their vehicle and crowded into a small "hotel," one of the many tiny hostels that show up now and then along the rural roads that thread through the region. When the owner asked why they had come, Kusimba, a native Kenyan, passed around some photos. They showed small shelters made of rocks, now mainly in ruins. Were there any structures like that around here?

2   Two young men nodded. They had been to a place like that when they were kids, they said, and agreed to take the archaeologists there.

The next morning, the group was bush- 3 whacking its way up Mount Kasigau. It was very hot. The two young guides had already gotten lost once, but they seemed to be sure of what they had seen, so everyone pressed on. And then, there it was: Tucked under the overhang of a smooth gray cliff were the remains of a long, squat stone building, much of which had now collapsed to expose a wooden framework.

For a long time historians thought elaborate 4 stone structures like this didn't exist in this part of the East African hinterland. Nineteenth-century European travelers described the scorching, scrubby bush region of Tsavo as hostile and practically uninhabited. The assumption was that it had always been that way—a place virtually without history. The supposedly barren interior stood in sharp contrast to the flourishing towns along the East African coast, which historians had long believed were founded by Arabs and Persians as early as A.D. 800. Known as the Swahili, these Muslim communities sprouted along the coastline of East Africa from southern Somalia to Mozambique, and their inhabitants prospered trading with their neighbors around the Indian Ocean. Even after much of the East African coast fell under the control of first the Portuguese in the sixteenth century, and later Omani Arabs and European colonizers, many Swahili towns thrived.

5   But over the past few decades new evidence has emerged suggesting that Swahili culture, while certainly shaped by Arabic immigrants, emerged from and also developed according to indigenous African traditions. Linguists have demonstrated that Swahili, though it contains many Arabic loan words, is derived from Bantu, an African language. Meanwhile, archaeologists have discovered that some Swahili towns were built on the foundations of older African villages.

6   The new thinking led Kusimba to reconsider the assumption that the people in the Kenyan interior were somehow separate and disconnected from those along the coast, and excluded from its economy. What, indeed, was going on in the Swahili hinterland and what ties did it have to the coast? These were the questions that sent Kusimba and his wife, Sibel Barut Kusimba, a Northern Illinois University archaeologist, to Tsavo in 1997. An area the size of Massachusetts, Tsavo became infamous in the 1890s when two lions terrorized workers building the rail line to Uganda, killing and eating 135 of them before being hunted down.

Now a national park, the area still teems with lions, elephants, rhinoceros, and many other kinds of wildlife. The Kusimbas were required to take an armed guard along for protection against the animals, and they were frequently diverted from areas they were interested in because of ranger investigations against poachers.

7   Over seven seasons of fieldwork, the Kusimbas ultimately documented 400 sites, everything from a few stone tools lying on the ground to big rock shelters and large-scale farming villages. The Kusimbas' project also included extended interviews with 18 elders from the local Wakasigau tribe, most of whom said their ancestors had been farmers, as most of them are today. The elders said farmers had shared the diverse landscape, which encompasses low-lying scrubby bushland and wetter hills that are good for crops, with herders and hunter gatherers, the original inhabitants. It was hardly barren. But they also reported that the last few centuries had been a time of many hardships, famine, migration, and violence.

8   When the Kusimbas asked about the rock shelter on Mount Kasigau, which carbon-dating showed was built about 300 years ago, they had a ready answer: farmers had probably used it to hide their livestock from Masai herders. But one man, an authoritative 82-year-old who had been the village circumciser until he became a born-again Christian, had a different explanation: people used the shelter to escape from Swahili slave raiders.

9   It was not an answer the Kusimbas expected, but for Chap it had the ring of truth. As a child he had heard stories of Swahili caravans stealing children.

10   Born in 1962 to Kenyan parents, Chap spent the first years of his childhood in Uganda, where his engineer father had moved the family to find work. When they returned to Kenya in

1967, his father's parents were concerned that their grandchildren, who had learned Luganda, the language of Uganda, did not speak their language, Lubukusu. So they insisted they stay with them in their village while Kusimba's father once again left to find work. It was there, listening to his grandparents' stories, that Chap's love of history first blossomed. Most of the stories were of how certain animals could outsmart other ones, but there were darker tales, too, of children being snatched and sold to the Swahilis. Later, Chap was struck by the conflicting views of the world represented by the stories; one depicted a safe and happy place, the other a threatening world roiled by dramatic environmental and social shifts. "The changing landscape described in folkloric stories might signal changing relationships due to warfare and slavery," he says, acknowledging that he is one of the relatively few archaeologists who admit folktales as a source of evidence.

11   At his Quaker school, Chap learned about the pioneering work of paleontologists Louis and Mary Leakey in Olduvai Gorge in neighboring Tanzania, where they found the fossil remains of Homo habilis, then considered the oldest human ancestor. The discovery anchored the continent's claim as the cradle of humankind, and deeply impressed the young Chap. "The very idea that you are sitting in the garden of Eden, and it is a real one, not something that is imagined in the Bible, that made a lot of sense at the time," he says.

12   In 1973, when Chap was in the fifth grade, his teacher arranged to take the class 150 miles to the Nairobi Museum. By what first seemed to be incredibly good fortune, Mary Leakey herself dashed by the group, and Chap's teacher attempted to tell her about the pupils' trip. "Mary just walked past my teacher and turned her into tears," Chap recalls. "I never forgot that embar-

rassment. I thought 'One day I will become an archaeologist for the sake of my teacher.'"

13   Just a decade later, while a student at Kenyatta University, Kusimba met Louis and Mary's son, Richard, who became an early mentor. Through Richard, Chap got his first experience at the early hominid site of Koobi Fora in Tanzania, and then came to the United States for graduate school at Bryn Mawr in 1988.

14   Within weeks of arriving, a professor asked Chap and a woman by the name of Sibel, who also had done a stint at Koobi Fora, to collaborate on a presentation about their experiences there. The two have been together ever since.

15   "Chap is much more interesting than I am," says Sibel archly, insisting that there is no grand narrative about the girl who grew up in Boulder, Colorado, the daughter of a Turkish physics professor and a Swiss mother. As a sixth grader, she devoured books on the Leakeys, painted watercolors of ancient hominids, and crafted a Rosetta Stone out of clay.

16   "I was into the art aspect of it," she says. In college, she toyed with many subjects, but ultimately found herself attracted to African history. She says she deliberated a long time before finally settling on archaeology and the study of African foragers.

17   "I guess it goes back to this interest in evolution I had as a kid. Who isn't interested in where we came from?" she asks.

18   Home base for the Kusimbas is the top floor of Chicago's Field Museum, far beyond the echoes of the children clamoring around the dinosaur bones in the main hall. To get to their lab, you have to hike for what seems like a mile through wide cement-floored corridors, past door after oak-trimmed door. The air here is tangy with the scent of old polish and formaldehyde, which, Sibel guesses, wafts up from the conservators' workshops. The Kusimba lab is

crammed with shelves and cabinets of dusty Ziplocs filled with bits of dung, pottery); and other material dug up in Kenya; in the center of the room, a long table is likewise covered with boxes and plastic bags full of items waiting to be examined.

19   Like many couples who collaborate, the Kusimbas have figured out who does what best. Chap, who has something of a reputation for bold ideas, generates the big hypotheses. Affable and charming, he shifts his large frame boyishly from one foot to the other as he tells stories. Sibel is self-deprecating and witty in conversation, and measured and philosophical in her writing; when not grading introductory anthro papers, she edits the couple's joint papers and pores over lithics. "Sometimes I wish I were a historian so I didn't have to go to all the trouble to dig this stuff up," she says wryly.

20   In the late 1980s, as Sibel began to steep herself in the literature on foragers, Chap turned to the study of the Swahili, and lived for almost a year with a Swahili family in Mombasa. Because of their identification with the slave trade and the presumption that they are of foreign descent, the Swahili have been somewhat excluded from Kenya's postcolonial national identity and complain of discrimination. Befriending a Swahili family was not an obvious move for Chap, who, though he does not advertise it, is a member of the Luhya tribe, one of the country's largest and most politically powerful ethnic groups. Chap has since drawn attention to the failure of Kenyan authorities to protect important Swahili archaeological sites, as well as the expropriation of land from Swahili villagers, who own coastal property that is becoming increasingly valuable as the country's tourism industry develops.

21   Between 1986 and 1997, Chap excavated Mtwapa, a mainland port town 15 miles north of Mombasa that he believes had between 8,000 and 15,000 inhabitants at its height in the fifteenth century. At Mtwapa he excavated a tomb holding eight skeletons—a very rare find. Significantly, Chap says, the morphology of those individuals more closely resembled those of Africans in the interior than Arabs. Though the sample is small, Chap says it demonstrates that the indigenous African population was also present in the town. These finds got him to wondering how far inland—into what historians had assumed was a barren and empty interior—such connections reached. Seeking a project that could fulfill both their interests, the Kusimbas hit upon the survey of Tsavo 75 miles in the interior.

22   For Sibel, Tsavo was an ideal place to investigate how hunter-gatherers had been able to persist until well into the twentieth century. Not only were there ample sites, but the couple's interviews provided critical insights into how modern-day foragers interact with their environment and neighbors.

23   At one forager site the Kusimbas excavated, the Kisio rock shelter, two levels of occupation emerged, one dating to about 1,000 years ago and the other to 150 years ago. Both had abundant faunal remains and lithic material found in the area—precisely what one would expect of a hunter-gatherer site. Both levels also had trade items, including European beads, pottery, and, in the more recent level, metal objects, including an arrowhead made of sheet metal, which was introduced to East Africa by the British in the nineteenth century. Here was critical evidence that people in the interior were indeed tied into the Indian Ocean trade both at a time when the Swahili towns were beginning to flourish and in later, historical times.

24   The Kusimbas hypothesize that for centuries starting around A.D. 1000 the herders, farmers, and foragers of the hinterland traded

freely with the people of the Swahili coast, procuring ivory and other items for the growing trade in the Indian Ocean. It was a mutually beneficial arrangement. The hunter-gatherers known as the Waata, respected for their excellent skills in elephant hunting and for the poison arrows they used, almost certainly supplied the caravans with elephant tusks in exchange for trade goods. Kasigau was an economically booming area right on the caravan route of the ivory trade.

25   But historical accounts, as well as the Kusimbas' informants, suggest that this ivory trade was later closely linked to the trade in slaves. As demand for slaves increased in the seventeenth century with the coming of the Portuguese, Swahili slave-raiding parties made the land unsafe. The Portuguese exported thousands of slaves from East Africa, but historians have long believed the slave trade did not make a significant impact until the early nineteenth century, when Omani Arabs set up massive labor-intensive spice plantations in Zanzibar, an island off the coast of Tanzania. Records are poor, so estimates of how many people were traded as slaves are controversial. According to the University of Chicago historian Ralph Austen, some 313,000 slaves were exported from East Africa in the nineteenth century.

26   But the Kusimbas see the dramatic effects of slave raiding as early as the seventeenth century. The farms on the edge of the hills in Tsavo were suddenly abandoned and herders disappeared from the plains. To avoid slave raiders, people retreated to remote places like Mount Kasigau, where they built the fortified rock shelters.

27   At Bungule 20, the large rock shelter Chap was led to by the two local men, the builders first created an earthwork mound on the lip of the cliff and then fortified the exterior walls with elaborate dry stonework. The entrance, instead of leading straight in, first runs along a narrow passageway outside of the building. There was also what appeared to be a secret back door. Chap imagines that it could have served as something like a house for guards, who would have alerted people in the vicinity if slave raiders tried to approach.

28   "To some extent I think it's fair to say that historians and archaeologists have really not faced up to the legacy of slavery before the nineteenth century," says Mark Horton, an archaeologist at the University of Bristol who has worked extensively in East Africa. "That's why [Chap's] work is so important, because what he's actually showing is that this relationship didn't actually just begin in the nineteenth century but goes a lot further back."

29   Hand in hand with the intensifying slave trade, Chap and Sibel say, went the overhunting of the elephant, which may also have contributed to the depopulation of the area. A decline in this keystone species, which consumes more than 100 pounds of both food and water daily, would have dramatically changed the ecology of the area. With fewer elephants, trees and grasses would have grown back, creating the shade required by the tsetse fly, whose bite can transmit a parasite that can be fatal to cattle and humans. In that case, herders no longer would have been able to live in the plains.

30   The result was a depopulated region that, to the explorers and travelers of the nineteenth century, seemed always to have been that way.

31   The Kusimbas have now turned their attentions to Mount Elgon, a volcanic mountain in western Kenya whose slopes rise gradually to 14,000 feet. Farmers, hunter-gatherers, and herders all lived here, says Chap. Just as at Mount Kasigau, the Kusimbas have begun surveying the area and will explore the economic,

social, ritual, and technological interactions among the groups currently living on the mountain. Part of their plans at Elgon also include establishing a field school for undergraduates, which will include classes in both archaeology and ethnography.

32   "Five years from now we will end up with three very complete data sets of adaptations in East Africa, one of which is coastal, another desert, and another mountainous with some of the most fertile land in Africa," Chap says.

33   The work at Mount Elgon represents some-thing of a homecoming for Chap. Much of his family still lives in the nearby town of Kimilili. His grandfather took him hunting on the mountain when he was just a child, and he saw many rock shelters and caves, including some with paintings. His grandfather told him that their ancestors had taken refuge from slave traders in the caves. But Chap says there's more drawing him to the place than a search for his roots.

"I think it's really the huge scientific poten-   34 tial," he says.

Evaluation of the Article
Difficulty Rating □ 1 □ 2 □ 3 □ 4 □ 5
(1 = easy; 5 = difficult)

What reading difficulties did you encounter? _____

_____

How did you handle these difficulties? _____

_____

Postreading Comprehension Development

Sentence Rewrite

To check your understanding of some of the key concepts of this essay, rewrite each of the following sentences in your own words, keeping the original idea. (See Chapter 1.)

1. But over the past few decades new evidence has emerged suggesting that Swahili culture, while certainly shaped by Arabic immigrants, emerged from and also developed accoding to indigenous African traditions. (5)

_____

_____

2. Because of their identification with the slave trade and the presumption that they are of foreign descent, the Swahili have been somewhat excluded from Kenya's postcolonial national identity and complain of discrimination. (20)

_____

_____

_____

3. The result was a depopulated region that, to the explorers and travelers of the nineteenth century, seemed always to have been that way. (30)

_____

_____

_____

Author's Main Idea

(See Chapter 3.)

1. The research question of interest to Chap Kusimba is stated in paragraph:

    ___ a. 5.

    ___ b. 6.

    ___ c. 7.

    ___ d. 8.

2. How does the discussion about Chap's childhood help serve the author's purpose for writing this article?

_____

_____

3. How clearly related is the title of the article to the main idea?

_____

_____

4. What title would have been equally, or more, appropriate?

_____

_____

Inferences, Metaphors, and Vocabulary in Context

(See Chapters 2, 6, and 7.)

1. Which of the following could be used to describe Chap and his wife, Sibel? Check all that apply. Be prepared to justify your answers.

____ a. careless

____ b. inquisitive

____ c. creative

____ d. sensitive

____ e. persistent

____ f. impulsive

____ g. argumentative

2. Considering the information from this article, how might we describe the relationship between archaeology and history?

a. Archeology uses scientific methods to document the past.

b. Historians try to disprove findings of archeologists.

c. Historians and archeologists fight to work in the same geographical areas.

d. Archeologists work to disprove findings of historians.

3. Which of the following does the author imply in paragraph 20? Be prepared to justify your answer.

a. Chap's family might have been guilty of discriminating against the Swahili.

b. Chap is insensitive to the feelings of other Kenyans.

c. Sibel had little interest in working in Mombasa with Chap.

d. The Swahili will sell their property as it increases in value.

4. Which of the following does the author imply in paragraph 29? Be prepared to justify your answer.
   a. There were few doctors in the region to treat anyone bit by a tsetse fly.
   b. Trading slaves for elephant ivory gained in popularity between the seventeenth and eighteenth centuries.
   c. Few villagers stayed in the region because of their fear of the slave trade.
   d. Elephants were not necessary to preserve the ecology of the region.

5. In your own words, explain the connection between paragraph (4) and paragraph (30).

   _____

   _____

6. One conclusion we can draw from this article is that:
   a. Archeologists contribute to our understanding of the history of groups of people.
   b. Archeologists usually work solo so their work is protected by museums around the world.
   c. Historians do not feel archeologists have much to offer to our understanding of the past.
   d. Archeology is primarily a science of oral communication.

7. The author's tone throughout most of this essay is:
   a. persuasive.
   b. humorous.
   c. somber.
   d. informative.

8. How do you think the author wants the reader to feel after reading the last paragraph of this selection? What are the reasons for your beliefs?

   _____

   _____

   _____

9. Using only the context and your knowledge of word structure, define each of the following words. Do not use a dictionary.

a. barren (4) _____

b. encompasses (7)_____

c. paleontologists (11) _____

d. affable (19)_____

e. expropriation (20) _____

f. ample (22) _____

g. excavated (21, 23) _____

h. procuring (24) _____

Recalling Details

(See Chapters 4, 5, and 6.)

1. Which of the following do we learn about Chap Kusimba? Check all that apply.

____ a. His father was a wealthy farmer in Uganda.

____ b. His early years were spent in Uganda.

____ c. He was influenced by Louis and Mary Leakey.

____ d. He knew the Swahili language when he went to live in Kenya.

____ e. He worked in Mtwapa for more than ten years.

____ f. His marriage to Sibel had been arranged by his family.

____ g. He was good at drawing conclusions from things he heard.

2. Indicate whether each of the following items is a major (MAJ) or minor (MIN) detail of this article. Be prepared to justify your answers.

____ a. Linguists have demonstrated that Swahili is derived from Bantu, an African language.

____ b. Tsavo became infamous in the 1980s when two lions terrorized rail line workers.

____ c. The Kusimbas documented 400 sites in Tsavo.

____ d. One man told the Kusimbas that people used a rock shelter on Mount Kasigau to escape from Swahili slave raiders.

____ e. Chap was born to Kenyan parents.

____ f. Most of the stories Chap heard as a child were about how certain animals could outsmart other ones.

_____ g. Louis and Mary Leakey did anthropological work in Tanzania.

_____ h. Chap met Richard Leakey while a student at Kenyatta University.

_____ i. The Kusimbas have figured out who does what best.

_____ j. Befriending a Swahili family was not an obvious move for Chap.

_____ k. Seeking a project that could fulfill both their interests, the Kusimbas hit upon the survey of Tsavo 75 miles in the interior.

_____ l. At one forager site the Kusimbas excavated, the Kisio rock shelter, two levels of occupation emerged.

_____ m. The hunter-gatherers known as the Waata were respected for their excellent skills in elephant hunting and for the poison arrows they used.

3. The pattern of organization used in paragraph 33 is:

   a. cause and effect.

   b. opinion and reason.

   c. simple listing.

   d. definition and explanation.

Critical Thinking: Reaction and Discussion

1. Return to the To Think About Before You Read section for this selection. Reconsider the objects you have listed. Are there others that tell more about your story, about who you are? Revise your list to make it even more about you.

2. With a group, discuss the question that follows. Be prepared to share with your class the major ideas resulting from this discussion.

   What role might archaeologists play when a government (federal, state or local) must determine whether to designate a particular site, such as a cemetery, as having historical significance. This determination would influence the government's decision on whether to preserve the land or destroy it and use it for some other purpose.

3. In the article, *Why History?* Paul Gagnon remarks, *"The value of history—that is, of our knowing and understanding as much of it as we can—may be summed up in three phrases: it matures us; it heartens us; it sets us free."*

In an essay of at least 250 words, discuss how Chap's work may have matured him, heartened him, and set him free.

 USING TECHNOLOGY FOR FURTHER UNDERSTANDING

Using the Internet, locate the archives of a history or national museum that interests you, such as the Smithsonian Museum, the Museum of London, or the National Museum of American History. Search the museum's website to locate ways in which archeology and history are blended in the exhibits. Write a report describing what you have found.

CHAPTER SIXTEEN

Political Science

A Social Science Analyzing Political Processes and Institutions

As Americans we need more than ever today to understand and cherish the political process. It is admittedly untidy. It is confusing. But it is the very essence of civilization.

—S. I. Hayakawa

Derivation: *politikos* —citizen

Key Concepts for the Study of Political Science

Before you read the following list of concepts, think about some issues and topics that you might study if you took courses in political science. In the space provided, list your ideas.

ACTIVIST.   An individual who is extensively and vigorously involved in political activity, either within or outside the party system.

BUREAUCRACY.   A large, complex organization composed of appointed officials.

CIVIL LIBERTIES.   The freedoms of speech, press, religion, and petition, together with freedom from arbitrary arrest or prosecution.

CIVIL RIGHTS.   The rights of citizens to vote, to receive equal treatment before the law, and to share equally with other citizens the benefits of public facilities.

FEDERALISM (OR FEDERATION).   A political system in which ultimate authority is shared between a central government and state or regional governments.

INTEREST GROUP.   An organization of persons that seeks to influence the making of public policy.

LOBBYIST.   A person, usually acting as an agent for a group, who seeks to bring about the passage or defeat of legislative bills, to influence their content, or to influence administrative actions.

PLURALISM.   A concept describing a society in which all affected interests vie through the political process to achieve their objectives, as opposed to one in which one interest or group dominates the process to the exclusion of others.

SEPARATION OF POWERS.   A principle of American government whereby constitutional authority is distributed among three branches of government—the legislative, the executive, and the judicial.

Now that you have read this list, what are some additional issues and topics that you might study if you took courses in political science? In the space provided, list your ideas.

- # SELECTION 19

Politics: Setting the Stage

■ W. PHILLIPS SHIVELY

Preview

Many decisions or events are said to be political. What does this mean? How does the power of particular individuals or institutions affect outcomes? Why can't we all get what we want? In this article the author introduces you to the field of political science and some of the complexities of the work political scientists do.

To Think About Before You Read

Following are a few environments in which you live or work, or groups to which you might be connected. For each, consider ways in which your experiences in that environment might be political. Cite one example of a decision made, or an outcome, that you think was the result of politics. Also decide if this outcome was what you had wanted.

Your family _____

_____

_____

Your job _____

_____

_____

Your community _____

_____

_____

Your college/university _____

_____

_____

Terms to Know Before You Read

constitute (9) to be the elements or parts of; compose

quasi (9, 10) having a likeness to something; resembling

Everyone knows something about politics, and many people know a great deal about it. It is an interesting, amusing, and moving spectacle that ranks not too far behind professional sports in the eyes of many. Political scientists, however, *study* politics and *analyze* it. This involves doing pretty much the same sorts of things that other people do who follow politics: we read the newspapers and listen to press conferences, take part in political campaigns, and so on. However, we also do some things differently. We usually try to see both sides of any question and to keep our emotions in low key, because emotions can cloud judgment. We borrow deliberately from other disciplines—such as economics, history, sociology, psychology, and philosophy—to help us understand what is going on politically. Above all, as you will see later in this chapter, we try to be precise about the meanings of the words we use. Many words having to do with politics—such as *liberal, represent,* and even *politics*—are quite complex, but most people use them unthinkingly. Political scientists are careful to analyze the varied meanings of such words and to use them precisely, partly because it is important to know exactly what we mean by the words we use and partly because careful examination of a richly complex word may teach us a lot about the things it describes.

W. Phillips Shivley, "Politics: Setting the Stage," *Power and Choice: An Introduction to Political Science,* 8th ed. New York: McGraw-Hill pp. 2–5, 13–16. Reproduced with permission of The McGraw-Hill Companies.

What do political scientists study? Over the 2 years, we have seen work in which political scientists:

* Measured just how much it actually costs a country to lose a war
* Devised a new system of voting in primaries that might have led to a different set of candidates for most presidential elections
* Analyzed and explained the various styles that members of the U.S. Congress adopt in dealing with their constituents
* Studied the spread of welfare reforms across the states
* Showed that the roots of successful government may go back to social institutions several centuries ago
* Showed why most nations will ignore warnings about surprise military action by hostile nations
* Studied why democracies almost never wage war on other democracies

These are the sorts of things political scientists do. In this book you will be introduced to the broad principles of what we have learned about politics, especially about the politics of democracies like the United States. I hope the study will sharpen and enrich the more general understanding of politics that you already have.

This first chapter, in particular, involves the 4 precise definition of several words with which you are already somewhat familiar. We must examine these definitions because you should start your study with some basic terms in place. You may also find it intriguing to see complexity in words, such as *politics,* that have probably not struck you before as being particularly complicated.

POLITICS

5 What is politics? What is it that makes an act political? Consider the following questions, all of which involve political circumstances. What do these have in common?

- How was Hitler able to take power through a series of supposedly democratic elections?
- Why does the U.S. Congress so often disagree with the president in framing energy policies?
- Why should workers sort letters the way their boss directs if they know a more efficient way?
- Why were southern blacks denied the vote and placed in segregated schools throughout the 1950s while at the same time their housing was not as segregated as that in the North?
- Should communists be barred from teaching in the schools?
- Should fascists be barred from teaching in the schools?
- Why does the United States have only two major political parties when most democracies have more?
- Should state and local governments have the right to force landholders to sell them land that is needed for public purposes?
- Was Henry Truman right to bomb Hiroshima and Nagasaki?
- Why do people so often feel guilty about not doing what their parents want them to do?

These questions deal with politics. The questions about bosses and parents may not have looked to you as if they belonged in this group, but their connection with politics should become clearer by the end of this chapter.

What is it that these questions have in common? There are two main things, and both have often been used as the defining characteristics of politics. First, all the questions involve the *making of a common decision for a group of people,* that is, a uniform decision applying in the same way to all members of the group. Second, all involve *the use of power* by one person or a group of people to affect the behavior of another person or group of people. Let us look at both of these in more detail.

POLITICS AS THE MAKING OF COMMON DECISIONS

Any group of people must often make decisions that will apply to all of them in common, as a group. A family must decide where to live, what sorts of rules to set for children, how to balance a budget, and so on. A class in a college or university (including the instructor as part of the "class") must decide what reading material to require, how students are to be graded by the instructor, how bright the light should be in the classrooms. A country must decide where to locate parks, what allies to seek out in war, how to raise revenue by taxing its citizens, how to care for the helpless, and many other things. Each of these requires the setting of common policy for the group, a single decision that affects all members of the group.

Not all human actions, of course, involve the making of a common policy for a group. When one brother teases another, he is not making a family policy, nor is a family member who decides to write the great American novel. A student who decides to read extra material on one section of the course (or, perhaps, to skip a bit of the reading) is not making a policy of the class. A person's decision to build a new house is not part of any common national policy, although the country may have policies—on interest rates, the regulation of building, land use, zoning, and so on—that affect this person's decision. Ford Motor Company's decisions on new-car styling are not part of a common national policy.

9   Those actions that contribute to the making of a common policy for a group of people constitute politics, and questions about those policies and the making of those policies are political questions. The political/nonpolitical distinction is not always easy to draw. The example of the Ford Motor Company, above, is tricky because Ford is so large that its decisions verge on being common policy for the whole United States, even though the company has no formal role in the nation's government. In other words, one might argue that because the U.S. government tolerates the concentration of our automobile industry among three giant corporations and because (as a result of this) the decisions of any one of the three bulk so large in American life, those decisions have a quasi-public character and are "sort of" political. In 1980, the quasi-public nature of large corporations was underlined when the government found that it had to become intimately involved in Chrysler Corporation's financing to prevent Chrysler from going out of business. Chrysler was so large that the economic health of the country was unavoidably bound to its economic decisions; therefore, the government decided it had no choice but to support Chrysler's loans. In this sense, decisions made

by the management of Chrysler were to a degree binding on the country as a whole and became, to some extent, U.S. political decisions.

Another tricky aspect of the political/non- 10 political distinction is that it is partly a matter of perspective. Ford's design decisions are not (except via Ford's quasi-public nature) political decisions for the *United States;* but they *are* political decisions for Ford's stockholders, managers, and workers, because they set a common policy for the company. A family's decision to build a house is not a political decision for the *country,* but it is a political decision for the *family* as a group inasmuch as it involves a common policy for the family. "Company politics" is involved in Ford's decision, and "family politics" is involved in the family's decision. Neither, however, is a national political decision. Society consists of groups within groups within groups. Ford Motor Company is a group within the United States, and a family may be a group within the larger group of those dependent on Ford. Politics exists within any of these groups whenever a decision that will apply to all the members of the group is made. Depending on which group you are thinking of, a given decision—the decision of the Clauski family to build a house—may be treated as either political or nonpolitical. The Clauski decision is political for the family as a group but not political for the nation.

POLITICS AS THE EXERCISE OF POWER

A second characteristic of politics, one that 11 runs through the questions at the start of this chapter, is that politics always involves the exercise of *power* by one person or persons over another person or persons. Power is the ability of one person to cause another to do what the first wishes, *by whatever means.* Politics always involves this: one person causing others to do what that person wants either by forcing or convincing them to do so. Looking back at the questions, we note that Hitler rose to high office by convincing many Germans to vote for him; the U.S. Congress disagrees with the president so often about energy policy because the president does not have much power either to force or to convince Congress to go along with his wishes in that area; and so on. In such ways, each of these questions involves the power of one person or persons over another or others.

12   The two defining characteristics of politics, then, are that (1) politics always involves the making of common decisions for groups of people *and* (2) those decisions are made by some members of the group exercising power over other members of the group. Power can consist of a wide variety of tools that help one person affect the actions of another. Power may be stark, as when a police officer stops a demonstrator from marching up the street; or it may be subtle, as when a group of poor people, by their very misery, elicit positive governmental action on their behalf.

13   Power may be exercised as *coercion* when we force a person to do something he or she did not want to do, as *persuasion* when we convince someone that that is what she or he really wishes to do, or as the *construction of incentives* when we make the alternative so unattractive that only one reasonable option remains. The ability to exercise any of these forms of power may be based on all sorts of things—money, affection, physical strength, legal status (the power of a police officer to direct traffic, for instance), the possession of important information, a winning smile, strong allies, determination, desperation (which helped North Vietnam

to defeat the United States in the 1970s), and many more. Any of these can help some people get other people to act as they wish.

14   It is not necessary to learn the specific bases of power listed. They are meant to provide a sense of the variety and complexity of power, not as an exhaustive list of its important sources. The point is that all politics involves the use of power, and such power may take varied forms. . . .

POLITICAL SCIENCE

15   Political science is the academic field that takes as its sole and general task the analysis of politics, especially the politics of the state. There has been continuing debate over how "scientific" political science should be. Some political scientists think that politics is so complex and involves such basic personal values that we should not try to pin it down to exact regularities. Rather, we should interpret each political event and idea more or less in and of itself, in a personal, subjective way. Such political scientists would model themselves upon historians, who interpret a particular sequence of events more or less in and of itself, seeking to retain the richness of its detail while making a general patterned interpretation of what process unfolded through the events.

16   Other political scientists think that their discipline should be more scientific than this, seeking out the basic essence of regularities across a whole set of events, even though this means sacrificing some of the rich detail with which each single event is laden. They think that the only way we will be able to explain and predict what happens in politics is to emphasize the underlying processes that a number of disparate events may have in common. These political scientists would model themselves on other social

scientists such as economists, who analyze events simply as instances of general processes, which they treat in the abstract. Economists, for instance, prefer to deal abstractly with supply-and-demand theories rather than analyze specifically what happens in a given used car lot.

17   The first type of political scientists are sometimes called "interpretivists" (or often "qualitative"), the latter "behavioralists" (or "quantitative"). Interpretive political scientists are most likely to deal in historical and philosophical aspects of politics and to seek detailed, nonnumerical information on a few cases. Behavioralists lean more to abstract, mechanical theories of politics and to statistical analyses of numerical information. They find numerical information especially attractive because it distills a set of complex details down into something very simple and basic—a number. Therefore, because behavioralists are looking for simple descriptions of basic processes, they see it as more useful to summarize party competition in many congressional districts with a single index number for each district than to try to digest masses of biography, newspaper accounts, and so on from a few congressional races.

18   This picture should not be seen as black and white. Political science does not consist of two warring camps, and most political scientists combine some element of "interpretivism" with some element of "behavioralism." However, there are different *degrees* of these among political scientists, which adds greatly to the variety of materials available in the field. . . .

THE PLEASURES OF POLITICS

19 I have led you through some rather dry material in this chapter because it was necessary to start you off with clarity on a number of concepts. Frequently throughout this book you will find that we are working toward greater precision than is found in everyday language; this usually requires abstraction and may also seem a bit dry. I hope, however, that as we do this, you will remember—and I can communicate—what a fascinating and dramatic thing we are studying.

20   "The use of power to reach collective choices"—think what this phrase means. We are talking about struggles for the souls of nations. The "use of power" has meant Thoreau going to prison to protest the United States' invasion of Mexico; underground resistance by the Catholic Church and the Communist Party against Nazi occupation troops in the Second World War; students braving police dogs and murderous assaults to integrate American businesses and public facilities in the 1960s; Mikhail Gorbachev and Boris Yeltsin juggling political coalitions to create democracy in the Soviet Union, where it had never been seen before. "Collective choices" have included the invention of democracy as a way to accomplish government by the people; the development of public education, park systems, public health; and also such horrors as the Nazis' murder of millions of Jews and other "undesirables."

21   The things we will be analyzing in the pages that follow involve real people devoting their energies to things they want and things they believe in. While you learn how to analyze what is happening in these events and to deal with the events dispassionately, I hope you will not forget the humanity that is moving through them.

> **Evaluation of the Article**
> Difficulty Rating ☐ 1 ☐ 2 ☐ 3 ☐ 4 ☐ 5
> (1 = easy; 5 = difficult)
>
> What reading difficulties did you encounter? _____
>
> _____
>
> How did you handle these difficulties? _____
>
> _____

Comprehension of the Discipline

1. Indicate whether, based on this article, the following statements are true (T) or false (F). Be prepared to justify your answers.

   _____ a. For something to be political, there must be political parties involved.

   _____ b. Political situations usually involve violence.

   _____ c. In political processes, some people will not have their preferences satisfied.

   _____ d. As a society becomes wealthier, politics will become less necessary.

   _____ e. Political behavior occurs in business situations.

   _____ f. Political scientists agree on how scientific their work should be.

   _____ g. People involved in politics never agree with one another.

   _____ h. It is often difficult to distinguish between political and non-political situations.

   _____ i. Political activity should result in everyone's thinking alike.

   _____ j. Successful political events occur only when all involved finally get what they want.

   _____ k. We can expect that there will never be an end to political activity among mankind.

2. Explain in your own words the role each of the following plays in political activity. Write several sentences for each.

a. Coercion:

_____

_____

_____

_____

b. Common decisions:

_____

_____

_____

_____

c. Collective choices:

_____

_____

_____

_____

d. Interpretivism:

_____

_____

_____

_____

3. In several sentences, explain what makes the following cartoon political.

_____

_____

Source: Bob Schochet, *Phi Delta Kappan* April 1992, 623.

_____

_____

_____

_____

_____

_____

_____

_____

4. Check each situation that could be considered political. Using this
   article, be prepared to justify your answers.

   _____ a. Your college's football team is having its first away game of
            the season.

   _____ b. Your state's Department of Environmental Protection is con-
            sidering building a toxic waste dump in your county.

   _____ c. Residents of a small town are voting on whether to build a
            community pool.

      d. A college professor has canceled class so that he may attend a professional meeting.

      e. The college president is meeting with union officials to discuss terms of a new faculty contract.

      f. A state employee has offered to work overtime to complete an important project.

      g. Executives of several divisions of a department store chain are meeting to decide on a series of layoffs.

      h. People protesting against abortion were forcibly removed from the front of a clinic when they wouldn't move voluntarily.

      i. Money for shelters for the homeless was voted on by the town council.

5. Briefly explain how the political study of human behavior appears to differ from:

   a. Psychological study: _____

     _____

   b. Sociological study: _____

     _____

6. Look at the charts and answer the following questions.

   a. Why might the information on these charts be of interest to political scientists? _____

     _____

   b. What can you conclude from this set of charts about each of the following:

    Views about rudeness in the United States: _____

    _____

    Views about the treatment of minorities: _____

    _____

    Views about the treatment of the disabled: _____

    _____

Views about the respect shown toward the elderly: _____

_____

_____

Which statement comes
closer to your own view?

A lack of respect and courtesy
is a serious problem and we
should try to address it
(79%)

A lack of respect
and courtesy is not
a serious problem
given all the issues
facing our society
(19%)

Don't know
(1%)

How about people who are rude and disrespectful?
Do you see this often, sometimes, or practically never?
How much does this bother you? Have you, yourself,
ever done something similar?

Percentage saying they:

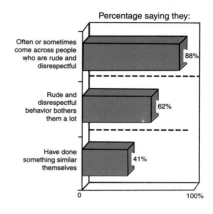

Often or sometimes
come across people
who are rude and
disrespectful — 88%

Rude and
disrespectful
behavior bothers
them a lot — 62%

Have done
something similar
themselves — 41%

0   100%

How about people who are kind and considerate? Do
you see this often, sometimes, or practically never?

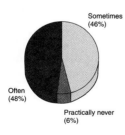

Sometimes
(46%)

Often
(48%)

Practically never
(6%)

As compared to the past, have the following things gotten
better, worse or stayed the same?

Percentage saying "gotten better":

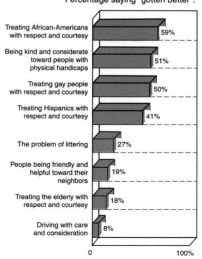

Treating African-Americans
with respect and courtesy — 59%

Being kind and considerate
toward people with
physical handicaps — 51%

Treating gay people
with respect and courtesy — 50%

Treating Hispanics with
respect and courtesy — 41%

The problem of littering — 27%

People being friendly and
helpful toward their
neighbors — 19%

Treating the elderly with
respect and courtesy — 18%

Driving with care
and consideration — 8%

0   100%

Source: *Public Agenda* January 2002. *http:www.publicagenda.org/specials/civility/civility1.htm.* Retrieved December 21, 2005.

READING

Critical Thinking: Reaction and Discussion

1. Review a recent issue of your student newspaper. Select one article that is about school politics, and answer the following questions:
   a. What makes this article political?
   b. Who has written it?
   c. What is the point of view that is expressed?
   d. What are some other points of view that people might have on this subject?
   e. What is your viewpoint on this subject?
   f. Why would you, or would you not, submit a letter to the editor expressing your viewpoint?

2. With a partner, examine a recent copy of the *New York Times* or another large city newspaper. Locate and read articles about the activities of politicians, and study the political cartoons. Then answer these questions:
   a. What image of politicians is conveyed in this paper?
   b. How does this image confirm or disagree with your own image of politicians?

USING TECHNOLOGY FOR FURTHER UNDERSTANDING

Use the Internet to see what you can find out about opinion polling.

1. What kinds of polls are taken online?
2. What are some of the other kinds of polls that are conducted offline but then reported on the Internet?
3. Who might make use of the information that seems to be available from polls?

Guidelines for Reading Political Science

Some things to bear in mind when you read political science are as follows:

ALL POLITICAL SYSTEMS ARE BASED ON IDEAS ABOUT THE RELATIONSHIP BETWEEN THE GOVERNMENT OF A NATION AND ITS CITIZENS. To understand the American or any other political system, you will need to know the set of beliefs about this relationship. That is, what are the government's beliefs about human rights? What is the extent to which the government believes it can control its citizens' everyday affairs? These beliefs guide how the country's government is structured. In some societies, the beliefs are directly stated in official documents such as a constitution. In others, they must be inferred from the actions of the government over time.

As You Read about Political Events, Knowing the Process of the Country's Political System Will Help You Understand How and Why Certain Events Occurred.   When you read about the political events in any country, you should try to identify the particular features of its political system. What role does public opinion play in the political process? Are there interest groups? How are campaigns and elections conducted? Is there a two- or a multiparty system or perhaps no party system at all? This information will enable you to comprehend why events occurred as they have in North Korea, for instance, and why they would have occurred differently in a country like Canada.

The Author's Personal Political Ideology Will also Bear on the Type of Information That Is Presented and What Is said About It. Unless you are reading mere statements of political facts (such as who the twenty-third president was or what socialism is), you will no doubt be reading material that reflects the author's bias. Most political scientists have their own views about what makes good government. These views will influence how they analyze certain governmental actions. A political scientist may write about a particular presidency, the fall of the Berlin Wall, or guerrilla warfare in South America. In each case, this writer chooses certain aspects to discuss. That choice, in itself, often reflects bias. For instance, one writer may choose to discuss Nixon's impressive foreign affairs record; another may choose to discuss his downfall and Watergate. As a careful reader, you will search for objectivity and note how the author's political ideology is reflected in the writing.

Another Source of Bias That Might Enter Political Science Writing Is the Author's Own Life Experience.   For instance, an author who was a citizen of the former East Germany and who witnessed the collapse of the Berlin Wall may interpret that event very differently from a person who lived in West Germany for a short time or who never was a citizen of either the former East or West Germany. Whenever you believe bias may have a bearing on the text you are reading, you will need to sort out as best as possible which statements are the result of personal views and which can be supported by facts.

Political Science Is, Indeed, a Science.   Political scientists look at events such as elections and revolutions and try to develop hypotheses or theories about what led to certain events and outcomes. You need to ask, then, whether the political scientist is being logical in the theories or hypotheses that are put forward. You should be sure there is enough supporting evidence for a particular explanation of an event. Critical readers will evaluate what is said and will challenge unsupported ideas.

POLITICAL SCIENTISTS USE A VARIETY OF TYPES OF DATA TO MAKE ANALYSES OR TO FORM THEORIES.   They might analyze demographics, such as age, ethnicity, education, or geographic location, of certain populations. Or they might study personal characteristics, such as level of involvement in community activities, church attendance statistics, and membership in particular organizations. From these data, they draw conclusions about the internal politics of groups, communities, organizations, and other segments of the population. These conclusions will enable them to make predictions about the future political activities of this population. Tables, charts, and graphs are often used to show these statistics. You should read these carefully.

POLITICAL SCIENTISTS MAY ALSO DRAW BROAD CONCLUSIONS BY LOOKING AT SPECIFIC EVENTS.   For example, they might make generalizations or draw conclusions about people's voting behavior during periods of large-scale unemployment that are based on the results of just one election during such a period. You, too, should look at each specific instance being described and attempt to see its broader implications. Your conclusions may be the same as the author's, or you may think of others. As you continue your reading, look for support for the generalizations and conclusions that you and the author have made.

Keep these guidelines in mind as you read the remaining articles from the field of political science.

● **SELECTION 20**

What Should We Know About American Government?

■ JAMES Q. WILSON

Preview

What makes the American system of government unique? It is called a democracy, but what, exactly, does that term mean? How is the United States different from other democracies? In the following article, you will read about features of American government that make it different from governments of other countries. While you read, consider how your life in this country might be different if some of these features were not present.

To Think About Before You Read

The United States is said to have a democratic form of government. What do you understand this to mean with regard to each of the following:

1. What rights do U.S. citizens have?

_____

_____

_____

_____

2. What obligations do U.S. citizens have?

_____

_____

_____

_____

3. What roles does public opinion play in governmental decision making?

_____

_____

Terms to Know Before You Read

demagogues (13) leaders who make use of popular prejudices and false claims and promises in order to gain power

centralized (16) concentrating power and authority in a center or central organization

Most Americans think they know how their government works, and many don't like it. A common view goes like this:

The president gets elected because of some slick television ads, although he has ducked all the tough questions. His party's platform is a meaningless set of words that gives you no idea what he will do in office. Once in the White House, he proposes bills and then Congress decides which to pass. Congress and the president do this not to solve problems, but to reward whichever interest groups have spent the most money getting them elected. The laws they enact are turned over to an all-powerful bureaucracy that administers them much as the bureaucrats see fit, adding a lot of needless red tape. If you don't like these laws, you can sue, but the courts will base their decisions on their own liberal or conservative preferences and not on any standards of justice or fair play. All of these people—presidents, members of Congress, bureau-crats, and judges—act without any real respect for the Constitution. No wonder our national problems don't get solved.

Almost every sentence in the preceding para-2 graph is either flatly wrong, greatly exaggerated, or seriously incomplete. If you want to find out why, read this book. By the time you are finished, you may still think our system has faults, but you will have a clearer idea of what they are and how they arose.

These criticisms contain enough truth, how-3 ever, to alert us to another reason for taking a course on American government. How our government operates is quite different from how other democratic governments, such as those in Western Europe, operate. We know that the president and Congress are often at logger-heads, that neither can exercise complete control over the bureaucracy, that judges often intervene to tell government agencies what to do, and that our politicians always seem to be involved in some scandal. We are also aware that other levels of government—cities and states—seem to compete with the federal government for the right to make certain decisions.

4   To most Europeans, all this would be absolutely baffling. In a country such as Great Britain, the legislature automatically approves almost any policy the chief executive (the prime minister) proposes, and does so without making any changes. The bureaucracy carries out the policy without resistance, but if something should go wrong, the legislature does not investigate the agency to see what went wrong. No citizen can sue the government in a British court; if one tried, the judge would throw the case out. There are no governors who have to be induced to follow the national policy; the national government's policies are, for most purposes, the *only* policies. If those policies prove unpopular, there is a good chance that many members of the legislature will not be reelected.

5   American government is not like any other democratic government in the world. Far from taking it for granted, students here should imagine for a moment that they are not young Americans but young Swedes, Italians, or Britons and ask themselves why American politics is so different and how that difference affects the policies produced here.

6   Consider these differences in *politics:*

  ⁂ In the United States, the police and the public schools are controlled by towns, cities, and states. In Europe, they are usually controlled by the national government.
  ⁂ If you want to run for office in the United States, you can do so by collecting the required number of signatures on a petition to get on the ballot in a primary election; if you win the primary, you then run in the general election. In Europe, there usually aren't any primary elections; instead, party leaders decide who gets on the ballot.

  ⁂ In the United States, fewer than one worker in five belongs to a labor union. In many European nations, a much larger proportion of workers belong to unions.
  ⁂ The United States has no large socialist, communist, or Marxist political party. In France, Great Britain, Italy, and elsewhere, socialist and Marxist parties are large and powerful.
  ⁂ The United States has many politically active persons who consider themselves born-again Christians. Such persons are relatively rare in Europe and certainly not a political force there.
  ⁂ In the United States, judges decide whether abortions shall be legal, which pornographic movies may be shown, and what the size of a congressional district shall be. In Europe, the legislature decides such issues.
  ⁂ When the prime minister of Great Britain signs a treaty, his nation is bound by it; when the president signs a treaty, he is making a promise only to try to get the Senate to ratify it.

7   Consider also these differences in *policies:*

  ⁂ The tax burden in the United States is about half what it is in Sweden and many other European nations.
  ⁂ The United States adopted federal policies to provide benefits to the elderly and the unemployed about a quarter of a century *after* such policies were already in effect in much of Europe.
  ⁂ The United States government owns very few industries. In parts of Europe, the government owns the airlines, the telephone system, the steel mills, the automobile factories, and even the oil companies.

❋ Throughout much of the 1980s and into the 1990s, the president and Congress could not agree on a budget—how much to spend, where to make cuts, and whether taxes should be increased; as a result, on some occasions the country had neither a budget nor the authority it needed to borrow money to keep paying its bills, and so the government partially shut down. In European democracies, this kind of deadlock almost never occurs.

8   How do we explain these differences? It is not that America is "democratic" and other nations are "undemocratic." Great Britain and the United States are both democracies—but two different *kinds* of democracies. The American kind is the product of two closely related factors: our constitutional system and the opinions and values of the people. We have the kind of constitution we do because the people who wrote it had certain beliefs about how government should be organized, and those beliefs are perpetuated and sharpened by the workings of the government created by that constitution.

9   In this book, we will not try to explain all the ways in which America differs from Europe. This book is not about comparative politics; it is about American politics. But keeping in mind the distinctive features of our system will, I hope, make the following chapters more interesting. You might try the following experiment. As you read this book, see how many of the differences listed above you can explain. You won't be able to explain them all, but you will be able to explain several.

THE MEANINGS OF DEMOCRACY

10   To explain why American democracy differs from democracy in Britain or Sweden, we must first understand what is meant by **democracy.**

That word is used to describe three different political systems.

11   One way the term *democracy* is used is to describe political systems in which all or most citizens participate directly in making governmental decisions. The New England town meeting, for example, comes close to fitting this definition of **direct democracy.** Once or twice a year all the adult citizens of a town come together to vote on all major issues and expenditures. In many states, such as California, a kind of direct democracy exists whenever voters are asked to approve or reject a specific policy, such as a plan to cut taxes or build a water system (a **referendum**), remove an elected official before his or her term has expired (a **recall**), or propose a new piece of legislation or a constitutional amendment (an **initiative**).

12   The second meaning of democracy was most concisely stated in 1942 by the economist Joseph Schumpeter: "The democratic method is that institutional arrangement for arriving at political decisions in which individuals [that is, officeholders] acquire the power to decide by means of a competitive struggle for the people's vote." This system is usually called a **representative democracy.** The Framers of the American constitution called it a **republic.**

13   Several arguments can be made in favor of representative democracy over direct democracy. First, direct democracy is impractical because it is impossible for all the citizens to decide all the issues: they don't have the time, energy, interest, or information. It is practical, however, to expect them to choose among competing leadership groups. Second, direct democracy is undesirable because the people will often make bad decisions on the basis of fleeting desires or under the influence of unscrupulous demagogues or clever advertising. Third, direct democracy makes it difficult

to negotiate compromises among contending groups; instead, one side wins and the other loses—even when there may have been a middle ground that both sides would have accepted.

14   You may think that these criticisms of direct democracy are unfair. If so, ask yourself which of the following measures (especially those that you feel strongly about) you would be willing to have decided by all citizens voting in a referendum. Abortion? Gun control? Federal aid to parochial schools? The death penalty? Foreign aid? Racial integration of public schools? The defense budget? Free trade? Most people, however "democratic" they may be, favor certain policies that they would not want decided by, in effect, a public opinion poll.

REPRESENTATIVE DEMOCRACY

15 In this book, we will use the word *democracy* to mean representative democracy, but we will not try to settle the argument over whether, or under what circumstances, direct democracy might be better. It is important to note, however, that representative democracy can exist only if certain conditions exist: freedom of speech and of the press (so that voters can learn about what their representatives are doing and communicate their preferences to them), freedom to organize (so that people can come forward as candidates for office), reasonably fair access to political resources (so that candidates can mount an effective campaign), a decent respect for the rights and opinions of others (so that the winners in an election are allowed to assume office and govern and the losers are not punished or banished), and a belief that the political system is legitimate (so that people will obey its laws without being coerced).

16   Broadly speaking, representative democracy can take one of two forms: the parliamentary system or the presidential system. The *parlia-*

mentary system, common to almost all European democracies, vests political power in an elected legislature. The legislature, in turn, chooses the chief executive, called the prime minister. So long as the prime minister has the support of a majority of the members of parliament, he or she can carry out any policy that is not forbidden by the nation's constitution. (Some parliamentary democracies do not have a written constitution. In Great Britain, for example, Parliament can do almost anything that it believes the voters will accept.) In a parliamentary democracy, political power at the national level is centralized; the prime minister and his or her cabinet make all the important decisions. The bureaucracy works for the prime minister. The courts ordinarily do not interfere. The theory of a parliamentary system is that the government should make decisions and then be held accountable to the voters at the next election.

A *presidential system* vests political power in 17 separately elected branches of the national government—a president and a congress. In addition, there may be an independent judiciary, as there is in the United States, that can disapprove of the actions of the president and Congress if they violate the Constitution. The president proposes legislation but has no guarantee that Congress will accept it, even if the president's party has a majority of members in Congress. The bureaucracy works for both the president and Congress; since its loyalties are divided, its actions are not always consistent with what the president or Congress wishes. Political power at the national level is decentralized and shared. The theory of a presidential system is that policies should be tested for their political acceptability at every stage of the policy-making process, not just at election time.

18 Some people believe that the presidential system, based on separate branches of government sharing power, makes it very hard to enact any policies at all. So many roadblocks are built into the system that the government is biased against taking action. Moreover, when government does act, so many people are involved in making the decision that it becomes difficult for the voters to hold anyone directly accountable for the result. If you don't like federal priorities, whom can you blame and vote against in the next election? The president? Your senator? Your representative?

19 To correct these features of the system, some critics have proposed that the United States change its constitution and make it more like a parliamentary democracy so that it will be easier for the government to act and easier for the voters to hold officials accountable for their actions at election time. But defenders of our constitution take a different view of the matter. The roadblocks in our constitutional system have not prevented our national government from growing about as fast, and adopting many of the same policies, as parliamentary democracies in Europe. And if the American government is not as big (measured by the taxes it levies, the money it spends, and the programs it enacts) as the governments of some European nations, maybe that is a good thing. Moreover, Americans may not be content with voting only once every four years to approve of or reject what the government is doing; they may want a chance to influence policy as it is being formulated—by writing their senator or representative, joining interest groups, marching on Washington, and bringing suit in court.

20 This book will not tell you whether to prefer an American-style presidential system or to yearn for a British-style parliamentary one. But it will tell you how our system works and explain why it works as it does. The primary reason it functions the way it does is the Constitution of the United States, which is where we shall start.

Evaluation of the Article

Difficulty Rating ☐ 1 ☐ 2 ☐ 3 ☐ 4 ☐ 5
(1 = easy; 5 = difficult)

What reading difficulties did you encounter? _____

_____

How did you handle these difficulties? _____

_____

Postreading Comprehension Development

Sentence Rewrite

To verify your understanding of some of the key concepts of this essay, rewrite each of the following sentences in your own words, keeping the original idea. (See Chapter 1.)

1. American government is not like any other democratic government in the world. (3)

   _____

   _____

2. Several arguments can be made in favor of representative democracy over direct democracy. (13)

   _____

   _____

3. The president proposes legislation but has no guarantee that Congress will accept it, even if the president's party has a majority of members in Congress. (17)

   _____

   _____

   _____

   _____

Author's Main Idea

(See Chapter 3.)

1. In your own words, state what you believe to be the author's major purpose for writing this article. Be prepared to justify your answer.

   _____

   _____

2. The paragraph that best introduces the author's purpose for the entire book is

    a. 8.

    b. 9.

    c. 10.

    d. 11.

Inferences, Metaphors, and Vocabulary in Context
(See Chapters 2, 6, and 7.)

1. Which of the following is probably true about British government?

    a. The prime minister doesn't have to explain policy changes to the people at the time they are implemented.

    b. National policies are popular policies because the people have voted on each policy before it is made into law.

    c. The courts play a major role in policy making.

    d. If the people don't like the policy changes being made, they can appeal to Britain's courts to overturn them.

2. Which of the following reflects an accurate picture of the decision-making processes in the United States in contrast to those of Europe?

    a. In Europe, the legislature has the final say, whereas in the United States the president does.

    b. In the United States, policies are determined mainly by the results of discussion and debate, whereas in Europe they are determined on the basis of authority and position.

    c. In Europe, decision makers seldom come to an agreement, so few policies are changed, whereas in the United States, agreement is achieved quickly, so policies are changed often.

    d. European government is more liberal, whereas that of the United States is more conservative.

3. Identify each of the following examples as being characteristic of democratic centralism (DC), direct democracy (DD), or representative democracy (RD). Be prepared to justify your answers.

    _____ a. A new municipal tax to be used for building a recycling plant was approved by the residents of West Sentura, New York.

    _____ b. The elected legislator believed his vote in favor of gun control legislation was what the people of his district wanted.

_____ c. The national government decided it would be good for everyone if the school year were made longer, so schools were scheduled to remain open eleven months per year.

_____ d. The voters in Highland Falls, Kansas, were asked to vote on a bond referendum for renovation of the town's senior citizen center.

_____ e. The town council rejected the builder's plans because the townspeople had argued against it, saying the new housing would increase traffic congestion significantly.

4. Using the context and your knowledge of word structure, write your own definition for each of the following words:

   a. loggerheads (3)_____

   b. induced (4)_____

   c. perpetuated (8)_____

   d. unscrupulous (13)_____

   e. contending (13)_____

   f. vests (16)_____

   g. decentralized (17)_____

   h. enact (18)_____

   i. accountable (19)_____

5. What is one inference that can be made from paragraph 8? Write your inference and the evidence for it in the spaces provided.

   Inference:_____

   _____

   Evidence:_____

   _____

6. What is the purpose of paragraph 17? Be prepared to justify your answer.

   _____

   _____

7. What is the purpose of paragraph 18? Be prepared to justify your answer.

_____

_____

8. The author's tone in this article is primarily
   a. informative
   b. scientific
   c. persuasive
   d. cynical

Recalling Details

(See Chapter 4.)

1. Indicate whether each of the following is true (T) or false (F) based on the selection. Be prepared to justify your answers.

   _____ a. Labor unions are more popular in the United States than in Europe.

   _____ b. France's public school system is under the control of the national government.

   _____ c. Italy does not have a socialist party.

   _____ d. It is harder for someone to get on a ballot in Germany than it is in the United States.

   _____ e. European lawmakers have the sole power to decide whether to make abortion legal.

   _____ f. There are more government-owned automobile factories in France than in the United States.

   _____ g. The United States is a democratic nation, whereas Great Britain is not.

2. In your own words, explain why the form of government in the United States is considered to be a representative democracy.

_____

_____

3. Read the following paragraphs. Decide whether all the desirable features of a representative democracy are present in the situation described. If not, indicate what is missing.

Gienka is a province of the country of Carka, and its population consists of 840,000 Buddhists. The Carkans sectored Gienka into a separate province because of their hatred of Buddhists and their desire to maintain separate religious and ethnic identities. When this separate province was formed, the Buddhists were stripped of their Carkan citizenship and were given papers identifying them as citizens of Gienka. Originally, Gienka was to have self-rule, governmental autonomy from Carka. But instead, the Carkan government appointed an interim president for the province.

A constitution provides for elections and majority rule in Gienka, and there are several political parties, but there have been no elections. The ruler of Gienka is genuinely concerned with the province but believes it will be many years before choosing new leaders will be possible. Riots and looting that followed a protest march demanding elections resulted in the police shooting thirty-eight adults and arresting many more. There is almost no history of political self-government in Carka for the last 800 years, but there is pressure to grant more individual rights and freedoms in both Carka and the new province of Gienka.

Your reactions: _____

_____

_____

_____

_____

_____

_____

_____

4. Read each of the following details selected from the Wilson article. Decide whether each is a major (MAJ) or minor (MIN) detail. Be prepared to justify your answers.

_____ a. In the United States, fewer than one worker in five belongs to a labor union. (6)

_____ b. The United States government owns very few industries. (7)

_____ c. Once or twice a year, all the adult citizens of a town come together to vote on all major issues and expenditures. (11)

_____ d. The courts ordinarily do not interfere. (16)

_____ e. Political power at the national level is decentralized and shared. (17)

_____ f. If you don't like the federal deficit, whom can you blame and vote against in the next election? (18)

_____ g. The roadblocks in our constitutional system have not prevented our national government from growing about as fast, and adopting many of the same policies, as parliamentary democracies in Europe. (19)

Critical Thinking: Reaction and Discussion

1. With a group, discuss the following question. Prepare to share your answers with the class.

   You are a president of Bombay County, Wisconsin. The people of your county have elected Daniel Carver as mayor, who promised (during his campaign) not to raise taxes. However, seven months after he took office, Carver has raised them. What should you do? What are your responsibilities as a citizen? What are your options? Was your job done once you voted?

2. Write an essay of at least 250 words in which you discuss whether you would prefer to be a leader or a follower in a team situation. Include your reasons for feeling this way.

3. With a partner, read the poem that follows. Discuss it with each other, then answer the questions.

   Citizenship

   The good citizen

   Loves God

   Loves the Empire

   Loves Canada

   Loves his own family

   Protects women and children

   Works hard

Does his work well

Helps his neighbour

Is truthful

Is just

Is honest

Is brave

Keeps his promise

His body is clean

Is every inch of a Man.

Alfred Fitzpatrick, *Handbook for New Canadians* (Toronto: Ryerson Press, 1919), p. 56. Retrieved February 25, 2006 from *http:fcis.oise.utoronto.ca/~daniel_schugurensky/assignment1/1919citizen.html.*

a. How does this poet's view of a good citizen contrast with your own? Are there other qualities you believe a good citizen should have?

_____

_____

_____

_____

b. What can you infer about the poet's attitude toward a citizen who is involved in the political life of his community?

_____

_____

_____

_____

c. What groups or individuals might disagree with this poet's idea of a good citizen? Why would they disagree?

_____

_____

_____

_____

🖳 USING TECHNOLOGY FOR FURTHER UNDERSTANDING

1. On the Internet, locate the home page for your state's government.

    a. What information do you find there that illustrates some of the points made in this article?

    b. What information does it contain that might be useful to a new resident of your state?

2. More than 30 percent of Americans registered to vote have identified themselves as independent voters, rather than Republican or Democratic. Many of these individuals want to hear each candidate's point of view on issues before choosing their candidate. Others are less concerned with the typical issues, such as the economy, abortion, and health care. They choose, instead, a candidate who runs on a platform of making changes in the electoral process itself. Such candidates often seek changes in one or more of the following:

    Campaign finance reform

    Proportional representation

    Initiative and referendum

    Terms limits

    Instant run off voting

    Select one of these five topics to investigate on the World Wide Web. Then with your class discuss the following:

    a. What are independent voters looking for in this aspect of the electoral process?

    b. Do you believe this issue is important enough to use as a basis for electing a candidate? Explain.

    c. Based on your research on the World Wide Web, what other concerns do these voters have about the electoral process?

    d. Do you share any of their concerns? Explain.

• SELECTIONS 21 AND 22 ALTERNATIVE VIEWPOINTS

Illegal Immigration

Mark Krikorian, *The Way to Go on Immigration* • Viewpoint 1

Edwin Meese III, James Jay Carafano, Ph.D., Matthew Spalding, Ph.D., and Paul Rosenzweig, *Not Amnesty, but Attrition: The Way to Go on Immigration* • Viewpoint 2

Preview

What follows are two articles on the topic of illegal immigrants in the United States. Each expresses concern about this issue, but the authors propose different solutions. All of the authors work at policy centers; Krikorian directs the Center for Immigration Studies. Individuals who are employed by the Heritage Foundation, a conservative research and educational institute, wrote the other article. The articles are designed to make suggestions about this issue and to convince policy makers that the proposed solutions are the ones that should guide any new legislation on this issue. Before you read them, you will have a chance to reflect on your own opinions on this topic.

To Think About Before You Read

What are your thoughts on illegal immigrants in the United States? Complete the Semantic Web in the space provided, indicating what you see as the problems, causes, effects, and solutions to illegal immigration in the United States.

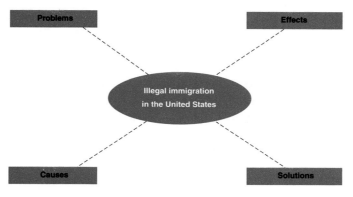

Terms to Know Before You Read

(Viewpoint 1)

Amnesty (title) a general pardon granted by a government, especially for political offenses

Hobson's choice (1) a choice without an alternative; the thing offered or nothing.

demure (3) modest

wonkish (5) from someone who studies excessively

vociferously (11) noisily

proactive (15) acting in advance to deal with an expected difficulty

precipitously (18) extremely rapidly

inadvertent (20) marked by unintentional lack of care

(Viewpoint 2)

remittances (6) sums of monies sent

exacerbates (8) increases the severity, violence, or bitterness of; aggravates

imperative (9) expressing a command or plea

leveraging (11) applying pressure to achieve a desired result

ameliorate (18) to make or become better; improve

repatriating (27) returning to the country of birth

Viewpoint I

The issue of what to do about illegal aliens living in the United States is often presented as a Hobson's choice: either launch mass roundups to arrest and deport 9-million-plus people, or define away the problem through legalization. The second option—amnesty—is the one President Bush chose in his January 7 speech on immigration. It also underlies many congressional proposals, from the McCain-Kolbe-Flake and Hagel-Daschle bills in the Senate to the House Democratic leadership's proposal unveiled in late January.

Few among the political elite entertain any [2] alternative. At a recent panel discussion on the president's immigration proposal, Margaret Spellings, the president's chief domestic policy adviser, reacted with a demure chuckle to the suggestion that we enforce the law.

The commentariat is more explicit. Not [3] content to politely ignore the notion of enforcing the law, the *Wall Street Journal,* for instance, has flatly asserted that it's not possible, a "fantasy" of the "extreme," "nativist," and "restrictionist" Right. Meanwhile, the Manhattan Institute's Tamar Jacoby wrote in *The New Republic* of "futile law enforcement" and how "the migrant flow is inevitable."

4   Fortunately for America there is a third way, between the politically impossible and disruptive approach of mass roundups on one hand, and the surrender of our sovereignty by the open-borders Left and its libertarian fellow-travelers on the other. This third way is attrition, squeezing the illegal population through consistent, across-the-board law enforcement to bring about an annual reduction in the illegal population rather than the annual increases we have seen for more than a decade. Over a few years, the number of illegal aliens would drop significantly, shrinking the problem from a crisis to a manageable nuisance.

OF VELVET FISTS

5   This isn't just a wonkish daydream. There is significant churn in the illegal population, which we can use to our advantage. According to a 2003 INS report, thousands of people stop being illegal aliens each year. From 1995 to 1999, an average of 165,000 a year went back home; the same number got some kind of legal status, about 50,000 were deported, and 25,000 died, for a total of more than 400,000 people each year subtracted from the resident illegal population. The problem is that the average inflow of new illegal aliens was nearly 800,000, swamping the outflow and creating an average annual increase of close to 400,000.

6   The solution, then, is to increase the number of people leaving the illegal population and to reduce the number of new illegal settlers, so that there is an annual decline in the total number. This is a measured, Burkean approach to the problem. It doesn't aspire to an immediate, magical solution to a long-brewing crisis, but rather helps us back out of an untenable situation that we helped create through our inattention to the law.

This begs the natural question: "But aren't 7 we already enforcing the law?" If not, as a *Wall Street Journal* editorial has asked, "Then what is it we've been doing for 20 years now?" The answer lies in the old Soviet joke: "We pretend to work and they pretend to pay us."

Since 1986, Congress has passed muscular 8 immigration laws and then made sure that they were not enforced. In that year, the Immigration Reform and Control Act (IRCA) was enacted, which traded an illegal-alien amnesty for a first-ever ban on the employment of illegal aliens. The point was to demagnetize the strong pull of good jobs—the main reason illegals come here in the first place.

More than 2.7 million illegals got legalized 9 up front, with promises of tighter enforcement in the future. But the law itself was hobbled such that it became unworkable. Only if employers had a means of verifying the legal status of new hires against Social Security or INS databases could the law succeed—but Congress refused to require the INS to start developing such a system. Instead, employers were expected to do the verifying themselves, by examining a bewildering array of easily forged documents, and then they were threatened with discrimination lawsuits by the Justice Department if they looked too hard. It would be hard to imagine a system more obviously intended to fail.

Eventually, even this handicapped setup was 10 sabotaged. After catching flak for workplace raids, the INS in 1998 decided to try a new approach to enforcing the hiring ban. Instead of raiding individual employers, Operation Vanguard sought to identify illegal workers at all the meatpacking plants in Nebraska through audits of personnel records. The INS then asked to interview those employees who appeared to be unauthorized—and the illegals ran off. The procedure was remarkably successful, and was meant to be repeated every two or three months until the whole industry was weaned from dependence on illegal labor.

11   Local police were very pleased with the results, but employers and politicians vociferously criticized the very idea of enforcing the immigration law. Nebraska's governor Mike Johanns organized a task force to oppose the operation; the meat packers and the ranchers hired his predecessor, Ben Nelson, to lobby on their behalf; and, in Washington, Sen. Chuck Hagel made it his mission in life to pressure the Justice Department to stop. The INS took the hint, and all but gave up on enforcing the hiring ban nationwide.

12   Nor is this the only example of tough-looking laws that go unenforced. In 1996, Congress passed a large immigration bill, which included a provision that sought to punish long-term illegal residence by barring illegals from future re-entry for three or ten years, depending on the length of the initial unlawful stay. Its scope was limited in any case, since it applied only to people who actually left the country and then tried to return, but it was denounced at the time by the usual suspects as "radical" and "draconian." But an examination of the law's results shows that, in its first four years, the bar prevented fewer than 12,000 people from re-entering the United States.

13   Even the expansion of border enforcement follows this pattern of ineffectuality. The Border Patrol has doubled in size since 1996, accounting for the lion's share of increased resources for enforcement. Its 10,000 agents are better equipped and doing a better job than ever before. But since, as any agent will tell you, the Border Patrol alone can't control illegal immigration, there's little danger that such increased capacity will actually curtail the flow. Again, a policy that appears tough, but isn't—a velvet fist in an iron glove.

NETWORKING

Why does this happen? It is a manifestation of 14 the yawning gap between public and elite opinion on immigration. The laws need to look tough, with promises of robust enforcement, to satisfy public concerns. But immigration's relatively low political importance for most people ensures that the elite preference for loose enforcement will be satisfied in the end.

But isn't the elite right in this case? Isn't immigration inevitable? Hardly. No one wakes up in Paraguay and decides, "Today, I will move to Sheboygan!" Immigration can take place only if there are networks of relatives, friends, and countrymen directing immigrants to a particular place. And these networks are a creation of government policy, either through proactive measures or through permitting networks to grow through non-enforcement of the law.

As an example, look at the Philippines and 16 Indonesia. Both are populous, poor countries on the other side of the world, and yet the 2000 Census found about 19 times more Filipino immigrants in the United States than Indonesians, 1.4 million versus 73,000. Why? Because we ruled the Philippines for 50 years as a colony and maintained a major military presence there for another 50 years, allowing extensive networks to develop, whereas we have historically had little to do with Indonesia.

17   Granted, interrupting such networks is harder than creating them, but it is not impossible—after all, the trans-Atlantic immigration networks from the turn of the last century were successfully interrupted, and atrophied completely. And, to move beyond theory, the few times we actually tried to enforce the immigration law, it worked—until we gave up for political reasons.

18   During the first several years after the passage of the IRCA, illegal crossings from Mexico fell precipitously, as prospective illegals waited to see if we were serious. Apprehensions of aliens by the Border Patrol—an imperfect measure but the only one available—fell from more than 1.7 million in FY 1986 to under a million in 1989. But then the flow began to increase again as the deterrent effect of the hiring ban dissipated, when word got back that we were not serious about enforcement and that the system could be easily evaded through the use of inexpensive phony documents.

19   As I've written in these pages before, when we stepped up immigration enforcement against Middle Easterners (and only Middle Easterners) in the wake of 9/11, the largest group of illegals from that part of the world, Pakistanis, fled the country in droves to avoid being caught up in the dragnet.

20   And in an inadvertent enforcement initiative, the Social Security Administration in 2002 sent out almost a million "no-match" letters to employers who filed W-2s with information that was inconsistent with SSA's records. The intention was to clear up misspellings, name changes, and other mistakes that had caused a large amount of money paid into the system to go uncredited. But, of course, most of the problem was caused by illegal aliens lying to their employers, and thousands of illegals quit or were fired when they were found out. The effort was so successful at denying work to illegals that business and immigrant-rights groups organized to stop it and won a 90 percent reduction in the number of letters to be sent out.

WAR OF ATTRITION

21   We know that when we actually enforce the law, eroding the illegal-immigration population is possible. So, what would a policy of attrition look like? It would have two key components. The first would include more conventional enforcement—arrests, prosecutions, deportations, asset seizures, etc. The second would require verification of legal status at a variety of important choke points, to make it as difficult and unpleasant as possible to live here illegally.

22   As to the first, the authorities need to start taking immigration violations seriously. To use only one example, people who repeatedly sneak across the border are supposed to be prosecuted and jailed, and the Border Patrol unveiled a new digital fingerprint system in the mid '90s to make tracking of repeat crossers possible. The problem is that short-staffed U.S. attorneys' offices kept increasing the number of apprehensions needed before they would prosecute, to avoid actually having to prosecute at all.

23   It would be hard to exaggerate the demoralizing effect that such disregard for the law has on the Homeland Security Department's staff. Conversely, the morale of immigration workers would soar in the wake of a real commitment to law enforcement. We've already seen a real-world example of this, too. I met with deportation officers in a newly formed "fugitive operations team" in Southern California who, unlike other immigration personnel I have spoken with, were actually excited about their jobs. They still have gripes, but the clear political commitment to locating and deporting fugitive aliens communicates to them that their

work is genuinely valued by their superiors all the way up to the White House.

24 Other measures that would facilitate enforcement include hiring more U.S. Attorneys and judges in border areas, to allow for more prosecutions; passage of the CLEAR Act, which would enhance cooperation between federal immigration authorities and state and local police; and seizing the assets, however modest, of apprehended illegal aliens.

25 But these and other enforcement measures will not remove most of the illegal population—the majority of illegals will have to be persuaded to deport themselves. Unlike at the visa office or the border crossing, once aliens are inside the United States, there's no physical place, no choke point at which to examine whether someone should be admitted. The solution is to create "virtual chokepoints"— events that are necessary for life in a modern society but are infrequent enough not to bog down the business of society.

26 This is the thinking behind the law banning the employment of illegal aliens—people have to work, so requiring proof of legal status upon starting a job would serve as such a virtual choke point. As discussed above, in the absence of a verification mechanism, such a system couldn't succeed. But the president signed into law at the end of last year a measure to reauthorize and expand the verification pilot programs that immigration authorities have been experimenting with since the mid 1990s.

27 Building on this fledgling system, we need to find other instances in which legal status can be verified, such as getting a driver's license, registering an automobile, opening a bank account, applying for a car loan or a mortgage, enrolling children in public schools, and getting a business or occupational license.

28 An effective strategy of immigration law en-

forcement requires no booby traps, no tanks, no tattoos on arms—none of the cartoonish images invoked in the objections raised routinely by the loose-borders side. The consistent application of ordinary law-enforcement tools is all we need. "Consistent," though, is the key word. Enforcement personnel—whether they are Border Patrol agents, airport inspectors, or plainclothes investigators—need to know that their work is valued, that their superiors actually want them to do the jobs they've been assigned, and that they will be backed up when the inevitable complaints roll in.

29 And, finally, this isn't root-canal Republicanism, bitter medicine we swallow for the greater good. Enforcement of the immigration law may not be popular among the elite, but actual voters across the political spectrum all are for it. As Alan Wolfe wrote in *One Nation, After All,* the difference between legal and illegal immigrants "is one of the most tenaciously held distinctions in middle-class America; the people with whom we spoke overwhelmingly support legal immigration and express disgust with the illegal variety."

30 If only our political leadership felt the same way.

Viewpoint 2

For the sake of national security, the rule of law, and responsible immigration policy, Congress and the President must take credible steps to reduce the number of individuals who are unlawfully present in the United States. Immigration reform must not encourage or exacerbate this problem.

2 In particular, any new initiative must not grant permission, as a matter of principle or policy, for unlawfully present persons to re-

main legally in the country. Such a program would undermine the credibility of efforts not only to control America's borders, but also to advance reasonable legal immigration reform.

3   A better alternative would be for policymakers to establish a comprehensive solution that fosters better national security, a growing economy, and a strong civil society. Part of this solution should be a realistic and reasonable program to assist unlawfully present individuals in returning to their countries of origin before applying for legal reentry to the United States.

WHY WE CARE

4   Estimates of the number of undocumented foreign workers in the United States vary widely.

  * In March 2005, a Pew Hispanic Center report estimated the number of currently undocumented U.S. residents at nearly 11 million, based on extrapolations of data from the U.S. Census Bureau's 2004 Current Population Survey and estimates that annual net growth of unauthorized migrants has averaged about 500,000 since 1990. Of the 11 million total, over 7 million were undocumented workers.

  * The Federation for American Immigration Reform estimates that 13 million illegal immigrants live in the United States, which translates into approximately 9 million unlawful foreign workers.

  * A widely cited (and challenged) estimate by a senior managing director at Bear Stearns calculates that as many as 20 million illegal immigrants could now reside in the United States. If correct, this figure implies that as many as 15 million undocumented workers could be employed here.

5   There are no signs that the overall trends of illegal entry and unlawful presence in the United States will change any time soon. As long as the economies of nations on or near our borders do not provide sufficient jobs to keep up with their population growth, their citizens will look elsewhere and seek to cross our border in search of work.

6   According to a Pew Hispanic Center study in 2003, individuals working in the United States sent almost $30 billion to their families in Latin America and the Caribbean. As the single largest form of direct foreign investment in the region, in many cases providing families with essential goods and services such as food and rent, remittances have become the economic engine of Latin America. Figures do not make distinctions between the sources of remittances, but contributions from undocumented workers are undoubtedly significant. As long as the unprecedented economic importance of remittances remains, individuals will seek access to the United States labor market by legal or illegal means.

7   Opportunities for undocumented workers in the United States encourage thousands to enter the United States illegally each month. At legal points of entry, such as seaports, airports, and established border crossings, the Department of Homeland Security (DHS) has implemented and is improving mechanisms for screening people and cargo to identify legitimate security threats, including terrorists, transnational criminals, and illicit cargo. However, many cross into the country at places other than the established points of entry, and the DHS cannot easily distinguish national security threats from other criminal activities along the territory and coastline between the legal points of entry.

8   The wave of illegal entry along this vast expanse significantly exacerbates the challenge of border security. Additionally, illegal border crossings put lives and property at risk for the individuals crossing, for those enforcing the law, and for local communities. In some areas, crime, property damage, and the risk of death from austere environmental conditions or reckless acts are becoming endemic. All of these factors force the DHS to deploy ever-greater resources to the point at which they are arguably less effective in achieving the department's primary purpose— safeguarding the nation against terrorists.

9   From a national security perspective, reducing illegal entry and unlawful presence in the United States is an imperative. Although border security efforts ought to be strengthened and expanded, it is doubtful that even dramatic additional investment in border security by itself will stem the tide of undocumented workers.

10   Rather than diverting exorbitant resources to the task of attempting to guard every mile of the border, why not make it in the interest of those seeking legitimate employment to enter this country through lawful means? This would make the task of policing borders and coastline more manageable. When the only individuals seeking to enter the United States illicitly are terrorists and transnational criminals, meeting the challenge of securing our borders will be more realistic. Under these conditions, everyone benefits—except the lawbreakers.

WHAT WE NEED

11   What is required is a comprehensive strategy that reverses decades of ignoring, indeed encouraging, the disregard of requirements for legally entering and lawfully residing in this country. An appropriate strategy would:

* **Require** and provide resources to enforce laws within the United States, including prosecuting benefits fraud, identity theft, tax evasion, and immigration violations.
* **Engage** the cooperation of federal, state, and local governments and non-governmental organizations.
* **Work** with other nations to enforce laws, to educate their citizens, and to develop more desirable legal alternatives for undocumented workers, such as allowing temporary workers to receive credit in their home countries' retirement systems.
* **Encourage** other nations to adopt sound governance and economic policies that will promote growth in their economies and negate the need for citizens to take low-paying jobs in the United States.
* **Enable** the private sector by allowing employers to identify lawful workers quickly and easily at a reasonable cost and in a manner that respects individuals' rights and privacy.
* **Create** alternatives to cumbersome, bureaucratic, government-run programs by leveraging the capacity of the private sector to develop innovative and effective solutions for bringing temporary workers to the United States and managing them.
* **Improve** the infrastructure at the points of entry and vastly enhance customer service for immigration and non-immigration support programs—such as visa issuance and monitoring and screening people and cargo—so that they speed rather than inhibit the legitimate flow of goods, people, and services across America's borders.

12   When the legal means of entry into the United States are perceived as more safe and ad-

vantageous for them, workers will have every incentive to respect the rule of law.

THE AMNESTY PROBLEM

13 A comprehensive system to encourage legal entry has little prospect for success unless the United States can reduce a thriving and prospering population of undocumented workers and benefit recipients. To address this issue, several policymakers have discussed the idea of a new "temporary worker program" that, among other things, would grant potentially millions of individuals who currently are unlawfully present in the United States the right to work legally in this country provided that U.S. employers could not find suitable American workers for the positions.

14 In recent months, proposals to this effect have been introduced in Congress. At issue in all of these proposals is the question of "amnesty." While most discussions oppose amnesty in general, consistent with long-standing principles of law and recent immigrant reform experience, there is no consensus on the exact meaning of the term.

15 Some define "amnesty" as the granting of American citizenship and stress that the reform proposals would not affect existing nationalization procedures. President Bush, for instance, has said: "I oppose amnesty, placing undocumented workers on the automatic path to 16 citizenship."

This use of the term is atypical. With respect to immigration, amnesty is most commonly defined as granting legal status to individuals unlawfully present in the United States, which all of the proposals certainly would do. It does not get around the amnesty problem to assert that an undocumented worker would not gain an unfair advantage in applications for citizenship or permanent worker (green card) status

over those foreigners who followed the law and applied for such status without working illegally in the United States.

17 While each of these proposals may have some merits, they are still fatally flawed in this respect: Regardless of the penalties imposed, any program that grants individuals who are unlawfully present legal permission to remain here rewards illegal behavior and will only encourage others to emulate them. As President Bush has also said, "Granting amnesty encourages violation of our laws, and perpetuates illegal immigration."

18 Any reform of U.S. immigration policies must adhere to the core set of principles that have governed laws in this area for decades. Programs that allow unlawfully present persons to remain in the country legally fail on at least three counts.

* Considerations of national security require the federal government to control entry and exit across U.S. borders. Any measure that would increase illegal entry would violate this principle. These programs would likely increase rather than ameliorate the problem and are thus unacceptable.
* Any changes in immigration policies should respect the sentiments of the American people. The fact that most Americans would not consent to special considerations for those who have willfully violated U.S. immigration laws should weigh heavily in congressional deliberations.
* The rule of law requires the fair, firm, and equitable enforcement of immigration policies. Rewarding unlawful behavior while disadvantaging those who have chosen to "play by the rules" violates the principal of fairness.

19   In short, any program that does not require lawbreakers to leave the United States and reenter through legal means if they wish to reside here will never satisfy the tenets of good immigration law and sound security practices.

PAST EXPERIENCE

20   There is, in fact, already ample evidence to suggest that these approaches will not work. In 1986, Congress enacted the Immigration Reform and Control Act, which contained an extensive if complex amnesty program that provided for temporary legal status in the United States, with few impediments against obtaining green card status for illegal aliens involved in agricultural work or who could show that they had been living in the United States for four years since 1982. Its drafters vastly underestimated the number of aliens who would seek to legalize their status. The overwhelmed authorities could justify denying only a small percentage of the claimants despite the widespread submission of fraudulent applications. Enforcement of the new provisions sanctioning employers who continued to hire undocumented workers was minimal.

21   In the three months following the announcement of the Administration's willingness to permit foreigners already working inside the United States to participate in its temporary worker program, the number of illegal aliens apprehended along the southwestern border soared 25 percent over the same period during the previous year. More generally, immigration generally promotes further immigration since new arrivals bring with them a network of familial and other ties. These connections in turn weigh favorably in nonresidents' decisions about whether or not to take up residence in the new country.

22   Nor is the American experience unique. For instance, Malaysian officials have concluded that, despite extensive enforcement measures, their recent amnesty program for undocumented foreign workers has not helped to reduce the number of illegal immigrants in their country.

23   Another case in point is a recent initiative in Spain. Aware of the problems that typically plague such amnesty programs, members of the European Union (EU) roundly denounced the Spanish government when it decided earlier this year to offer amnesty and one-year residence and work permits to illegal immigrants who could prove that they had lived in Spain for at least six months, had no criminal record, and had a firm offer of employment in Spain for at least six months. EU members fear that the Spanish program, which ended in early May 2005, will encourage foreigners seeking work in Europe to enter Spain first and then, exploiting the right of residents of one European state to live and work anywhere in the EU, to settle in other European countries.

AN ALTERNATIVE PROPOSAL

24 For any package of immigration reforms to be considered credible, it must address the significant population of persons unlawfully present in the United States. As an encouragement for illegal residents to gain legal status and as a deterrent to potential future lawbreakers, U.S. law must insist that individuals currently in the country who have violated immigration statutes must leave and apply for admission through legal means. Combined with the consistent enforcement of immigration laws within the United States and the enhancement of the legal alternatives for entering and residing in the country, this requirement will serve as a powerful disin-

centive to most, other than perhaps terrorists and transnational criminals, from attempting to cross America's borders illicitly.

25   The challenge is to create policies that can be fairly and practically implemented. It is unrealistic to assume that millions of undocumented workers will simply leave, just as it would be practically impossible to force each of them to return to their countries of origin.

26   The responsible course of action is to establish return programs that, except for repeat offenders and felony-criminal offenses, are voluntary in nature. These must be supported by humanitarian initiatives that protect the safety and legal rights of individuals, regardless of immigration status. At a minimum, reforms should:

* **Require** the Administration to enter into compacts with key nations to facilitate the return of their citizens and reward nations that develop robust programs that assist in significantly reducing the unlawful population in the United States.
* **Engage** non-governmental organizations and stakeholders in establishing humanitarian support programs to assist undocumented workers in returning to their host countries.
* **Establish** that unlawfully present individuals who voluntarily leave the United States, have no criminal record, and register with authorities before leaving through the US-VISIT program can apply for legal entry to the United States without prejudice.
* **Create** a national trust fund based on voluntary contributions to assist in covering the expenses of returning undocumented workers to their host countries.

CONCLUSION

27   Immigration reform should be a matter of national priority. To be successful, reforms must include a comprehensive package of measures to reduce illegal entry into the United States as well as to reduce the current population of unlawfully present persons. The cornerstone of any such initiative must be a fair and practical program for repatriating foreign persons who are illegally present in the United States.

Evaluation of the Articles

Difficulty Rating □ 1 □ 2 □ 3 □ 4 □ 5
(1 = easy; 5 = difficult)

What reading difficulties did you encounter? _____

_____

How did you handle these difficulties? _____

_____

Postreading Comprehension Development

1. On the lines provided, write a main-idea sentence for each of the two articles, using the starter sentence provided.

   Author: Krikorian *The author wants me to understand that:*

   _____

   _____

   Authors: Meese et al. *The authors want me to understand that:*

   _____

   _____

2. In which paragraph do the specific recommendations for solving the problem of illegal immigration begin in Krikorian's article?
   a. 21
   b. 22
   c. 23
   d. 24

3. In which paragraph do the specific recommendations for solving the problem of illegal immigration begin in the article by Meese et al?
   a. 23
   b. 24
   c. 25
   d. 26

4. In your own words, what do you see as important differences between these recommendations in terms of each of the following:
   a. the role of employers: _____

   _____

   _____

   b. the role of the federal government: _____

   _____

   _____

c. the consequences to illegal immigrants: _____

_____

_____

d. the expected results of the plan: _____

_____

_____

5. Why do you think these articles wait until midpoint to begin making specific recommendations? Write your explanation on the lines provided.

_____

_____

6. What are some major details the author/s gave to support his/their point of view? List four major details sentences from each article. Next to each detail, identify the type of detail it is.

Author: Krikorian

a. Major Detail: _____

   Type of detail: _____

b. Major Detail: _____

   Type of detail: _____

c. Major Detail: _____

   Type of detail: _____

d. Major Detail : _____

   Type of detail: _____

Authors: Meese et al.

a. Major Detail: _____

Type of detail: _____

b. Major Detail: _____

Type of detail: _____

c. Major Detail: _____

Type of detail: _____

d. Major Detail : _____

Type of detail: _____

7. Krikorian refers to the current policies as "a velvet fist in an iron glove." What details does he provide in his article that justify this metaphor?

_____

_____

8. How effective were the statistics used in each article? Give reasons for your opinions in the space provided.

Author: Krikorian _____

_____

Authors: Meese et al. _____

_____

9. In your opinion, which author/s did the best job of offering a well-designed plan to address illegal immigration? Explain your answer on the lines provided.

_____

_____

_____

Critical Thinking: Reaction and Discussion

1. Refer back to the To Think About Before You Read section at the beginning of these articles. How did reading and thinking about these articles effect your ideas? Take another look at the Semantic Web you created before reading these articles and add any new ideas you have for each of the four sections.

2. Both of these articles have rejected amnesty as a solution to the problem of illegal immigration. What do you think? Should illegal immigrants currently in the U.S. be given amnesty? How would this work? Who would benefit? What, if any, would be some undesirable outcomes? With a group, discuss the following topic. Be prepared to share your conclusions with your class.

   Illegal immigrants currently in the U.S. should (should not) be given amnesty.

3. With a group, prepare a set of questions you could use to interview someone who has immigrated to the United States during the past five to ten years. Decide what it is you want to know, and create your questions with these goals in mind. Then interview two individuals. Be prepared to share your findings with the class.

USING TECHNOLOGY FOR FURTHER UNDERSTANDING

1. In 2005, President George W. Bush proposed a "guest worker program." Use the Internet to locate information on his proposal and comment on ways it differs from and/or is similar to the proposals the authors make in their articles.

2. Select one issue that is listed below and use the Internet to locate different viewpoints on it. Create a Contrast Box (Chapter 5) that shows these different positions. Beneath the box, list the websites you have used. Beneath the website list, write your conclusion on this issue.

   Legal driver's licenses for illegal immigrants
   Education in public schools for illegal immigrants
   In-state college tuition for illegal immigrants
   Professional work visas for illegal immigrants
   Free health care for illegal immigrants
   English as the official language in the U.S.

APPENDIX

Readability Levels for Essays*

Psychology

What Psychology Is   12.0
Understanding the Terrorist Mind-Set   12.0
The "Perfect" Trap   9.1
Television Addiction Is No Mere Metaphor   11.0

Sociology

The Sociological Perspective   11.5
Blown Away by School Violence   10.7
Here Comes the Groom   11.8
The Threat of Same-Sex Marriage   10.6

The Sciences

The Nature of Science   12.0
The Drunken Monkey Hypothesis   12.0
Natural Disasters: Earthquakes and Tsunamis   12.0

Business

Making Work Meaningful   12.0
Who Are the Pirates?   12.0
Coke's Sinful World   12.0
El Millonario Next Door   12.0

History

Why History?   11.0
Kidnapped, Enslaved, and Sold Away, (c. 1756)   9.6
A Place Without History   12.0

Political Science

Politics: Setting the Stage   12.0
What Should We Know About American Government?   11.6
The Way to Go on Immigration   12.0
Alternatives to Amnesty: Proposals for Fair and Effective Immigration Reform   12.0

*Based on the Flesch-Kincaid Grade Level formula.

CREDITS

Approach, 4/e. Published by Allyn and Bacon, Boston, MA. Copyright © 1999 by Pearson Education. Reprinted by permission of the publisher. **pp. 409–11** "Blown Away by School Violence," by Donna Harrington-Lueker, from *The Education Digest*, November 1992. Excerpted with permission of American School Board Journal, Copyright © 1992, National School Boards Association. All rights reserved. **pp. 420–23** Andrew Sullivan, "Here Comes the Groom." Reprinted by permission of *The New Republic*, © 1989, The New Republic, LLC. **pp. 423–27** Msgr. Robert Sokolowski, "The Threat of Same-Sex Marriage," *America*, Vol. 190, No. 19 p. 12. Copyright 2004 America Magazine. All rights reserved. Reproduced by permission of America Press. For subscription information, visit www.americamagazine.org **pp. 438–42** Excerpt from *Science for All Americans* by American Association for the Advancement of Science, copyright © 1989, 1990 by American Association for the Advancement of Science. Used by permission of Oxford University Press, Inc. **pp. 450–54** Dustin Stephens and Robert Dudley, "The Drunken Monkey Hypothesis." Reprinted from *Natural History*, Dec 2004/Jan 2005; copyright © 2005 Natural History Magazine, Inc. **pp. 466–67** Chernicoff, S. and Haydn, A., "Earthquakes and the Earth's Interior," *Essentials of Geology*, 3/e, HMCO, 2003, pp. 197–202, including Figure

10–3, "The Anatomy of an earthquake." Copyright © 2003 by Houghton Mifflin Company. Reprinted with permission **pp. 481–87** Roger E. Herman and Joyce L. Gioia, "Making Work Meaningful: Secrets of the Future-Focused Corporation," originally published in the December 1998 issue of *The Futurist*. Used with the permission of the World Future Society, 9910 Woodmont Avenue, Bethesda, MD. 20910. www.wfs.org **pp. 493–98** Jack Bishop, "Who are the Pirates? The Politics of Piracy, Poverty, and Greed in a Globalized Music Market," *Popular Music and Society*, Vol. 27, No. 1, 2004, pp. 101–106. Reprinted by permission of Taylor & Francis Ltd, <http:www.tandf.co.uk/journal **pp. 506–10** Paul Klebnikov, "Coke's Sinful World," *Forbes*, 12/22/2003, Vol. 172 Issue 13, pp. 86–92. Reprinted by Permission of Forbes Magazine © 2005 Forbes Inc. **pp. 519–26** Tyce Palmaffy, "El Millionario Next Door," *Policy Review*, July/August, 1998, p. 30–35. Reprinted by permission. **pp. 536–42** "Why History?", by F. Otnes. This article is reproduced from our March/April 1991 issue of *American History Illustrated* with the permission of PRIMEDIA Special Interest Publications (History Group), copyright American History Illustrated. **pp. 551–55** *The Interesting Narrative of the Life of Olaudah Equiano, or Gustavus Vassa, the African*, [London, 1784.], in David

Northrup, ed., *The Atlantic Slave Trade* (Lexington, MA: D.C. Heath, 1994), pp. 74–80. **pp. 563–68** Reprinted with permission of *Archaeology Magazine*, Volume 58, Number 5 (Copyright the Archaeological Institute of America, 2005) **pp. 578–82** W. Phillips Shively, "Politics: Setting the Stage," *Power and Choice: An Introduction to Political Science*, 8/e. New York: McGraw Hill, pp. 2–5, and 13–16. Reproduced with permission of The McGraw-Hill Companies. **pp. 592–96** Source: Wilson/DiIulio, "The Study of American Government," pp. 3–5, from *American Government*, 7th edition. Copyright © 2005 by Houghton Mifflin Company. Reprinted with permission. **pp. 606–10** Mark Krikorian, "Not Amnesty, But Attrition," *National Review*, 3/22/2004, Vol. 56 Issue 5, pp. 38–41. © 2004 by National Review, Inc., 215 Lexington Avenue, New York, NY 10016. Reprinted by permission. **pp. 610–15** "Alternatives to Amnesty: Proposals for Fair and Effective Immigration Reform" by Edwin Meese III, James Jay Carafano, Ph.D., Matthew Spalding, Ph.D., and Paul Rosenzweig, *The Heritage Foundation*, June 2, 2005. Reprinted by permission. **pp. 578–82** Source: Sylvia Mader, *Biology: Inquiry Into Life* (Dubuque, IA: Wm. C. Brown Publishers), Figure 17.16. Reproduced with permission of The McGraw-Hill Companies.

INDEX

A

Abridged dictionaries, 61, 66
Academic self-esteem and assessment
    survey, 3–6, 334–336
Active (positive) listening, 296–301
    See also Listening
Activists, 576
Affixes, 54–60, 62
Agrarian society, 534
Alienation, 392
American government, 591–596
Anthropology, 398
Antonym context clues, 42–44
Appearance of speaker, 299
Archaic words, in dictionary, 65
Arguments, 111, 112
Arrays:
    hierarchical, 169–171
    linear, 171–172
Assessments:
    of academic self-esteem, 3–6, 334–336
    of new knowledge, 333–335
    of reading comprehension, 29–30
    of textbooks, 11–14
Assets, 478
Assumptions, author, 241, 243
Authoritativeness of Web resources, 240,
    241
Authors:
    bias and assumptions of, 241, 243
    focus of, 84, 91
    mood and tone of, 212–219, 221
    organization of, 137
    qualifications of, 201
    restating ideas of, 18–19
    style of, 207–212
    See also Main ideas; Point of view

B

Background essays:
    business, 480–487, 492–498,
        505–510, 518–526
    history, 535–542, 550–555, 562–568,
        591–596, 605–615
    psychology, 341–351, 352–364,
        365–376, 377–390
    readability levels for, 621
    sciences, 436–442, 449–455, 464–470
    sociology, 394–407, 408–418,
        419–427

Background knowledge, 29–30
Balance of trade, 478
Bar graphs:
    details on, 276–277
    inferences from, 283
    previewing, 262–264
    as visual aid type, 251, 252
    See also Graphs
Basco, Monica Ramirez, 365–376
Base (root) words, 54–60, 62
Behavior, 340
Bias, author, 241, 243
    See also Point of view
Biology, 435
Body language, 296
Borum, Randy, 352–364
Bureaucracy, 576
Business, 477–532
    background essays in, 480–487,
        492–498, 505–510, 518–526
    comprehension of essays on, 488–489,
        498–503, 511–516, 526–531
    critical thinking about, 490, 503–504,
        516–517, 531–532
    detail recall from, 502–503, 514–516,
        530–531
    guidelines for reading, 490–491
    inferences and metaphors in, 500–501,
        512–514, 528–530
    key concepts for study, 478–479
    main ideas in, 499, 511–512, 527
    previewing essays on, 480–481,
        492–493, 505–506, 518–519
    readability levels for essays in, 621
    rewriting sentences from, 498–499,
        511, 526–527
    visual aids for, 491
    visual aids related to, 491
    vocabulary in context, 500–501,
        512–514, 528–530
    vocabulary terms for, 478–479, 493,
        506, 519
    Web resources for, 490, 504, 517, 532

C

Carafano, James Jay, 605, 610–615
Cartoons, political, 585
Cause and effect pattern, 138, 148–151,
    548
Cause pattern, 148–149

Chapters:
    assessment of learning, 28–29
    defined, 76
    introductions to, 11–12
    predicting content in, 329–330
    previewing, 14, 329–330
    questions related to, 12
    reading strategies, 76, 81
    subtopics in, 76, 78–81, 310
    summaries of, 12
    titles and subtitles for, 11, 76–77
Charts, 249–251
    defined, 12
    drawing conclusions from, 287
    flowcharts, 171–172, 250–251
    inferences from, 283
    sciences essays, 447
    software for creating, 561
    tree charts, 249
    See also Visual aids
Chernicoff, S., 464–470
Chronological order, history, 548
Circle graphs:
    as comprehension aid, 258
    connecting to text, 279
    example of, 247
    inferences from, 284
    predictions from, 270–271
    purpose of, 279, 521
    See also Graphs
Civil liberties, 576
Civil rights, 576
Classification, 142
Class (social), 392
Clauses, dependent and independent,
    19, 20–23
Clues, context, *See* Context clues
College vs. high school, 8, 10
Colors in visual aids, 272
Common-sense beliefs, 403–406
Common-sense context clues, 49–50
Communication:
    barriers to, 299–300
    connecting with speaker, 296–297
    non-verbal, 296
    positive listening, 296–301
    tone of, 213
Comparison and contrast box, 172–173
Comparison and contrast patterns,
    144–146

Comparison and contrast patterns (*cont.*)
    as organizational pattern, 138, 144–146
    signal words for, 144
    visual aids and, 172–175
Comparison pattern, 144
Competition, 478
Complete predicates, 20
Comprehension, *See* Reading
    comprehension
Computers:
    addiction to, 383–384
    software for graphics creating, 561
    spell checkers on, 69
    See also Web resources
Concentration, 297–298
Concept maps, 165–167
Conclusions, 229–236
    defined, 229–230
    drawing from critical reading, 229–236
    drawing from visual aids, 281–289
    drawing from Web resources, 241,
        243–244
    evidence for accepting, 234–236
    identifying, 231–234
    and prior knowledge, 285
    reflections on, 234, 236
Confusion, 300
Conjunctions, 19
Consumerism, 478
Content choices, 188–189
Context, 37, 61
Context clues, 37–53
    antonym clues, 42–44
    benefits of, 37–40
    common-sense clues, 49–50
    contrast clues, 42–44
    definition clues, 45–46
    example clues, 46–48
    experience clues, 49–50
    illustration clues, 46–48
    processing for use, 40–42
    restatement clues, 44–45
    review of, 50
    summary activity on, 51–53
    synonym clues, 44–45
    types of, 42–53
    usefulness of, 42–53
    See also Vocabulary
Contrast context clues, 42–44
Coordinating conjunctions, 19
Cornell method of notetaking, 312–315
Critical reading, 182–245
    analysis of Web-based material,
        236–244
    applying understanding of, 220, 245
    author qualifications and, 201
    author style and, 207–212
    choices and, 182–183, 196
    content choices and, 188–189

defined, 183
drawing conclusions from, 229–236
evidence to support opinions, 197–201
explanation and examples of, 183–188
fact vs. opinion in, 189–206
inferences in, 221–229
judging facts and opinions in,
    189–206
language choices, 188–189
mood and tone identification in,
    212–219, 221
points of view in, 202–206
of Web resources, 236–244
Critical thinking:
    about business essays, 490, 503–504,
        516–517, 531–532
    about history essays, 547, 560–561,
        573–574, 619
    about political science essays, 588,
        602–604
    about psychology essays, 349, 364,
        375–376, 389–390
    about sciences essays, 445–446,
        460–461, 476
    about sociology essays, 402–406, 418,
        431–433
    choices and, 182–183
    content choices and, 188–189
    language choices and, 188–189
Cross-referencing notes, 319
Csikszentmihalyi, Mihaly, 377–390
"Curve of forgetting," 321

D
Dated notes, 310
Decision-making strategies, 175
Definition and explanation pattern, 138,
    142–144
Definition context clues, 45–46
Definitions of words, 40–53, 68
    See also Context clues; Dictionaries
Dependent clauses, 19, 20–23
Descriptive details, 111, 112
Details, 107–136
    applying understanding of, 134
    in business essays, 502–503, 514–516,
        530–531
    citing facts or statistics, 111, 114
    descriptions as, 111, 112
    examples or illustrations as, 111, 113
    in history essays, 559–560, 572–573
    identifying types of, 115–118
    listening for, 297–298
    major and minor, 123–134
    map of, 130
    need for, 107–108
    notetaking, 310, 318–319
    organizational patterns of, 154–155,
        162–175

outlining steps or procedures, 111,
    112–113
paragraphs providing, 111, 114,
    130–134
in political science essays, 600–602
predicting from main-idea sentences,
    119–122
in psychology essays, 363–364,
    374–375, 388–389
questions answered by, 118–119,
    126–128
reasons for, 111, 112
in sciences essays, 459–460, 474–476
sentences providing, 110–111,
    119–122, 124–126
in sociology essays, 415–418, 428
types of, 111–118
visual aids and, 272–277
Deviant behavior, 392
Diacritical markings, in dictionary, 64–65
Diagrams:
    connecting to text, 278
    defined, 12
    examples of, 255–256, 257, 260
    notetaking and drawing of, 311
    Venn diagrams, 174–175
    See also Visual aids
Dialect, 299
Dictionaries, 61–70
    abridged, 61, 66
    entry features and function, 64–68
    personal use of, 70–71
    prior knowledge about, 63–64
    pronunciation checked in, 69
    spelling checked in, 69
    structure and meaning in, 64–66
    supplementary sections in, 66
    types of, 61, 63
    vocabulary strategies with, 61–70
    words defined with, 68
    words defined without, 40–53
    word usage checked in, 69
Difficulty of material, and reading speed,
    15–16, 446
Discussion, 349, 433, 462
    See also Reading comprehension
Distractions, elimination of, 16
Distributed review, 320
Drawing conclusions:
    from critical reading, 229–236
    from visual aids, 281–289
    from Web resources, 241, 243–244
    See also Conclusions
Drawings as visual aids, 255–256, 257,
    311

E
Earthquakes and the earth, 464–467
Economics, 397–398

Editing your notes, 318–319
Effective listening, *See* Listening
Effect pattern, 149–150
Eisenhower, John, 541–542, 545
Embedded ideas, 18, 22–25
Encoding, for notetaking, 305
End-of-line divisions, in dictionary, 64
Entrepreneurs, 478, 518–526
Entries, in dictionary, 64–68
Environment, 340
Environmental science, 435
Epoch, 534
Equiano, Olaudah, 550–555
Essays:
    identifying organizational patterns in,
        162–164
    readability levels for, 621
    See also Background essays
Ethnocentrism, 534
Etymology, in dictionary, 65
Evidence:
    conclusions from, 234–236
    for inferences, 222–224
    for opinions, 197–201
Example context clues, 46–48
Examples, as details, 111, 113
Exams, preparation for, 31–33
Experience context clues, 49–50
Expert opinions, 197, 199–201
Eye contact, 296

F
Facts:
    characteristics of, 189–190
    criteria to judge, 201–207
    critical reading of, 189–206
    details that cite, 111, 114
    distinguishing opinions from, 197–201
    in history essays, 549
    in paragraphs, 194–195
    in sentences, 193–194
    Web resources on, 240–241
Federalism, 576
Federation, 576
Film, mood and tone in, 218–219
Fixed costs, 478
Flowcharts, 171–172, 250–251, 288
    See also Charts
Focus, author, 84, 91
Footnotes, 254, 549
Forgetting curve, 321
Fukuyama, Francis, 541, 544

G
Gagnon, Paul, 538, 543
Gay marriage, 419–427
Generalizations, 198
General main-idea sentences, 99–103
Geology, 435

Gioia, Joyce L., 480–487
Global music piracy, 492–498
Glossaries, 12–13
Government, *See* Political science
Grammar, 240, 241
Graphic organizers, 162–175
    choices of, 175–179
    comparison and contrast box, 172–173
    concept maps, 165–167
    hierarchical array, 169–171
    linear array, 171–172
    as memory aid, 164
    semantic webbing, 167–169
    Venn diagrams, 174–175
    See also Visual aids
Graphs, 251–253
    connecting to text, 279
    defined, 12
    details, 274–276
    drawing conclusions from, 281–289
    inferences from, 282, 283–284
    line, 251–252
    previewing, 262–265
    software for creating, 561
    See also Bar graphs; Circle graphs;
        Visual aids
Guidelines for reading:
    business essays, 490–491
    history essays, 547–549
    political science essays, 588–590
    psychology essays, 349–351, 352–355
    sciences essays, 446–447
    sociology essays, 406–407
    textbook marking, 323–331
Guide words, in dictionary, 66

H
Haley, Alex, 540–541, 544
Harrington-Lueker, Donna, 408–418
Haydn, A., 464–470
Hearing, 292–293
    See also Listening
Henslin, James M., 394–407
Heritage, 534
Herman, Roger E., 480–487
Hierarchical array, 169–171
High school vs. college, 8, 10
Hispanic entrepreneurs, 518–526
Historical references, 198
History, 533–574
    background essays in, 535–542,
        550–555, 562–568, 591–596,
        605–615
    comprehension of essays on, 542–547,
        555–560, 568–573, 616–619
    critical thinking about, 547, 560–561,
        573–574, 619
    derivation of term, 533
    detail recall from, 559–560, 572–573

    guidelines for reading, 547–549
    inferences and metaphors in, 557–559,
        570–572
    key concepts for study of, 534
    main ideas in, 556, 569–570
    media resources on, 574
    previewing essays on, 535–536, 550,
        562–563, 605–606
    readability levels for essays in, 621
    rewriting sentences from, 555–556,
        568–569
    visual aids for, 546, 548, 552
    vocabulary in context, 557–559,
        570–572
    vocabulary terms for, 533, 534, 536,
        550, 563
    Web resources for, 547, 561, 619
Homosexual marriage, 419–427
Hypotheses, 189, 340

I
Ideas:
    embedded in text, 18, 22–25
    identifying essential, 18–19
    notetaking on, 310
    reading comprehension of, 17–19
    restatement of, 17–19
    See also Main ideas
Illustrations, 46–48, 111, 113
Imagination and history, 547
Immigrants, 534
Immigration reform, 605–615
Independent clauses, 19, 20–23
Indexes (textbook), 13
Industrial Revolution, 534
Inferences, 221–229
    in business essays, 500–501, 512–514,
        528–530
    in everyday life, 222
    explained, 221–222
    in history essays, 557–559, 570–572
    identifying possible, 225–228
    identifying support for, 222–224
    making and understanding, 224
    in political science essays, 598–600
    in psychology essays, 361–363,
        373–374, 386–388
    in sciences essays, 457–459, 471–474
    in sociology essays, 413–415
    from visual aids, 281–284
Inferential reading, 221–222
Inflected form of word, in dictionary, 65
Information:
    distributed review of, 320
    memory for, 162–164, 320
    notetaking, and room for additional,
        310
    organizational patterns for recall,
        162–164

Information (*cont.*)
  outside sources of, 29–30
  recency of, 201, 202, 240, 241
  sources of, 29–30, 201–202, 448, 548
  See also Web resources
Informed opinions, 197–198
Instructors and speakers:
  connecting with, 296–297
  high school vs. college, 8, 10
  point of view, 298
  style of, 299–300, 301–304
Interest groups, 576
Internet, *See* Web resources
Interpretive, historical writing as, 549
Intuitive decision-making strategies, 175

J
Jargon, 299

K
Klebnikov, Paul, 505–510
Knowledge:
  outside sources of, 29–30
  postreading assessment of, 29–30
  See also Prior knowledge
Krikorian, Mark, 605–610, 616–618
Kubey, Robert, 377–390

L
Labor unions, 478
Language choices, 188–189
Law of demand, 478
Learning:
  and academic self-esteem, 3–6, 334–336
  environmental controls and, 6–10
  listening with intention of, 299–300
  postreading assessment of, 29–30
  schedule creation for, 6–8
Lectures:
  graphic creation from, 323
  identifying usable notes from, 305–309
  listening strategies for, 296–301
  notetaking during, 304–305, 312–313, 315–318
  prior knowledge of subject, 297
Legibility of notes, 311, 318
Lesbian marriage, 419–427
Linear array, 171–172
Line graphs, 251–252, 272
  See also Graphs
Lines, visual aids, 272
Listening, 292–332
  applying understanding of, 332
  becoming a good listener, 292–293, 294–295
  choices about, 182–183
  and concentration, 297–298

and confusion, 300
connecting with speakers, 296–297
controlling the experience of, 301
defined, 293
hearing distinguished from, 292–293
instructional styles and, 299–300, 301–304
intent to learn and, 299–300
and notetaking, 304–323
positive habits of, 293–294
strength analysis of, 295–296
and textbook marking, 323–331
  See also Critical reading
"Listening between the lines," 298
Lobbyists, 576

M
Macro-level sociology, 393
Main ideas, 83–106
  applying understanding of, 106
  in business essays, 499, 511–512, 527
  in history essays, 556, 569–570
  identifying sentences containing, 93–99
  listening for, 297–298
  longer reading selections and, 94
  maps of, 91, 92, 98–99, 102
  notetaking on, 305, 310
  organizational patterns and, 154–155
  in political science essays, 597–598
  progression from topics to, 84–86
  in psychology essays, 360–361, 372, 385–386
  in reading strategies, 83–86, 94
  in sciences essays, 448, 456, 471
  in sociology essays, 413, 427
  testing sentences of, 99–104
  topics distinguished from, 83–86
  See also Ideas; Main-idea sentences
Main-idea sentences, 86–106
  creating, 89–99
  locating in paragraphs, 86–89
  predicting details in, 119–122
  and question formulation, 99–105
  reading strategies, 85–94, 99–105
  testing, 99–104
Major details, 123–134
  identifying sentences with, 124–126
  questions answered by, 118–119, 126–128
  recognizing paragraphs with, 130–134
Management, 478
Management of time, 6–8
Maps:
  concept, 165–167
  details in, 130
  main-idea, 91, 92, 98–99, 102
Marketing, 478
Marking textbooks, 323–331

Master words, 60, 62
McCullough, David, 537–538, 543
McNeill, William H., 537, 543
Meaningful work, 480–487
Media resources:
  history and, 574
  psychology, 390
  sociology and, 402
  See also Web resources
Medieval, 534
Meese, Edwin III, 605, 610–615, 616–618
Memory:
  "curve of forgetting," 321
  distributed review, 320
  organizational patterns to aid, 164–175
Mergers, 478
Message, evaluation of, 298
Metaphors:
  in business essays, 500–501, 512–514, 528–530
  in history essays, 557–559, 570–572
  in political science essays, 598–600
  in psychology essays, 361–363, 373–374, 386–388
  in sciences essays, 457–459, 471–474
  in sociology essays, 413–415
Micro-level sociology, 392
Minor details, 123–134
  identifying sentences with, 124–126
  questions answered by, 118–119, 126–128
  recognizing paragraphs with, 130–134
Monarchy, 534
Mood, 212–219
  in film, 218–219
  identifying, 215–218
  overview, 212–213
  in reading, 212–219, 221
Motivation, 340
Music piracy, 492–498

N
Narrowed topics, 74–76, 80, 81, 84, 91
Nationalism, 534
Natural sciences, 397
New knowledge, assessment of, 333–335
Nonstandard words, 65
Non-verbal communication, 296
Norms, 392
Notes:
  accuracy checking, 319
  cross-referencing, 318
  distributed review, 320
  editing, 318–319
  effective use of, 318–323
  footnotes, 254, 549
  key point summaries, 319–320

and question formulation, 321–322
review of, 314–315, 320, 330
as textbook notations, 323–331
Notetaking, 304–323
applying understanding of, 332
basic principles of, 310–311
choices about, 322–323
Cornell method of, 312–315
current strategies, 304–305
graphics used in, 323
identifying usable lecture notes,
305–309
listening and, 298–299
marking system development, 330
outline method of, 315–317
preferences in, 309
process for, 305, 311–312
review of, 330
systems of, 312–318
textbook-notation strategies, 323–331
using notes effectively, 318–323
wait time used for, 305

O
Obsolete words, 65
Online resources, *See* Web resources
Opinion and reason pattern, 138,
146–148
Opinions, 189–206
characteristics of, 190–191
criteria to judge, 201–207
evidence to support, 197–201
expert, 197, 199–201
facts distinguished from, 189–206
history essays, 549
identifying, 193–195, 199–201
information sources for, 201–202
informed opinions, 197–198
in paragraphs, 194–195
point of view as, 202–203
in sentences, 193–194
of speakers, and listening, 298
support for, 197–201
unsupported, 198–201
Organization, writer's, 137
Organizational patterns, 137–181
applying understanding of, 180–181
cause and effect pattern, 138, 146–148
choices about, 175–179
comparison and contrast pattern, 138,
144–146
concept maps and, 165–169
definition and explanation pattern,
138, 142–144
details and detail recall, 154–155,
162–175
graphic organizers and, 162–175
hierarchical array and, 169–171
identifying, 140–164

linear array and, 171–172
main ideas and, 154–155
as memory aid, 164–175
multiparagraph essays and, 162–164
opinion and reason pattern, 138,
146–148
overview of, 138
paragraphs and, 156–164
predicting, 155–162
prior knowledge of, 138–140
problem and solution pattern, 138,
151–153
semantic webbing and, 167–169
simple listing pattern, 138, 140–142
textbooks, 11
thesis and proof pattern, 138, 146–148
types of, 138
Venn diagrams, 174–175
Organizations, 478
Origin of words (etymology), 65
Otnes, F., 535–542
Outline method of notetaking, 315–317

P
Palmaffy, Tyce, 518–526
Paragraphs:
addition of supporting sentences to,
108–110
creating main-idea sentences for,
94–99
critical reading, fact vs. opinion,
194–195
details in, 111, 114, 130–134
main-idea maps for, 91, 92, 98–99,
102
main-idea sentences in, 86–89
organizational patterns in, 156–164
topics in, 83–89
Participant observation, 393
Parts of speech, in dictionary, 65
Patterns, 272, 447–448
See also Organizational patterns
Pauk, Walter, 312
Perception, 340
Perfectionism, 365–376
Personal experience, 198
Perspective, 202–206
See also Point of view
Photographs, 12, 254, 261
Physical appearance of speaker, 299
Physics, 435, 464, 467–470
Piracy of music, 492–498
Pluralism, 576
Pocket dictionaries, 63
Point of view, 202–207
in history essays, 549
identifying, 203–206, 237–238
listening for, 298
as opinion, 202–203

personal response to, 206
in political science essays, 589
in sociology essays, 431
in Web resources, 237–244
Political cartoons, 585
Political science, 575–619
background essays in, 575–582,
591–596, 605–616
comprehension of essays on, 583–587,
597–602
critical thinking about, 588, 602–604
derivation of term, 575
detail recall from, 600–602
guidelines for reading, 588–590
inferences and metaphors in, 598–600
key concepts for study of, 576
main ideas in, 597–598
previewing essays on, 577–578,
591–592, 605–606
readability levels for essays in, 621
rewriting sentences from, 597
as social science, 397
visual aids related to, 585, 587
vocabulary in context, 598–600
vocabulary terms for, 575, 576, 578,
592, 606
Web resources for, 588, 604, 619
Politics, 575–582
Position of author, *See* Point of view
Positive listening habits, 293–294
See also Listening
Postreading, *See* Reading comprehension
Powers, separation of, 576
Predicates, 19, 20–23
Predictions:
of chapter content, 329–330
of details from main-idea sentences,
119–122
of information from visual aids, 265,
267
listening strategies for, 298
of organizational patterns, 155–162
of topics, 79–81
Prefixes, 54–60, 62
Preliminary schedule, 9
Prereading, *See* Previewing
Previewing:
in business essays, 480–481, 492–493,
505–506, 518–519
chapters, 14, 329–330
and communication effectiveness, 299
graphs, 262–265
in history essays, 535–536, 550,
562–563, 605–606
overview, 76–79
in political science essays, 577–578,
591–592, 605–606
in psychology essays, 341, 352–355,
365–366, 377–379

Previewing (*cont.*)
  in sciences essays, 436–438, 446–447,
    449–450, 464–465
  in sociology essays, 394, 408, 419–420
  tables, 265–269
  for topic recognition, 76–79
  visual aids, 262–271
Primary sources, history, 548
Prior knowledge:
  of dictionaries, 63–64
  drawing conclusions from, 285
  and inferences, 222–223, 281
  and informed opinions, 198
  of lecture subjects, 297
  of organizational patterns, 138–140
  predictions from, 79–81
  topical, 14–15, 79–81, 297
  of visual aids, 256, 267, 281, 285
Problem and solution pattern, 138,
  151–153
Procedural details, 111, 112–113
Process, on flowchart, 250–251
Production, 479
Professors, *See* Instructors and speakers
Profit, 479
Pronunciation, in dictionary, 64–65, 69
Psychology, 339–390
  Anticipation/Reaction Guide,
    352–355
  background essays in, 341–351,
    352–364, 365–376, 377–390
  comprehension of essays on, 347–348,
    359–364, 371–375, 385–389
  critical thinking about, 349, 364,
    375–376, 389–390
  derivation of word, 339
  detail recall from, 363–364, 374–375,
    388–389
  discipline of, 341–351
  guidelines for reading, 349–351
  inferences and metaphors in, 361–363,
    373–374, 386–388
  key concepts for study of, 340
  main ideas in, 360–361, 372, 385–386
  media resources, 390
  previewing essays on, 341, 352–355,
    365–366, 377–378
  readability levels for essays in, 621
  rewriting sentences from, 359,
    371–372, 385
  as social science, 398
  visual aids for, 356
  vocabulary in context, 361–363,
    373–374, 386–388
  vocabulary terms for, 339, 340, 355,
    361–363, 366, 373–374, 379,
    386–388
  Web resources for, 349, 364, 376
Purposes for reading, 15

Q
Qualifications of authors, 201
Question formulation:
  applying understanding of, 106
  from chapter material, 12
  details as answers to, 118–119,
    126–128
  during listening, 298
  from main-idea sentences, 99–105
  from notes, 321–322
  during reading, 17, 82

R
Ravitch, Diane, 538–539, 544
Readability levels for essays, 621
Reading, 3–35
  and academic self-esteem, 3–6,
    334–336
  applying understanding of, 34–35
  assessment of learning from, 29–30
  background knowledge for, 29–30
  conclusions from, 229–236
  inferential, 221–222
  learning environment for, 6–10
  preparation for, 14–16
  purpose for, 15
  speed of, 15–16, 446
  and test preparation, 31–33
  textbook, prior to notation, 330
  See also Critical reading
Reading comprehension, 10–31
  applying understanding of, 34–35
  assessment of, 28–29
  business essays and, 488–489,
    498–503, 511–516, 526–531
  history essays and, 542–547, 555–560,
    568–573, 616–619
  identifying ideas, 17–19
  monitoring mental alertness, 17–18
  outside sources for, 29–30
  political science essays, 583–587,
    597–602
  preparation to read, 14–16
  psychology essays and, 347–348,
    359–364, 371–375, 385–389
  and question formulation, 17, 82
  sciences essays and, 442–445,
    455–460, 470–476
  self-monitoring strategies, 28–29
  sociology essays and, 399–402,
    412–418, 427–431
  strategies for improving, 10–30
  textbook exploration and assessment,
    11–14
  topic knowledge and, 72, 74, 81–82
  visual aids and, 257–258
Reading guidelines:
  for business essays, 490–491
  for history essays, 547–549

for political science essays, 588–590
for psychology essays, 349–351,
  352–355
for sciences essays, 446–447
for sociology essays, 406–407
Reading strategies, 72–106
  applying understanding of, 106
  for chapters, 76, 81
  for main ideas, 83–94, 98–105
  for paragraphs, 91, 92, 98–99,
    102
  predictions from prior knowledge as,
    79–81
  previewing as, 76–79
  question formulation and, 17, 82
  for sentences, 85–94, 99–105
  for subtopics, 76, 78–81, 310
  for topics, 73–85
  See also Details; Visual aids
Reasons, details offering, 111, 112
Recall of details, *See* Details
Recency of information, 201, 202, 240,
  241
Record ideas, for notetaking, 305
Regional words, in dictionary, 65
Remembering, *See* Memory
Repetition, 81–82
Research, 197–198
Restatement:
  context clues, 44–45
  of ideas, 17–19
  rewriting sentences as, 25–27
Revenues, 479
Review of notes, 314–315, 320, 330
Revolution, 534
Rewriting sentences:
  from business essays, 498–499, 511,
    526–527
  from history essays, 555–556,
    568–569
  from political science essays, 597
  from psychology essays, 359, 371–372,
    385
  as restatement, 25–27
  from sciences essays, 448, 455, 470
  from sociology essays, 412, 429–430
  See also Sentences
Roles, 392
Roots of words, 54–60, 62
Rosenzweig, Paul, 605, 610–615

S
Schedules, creating, 6–9
School violence, 408–418
Sciences, 434–476
  background essays in, 436–442,
    449–455, 464–470
  comprehension of essays on, 442–445,
    455–460, 470–476

critical thinking about, 445–446, 460–461, 476
defined, 396–397
derivation of term, 434
detail recall, 459–460, 474–476
goals of, 398–399
guidelines for reading, 446–447
inferences and metaphors in, 457–459, 471–474
key concepts for study, 435
main ideas in, 456, 471
nature of, 436–442
political science as, 589–590
previewing essays on, 436–438, 449–450, 464–465
readability levels for essays in, 621
rewriting sentences from, 455, 470
visual aids for, 447, 462, 467
vocabulary in context, 457–459, 471–474
vocabulary terms for, 434, 435, 450, 465
Web resources for, 446, 463, 476
See also Political science
Scientific decision-making strategies, 175
Secondary sources, history, 548
Selection, for notetaking, 305
Self-esteem, academic, 3–6, 334–336
Self-monitoring, 17–18
Semantic webbing, 167–169
Sentences:
    addition of supporting, to paragraphs, 108–110
    details provided by, 110–111, 119–122, 124–126
    embedded ideas in, 18, 22–25
    fact vs. opinion in critical reading of, 193–194
    general vs. specific, 99–103
    identifying essential ideas in, 18–19
    main-idea, 86–106
    types of, 20–22
    See also Main-idea sentences; Rewriting sentences
Separation of powers, 576
Shadings in visual aids, 272
Shively, W. Phillips, 577–582
Shorthand system, 310
Signal words:
    for cause and effect patterns, 148
    for comparison and contrast patterns, 144
    for context clues, 42
    for definition and explanation pattern, 143
    for opinion and reason pattern, 148
    for problem and solution patterns, 151
    for simple listing patterns, 140–142
    for thesis and proof pattern, 147

Simple listing pattern, 138, 140–142
Simple predicates, 20
Slang, in dictionary, 65
Slant, *See* Point of view
Slave trade, 550–555
Social class, 392
Social institutions, 392
Socialization, 392
Social sciences, 397–398
Socio-economic class, 392
Sociology, 391–433
    background essays in, 394–407, 408–418, 419–427
    common-sense beliefs, 403–406
    comprehension of essays on, 399–402, 412–418, 427–431
    critical thinking about, 402–406, 418, 431–433
    derivation of term, 391
    detail recall from, 415–418, 428
    guidelines for reading, 406–407
    inferences and metaphors in, 413–415
    key concepts for study of, 392–393
    main ideas in, 413, 427
    media resources on, 402
    perspective of, 394–407
    previewing essays on, 394, 408, 419–420
    readability levels for essays in, 621
    rewriting sentences from, 412, 429–430
    as social science, 398
    visual aids for, 408, 417, 433
    visual aids related to, 408, 417
    vocabulary in context, 413–415
    vocabulary terms for, 391, 392–393, 394, 420
    Web resources for, 402, 418, 432
Sokolowski, Robert, 419, 423–427
Solid lines as visual aids, 272
Sources of information, 29–30, 201–202, 448, 548
Spalding, Matthew, 605, 610–615
Speakers, *See* Instructors and speakers
Special effects, visual aids, 272–277
Specialized dictionaries, 63
Specific sentences, 99–103
Speed of reading, 15–16, 446
Spell check, computers, 69
Spelling, 69, 240, 241
Statistics, 111, 114, 197–198
Steps, outlining, 111, 112–113
Stereotypes, 198
Stopping, on flowchart, 250–251
Strategic reading, *See* Reading strategies
Studying and notes, *See* Notes
Style:
    of authors, 207–212
    of instructors and speakers, 299–300, 301–304

Subject, of sentence, 19, 20–23
Subtitles, 11, 76–77
Subtopics, 76, 78–81, 310
Suffixes, 54, 55–60, 62
Sullivan, Andrew, 419–423, 427–429, 431
Summaries of chapters, textbook, 12
Supporting sentences, 108–110
Swahili culture, Kenya, 562–568
Sweeping generalizations, 198
Synonym context clues, 44–45
Systematic decision-making strategies, 175

T

Table of contents, textbook, 11
Tables:
    creating, 257
    details in, 273–274
    drawing conclusions from, 286–287, 289
    footnotes on, 254
    inferences from, 282–283
    previewing, 265–269
    as visual aids, 253–254, 255
Teachers, *See* Instructors and speakers
Technical language, 299
Technology, 435
    See also Computers; Media resources; Web resources
Television, 377–390
Terms, *See* Vocabulary
Terrorism, 352–364
Tests, preparation for, 31–33
Text, connecting with visual aids, 277–281
Textbooks:
    assessment of, 11–14
    context for, 37–40
    features and parts of, 11–14
    graphic aids for, 12, 323
    and listening, 323–331
    marking guidelines, 323–331
    notations in, 323–331
    notetaking on, 311, 318
    preparation to read, 14–16
    rewriting key sentences from, 25–27
    underlining key points in, 323–331
    See also Chapters; Organizational patterns
Theories, 189
Thesis and proof pattern, 138, 146–148
Thesis statements, 90, 189
Thought process, 134
    See also Critical thinking
Timelines, 254, 256
Time management, 6–8
Titles, 11, 76–77

Tone, 212–219
  examples of, 214
  in film, 218–219
  identifying, 215–218
  overview, 212–213
  in reading, 212–219, 221
Topics, 73–85
  applying understanding of, 106
  defined, 73
  main ideas distinguished from, 83–86
  narrowed, 74–76, 80, 81, 84, 91
  predicting, 79–81
  previewing, 76–79
  prior knowledge of, 14–15, 79–81, 297
  progression to main ideas from, 84–86
  reading comprehension and, 72, 74, 81–82
  recognizing, 74–82
  repetition as clue to, 81–82
  subtopics, 76, 78–81, 310
Trade, balance of, 478
Tree charts, 249
Tsunamis, 464, 467–470
TV, 377–390

U
Unabridged dictionaries, 61
Uncertainty and notetaking, 310–311
Underlining in textbooks, 323–331
Unsupported opinions, 198–201

V
Venn diagrams, 174–175
Violence, school, 408–418
Visual aids, 246–291
  applying understanding of, 291
  for business essays, 491
  charts as, 249–251
  choices about, 175–179
  colors, shadings, or patterns on, 272
  comparison and contrast patterns, 172–175
  comprehension aided by, 257–258
  concept maps as, 165–167
  connecting to text, 277–281
  creating, 257
  details of, 272–277
  diagrams as, 12, 255–256, 257
  drawing conclusions from, 281–289
  drawings as, 255–256, 257

hierarchical array as, 169–171
for history essays, 546, 548, 552
illustrations as, 46–48, 111, 113
inferences from, 281–284
informed opinions and, 198
linear array, 171–172
line styles on, 272
notetaking and use of, 323
photographs as, 12, 254, 261
for political science essays, 585, 587
predicting information from, 265, 267
previewing, 262–271
prior experience with, 256
and prior knowledge, 256, 267, 281, 285
for psychology essays, 356
purpose of, 277
reading strategies, 262
for sciences essays, 447, 462, 467
semantic webbing, 167–169
sharing with others, 271–272
fosr sociology essays, 408, 417, 433
special effects in, 272–277
tables as, 253–254, 255, 257
in textbooks, 12
timelines as, 254, 256
types of, 249–256
value of, 246–249
and Web content, 241, 243
  See also Graphs
Visualization, sciences essays, 447
Vocabulary, 36–71
  applying understanding of, 71
  in business essays, 478–479, 493, 506, 519
  concept maps for key vocabulary, 165–167
  context for, 37, 61
  dictionaries and, 61–70
  in history essays, 533, 534, 536, 550, 563
  and notetaking, 310
  in political science essays, 575, 576, 578, 592, 606
  in psychology essays, 339, 340, 355, 361–363, 366, 373–374, 379, 386–388
  in sciences essays, 434, 435, 447, 450, 465
  in sociology essays, 391, 392–393, 394, 420

word structure and meaning, 54–61
  See also Context clues

W
Wait time, 305
Watkins, T. H, 539–540, 544
Webbing, semantic, 167–169
Web resources:
  authoritativeness of, 240, 241
  on business, 490, 504, 517, 532
  critical reading of, 236–244
  drawing conclusions from, 241, 243–244
  fact vs. opinion on, 240–241
  on history, 547, 561, 619
  point of view in, 237–244
  on political science, 588, 604, 619
  on psychology, 349, 364, 376
  recency of, 240, 241
  on sciences, 446, 463, 476
  on sociology, 402, 418, 432
  See also Media resources
Wilson, James Q., 591–596
Word processing programs, spell check, 69
Words, 40–65
  affixes, 54–60
  archaic, 65
  context clues, 40–53
  definitions of, 40–53, 68
  etymology, 65
  nonstandard, 65
  notetaking, 310
  obsolete, 65
  origins of, 54–55, 65
  prefixes, 54–60
  prior knowledge about, 63–64
  pronunciation of, 69
  roots of, 54–60
  slang, 65
  spelling, 69
  structure and meaning of, 54–61, 62
  suffixes, 54, 55–60
  usage of, 69–70
  vocabulary strategies, 54–61
  See also Dictionaries; Signal words
Work as meaningful, 480–487
World Wide Web, See Web resources
Writers, See Authors
Writer's organization, 137